THE
GREAT PLAINS
REGION

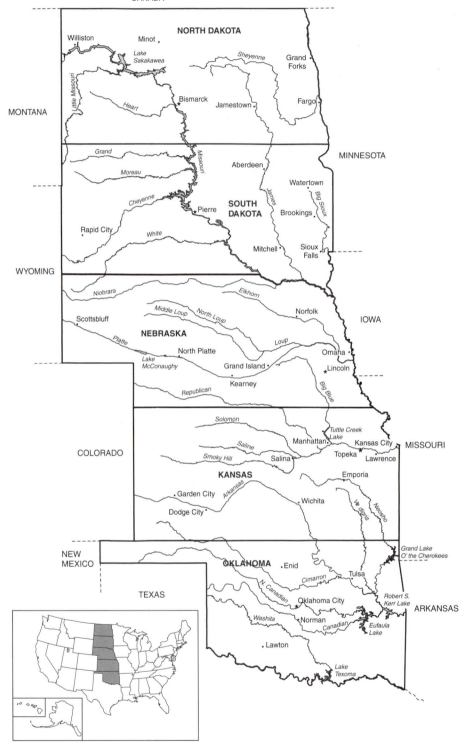

THE
GREAT PLAINS
REGION

The Greenwood Encyclopedia of
American Regional Cultures

Edited by
Amanda Rees

Foreword by William Ferris, Consulting Editor

Paul S. Piper, Librarian Advisor

GREENWOOD PRESS
Westport, Connecticut • London

Library of Congress Cataloging-in-Publication Data

The Great Plains Region : the Greenwood encyclopedia of American regional cultures / edited by Amanda Rees ; foreword by William Ferris, consulting editor.
    p. cm.
   Includes bibliographical references and index.
   ISBN 0–313–33266–5 (set: alk. paper)—ISBN 0–313–32733–5 (alk. paper)
   1. Great Plains—Civilization—Encyclopedias. 2. Great Plains—History—Encyclopedias.
3. Great Plains—Social life and customs—Encyclopedias. 4. Popular culture—Great Plains—Encyclopedias. 5. Regionalism—Great Plains—Encyclopedias. I. Rees, Amanda. II. Series.
F591.G75 2004
978'.003—dc22   2004056069

British Library Cataloguing in Publication Data is available.

Library of Congress Catalog Card Number: 2004056069
ISBN: 0–313–33266–5 (set)
     0–313–32733–5 (The Great Plains Region)
     0–313–32954–0 (The Mid-Atlantic Region)
     0–313–32493–X (The Midwest)
     0–313–32753–X (New England)
     0–313–33043–3 (The Pacific Region)
     0–313–32817–X (The Rocky Mountain Region)
     0–313–32734–3 (The South)
     0–313–32805–6 (The Southwest)

First published in 2004

Greenwood Press, 88 Post Road West, Westport, CT 06881
An imprint of Greenwood Publishing Group, Inc.
www.greenwood.com

Printed in the United States of America

The paper used in this book complies with the
Permanent Paper Standard issued by the National
Information Standards Organization (Z39.48–1984).

10 9 8 7 6 5 4 3 2 1

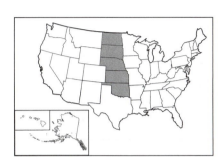

CONTENTS

Contents

FOREWORD

Region inspires and grounds the American experience. Whether we are drawn to them or flee from them, the places in which we live etch themselves into our memory in powerful, enduring ways. For over three centuries Americans have crafted a collective memory of places that constitute our nation's distinctive regions. These regions are embedded in every aspect of American history and culture.

American places have inspired poets and writers from Walt Whitman and Henry David Thoreau to Mark Twain and William Faulkner. These writers grounded their work in the places where they lived. When asked why he never traveled, Thoreau replied, "I have traveled widely in Concord."

William Faulkner remarked that early in his career as a writer he realized that he could devote a lifetime to writing and never fully exhaust his "little postage stamp of native soil."

In each region American writers have framed their work with what Eudora Welty calls "sense of place." Through their writing we encounter the diverse, richly detailed regions of our nation.

In his ballads Woody Guthrie chronicles American places that stretch from "the great Atlantic Ocean to the wide Pacific shore," while Muddy Waters anchors his blues in the Mississippi Delta and his home on Stovall's Plantation.

American corporate worlds like the Bell system neatly organize their divisions by region. And government commissions like the Appalachian Regional Commission, the Mississippi River Commission, and the Delta Development Commission define their mission in terms of geographic places.

When we consider that artists and writers are inspired by place and that government and corporate worlds are similarly grounded in place, it is hardly surprising that we also identify political leaders in terms of their regional culture. We think of John Kennedy as a New Englander, of Ann Richards as a Texan, and of Jimmy Carter as a Georgian.

Because Americans are so deeply immersed in their sense of place, we use region like a compass to provide direction as we negotiate our lives. Through sense of place we find our bearings, our true north. When we meet people for the first time, we ask that familiar American question, "Where are you from?" By identifying others through a region, a city, a community, we frame them with a place and find the bearings with which we can engage them.

Sense of place operates at all levels of our society—from personal to corporate and government worlds. While the power of place has long been understood and integrated in meaningful ways with our institutions, Americans have been slow to seriously study their regions in a focused, thoughtful way. As a young nation, we have been reluctant to confront the places we are "from." As we mature as a nation, Americans are more engaged with the places in which they live and increasingly seek to understand the history and culture of their regions.

The growing importance of regional studies within the academy is an understandable and appropriate response to the need Americans feel to understand the places in which they live. Such study empowers the individual, their community, and their region through a deeper engagement with the American experience. Americans resent that their regions are considered "overfly zones" in America, and through regional studies they ground themselves in their community's history and culture.

The Greenwood Encyclopedia of American Regional Cultures provides an exciting, comprehensive view of our nation's regions. The set devotes volumes to New England, the Mid-Atlantic, the South, the Midwest, the Southwest, the Great Plains, the Rocky Mountains, and the Pacific. Together these volumes offer a refreshing new view of America's regions as they stretch from the Atlantic to the Pacific.

The sheer size of our nation makes it difficult to imagine its diverse worlds as a single country with a shared culture. Our landscapes, our speech patterns, and our foodways all change sharply from region to region. The synergy of different regional worlds bound together within a single nation is what defines the American character. These diverse worlds coexist with the knowledge that America will always be defined by its distinctly different places.

American Regional Cultures explores in exciting ways the history and culture of each American region. Its volumes allow us to savor individual regional traditions and to compare these traditions with those of other regions. Each volume features chapters on architecture, art, ecology and environment, ethnicity, fashion, film and theater, folklore, food, language, literature, music, religion, and sports and recreation. Together these chapters offer a rich portrait of each region. The series is an important teaching resource that will significantly enrich learning at secondary, college, and university levels.

Over the past forty years a growing number of colleges and universities have launched regional studies programs that today offer exciting courses and degrees for both American and international students. During this time the National Endowment for the Humanities (NEH) has funded regional studies initiatives that range from new curricula to the creation of museum exhibits, films, and encyclopedias that focus on American regions. Throughout the nation, universities with regional studies programs recently received NEH support to assist with the programs that they are building.

The National Endowment for the Arts (NEA) has similarly encouraged regional initiatives within the art world. NEA's state arts councils work together within regional organizations to fund arts projects that impact their region.

The growing study of region helps Americans see themselves and the places they come from in insightful ways. As we understand the places that nurture us, we build a stronger foundation for our life. When speaking of how she raised her children, my mother often uses the phrase "Give them their roots, and they will find their wings." Thanks to *American Regional Cultures*, these roots are now far more accessible for all Americans. This impressive set significantly advances our understanding of American regions and the mythic power these places hold for our nation.

William Ferris
University of North Carolina
at Chapel Hill

PREFACE

We are pleased to present *The Greenwood Encyclopedia of American Regional Cultures*, the first book project of any kind, reference or otherwise, to examine cultural regionalism throughout the United States.

The sense of place has an intrinsic role in American consciousness. Across its vast expanses, the United States varies dramatically in its geography and its people. Americans seem especially cognizant of the regions from which they hail. Whether one considers the indigenous American Indian tribes and their relationships to the land, the many waves of immigrants who settled in particular regions of the nation, or the subsequent generations who came to identify themselves as New Englanders or Southerners or Midwesterners, and so forth, the connection of American culture to the sense of regionalism has been a consistent pattern throughout the nation's history.

It can be said that behind every travelogue on television, behind every road novel, behind every cross-country journey, is the desire to grasp the identity of other regions. This project was conceived to fill a surprising gap in publishing on American regionalism and on the many vernacular expressions of culture that one finds throughout the country.

This reference set is designed so that it will be useful to high school and college researchers alike, as well as to the general reader and scholar. Toward this goal, we consulted several members of Greenwood's Library Advisory Board as we determined both the content and the format of this encyclopedia project. Furthermore, we used the *National Standards: United States History* and also the *Curriculum Standards for Social Studies* as guides in choosing a wealth of content that would help researchers gain historical comprehension of how people in, and from, all regions have helped shape American cultures.

American Regional Cultures is divided geographically into eight volumes: *The Great Plains Region*, *The Mid-Atlantic Region*, *The Midwest*, *New England*, *The Pacific Region*, *The Rocky Mountain Region*, *The South*, and *The Southwest*. To ensure that cultural elements from each state would be discussed, we assigned each state to a particular region as follows:

The Great Plains Region: Kansas, Nebraska, North Dakota, Oklahoma, South Dakota

The Mid-Atlantic Region: Delaware, District of Columbia, Maryland, New Jersey, New York, Pennsylvania, West Virginia

The Midwest: Illinois, Indiana, Iowa, Michigan, Minnesota, Missouri, Ohio, Wisconsin

New England: Connecticut, Maine, Massachusetts, New Hampshire, Rhode Island, Vermont

The Pacific Region: Alaska, California, Hawai'i, Oregon, Washington

The Rocky Mountain Region: Colorado, Idaho, Montana, Utah, Wyoming

The South: Alabama, Arkansas, Florida, Georgia, Kentucky, Louisiana, Mississippi, North Carolina, South Carolina, Tennessee, Virginia

The Southwest: Arizona, Nevada, New Mexico, Texas

Each regional volume consists of rigorous, detailed overviews on all elements of culture, with chapters on the following topics: architecture, art, ecology and environment, ethnicity, fashion, film and theater, folklore, food, language, literature, music, religion, and sports and recreation. These chapters examine the many significant elements of those particular aspects of regional culture as they have evolved over time, through the beginning of the twenty-first century. Each chapter seeks not to impose a homogenized identity upon each region but, rather, to develop a synthesis or thematically arranged discussion of the diverse elements of each region. For example, in turning to the chapter on music in *The Pacific Region*, a reader will discover information on Pacific regional music as it has manifested itself in such wide-ranging genres as American Indian tribal performances, Hawaiian stylings, Hispanic and Asian traditions, West Coast jazz, surf rock, folk scenes, San Francisco psychedelia, country rock, the L.A. hard-rock scene, Northwest "grunge" rock, West Coast hip-hop, and Northern California ska-punk. Multiply this by thirteen chapters and again by eight volumes, and you get a sense of the enormous wealth of information covered in this landmark set.

In addition, each chapter concludes with helpful references to further resources, including, in most cases, printed resources, Web sites, films or videos, recordings, festivals or events, organizations, and special collections. Photos, drawings, and maps illustrate each volume. A timeline of major events for the region provides context for understanding the cultural development of the region. A bibliography, primarily of general sources about the region, precedes the index.

We would not have been able to publish such an enormous reference set without the work of our volume editors and the more than one hundred contributors that they recruited for this project. It is their efforts that have made *American Regional Cultures* come to life. We also would like to single out two people for their help: William Ferris, former chairman of the National Endowment for the Humanities and currently Distinguished Professor of History and senior associate director for the Center for the Study of the American South, University of North Carolina at Chapel Hill, who served as consulting editor for and was instrumental in the planning of this set and in the recruitment of its volume editors; and Paul S. Piper, Reference Librarian at Western Washington University, who in his role as librar-

ian advisor, helped shape both content and format, with a particular focus on helping improve reader interface.

With their help, we present *The Greenwood Encyclopedia of American Regional Cultures.*

Rob Kirkpatrick, Senior Acquisitions Editor
Anne Thompson, Senior Development Editor
Greenwood Publishing Group

INTRODUCTION

Regions are important and complex textured threads in the tapestry of any nation's culture. A slippery, silky mixture of nature, culture, and specific historical moments, regions offer one framework for understanding who people are (identity), what happened to whom (history), how they make sense of their local environment (space and place), and what they can look forward to (the future). Regions are tools to organize similarities in one area of a very large and complex national and global surface. Regions are elusive and attractive cultural phenomena because they are never fixed or unchanging.

Regions often do not make sense on their own; indeed, people need other regions placed in relationship to their region of study so that they can compare and contrast and ultimately draw a boundary line between them. For example, understanding the American North and its meaning in American culture is a great deal harder if the American South is not included. This relationship raises the question: where is the Great Plains in relation to other regions, and how do regional dwellers understand that relationship? For some, the Plains is merely an extension of the Middle West or Midwest; for others, the Plains forms the eastern part of the much larger region of the American West. For yet others, the Great Plains is a distinct and important part of the American regional fabric.

In understanding the Great Plains region, three characteristics need to be appreciated: first, the region's environmental context; second, the ways in which the region's populations have been in flux since prehistoric settlement; and finally, the ways in which regionalism itself and the Great Plains region have been understood and studied in the twentieth century.

ENVIRONMENTAL CONTEXT

What and where is the Great Plains region? To a person who is entering the Plains, it seems to stretch without boundaries, with enormous skies and expansive, open uninterrupted landscape. Indeed, in terms of its physical definition, the political defined boundaries of North Dakota, South Dakota, Nebraska, Kansas, and Oklahoma are too limiting. Regions are not merely the result of the physical environment, they are also a result of culture. However, this is equally slippery. For example, a sense of region is not always shared equally amongst inhabitants. In my own work on Great Plains regionalism, I asked Plains inhabitants about the ways in which they think of their own region. Though some responded that they lived in the Great Plains others saw themselves living in what they termed the High Plains, while others saw no distinction between themselves and the more general term the Midwest. Thus, not everyone in the Dakotas, Nebraska, Kansas, and Oklahoma recognizes herself or himself to be in the Great Plains. However, when asked to describe their region, residents often share similar definitions of their region as shaped by climate, economics, history, and culture. Regions are rarely simple to identify or embrace. However, they are a fascinating and useful tool to understand how places came to be, how they function, what makes them special, and what issues connect them to other places. East to west, an environmentally defined region stretches from around the ninety-eighth meridian (altitude 2,000 feet; though some choose the one hundredth meridian), to the Rocky Mountains (altitude 7,000 feet) in the west. This eastward-sloping, treeless, semiarid, shortgrass plateau's annual rainfall is between thirteen and twenty inches, and the region's continental climate creates an environment of extremes, excessive heat and cold, and violent weather patterns. But the physical extension of the region is only one way in which this landscape can be understood. Indeed, as Sonja Rossum and Stephen Lavin's work on mapping the region shows, maps of cultural characteristics of the region are usually smaller and are differently shaped from environmentally defined maps.[1] In this exploration of the Great Plains we draw together architecture, art, ecology and the environment, ethnicity, fashion and dress, film and theater, folklore, food, language, literature, music, religion, and sports and recreation not to visually map the region but to use narrative to map this space that embraces the regional definition of North and South Dakota, Nebraska, Kansas, and Oklahoma and also extends beyond these state boundaries.

LIVING IN THE REGION

Since the earliest settlement on the Plains, the region's population has been in flux. For example, evidence suggests that the first human occupation of the Plains occurred at the end of the last ice age (around 10,000 B.C.E.). However, between 5000 and 2000 B.C.E. a long and severe drought made the region uninhabitable. In the two hundred years since the United States purchased the Plains as part of the Louisiana Purchase in 1803, the peak of the region's population was recorded in the 1950 census, and since that point it has exhibited a profound decline in its most rural sections. Over the long haul, this region's environment has both welcomed and repelled its human inhabitants, but the population decline since the middle of the twentieth century has had a profound impact on the region.

HOW REGIONALISM AND THE GREAT PLAINS REGION HAVE BEEN UNDERSTOOD IN THE TWENTIETH CENTURY

Today, according to surveys, the last place American and international tourists seek to explore is the Great Plains. Indeed, if tourists have to travel through this region, they seek to fly over it or drive through at night, and regardless of how they manage to move through this space, they are always in a hurry. But this strong dislike and disregard of the region was not always the case.

Unlike contemporary attitudes that seem to dismiss the region, Americans' sense of regionalism and of the Great Plains in particular was very different in the post–World War I period. Indeed, many people both inside and outside the region saw the concept of regionalism as the answer to the decadence of modernism, the utter devastation of World War I, the economic depression agriculture suffered after the war, the rise of fascism in Europe, and powerful American financial and political centers of the East. Regionalists believed that a return to regionalism offered something urban America lacked, namely, being in touch with its roots.

During this interwar period, the Great Plains region was distinguished in academic writings and conferences and literary writings, as well as in the arts and film. Historian Walter Prescott Webb, who defined the Great Plains as a distinct, environmentally unified region, described it in this way: "The Great Plains environment, as defined in this volume, constitutes a geographic unity whose influences have been so powerful as to put a characteristic mark upon everything that survives within its borders."[2] Indeed, in 1942, two conferences on the Great Plains were held in New York and Nebraska.[3] The region was articulated in the popular imagination by authors such as John Steinbeck, artists such as John Steuart Curry, and directors such as John Ford in his powerful interpretation of Steinbeck's *Grapes of Wrath*. This refocusing on American regionalism, together with the spectacular environmental, ecological, and cultural devastation brought on by the combination of the Great Depression and the Dust Bowl, worked to shape an especially powerful and long-lasting sense of the American Great Plains.

During this period, the Great Plains was understood and represented in terms of its physical and environmental characteristics. The environmental constraints that dominated the region's migrants in the nineteenth century were a primary lens through which to understand the region. This environmental lens drew upon climate, physiognomy, flora, and fauna to distinguish itself from other regions.[4] There were also efforts by sociologists to work in the same way to unify the region by looking at the social environment. As the regional scholar Frederick Luebke has claimed, the works of historians and sociologists were often underpinned by the work of geographers who also sought to articulate regional homogeneity.

However, by the 1950s, regionalism in American culture had fallen out of favor because Cold War ideology rejected regional division, differentiation, and diversity in exchange for the celebration of and study about national unity. As the economic and ecological ravages of the Dust Bowl abated and the war years ended, a period came when many commentators considered regionalism finished. In 1957, writer Wright Morris declared regions dead: "The only regions left are those the artist must imagine. They lie beyond the usual forms of salvage. No matter where we go, in America today, we shall find what we left behind."[5]

However, the wholesale rejection of regionalism was somewhat mitigated in the 1960s. In the midst of much civil rights tension, culture was understood to be the shaper of regionalism, and the focus of regional study shifted to the ways in which different groups brought their cultural sensibilities to a region, and how cultural traditions diffused through these regions. In Great Plains research the role of the immigrant cultures to the region became a major focus, cultural and regional geographers began to map food culture, religion, and linguistics as markers of culture and regionalism, and the role of the environment was placed into a cultural context. One of the leaders of cultural regionalism, historian Frederick Luebke, made the case that

> The effect of the older scholarship was to reveal regional uniformities, just as the newer scholarship stresses interregional variation. Each discerns relationships that are beyond the analytical power of the other. Regions are therefore best conceptualized in terms of the interplay between environment and culture; they are best described and analyzed through appropriate comparisons in time, space, and culture.[6]

As Luebke suggested, the environment could not be forgotten in the desire to incorporate culture. This view took on more significance in the decade after Earth Day in 1970. With the rise of the environmental movement and a critical stance on region, nature was reintroduced into Great Plains regional discussions in such powerful works as Donald Worster's *Dust Bowl*. In addition to this mix of nature and culture, regions have gained entry into the popular imagination in the last thirty years with new regional magazines such as *Midwest Living*, as well as regional festivals and the packaging and marketing of local regions by state tourism agencies and local chambers of commerce. Though there is no regional magazine that represents the Great Plains, there is an increasing interest in local history and the proliferation of state humanities councils in the Plains, and there are at least three regional study centers: the Center for Great Plains Studies at Emporia State University, Emporia, Kansas, the Institute for Regional Studies, North Dakota State University, and the Center for Great Plains Studies, University of Nebraska at Lincoln.

At the beginning of the twenty-first century, this text works to draw together a rich quilt of environmental and cultural activities to demystify one of the most challenging regions in the United States, the Great Plains. Hopefully, this text will encourage a slower pace, a lingering to explore this enormous, complicated, and ever-changing place.

THEMES IN GREAT PLAINS REGIONAL STUDY

Though Steve Martens and Ronald Ramsay do not make claims for a specific regional architecture, they reveal Great Plains built space as humble, modest, restrained, and presenting a beautiful aesthetic. The Great Plains has hosted built environments that utilize regionally grown or quarried materials: grasses, earthen-walled buildings, sod huts, local stone, petrified wood, and brick made from local clay. One of the technologies that had a profound influence on regional architecture and reshaped it in its wake was the railway. It drew late-nineteenth-century architecture away from local materials toward wooden balloon frames and eastern styles that were shaped by a more humid eastern environment where forests were more plentiful. In addition to local and imported materials and styles, ethnic enclaves of nonnative immigrants brought their traditions directly from Hungary, Russia, Finland, and Iceland. One of the great gifts that Martens and Ramsay's chapter brings to the reader is a subtle articulation of landscape that incorporates grain elevators, the arrangement of agricultural buildings in rural space, and small Plains town urban spaces. They also suggest that at least some of these spaces have, since the 1970s, received increasing attention from preservationists who seek to celebrate regional architecture.

Like Martens and Ramsey, William Tsutsui and Marjorie Swann argue that the Great Plains region does not reveal a single style of art but instead several distinctive elements and common concerns. Native American traditions have been a powerful shaper of state artistic identity in the Plains, especially in states with larger Native populations, Oklahoma and South Dakota in particular. Perhaps one of the more remarkable early Plains representations from the exploration period can be found in the physically enormous work of John Banvard. In 1840, Banvard created what was then called the largest painting executed by humans. Rising to the challenge of representing this dramatic and extensive region, he created a three-mile-long panorama of Plains topographical scenes that amazed audiences in the East and Europe. The isolated experience of Plains life influenced artists in two ways. First, some left the region for professional advancement elsewhere. Second, others found that the isolation offered the possibility of an expressive range that might not be found in the urban centers where other artists congregated. Finally, for those who stay in place, the painter Robert Sudlow points out that this extensive rural space offers the artist no subject, but it does offer both space and weather. The challenge is that of conveying presence rather than absence in this vast landscape and, second, representing a vast and complex horizontal distance rather than the more traditional focus on the vertical. This unique landscape and demanding climate offer contemporary artists a number of fascinating representational challenges.

In his examination of ecology and environment, John Opie tells the story of a 6,000-year-old grassland. The environmental characteristics that define the Plains cover one-fifth of the lower forty-eight states and include the Dakotas, Nebraska, and Kansas, as well as eastern Colorado, Oklahoma, and Texas. Opie explores a number of major periods in the life of the Plains environment from Native American experiences to Euro-American settlement and the lack of water, the rise of irrigation technology, and the issues of sustainability and conservation. Opie concludes by asking how the region's environmental future is being imagined: should agriculture be rejected and the landscape returned to the buffalo, or should a new agricultural system be developed that rejects large-scale farming for small-scale agriculture that can weather large-scale economic booms and busts and exist more easily in a landscape of environmental extremes?

Though the stereotypical vision of Plains ethnicity seems to suggest similarity rather than diversity, A. Dudley Gardner reveals a complex patchwork of ethnic groups. Gardner divides his analysis of ethnicity between peoples before the

Louisiana Purchase (1803), and after 1803, when Napoleon sold the region, among other lands, to the U.S. government. The early period covers early Native presence, the influence of Spanish and Old World technology, such as the gun, introduction of the horse, disease epidemics, the removal of eastern Indians into the Plains, Scottish and French influence from the trapping trade, and escaped slaves. The period after 1803 includes the movement of African American farmers to Kansas, Scandinavian settlers who settled primarily the northern Plains, Icelanders, Russian Germans, religious groups such as Hutterites and Mennonites, and Pennsylvania Dutch, Jewish, Japanese, and Chinese immigrants. Gardner then turns to the latter part of the twentieth century and the rise of immigration from Vietnam, Laos, and Cambodia, as well as Filipinos, Asian Indians, Middle Eastern immigrants, and the dramatic rise of Hispanic populations, who are often centered on the meat-packing industry in the region. Gardner concludes with a discussion of the extraordinary rise of Native populations in the contemporary region.

Like architecture, dress has historically stood in direct relation to the limitations of climate and, in the region, the availability of local materials prior to the arrival of mass-manufactured clothing in the 1850s. Before many Plains tribes glimpsed their first white person, manufactured elements, beads, ribbons, and woven woolen fabric from the East and even from Europe were an important part of intertribal trading regimes and regional dress practices. Regional dress provides a unique window into the struggles between a centralized federal authority and people in the region. Not only was Native dress radically altered, but centralized federal authority also made decisions about army dress. Decisions made in Washington, D.C., were rarely shaped by knowledge of Plains life, the intense summer humidity, and the equally intense dry cold of winter. Author Laurel Wilson also outlines the impact of incoming fashions seized upon by Plains women. She offers a nuanced interpretation of the constant battle between comfort and the ability to fulfill the demands of a rural agricultural life and the demands of contemporary propriety in public places. Wilson explores dress related to regional occupations such as the cowboy and offers a thoughtful conclusion on contemporary regional dress.

Film and theatrical representations of the Plains have long held in tension a complicated set of themes such as the relationship between nature and culture, the relationship between its Euro-American and Native populations, and political violence surrounding the Civil War and reveal a fascinating visual record, interpretation, and reinterpretation of the Great Plains. The drama of environmental extremes is represented in the tornadoes in films from *The Wizard of Oz* to *Twister*, and the environmental and cultural pain of the Dust Bowl is revealed both in fiction and documentary films, such as *The Grapes of Wrath* and *The Plow That Broke the Plains*. Ronald Wilson argues that like regional artists, filmmakers are also drawn to the drama of the region, from the extensive and relentlessly flat landscape of Kansas in *Paper Moon* to the spectacular and often confusing terrain of the Dakota badlands in *Badlands*. Wilson explores the ways in which Plains Indians have been represented throughout the twentieth century, as well as the rich vein of migration and the concept of westward expansion. Perhaps one of the more surprising findings is that a generous number of films have focused on the proslavery/abolitionist drama surrounding the very bloody Quantrill's Raid on Lawrence, Kansas, about which eight movies were made between 1914 and 1999.

This chapter ranges from silent movies and cowboy features to contemporary representations of Plains life revealed in such satirical films as Alexander Payne's *About Schmidt*. Wilson concludes with a discussion of the life of the theater in the region, with particular attention to William Inge.

Plains folklore offers yet another set of tensions that surround survival in the Great Plains region. Amanda Rees offers a sense of Plains folklife and the varying ways in which folklorists worked to understand the life of the folk. Native oral traditions span stories of the beginning time when the world was forming and of the beginnings of tribal society and the establishment of tribal traditions and codes of behavior. They also reveal heroes and traditional characters such as the trickster who in turn reveal relations between Native and immigrant populations and the impact of Euro-American diseases such as smallpox. There are the stories of big men in a big country who work to tame the region to provide an abundance of agricultural, mining, or oil products. Big animals and big fauna are also characteristic of both nineteenth- and early-twentieth-century folklore narratives, as well as incredible roadside attractions that feature "the largest prairie dog in the world" or the "biggest pheasant in the world." But it is in the small-scale family-oriented folklore often associated with objects such as quilts or charm strings that the transfer of regional folklore in contemporary society can be best identified, and these small but important items reveal stories of social relations between Native populations and immigrants or between young girls. The stories of local heroes and outlaws become powerful reminders of what Plains people choose to value and remember about their past. Occupational folklore is also an important part of understanding the ordinary lives of Plains folk, such as the traditions that surround how and who counts the cattle. Plains folklore reveals the ways in which early settlers made sense of the new environment they were in and, more recently, how ethnic traditions have developed into large-scale folk celebrations in the region, such as the Czech festivals that dotted Nebraska in the mid-twentieth century and the late-twentieth-century rise of Scottish folk celebrations in western South Dakota.

According to food geographer Barbara Shortridge, beef and pie distinguish Great Plains food traditions, traditions that support both the agricultural base and the region's ethnic heritages. Foodways or traditions, Shortridge argues, reveal a high caloric intake to supply the needs of hardworking farmers, and this heritage still pervades food traditions today, though only a very small percentage of the region's population is engaged in agriculture. Place-specific dishes and their preparation are discussed, including such items as bierocks, chicken-fried steak, and the Jell-O salad, an often highly constructed molded gelatin salad that can be found at the Thanksgiving dinner table and on restaurant buffets. She reveals the secrets of the slow-cooking tradition that underpin hot dishes such as casseroles incorporating such ingredients as condensed cream soup, ground beef, Tater Tot brand frozen potatoes, or perhaps tuna, rice, or noodles. Regional ethnic traditions are revealed from the pan-Indian tradition of fry bread to the Czech kolache. Shortridge shares her research on Plains foodways. Having asked Great Plains residents to provide a hypothetical menu for a meal that represents their part of the state and that they would serve to out-of-town guests, Shortridge presents a tour of a Plains dinner table with beef, starches, vegetables, salads, dessert, and beverage that offers a thoughtful sense of what people eat on the Plains and why.

The discussion by Pamela Innes of regional linguistics opens a window onto the health of Native American languages, the effects of languages on the culture in both the nineteenth and twentieth centuries, and how Old World and recently introduced languages are faring. In the contemporary Great Plains, there are nine major Native language families, with multiple languages within most of these families, and Innes characterizes those families and languages that are thriving, those that are close to extinct, and the language programs at work in revitalizing language traditions. Innes explores the movement and influence of languages from Europe, the Middle East, Africa, and East, Southeast, and South Asia. She concludes with a discussion of Black English Vernacular in the region and the rich and subtle subregional varieties of English spoken on the Plains.

Plains writers, poets, novelists, and nonfiction authors reveal a rich tension between a romantic belief in community and a profound sense of endless potential wasted against natural and cultural environments. From early exploration journals and migrant diaries to present-day accounts, Stacy Coyle argues that the landscape, the biology, and the botany of the place have dominated Plains writing, with a particular focus on the grasses that seem to create a feeling of being at sea. Coyle explores a strong sense of impermanence that pervades the region and refers to poet William Stafford's image of a phone call to a farm on the Great Plains. He reaches someone, but that person is the last tenant in the region. Coyle concludes by articulating what she sees as a pervading sense of pessimism about the region's survival and a sense that this may indeed be the last generation in the region.

The Great Plains is rich in both musical traditions and the hybridization of musical traditions, and Paula Conlon, Addie deHilster, and T. Chris Aplin nod to traditions and hybridizations in their examination of regional Great Plains music. They move from Native music and dance to polka, jazz, country and western, bluegrass, rock and popular, and classical music. Perhaps one of the more telling examples of hybridization, the mixing of genres in unique and interesting ways, can be found in polka music, which was brought to the region by eastern European immigrants and made famous in the American popular consciousness through the work of Lawrence Welk and his mid-twentieth-century television programs. The region embraced very specific "country-of-origin" styles such as polkas by Slovenian, Czech, German, and Polish performers. Mexican and Mexican American musicians in nineteenth-century Texas then embraced these traditions. The Tejano style mixed Mexican instruments with the accordion (a traditional European instrument) and German and Czech songs. The Tejano tradition then spread north into the Plains.

The Great Plains is one of the most churched regions in the United States, with 60 percent of residents claiming membership in a religious group and attending church regularly. Steve Foulke reveals that one of the most important issues that shapes Plains religious practices is the declining rural population. Foulke explores Native American religious history, as well as the complexity of Christian traditions that spread across the region and the more urban non-Christian traditions located in the metropolitan peripheries of the region. Foulke's work ranges from the impact of the region's largest religious denomination, Catholicism, claimed by a third of the population, to the smallest Anabaptist strains, the Hutterites and Amish, who retain distinctive religious and cultural traditions in the Dakotas and Kansas, respectively. Foulke concludes with a discussion of the rise of megachurches in such communities as Overland Park, a suburb of Kansas City, and Oklahoma City whose enormous congregations of up to 10,000 people contrast dramatically with the decrease in the Plains rural population, the aging in place of that declining population, and the struggle to locate clergy, all of which present an enduring challenge to parish life in the region.

"Sports for sports sake" is the Great Plains sports philosophy according to Thomas Wikle and John Rooney Jr. In contrast to urban areas, rural Plains schools have small enrollments and provide opportunities for most interested students. Plains participation for almost every major team sport is well above the national average, participation is valued over quality and success, and women's athletics is celebrated. Professional sports are not represented well in the region, minor-league and semiprofessional teams have established themselves, and intercollegiate sports have also taken an important role in Plains culture. Indeed, intercollegiate football forges powerful links between alumni and their alma mater, and Nebraska and Oklahoma provide particularly powerful examples. In addition, collegiate basketball and baseball are particularly strong in the central Great Plains. Recreational tourism does not provide a strong magnet for tourists, in part because of the large distances that separate recreational amenities, and Wikle and Rooney argue that for many, the Plains is a region of transit rather than destination. In relation to recreation, federal and state agencies as well as municipalities manage regional recreational activities and recreational lands. Water recreation is abundant on a large number of federally funded reservoirs. Hunting is twice as popular as the national average and occurs in private and state-managed lands, in particular for waterfowl in the northern Plains.

CONCLUSION

The Great Plains is a challenging place for visitors to make sense of, and this collection of chapters reveals a rich and timely tapestry of often complicated regional cultural activities, especially because much of the analysis of Great Plains regional cultural practices has never been collected in one place. Environmental extremes, the forcible removal of Native populations to the region and within the region, the in-migration of non-Native Euro- and African Americans, the dramatic environmental, economic, and cultural impact of the 1930s Dust Bowl, and the region's low population density and population decline, hand in hand with its isolation from large metropolitan centers, together have profoundly shaped cultural life in the region. The ways in which the Great Plains has been represented and the general waxing and waning in regionalism have also shaped people's understanding of regional life in the Plains. The various lenses of architecture, art, ecology and the environment, ethnicity, fashion, film and theater, folklore, food, language, literature, music, religion, and sports and recreation, suggest a slower, more thoughtful navigation of this place and a joyful exploration of this dramatic region, the Great Plains.

BIBLIOGRAPHY

Briggs, Harold E. "An Appraisal of Historical Writings on the Great Plains since 1920." *Mississippi Valley Historical Review* (June 1947): 83–100.

Luebke, Frederick C. "Regionalism and the Great Plains: Problems of Concept and Method." *Western Historical Quarterly* 15 (January 1984): 19–38.

Rossum, Sonja, and Stephen Lavin. "What Are the Great Plains? A Cartographic Analysis." *Professional Geographer* 52, no. 3 (August 2000): 543–552.

Steiner, Michael, and Clarence Mondale. *Region and Regionalism in the United States: A Source Book for the Humanities and Social Sciences.* New York: Garland Publishers, 1988.

Steiner, Michael C., and David M. Wrobel. *Many Wests: Place, Culture, and Regional Identity.* Lawrence: University Press of Kansas, 1997.

Webb, Walter Prescott. *The Great Plains.* Boston: Ginn and Company, 1931.

Worster, Donald. *Dust Bowl.* New York: Oxford University Press, 1979.

ARCHITECTURE

Steve Martens and
Ronald L. M. Ramsay

Buildings serve practical purposes, but people who design and construct buildings make judgments and choices that reveal heritage, aspirations, cultural values, and priorities. In addition to functionality, architecture embodies individual preferences, human values, cultural meanings, and a shared worldview. Buildings reveal regional differences and variations that are useful in understanding a region's culture. Great Plains architecture has evolved over time to reflect distinctive aspects of local culture and regionally specific ways of expressing national tastes and trends. Historically, the term "architecture" was reserved for important buildings designed and built according to the judgment of people who called themselves "architects." Increasingly, the terms "buildings" and "architecture" are used interchangeably to reflect a growing awareness among scholars that small and seemingly simple buildings created by different processes may also be exceptionally appropriate in responding to the environment.

Great Plains architecture is one visible manifestation of the concept of cultural diffusion, that is, the way material culture changes as it spreads. As people moved westward into a new environment, they brought with them familiar ways of designing and constructing buildings that often reflected places from which they came. Aspects of imported historical architectural traditions continue in the present day, and variations from place to place provide fascinating examples of regional distinctiveness. Regional variations in architecture are further reinforced by prosaic and spiritual expectations and by demands of the physical environment. Perhaps one of the most notable patterns in Great Plains' architecture is that there is greater cultural consistency from east to west (along transportation routes) and more "striated" from north to south, where culture is impacted most by climate variations.

VERNACULAR, FOLK, AND POPULAR ARCHITECTURE IN THE GREAT PLAINS

Architecture (including buildings, landscapes, and other constructions) often reveals the process by which it was designed and constructed. Buildings may be created by indigenous or *folk* traditions that are well learned from prior experience and evolve slowly over a long time based on people's familiarity with a place or even upon common wisdom that is passed along by storytelling and oral tradition. Second, buildings may be created by vernacular or commonplace processes that people learn from hands-on practice and observation. Architecture of this second kind includes *popular* designs that borrow freely from tastes, styles, and preferences shared by many people, but also reflect substantial ingenuity, innovation, and change over time. Vernacular designers and builders often gain experience through apprenticeship, learning from a more experienced mentor. Buildings designed and constructed by a vernacular process, with its basis in prior experience and environmental adaptation, are prevalent on the Great Plains landscape. Last, buildings may be products of design by architects who have been formally educated according to national and international trends of *academic* style and design theory. As building technology has become ever more complex in the twentieth and twenty-first centuries, public buildings are increasingly designed by architects or teams of architects who work with other related design specialists. Whichever of the three processes is used to design and construct a building, the end result reflects cultural preferences and local conditions of the regional context.

The large majority of buildings on the Great Plains landscape may be referred to as vernacular; that is, they were designed and built by people who were not trained in architecture schools. Instead, most builders of rural architecture were carpenters, farmers, or small-town businesspeople who learned about constructing buildings from observation and experience. This should in no way diminish the appreciation of rich, imaginative architecture that was built according to a commonplace tradition. Buildings designed by nonarchitects are much more prevalent on the Plains as sources to learn from than are "high-style" buildings that people would immediately recognize as architecture, but commonplace buildings are no less relevant to the understanding of the culture of building on the Plains. Buildings on the Great Plains landscape are full of meanings about the variety of things that are truly important to people who live there.

The process of genetic hybridization, intuitively applied, is very much like the way in which commonplace buildings and vernacular landscapes developed throughout the Great Plains region. Buildings that successfully satisfied requirements of their context and cultural setting were repeated with small variations, and over time some consistent characteristics became clearly recognizable. Like seeds that hybridize in adapting to local environment, the cumulative effect of "unimportant" incremental decisions produces the richly varied buildings and landscape on the Great Plains today. Vernacular buildings evolved slowly over time, and for that reason they often employ material knowledgeably, in a way that is well suited to the cultural and environmental context where the material is to be used. Buildings differ from place to place because they are a combination of local tradition, resources, custom, and culture. The built environment evolves through shared experience specific to a particular location or time. Scholars of vernacular or commonplace architecture often find such patterns of similarity among aesthetically beautiful and sophisticated commonplace buildings to be more revealing than stylistic labels attached to unique, one-of-a-kind buildings.

A popular misconception about vernacular buildings is that they do not allow for meaningful innovation. Rural people on the Great Plains have a deep-seated faith in innovation, a cultural value that is fundamental to the way they solve problems and construct buildings. Builders of Great Plains landscapes felt strongly that things they constructed should function well and should look durable and handsome. Decisions about design tended to emphasize efficiency and conservative, commonsense judgment. Buildings created by vernacular tradition often have a magnificent simplicity or beauty by any standard of architectural evaluation. Houses, churches, and agricultural buildings designed by this vernacular process satisfied cultural aspirations of people who originally used them, and they continue to have meaning and appropriateness in their context.

Architecture of the Great Plains should not be regarded as hidebound or excessively constrained by tradition and precedent. Experimentation and innovation are associated with the work of many architects and builders on the Plains who have sought new and imaginative ways to satisfy needs and expectations of a client or community. Oklahoma-based architect Bruce Goff (1904–1982) is noted for using commonplace building materials in daring and original ways. Free, unconstrained experimentation with style is clearly evident in imaginative buildings of the Prairie school, which aspired to an entirely new and "American" way of arranging space and ornamenting buildings. Builders of commonplace, vernacular buildings from barns to grain elevators engaged in a conscious process to refine and improve performance or to use familiar materials in more efficient ways. Among academically trained architects of the late twentieth century, the aspiration to innovate and to solve each design problem as though it was entirely unique and original became a virtual obsession on the Great Plains, as it has become elsewhere.

THE CULTURAL CONTEXT OF ARCHITECTURE IN THE GREAT PLAINS

As culture spreads from one location to another, factors of cultural preference interact with circumstances of physical environment to influence the form, character, and meaning of architecture. The human desire to express culture based on prior experience is a powerful and compelling trait. A prevailing viewpoint among people who study architecture and cultural geography is that "when environment and culture collide, culture usually wins."[1] Increasingly, people understand that while culture may adapt to a new environment, it is just as likely that environment may adapt (or be adapted) to suit culture. People who have lived for many years on the Great Plains have a genuine awareness of the frailty of human cultural endeavor in the face of natural forces like tornadoes, floods, droughts, and blizzards. Residents of the Great Plains region were reminded of this principle during the Dust Bowl years of the Great Depression, a brutal time of cultural adjustment after unsustainable forms of human agriculture had been imposed on the Plains. Human vulnerability in a challenging environmental context is a matter of cultural awareness that is clearly reflected in the built environment of the Plains, its architecture, and constructed landscapes like the shelterbelt system of tree planting that exists as part of the legacy of the Dust Bowl.

Each culture that moved onto the Great Plains found it necessary and appropriate to adjust building practices to environmental conditions encountered in the new setting and to modify the physical environment to better suit human needs for shelter, community, and intellectual and spiritual expression. People who share a set of cultural traits tend to transmit or spread their preferred way of doing things in two main ways. Sometimes culture groups relocate geographically and transport various aspects of culture from their remembered homeland to a new setting with only minimal modifications. The phenomenon of *relocation diffusion* is demonstrated by discrete immigrant groups that relocated to the Great Plains in the nineteenth and early twentieth centuries and brought with them artifacts of culture familiar in their homelands. Often, they settled in new enclaves where neighbors shared many of these same culture traits, so on the Great Plains there is a fascinating range of discrete local cultures with architectural traditions that seem oddly out of place when they are compared with other parts of the United States. Because of the late date when the Plains were occupied by non-Native immigrants, ethnic enclaves of Americanized German Hungarians, Germans from Russia, Finnish Americans, Icelandic Americans, and other culture groups are conspicuous and surprisingly distinct across the Plains, crafting buildings exactly as they had in "the old country." Many visitors are astonished to find a house copied verbatim from the Rhineland in Kansas or to discover the onion-domed spires of a Ukrainian Greek Orthodox church in a small North Dakota town, vestiges of a connective house-barn elsewhere, or an early mosque or synagogue in a small town on the Plains.[2]

Architecture and other cultural expressions also transform across time and space by a process termed *contact diffusion* or *contagion diffusion*, in which tastes and inclinations of one culture group are influenced and modified in response to one's neighbors. Each distinct culture group may modify some of its cultural practices (and its buildings) based on familiarity with things its neighbors are doing. These cultural adjustments lead to mixing, as implied by the melting-pot metaphor, and to assimilation of subcultures by a dominant culture. Buildings express prosaic and practical aspects of the relationship between culture and environment, reinforcing social relationships and reflecting reasoned, intellectual understanding of the world. Architecture may also express a view of the world in more poetic, spiritual ways that reach into the soul of shared human experience. People grow in their ability to understand culture when they practice looking thoughtfully at buildings and trying to understand cultural values that influenced people who designed and built them. As people look at examples of the range of buildings on the Plains, they may understand them better in terms of the practical, intellectual, and spiritual aspirations of their designers and builders.

Many things that people create as part of their shared cultural heritage reveal aspects that are neither practical nor intellectually logical, but are instead an unself-conscious expression of the human spirit. Anthropologists confirm that all cultures engage in a search for beauty and aesthetic perfection. Consistent with the harshness of the Great Plains environment and the preciousness of scarce resources, a cultural aesthetic has emerged that highly values efficient, minimalist expression of functional performance and shows preference for simplicity, modesty, humility, and restraint in the way architecture is ornamented and composed. It may be fairly said that overt "beauty" as an applied form of decoration tends to be tolerated only grudgingly on the Plains.[3] On the basis of ethnic background and religious heritage, many residents of the Plains also share a cultural inclination toward humility, modesty, and restraint and strive to avoid "putting on airs" with overt expressions of culture and taste. Still, a restrained and beautiful aesthetic quality is apparent in many buildings on the Plains.

PHYSICAL CONTEXT AND MATERIAL AND PRACTICAL ASPECTS OF GREAT PLAINS ARCHITECTURE

Background factors and conditions inherent in Great Plains settlement influenced the architecture that emerged in the region. The physical environment of the Great Plains can be nearly as harsh, extreme, and changeable as that of any other place on the planet. An examination of buildings should consider how well they use resources at hand to modify the physical environment and enhance human activity in ways that are comfortable, convenient, and sustainable. European culture came to influence habitation on the Great Plains fairly late, relative to other regions of the United States. Many social groups who came to the Plains also had prior experience with other harsh environments that afforded lessons that were applied to facilitate successful habitation on the Plains. As Euro-American culture spread onto the Plains, materials and building techniques, too, were imported through the network of transportation, notably the railroads.

Geographically and climatically, the Great Plains extends well beyond the political boundaries of North and South Dakota, Nebraska, Kansas, and Oklahoma, encompassing land from western Missouri and Minnesota to eastern Montana in one direction and from Texas to the Canadian prairie provinces of Manitoba and Saskatchewan in another. Throughout history and prehistory, people who arrived on the Plains were impressed and often intimidated by the semi-arid climate and the harshness of climatic swings that can vary from minus 50 degrees Fahrenheit (minus 45 degrees Celsius) to 120 degrees F (49 degrees C) in any one location seasonally, with recorded diurnal temperature swings of as much as 70 degrees F (39 degrees C) on a particular day. Sustained high wind is a common condition, as are periods of prolonged lack of precipitation or drought. Weather and climate contribute to diminished, short-grass vegetative cover, with tree cover limited mostly to the bottom of river valleys. Weather events like tornadoes and blizzards are unforgettable experiences on the unprotected, open Plains. Buildings and communities have struggled to adjust to the variability and uncertainties of weather and climate. Many resources and building materials that people found abundantly in other locations were scarce on the Plains or were available only through great effort and expense.

A broad range of material options was exploited on the Plains, as elsewhere, when materials suiting local taste were available in a particular locale (either naturally occurring or by importation). Authors such as David Erpestad and David Wood discuss materials used for buildings in specific locations on the Plains in appropriate detail.[4] Earthen-walled (mass-wall) building methods were being used very effectively by indigenous, Native American populations at the time of Euro-Americans' first explorations of the Plains at the turn of the nineteenth century.

In fact, Lewis and Clark's 1804–1806 Corps of Discovery was received at a village of Mandan-Hidatsa earth lodges in the first winter of their exploration. Regionally appropriate traditions of building with rammed earth, adobe, and sod were reintroduced by immigrants with prior experience in Ukraine and continued as late as 1910, using the scant resources that were readily available to create shelter of surprising environmental comfort and cultural sophistication.

As new enclaves and communities were established on the Plains, resources of naturally occurring local stone were exploited, including limestone, sandstone, granite fieldstones and metamorphic quartzite, calcite "chalk rock," and even (occasionally) petrified wood. Locally available stone was harvested early on for foundations and for entire buildings: limestone and flint rock in eastern Kansas, quartzite in eastern South Dakota, and rough sandstone slabs or gathered fieldstones in western North Dakota. Cut stonework and brick masonry (building techniques often associated with high-style academic architecture in Europe and the eastern United States) are found on the Plains from the earliest buildings by itinerant builders to high-style architectural edifices of the Romanesque period and late modernism. Building stone was quarried in a few important locations on the Plains and was later imported, enabling the late-nineteenth-century architecture of the Plains to emulate styles that were popular in distant locations. Immigrant populations who had prior experience with brickwork were attuned to available clay resources, although a shortage of wood for firing kilns limited production of brick somewhat within the region until other fuel sources became available. Nonetheless, when brickyards became established (in brick-making centers like Sioux City, Iowa, Hebron, North Dakota, and Belle Fourche, South Dakota, as well as at local production sites in many communities scattered throughout the Plains), architects and builders rapidly exploited the design potential of this fire-resistant material in civic and commercial buildings. Architectural cast terracotta was another clay material that was imported by rail for cladding and ornament on buildings in the 1910s and 1920s.

As in other settlement regions, oak, hickory, elm, and cottonwood trees were harvested (where wood was readily available) to make building frames and trimwork. The shortage of lumber resources compared with other regions of North America necessitated judicious use of this relatively scarce resource. Indigenous populations of Native Americans from Oklahoma to North Dakota devised wise strategies for using scarce wood resources and even grasses to make shelters that were comfortable, durable, and even transportable. In a few scattered enclaves, builders from European traditions (such as the Finnish Americans and Scandinavian immigrant populations) revived the familiar technology of notched log construction from their homelands. Early French fur traders and Métis on the northern boundary of the Plains employed *pièce en terre, poteaux en terre* (post in the earth), and *pièce sur sole* (posts on edge beam) construction techniques. (These antiquarian building techniques can be observed in the reconstructed Gingras Fur Post state historic site near Walhalla, North Dakota.) German Hungarians and other eastern European people sometimes constructed lightweight frames of wattle and daub (woven branches with stucco plaster). Lightweight, balloon frame construction, widely adopted in all parts of the United States in the 1880s and 1890s (the time when the Plains was being most intensively settled by immigrants), was a lightweight, relatively transportable building technology especially well suited to importation through railhead lumberyards to fabricate boomtown false-fronted commercial buildings on the main streets of many small towns.

Riverboats delivered precious manufactured materials to Great Plains communities in the earliest years. Metal and glass became available on the Plains only after transportation networks had extended the distribution of these industry-intensive materials into the region from the East. The dependency of the railroads on iron and even wood for the construction of rail beds and bridge trestles and for power is especially ironic since the iron horse soon became the conduit that brought these materials onto the Plains. Until the distribution networks were well established, glass and ironwork tended to be reserved for structural applications. Cast iron, wrought iron, and structural steel were used in various combinations for packaged bridge designs on the Great Plains, as elsewhere. Pressed metal found its way into the fabrication of elaborate cornices, window trim, decorative storefronts, and interiors as a less expensive substitute for heavy, hand-cut ornamental stone. As an exterior cladding material over wood-frame buildings, factory-stamped, galvanized pressed sheet metal or "tin" (from manufacturers like Mesker Brothers in Evansville, Indiana, and George Mesker of St. Louis, Missouri, but also from regional manufacturers like Fargo Ornamental Iron and Metal) is surprisingly prevalent on the Great Plains. For less than a third of the cost of stonework, this system of exterior cladding could be easily assembled over a light wood-frame building by any carpenter, working with stock catalog pieces. Pressed metal was especially popular as a system of applied ornament for cornices and trim on classical revival–style commercial buildings after the Chicago Columbian Exposition of 1893.

Naturally occurring materials for portland cement are relatively scarce on the Plains. This scarcity limited the use of concrete as a building material until the transportation network was well established. Nonetheless, for fire-resistant buildings of larger scale, concrete has been extensively used on the Plains since 1915 for building frames and pavements. Because of extensive hand labor for formwork and placement, this heavyweight building technology was used on many public works projects throughout the Great Plains region during the Great Depression. Concrete also played an important role in the built environment through its utilization in the highway transportation system, reflected in U.S. Route 66 through Oklahoma, the Lincoln Highway (U.S. Route 30), and other cross-country thoroughfares that predated the interstate highway system of the 1950s and 1960s. Concrete building construction is closely associated with the expression of postwar modernism in the latter half of the twentieth century.

Other background conditions and circumstances specific to the Great Plains impacted the spread and development of architecture. It would be difficult to overstate the impact of railroads on every aspect of Great Plains architecture, from landownership patterns and speculative town planning to mobility of architects and availability of construction materials. The earliest settlers worked as much as possible with materials at hand that could be harvested directly from their surroundings. Even before railroads, a network of riverboats brought processed industrial goods like cast iron to fledgling towns like Washburn, North Dakota, on the upper Missouri River. Simultaneously with their delivery of new immigrant populations, railroads began delivering materials like iron, glass, and lumber from which more durable communities could be constructed. Railroads encouraged east-to-west development and cultural communication, while patterns of cultural similarity from north to south are far less evident.

Culture and architecture dispersed from earlier-developed towns and urban centers like Kansas City on the eastern boundary of the Plains. Exploitation of mineral resources, oil, coal, grain, cattle, and other commodities fed the transfer of resources from the Plains in exchange for prepackaged artifices of culture from industrial centers. Railroads were the essential lifelines for this two-way exchange of commodities, industrial goods, and culture, and a consequent perception of dependency soon took hold on the Plains. Cycles of economic boom and bust and the general extent to which small towns were speculatively overbuilt by railroad entrepreneurs led to patterns of unevenness and abandonment in the growth of communities. In virtually every newly formed community, the earliest artifices of economic development were the railroad depot and baggage shed, the lumberyard, the grain elevator, and the railroad hotel. Most communities on the Plains were platted and laid out by railroad speculators, who determined the location of commercial lots, schools, and residential neighborhoods. Each railroad company had its own formula for arranging lots and naming streets. Over time, these earliest patterns were extended or obscured in larger, growing communities, but the patterns are still clearly visible in many smaller towns.

INDIGENOUS TRADITIONS OF DISTINCT NATIVE AMERICAN POPULATION GROUPS

Important lessons about the relationship between architecture and culture can be learned from careful study of the indigenous traditions of Native Americans before contact with European immigrants. Several regionally distinct building types developed by Native Americans on the Great Plains were excellent adaptations of available material technologies to the harsh and variable environmental conditions on the Plains. Three principal types of buildings devised by Native Americans on the Plains before contact with the different culture of European immigrants—the earth lodge, the grass house, and the tipi—also reflected indigenous peoples' sacred beliefs. For Native American people, buildings were not just practical forms of shelter, but also repositories for a culturally shared and consistent way of seeing humankind's place within the cosmos. Early scholarship about these sophisticated building types tended to emphasize their material and performance characteristics. More recently an excellent book by Peter Nabokov and Robert Easton gives proper attention to the symbolic and cultural underpinnings connected with the buildings and recognizes that they are an embodiment of cultures that survive in the present and continue to have cultural meaning and relevance transmitted through oral history.[5] In light of their importance and cultural complexity, these buildings are well worth the effort to try to understand them more completely.

From 700 C.E. onward, earth lodges were found throughout the Plains from the Republican River basin of Kansas-Nebraska to the upper Missouri River, where Lewis and Clark were hosted by Mandan-Hidatsa people in the winter of 1804. Earth-lodge dwellings modeled after those of the Pawnee, Mandan-Hidatsa, and Arikara can be seen in reconstructed form at the Knife River Indian Villages National Historic Site in North Dakota. Considerable archaeological investigation has been made of the sedentary lodge village complexes, which eventually were modified with dry-moat and stockade fortifications (as at the On-a-Slant Village and Double-Ditch sites on the upper Missouri). Customarily, erecting the lodges (except for lifting the four principal lodge poles) was principally the responsibility of tribal women. In the historical period, dwelling lodges were generally round, with four main posts that supported a rectangular framework of primary beams and secondary timber supports that extended to the ground. Thick earthen domes were then formed over the framework, enclosing a well-structured and well-ventilated interior large enough to contain food stores and horses in addition to the full range of domestic items. The stable societies that dwelt in these sedentary groupings of buildings practiced advanced agricultural techniques and maintained productive, well-tended gardens nearby.

Another Native dwelling form, the tipi, was highly efficient and transportable and was usually erected in village groupings arrayed in circular configurations. Tipis were used in the southwestern and western regions of North America, where, before the arrival of the Spanish, they were transported by dogs on *travois*. The tipi is the building form most closely associated with indigenous Plains peoples after the time of European contact, especially the mobile Siouan peoples (Lakota-Dakota-Oglala), Cheyenne, Crow, and Blackfeet, who altered the traditional transport technology to utilize horses, which could accommodate much larger conical tipis. So powerful was the attraction of this highly mobile building type that after the 1700s the Cheyenne largely abandoned sedentary earth-lodge culture in favor of a more mobile hunter-warrior social organization. The structural framework of the tipi was based on a circular (or, more accurately, egg-shaped) array of peeled

Inside a lodge at the Knife River Indian Villages National Historic Site. Photo by Jason Lindsey. Courtesy North Dakota Tourism.

lodge poles with either three or four principal poles erected first in sacred orientations. Painted buffalo-skin (and later canvas) covers were decorated based on sacred visions rather than the willfulness of human design. Reconstructions of the tipi building type can be seen at fur-trading reconstructions such as Fort Union National Monument on the North Dakota–Montana border. Traditional decorated tipi skins of hide and canvas are in collections of some regional museums, although display, in many instances, is limited by the objects' sacred associations.

At the time of Francisco de Coronado's incursions in the 1540s, woven, thatched, or braided grass houses were being erected and occupied by the Caddoan-speaking people of the southern Plains, including native Wichita in western Oklahoma. Buffalo-grass houses were constructed in a circular form with sewn thatch bundles over a framework of bent poles, tied ceremonially at the top. The process of building respected a clear division of labor by gender (as it did in most other Native American dwelling types). Shaping domestic space was the social domain of women. Larger versions of grass houses were occasionally used as dance lodges, and this late form of a traditional building was also found in both North and South Dakota. A few traditional grass lodges survived on western Oklahoma's Wichita reservation until about 1915.

Native people created architecture that was both useful and symbolically important. Their buildings were sometimes mobile and portable, were always environmentally well adapted, and reinforced ritualized social relationships, symbolic meanings, and sacred configurations of space. Aspects of their highly successful buildings were occasionally emulated by later settlers on the Plains. Traditional and sacred buildings pose appropriate questions about whether design is a product of the intellectual will of a person who makes the building, or whether design emerges from spiritual sources for which the individual is merely a conduit. For many Native Americans, architecture was (and remains) a principal means by which members of a community grew to better understand enduring cultural relationships. Buildings may be seen as a means of cultural communication, not only as a spatial commodity or an artifact of the past.

Sites that are sacred to Native people (occasionally marked by pictographs, stone markers or *petroforms*, and ceremonial placement of tobacco) are among the important cultural features of the Great Plains. Native Americans on the Plains also built and used a variety of ceremonial structures, including sweathouses, ritual shrine enclosures, covered arbors, and sun-dance lodges. At the turn of the twenty-first century, scholars have written insightfully about an encouraging revival of Native traditions learned from oral cultural traditions. Much more than "myth" or "legend," these oral traditions of transmitting cultural meanings (underpinning the process by which indigenous buildings are constructed) link the making of shelter with prior experience and understanding of the world. Today, interest in the ritual process of constructing Native American dwellings and other building types is being rekindled. Though Native experiences with housing environments constructed by the U.S. government have been broadly unsuccessful, contemporary experience with tribally sponsored education facilities and even casino resorts reflects a somewhat encouraging revival of awareness of buildings as a form of cultural expression and heritage.

REGIONALLY IMPORTANT, FUNCTIONAL BUILDING TYPES OF THE GREAT PLAINS

Waves of European immigrants onto the Plains brought with them familiar folk traditions of constructing buildings and organizing communities. Some immigrants endeavored to form agricultural villages on the Plains for a brief time, but the distinctly American township-range-section method of dividing land according to a strict system of gridded acreages within thirty-six-section townships soon became the prevalent pattern on the landscape. Farms and villages were placed within this unrelenting Cartesian framework. A few divergent approaches were explored, including the development of several expansive, corporate "Bonanza farms" comprised of from 10,000 to 30,000 acres in the Red River valley of North Dakota in the period 1890 to 1910.

Commonplace, functional buildings introduced to the Plains by immigrant cultures matched requirements of a particular type of building with a shape, configuration, and material palette to optimally fulfill that purpose. Some immigrants clung to familiar folkways of constructing barns and farmhouses. Often they applied the available material technology of sod construction to make dugouts, "soddies," rude claim shanties, or earthen-walled buildings. In some instances, much more advanced folk techniques for building with stone, adobe, or straw were employed. Examples of these distinctively Plains techniques survive in only a few locations. As an aid to interpretation, the Lawrence Welk boyhood home near Strasburg, North Dakota, displays its underlying fabric of unfired earthen blocks that were part of the Welk family's heritage as Germans from Russia. Other Germans in eastern Kansas employed locally harvested rubble stone to build houses with visibly distinctive arrangements of rooms, exterior form or roof shape, and patterns of door and window openings. Often these imported traditions are concealed beneath a surface coating of stucco plaster or wood cladding. Remarkable surviving straw-bale houses, built by pioneering families in the northwestern Sand Hills region of Nebraska, have been the subject of recent research interest as an innovative use of a recognized material to solve a critical need in a sustainable way. Scattered surviving examples of folk building techniques give useful insight into the power of culture to influence people's judgments about architecture.

Michael Koop and Steven Ludwig's analysis of German–Russian Folk Architecture in Southeastern South Dakota is an excellent videotape, available from several regional libraries on the Plains, and illustrates the broad range of construction techniques employed by immigrants.[6] Similar folk techniques used throughout the Plains can be found from Kansas to North Dakota. Though the buildings appear simple and are sometimes lumped together under the misnomer of "sod" buildings, they employ and extend the wisdom of prior experience in the harsh environment on the steppes of Russia (including the custom of building with *mistholz* blocks molded from straw and manure). One account of a visitor to the Frank and Veronica Hutmacher stone-slab farmhouse in western North Dakota characterizes the home as warm, comfortable, and sheltering on the coldest winter days and cool and secure against fire and wind in the heat of summer.[7] Vestiges remain of the house's original, worshipful "Lieberherrgottseck" (God's corner) shrine with icons of the Catholic faith. Interior paint colors (e.g., bright pink, deep sky blue, chartreuse) are another good source of insight into the cultural associations of a folk

Lawrence Welk Homestead, Strasburg, North Dakota. Photo by Bruce Wendt. Courtesy North Dakota Tourism.

house. Surviving examples of these powerful and primal folk building traditions are rapidly disappearing from the Plains, and any serious student of the built environment should feel privileged to have the opportunity to experience such buildings firsthand. Regional libraries have endeavored to preserve a visual record of them through collections of historical documentary photographs.

ARCHITECTURE AND THE REALM OF DOMESTIC LIFE IN THE RURAL COUNTRYSIDE

Homestead and timber-claim settlement of farms on the Plains often necessitated construction of a temporary "claim shanty," dugout, or modest sod shelter.[8] The earliest permanent farmhouses generally consisted of simple single-pen or double-pen structures (with one or two rooms, respectively). Throughout the 1800s, T- or L-shaped farmhouse plans were commonplace throughout the Midwest and onto the Plains, with a strong orientation of interior spaces toward the farmyard and advancements in food-processing facilities in the kitchen. The tall American Foursquare or "Cornbelt Cube" farmhouse is far less common (and less environmentally appropriate) on the Plains than it is in the traditional Midwest. Owing to the prevalence of balloon-frame construction and the central role of lumberyards as a source of building materials for virtually every farm home from the 1870s onward, light wood framing is almost universal in farm homes and agricultural outbuildings, as it is for single-family homes in towns on the Plains. Today, ramblers and one-story ranch-style farmhouses are ubiquitous throughout the Great Plains landscape. Even so, the legacy of cultural heritage is well known to farm families on the Plains, and surviving examples of old-fashioned ways of building are still fondly remembered and occasionally shown with pride to young members of future generations.

The farmhouse was much more than a center of domestic life. It was a working building on the farm. Kitchens (or small, detached "summer kitchens" that allowed cooking to be separated from other living spaces in hot weather) served double duty in canning and otherwise preparing foods for storage. Pattern-book architecture had some impact on the design of farm homes at the time of settlement, but the pattern books and pamphlets were much more influential after 1900. In the nineteenth century, pattern books for residential design were widely distributed by architect-builders like A. J. Downing (1815–1852) and George and Charles Palliser & Co. (1878–1911), although these publications seem to have had less application on farms than in rural towns and villages. The Progressive Country Life movement at the start of the twentieth century employed the land-grant university extension service to promote improvements in the dwelling environment of farm families. Publications like Robert Morris Copeland's *Country Life* and pamphlets promulgated by Liberty Hyde Bailey from Cornell University's College of Agriculture soon found their way into extension publications from land-grant universities on the Plains. The idea of domestic science was especially applicable to improving the quality of life for farm families on the Plains. Frequently these design prototypes were modified and adapted to unique local requirements by carpenter-builders or farmers themselves. Popular women's journals were also a source of design ideas for residences in towns and rural settings, as is evidenced by similar pattern houses that crop up in several locations. Perhaps a surprising influence on the process of designing and building rural architecture—houses in particular—was the successful marketing of precut buildings by mail-order suppliers like Sears, Roebuck and Company. Sears houses can be correctly identified by many homeowners, and this heritage is passed along from one generation to the next by word of mouth.

PRACTICALITY AND "SYSTEMATIC" WORKING BUILDINGS

Farmers, ranchers, and other people who live on the rural Plains have gained reputations as tinkerers who are fond of experimenting and refining solutions to practical problems. This same method was applied to their architectural problem solving. Large barns are one of the building types closely associated with mixed farming from the traditional midwestern states, and large barns were very commonplace in most parts of the central and northern Plains, beginning with land booms in the 1850s, 1870s, and 1890s that anticipated forms of agriculture similar to those in the places early settlers had come from. Recognition of the need to create large hay storage mows in livestock barns, for example, led to the development of a wide variety of construction systems. Many such barn-building technologies were even patented and marketed by their inventors through popular journals. They include barns framed with complex wood trusses, glue-laminated Gothic-arched wood timbers, and in recent times, even pole barns and steel-framed loafing sheds with precast concrete feed bunks for livestock. Round livestock barns (often promulgated by agricultural colleges) remain a novelty building type scattered throughout the Plains, but large barns are observed to be rapidly disappearing from the landscape. Today, combination barn/machine sheds, grain storage structures, and Quonsets or other machine storage buildings are the principal functional types on farms. Extension services at many land-grant universities, and even local lumberyards, continue to develop and distribute packaged designs for many agricultural building types.

Though most farmers would scoff at the notion that farm buildings are in any way "architectural," the simplified, functional forms of ensembles of farm buildings are striking on the landscape. Various types of working buildings and specialized storage buildings evolved on farms and in small towns, where they support either the agricultural infrastructure or other aspects of rural community. Architecture of this sort is expected to be functionally well suited to a particular activity. Rural architecture should also be understood to include groupings of farmstead buildings and even alterations to the physical landscape, such as shelterbelt windbreaks and livestock confinement structures. Careful study of these features of the built environment can tell (through their shapes, materials, and construction details) a good deal about how they were envisioned to function for a specialized agricultural purpose.

Adjacent to an active or abandoned rail line, the grain elevator is perhaps the ubiquitous building type most readily associated with the Great Plains. Reflecting its function, an elevator is a vertically structured grouping of bins for storing various small grains, served by an elevator lift mechanism for sorting called a grain leg. Within these broad functional requirements, myriad variations in color, material, shape, arrangement, and construction technology may be noted. From about 1870 until well into the twentieth century, most elevators were built of wood side walls consisting of dimensionally milled lumber laid crib fashion, that is, placed flat and nailed together to contain the outward pressure of grain. In more recent times, many newer grain storage structures have been constructed of combustion-resistant, slip-formed concrete or corrugated steel. Numerous photo essays and publications in the popular press have surveyed this distinctive architectural type and have characterized it as "the skyscraper of the prairie."

Bridges and buildings of engineered efficiency, constructed for practical purposes of mining, telecommunications, water management, and myriad other purposes, also help tell the story of life on the Plains through their prosaic and efficient forms. On the basis of scale alone, coal-fired power plants that feed the power grid from several Plains states, together with the impoundment dams along the Missouri River and other watercourses on the Plains, assert a cultural commitment to harvest and manage scarce resources for export. Another important facet of the architectural fabric of the Great Plains are the lumberyards. A critical type of working building visible on the Plains, they were necessarily large sheds that covered rows of stock and often employed features of style in their ventilation and front offices. Well-written studies have been published that can help guide understanding of commonplace buildings like lumberyards and train depots—buildings that were entwined with the growth and daily commercial exchange of communities on the Plains.[9] All these various types of practical "working" buildings were systematically constructed for functional efficiency and were expected to be economical and straightforward. While efficiency and practicality are values perhaps more pervasively associated with American civilization than with nearly any other culture, people who dwelt on the Plains were especially conscious of these values in their architecture.

EXPRESSION OF COMMUNITY IN THE ARCHITECTURE OF SMALL TOWNS

As various culture groups settled and intermingled on the Great Plains, they applied judgments about the kind of physical environment they wished to inhabit in thoughtful and self-conscious ways in forming coherent communities. Designers, builders, and property owners all made conscious and unconscious choices about scale, context, and expression in their commercial architecture. For example, building an elaborately styled, Romanesque brick bank building on the corner of Main Street in a recently platted railhead town in North Dakota was a way of overtly declaring, "We are making a commitment to the financial success of immigrant farmers who will earn a living from the surrounding area." Socially well-established businesspeople and investors who relocated from Ohio to establish a new community in Kansas probably sought to express stability and social standing in the Episcopal or Methodist churches they built, and eventually in classical revival lodge halls where they could gather with similarly progressive and upwardly mobile business associates to celebrate their status in the community. Civic and commercial buildings that accurately applied principles of architectural style confirmed the good taste and aspirations for success of their builders. City government buildings and county courthouses were prominent opportunities to demonstrate, through their display of architectural style, that an emerging community was optimistic, well connected, and up-to-date in carrying out the business and rituals of the democratic process.

Other public buildings constructed for purposes of education or health care may best be examined by looking at them in historical periods that reflect scale and economic viability of the community, but also changes in thinking about practical matters like lighting, ventilation, sanitation, and physical and intellectual well-being. Because nearly all communities needed a school to assure their viability, architects tended to work in a systematic way in solving similar problems from one place to the next while trying to assure that each community retained a distinctive identity and sense of local pride. Planning of schools and hospitals was substantially influenced by national publications and civic movements to improve social institutions. Because architects who were versed in the latest thinking about these building functions tended to design several such buildings, similarities of building form, style, and material are often evident. Architect Charles Shaver (1899–1970), for example, executed a substantial amount of school-building design work in Kansas, and other architects who worked regionally tended to specialize in a similar way. Designing projects that were somewhat "repetitive" also enabled architects to reliably assure a school or hospital board of probable costs for construction.

Commercial buildings of Main Street in most small Plains towns were typically limited to two or three stories in scale. Larger regional service centers are widely spaced and conspicuously different in architectural scale. Design principles of commercial buildings on the Plains provided a canvas against which architects and property owners could apply the latest architectural styles in the interest of merchandising success. Richard Longstreth has authored an insightful reference handbook for discerning design principles of Main Street buildings and interpreting the buildings of Main Street from the standpoint of their form and scale, stylistic period, and social factors that entered into their builders' judgments.[10]

THE REALM OF PLEASURE AND RECREATION

The prosaic, practical side of Plains life and architecture might tempt people to overlook types of commonplace and architecturally designed buildings whose principal purpose is to fulfill the human need for recreation, enjoyment, fantasy, and whimsy. These are not cultural values that are immediately associated with Great Plains life, but an undercurrent is apparent on the Plains that seeks such diversions from the hardship of daily life. Buildings constructed for tourism and outdoor recreation capture people's attention in wayside parks and along highway thoroughfares like the famous Route 66. Functional building types like the diner, motor hotel, and drive-through restaurant evolved on the Plains to meet the needs of automobile travelers. In the 1920s, an impressive summer resort connection existed between Oklahoma and Minnesota. Buildings along the Lincoln Highway (U.S. 30) and U.S. Route 66 chronicle out-migration in the 1930s and tourism in the 1950s. Since the 1960s, the interstate highway system has reshaped the landscape of the Great Plains in a manner comparable to the transcontinental railroad a hundred years earlier. Today universal buildings emerge and evolve along the corridor of interstate highways, where space is treated strictly as a commodity, and where architecture is sold by the square foot.

Eccentricity and idiosyncratic building designs for dance pavilions, casinos, and resorts all defy the practical, prosaic side of human nature. On the Plains, such buildings provide a whimsical diversion from the austere realities of daily life. Franchised gasoline service stations were devised as systematic solutions for each of the various oil-company chains at a time when "full service" was a requirement and expectation for long-distance, cross-country travel. The scale and range of services offered by these working buildings—many of which are now abandoned relics of the past—capture a visitor's imagination with respect to a vanished lifestyle in remote and isolated settings. Opera houses and their successors, movie theaters, are a conspicuous part of the architectural infrastructure of many communities. The principal purposes of these recreational and cultural buildings were to bring entertainments from the outside and to feed fantasies of local residents. Such buildings often embody outlandish and unexpected styles like the moderne in otherwise pragmatic community settings. Dance pavilions or ballrooms (well known to locals by names like the Cotillion Ballroom, Red Willow Lake Pavilion, Sokol Park Hall, White Eagle and Archer Ballrooms, and Rainbow Gardens) were places where residents of the Plains gathered to escape isolation and celebrate music and dance as forms of social communality. Whether catering to rock-and-roll, polka, or country and western, these buildings (and the extent to which they are locally and regionally known) tell something of the cultural aspirations and recreational diversions of people who lived in isolated Plains settings.

Another institutional aspect of cultural infrastructure on the Great Plains is the consistent presence of fraternal organizations and lodge hall buildings that often became a center of community social life. Lodge members of the Ancient Free and Accepted Masons (especially Scottish Rite lodges), the International Order of Oddfellows, the Order of the Eastern Star, and the Knights of Columbus were all influential movers and shakers of the community. Other communities reinforced ethnic heritage by establishing meeting halls for Czech/Bohemian lodges or Sons of Norway. If a town could not afford a separate opera house, the lodge hall often performed double duty in serving this need. During the first fifty years of Great Plains settlement, it was essential for local architects to be well connected through lodge membership and other similar social affiliations. For the common traveler and local businessperson alike, United Commercial Travelers (UTC) sample rooms were often connected with a railroad hotel. As one of the most reliable sources of merchandise to growing rural communities, traveling salesmen carried sample cases from which they could display physical samples of merchandise available on order to local business merchants. Buildings of this type cross perceived boundaries between commercial, civic, and recreational purposes.

EMERGENCE OF ARCHITECTURE AS A PROFESSIONAL DISCIPLINE

On the Great Plains, as in other regions of the United States, there was a tendency over time for an increasing number of buildings to be designed by academically trained architects. Academic or "high-style" architecture refers to buildings designed by architects with this kind of specialized training. Making such a distinction should not imply that vernacular buildings lack beauty, elegance, or sophistication, but merely that as buildings have become larger and more complex, they have tended to be designed by persons with some form of specialist training. The earliest architects who worked in communities on the Great Plains gained their specialized expertise in a hands-on manner, becoming respected as architects by earning a reputation for quality in design and construction. Building designers often started their careers as carpenters or cabinetmakers, then became contractor-builders, and later identified themselves as qualified architects. Early architects gained pragmatic experience through this school of hard knocks that was sufficient to make the transition from builder to designer of buildings. As builders moved from one geographic region to another, they often changed careers and moved upward on the hierarchy of professionalization by identifying themselves as architects.

Each new generation of architects was influenced by their educational experiences and their judgments about changing context. Just prior to 1900, working alongside (and in competition with) architects who emerged from a hands-on training experience were architects who had been educated at established schools in Europe and in the eastern United States (principally Cornell, Harvard, and MIT). These academically trained architects recognized the opportunity to ply their art on large-scale public and institutional buildings like governmental and university buildings, places of worship, fraternal lodges, and commercial buildings. Prior to 1900, architects came to the Great Plains almost entirely from somewhere outside the region. They brought with them lessons and experiences with style they had adopted in other settings. Joseph E. Rosatti (1888–1968), influenced by his work experience with Louis Sullivan in Michigan, brought with him to North Dakota a way of designing that he applied to several small-town banks. Architects' careers and the work they created were largely molded by their education and early professional experience.

After the period of in-migration (when all architect builders came to the Plains with experience gained elsewhere), a generation of architects arose who were born and bred on the Plains and who supplemented their applied experience by earning a degree or certificate in mechanic arts or architectural drafting at state land-grant universities that emphasized "agriculture and mechanic arts." The educational trend for architects in the 1870s and 1880s was based more strictly on theoretical classroom-studio architectural education, modeled after the Beaux Arts *atelier* system by which European architects had been educated. Programs of this type emerged first at eastern schools like Cornell and were then emulated by schools in the Midwest and Great Plains (e.g., Iowa State, Minnesota, St. John's, and Kansas State). The work of academically trained architects, who learned the process of building design from programs of architecture at established academic institutions, reflects the trend after 1900 toward increasingly specialized training in the "learned professions."

As schools of applied art and science were established in the Plains region (largely promulgated by the Morrill Act of 1862, which provided for land-grant universities), programs in architecture began to be established in academic settings like Kansas State University (1877), the University of Nebraska (1894), Oklahoma State University (1909), and North Dakota State University (1914). At about the same time or soon thereafter, architectural programs with a core emphasis on humanities and fine arts were established at the University of Kansas (1913) and the University of Oklahoma (1926). Given the sparseness of architect-designed buildings on the Great Plains landscape, it is somewhat surprising to find so many professional programs in architecture at institutions of higher education on the Plains. By the late twentieth century, practice of the profession of architecture was effectively regulated by law in all states in the United States and limited, for all intents and purposes, to persons who graduated from accredited university programs.

HOW ARCHITECTS WORKED: HIGH-STYLE ARCHITECTURE AS A FORM OF CULTURAL EXPRESSION

Academically designed architecture spread onto the Plains from established seats of wholesale, retail, and commercial enterprise, fanning out from its starting points like stains spreading on a carpet. Owing to their earlier dates of statehood, eastern Kansas and Nebraska were the first areas of the Plains to have a well-established architectural infrastructure, followed by settlements in the eastern Dakotas and in Oklahoma after the Land Rush of 1889. From early communities perched on the eastern edge of the Plains, architecture spread westward along with other features of settlement, following primarily the transportation routes of the railroads.

Several factors motivated the spread of architecture as a learned and specialized profession onto the Great Plains as an aspect of culture. At the time when most communities were being founded on the Plains, around 1860 in Kansas and Nebraska, the 1870s in Dakota Territory, and 1905 in Oklahoma, one factor was the growing awareness of competition from established communities in the states just to the east. After the 1910s, marketing and delivery of architectural services changed when automobiles improved access to communities off the railroad main line. Coinciding with the first architectural licensing laws (beginning in 1917 in North Dakota and as late as 1949 in Kansas), practice laws attempted to draw a line in the sand that would exclude perceived "carpetbagging" architects based in more easterly states from competing on the Plains.

The broad range of social and cultural affiliations brought architects into contact with their peers in a community and, at times, served as an entrée into neighboring towns and cities. Members of one church's building committee will invariably seek advice from a neighboring congregation that has recently gone through the process of seeking and selecting an architect. Association of an architect with a few buildings of the same type (churches, schools, and libraries, among others) at times made a specialist out of a general practitioner. Schools and courthouses particularly lent themselves to repetition. Architect T. D. Allen (1829–1924), a specialist from outside the region in the 1890s, peppered the region with school designs, many of them virtually identical. Charles E. Bell (c. 1870–1932) eventually parlayed his experience with repetitive courthouse designs into the commission for the South Dakota state capitol building in Pierre. A sound strategy for marketing architectural services was important to establishing the profession of architecture on the Great Plains. Architects were mobile, but the predominant movement was from east to west, along with the spread of other manifestations of culture. During the first hundred years, most communities on the Plains were barely large enough to sustain a full-time architectural practice, so many architects utilized rail connections for more regionally distributed outreach to satellite communities.

Buildings can be retrospectively classified based on stylistic traits. Beyond the fundamental issue of taxonomy, though, styles often embody social and cultural values and preferences. Architects and property owners often made their design judgments based not so much on "what style is popular this year" as on their answer to the aesthetic question they sought to explore through achitecture, "Does the design of my building reflect the values of durability, permanence, whimsy, progressive thinking?" or whatever the shared cultural values were that the builder sought to convey to neighbors and the larger community. Architects tended to graft their work onto a style that was individually familiar to them, a design style imported and applied to a new regional context. On the Great Plains, style took root and flourished in response to conditions of "local soil" and distinctive characteristics of communities as they established themselves in the region.

PREVALENT ARCHITECTURAL STYLES ON THE PLAINS

Architectural styles are not a strictly regional phenomenon. In fact, nationally popular styles are based, in part, on the dates when that region was settled and when major economic booms or calamitous disasters took place. (Growth spurts in buildings often followed on the heels of natural or human-caused disasters.) Labels for architectural styles have gradually emerged through scholarly analysis and have become quite precise in their meanings. Like other cultural trends that transform as they spread, architectural styles may be seen as applied motifs in many Great Plains buildings, where a degree of eclectic mixing and liberal combining of stylistic features occurs. Architectural firms often exhibited a preference for certain familiar styles, based on the architects' education and the range of information to which they were exposed. The influence of each style on architecture of the region roughly corresponded with the chronological sequence in which styles emerged nationally.

Various design characteristics ranging from material details and construction techniques to abstractions of proportion, rhythm, and scale, all combine to make up what architectural historians refer to as an architectural style. Owing to the rapid pace of advancing settlement, styles that had been fashionable for much longer periods of time in established communities to the east were employed for only five or ten years on the Plains. Architect-designed landmark buildings tell the story of architecture as one visible form of cultural expression that reflects changing circumstances throughout the decades when communities were established on the Plains.

CIVIC INFRASTRUCTURE AND CLASSICAL REVIVAL ARCHITECTURE IN THE EARLY PERIOD (1860–1890)

Throughout the 1860s and 1870s, architecturally designed buildings were only rarely constructed on the Plains. The earliest buildings, such as railroad hotels, military forts, rural churches, and schools, were almost invariably designed and built by itinerant craftsmen. Academically styled buildings designed by architects began to appear in eastern Kansas and Nebraska in the 1860s, when national tastes tended to prefer buildings with tall proportions and applied ornament, like the Victorian Gothic, French Second Empire, and Italianate. These styles were reflected in the first territorial capitol buildings and in early state capitols. The Kansas state capitol, for example, was built in phases from 1866 to 1879 and was completed with a crowning dome only in 1903. This patient, "build it as you grow" mentality is reflected in other Great Plains state capitols from Oklahoma to North Dakota. A Supreme Court wing was eventually added to the North Dakota capitol in 1982 (Foss Associates and Ritterbush Associates, architects), and the dome of the Oklahoma capitol was completed in 2003.

State capitols and other state institution campuses were often begun without a clear architectural vision of the end product, so much of the order and organization of capitol complexes was imposed after the fact by the discipline of landscape architecture. Designed order and master planning began to be applied to these campuses in the 1890s, largely through the influence of academically trained landscape architects like H.W.S. Cleveland (1814–1906), who is often associated with Frederick Law Olmsted. Cleveland had a profound influence on designed landscapes and ordered beauty of campuses in the region, as did the later landscape architecture firm of Anthony Morrell (?–1924) and Arthur Nichols (1881–1970) in the 1920s and 1930s. In the 1880s and 1890s, Cleveland designed picturesque Elmwood Park and Forest Lawn Cemetery in Omaha, Highland Cemetery in Junction City, Kansas, and the National Military Veterans' Home in Leavenworth, Kansas. At about the same time, regional landscape designer Maximillian Kern (dates unknown) developed an innovative design for the land-grant university campus at Kansas State University, a precedent that influenced thinking in the region for the layout of campuses from state capitol grounds to universities and state mental hospitals.

In the 1880s, buildings for state institutions were much prized and sought-after architectural commissions. Competition for such public facilities was intense between communities. Campus complexes of state institutions were extremely important opportunities to proclaim the commitment of the community and the backing of state governmental and business leaders. Communities fought and squabbled for state institutions. Newly formed state governments in each of the recently formed Plains states were in a position to virtually guarantee success for emerging communities where they located state institutions. Historicist styles expressed an aspiration to the "proven" architectural tastes and cultural values of established European civilizations, combined with a fondness for "filigree" on the part of Scots-Irish New Englanders who were among the first speculative investors in public infrastructure on the Plains. (For example, see the substantial body of work by Wallace L. Dow [1844–1911] on the campus of the University of South Dakota in Vermillion, the state penitentiary at Sioux Falls, and the state mental hospital in Yankton.) State mental hospitals, disease sanitoria, county poor farms, and old soldiers' homes were all planned from the dual standpoint of efficiently using public dollars and a keen awareness of Progressive notions that a well-designed setting could foster health and well-being.

A striking number of state institutions were established on the Great Plains between 1870 and 1910. Stylistically, the proclivity in state institutions and campus complexes was toward expressing durability—not just proclaiming what was fashionable, but what was solidly fashionable, a taste for imposing buildings that sought to express permanence. Architects focused their clients' dollars on building instant tradition and creating a strong sense of place almost overnight. As the regional economy rebounded after 1900, architectural commissions for important public projects revived. In the first decade of the century, and continuing to about World War I, neoclassical motifs prevailed for civic and commercial architectural tastes in most Plains communities. Notable exceptions include the South Dakota veterans' Old Soldiers' Home in Hot Springs (designed in a simplified mission style by architect Thomas R. Kimball [1862–1934], with G. E. Kessler [1862–1923] of Kansas City serving as landscape architect), and the Sullivan-influenced designs of William L. Steele (1875–1945). Kimball also had significant regional influence on campus planning and landscape design.

The aspiration for healthful campus environments after 1905 reflected a progressive "domestic science" approach. Space between buildings, ventilation egress, and lighting all demonstrate increased awareness of recurrent influenza epidemics and other public health issues related to the built environment. Outside specialists were brought in, and design was influenced by progressivism, public health issues, fresh air, sunshine, and air movement. Dormitories were placed based on perceived health benefits. The regional firm of Morrell and Nichols devised landscape master plans for many state campuses in the 1920s, 1930s, and 1940s.

COMMUNITIES TAKING HOLD: THE SECOND PERIOD OF ARCHITECTURE ON THE PLAINS (1890–1910)

If the choice of architectural style was an open question before 1890, it was largely settled by the emergence of the Romanesque revival style popularized by Henry Hobson Richardson (1838–1886) and regional architects who emulated his design principles. Richardsonian Romanesque, with its half-arches, heavily textured and aggressively patterned surfaces, and logically functional interior planning, is arguably the first truly "American" architectural style. The Richardsonian style gained widespread popularity across the eastern United States and Midwest, from whence many town builders on the Plains originated. Atchison, Kansas, is especially well represented by buildings in this style, including the Atchison County Courthouse, the Atchison Post Office, and a magnificent railroad depot for the Atchison, Topeka, and Santa Fe line.

Kansas architect Charles W. Squires (1851–1934) designed numerous, excellent buildings in the Romanesque style in this period (First Presbyterian Church in Emporia), as did the firm of Proudfoot and Bird (Wichita Old City Hall), Charles Sedgwick (1871–1946?) from Minneapolis (old Arkansas City, Kansas High School), and Louis S. Curtiss (1865–1924), chief architect for the Atchison, Topeka, and Santa Fe railroad. Romanesque architecture made effective use of locally available building stone in eastern Kansas, as it did in the vicinity of Sioux Falls, South Dakota (e.g., the superb Minnehaha County Old Federal Courts building, Wallace L. Dow, architect). On the northern Plains, excellent Richardsonian buildings like the Grand Forks, North Dakota, Metropolitan Opera House and Morton County Courthouse in Mandan, North Dakota, were the exception rather than the rule. The fact that so many well-designed Romanesque buildings survive today is a testament both to their handsomeness and their rugged durability. At the turn of the twenty-first century, much of this architectural heritage has been renovated and adaptively used for new functions, as is the case with the Cass Gilbert–designed Northern Pacific Railroad depot in Fargo (1893; renovated 1983). Gilbert (1858–1934) was one of America's foremost architects at the turn of the century, with design responsibility for New York's Woolworth Building, the Minnesota state capitol, and numerous federal and civic commissions.

Murals of corn and grains cover the Corn Palace in Mitchell, North Dakota. Each harvest time the murals are replaced with fresh corn and a new theme of pictures. Eleven different shades of corn are used in the designs. Courtesy South Dakota Tourism.

The most architecturally influential event of all in 1893 was the impact on public thinking that resulted from the Columbian World Exposition that year in Chicago, the occasion for which its principal architect Daniel H. Burnham (1846–1912) coined the admonition "make no small plans." The Columbian Exposition was a world's fair that embodied a great many architectural aspects. The fairgrounds were planned and organized as the best early example of the planning principles of the City Beautiful movement, focusing on the purposeful and formal relationship between public buildings. Each state constructed a demonstration pavilion at the fair to show the economic bounty and commercial potential of the state. These architectural conceptions were revived in popular buildings like the iconic 1892 Corn Palace (Mitchell, South Dakota), and other grain palaces built to promote agriculture on the Plains.

Architecturally, the Columbian Exposition used classical revival motifs as a celebration of the republican values and democratic virtues of earlier civilizations. It would be difficult to overstate the extent to which this exposition struck a chord with visitors to Chicago from all over the Plains and influenced the style of buildings for at least the next thirty years. (At the time of the fair, Chicago architect Louis Sullivan declared that the conservative vocabulary of the Columbian Exposition would set back American architecture for at least fifty years.) There is no denying, though, the extent to which the "Great White City" of Corinthian columns, domes, colonnades, and classically inspired cornices at the Columbian Exposition appealed to laypeople on the Plains, who set about working with their architects to liberally apply this vocabulary, largely in the form of pressed metalwork that reproduced stone decorative motifs in a much more economical way.

From 1900 to the beginning of the Great Depression in 1929, public architectural commissions glorified democratic virtues throughout the Plains through the design of county courthouses, federal courthouses and post offices, and Carnegie libraries. As architects perfected the "formula" for these commissions, firms like Beuchner and Orth executed more than a dozen classically inspired courthouses throughout North Dakota. Carnegie libraries, gifts to individual communities in the name of steel baron Andrew Carnegie, are visible and prized investments in learning and culture as well as distinctive and well-detailed buildings architecturally. Regionally important architects designed a series of diminutive library buildings, many of which continue to serve their communities nearly one hundred years after they were built. These buildings are an example of architects playing freely with a well-understood vocabulary, rather than evidence of stylistic mimicry.

BUILDINGS OF RELIGIOUS FAITH

In addition to their spiritual purpose, church buildings reflect a range of cultural and intellectual meanings and civic relationships. Churches were designed based on liturgical rites and religious traditions of the particular faith, often with a strong connection to ethnic and cultural origins. From the earliest years of Euro-American presence on the Plains, some churches were designed by architects based on stylistic precedents, other churches were based on standard designs disseminated from the central diocesan or synod office, and still others were handcrafted based on the design judgment of a carpenter-craftsman.

From about 1890 to 1920, a group of surprising buildings emerged on the Plains that deserves special mention. Series of similar, but varied, church buildings were designed and built throughout this period as the product of rich collaborations between architects, church leaders, and builder-craftsmen based on traditional liturgical rituals.

Rural Churches

Early rural church buildings reinforced ethnic distinctions, group identity, rank, and social priority among institutions. A typical account is that of a small, rural Norwegian Lutheran church (built near LaMoure, North Dakota, in the 1880s) whose congregation ordered stained-glass windows that were fabricated in Minneapolis, shipped to Fargo by the Northern Pacific Railroad, and then transported to the church site by horse and wagon. The North LaMoure Lutheran Church was demolished in 2002, and the stained-glass windows were rededicated in a new, multidenominational church building in more urban West Fargo. Church artifacts have been similarly relocated from other demolished church buildings to newly constructed Episcopal, Catholic, and Protestant churches elsewhere in the region, including the contemporary Charles Moore/Arthur Anderson design of Fargo's Gethsemane Cathedral. In 2000, the National Trust for Historic Preservation and its statewide affiliate Preservation North Dakota initiated a program, "Prairie Churches of North Dakota," to encourage preservation of rural churches as an irreplaceable feature of Great Plains culture and architectural heritage.

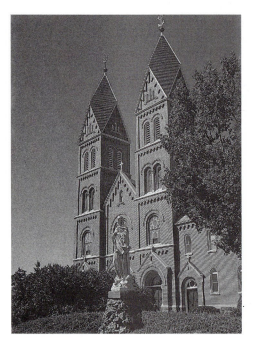

Assumption Abbey, Richardton, North Dakota. Photo by Dawn Charging. Courtesy North Dakota Tourism.

Notable among these was the collaboration on the northern Plains between architect George Hancock (1849–1924), Rev. B. F. Cooley, and stonemason Andrew Maconachie to build a series of picturesque, handcrafted Episcopal stone churches in the pure English Gothic style. A somewhat comparable collaboration evolved between Catholic missionary priest Vincent Wehrle (1855–1941), later bishop of the Bismarck diocese, and Milwaukee architect Anton Dohmen (1861–1951). Similarly close working relationships can be illustrated elsewhere on the Plains between clerics, congregations, and architects. These fertile collaborations are fascinating object lessons about the relationship between specialized designers and the desire of a local congregation to express its own culture, heritage, and liturgical traditions.

Monumentally scaled churches were built in unexpectedly remote locations to anticipate waves of immigration and to appeal to German-speaking Catholic immigrants from Hungary, Ukraine, and the Volga region. The Wehrle-Dohmen collaboration, in particular, produced several local churches and two monumental buildings of landmark significance, Assumption Abbey in Richardton, North Dakota (1906), and St. Anthony of Padua Church in Hoven, South Dakota. These expansive and powerful buildings in Great Plains landscapes that most people would regard as remote may be seen as precedents for the austere modernist work of internationally renowned architect Marcel Breuer (1902–1981) at Annunciation Priory (1963) and the University of Mary (1968) on the bluffs of the Missouri River south of Bismarck.

Particularly in churches built before 1950, the religious denomination can often be discerned by the layout and stylistic embellishments of the church building. While many Protestant and most Catholic churches were based on the axial, linear basilica plan, there are interesting exceptions, such as the Greek cross Orthodox churches built by Ukrainians and Germans from Russia. "Akron Auditorium"–plan churches were organized radially, with flexible room dividers, and provided spaces for the social service mission of these congregations. An excellent example of one such Akron Auditorium–plan Methodist church can be found in Marysville, Nebraska, but other examples abound, often recognizable by their distinctive corner entrances. A noteworthy and precedent-setting religious building is the Akron Auditorium–plan Methodist Episcopal church in Aberdeen, South Dakota, by the Cincinnati firm of Brown and Davis (1908).

HOPEFULNESS AND THE GREAT CREATIVE IMPULSES OF THE 1910s, 1920s, AND 1930s

Largely because residents of the Great Plains perceived (with much legitimate cause) that they were subjects of economic exploitation by eastern, urban, and banking interests, Plains states were formed in the crucible of Progressive politics, with a view toward protecting Plains inhabitants from unfair exploitation. Rethinking the rules of government and social relationships led indirectly to rethinking architecture as part of the Progressive Country Life movement. Scientific living and awakening of aspirations for "the good life" caused architects to approach design with a clearer view of how well the building would support activities of its users and improve their quality of life. Cultural manifestation of social values through architecture is visible in the state mill and elevator, state brewery, and numerous power and grain cooperatives formed on the Great Plains. Much of the architectural legacy of the twentieth century reflects these regionally distinct relationships on the Plains.

THE PRAIRIE SCHOOL AND ITS INFLUENCES

The 1910s were a time of growing confidence in new styles and new ways of thinking about architecture, influenced by ideas of the Prairie school. With Frank Lloyd Wright (1867–1959) as its principal proponent, the Prairie School Movement advocated a strong emphasis on horizontality, integration of mechanical systems, new systems of geometric ornament based on symbolic treatment of vegetative forms, and organizations of activities that were only loosely suggested by space-dividing partitions. Wright and the major regional firm of Purcell and Elmslie (1907–1921) professed that architecture of this character was well suited to the horizontal landscapes of the midwestern prairie and the Great Plains. In the teens, Wright executed projects like the Henry J. Allen House in Wichita (1917–1919), and Purcell and Elmslie was responsible for the O. L. Bronson and Company Bank in Mitchell, South Dakota, but their greater influence was probably the impact their work had on second-tier regional firms that studied the work of the Prairie school masters in publications like the *Inland Architect* and the *Western Architect*.

William Gray Purcell (1880–1965) and George Grant Elmslie (1868–1952) executed a substantial amount of very influential work on the northern Plains, in both cities and smaller communities. Progressive-era buildings spread from Chicago under the influence of architectural giants like Louis Sullivan (1856–1924) and Frank Lloyd Wright. Progressive-era, Sullivanesque-Wrightian designs were carried out by second- or third-tier disciples of that movement. These firms and individual architects may have had no direct connection, but were inspired by published literature in journals. They then applied the design principles in their own projects, like Perkins and McWayne's Lennox, South Dakota, City Hall (1920) and William A. Wells' Colcord Building in Oklahoma City (1910). In a somewhat more politically detached, retrospectively classical revival vein, architect Solomon A. Layton (dates unknown) also designed the first phases of the Oklahoma state capitol building beginning in 1917. From his practice based in Sioux City, William L. Steele designed the Woodbury County Courthouse, a city hall building for Holdrige, Nebraska, and the Charles Mix County Courthouse in Lake Andes, South Dakota.

Architects were relatively mobile, and those who established practices on the Plains during the Progressive era did so by informed judgment. William A. Wells' (1878–1938) path to a career in architecture may have been set early in life by his

Nebraska State Capitol Building. Courtesy Nebraska Division of Tourism.

maternal grandfather, a builder in Iowa. By 1901, Wells was taking classes at the Chicago Art Institute, giving his local mailing address as "c/o Frank Lloyd Wright's architecture studio in Oak Park." Wells relocated from Chicago to Omaha and later to Oklahoma Territory, where he designed the Oklahoma County Courthouse (1904–1905) in the Richardsonian Romanesque style, befitting its stability and permanence as a public edifice. A short time later he designed the Pioneer Telephone Building under the influence of the Chicago school/Sullivanesque (1907). Wells also designed houses in the style of George W. Maher (1864–1926), skillful and influential innovator of Prairie school motifs and systems of ornament, so he was influenced by very eclectic architectural tastes.

A good deal of architectural innovation flowered on the Plains in the 1920s, including projects inspired by Wright himself (Richard Lloyd Jones house in Tulsa by Frank Lloyd Wright, 1929), a suburban Kansas City, Kansas, house by Clarence E. Shepard (1870–1949), and Coughlin Campanile at University of South Dakota, Brookings (Robert A. Perkins [1882–?]; Perkins and McWayne, 1929). This new direction in "streamlined" architectural design was propelled by projects like First United Lutheran Church of Grand Forks, North Dakota, and Boston Avenue United Methodist Church in Tulsa (Rush, Endacott, Rush, 1929; a project for which the budding designer Bruce Goff was reportedly the lead architect) and culminated in Bertram Grosvenor Goodhue's (1869–1924) art deco remarkably pure design for the new Nebraska state capitol (1922–1932). As the result of a national design competition, architects Holabird and Root were commissioned to work with William F. Kurke (1889–1965) and Joseph Bell deRemer (1871–1944) on a simplified moderne high-rise tower for the new North Dakota state capitol building (completed in 1934). Given the horizontality of the landscape, many visitors to the Plains find it surprising that Lincoln, Nebraska, and Bismarck, North Dakota, display such strikingly tall skyscrapers for state government.

Though the decade of the 1930s was a time of hardship in all parts of the country, effects of the Great Depression were almost certainly more profound on the Great Plains than anywhere else. Out-migration, abandonment, public works, and land reclamation all had impacts on the architecture of the Plains region. Architects struggled to survive by competing for projects promulgated by the federal government under Franklin Roosevelt's various New Deal programs. Programs like the Works Progress Administration (WPA) and Public Works Administration (PWA) resulted in a great many architecturally sensitive buildings that survive today, but are sadly underappreciated. Site-cast concrete swimming pool structures, split-stone park shelters, and other similar (usually small) constructions are ubiquitous in small towns throughout the Plains, and a careful eye can pick them out.

Remarkable WPA rustic buildings at Custer State Park in South Dakota (Harold Spitznagel, architect, 1938), depression-era projects by Thomas R. Kimball (1862–1934), WPA moderne recreational facilities like S. Marius Houkum's (1891–1980) Fargo Auditorium and swimming pool, and the marvelous Turner Falls State Park in Oklahoma and Turtle River State Park in North Dakota all provides insight into the range of design skills brought to these public works projects by capable and talented architects. Depression-era buildings of the WPA, PWA, and FERA agencies and landscapes constructed under the auspices of the Civilian Conservation Corps (CCC) illustrate how the cultural expression of architecture can uplift and ennoble. The system of windbreak shelterbelts that still contributes to managing erosion on all parts of the Plains is a human-made landscape design feature that grew directly out of the "dirty thirties." Some of the most important regional work that synthesizes architecture and landscape architecture is evident in the depression-era WPA and CCC park designs and recreational building designs that bring together the Arts and Crafts–inspired rustic vernacular in a wholly original way that honestly reflects the uniqueness of regional and even local culture. Thankfully, a handful of the investments made in public infrastructure during the 1930s are becoming appreciated once again.

INTERNATIONALISM AND AMERICAN ARCHITECTURE AS WORLD CULTURE

As a consequence of rationing and the uncertainties of World War II, very little building construction occurred on the Plains during most of the 1940s. The few exceptions from before and after the war include the Wright-influenced Barry Byrne (1883–1967) design of Ss. Peter and Paul Catholic Church in Pierre, South Dakota. Also noteworthy is the 1948 streamlined moderne design of the Crocker Theater in Ulysses, Kansas, identified by David Sachs and George Ehrlich as "a well-preserved example of the pragmatic but optimistic commercial architecture of the post-war period."[11]

The 1950s and 1960s gave rise to new directions in architecture that expressed cultural values growing out of postwar prosperity and opportunity. Edward J. Schulte's (dates unknown) design of the Salina, Kansas, Sacred Heart Cathedral (1952–1953) is well proportioned and energetic. The H.C. Price Tower in Bartlesville, Oklahoma, is a building of international reputation, the most complete and sophisticated high-rise building ever completed by Frank Lloyd Wright. Bruce Goff continued to experiment with avant-garde uses of material and unfamiliar, organic building forms (like the Bavinger House in Norman, Oklahoma, 1955) that intentionally challenge public taste. Goff's architecture shows another side in appealing to popular tastes and values through his design for Hopewell Baptist Church (Oklahoma City, 1953), which uses oil-field pipe assembled into exterior trusses by members of the congregation. This unconventional church design is reminiscent of Native American traditions and at the same time invokes the industrial craft of oil-field workers.

The concluding forty years of the twentieth century were characterized by larger-scale architecture that was more corporate, both in the needs and preferences of its clients and in the more complex, team-oriented manner by which large architectural commissions were accomplished. As often as not, the name of an in-

Frank Lloyd Wright's H.C. Price Tower, Bartlesville, Oklahoma. Courtesy Oklahoma State Historical Society for Preservation Oklahoma.

dividual designer is no longer associated with a particular building. Instead, the name of a large architectural firm or joint venture with multiple firms conceals the design contributions of individual architects. This is true of excellent design work done regionally and internationally by firms like Dana-Larson-Roubal and Helmut-Obata-Kassebaum. The work of some architects has run counter to the trend. Among them are the Oklahoma City Theater (1970) by John Johansen (1916–), the whimsically Wrightian King Louie Bowling Alley in Overland Park, Kansas (Manuel Morris and Associates, 1948 and 1965), and even Michael Graves' (1934–) unbuilt proposal for a Fargo-Moorhead Cultural Bridge (perhaps the best-publicized building that was never constructed on the Plains). Philip Johnson's (1906–) design of a Lincoln, Nebraska, residence and his 1964 modernist design for the Sheldon Memorial Gallery at the University of Nebraska at Lincoln are period pieces of the modern era. I.M. Pei Partners' 1976 National Bank of Commerce in Omaha explores principles of the modernist movement in a more intriguing way. Sir Norman Foster's (1935–) 1994 addition to the 1931 art deco Joslyn Art Museum in Omaha is a refreshing study of material, texture, and the play of natural light on rich surfaces.

The last quarter of the twentieth century was also an important time for a new initiative to celebrate the rich variety of Great Plains architecture. As a way of extending the life of architecturally important buildings from the past, important historic preservation and adaptive use projects have been realized, like the revitalization of Omaha's warehouse district, the adaptation of Fargo's International Harvester branch house as a new home for regional collections of the Plains Art Museum, and the adaptive use of historic train depots in many Great Plains communities from Minot, North Dakota, to Shawnee, Oklahoma. These are all excellent examples of communities recognizing a valuable and useful cultural resource and then extending the life of culturally invested architecture through wise resource conservation.

The growing interest in preservation of historic buildings reinforces several important themes of regional architecture on the Plains. First, preservation wisely conserves scarce resources by extending the useful life of buildings. Second, preserving landmark buildings gives a community its unique identity and encourages continuity in the architectural fabric of community. Visible buildings that are part of a community's shared heritage (like the Corn Palace or a Carnegie library or many rural churches) enhance opportunities for future generations to celebrate regional cultural identity. Despite American culture's fondness for things that are new and that show people are in step with other up-and-coming metropolitan centers, there is growing awareness that buildings hold greater cultural meaning than is embodied solely by the space they contain.

LANDSCAPE ARCHITECTURE

Though it has been touched upon earlier, as a separate discipline landscape architecture has its own visible presence on the Plains, ranging from land division and town planning to campuses for institutional buildings to high-style design by nationally recognized masters of the discipline. Public parks and cemeteries were influenced by the design vocabulary of H.W.S. Cleveland. The firm of Morrell and Nichols successfully implemented campus designs and master planning for North Dakota state institutions. The International Peace Garden on the border between North Dakota and Manitoba is a contemporary work of landscape architecture that receives increasing visibility. A landscaped and waterscaped mall design for the central commercial district of Omaha was accomplished in the 1970s by collaboration between landscape architect Lawrence Halprin Associates and the Omaha firm of Bahr, Vermeer, Haecker. Butzer Design Partnership's (2000) Oklahoma City National Memorial is a contemporary landscape of international significance commemorating lives lost in the terrorist bombing of the Murrah Federal Building.

CONCLUSION

Careful attention to the broad range of buildings on the Great Plains, including buildings designed by architects and those ubiquitous buildings constructed by vernacular or folk processes can help one learn a good deal about the cultural values of people on the Plains and provide useful lessons about how culture and environment adjust to accommodate human activity and cultural values. As an expression of culture, architecture differentiates the Plains from other regions in the way people apply their traditions to a severe but well-understood environmental context. Architecture on the Plains is often regarded as austere and practical, but there is also an undercurrent of appreciation for beauty of a pragmatic or handsome sort, and even for occasional eccentricity.

In examining the architectural history of the Great Plains, one discovers that many "old-fashioned" ways of employing local materials or designing buildings had a sustainable, environmentally appropriate "fit," adapted over time to a particular place. Appreciating the spiritual beauty of a well-executed design is a value shared by all cultures. Discovering cultural values that underscore the Great Plains' regional aesthetic is an aspect of the way people look at architecture that enables them, through practice, to recognize beauty in all its variations. Appreciation of the built environment is not the narrow privilege of architects and historians; it is part of the birthright of all people who are willing to spend time exploring the rich diversity of Great Plains culture.

RESOURCE GUIDE

Printed Sources

The Society of Architectural Historians has undertaken development of a series of architectural guidebooks for each state, published by Oxford University Press, called *Buildings of the United States*. At the time of this writing, volumes for all Great Plains states are pending.

Arthur, Eric, and Dudley Witney. *The Barn: A Vanishing Landmark in North America*. New York: M. F. Feheley and Arrowood Press, 1988.

Beedle, Peggy Lee, and Geoffrey M. Gyrisco, eds. *The Farm Landscape*. Madison: State Historical Society of Wisconsin, 1996.

Blouet, Brian W., and Frederick C. Luebke, eds. *The Great Plains: Environment and Culture*. Lincoln: University of Nebraska Press, 1979.

Blumenson, John J. G. *Identifying American Architecture: A Pictorial Guide to Styles and Terms, 1600–1945*. Nashville: American Association for State and Local History, 1977. Rev. ed. New York: W. W. Norton and Co., 1981.

Brandhorst, L. Carl. "Limestone Houses in Central Kansas." *Journal of Cultural Geography* 2 (fall/winter 1981): 70–81.

Carlson, Alvar W. "German-Russian Houses in Western North Dakota." *Pioneer America* 13 (September 1981): 49–60.

Chiat, Marilyn J. *America's Religious Architecture: Sacred Places for Every Community*. New York: John Wiley and Sons, 1997.

Cook, Jeffrey. *The Architecture of Bruce Goff*. New York: Harper and Row, 1978.

Coomber, James, and Sheldon Green. *Magnificent Churches on the Prairie: A Story of Immigrant Priests, Builders, and Homesteaders*. Fargo: North Dakota Institute for Regional Studies, 1996.

Cronon, William. *Nature's Metropolis: Chicago and the Great Midwest*. New York: W. W. Norton and Co., 1991.

Danbom, David. *Born in the Country: A History of Rural America*. Baltimore: Johns Hopkins University Press, 1995.

De Long, David G., Helen Searing, and Robert A. M. Stern, eds. *American Architecture: Innovation and Tradition*. New York: Rizzoli International Publications, 1986.

Domer, Dennis. "Genesis Theories of the German-American Two-Door House." *Material Culture* 26, no. 1 (spring 1994): 1–36.

Erpestad, David, and David Wood. *Building South Dakota: A Historical Survey of the State's Architecture to 1945*. Pierre: South Dakota State Historical Society Press, 1997.

Fitch, James Marston. *American Building I: The Historical Forces That Shaped It*. Boston: Houghton Mifflin, 1966.

Grant, H. Roger. *Living in the Depot: The Two-Story Railroad Station*. Iowa City: University of Iowa Press, 1993.

Hart, John Fraser. *The Look of the Land*. Englewood Cliffs, NJ: Prentice-Hall, 1975.

Harvey, Thomas. "Railroad Towns: Urban Forms on the Prairie." *Landscape* 27, no. 3 (1983): 26–34.

Hudson, John C. "Frontier Housing in North Dakota." *North Dakota History* 42 (fall 1975): 4–15.

———. *Plains Country Towns*. Minneapolis: University of Minnesota Press, 1985.

Jackson, John Brinkerhoff. *Discovering the Vernacular Landscape*. New Haven, CT: Yale University Press, 1984.

Koop, Michael H., and Steven Ludwig. *German-Russian Folk Architecture in Southeastern South Dakota*. Film Transcript. Vermillion: South Dakota State Historic Preservation Center, 1984.

Krinsky, Carol Herselle. *Contemporary Native American Architecture: Cultural Regeneration and Creativity*. New York: Oxford University Press, 1996.

Lewis, Peirce F. "Common Houses, Cultural Spoor." *Landscape* 19, no. 2 (1975): 1–22.

Lindgren, H. Elaine. *Land in Her Own Name: Women as Homesteaders in North Dakota*. Fargo: North Dakota Institute for Regional Studies, 1991.

Longstreth, Richard. *The Buildings of Main Street: A Guide to Commercial Architecture*. Washington, DC: Preservation Press for National Trust for Historic Preservation, 1987.

Martin, Christopher. "Skeleton of Settlement: Folk Building in Western North Dakota."

In *Perspectives in Vernacular Architecture, III*, ed. Thomas Carter and Bernard L. Herman, 86–98. Columbia: University of Missouri Press, 1989.

McMurry, Sally. *Families and Farmhouses in Nineteenth Century America*. New York: Oxford University Press, 1988.

Meinig, D. W., ed. *The Interpretation of Ordinary Landscapes*. New York: Oxford University Press, 1979.

Murphy, David. "Building in Clay on the Central Plains." In *Perspectives in Vernacular Architecture, III*, ed. Thomas Carter and Bernard L. Herman, 74–85. Columbia: University of Missouri Press, 1989.

Nabokov, Peter, and Robert Easton. *Native American Architecture*. New York: Oxford University Press, 1989.

Newsom, D. Earl. *Stillwater, One Hundred Years of Memories: A Pictorial History*. Norfolk, VA: Donning Company, 1989.

Noble, Allen G. "The North American Settlement Landscape." In *Wood, Brick and Stone*, vol. 1, 134–170, and vol. 2, 67–125. Amherst: University of Massachusetts Press, 1984.

———. "Pioneer Settlement on the Plains: Sod Dugouts and Sod Houses." *Pioneer America Society Transactions* 4 (1981): 11–19.

Oklahoma State University School of Architecture, and Cecil D. Elliott, eds. *Oklahoma Landmarks: A Selection of Noteworthy Structures*. Stillwater: Oklahoma State University, 1967.

Peterson, Albert J. "The German-Russian House in Kansas: A Study in Persistence of Form." *Pioneer America* 8 (January 1976): 19–27.

Peterson, Fred W. *Homes in the Heartland: Balloon Frame Farmhouses of the Upper Midwest, 1850–1920*. Lawrence: University Press of Kansas, 1992.

Pregill, Philip, and Nancy Volkman. *Landscapes in History: Design and Planning in the Eastern and Western Traditions*. New York: John Wiley and Sons, 1999.

Ramsay, Ronald L. M. "Historical Development of the Architectural Profession on the Northern Great Plains." Master's thesis, University of Texas at Austin, 1992.

Rau, John E. "Czechs in South Dakota," In *To Build in a New Land: Ethnic Landscapes in North America*, ed. Allen G. Noble, 285–306. Baltimore: Johns Hopkins University Press, 1992.

Sachs, David H., and George Ehrlich. *Guide to Kansas Architecture*. Lawrence: University Press of Kansas, 1996.

Scott, Quinta. *Along Route 66*. Norman: University of Oklahoma Press, 2000.

Sherman, William C. *Prairie Mosaic: An Ethnic Atlas of Rural North Dakota*. Fargo: North Dakota Institute for Regional Studies, 1983.

Sherman, William C., and Playford V. Thorson, eds. *Plains Folk: North Dakota's Ethnic History*. Fargo: North Dakota Institute for Regional Studies, 1988.

Smith, G. E. Kidder. *The Architecture of the United States*. Vol. 3, *The Plains States and Far West*. Garden City, NY: Anchor Books/Doubleday, 1981.

Tishler, William H., ed. *Midwestern Landscape Architecture*. Urbana: University of Illinois Press, 2000.

Upton, Dell, ed. *America's Architectural Roots*. Washington, DC: National Trust for Historic Preservation, 1986.

Upton, Dell, and John Michael Vlach, eds. *Common Places: Readings in American Vernacular Architecture*. Athens: University of Georgia Press, 1986.

Vogel, John N. *Great Lakes Lumber on the Great Plains: The Laird, Norton Lumber Company in South Dakota*. Iowa City: University of Iowa Press, 1992.

Vrooman, Nicholas Churchin, and Patrice Avon Marvin, eds. *Iron Spirits*. Fargo: North Dakota Council on the Arts, 1982.

Welsch, Roger L. "Nebraska's Round Barns." *Nebraska History* 51 (spring 1970): 48–92.

———. "Shelters on the Plains." *Natural History* 86 (May 1977): 48–53.

Web Sites

Center for Great Plains Studies
www.unl.edu/plains/

Germans from Russia stone-slab architecture in North Dakota
www.lib.ndsu.nodak.edu/grhc/history_culture/history/hutmacher.html

Kansas State Historical Society
www.kshs.org/

National Trust for Historic Preservation
www.nationaltrust.org

Nebraska Statewide Inventory of Historic Properties
www.nebraskahistory.org/histpres/nehbs.htm

North Dakota Institute for Regional Studies
www.lib.ndsu.nodak.edu/ndirs/

Oklahoma Landmarks Inventory
www.ok-history.mus.ok.us/enc/org

Preservation North Dakota (See especially the "Prairie Churches" initiative.)
www.prairiechurches.org

Route 66 Preservation Organization
www.oklahomaroute66.com

Society of Architectural Historians' Buildings of the United States series
www.sah.org/bus.html

Videos/Films

Fort Totten: Military Post and Indian School. Bismarck: State Historical Society of North
Dakota, 1986.
German-Russian Folk Architecture in Southeastern South Dakota. Dir. Michael H. Koop and
Steven Ludwig. Vermillion: South Dakota State Historic Preservation Center, 1984.
Northern Lights. Dir. John Hanson and Rob Nilsson. Minneapolis, MN: New Front Films,
1978.

Organizations, Museums, Special Collections

Center for Great Plains Studies
1155 Q Street
PO Box 880214
Lincoln, NE 68588-0214

North Dakota Institute for Regional Studies
1305 19th Avenue N.
Fargo, ND 58105

Also see collections of the state historical societies for each state on the Great Plains.

ART

William M. Tsutsui and Marjorie Swann

For much of its history, the Great Plains region has been perceived as a cultural wasteland, a frontier devoid of art and civilization, a no-frills backwater at the very heart of America. The Plains was "a desert of newness and ugliness and sordidness," Willa Cather wrote at the turn of the twentieth century, lacking "all that is chastened and old, and noble with traditions." What is more, the flat and featureless Plains seemed a place uniquely unsuited to artistic depiction and alien to traditional notions of aesthetics. "There seemed to be nothing to see," one of Cather's pioneer characters lamented, "no fences, no creeks or trees, no hills or fields." "The challenge for prairie painters," a scholar later reflected,

> has been to see and represent presence rather than absence. This has required skill and vision to move from the dominance of the vertical, so central to previous aesthetic notions, toward an accommodation of the horizontal. . . . Above all, it has challenged a capacity to represent distance, . . . to accommodate a world in which foreground, middle distance, and background refuse to keep their assigned places, intertwining in an elaborate choreography that has . . . confused and dislocated those who have entered this country's grass-filled interior.

Perhaps as a consequence, the art of the Great Plains has not been a subject much examined by academic art historians. The artistic heritage of the Dakotas, Nebraska, Kansas, and Oklahoma is often simply ignored in surveys of American art or else considered peripherally in treatments of neighboring areas—the Southwest, the Rocky Mountain states, Chicago and the Upper Midwest—with more celebrated artistic traditions. Nevertheless, the states of the Great Plains, neither as deficient in culture nor as unaccommodating to artistic expression as most previous observers have assumed, can boast a long, vibrant, and diverse art history.[1]

This chapter provides a chronological overview of the visual arts on the Great Plains, beginning with the art of the Plains Indians prior to white settlement and continuing up to the present day. The emphasis in this chronological narrative, which documents the steady development of artistic activity in the region since the nineteenth century, is on painting, printmaking, and sculpture. This chapter treats those forms of art—photography, quilting, folk arts, ceramics, and so forth—that have only attracted widespread scholarly recognition during the past several decades. The chapter concludes with a concise analysis of the major historical factors that have shaped the artistic heritage of the region and contributed to the evolution of a rich and varied art culture on the Great Plains.

ART OF THE PLAINS INDIANS

Most scholars who have surveyed the history of art on the Great Plains have begun their narratives with those nineteenth-century Euro-American painters who accompanied the great expeditions of discovery across the region. Many works, even standard sources, completely ignore the Native American heritage on the Plains. The chapter on art in the 1941 Works Progress Administration (WPA) guide to Oklahoma, for example, makes no mention of Indian art and instead locates the state's artistic genesis in the passage of George Catlin (1796–1872) through the Wichita Mountains in 1834. Other studies have given the traditions of Plains Indian art only passing attention or have dismissed them condescendingly. "Naturally," one 1978 overview of Nebraska art conceded, "the first artists who worked in this area were the various groups of native Americans. When one views examples of some of their art forms, one can hardly call them primitive peoples." In numerous accounts, Native Americans are figured less as the creators of art than as the colorful subjects of others' depictions. According to a 1961 catalog of historical Kansas art, "The Indians, of course, provided an exotic strangeness, and the works of art concerning them are boundless." As the Lakota painter Arthur Amiotte (b. 1942) has accurately concluded, "Generally speaking, little attention is ever given to the artistic accomplishments of the Indians of North America; for, in essence, at the time of discovery they were considered non-entities or as part of the land to be subdued."[2]

Such attitudes notwithstanding, the Plains Indians had rich artistic traditions, what Dorothy Dunn called "a spirited and vigorous art, unique in history." As early as 1540, Francisco de Coronado observed painted buffalo-hide robes from the northern Plains, and in the subsequent centuries, as horses and firearms introduced from Europe radically altered the Native lifestyles in the region, a sophisticated artistic culture evolved. The more than two dozen tribes of the Great Plains— Lakota, Kiowa, Arapaho, Pawnee, Mandan, and others—developed what some scholars have labeled an "eminently portable" art, well adapted to the nomadic, buffalo-hunting societies of the American prairies and using buffalo hides as the medium for virtually all their creations. The Plains Indian tradition came to encompass "a multitude of visual arts in skin, hide, quillwork, featherwork, painting, carving and beadwork."[3]

The art of the Plains Indians was personal as well as ceremonial, an "expression of individual identity and achievement through adornment of oneself and one's possessions." All members of Plains Indian communities participated in the mak-

George Catlin's engraving, *The Snow-Shoe Dance*. Number Fourteen from North American Indian Collection. Courtesy Denver Public Library Western History Collection, George Catlin.

ing of art. Men painted robes, shields, and tipis with animated life scenes, alive with figures and animals, in a flat, pictographic, almost abstract style. Such work, according to Dunn, "although deeply religious in some instances, was not primarily for appeasement or supplication of unearthly powers, but rather for demonstrating personal achievements to gain prestige within the tribe and to proclaim invincibility before enemies." Plains Indian men also made elaborate hide paintings known as "winter counts," pictorial records of family or community history that recorded the events of passing years. Indian women, who, unlike the men, often worked communally, specialized in abstract patterns in the painting of garments, tipis, and parfleche articles. Quillwork was also the province of women and was considered a sacred art, originally transmitted to Indian women from a divine source. Just as men used painting as a social marker and a form of personal aggrandizement, so art was central to the workings of female society. As Janet Berlo and Ruth Phillips note, "On the Great Plains, a woman's path to dignity, honor, and long life lay in the correct and skilled pursuit of the arts."[4]

As a "dynamic and restless" indigenous tradition, the art of the Great Plains Indians was affected significantly by contact with white artists and traders. Exposure to Euro-American artists like Catlin and Karl Bodmer (1809–1893) in the nineteenth century encouraged some Plains Indians to experiment with Western techniques (including perspective) and genres (such as portraiture). New materials were also introduced. Plains Indian men were soon drawing their stylized images of battles and hunts with pencil and paper, often using the distinctive lined pages of ledger books. Even in the late eighteenth century, commercial pigments were

Karl Bodmer's *Horse Racing of Sioux Indians, Near Fort Pierre*. Engraved by Rawdon, Wright & Hatch, circa 1837–1859. Courtesy Library of Congress.

highly sought after for hide painting. Trade beads—easier to work with and more colorful and durable than porcupine quills—had a profound impact on the artistic endeavors of Indian women from the early nineteenth century.[5]

Despite the vibrancy of Plains Indian art, many of its traditional practices and purposes were upset by conquest, accelerated white settlement, and the transition to reservation life. In some parts of the Great Plains, scholars have concluded that the Native American heritage had only the slightest impact on later artistic activities. The 1939 Nebraska WPA guide, for instance, declared that "the art of the Indians . . . had little bearing on the later cultural development of the State," while Kansas art expert John Helm (1900–1972) concluded that "early art in Kansas and the plains region has had little effect on subsequent developments here."[6] In other parts of the Great Plains, however, and especially in areas with significant Native American populations, the legacy of Plains Indian art has proven far different. In Oklahoma and, to a lesser extent, South Dakota, Indian traditions were foundational to the states' artistic identities in later decades and became the basis for nationally important developments in the creation of a dynamic, modern Native American art in the twentieth century.

THE ARTIST EXPLORERS

The first non-Indian artists in the Great Plains were the painters who traveled through the region as members of the many government-sponsored and private expeditions of the nineteenth century. Known generally as the artist explorers, these men documented the Plains topographically and ethnographically in their paintings and sketches, creating images of the inland frontier and its Native inhabitants for curious audiences in the urban East and in Europe. Although their work has often been criticized artistically, and later commentators have found fault with their frequently superficial visions of the land and its peoples, the artist explorers left an important visual and historical record of the Great Plains in the decades before white settlement and in the earliest years of pioneer life. As one scholar has described it, "In the nineteenth century, the first and foremost task of the art of the region was to confront the great experience of western space, its native American inhabitants, and those Caucasians who intruded upon, colonized, and conquered that space."[7]

The "first painting done on Nebraska soil," along with its Kansas counterpart, was the work of Samuel Seymour (1775–1823), an artist of "modest, if not meager, talent" who accompanied Major Stephen Long's surveying party to the Rocky Mountains in 1819–1820. Seymour's charge, like that of many of his successors in Plains exploration, was to "furnish sketches or landscapes, whenever we meet with any distinguished for their beauty and grandeur, . . . paint

Alfred Jacob Miller's *Preparing for a Buffalo Hunt*. Courtesy The Walters Art Museum, Baltimore.

miniature likenesses, or portraits, if required, of distinguished Indians, and exhibit groups of savages engaged in celebrating their festivals or sitting in council." A decade after Seymour's sojourn, George Catlin, a Philadelphia lawyer and artist, first traveled to the Plains. Inspired by his contacts with Native Americans and moved by the ongoing loss of their traditional lifestyles, Catlin dedicated the rest of his creative life to documenting the vanishing manners and customs of the Plains Indians. While "his ability was below his aim and his vision," Catlin's paintings—along with the watercolors of the Swiss artist Karl Bodmer, who was employed on Prince Maximilian of Wied-Neuwied's expedition of 1833–1834—constituted a "comprehensive and meticulous documentation of the Great Plains and the tribes living there." The ongoing demand for images of the western frontier was addressed by the dramatic, exoticized oils of Alfred Jacob Miller (1810–1874), who followed the Overland Trail in 1837, and the sweeping landscapes of John Mix Stanley (1814–1872), who was a member of several expeditions, including the Pacific Railroad Survey of 1853. By the time that Albert Bierstadt (1830–1902) crossed the Plains in 1859, exclaiming that "the wildness and abandon of nature here is very attractive to an artistic eye," the number of artists traveling west had increased dramatically. In the 1860s and 1870s, painters and illustrators dispatched from the East were busily supplying popular periodicals like *Harper's Weekly* and *Frank Leslie's Illustrated Newspaper* with the latest images of land, life, and settlement on the Great Plains frontier.[8]

In depicting the Plains, the artist explorers were forced to confront not just the harshness of the land and the rigors of the frontier, but also the established conventions of Victorian landscape painting. To those trained in the European tradition, the flat Plains scenery was oppressive and unpromising aesthetically, completely lacking in the vertical elements necessary for pleasing compositions. Some artists simply suffered through the monotony of the Plains, awaiting the ultimate aesthetic reward of the Rocky Mountains. Other painters, however, rose to the challenge: "they managed in a variety of ways not only to confront these problems but also to overcome them, and their resolutions in turn helped provide identity to a landscape that seemed so devoid of definition." Indeed, the very lack of artistic promise in the unrelenting horizontality of the Plains may have encouraged innovation among the artist explorers. As Donald Bartlett Doe has reflected, "early paintings and drawings of this region offer a freshness of vision simply because European Art offered no real formal precedent for the American artist as he faced the enormous sweep of the Great Plains."[9]

The artist explorers thus contributed to the establishment of an American landscape tradition, as well as providing later generations with a valuable historical record. As Oscar Jacobson (1882–1966) wrote in a survey of early Oklahoma art, "The paintings and drawings of the first white artists . . . are very important historically and, in some cases, possess artistic value, providing us with the only visual information concerning the country and the people before the invention of the camera." Moreover, through their oils, watercolors, and sketches, artists like Catlin and Bodmer created powerful and abiding visual stereotypes of the Great Plains and the western frontier for distant audiences in America and Europe. In later years, these stereotypes were reinforced and further elaborated by successful illustrators such as Frederic Remington (1861–1909) and Charles Marion Russell (1864–1926). Yet in terms of the artistic development of the Plains region itself, the legacy of the artist explorers was actually quite limited. John Helm observed in 1956, "The first white artists who visited this region were naturally European or eastern trained and brought that viewpoint with them. Their work, often in the nature of reporting, is usually remarkably well designed [but] is, naturally, a transplanted art and shows little effect of the country upon the artist." As Norman Geske nicely put it, the artist explorers "came and went, taking with them the record of their observations."[10]

ART AND CIVILIZATION ON THE FRONTIER

Many historians have suggested that the fine arts were slow to take root on the nineteenth-century Great Plains frontier. The epic struggles of the first generations of pioneers have often been thought incompatible with the cultured life and the presumed frivolities of painting, drawing, and sculpture. "The early days of settlement are never, as a rule, the days of achievement in any of the arts," one standard survey declared. "Too much energy is devoted to the immediate problems of sustaining life in a primitive environment to allow the demands of creative concentration." "In the three or four decades following the establishment of Kansas territory in 1854," the historian Robert Taft wrote,

> few Kansas artists attempted to depict life in Kansas. . . . To be sure, there was cultural growth, especially in the fields of education, of journalism, and of music, but on the whole the energy of these earlier Kansans was directed chiefly to the establishment of farms, homes and villages, to the building of railroads, to combating inclement weather and voracious insects and to a participation—at times a quite vociferous and rugged participation—in the politics attendant upon the formation of a new territory and state created on the virgin and spacious plains of the great West.[11]

But despite the many "crudities and harsh necessities of frontier life," art was never completely ignored, even in the earliest days of settlement on the Plains. Homesteaders' wives, eager to re-create the gentility and domesticity of eastern parlors, hung the coarse walls of their sod houses with etchings, photographs, and pictorial calendars; art clubs and private academies sprouted in frontier towns; and art instruction flourished in small prairie schools and in the region's fledgling colleges and universities. Indeed, the appreciation and creation of fine art was extremely important on the frontier because artistic endeavor conveyed an aura of culture, civility, and permanence in the young Plains settlements that were considered rough, uncouth, and barely civilized by the refined urbanites of the East. Impatient to dispel the persistent notion that the Great Plains was a cultural desert, alive only with "gaudily painted red-skins and stampeding herds of long horned cattle," the pioneer generations embraced artistic activity as a natural, inseparable part of the larger crusade for progress, civilization, and prosperity. Sarah Wool Moore (1846–?), a Vienna-trained painter and one of the first art instructors at the University of Nebraska, argued in 1888 that

> "As long as every man is engaged in collecting the materials necessary for his own subsistence there will be neither leisure nor taste for higher pursuits"; but, the prosperity of a state once assured, the mind relaxes its strenuous endeavor and that beneficent and instructive hunger for beauty makes itself felt. Then the artist and the artistic artisan come to the front; the state demands them and develops them, and their growth reacts again upon its prosperity, giving it an impulse from within—the best pledge of vitality, the most substantial evidence and enduring monument of civic or territorial importance.[12]

Although one chronicler has described the early history of South Dakota culture as "a succession of writers and painters coming and going, rarely staying," a number of trained, professional, and even nationally recognized artists settled on the Plains in the latter half of the nineteenth century. As Norman Geske has noted, however, "The artist who came to the frontier, not to marvel at the sights but to stay and make a living, had a meager time of it. The portrait painter [and] the professor of art . . . were not here in response to a thriving market or a sophisticated urbanism. They were 'pioneers' who came here out of a need for new opportunities or a settled livelihood and, in some instances, out of a missionary zeal to bring culture and enlightenment." The first resident Kansas artist to enjoy a "reputation almost national" was Henry Worrall (1825–1902), a native of England who began his career in Cincinnati before arriving in Topeka in 1868. Though he boasted little art training, Worrall was a contributor to *Harper's Weekly*, a successful book illustrator, and the designer of the Kansas agricultural pavilion at the 1876 Philadelphia Centennial Exposition. Another notable migrant to the Plains was John Banvard (1815–1891), an artist, poet, and showman who settled in Watertown, South Dakota, in 1881. Banvard gained international acclaim in the 1840s with "the largest painting ever executed by man," a three-mile long panorama of topographical scenes along the Mississippi River. The huge painting, scrolled through large mechanical cylinders for audiences, was displayed throughout the United States and Europe and earned the fulsome praise of Queen Victoria, Charles Dickens, and more than 400,000 viewers in New York City alone. Banvard took refuge in the Dakotas from his debts, and his final work was a diorama, exhibited in Watertown, of General William Sherman's 1865 burning of Columbia, South Carolina. A virtual work of performance art, complete with sound and light effects, "it was a one man show, with John Banvard operating the immortal works, winding windlasses, pulling ropes, firing rockets, . . . ringing bells, and doing divers other things to multiply the illusion and augment the tumult."[13]

A number of immigrant artists from Europe also came to the nineteenth-century Plains, bringing Continental training and sensibilities to the frontier. Stanislas Schimonsky (dates unknown), a native of Schleswig-Holstein, farmed and painted near Bellevue, Nebraska, in the 1850s. Henriette Clopath (1862–1936), a Swiss impressionist painter who studied in Dresden, Munich, and Paris, operated a studio in early Tulsa and offered private art instruction. A particularly important figure was Birger Sandzén (1871–1954), a Swede classically trained in Stockholm and Paris, who was lured to Kansas by Carl Swensson's *I Sverige* and its enthralling description of the small Swedish settlement of Lindsborg. Finding employment at Bethany College, Sandzén spent more than sixty years in Lindsborg and became a leading force in Kansas art, a celebrated painter and printmaker, and "so thorough a Kansan that he is our most characteristic and dynamic artistic force." Sandzén also trained a number of artists who would have a significant impact on Great Plains art, including Samuel Holmberg (1885–1911), founder of the art program at the University of Oklahoma, and his successor Oscar Jacobson, who became a major figure in Oklahoma and Native American art circles.[14]

The first generation of artists born on the Plains began to make its mark on the region's artistic life in the late nineteenth century. George M. Stone (1858–1931), known as the "Millet of the Prairies," was born near Topeka in 1858 and studied in Paris before returning to Kansas to paint portraits and operate a private art academy. Susette La Flesche Tibbles (1854–1903), an Omaha Indian, was a native of Bellevue, Nebraska, and a longtime resident of Lincoln. Tibbles provided the illustrations for Fannie Reed Giffen's 1898 book *Oo-Mah-Ha Ta-Wa-Tha*, said to be the "first artistic work by an American Indian ever published." Though lacking in formal training, Augusta Metcalfe (1881–1971), a native of Kansas who settled in Oklahoma in the 1880s, was a prolific painter, "capturing the spirit of a hard land and a hard people" in her oils of southern Plains pioneer life. The works of Stone, Metcalfe, and other aspiring artists on the frontier belie the notion that "After the subsidence of interest in the pioneer phase by visiting artists, native [Plains] art

Smokey River at Twilight, by Birger Sandzén, 1928. Linoleum-cut block print, 9 × 12 inches. Courtesy Birger Sandzén Memorial Gallery Collection, Lindsborg, Kansas.

was mainly an activity of more or less amateur practitioners among the house painters, 'cafe muralists' and small-town art teachers with more enterprise than talent."[15]

Although the National Academician John Noble (1874–1935) once proclaimed that "Kansas does not breed expatriates," many aspiring artists in the nineteenth century and afterwards left Kansas—and the rest of the Great Plains—for educational and professional opportunities elsewhere. Noble, while a "true son of the Plains" who always maintained ties to his Kansas home, was trained and found fame as a landscape painter in Paris and the art centers of the East. Such a pattern was not uncommon: the acclaimed painters Fern Coppedge (1883–1951), Henry Varnum Poor (1888–1970), Van Dearing Perrine (1869–1955), and Gladys Nelson Smith (1890–1980) were all Kansas natives who pursued their successful creative careers on the east or west coasts. Two celebrated early "expatriates" from South Dakota were the sculptors Gilbert Risvold (1881–1938) and James Earle Fraser (1876–1953). Fraser, perhaps the most popular American sculptor in the early twentieth century, created *End of the Trail*, the now iconic statue of a dispirited Indian warrior, and designed the buffalo and Indian-head nickel, once described as the "most American of coins." Among what one author termed the "exodus of Nebraskans to the art schools in the East and Europe" was Robert Henri (1865–1929), the innovative and influential painter who was a leader in "the Eight" and the Ashcan school. Although "without doubt, the most famous and important of the artists associated with the state," Henri—born Robert Henry Cozad—spent only nine childhood years in Cozad, Nebraska, the town founded by his father, a storied frontier gambler and land speculator. Another prominent Nebraska émigré was Angel DeCora (1871–1919), born on the Winnebago Reservation, who became an independent illustrator in Boston and New York and taught art at the Carlisle Indian School. Howard Pyle, the dean of American illustrators and one of DeCora's teachers, was once asked if he had ever instructed a real genius. "Yes," Pyle allegedly replied, "But unfortunately she was a woman, and still more unfortunately, an American Indian."[16]

WOMEN AND ARTS ON THE FRONTIER

Although art historians have generally concerned themselves primarily with professional, formally trained male artists, the fine arts were usually regarded as the preserve of women in the frontier societies of the Great Plains. The painter Kenneth Adams (1897–1966) recalled of his native Topeka in the early twentieth century that "when I started taking . . . private painting lessons, I was looked upon as perhaps just a little odd. That women painted, and painted china and that sort of thing [was accepted], but it was not a masculine occupation, painting." Many later commentators have completely ignored the early artistic endeavors of Plains women or else dismissed them condescendingly, treating popular female forms like quilting, pyrography, and china painting as mere dilettantish recreation. As Oscar Jacobson wrote in 1954, discounting the very possibility that the amateur women's art of the Plains could hold aesthetic value, "I have yet to be introduced to any young lady who does not tell me that she has an aunt or a grandmother who paints beautifully, though she has never taken a lesson. This is probably greatly exaggerated, but the fact remains that, in early Oklahoma, there were many 'ladies who painted' as a cultured accomplishment."[17]

Women on the Great Plains frontier did not just create art—from exquisite oils and watercolors to "quilts, hats, and yarn-and-cardboard mottoes to hang on the wall"—but were also instrumental in promoting art appreciation, education, and collecting. In addition to the many talented female artists who emerged from the Plains, women dominated the teaching of art in the region's schools, colleges, and universities. This was particularly apparent at the University of Nebraska, where a series of able art instructors—Sarah Wool Moore, Cora Parker (1859–1944), and Sara Shewell Hayden (1862–1939)—built a strong curriculum and stimulated public interest in art in the late nineteenth and early twentieth centuries. Circumstances were similar at South Dakota Agricultural College (later South Dakota State University), where Ada Caldwell (1869–1937), a graduate of the Art Institute of Chicago and an accomplished landscape painter, worked "to cultivate a taste and a desire for beauty" and trained a number of prominent artists, including Harvey Dunn (1884–1952) and Gilbert Risvold.[18]

ART CULTURE ON THE GREAT PLAINS

By the first decades of the twentieth century, a broad, active, and increasingly well-established art culture had emerged on the Great Plains. Although there remained a few "remote and lonely places where Art has not penetrated," amateur artists proliferated, trained painters both native born and immigrant established studios and academies, and organizations devoted to promoting the visual arts sprouted in the cities and larger towns. Plains colleges and public schools early embraced art education, and many of the first formally trained artists in the region were affiliated with educational institutions. Art classes were first offered at Baker University in Kansas in 1858, at the University of Nebraska in 1877, at South Dakota Agricultural College in 1887, and at the University of Oklahoma in 1908. Alfred Montgomery (1857–1922), the so-called farmer painter, introduced art instruction in Topeka high schools in 1887; in Oklahoma, mission schools taught art from 1889; and in 1905, Martha Avey (1872–1943) was appointed the first art supervisor of the Oklahoma City public schools. As one Nebraska observer declared, "Educators no longer look upon art, music and the cultural subjects as expensive luxuries in the public schools, and as a waste of time as well. There seems to be an awakening consciousness of the need of the finer things of life in every community."[20]

Women's Clubs and the Spread of Fine Arts

Some of the most important work in promoting the fine arts in the young states of the Great Plains was undertaken by women's clubs, both the myriad associations formed in towns large and small and the powerful state federations into which they were organized. According to Nan Sheets (1885–1976), an influential figure in the Oklahoma City art community, "It was the club women responsible for these organizations who brought the first art exhibitions into the new State of Oklahoma. They encouraged local talent, gave scholarships to art students, and in every way possible promoted art activities. . . . It was the club women who started collections of art for their respective cities and voiced the need for suitable buildings to house them. Out of the pioneer work of these women an awareness of art was aroused over the entire state." In Kansas, clubs established an "extensive and valuable collection," the Aplington Art Gallery, which was displayed widely "to diffuse throughout our state a knowledge and love of what is best in art." In South Dakota, the Federation of Women's Clubs led a successful campaign in 1908 to include interior decoration and murals "befitting the wealth, culture and dignity of a great commonwealth" in the new state capitol. Such efforts, along with those of clubwomen across the region, were fundamental in creating a public awareness, understanding, and appreciation of art in the rough-and-ready settlements of the frontier Plains.[19]

In addition to a number of women's clubs (see sidebar), several other important groups dedicated to promoting the fine arts were founded in the late nineteenth century. The Kansas State Art Association, established in 1883, opened a modest museum, sponsored annual exhibitions, and operated an art school in Topeka. In Omaha, art study clubs were formed in the 1870s, and major public exhibits had begun by the end of the decade. In 1888, the Western Art Association was chartered in the city; boasting 300 members, the association held annual exhibitions and in 1881 opened the Omaha Academy of Fine Arts, with J. Laurie Wallace (1864–1953), a student of Thomas Eakins and a noted portraitist, as the principal instructor. Among the most important (and longest-lived) art organizations of the frontier Plains was the Nebraska Art Association, founded in Lincoln in 1888 as the Haydon Art Club. Aspiring to stage "exhibitions of original works in oil, water color, statuary, bric-a-brac, ceramics and curios . . . to purchase from time to time for a permanent Art Gallery original works of art, to encourage art education in the public schools, and to establish and maintain a state college of fine arts," the association was closely affiliated with the University of Nebraska and had more than 1,000 members by the turn of the twentieth century. The association's first public exhibition, held in 1888 in the Lincoln post office, featured just one painting, *The Wise and Foolish Virgins* by the now-obscure German artist Karl von Piloty. Despite the relatively expensive entrance fee of fifty cents a person, thousands attended the show, including whole classes of schoolchildren and trainloads of visitors on special railway excursions from distant Nebraska towns.[21]

Although collections of original art were hardly common on the frontier Plains, a number of individual and institutional collectors had begun to appear by the early twentieth century. The Nebraska Art Association purchased its first painting, a "moody tonalist landscape" by Leonard Ochtman (1854–1934), in 1898. In South Dakota, the Yankton State Hospital began amassing a large collection of watercolors for the enjoyment and edification of its patients in 1906. On the southern Plains, "men made wealthy by oil, ranching, and other industries encouraged art by buying the work of painters" in the decades prior to World War I. The most famous early collection, however, was in Omaha, where George Lininger (1834–1907), a baron in the farm implement trade, accumulated a diverse and extensive group of artworks after traveling to Europe in the early 1880s. Lininger constructed a large public gallery for his collection in 1888, but following his death in 1907, the gallery closed and the artworks were dispersed at auction. As one historian noted, "George Lininger had an ambition to stimulate art in the midwest and his gallery fulfilled that dream. But after his death, one Omahan recalled, a void existed: '[Gone were the] pleasant, leisurely days when on Thursday and Sunday the townsfolk make their way to the . . . gallery, on an average of one thousand per month, there to spend a little while in the atmosphere of quiet and beauty.' "[22]

In the absence of public museums or even many private collections like Lininger's, expositions and fairs were important venues for displaying original art and showcasing the work of local artists on the Great Plains. Although some complained that "the early fairs in Dakota territory ran heavily to hand-painted china," state and county fairs, as well as Chautauqua art displays and lectures, focused attention on the fine arts, especially in rural areas. Larger events like the Interstate Fair and Exposition of 1886, which brought three hundred paintings from Chicago and Milwaukee to a marquee in Omaha, attracted tens of thousands of art admirers. National expositions allowed Plains states to show off their homegrown artists and boast of the cultured, refined development of their frontier settlements. At the 1893 Chicago World's Fair, for example, the South Dakota pavilion featured a large allegorical oil painting with a huge female figure representing the young state brandishing "a sheet proclaiming 'Free Homes' before an unlikely assortment of ethnic types." As one critic evaluated the Kansas art exhibit at the 1893 fair, "If many things bordered on the naive, the absurd, the gauche, the unfinished, if it all shouted aloud the lack of home-grown tradition, if it was but doubly provincial in its efforts to imitate the grandeurs of other climes, nevertheless it breathed an aspiration for democratic self-expression, a sort of virile self-confidence that is lacking in many a more stream-lined creation of later years. . . . Never before or since have the people of Kansas been so self-expressive."[23]

In spite of all the hindrances to the development of a vibrant artistic culture on the Great Plains—"relatively late settlement, persistently low population densities, and great distances," among other things—the pioneer generations patiently cultivated art, as well as corn, wheat, and alfalfa. One early Oklahoma artist reminisced bittersweetly that "Throughout the territorial period and into the early years of statehood Oklahoma art and artists matured to a level that not even harsh conditions could destroy." If the Plains frontier was not nearly as urbane and polished as the cities of the East or the salons of Europe, it did aspire, endeavor, and, eventually, succeed in the pursuit of a cultured lifestyle. As the historian Howard Lamar appropriately concluded, "It seems safe to say that . . . in the Great Plains between the 1880s and 1910, [the] art-oriented world was larger, more accessible, more comprehensible, and far more democratic and citizen-minded than may have been realized."[24]

REGIONALISM AND THE DEPRESSION (1920s AND 1930s)

The period between the two world wars brought widespread national attention to artistic developments in the Great Plains. For the first time (and, some would argue, the last as well), influential artistic movements emerged from the American heartland, including the Plains states. Rather than belatedly receiving the second-hand artistic fashions of the East and Europe, Plains artists of the 1920s and 1930s were at the forefront of developments in American art, particularly the Regionalist movement and the renaissance of Native American painting. At the same time, as art gained a higher public profile and was more thoroughly ingrained in daily life, it also became a more controversial and contentious subject. Such tensions became particularly obvious when artistic depictions of the region and its lifestyle diverged from deeply cherished values, ideals, and myths of the proud (and often rather defensive) residents of the Plains.

The interwar artistic dynamism on the Great Plains sprang from a number of sources. By the 1920s, the experience of more than fifty years of art promotion in the region—the accumulated efforts of schools, women's clubs, art lovers, and pioneering artists—had stimulated public interest in art and contributed to the significant growth of local artistic talent. Simultaneously, national trends began to favor subjects, styles, and values associated with the rural Midwest and the Great Plains. In the wake of World War I, artists and critics across the country turned increasingly to realistic portrayals of homegrown subject matter, what became known as the "American scene." According to art historian Charles Eldredge, "the pre-war achievements of vanguard non-objective artists were challenged by new concerns for representation and for subject matter, often local or regional. After the horrors of military conflict, a generation of creative artists seemingly looked homeward, there to cultivate their own gardens after the disillusionments of world war." That artists disenchanted with the charms of Europe should look to the American heartland is hardly surprising: especially with the onset of the Great Depression, many Americans sought spiritual refuge in what seemed a simpler, gentler, and more comprehensible place and time. "American culture suddenly rediscovered the territory west of the Hudson River," one scholar observed. "At a time of national crisis, all things distinctively American became precious affirmations of an imperiled identity."[25]

This nostalgic embrace by American artists of an idealized midwestern idyll— "the old swimming hole, the shack in the woods, and the Fourth-of-July oration down in the town square"—was known as Regionalism. The movement's most outspoken and influential champion was the art critic Thomas Craven (1888–1969), a native of Salina, Kansas. Although branded as nationalistic, reactionary, and even homophobic by later detractors, Craven advocated a "new and emancipated tradition of art in North America," freed from the domination of East Coast elites, European fads, and the imported excesses of abstraction:

If we are ever to have an indigenous expression, it will be an art proceeding from strong native impulses, simple ideas, and popular tastes. . . . If the mechanized United States has produced no plastic art of any richness or vitality, it is because she has borrowed her art from foreign sources, and refused to utilize the most exciting materials that have ever challenged the creative mind, . . . the immensity of New York; . . . the tractors in the Kansas wheat fields; the cow gentlemen of the Southwest; the Rockies. . . . [26]

Benton, Wood, and Curry

The most acclaimed standard-bearers of Craven's Regionalist creed were a triumvirate of native midwestern painters: Thomas Hart Benton (1889–1975) of Missouri, Grant Wood (1892–1942) of Iowa, and the Kansan John Steuart Curry (1897–1946), born in rural Jefferson County. Uninterested in working on the family farm—he later admitted that "I got tired of pitching wheat bundles and . . . tossing a paint brush is more to my taste"—Curry studied at the Art Institute of Chicago and with the leading illustrator (and fellow Plains expatriate) Harvey Dunn. Settling in Connecticut, Curry labored in obscurity until 1928, when his painting *Baptism in Kansas*, an overwrought image of the "religious fanaticism of the hinterland," received glowing praise from New York critics and earned him the patronage of the society art doyenne Gertrude Vanderbilt Whitney. Hailed as refreshingly original, unaffected, and authentic—"a new artist who is trying to express the true meaning of American life, who draws inspiration from the very soil he treads"—Curry was lionized as "the first of our painters to give significant expression to the poetic aspects of the Middle West." "Kansas," the *New York Times* critic Edward Alden Jewell declared, "has found her Homer."[27]

But for all the encomiums of metropolitan trendsetters, the folks back home proved "reluctant to embrace an artist, even a native son, who favored images that cast Kansas in an unfavorable light." Curry's paintings of fundamentalist rituals, looming tornadoes, rampaging floods, and backwoods manhunts may have struck many East Coast urbanites as glimpses into the authentic heart of Kansas, but Kansans themselves bristled at Curry's frequently sensationalized images. In 1931, an exhibition of Curry's canvases, organized by New York art dealer Maynard Walker (himself a native of Garnett, Kansas) and Emporia newspaperman William Allen White, toured the state in a blaze of publicity. Not a single painting was sold, however, and the local reactions were chilly. "I feel Mr. Curry has a great force in delineating the subjects he has chosen," wrote Elsie J. Allen of Wichita, the wife of a former governor, "but to say he portrays the 'spirit' of Kansas is entirely wrong. To be sure we have cyclones, gospel trains, the medicine man. And the man hunt, and we have had an automobile tip over a bank and kill a man. . . . But why paint outstanding friekish [*sic*] subjects and call them the 'spirit' of Kansas?" Curry's "friekish" works may have satisfied the stereotypes and nostalgic dreams of New York audiences, but they conflicted with the image Kansans cherished most deeply of themselves, as progressive, modern, and anything but provincial participants in the cultured mainstream of American life. That neither East Coast myths of the heartland nor Kansans' myths of themselves fully reflected reality was irrelevant; in the end, Curry, the "hometown boy made good," found fellow Kansans his harshest critics.[28]

Other Artists of the Period

Not all Plains painters who worked in the Regionalist idiom faced as frosty a public reception as that accorded John Steuart Curry. An important reason for this was the fact that most interwar artists in the region were far less apt to indulge in "the mythologizing and the occasional condescension" that characterized the work of Curry and his fellow Regionalist torchbearers, Benton and Wood. Plains artists of the 1920s and 1930s generally favored an unromanticized vision of the land and its people, an approach that portrayed the harsh reality of Great Plains life—especially during the Great Depression and the Dust Bowl—with directness and honesty, but also with respect, compassion, and affection. As one observer wrote of the Lincoln artist Gladys Lux (1899–2003):

> There is a genuine sentiment that Miss Lux tries to paint into her Nebraska subjects. She grew up on a Nebraska farm and she sees more than the superficial beauty of the landscape. As she herself expressed it, "Nebraska is full of pain and grief," and she feels that one must know this in order to understand the real beauty of Nebraska. She wants to express a love for the land that is stronger than drouths or depression. And she is too proud of Nebraska to feel that she has to hide its faults and put its best foot forward. That is why she can paint subjects like drouth-killed trees without insulting Nebraska.

Across the Plains, artists sought beauty and inspiration in the landscape and the workaday world around them, and many won regional and national recognition for their efforts. In Nebraska, Dwight Kirsch (1899–1981), Terence Duren (1906–1968), and Aaron Gunn Pyle (1903–1972), a Chappell farmer who had studied with Thomas Hart Benton and sensitively documented his small town in egg tempera, were noted Regionalists. The painter Oscar Jacobson and the Oklahoma A&M professor Doel Reed (1895–1985), the foremost aquatint etcher of his generation, captured the red earth and brooding skies of the southern Plains. In Kansas, a group of talented printmakers—C. A. Seward (1884–1939), Herschel Logan (1901–1987), and Norma Bassett Hall (1889–1957), among others—celebrated the glories of the landscape and recorded the hardscrabble reality of depression-era life. In North Dakota, the university art instructor Paul Barr (1892–1953) and Einar Olstad (1876–?), a Norwegian rancher and blacksmith with little formal training, painted the local scene, and their oils proudly represented the state at the 1939 New York World's Fair.[29]

The Plains artist embraced most heartily by hometown audiences was almost certainly Harvey Dunn, the creator of countless monumental scenes of pioneer life and a native son beloved by generations of South Dakotans. Born in 1884 on a homestead near the small town of Manchester, Dunn studied at South Dakota Agricultural College with Ada Caldwell, who encouraged the aspiring artist to enroll at the Art Institute of Chicago. After apprenticing with Howard Pyle, Dunn went on to become one of America's most successful illustrators, establishing a studio and art school in New Jersey and serving as an army battlefield painter during World War I. In spite of his cosmopolitan career path, Dunn, in the words of his biographer, Robert Karolevitz, "maintained an invisible but gripping tie to the prairies of South Dakota." As Dunn himself admitted, "I find that I prefer painting pictures of early South Dakota life to any other kind. . . . May I garble a very old saying: 'Where your heart is, there is your treasure also.' " Dunn's paintings of the frontier Dakotas were far from documentary images; they did not portray the world as it was or exhibit scrupulous fidelity to everyday reality, but injected the story of settlement on the northern Plains with drama and sentiment. "Paint a little less of the facts and a little more of the spirit," Dunn once advised young artists. "Let it be an expression rather than a description. . . . Don't be subtle, be obvious. Paint more with feeling than with thought. If you paint a farmer, that farmer must be all the farmers of America rolled into one, with all their dirt and sweat and fatigue." Dunn depicted the pioneers as heroic presences, as larger-than-life characters who valiantly contended with the land, the elements, and the endless horizon in taming and cultivating the Great Plains. Unlike John Steuart Curry's "friekish" oils, which undermined the cultured aspirations of depression-era Kansans, Dunn's paintings resonated with his fellow Dakotans and became iconic images of rugged, stalwart individualism on the harsh Plains frontier. By looking homeward with rose-colored glasses, sanctifying on canvas the ideals and myths held most dear by the region's residents, Harvey Dunn won the popular acceptance and acclaim that eluded Curry and many other Great Plains Regionalists.[30]

TRADITIONAL INDIAN PAINTING

Beyond Regionalism, the other major artistic movement to emerge on the Plains in the early twentieth century was a revival of Native American art known as "traditional Indian painting." It is hardly surprising that such a development took place in the region, given the heritage of Plains Indian art (especially hide painting and later ledger-book work) and the fact that almost one-third of all Native Americans were resident in Oklahoma in the decades prior to World War II. The twentieth-century renaissance began in Anadarko, Oklahoma, in 1914, when St. Patrick's Mission School began offering art classes to young reservation Kiowas. In 1918, Susie Peters, a field matron of the U.S. Indian Service, started supplying the aspiring artists with materials and providing informal private tutoring. Recognizing the talent of her most promising students, Peters arranged for James Auchiah (1906–1974), Spencer Asah (1905–1954), Jack Hokeah (1902–1973), Stephen Mopope (1898–1974), and Monroe Tsatoke (1904–1937)—later labeled the Kiowa Five—along with one woman, Lois Smokey (1907–1981), to attend the University of Oklahoma and study art under Oscar Jacobson. With scholarships provided by a Ponca City oilman, the Kiowas arrived in Norman in 1927. Jacobson and his colleague Edith Mahier gave the students remarkable creative freedom; materials, studio space, and plentiful encouragement were provided, but "the imposition of Western standards was to be studiously avoided." Jacobson organized an exhibition of his students' works that traveled across North America and Europe and was displayed at the International Folk Art Congress in Prague in 1929. The flat, colorful paintings of the Kiowa artists, which depicted traditional Indian motifs (especially ceremonial dancing) in a strikingly modern, decorative style, proved compelling to both Indian and non-Indian audiences. "They were the first to be able to develop their art without losing the essential elements of their traditions,"

The Procession, 1958, by Stephen Mopope, Kiowa, 1900–1974. Watercolor, Museum purchase. Courtesy The Philbrook Museum of Art, Tulsa, Oklahoma.

Jacobson enthused. "They enriched it with a personal expression; they breathed life into the rigid impassive figures; they possess[ed] an extraordinary natural flair for color and for composition." The influential, pioneering work of the Kiowa Five at the University of Oklahoma sparked "a prairie fire of enthusiasm" for Indian painting and was one of the first momentous steps in the development of a modern Native American art in the Plains region and beyond.[31]

THE DEPRESSION AND PLAINS ART

Despite the raging debates over Regionalism and the resurgence of a vital Plains Indian art, the depression years were particularly difficult ones for painters, printmakers, and sculptors. Oklahoma City's only fine-art dealer closed up shop in the 1930s; as artist Leonard Good (1907–2000) later recalled, "The dust bowl was supersaturated with grit and times were really rough." In the Dakotas, the only artistic activity was said to be on college and university campuses. Some sought to make light of the trying times: the 1933 Beaux Arts Ball, a benefit for the Nebraska Art Association, "adopted a 'depression' theme, and participants were asked to select the oldest and shabbiest costumes from the family wardrobe." Artists became more resourceful—and desperate—in the straitened circumstances: for example, the prominent Lincoln artist Elizabeth Dolan (1871–1948), who had executed a mural in the new Nebraska state capitol in 1930, sold small easel works for five dollars each from the front windows of the local Sherwin Williams paint dealer. Even the wealthy Wichita art patron and amateur artist Edmund Davison (1877–1944) grew despondent in the 1930s: "The universal economic chaos has for the time being practically killed all interest I have in art—yours, mine or anybody's. It all seems so utterly futile now." As one Kansas newspaper reported in the depths of the depression and the Dust Bowl, "The artist who attempts to earn his or her living from the profession is rarely to be found in Kansas."[32]

That art on the Plains survived and, in some ways, even flourished during the 1930s was due in no small part to unprecedented levels of federal government patronage and institutional support. Under New Deal relief programs, an alphabet soup of new agencies—the PWAP (Public Works of Art Project), the FAP (Federal Art Project), the Treasury Department's Section of Fine Arts, and a variety of other bodies related to museums, crafts, and public art—employed Plains artists, commissioned sculptures and murals, and funded new galleries and public art collections. In 1933–1934, the Nebraska PWAP gave jobs to thirty local artists, who created 180 paintings, drawings, and prints for display in government buildings. In South Dakota, only about a dozen artists were employed by the FAP in 1936–1938, but projects included wood carvings for public schools, illustrated portfolios of Sioux arts, and murals for eight courthouses, libraries, and other civic structures. The North Dakota FAP, under the direction of skilled potters Laura Taylor (?–1959) and Charles Grantier (1909–1979), produced a wide range of decorative and functional ceramics from local clays. Although government officials frequently complained that there were not enough competent artists in Oklahoma to fully staff the relief programs, federal funds underwrote projects to market Indian crafts and, in 1935, established the Oklahoma City Gallery to display, teach, and promote the fine arts. In what was probably the most visible (and controversial) element of the New Deal art programs, more than eighty post office murals were commissioned across the Great Plains between 1934 and 1943. The creation of these original works of art in towns from Yukon, Oklahoma to Lisbon, North Dakota, by distinguished regional artists including Kenneth Adams, Ethel Magafan (1916–1993), and Birger Sandzén was to some observers the ultimate in enlightened government patronage, while to other, more skeptical critics, it was the ultimate in federal profligacy.

The experience of the depression and government relief did not lead all Plains artists to despair and resignation, but awakened in many a new crusading spirit. In the 1930s, artists across the nation embraced the idealistic notion of democratizing art by making it available to a broader public and by encouraging the diffusion of high-quality original works beyond museums, galleries, and the homes of the wealthy. This commitment to art that was accessible—financially as well as aesthetically—influenced many artists to move away from traditional easel painting and toward forms like printmaking. "If the only pictures available for homes were oils and water colors," the Kansas artist Birger Sandzén explained, "the sheer cost of these would necessarily sharply limit the possession of good pictures to the well-to-do. However, practically everybody can afford a good print." Thus prints were a "valuable vehicle to bring Kansas art to the home," an effective way for artists "to enable people of average income to acquire art objects, and to afford school children an opportunity to become acquainted with good pictures." Driven by this philosophy, printmaking flourished on the Great Plains between the world wars. This was particularly true in Kansas, where the Prairie Print Makers, a nationally prominent group that aimed "to further the interests of both artists and laymen in printmaking and collecting," was founded in 1930. The democratic urge in art circles took other forms as well. Sandzén, for instance, opened his Lindsborg studio to all visitors and talked to dozens of women's clubs and civic groups each year. In Nebraska, an enterprising Lincoln housewife arranged in 1935 to take small exhibitions of original paintings and prints to rural areas around the state in the trunk of her Ford sedan. By 1937, this modest program of "art on wheels" had received funding from the Carnegie Corporation of New York, and by 1939, it was estimated that more than 160,000 Nebraskans had seen the traveling displays.[33]

THE DEVELOPMENT OF ART INSTITUTIONS

The institutional structure for art on the Great Plains also continued to develop in the interwar decades. Most obviously, the number of museums and public galleries increased steadily. In Kansas, the Mulvane Museum opened in Topeka in 1924, the Thayer Collection at the University of Kansas in 1926, and the Wichita Art Museum in 1935. The Joslyn Memorial, later described as a "marble tomb of a museum" by Nebraska painter Grant Reynard (1887–1968), was dedicated in Omaha in 1931. The first significant gallery in Oklahoma seems to have been the Laura A. Clubb Art Collection, an assemblage of two hundred European paintings hung in the lobby and corridors of the Clubb Hotel in rural Kaw City. The wife of a rancher made rich by oil, Laura Clubb began collecting in 1922. "When she bought her first painting . . . for $12,500, it is said that her husband protested, 'I could have bought a trainload of cattle for that!' " Oil money also provided for the founding of two significantly more important museums in Tulsa, the Philbrook (1939), housed in the mansion of oilman Waite Phillips, and the Gilcrease (1942), dedicated to preserving the "artistic, cultural and historical records of the American Indian."[34]

Even during the depression, art continued to find a place in the curricula of Plains educational institutions. One Oklahoma observer testified that "By 1930 the civilizing influence of art had definitely established itself in state supported public schools and universities." In Nebraska, nine colleges and universities offered instruction in art or art history in 1932, with more than 1,000 students across the state enrolled. Fifteen Nebraska towns and cities provided high-school art classes, even in the depths of the region's economic and agricultural slump; Grand Island alone boasted three art teachers and annual enrollments of 275 students in the high-school art department. A particularly noteworthy program was established at Bacone College in Muskogee, Oklahoma. Intended to "foster appreciation of Indian art forms and the richness of native materials," the Bacone School of Art was directed by a series of influential Native American painters—Acee Blue Eagle (1909–1959), Woody Crumbo (1912–1989), and Dick West (1912–1996)—all former students of Oscar Jacobson at the University of Oklahoma. These talented artists and teachers turned Bacone into one of the most important centers of Native American art in the nation and trained generations of students in the dynamic techniques of "traditional Indian painting."[35]

The continued vitality of Great Plains art during the depression years was due not only to institutions and federal patronage, but also to a number of extremely active, committed, and creative individuals who ceaselessly promoted regional art and artists. In Kansas, Sandzén was a major presence, but it was C. A. Seward, a native Kansan, celebrated lithographer, and one of the first commercial artists in

Wichita, who was the "catalytic agent [in] the development of a true Kansas art." Seward mentored and encouraged young local talent—including the printmaker William Dickerson (1904–1972) and the sculptor Bruce Moore (1905–1980)—and was a leader in the establishment of both the Kansas Federation of Art and the Wichita Art Museum. In Oklahoma, Nan Sheets was credited with doing "more than any other person to awaken interest in and enthusiasm for art." An accomplished painter, Sheets was the state's FAP director and was instrumental in the founding of the Oklahoma City Gallery. Her home became something of a salon for Oklahoma's cultural elite, "a refreshing oasis in a young state's rather sterile cultural climate," as one admirer called it. The other major force in Southern Plains art was Oscar Jacobson, who from his position at the University of Oklahoma not only shepherded a revival in Native American art, but also patiently nurtured the artists, nascent art organizations, and art-minded public of the "young state." As one biographer concluded, "He was the constant champion for the western regions of the country reminding or calling to the attention of the eastern establishment that real culture existed out there and the days of [the] so-called wild west had departed and a sensibility equal to that of the East had sprung up in its stead, or at least along side its remnants."[36]

The coming of World War II, like the depression, had a dampening effect on art activities. "The general atmosphere is just now very unfavorable for us artists," Birger Sandzén lamented in 1942. "Very few people have time to think of art." But by the early 1940s, Great Plains art activists like Sandzén could claim real achievements in promoting, creating, and defining a place for the fine arts in the region. Despite the consequences of the depression and the Dust Bowl, many Plains artists and critics were openly optimistic about the artistic prospects for the nation's heartland. "Now at last the middle west—Kansas, Nebraska and Oklahoma—is producing artists who cannot be ignored," Wichita art patron Faye Davison (?–?), wife of Edmund Davison, wrote in 1933. "In fact it may be from this very middle west the vital art of the future will come. Far removed from the eastern and western extremes, this section of the country has been forced to develop an individual art drawn from vast plains and pioneer peoples." As John Helm resolutely declared in 1936, "If there is to be an American renaissance within this decade it will be more likely to germinate and develop in Kansas soil than in that of any other state in the union." The national prominence of Regionalism and the dogged tenacity of Plains artists through the "dirty thirties" made such rosy pronouncements—unthinkable just a few years earlier—seem at least conceivable.[37]

A bright future for Plains art also appeared within reach in the early 1940s because, for the first time since the wagon trains rolled across the prairies, art seemed broadly relevant and even important to midwestern society. In the decades since the opening of the frontier, painting, printmaking, and sculpture had evolved from the genteel stuff of women's clubs, society soirées, and prim front parlors to topics of more general concern, discussed in newspapers and barrooms as well as in university studios, high-school classrooms, and public art galleries. That art was controversial, rousing contention and debate often broad and deep, shows how far art—and the public's engagement with art—had progressed in less than a century. This was nowhere more obvious than in Topeka, where between 1937 and 1941 John Steuart Curry was commissioned to paint a series of murals on the walls of the Kansas State capitol. What had been promoted as a belated homecoming for the expatriate artist-hero turned into an extended and bitter conflict. Curry's *Kansas Pastoral*, an idyll of midwestern farm life, was roundly criticized for its inaccurate depictions of pigs' tails and bulls' legs. *The Tragic Prelude*, Curry's now-iconic image of a fiery John Brown, rifle in one hand, Bible in the other, engendered even more vitriolic attacks from newspapers, women's groups, and legislators. Although the storm in Topeka left Curry shattered and Kansas branded as narrow, unimaginative, and aesthetically ignorant in the national media, the Kansas mural controversy highlighted how visible, compelling, and significant art had become in Great Plains life. As one Oklahoma artist succinctly put it, looking back on the experience of the 1930s, "Art had reached its respectable voting age along with the state itself."[38]

GREAT PLAINS ART SINCE 1945

For all the optimistic prewar prognostications, the Great Plains did not emerge as the vibrant heart of the nation's artistic community in the wake of World War II. In the changed circumstances after 1945, the Regionalist idiom and its midwestern stronghold, both of which had seemed so authentic, stable, and reassuring in the 1930s, suddenly looked naïve, conventional, and decidedly provincial. As one chronicler of Oklahoma art observed in the early 1960s:

Twenty years ago the picture titles in the art catalogs revealed the primary interest of the artists to be in the local scene, but as artists have been exposed to a kaleidoscopic variety of experiences there is a difference in the catalogs issued after 1940. During World War II servicemen saw the new directions in European art; many returned to study under the G.I. Bill or other such scholarships. With the perfection of truer and cheaper printing processes, art books with excellent color reproductions became available and added scope to the students' education. These factors, and an awareness of the stimulating vistas opened by science, have created new approaches to art.

In the radically altered political and cultural landscape after 1945, America's ascent as a world power, postwar reengagement with European artistic fashions, and the rise of abstract expressionism—whose emphasis on spontaneity, emotion, and the collective unconscious was the virtual antithesis of Regionalism—combined to leave the Great Plains and its artists well outside the evolving artistic mainstream.[39]

As New York City emerged as the center of national (and even global) artistic trends, the postwar Great Plains returned to its familiar position among America's cultural backwaters. As *American Artist* magazine reported in October 1955, capturing well the metropolitan stereotype of the Plains, "A few years ago we heard a story, probably apocryphal, to the effect that when a famous company was running a series of ads featuring an artist from each of the states, an impasse was reached at North Dakota: there were no important artists in—or from—North Dakota." The prominent historian Allan Nevins, speaking in 1954 at the commemoration of Kansas's territorial centennial, decried the state's lack of cultural achievements: "All in all, Kansas life of today is as yet deprived of the enrichment by sculpture and music, painting and poesy, which might perpetuate nobilities of the past and nourish dreams of the future." Few Plains artists felt compelled by such slights to defend their region's long and rich artistic heritage. Indeed, most Plains artists and critics came to accept their own marginalization and implicit inferiority in the post-war hierarchy of cutting-edge contemporary art. "Would any artist remain in western North Dakota—or in any small town—if he were any good?" one prominent North Dakota scholar and poet lamented in 1965. "On the other hand, is any good artist encouraged to stay? Is there a public capable of giving him the kind of support which would keep him there?" In the decades after World War II, many Plains artists labored vigorously to distance themselves from anything that might be considered provincial in favor of cosmopolitan styles and the secondhand isms of the international art scene. In the headlong rush to embrace abstraction, notions of a universal "modern art," and the cultural hegemony of the East and West Coasts, postwar artists lost touch with the Great Plains' artistic heritage and with a sense of what made the life, landscape, and culture of the region distinctive.[40]

Modern and Conservative Style Controversies

Although the Plains art elite—critics, patrons, and cognoscenti—as well as many (if not most) trained artists in the region, were carried away in the postwar torrent of fashionable isms, some artists and a large slice of the general public remained strongly inclined toward realism, the Regionalist style, and a more accessible, humane art. A fascinating 1931 study of the artworks in 388 North Dakota homes revealed not "a single copy of any modernistic painting, nor of any immoral or suggestive picture. . . . This would indicate that modernistic, and certainly futurist and cubist art [have] made no appeal to the mass of people and that these productions are as yet in an experimental stage, surviving because of the sympathetic interest of a limited number of patrons." A similar survey conducted in 1961 found that while "modernistic art" had made some progress in North Dakota, its audience was not large or broadly distributed throughout society, but was predominantly urban, well educated, and relatively high income. In Oklahoma, debates over styles divided the artistic community, as well as the public consumers of art. The Association of Oklahoma Artists, a group formed in 1916 by Oscar Jacobson, fractured in 1939: "Devotees of the tried-and-true pictorialism argued against more adventurous moderns who either distorted natural appearances for decorative or expressive purposes or banished recognizable elements completely. To be 'realistic,' 'figurative,' 'non-objective,' or whatever required a serious decision. Each artist would have to declare an allegiance to the academies or join the avant-gardes. The association's officers decided to split its awards and offer identical prizes for two types of creativity." By the 1960s, the aesthetic divide spread to museums, and a group splintered from the fashionable Oklahoma City Gallery: "Two camps evolved from the art lovers in the community: the 'moderns,' who embraced the spirit of a new artistic era, and the 'conservatives,' who insisted that art retain elements of representation of real objects. So passionate were these two camps that a Museum of Conservative Art was founded in 1968 at the Red Ridge Estate to concentrate exclusively on representational art." The furor over "modern art" extended to classrooms as well. As one commentator wrote of the University of Nebraska:

> [After World War II,] students who had been copying casts were now set to "fingerpainting," as it was somewhat derisively termed by the few realists left.

The studies of anatomy and perspective were almost dropped from the curriculum in favor of the new freedom. "Modern" art thrust itself at one from every advertisement, from television, from gallery and printed page. As one critic put it, "it had almost superseded religion." No other subject matter, unless it was politics, presented so many opportunities for argument, for debate, and for disagreement.[41]

Postwar public art proved a particularly acute source of aesthetic contention. Artists and art elites wedded to abstraction clashed with a taxpaying public that demanded a more readable, compelling mode of artistic expression. In 1976, for example, controversy swirled around the Nebraska I-80 Bicentennial Sculpture Project, a series of large roadside works strung along Interstate 80, "a sculpture garden approximately 500 miles long." The eight pieces, all nonobjective and designed by prominent artists (none of them native Nebraskans), were touted by boosters as potent symbols of sophistication and culture that would elevate the state in the eyes of the nation. The critics of the sculptures were numerous and vocal: "This art, and I use the term loosely, does not fit in our landscape, industry or history," one Nebraskan wrote. "It has no bearing whatsoever to anything; it is one person's nightmare and one person only. Why must the public put up with it?" "People simply do not like abstract art," another complained. "Cultural snobs are forcing these upon us." In Huron, South Dakota, the public reacted strongly to the 1979 installation of *Hoe-Down*, a nonrepresentational wood and steel sculpture by the California artist Guy Dill, in front of the city's new federal building. A group of irate local citizens "undedicated the sculpture, auctioned it off for the price of a peanut (a symbolic gesture; the sculpture remains)," and successfully lobbied one of the state's U.S. senators to freeze temporarily all federal funding for public art.[42]

Even in Plains Indian art, "modern" styles had an important and controversial impact after World War II. The most influential Native American artist "merging the old with the new" was Oscar Howe (1915–1983), a Yanktonai Sioux born on the Crow Creek Reservation in South Dakota in 1915. After an unhappy childhood marked by illness, Howe studied from 1935 to 1938 with Dorothy Dunn at the Studio of the Santa Fe Indian School, a leading institution in the development of "traditional Indian painting." Howe executed murals for the Federal Art Project during the depression and, following service in Europe in World War II, received a master of fine arts degree from the University of Oklahoma and served on the faculty of the University of South Dakota. Howe's paintings, alive with motion and color, integrated "modern techniques with the traditions of the Sioux and of the land which produced him." Although Howe himself steadfastly denied any Western influence on his style, critics have generally stressed the creative fusion in his painting: "Taking the artistic expressions of modern art (particularly Cubism), Howe synthesized these elements with the traditional approach of Sioux symbolism and the tutored style of The Studio in order to emerge with a hybrid style which was new, innovative, striking, theatrical, and aesthetically pleasing." Indeed, in 1958, a work Howe submitted to the Philbrook Museum's thirteenth Indian Art Annual was rejected by the jury as too abstract to constitute "traditional" Native American painting. Howe's now-famous response, called by one scholar a "declaration of emancipation" for modern Indian art, encouraged generations of

Native American artists to experiment, innovate, and create new traditions: "There is much more to Indian Art than pretty, stylized pictures. . . . Are we to be held back forever with one phase of Indian painting, with no right for individualism, dictated to as the Indian always has been, put on reservations and treated like a child, and only the White Man knows what is best for him?"[43]

Place of the Fine Arts in the Plains after 1945

For all the postwar contention and stylistic fluidity, the fine arts became increasingly prominent features in Great Plains life in the decades following 1945. Artists both amateur and professional proliferated across the region. The growth of individual participation in the arts was particularly striking. A 1954 study of North Dakota observed that "There has been, during the past few years, a great upsurge of interest in the arts as a hobby, a recreation, a means of relaxation." Women's clubs were active promoters of this trend; in Kansas, the state federation encouraged its members, "Be involved in Creativity—the glorious adventure that lets man approach the image of God—the exhilarating experience that raises man above the animals." Local artists' guilds, painting clubs, and art associations flourished; in western South Dakota alone, a dozen such organizations—from the Spearfish Paint and Palette Club to the Rapid City Hobbyettes—mushroomed between 1950 and 1965. Art education was adopted in virtually every school, college, and university on the Plains. More private galleries and public museums seemed to sprout with every passing year. The South Dakota Museum of Art was established by the State Federation of Women's Clubs in 1970. The Sheldon Museum at the University of Nebraska at Lincoln opened its doors in 1963, while the Museum of Nebraska Art, incorporating the state's official collection, was dedicated in Kearney in 1986. Where formal gallery space was unavailable, enterprising local artists improvised. The Bismarck Art Association, for example, hung shows in the Steak House Restaurant at the Grand Pacific Hotel, "a split-level dining room with a large charcoal grill as part of its decor." "When [the] Steak House and exhibits of originals begin operation," the *Bismarck Tribune* exclaimed in 1955, "rare and well done describe both food and fancy!"[44]

New Funding and Interest in Art

A significant boost to artistic activity, particularly in rural parts of the Great Plains, was provided by state arts commissions and councils, which were formed across the region in the 1960s. Funded by state governments and federal appropriations channeled through the National Endowment for the Arts, these organizations undertook a wide variety of programs to stimulate art appreciation and support regional artists. Through artist-in-residence projects, sponsorship of traveling exhibitions, grants to local agencies, and hundreds of other focused initiatives, the state arts commissions and councils contributed broadly to the vigorous postwar expansion of artistic creativity on the Plains. Taking responsibility for "developing the arts where they are not," the state bodies have been particularly concerned with bringing opportunities for viewing and creating art to underserved groups (such as Native American and Hispanic populations) and smaller communities, especially in rural areas. As one commentator concluded in 1989, "The arts councils and arts commissions, together with the almost universal availability of the television and the automobile, have succeeded in making the arts accessible to virtually everyone across the vast sweep of the Great Plains."[45]

With such grassroots energy and widespread engagement with the arts across the Great Plains, an artistic reaction against trendy isms, metropole envy, and "the international march toward homogeneity and the loss of particularity" was all but inevitable. An aesthetic and intellectual break from the postwar mainstream of "modern art" and a conscious return to regional subject matter and a representational style began in the 1970s and accelerated in the 1980s. At the core of this artistic homecoming was the belated rediscovery of a "sense of place," the "renewed acknowledgment of the centrality of landscape, climate and local traditions" to the lifestyle and culture of the Plains. "Over the past two decades," one perceptive observer wrote in 1988, "poets, painters, and photographers have begun to celebrate once again the beauty of the Kansas landscape. . . . Kansans now have 'permission' to appreciate their physical environment." In the works of the Nebraskans Hal Holoun (b. 1939) and Keith Jacobshagen (b. 1941), the Kansans Robert Sudlow (b. 1920), Walter Hatke (b. 1948), and Phil Epp (b. 1946), and many others throughout the region lay a renewed appreciation of the Plains landscape and an imperative "to attend to roots, to notice what is about us, to involve ourselves deeply in our own locations, to recognize that in some hidden way we are the products of our places."[46]

Economics also played a part in the resurgence of a distinctive, regionally rooted, and vibrant Great Plains art. The potential value of cultural amenities and a dynamic arts community as inducements to tourism and central elements in the region's quality of life became increasingly obvious during the 1970s and 1980s. The South Dakota Arts Council, for example, was chartered with the objective of economic development explicitly delineated: "The South Dakota Legislature, being aware of the impact of culture on a stable economy, desires to stimulate, encourage, and give recognition and assistance to the fine arts." In North Dakota, the economic impact of the arts in 1985 was estimated at more than $5 million; in Nebraska, almost two million people—more than the entire population of the state—attended arts events in 1966. As the executive director of the Nebraska Arts Council declared in the 1970s, revealing the profound intertwining of economics and the arts, as well as a lingering inferiority complex on the Plains, "The arts have grown tremendously in Nebraska in the past few years. . . . A $38 million business is one Nebraskans can, and should, be proud of—one that should help lay to rest the misconception back east that Nebraska is a cultural desert." Art could thus be enriching financially as well as culturally, and an accessible regional art, rooted in the landscape, history, and culture of the Great Plains, seemed to appeal to local audiences and tourists alike.[47]

Among the most ambitious artistic developments on the Great Plains since World War II is the Redlin Art Center, a lavishly appointed museum established in 1997 beside Interstate 29 in Watertown, South Dakota. Home to hundreds of patriotic and unapologetically sentimental paintings of charming Dakota homesteads, blazing sunsets, and cozy hunting lodges by hometown hero Terry Redlin (b. 1936), the center has lured more than 250,000 visitors a year to its galleries and fully stocked gift shop. Although critics have dismissed Redlin's commercialized creations, and his nostalgic mythologizing harkens back to the canvases of his fellow South Dakotan Harvey Dunn, his work has enjoyed enormous popularity and has been hailed by Senator Tom Daschle as "some of the most enduring images of rural life that we will ever see."[48] In the end, the successes of Great Plains enterprises like the Redlin Art Center concretely demonstrate the potent convergence of art, commerce, and a renewed popular yearning for authenticity and a sense of place at the turn of the twenty-first century.

NEW UNDERSTANDINGS OF GREAT PLAINS ART

Since the 1970s, in tandem with the revival of a distinctive, locally grounded Great Plains art, scholars, collectors, and artists themselves have begun to reexamine and reappraise the artistic heritage of the region. New understandings of what constitutes art and who is regarded as an artist have broadened and enriched the received narratives of Plains art history and challenged many assumptions about the region's cultural development. Through expansion of the boundaries of what is considered "art" and an "artist," a fuller comprehension of the complex evolution of the visual arts on the Great Plains has begun to emerge.

Although the time-honored image of the Great Plains artist—a white man, formally trained in the European artistic tradition—is tenacious, it is now apparent that the artists of the region during the past 150 years have been a far more diverse lot. Plains women artists have received increasing critical acclaim and popular attention since World War II, and during the past several decades, historical research has revealed the important contributions of pioneering female painters, sculptors, and printmakers. Once obscure figures like Ada Caldwell, Elizabeth Dolan, Nan Sheets, the Kansan Mary Huntoon (1896–1970), and the Oklahoman Olinka Hrdy (1902–1987) are now rightly honored as some of the region's most proficient and influential artists, teachers, and activists. While the presence of creative Native Americans in Great Plains art has long been difficult to ignore, the role of African Americans and other racial minorities has only recently begun to be explored. Prominent artists like painter Aaron Douglas (1898–1979), born in Kansas, educated at the University of Nebraska, and a leader in the Harlem Renaissance, and photographer Gordon Parks (b. 1912), a native of Fort Scott, Kansas, are now proudly regarded as products of the Plains. Asian Americans, many of whom (like Kansas State University ceramicist Yoshiro Ikeda [dates unknown]) work in the region's postsecondary institutions, have been critically and popularly acknowledged. Though racial diversity is not historically one of the defining characteristics of Plains artists, or indeed of the Plains themselves—North Dakota, for example, had only 201 black residents in 1940—even a cursory survey reveals that the region's creative talent has clearly not been monopolized by white male artists.

Many forms traditionally viewed as crafts and not considered "true" art have been reassessed as significant components of the artistic heritage of the Great Plains. A number of these forms, implicitly denigrated and often simply ignored by later art historians, were associated with Plains women. China painting, for instance, was widely practiced in the region in the late nineteenth and early twentieth centuries but has only relatively recently become the subject of serious historical study. Quilting is another excellent example. Before a resurgence of interest in quilting in the 1980s—spurred to a large extent by the women's movement and feminist scholarship—the practice was generally regarded as "a subsistence activity of farm wives, an immigrant tradition, or an avocation of middle-class homemakers." By the 1990s, as the creative work of women and textile art in general were gaining more critical and scholarly respect, quilts came off beds and out of cedar chests to hang on the walls of major museums and fashionable urban galleries. New research has revealed the diversity of quilting traditions on the Plains—including the work of African American and Indian artists—and documented the national importance of prominent quiltmakers like Rose Kretsinger (1886–1963) of Emporia, Kansas, and Camille Nixdorf Phelan (1882–1946) of Oklahoma City.[49]

Although once derided as "uninspired and uninspiring artifacts," folk arts—traditional forms, often rooted in immigrant communities, that "reflect and conform to community aesthetics and values"—have attracted new interest since the 1970s. As critics, collectors, and the public have sought a more authentic, distinctive, and regionally specific art, the work of Plains folk artists—from Czech egg decorators in Kansas to the fabricators of Russian German grave crosses in North Dakota and to Oklahoma bootmakers—has found new audiences and admirers. As one scholar noted in 1989, the folk arts "are not only a link to our past but also a testament to the vitality of traditional life [on the Plains] today. If we need to find a symbolic rock of stability on our vast prairie lands that anchors us to both the past and the present, it is folk tradition." "Nonacademic," self-taught artists working outside a specific folk art tradition, like the South Dakota farmwife and trompe l'oeil painter Myra Miller (1882–1961) and the celebrated Elizabeth "Grandma" Layton (1909–1993) of Wellsville, Kansas, have also been the subject of new inquiry by art historians. Particular attention has been devoted to the region's "grassroots" or "outsider" art, the generally fantastical creations of what one pundit has described as the "noble savages of the art world." A nontraditional form that is "not rooted in community tastes, often politically motivated, and inventive in its imagery and use of materials," grassroots art has flourished on the Great Plains. Some of the noteworthy works in the region—S. P. Dinsmoor's (1843–1932) curious Garden of Eden in Lucas, Kansas, Jim Reinders' (b. 1927) iconic Carhenge in western Nebraska, Ed Galloway's (1880–1962) monumental concrete totem pole on a side road in rural northeast Oklahoma—are now widely judged to be among the most important examples of grassroots art in the nation.[50]

Other previously overlooked art forms have also begun to receive long-overdue recognition. Artist-craftsmen such as the multitalented Lester Raymer (1907–1991) of Lindsborg, Kansas, and artist-decorators such as the Kansan Adam Rohe (1844–1923), who was responsible for the original design of the Mitchell Corn Palace in South Dakota, and the Danish immigrants Charles Hansen (1868–?) and James Willer (1886–1944) in Nebraska have only recently been recognized as important figures in the history of Plains culture. Art pottery has long been a

Ed Galloway's Totem Pole, Lawrence/Baldwin City, Kansas. Courtesy of Carolyn Comfort.

commercially and artistically significant activity in the region, and collectors have assiduously documented major Plains producers like Frankoma (Oklahoma), Dryden (Kansas), and the Dakota potteries Rosemeade, Dickota, and University of North Dakota School of Mines. The rich heritage of Plains photography has also been revealed during the past several decades. Historians have begun to record the work of the hundreds of frontier photographers (including many women) in the region, and Solomon D. Butcher's (1856–1927) evocative portraits of Nebraska homesteaders in the 1880s and 1890s have been acknowledged as the "major visual chronicle" of pioneer life in America. Other noted photographers from or of the Plains—the Dakotan Levon West (1900–1968), who was a trailblazer in color photography under the pseudonym Ivan Dmitri; Wright Morris (1910–1998), whose haunting images of small-town Nebraska captured "a world caught between change and changelessness"; the Farm Security Administration artists (including Arthur Rothstein [1915–1985] and Dorothea Lange [1895–1965]) whose photographs of Dust Bowl Kansas and Oklahoma became enduring symbols of the "dirty thirties"; the acclaimed photojournalist W. Eugene Smith (1918–1978), originally from Wichita; and influential contemporary landscape photographers like the Kansans Terry Evans (b. 1944) and Larry Schwarm (b. 1944)—have been the subject of major exhibitions and increasing scholarly study.[51]

In short, a more inclusive approach to art on the Great Plains has uncovered unexpected diversity, creativity, and dynamism in the region's culture during the past century and a half. Looking beyond the elite traditions of painting, sculpture, and printmaking, as well as the long-standing stereotype of the professional artist, scholars can now recognize that the arts have been more broadly based, meaningful, and indeed intrinsic to Great Plains society than was previously assumed.

DEFINING THE ART OF THE GREAT PLAINS

Given the richness and diversity of the region's cultural heritage, specifying precisely what constitutes "Great Plains art" is almost certainly impossible. All observers seem to agree that no single style has been shared by Plains artists, nor can the region's painters, printmakers, sculptors, photographers, and craftspeople be readily classified as members of one particular school. As Norman Geske has written, in a statement that applies equally as well to the Great Plains as a whole as to Nebraska, "It is obvious enough that 'the art of Nebraska' is a concept that is largely meaningless, certainly in a geographic sense but also in terms of social and cultural history. We cannot assume, local patriotism aside, that what has happened within the boundaries of this state is substantially different in kind or quality from similar artistic developments to the north, south, east, or west of us." David Park Curry has put it even more concisely: "A geographic boundary does not necessarily create a cohesive group or a pervading style." Despite this fact, numerous scholars, critics, and artists past and present have expounded confidently on a real, if rather hazily defined, Great Plains art. Indeed, while a rigorous definition is elusive, it is possible to delineate several distinctive elements that have shaped the art of the Plains and to identify a variety of common concerns, characteristic themes, and shared influences that have been widespread, even if not universal, among the region's artists.[52]

Many commentators have suggested that the heritage of the pioneers and the experience of frontier life profoundly shaped the visual arts of the Great Plains. To some, it was stout "pioneer virtues"—"qualities of courage, endurance, and a sense of justice," to name but a few—that fired artistic activity in the region. For others, it was the myriad challenges and opportunities of the frontier—which gave rise to a determined temperament, a freedom from time-honored traditions, and an openness to change and a certain creative vigor—that have made the art of the region distinctive. "It is here on the plains of the Dakotas," one observer contended, "where our heritage is but a generation or two away, that the arts can and will flourish in their finest sense. . . . It is here in South Dakota where the earth is so much a part of our lives . . . and where we deal with one another openly and without pretense . . . that the arts have some meaning, some expression of our condition that says something about us and our times." The frontier experience was also undoubtedly a major factor in the unusually high profile of women in the cultural development of the Plains. The female artists of the region, art historian Joni Kinsey has convincingly argued, "were at the forefront of a developing professionalism that gender bias often denied to women elsewhere. . . . Perhaps because institutions were slower to mature [on the Great Plains], women had a longer and consequently greater impact on the development of the fine arts. Lack of male competition may have been another reason why women commanded positions as artists and cultural entrepreneurs in the early years, perhaps because of a gender bias *against* artistic culture that would have relegated it largely to females." Pioneering women artists were thus not simply pathbreakers in the settlement of the Plains but "were part of a frontier of a different sort—one that challenged traditional boundaries of profession, gender, and forms of visual representation."[53]

An enduring sense of isolation that derived from the region's low population densities, great distances, dearth of major metropolitan areas, and remoteness from the trendsetting East and West Coasts was another major influence on the evolution of art on the Great Plains. From the late nineteenth century to the present, this isolation has proven challenging for artists financially, intellectually, and psychologically. Many promising young painters and sculptors have sought what Harvey Dunn called the "glimmering along the horizon," leaving the Plains for training, professional opportunities, and more stimulating community life in New York, Chicago, Taos, or Paris. As late as 1985, one North Dakotan complained that "there are few collectors, poorly funded museums, no critical press and no commercial art galleries at this time that encourage regional artists." A noted critic of Kansas art once remarked that "The rancor I detect in many Kansas artists may be attributable to their relative isolation, to struggling on or being forced to escape from a demanding, rigorous way of life." Yet many commentators have also asserted that isolation from the established art centers, colonies, and academies has had a positive impact on Great Plains artists, allowing for greater creativity, individuality, and expressive range. "Kansas possesses no time-honored art culture," Gertrude Dix Newlin observed in 1951. "Instead, among the young painters, we see the growing desire to throw off the European yoke, seek new paths, and find for themselves a significant expression of the new age. . . . In this Middle-Western state the artist is free to express himself with all the originality and force he possesses." As another sympathetic historian later noted, "Nebraska inspires an earthiness, a freedom, and a diversity."[54]

An abiding characteristic of the artistic culture of the Plains has been a lack of private patronage of the visual arts. For all the noted patrons and collectors in the region—Frank Hall in Lincoln, Edmund Davison in Wichita, Thomas Gilcrease in Tulsa—financial support for local artists has always been scant. "Exhibitions have passed us by and art patrons have been an almost unknown quantity," one supporter of Kansas art wrote in 1933. A fascinating case of patronage on a small scale was that of the Sioux painter Andrew Standing Soldier (1917–1967), whose supporter, the Gordon, Nebraska, car dealer Doug Borman, negotiated commissions, arranged for provisions, and supplied studio space in his showroom. But such situations have been rare indeed for Plains artists. As a jaded Oklahoma painter noted, most wealthy art buyers tended to look down on the "local talent": "Evidently the people who would like to have owned the paintings could not afford them, and patrons who could easily have bought them preferred shopping in more prestigious art marts." Under such circumstances, the government became more significant as a sponsor of the arts on the Great Plains than appears to have been the case in other parts of the nation. Through depression-era relief programs, arts faculties at colleges and universities, collecting by public museums, commissions in public buildings, and support from state arts councils, government entities, federal, state and local, have been active, generous, and important patrons in the region since the 1930s.[55]

As generations of critics and artists have attested, the art of the Great Plains has been affected most deeply by the unique landscape and dramatic climate of the region. During the past century and a half, artists have sought a hidden beauty on the Plains, forged a spiritual identification with the land and sky, and cultivated a genuine sense of place in a forbidding and unaccommodating environment. Artists have, to be sure, approached the Plains landscape's "solemn magic," what one commentator has called the "language of the Kansas atmosphere and the Kansas sky," in disparate and profoundly individual ways. Birger Sandzén, one noted critic observed, "has come from the plains where things grow rank and strong, from Kansas where he has interpreted ugliness, disharmony, monotony in terms of beauty and yet faithfully and with affectionate wisdom." For some artists, art reflected the struggle with a hostile environment and the uncertain triumph of human culture on the Great Plains. "North Dakota is a state where man and his machines are engaged in a constant struggle with nature for survival," the painter Ross Shattuck explained. "To wrest a living from its soil requires a lot of stamina. I wanted to present it as a place seemingly bleak and barren but suggestive of the rugged beauty of limitless distances and the challenge of rigorous elemental forces." The sweeping prairies, endless skies, and explosive storms of the Plains influenced the work of other artists in even more fundamental ways. According to one appraisal of the South Dakota artist Signe Stuart (b. 1937), "Her long sojourn in a part of the United States that is marked by particularly stark confrontations of earth, sky, and weather, by the echoes of previous civilizations and of humankind's efforts to utilize nature's resources, is all imbued into her work. The breeze that often seems to rush through her paintings, their broad expanses and gradations of color and shape, are her gestures to the prairie and to the life we have wrought upon it." For a number of artists, the lack of aesthetic promise on the Plains—"the very inadequacy of the landscape"—has become a creative asset. This sentiment was strongly affirmed by the Kansas painter Robert Sudlow: "Kansas in particular is understated. I like to take students out here because there's not that 'subject'—a lighthouse or a mountain or something very picturesque—but there's space and there's the weather, which is always in flux. The things that are here are a kaleidoscope of change. Kansas is a microcosm. Everything is here, but it is secret. And the more secret it is, the more precious it is."[56]

The importance of landscape to Great Plains art is further demonstrated by the long-standing pattern, surprisingly common in the region, of using the land itself as canvas and palette in the creation of art. The most famous example of this is, of course, Mount Rushmore, the monumental (if aesthetically undistinguished) portrait of four U.S. presidents carved out of a South Dakota granite cliff by Gutzon Borglum (1867–1941) between 1927 and 1941. Hailed by the state as a tourism godsend, damned by environmentalists and Native Americans as a desecration, and largely ignored by art historians and critics, Mount Rushmore is a powerful statement of American settlement, ownership, and mastery of the Black Hills and, indeed, of the entire Great Plains region upon which Borglum's gargantuan sculptures gaze. Other examples of utilizing the land in art, some well known and others obscure, abound on the Plains. The North Dakotan Ida Prokop (1902–1990), for instance, transformed pheasant feathers and dried local plants into her celebrated *Prairie Pictures*. At the University of North Dakota School of Mines and other art potteries, ceramicists have used native clays and glazes made from local minerals to craft distinctive regional products. At the Mitchell Corn Palace, a South Dakota institution since 1892, tons of Plains corn, oats, and flax are consumed each year in the creation of massive grain murals. Even contemporary artists like the South Dakota sculptor Carol Hepper (b. 1953), who used wood and bone scavenged off the prairie, and Kansas "crop artist" Stan Herd (b. 1950), who manipulates plantings and earthworks to make murals on the land, have contributed to the creative blurring of landscape and art that has become characteristic of the Great Plains.

For a number of observers, however, the defining feature of Great Plains art is even more basic and more intangible than a deep and enduring connection with the land. According to John Helm, the artists of the region share an "interest in the local scene and honesty in portraying it." To the art historian Donald Bartlett Doe, Plains artists were marked by "authenticity," a "common interest in their physical surroundings," and "a reluctance to mythologize the landscape." As one Kansas chronicler put it, "Kansas artists in no way resemble [each other] except in their sincerity, but it is sincerity that characterizes art in Kansas." These commentators and many others have sensed in Plains art, if not a specific style, then a characteristic directness and honesty, an attachment to the immediate and the local, an understanding of and affection for the region, and, perhaps above all, a singular "fidelity to place." The Nebraska artist Grant Reynard may have captured the indefinable essence of Great Plains art as well as anyone in his poetic description of a journey across his home state:

> Flattest prairies, farms that stretched horizons
> Cottonwoods, spare placed, simple houses,
> All the country blistered by the sun.
> But this was my own state, my native land,
> Everywhere that I could look lay beauty
> Art was everywhere in simple things.[57]

RESOURCE GUIDE

Printed Sources

Barr, Paul. *North Dakota Artists*. Grand Forks: University of North Dakota Library, 1954.

Geske, Norman. *Art and Artists in Nebraska*. Lincoln: Sheldon Memorial Art Gallery, University of Nebraska–Lincoln, 1983.

Good, Leonard. "Oklahoma's Art in the 1930s: A Remembrance." *Chronicles of Oklahoma* 70 (summer 1992): 194–209.

Huseboe, Arthur, with a section on Sioux Indian arts by Arthur Amiotte. *An Illustrated History of the Arts in South Dakota*. Sioux Falls: Center for Western Studies, Augustana College, 1989.

Kinsey, Joni. *Plain Pictures: Images of the American Prairie*. Washington: Smithsonian Institution Press, 1996.

Stuart, Joseph. *The Art of South Dakota*. Brookings: South Dakota Memorial Art Center, South Dakota State University, 1974.

Tsutsui, William, and Marjorie Swann. "Kansans and the Visual Arts." *Kansas History* 25 (winter 2002–2003): 272–295.

Wycoff, Lydia, ed. *Visions and Voices: Native American Painting from the Philbrook Museum of Art*. Tulsa: Philbrook Museum of Art, 1996.

Web Sites

Goddard, Stephen, *The Prairie Print Makers*, Spencer Museum of Art Printroom
http://www.ku.edu/~sma/ppm/ppm.htm

Goddard, Stephen, *Remembering the Family Farm: 150 Years of American Prints*, Spencer Museum of Art Printroom
http://www.ku.edu/~sma/barns/barnhome.htm

Organizations

Beach Museum of Art
Kansas State University
701 Beach Lane
Manhattan, KS 66506
http://www.ksu.edu/bma/

An important collection of prints, paintings, and three-dimensional works by Kansas and regional artists.

Gilcrease Museum
1400 North Gilcrease Museum Road
Tulsa, OK 74127-2100
http://www.gilcrease.org

One of the world's largest collections of western art, including important works by the "artist explorers," Oklahoma artists, and the "Kiowa Five" and other Native American artists.

Grassroots Art Center
213 South Main Street
Lucas, KS 67648
http://skyways.lib.ks.us/Kansas/towns/Lucas/grassrootsartcenter.htm

Displays include stone carvings, metal totems, and concrete sculptures by a number of important self-taught, "outsider" artists.

Museum of Nebraska Art
University of Nebraska–Kearney
2401 Central Ave.
Kearney, NE 68847
http://monet.unk.edu/mona/

Home of the Nebraska Art Collection, recognized by the state legislature as the official visual art collection of the state of Nebraska.

Philbrook Museum of Art
2727 South Rockford Road
Tulsa, OK 74114
http://www.philbrook.org

Holdings include important collections of traditional and modern Native American art from the Plains region.

South Dakota Art Museum
South Dakota State University
Medary Avenue at Harvey Dunn Street
Brookings, SD 57007
http://www3.sdstate.edu/Administration/SouthDakotaArtMuseum/

Holdings include major collections of works by South Dakota artists, including the paintings of Harvey Dunn and Oscar Howe.

State Historical Society of North Dakota Museum
North Dakota Heritage Center
612 East Boulevard Avenue
Bismarck, ND 58505-0830
http://www.state.nd.us/hist/index.html

Collections include paintings, sculptures, and photographs by North Dakota artists (including Ida Prokop and Einar Olstad) as well as important holdings of North Dakota pottery.

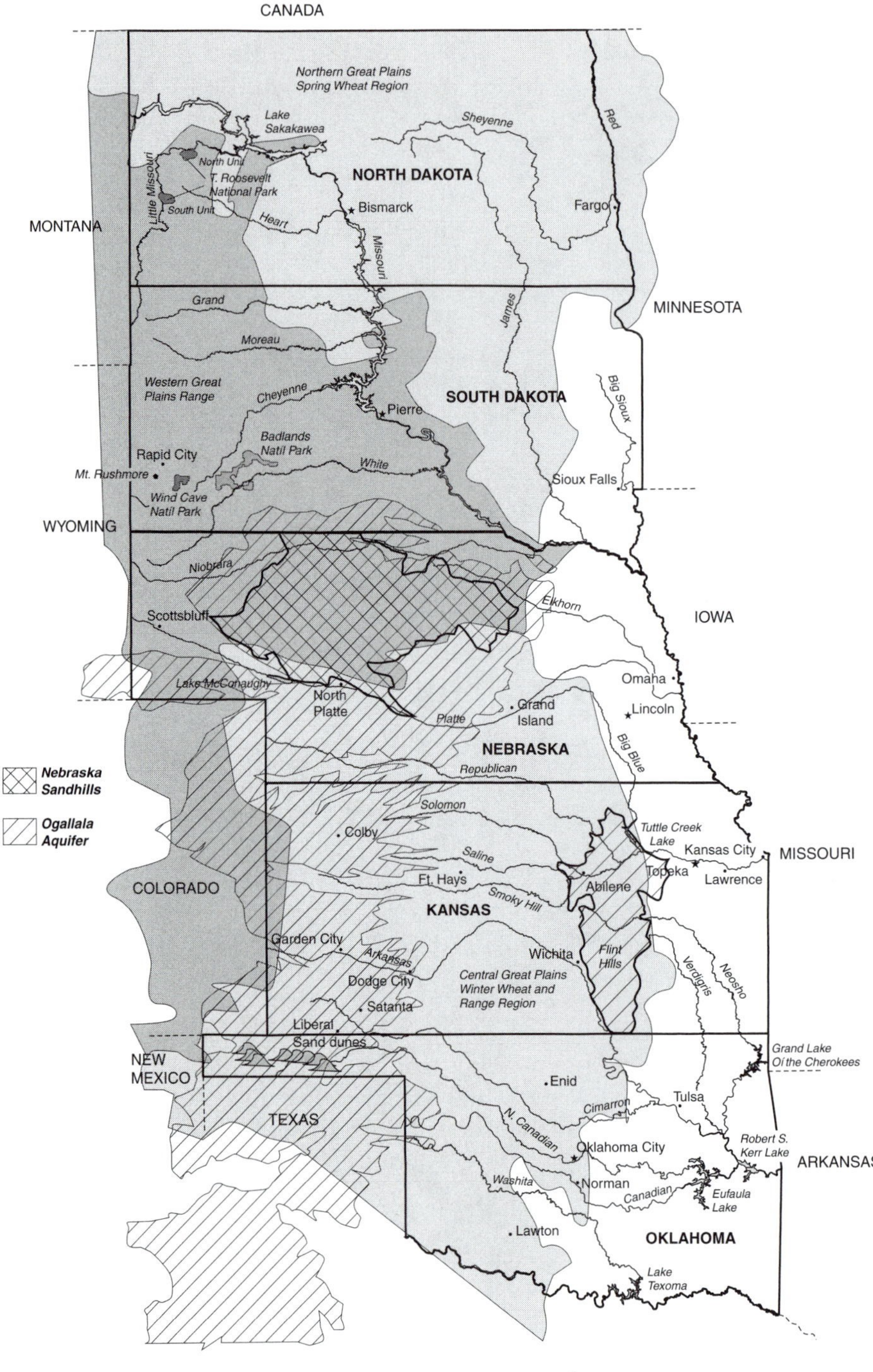

CANADA

Northern Great Plains
Spring Wheat Region

Sheyenne

Red

Lake
Sakakawea

NORTH DAKOTA

Little Missouri

North Unit
T. Roosevelt
National Park

★ Bismarck

MONTANA

South Unit

Heart

Missouri

Fargo

Grand

MINNESOTA

Moreau

SOUTH DAKOTA

Western Great
Plains Range

Cheyenne

★ Pierre

James

Big Sioux

Rapid City •

Badlands
Natil Park

White

Mt. Rushmore •

Wind Cave
Natil Park

Sioux Falls

WYOMING

Niobrara

Elkhorn

IOWA

Scottsbluff

Lake McConaughy

North
Platte

Platte

• Grand
Island

Omaha •

★ Lincoln

NEBRASKA

Republican

Big Blue

|⊠| **Nebraska**
Sandhills

Solomon

• Colby

Saline

Tuttle Creek
Lake

Kansas City

MISSOURI

|⧄| **Ogallala**
Aquifer

Ft. Hays •

Smoky Hill

Abilene •

Topeka ★

Lawrence

COLORADO

KANSAS

Garden City •

Arkansas

Wichita •

Flint
Hills

Verdigris

Neosho

Dodge City •

• Satanta

Central Great Plains
Winter Wheat and
Range Region

Liberal •

Sand dunes

Grand Lake
Ol the Cherokees

NEW
MEXICO

• Enid

Cimarron

• Tulsa

TEXAS

N. Canadian

Oklahoma City •

Robert S.
Kerr Lake

ARKANSAS

Washita

• Norman

Canadian

Eufaula
Lake

• Lawton

OKLAHOMA

Lake
Texoma

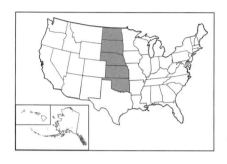

ECOLOGY AND ENVIRONMENT

John Opie

Covering more than a million square miles, about one-fifth of the entire lower forty-eight states, the Plains region has been compared to the pampas of Argentina, the savannas of Africa, and the steppes of central Asia. To the north, this world-quality grassland extends well into Canada. It includes most of the Dakotas, Nebraska, and Kansas, as well as the eastern half of Colorado. To the south, it includes much of Oklahoma and a third of Texas, including the Llano Estacada (Staked Plains) Panhandle country, famed as the original Cattle Kingdom region. Along its western border, the Plains is stopped short by the rise of the front range of the Rocky Mountains. Its eastern border is harder to define. One of the environmental measures of the Great Plains is climate, in this case, rainfall. The amount of rainfall controls the native grasses that prevail, yet another environmental definition of the Plains.

The Great Plains is mostly a short-grass region, bordered on the east by a transitional zone that leads to the great midwestern tallgrass prairies. Rainfall varies season by season, year by year, but Plains rainfall in a good year runs between twelve and twenty inches a year, fine for wheat but not enough for corn. These variations create a fuzzy eastern border that runs roughly through the middle of the Dakotas in the north, Nebraska and Kansas in the middle, and Oklahoma and Texas, where it peters out in the overheated sagebrush of south central Texas. This is approximately between the ninety-eighth and one-hundredth north-south meridian and neatly splits the lower forty-eight states in half. It is convenient to keep in mind these three zones: eastern tall grass prairie, a broadly transitional midgrass zone, and the western short-grass plains. Today these three grasslands are the eastern corn and soybean zone, the Plains soft and hard wheat belt, and the western cattle rangelands. Their 334 million tons of wheat, oats, barley, rye, sorghum, and corn are roughly 25 percent of the world's total production of these grains. It is not entirely rainfall that controls these different zones today; overgrazing in the west, first by buffalo and later cattle is also a factor. The zones also shift depending on climate. The tall grasses worked west during heavy rains, as in the 1880s, or retreated during the big and little Dust Bowls of the 1930s, 1950s, 1970s, and 1990s. One historic measure of the boundaries of the Great Plains comes from post–Civil War nineteenth-century frontier settlers and the first farmers. After getting over the shock that a treeless region could enjoy fertile soil, they discovered that the Plains, with the right rain during the right season, was fine wheat country. But when it did not rain, which was often, they tried to survive in a troubled region.

CHARACTERISTICS OF THE GREAT PLAINS

For thousands of years, native grasses covered the Great Plains. The perpetual winds turned the landscape into a waving sea of grass: blue and sideoats grama, big and little bluestem, buffalo grass, sloughgrass, dropseed, three-awns, fescue, wheatgrass, and switchgrass, to name a few. Amid these grasses lived a mass of animal life: the famous bison (called buffalo) and pronghorn antelope, but also badgers and gophers, mice, prairie dogs and prairie chickens, jackrabbits, foxes and coyotes, and deer, together with crowds of blackbirds, buntings, doves, chickadees, magpies, meadowlarks, crows and buzzards, ducks and geese, grouse and quail, herons, falcons, owls, hawks and eagles, and sandhill cranes. Lewis and Clark, in their famous 1804–1806 expedition that crossed the Plains up the Missouri River, were amazed at the abundance of animal life: on September 17, 1806, they wrote of herds of buffalo, "which were in such multitudes that we cannot exaggerate in saying that in a single glance we saw 3,000 of them before us," as well as large numbers of antelope. On October 19, "we counted 52 herds of buffalo, and three of elk, at a single view." The next spring, on April 17, 1804, "around us are great quantities of game, such as herds of buffalo, elk, antelopes, some deer and wolves, and tracks of bears."[1] They also reported on an amazing soil fertility of grasses, legumes, forbs, and scrub gamble oak trees and were astonished by large flocks of birds that filled the sky and even masses of insects such as bees. Their observations included many new species of plants and animals. The Plains were a vast new Garden of Eden.

Climate

So far rainfall, a nonliving force, and living entities such as short grasses and wheat have been mentioned. There is, of course, much more to the Great Plains. Living and nonliving forces must be distinguished. Nonliving impacts include weather. Plains seasons are extreme. Severe winters can have temperatures that dip to 10 to 20 degrees F below zero. Summers are mostly blazingly hot, often more than 100 degrees F, under clear skies, with only an occasional drop of rain. On the other hand, spring, late summer, and fall are tantalizingly beautiful and temperate.

The Great Plains is also an extremely windy region, mostly from the west or north. Soil and sand constantly blow across the landscape where the grasses or crops do not hold them in place. Settlers and farmers from the earliest days complained about perpetual winds; the nonstop blowing drove some of them crazy and into violent acts. Elsewhere in the world, such infuriating winds are given names, like Israel's *hamsin* and France's *mistral*, and human acts of violence during windy seasons are treated more lightly in the courts. On the Plains, the wind is simply "the Wind."

Two views of the same tornado at Goddard, Kansas, May 26, 1903. Figure 135 of *Meteorology* by Willis Milham, 1912. Courtesy Historic NWS Collection.

The combination of extreme temperatures and winds makes the Great Plains a region of great storms, which some call the grandest storms in the United States. Wintry blizzards pile up mounds of snow, freeze cattle standing on their feet, send fingers of snow through the smallest cracks in walls, windows, and doors, strand homes and farms, and leave luckless travelers dead in their tracks. In other seasons, great towering thunderstorms flick lightning across the landscape and send unpredictable downpours that flood farm fields for a short time of nourishment.

The Great Plains is notorious for dust storms, which usually last two to five years in cycles of approximately twenty years. During these periods, rainfall ranges from six inches a year to no rain at all, the grasses or crops die, and the soil is free to blow away. The Dust Bowl of the 1930s was the most famous, although it was not the greatest ever measured. It forced tens of thousands of farmers—500,000 people in all—to abandon their homes and their land. Dust—blowing soil—piled up against fences and buildings, filled the sky in great brown clouds up to 10,000 feet high, and deposited its powder on buildings, automobiles, and furniture as far east as the Atlantic coast. Some scientists say that dust storms should be considered "normal weather" for the Great Plains instead of other standards. Other historic threats that were actually natural processes were plagues of locusts and wildfires that burned and refreshed thousands of acres at a time.

Soil

The surface of the Great Plains appears to be amazingly flat. The most common markers are grain elevators that dominate small, dying towns. In reality, the Plains is tilted slightly, perhaps fifteen feet per mile, from the Rocky Mountains east by southeast toward the Gulf of Mexico. Plains altitudes range from 2,000 to 5,000 feet above sea level. Much of the surface is world-class dirt that enticed settlers onto the otherwise difficult Plains. A significant part of the soil above the Ogallala Aquifer is windblown dust, or loess mantle. Over several thousand years, countless dust bowls of transitory loess deposited the incredibly rich clay soil prized by nineteenth and twentieth-century pioneers and immigrants. Such soil has been named "chernozem," a Russian word for black or dark brown earth (*chernyi* means a dark brown-black color), a rich and fertile substance.

The Plains chernozem accumulated during 6,000 years to be several feet deep and once seemed inexhaustible to farmers and scientists. In some places like southwestern Kansas and north central Nebraska, the outcome was not fertile soil, but sweeping sand dunes. The famous Nebraska Sand Hills, as large as Massachusetts, Connecticut, and Rhode Island combined, put some truth into the fable of the Great American Desert. Nevertheless, the impact of the widespread belief that Plains soil was unbeatable on American and world history cannot be overestimated. As late as 1900, the U.S. Bureau of Soils claimed that "The soil is the one indestructible, immutable asset that the nation possesses. It is the one resource that cannot be exhausted, that cannot be used up." This may have been a wild promotional statement or whistling in the dark. Pioneering soil historian Edward Hyams notes: "Should anything happen to inhibit the work and multiplication of ammonifying bacteria, the soil fungi, and the nitrogen-fixing bacteria, all [land] life on the planet would come to an end in a matter of months."[2]

People cannot live by pulverized rocks alone. The soil that produces food is more than an inanimate matrix of rocks and minerals. It is an organic living entity: bacteria, fungi, and microbes on one scale, insects, roots, the all-important earthworm, and animals like the mole on a larger scale. The rock particles, mixed with the one necessary ingredient, water, provide the medium in which organic matter flourishes. The end result is often called humus. Plains farmers called it sod. It is the work of nitrogen-fixing bacteria, as well as fungi, rocks, minerals, atmosphere, water, and decaying plant and animal matter.

Humanity's utter dependence upon the thin layer of rocky debris called soil is summed up in "Albrecht's dilemma," after the pioneering Missouri soil scientist William A. Albrecht. The irony of soil is its fluidity. In order to feed themselves, humans intervene in nature by plowing up virgin soil and planting crops that produce more useful food than would naturally grow on the land, but in the process they speed up the depletion of nutrients from the soil by means of high levels of mineral solutions to feed their plants. The brief geological moment of productive soil—"a temporary interlude for rocks and minerals on their way to solution and to the sea"—is dangerously hastened by necessary human interference.[3] Erosion from aggressive farming speeds up the loss. Great Plains soil is predestined to flow eventually to rivers and the sea just as much as the rocks inevitably broke from mountains to become soil. On the High Plains, today's soil and wind erosion matches or surpasses that of the horrific Dust Bowl years.

Ecologically minded scientists learned that good sod (humus) on the Great Plains is a miraculous ecological balance between the right chemical salts and the presence of the right amount of water. Farmers knew this already without the jargon. Fortunately for humans, the sod is extremely interactive with the plants that must feed upon it. Soil is potent, a vigorous and flowing medium, at one time the nourishment for the grassland sea and now set to the plow for wheat, soybeans, or sorghum. Calcium, magnesium, potassium, sodium, and hydrogen, as well as nitrate and phosphate, in the top six to eighteen inches of the ground, mixed with the right amount of moisture, are necessary for the electrochemical exchanges between the roots of plants and ingredients in the soil. All the grains, every seed and every morsel of the fruits and vegetables that humans consume depend upon these exchanges. As a secondary result, humans can also have meat to eat—beef, lamb, pork, and chicken—because these animals consume the plants, many inedible by humans. Animal and human survival depends upon the ionization that makes the plants grow.

Root hairs, like the ones the weekend gardener sees in transplanting tomatoes or azaleas, are enveloped in hydrogen carbonate. Hydrogen is a hyperactive element, and the plant in the hydrogen exchange between soil and root acquires the solid nutrients in the form of salts. The higher the concentration of chemical dynamics in the soil, the larger and better the crops. Farmers struggled to find the delicate balance: if the soil lacks the nutrients or has too many salts, or if moisture is too high or too low, plant growth is limited, as in the worn-out lands of Appalachia, or virtually nonexisten. as in Nevada's Great Basin.

An enduring soil has consistently offered each human civilization its long-term security, its ecological capital that deserves to be reinvested rather than squandered. Good life-giving soil maintains a proper physiochemical-electrical balance. The old phrase "salt of the earth" turns out to be remarkably accurate. European settlement on Plains soils, according to Edward Hyams, sacrificed the region's remarkable fertility and stability in its soil to the American commitment to individual freedom (e.g., private property) at all costs.[4]

Unlike hydrogen, nitrogen is underactive. It does not easily combine with other elements for plants to absorb through their roots. Yet nitrogen is essential to every family of living things on earth. The process through which plants acquire nitrogen, which exists in the atmosphere, is called "nitrogen fixing." Strange nodules, called warts or galls, on the roots of legumes like beans, peas, and clover are filled with millions of bacteria. The plants give bacteria their energy through carbohydrates; the bacteria in turn capture nitrogen from the air and make it available to the plant. Once captured by the bacteria, the nitrogen takes the form of nitrates, which plants capture chemically and convert into proteins. Animals and humans in turn consume these proteins. This is a symbiotic relationship, since neither plants nor bacteria alone can achieve nitrogen fixation. Of the importance of nitrogen fixing, journalist Peter Farb wrote in 1959, "Should some calamity overtake these bacteria, or a sudden change occur in the environment of the planet, that their numbers might be so seriously reduced . . . [the event would] collapse our superstructure of life, which is hinged to the nitrogen fixed by these microbes."[5]

A good little bluestem acre on the arid Great Plains includes two and one-half tons of plant material in the first six inches of soil. The roots absorb the nitrates, other mineral compounds, and soil matter and hold the plant in place. As a perennial, little bluestem roots are centers of plant food storage. Farmers quickly learn not to cut their bluestem less than four inches above the surface nor to allow their animals to graze it down excessively, or the underground sod would suffer, since the aboveground growth produced the sugars and starches the roots needed. The dense roots of quality bluestem withstand drought and can carry cattle through dry spells and winter. Prairie sod is a final synthesis of the best of the Great Plains.

Grasses

Travelers who rush across the Plains in their vans see only a monotonous world. If they paused and took a side dirt road to one of the few remaining reserves of original prairie, got out of their vehicle, and strolled into the grassland, the variety, colors, sizes, and shapes of the original Great Plains might astonish them. Even the names are wonderful: turkeyfoot bluestem, weeping lovegrass, sideoats and hairy grama, sand dropseed, smooth brome, sand reedgrass, windmillgrass, plains beebalm, the prehistoric foxtail millet, the poisonous wooly loco and lambert crazyweed, weeds like curlycup gumweed, the pretty maximilian sunflower and threadleaf groundsel (the latter poisonous), and the widespread Plains blue grama and buffalo grass. The best time to visit would be early morning, though boots and jeans would get soaked as one waded through the wet dew of hip-high plants.

The classic prairie emerges in late July and early August. The weather is hot and dry, and the stems and leaves of the grasses, like big bluestem, have lengthened and outgrown early-flowering forbs or nongrass prairie plants (broadleafed herbs, like prairie catsfoot and wildflowers). Where it has not been farmed, the sweeping windblown grassland is like an organic kaleidoscope, a veritable flower garden. There are multiple layers competing for space and sun, soil and water. Against a luxurious silver-green background, the summer-blooming plants—larkspur, roses, coneflowers—are met in midsummer by the first yellows and golds of the autumn-blooming forbs, such as ironweed, gentians, asters, sunflowers, and goldenrods. The midcontinent grasslands are so vast that one could follow changing climate zones for a thousand miles from south to north or east to west, depending on altitude, geography, and season.

Water

One nonliving feature is in short supply on the Plains. Compared to the Midwest and the East, the Great Plains lacks any bounty of water from major rivers. The Missouri River edges along the northern Plains. In its natural condition, it contributed little to farming in the Dakotas, although modern dams and reservoirs store water for irrigation. The Platte River that splits the Plains roughly into north-south halves is a shallow, braided stream that fights storage and irrigation. Other rivers on the map, such as the Republican and Cimarron in Kansas, actually run dry more often than not in the modern era. The Pecos and Rio Grande are not in the picture. Many Plains farmers failed simply because of the lack of water.

Today one of the major sights on the Plains is the great crop circles of wheat, sorghum, soybeans, and corn, all watered by center-pivot sprinklers that look like mechanical centipedes as they circle the fields. But a vast body of groundwater rarely reached the surface, except in central Nebraska, and is not part of the original Great Plains. It is a later story.

Environmental Perspectives

Regardless of garden or desert from the viewpoint of the opportunity for successful farming, the Great Plains today is also recognized by scientists as one of the world's greatest natural ecosystems. Or it once was. The pioneering mapper of the world's ecosystems is Robert G. Bailey of the U.S. Forest Service in Fort Collins, Colorado. He is among many scientists who believe that the Great Plains cannot be defined only by state and county lines, highway maps, and agricultural needs. He divides the Great Plains into roughly two north-south units through the middle of Oklahoma and the Texas Panhandle. He looks at weather, geology, soils, plants, and animals.

Bailey concludes that all of the Plains is a part of America's "Dry Domain" that is similar to steppes elsewhere in the world. Bailey's approach has been used by the Sierra Club to identify the Great Northern American Prairie, the biggest of the United States' fifteen great "ecoregions," all with important natural features, and all in environmental trouble. The Defenders of Wildlife concluded in its own study that the Great Plains has experienced the virtually complete (99 percent) disappearance of the original grasses to single-crop (monoculture) agriculture, together with increasing aridity that suggests "desertification" during the twenty-first century. It emphasized that the region once was "a biome unique to North America, a mosaic of many different plant communities covering an immense expanse of the continent. Millions of bison thundered across these prairies, and fires roared over thousands of square miles."[6]

This is not the only viewpoint. For example, in 1981, the Soil Conservation Service (now the Soil and Water Conservation Service) of the U.S. Department of Agriculture would have agreed only in part with Bailey, since it included current land use, meaning crop farming and grazing, together with elevation and topography, climate, water, soils, and potential natural vegetation. These were applied less as Bailey's natural Great Plains than as measures for successful farming.[7]

For the Soil Conservation Service, the Great Plains involved three major regions: a Northern Great Plains Spring Wheat Region, where the land was virtually all dryland farms and ranches that depended upon limited rainfall; a Western Great Plains Range and Irrigated Region, mostly cattle ranges, dryland farming, and irrigation farming, that primarily grew feed grain for livestock; and a Central Great Plains Winter Wheat and Range Region, with better opportunities for wheat, alfalfa, corn, and cotton farming, much of which was under irrigation since rainfall was light, erratic, and concentrated in the summer. A think tank, the Heinz Center for Science, Economics, and the Environment, published a 2002 study that saw a highly productive Plains farmland with a monetary value second only to that of California (but almost entirely in the eastern and southern Plains), but also a farmland at risk because of soil consumption and heavy chemical use. It also looked at the Plains as overused cattle grassland.[8]

ORIGIN OF THE GREAT PLAINS

Measured by geological time, today's Great Plains is a fast-moving blip in time, with its human history a smaller blip yet. Nothing on the Plains is long lasting or entirely durable. Most of its features are imports from elsewhere. Several times during the last half billion Earth's years, it was the floor of vast inland seas that flowed openly from the Arctic through today's Caribbean. The last great flooding took place 60 million years ago. Today's Hudson Bay is the last large shallow remnant of this ancient sea. Called by geologists the Rocky Mountain Trough, these inland seas were often one thousand miles wide and three thousand miles long. Each time they came, they laid down hundreds or thousands of feet of sediment, sometimes limestone filled with fossils, sometimes sandstone that still shows the ripples of dunes.

The limestone Flint Hills of eastern Kansas, for example, are the deep remains of shellfish deposits immeasurable on any human time scale. These thick layers surfaced many times when the seas withdrew during different geological eras. Some were eroded to slivers of nothing. The sandy dunes of the Oklahoma Panhandle country, for example, were overflowed about 580 million years ago (late Cambrian), only to surface again 400 million years ago and stand dry for 50 million years. The waters returned for 75 million years, leaving several thousand feet of limestone and shale. During the Pennsylvania period that began 275 million years ago the landscape surfaced briefly for 25 million years with heavy erosion and then was covered by Permian and Triassic seas that, when they departed, left behind one or two thousand feet (depending on the region) of red sandstones and shales.

The Plains region again descended under a Jurassic and Cretaceous sea from 150 million to 65 million years ago. "These tens of thousands of feet of level 'layer-cake geology' would have made Oklahoma one of the highest places on Earth were it not for thousands of millennia of erosion by water and dust-storm winds when the land stood above the seas. It is not clear when the region will slip below the waters again, but the record is promising."[9] This geological cycling is still in process. During the Jurassic period 200 million years ago, there may have been a climate similar to that of modern times—dry and extreme—that lasted for 20 million years.

Events at the western edge of today's Plains, the Rocky Mountains, must be considered. Overall, the rise of the Rocky Mountains led to erosion that flowed eastward to make up the top fifty to three hundred feet of the Plains landscape. The Rockies were once no more than gently rolling hills until the mountain-building period called the Laramide orogeny 70 million years ago, during the Cretaceous period. The ancestral Rockies rose quickly, expelled their seas, and became high rolling country. Yet eroding water was abundant in a moist and semitropical climate, and soon the countryside became valley floors and mountain peaks, all thou-

Agate Fossil Beds National Monument, Grass Plains, Nebraska. Courtesy Agate Fossil Beds National Monument.

sands of feet above sea level. Then the Pleistocene ice ages between 500,000 and 100,000 years ago carved out the rugged region seen today in Colorado's Rocky Mountain National Park. At this point begins the story of the Plains soils mentioned earlier, an unthinkable tonnage of rocks and gravel and grit from the west.

Even the climate in large part is literally shaped by the Rocky Mountains. Originally nothing stood between the flow of moisture-laden winds from the Pacific Ocean that once intruded just on the other side of the Rockies. Damp air was yet another migrant onto the Plains. Ten to five million years ago, the Great Plains from South Dakota to Texas could not have been more different from today's semiarid geography. It was a moist, low-lying, semitropical region with heavy vegetation (this could happen again in some distant future). But as the Rockies rose, first as a high plain, then as soft mountains, and later as today's rugged chain, they cut off moist air and rain from the west.

Today the Great Plains stands in what is called the rain shadow of the Rockies that forces clouds to give up their burden well before Plains farmers look hopefully for rain clouds. Today's human-induced climate change is already shortening any stability for the Plains. If today's grassland had not been transformed into fields of wheat, corn, soybeans, and sorghums, people might have been seeing grassland that had existed at least once before, 200 million years ago. But in between, a little more than a million years ago, a worldwide cooling that lasted well into the nineteenth century brought more arid and extreme climates than those of today. Even more dust storms swept the landscape and moved more dust into today's rich loess soil. The region was truly a drifting, duneland Sahara or Mongolia. Today's Plains climate, despite its toughness, is a softer version of an earlier day.

HUMANS ON THE GREAT PLAINS ENVIRONMENT: A DIFFICULT PLACE

Native Americans

The short grasses, the hot dry summers, the bitter winters, the nearly ceaseless wind, and sudden weather changes forced the first humans to stay primarily nomadic hunters. Despite uncertain information, it appears that a variety of early peoples—Paleo-Indians—existed on the Plains well before 11,000 B.C.E. Using stone-pointed spears, as well as slings and clubs, they participated in the extinction of great mastodons, ground sloths, giant beavers, giant cats, and even camels. Climate change probably shaped the extinctions as well, as the so-called Wisconsinan glacier continued its retreat. A successful team killing of a mammoth was a major event. When the band gathered around the massive carcass, they gorged on the meat, made leatherwear, and forged badly needed tools, more weapons, and religious and decorative items from the bone and ivory. Plains Indians only rarely settled into agriculture—corn, squash, and beans along streambeds—compared to other First Nations in the eastern, midwestern, and southwestern regions of North America.

Beginning around 9000 B.C.E., the Plains, as its grasses became more abundant, abounded with large herds of bison. Today's major grasses appeared on the scene: blue grama, western wheatgrass, threadleaf sage, and others. The bison were never domesticated, unlike cattle, sheep, goats, and pigs in the Old World, but humans used them as the intermediaries for grasses inedible by humans. Bands of humans learned to exploit the great herds that seasonally moved from dry to moist areas of the Plains. The keys to animal existence were grasses and water. The bison searched for them, and humans followed the bison. Every part of the bison was used: horns, hooves, bones, skin, hair, entrails, blood, and muscles.

Like European Plains settlers in the nineteenth and twentieth centuries, these First Nations also adopted new technologies to improve their capacity to sustain themselves on the harsh Plains. The bow and arrow revolutionized hunting around 2000 B.C.E. There is evidence that Plains conditions in the fifteenth century C.E. became extreme—higher temperatures and less rainfall—during increasingly arid summers, when the soil was laid bare and enormous dust storms rolled across the Plains. Large areas of the Plains were abandoned.

Over time, these bands became the Blackfeet, Cree, Assiniboine, Shoshoni, Arapahoe, Gros Ventre, Crow, Hidatsa, Salishan, Northern Cheyenne, and Flathead, to mention only the northern tribes. The middle Plains included the Southern Cheyenne, Sioux, Ponca, Oto, Arikara, Comanche, Kiowa, and Pawnee. Some of the latter settled into farming in today's Nebraska. Further south were the Kansa, Osage, Plains Apache, and other Pawnee. The Plains Indians probably never totaled more than 10,000, although they controlled an area several times larger than New England. Sometimes these First Nations cooperated for the common good; sometimes they fought for dominance.

After 1700 C.E., the acquisition of white people's horses and guns created a second revolution with even more environmental impact. This marked the beginning of the decimation of the bison with wasteful killings, such as "bison jumps" in which entire herds were driven over cliffs. The nomadic Comanche, like the Bedouin of Arabia on their camels, became mounted warriors on their horses, noted for their savage ferocity, cruelty, and implacability, even displacing the Apache, who had dominated the central Plains since 1500. The Comanche roamed, raided, and claimed control of vast areas of the central Plains. Indians with guns could quickly dominate less-well-equipped tribes. Ironically, the horse had been native to prehistoric America, but was long extinct. Entire bands of horses, whether wild and feral or broken for human use, could perish in a particularly severe Plains winter. Historian Theodore Binnema noted that the horses of the Blackfeet were sometimes in such poor condition that they substituted dogs.[10] The Cree and Assiniboine replenished their herds by hit-and-run raids on other tribes. Battles for horses became particularly aggressive between the Cree and Blackfeet in the 1780s. A few decades later, the Blackfeet, Cheyenne, and Dakota Sioux offered some of the greatest resistance to white human's invasions.

The environmental story of the nineteenth century begins with the buffalo—more accurately, bison. There were often two great Indian hunts a year—June through September and November into April. These were not only a desperate search for meat, but also for hides, hair, sinew, horns, and even hooves. These were transformed into clothing, sleeping robes, tools, cooking utensils, and sheltering walls. Bands of Indians, families and all, might travel a thousand miles during a hunting season. Fighting might break out as bands crossed into territories claimed by other tribes. A successful hunt meant a gorging feast of fresh meat, with some saved as jerky. The Pawnee, for example, also ate elk, deer, beavers, raccoons, badgers, dogs, rabbits, squirrels, and occasionally fish.

The millions of bison on the Great Plains were greatly disturbed after the Civil War by four transcontinental railroad lines that carved up their normal migration patterns. Great meaningless massacres were carried out by outrageous eastern "hunting parties" shooting at will from their railroad cars. The weapon of choice was the powerful long-range Sharps rifle. At their peak, there were more than 4 million bison on the Plains. Indians and whites both saw the bison, in Walter Prescott Webb's words, as "the easiest victim to the hunter, whether the redman with bow and arrow or the white man with his long-range buffalo gun."[11] Once down to a few hundred animals, the bison made a comeback in the late twentieth century, helped by human protection and commercial use.

Fantasies about the Plains from the First European Ventures

Europeans had fantastic and contradictory expectations of the Great Plains. Was it the Great American Garden or the Great American Desert? The Spanish expedition led in 1540–1541 by Francisco de Coronado strayed as far as central Kansas seeking the mythical Seven Cities of Cibola, a vast interior region of wealth and beauty. Zebulon Pike's 1806–1807 exploration of the Arkansas basin described the Plains as "prairie," by which he meant an English "natural meadow." But he also compared "these vast plains of the western hemisphere" with the "sandy deserts of Africa . . . on which not a speck of vegetable matter existed." Pike's negative view reinforced the Jeffersonian policy that American settlement would stop at the Mississippi River. The English botanist John Bradbury, in Henry Brackenridge's 1814 expedition, concluded that "In process of time, it [the Plains] will not only be peopled and cultivated, but . . . will be one of the most beautiful countries in the world." Brackenridge, however, saw "extensive tracts of moving sands similar to those of the African deserts."[12] Stephen Long's 1819–1820 expedition that crossed the Plains as far as the Rocky Mountains came to the same desolate conclusion.

These views led Secretary Joseph Henry of the Smithsonian Institution to state that "the whole space to the west, between the 98th meridian and the Rocky Mountains, denominated the Great American Plains, is a barren waste." He added that there was "scarcely an object to break the monotony" of the landscape. It was "a country of comparatively little value to the agriculturalist." The native peoples were, it was said, "merely marginal nomads . . . ekeing out a precarious and poverty-stricken existence." On the other hand, the expansionist Missouri senator Thomas Hart Benton insisted that the Plains would be the rich heartland of a new American empire that would compare with the Persians and Rome. After the Civil War, military leaders of railroad surveys, such as William B. Hazen in 1874, described the Dakota country as "almost totally useless." The Plains were labeled the Great American Desert, "transfixed by a fiery sun, and baked into sterility." But others, like George Armstrong Custer and F. V. Hayden, described the northern Plains as fit for nearly every conceivable type of agricultural pursuit.[13] The controversy over garden or desert died down as postwar settlers successfully moved into the Dakotas, Nebraska, and Kansas, at least for a time.

In a complete turnaround from Coronado, Pike, Long, and Sherman, a newly arrived Plains wife could write, "We must pronounce this the most charming country our eyes have ever beheld. Beautiful rolling prairie, undulating like the waves of the sea, high limestone cliffs with immense bottom-lands, stretching into thousands of acres as rich as it is possible for it to be, high tablelands, with a soil a number of feet in depth." In 1831, Joshua Pilcher told Congress that anyone who saw the open grasslands as an impossible obstacle "must know little of the American people, who supposes they can be stopped by any thing in the shape of . . . deserts." A western booster agreed: "The skill and enterprise of American farmers will find the means of obtaining comfort and wealth in those regions, both of Kansas and Nebraska, which many are disposed to condemn as worthless." Indiana senator G. S. Orth, member of an 1867 Republican junket onto the Plains, announced that "Our good 'Uncle Sam' has come here, and he brings with him science and civilization. He intends to plant permanently a part of his great family; for he is now founding empires." A journalist announced that the Great Plains offered "a garden three times the area of France."[14]

Settlers Venture Warily onto the Plains

To reach plush California and green Oregon, the first American migrants barely paused to feed their animals on the Plains. They could not even collect wood for fires or wagon repairs. Water could be scarce. They confirmed the stories that the harsh central plains, a thousand-mile-wide windswept grassland, devoid of trees and other landmarks, scorched in the summer and storm swept in the winter, had to be crossed as one would cross the Atlantic Ocean or the Sahara Desert. Crossing the Plains was a one-way passage, to be completed as rapidly as possible across the apparently worthless but difficult plains, mountains, and deserts.

After the Civil War, the desert was claimed as America's garden, the last frontier aside from frozen Alaska, the final step that would complete Americans' Manifest Destiny to conquer, domesticate, and inhabit the wild continent. The boomer psychology of Pilcher and others meant that the Plains surprised settlers with its unexpected hardships.

The first to arrive, however, were not farmers, but a new breed of ranchers who managed cattle on horseback over large areas of land instead of the eastern pattern of fenced cattle on small acreages. For only a brief period, little more than a decade in the 1870s and 1880s, the Cattle Kingdom prospered on the Empire of Grass across much of the Great Plains. From it came the harsh, but romanticized, image in literature, movies, and television of the solitary cowboy, riding his horse, with his broad-brimmed hat, soiled chaps, long duster, worn saddle, jingling spurs, rope, and Colt six-shooter—the guitar-strumming Tom Mix, the valiant John Wayne, and the deadly Clint Eastwood.

Most of the ranching had Spanish and Texas origins that became Americanized and industrialized. Over time, the mean and sinewy free-ranging Texas Longhorn became through interbreeding the docile steer fattening on the open range. By 1880, more than 11 million cattle had taken the place of the Plains bison. Most famous were the great cattle drives of thousands of head from the southern Plains—valued in the south at $5 a head but sold for as high as $40 in the northern markets for eventual arrival at the great processing yards and plants in Chicago. This innovation came from the McCoy brothers, drovers in Texas, who looked to the extension of railroads, especially into Abilene, Wichita, and Dodge City, Kansas. Between 1866 and 1880, nearly 5 million cattle arrived along the famous trails.

The era of the great cattle drives and the Cattle Kingdom itself fell before external forces like the economic panics of 1873 and 1893, in which prices collapsed, and local changes like the invention of barbed wire and the windmill, the expansion of farmers drawn onto the Plains by the 1862 Homestead Act, and the severe drought of 1883–1884, which was followed by the fierce winter blizzards of 1886–1887 that killed tens of thousands of cattle. The Great Plains was not a forgiving place.

For incoming eastern farmers, the midcontinent grassland, treeless and short of water, was a novelty. No one put it better than Walter Prescott Webb in 1931, who described an "institutional fault line" between eastern timberland farming and the absolute shift to a western way of life. He added, "East of the Mississippi civilization stood on three legs—land, water, and timber; west of the Mississippi not one but two of these legs were withdrawn,—water and timber,—and civilization was left on one leg—land. It is small wonder that it toppled over in temporary failure."[15]

One of America's premier geographers, Carl Ortwin Sauer, would agree. He argued that the midcontinent grasslands were where the nation's frontier history really began. In the eastern forests, the first waves of white settlers deadened trees, cleared openings, and planted fields in ways little different from generations of European forebears. If frontier means an encounter with strange conditions that require new responses, then the American frontier began not at the Atlantic coastline or Appalachian Mountains, but at the "prairie peninsula" that edged onto today's Indiana–Illinois state line. The midland grasslands marked the starting point for a distinctively American history and American space.[16]

Waves of farm families, filled with Jeffersonian idealism and the sacred mission of Manifest Destiny, moved onto the Plains during the second half of the nineteenth century. To their surprise, they were often forced back by the lack of rain or groundwater. To the aspiring young husband and wife of a farm family, rumors of a grassland that was vast but lay under rainless skies were not encouraging, despite the national passion that the American Everyman deserved his God-given share of the virtually free land carved out of the public domain. They learned that the myth of the desert was not entirely a myth. Like troops sacrificing themselves on the battlefield, fresh waves of farmers seemed always ready to step forward. When they lost their crops under a rainless bleaching sun and began to starve, newly settled farmers felt betrayed.

The vaunted American farmer seemed unable to conquer the drought-prone Great Plains. In the 1870s, he (sometimes she) lived under conditions of extremely high risk. He was undertooled, underinformed, and undercapitalized. A single incident of a broken axletree or smashed kneecap, bad seedcorn or a rainless June, could put him out of business. Paradoxically, settlers also believed that they had betrayed the American dream by their failure. They believed that it was unpatriotic (and possibly even sinful) to desert their homesteads. This was not a strange attitude in the age of Manifest Destiny; God, after all, was on America's side.

The Great American Opportunity

Anyone who flies over the Plains sees a vast landscape of squares and rectangles that illustrates America's remarkable history of government land sales to excited farmers. In 1785, two years before the Constitutional Convention in Philadelphia,

Thomas Jefferson pushed through the Continental Congress, meeting in New York, an ambitious plan to give every American a piece of land upon which he (rarely she) could establish a satisfying, prosperous, and independent life. It was the fulfillment of the phrase "the pursuit of happiness" that would appear in the Constitution. The Ordinance of 1785 set out the mile-square sections of 640 acres that would define the Plains. This settlement plan—selling the nation's public domain into private hands—held true until 1935, with many modifications, including the sale of quarter sections of 160 acres.

Second only for Plains settlers was Abraham Lincoln's Homestead Act of 1862, which offered a quarter section free to a farm family after it had successfully settled for five years. Nowhere else did the geometry of land sales take place so vividly. Homesteading began in the 1870s and continued into the 1910s and 1920s. However, on the Plains, the American dream often turned into much more of a nightmare.

Newly arrived settlers learned painfully that less corn, the American farmer's crop of choice, would grow on 160 acres in western Kansas than sprang forth on 40 acres in Illinois or Iowa, despite more hard labor and personal risk. They reluctantly shifted from corn to spring wheat or the strange new hard red winter wheat—Turkey Red—imported by newly arrived Russian German Mennonite communities.

Settlers also learned dryland farming techniques—holding rainfall moisture in the soil—from these immigrant communities. Back east, 20 or 40 or even 80 acres could be worked with hand tools, a plow, and horses, but not 320 acres in a half section or 640 acres in the full section required to prosper on the Plains. This new dryland farming required far bigger farms to field a decent crop, and new machinery to cultivate the bigger farm.

The open country demanded technological innovation and dramatically new farming practices. A clearheaded newly arrived farmer saw a treeless, arid, and desolate landscape. What features in the land would allow him to apply new skills and tools to guarantee his survival? He knew that he could plow the flat land, and that the deep soil was extremely fertile. The potential for success seemed better with the appearance of John Deere's moldboard iron-tipped plow. Word spread that it "cut through the sod like a hot knife through butter."

Joseph Glidden's barbed wire for fencing gave the farmer another necessary boost in a woodless country. The barbed-wire revolution cannot be overstated—the business grew from 10,000 pounds in 1874 to more than 80 million pounds in 1880 and more than 300 million pounds in 1900, while prices fell from $20 per hundred pounds to $1.80 per hundred pounds in the same period. House building was also revolutionized with the economical balloon-frame house (still today's standard technology) instead of the log cabin or terrible sod hut.

Daniel Halladay's self-regulating windmill, which could be constructed from an $80 kit and barnyard spare parts, relieved farmers from hand-dug wells and droughty conditions. The familiar windmill can still be seen in the Plains, its blades and vane perched on a steel skeleton over a simple pump and narrow shaft to the water. One of its most attractive new features was its rudderlike vane that automatically turned it into the wind. The best version was self-lubricating so that the farmer did not have to climb up and oil it in a blizzard. Yet a standard eight-foot windmill could only pump from about thirty feet below ground and water only the household, the barnyard, the kitchen garden, and perhaps ten acres of wheat or corn.

After the Civil War, Cyrus McCormick began selling a workmanlike mechanical reaper. It alone multiplied eightfold the land a farmer could harvest and seemed destined to guarantee success for dryland farming. Expensive and bulky steam tractors could not replace horses as well as Henry Ford's inexpensive gasoline-powered Fordson tractor in the early twentieth century. Back east, the new roller process for milling wheat for bread encouraged larger plantings on more land. The new mechanized equipment seemed designed for flat open country. Large-scale farming covered hundreds of acres instead of tens of acres.

Railroads, instead of only racing across the Plains to the West, early in the twentieth century had spread across the landscape to connect Plains commodities with their eastern markets. Not until 1912 did the Santa Fe Railroad edge onto the sweeping sunburned grasslands of southwestern Kansas by building a branch line from Dodge City to Satanta along the old Dry Fork of the Santa Fe Trail. Before this, settlers creaked and bounced their wagons into the region by following the ruts of the centuries-old trail. There were no broad and smooth-flowing rivers, like the Ohio or the Mississippi, to carry a raftload of a farm family and its animals and tools into the central High Plains. Roads and bridges (across dry washes) did not exist before 1912 in the sandy country on the north bank of the Cimarron River. Wandering families simply rattled out cross-country. During the 1870s, the Santa Fe Railroad had run its new Pacific-bound line along the Arkansas River thirty-five miles to the north, but that was a hard, jouncing, two-day, roadless wagon ride away from farmsteads along the Cimarron. The Santa Fe was more intent on getting across the hot and dry Plains than in serving its cash-poor population and sparse resources.

THE PROBLEM OF THE GREAT PLAINS: LACK OF WATER

Despite these remarkable innovations and farmers' dedication to new techniques, settlers were still forced back by the lack of rain or groundwater. Water became the Plains obsession. The trick was to make a small amount of water go a long way. But wheat or corn for cash and survival needed more than a trickle. Irrigation was known to succeed in California and among the industrious Mormons around the Great Salt Lake, but where was the water across the western Plains? Year-round streams were rare, and their banks were quickly captured by the first round of settlers, who claimed exclusive "riparian rights."

Congress tried to legislate an environmental fix by imposing an eastern landscape of trees and meadows on the short-grass Plains. The Timber Culture Act of 1873 promised to give free title to 160 acres to each farmer who planted trees on one quarter of his (sometimes her) claim. He had to keep them growing on forty acres for ten years, in which time it was believed (mistakenly) that the trees would eventually spread and improve the climate. Both trees and climate change failed.

In 1877, Congress tried again with the aptly named Desert Land Act, which discounted a full section of 640 acres to settlers who would water their land. Not a few farmers achieved their discount by plowing a row of furrows uphill and downhill and calling them "irrigation ditches." A saying went around that "water runs uphill to money." It also became abundantly clear that the celebrated 1862 Homestead Act, which restricted settlers to an inadequate 160 acres, failed to suit conditions west of the ninety-eighth meridian. The five years of farm residency it required before they received free title was soon labeled "the period of starvation." The 1912 passage of the Three-Year Homestead Act admitted that the point of starvation was far short of five years.

The Desert Becomes a Temporary Garden, but Climate Wins Out

Then a miracle happened. In 1844, the western booster Josiah Gregg had effused that "the extreme cultivation of the earth might contribute to the multiplication of showers."[17] Now for a decade—approximately 1878 to 1887—extraordinarily heavy rains fell on the entire Great Plains country west of the ninety-eighth meridian from Texas to Canada. Frontier farmers rushed onto the Plains because they believed that they could manufacture rainfall. Mormon settlers had already happily reported that the level of the Great Salt Lake had risen when they began irrigating and cultivating nearby land. On the Plains, ordinary sodbusting—plowing open rows of soil in the ancient grassland—altered the forces of nature. "Rain follows the plow" became the popular slogan. These farmers, together with government agents, private boosters, and the American public at large, concluded that the weather could be permanently changed. The power of ordinary but Bunyanesque Americans to dictate favorable geographic change was not a strange claim in the age of Manifest Destiny.

The theory of increasing rainfall by plowing the land took hold as "scientific truth" when it was endorsed by Joseph Henry of the Smithsonian Institution, the new American Association for the Advancement of Science (AAAS), and the most famous explorer-scientist of the day, F. V. Hayden, director of the U.S. Geological Surveys of the Territories. In 1880, a Nebraska soil scientist, Samuel Aughey, concluded, "after the soil is broken, a rain as it falls is absorbed by the soil like a huge sponge."[18] Then the soil evaporates a little moisture into the atmosphere each day, receiving it back at night as heavy dew. Farmers and boosters, especially on the central Great Plains, were delighted with the new science.

This theory was not bad science for its day, but it was inadequate science for climate modification. In addition, it was widely believed that the spread of the railroads and telegraph also brought rains, since the iron and steel rails and electric wires modified natural electrical cycles in an arid zone to induce the fall of moisture. Civil War veterans also remembered that artillery fire, such as that at the Battle of Gettysburg, had seemingly contributed to deluges that followed. If Sherman would use more cannon to clear the Plains of Indians, it might have the added benefit of bringing rain.

The wonderful combination of more rainfall, better crops, cheap fertile land, and the beginning of an interlaced network of railroads was too good to resist. In 1878–1879, the land office at Bloomington, Kansas, which covered southwestern Kansas, entered homesteads totaling more than 307,000 acres. The spell of good rain encouraged a Chicago newsman to say in 1884 that "Kansas was considered a droughty state, but that day is past, and her reputation for sure crops is becoming widely known. . . . Land is cheap and a good home can be made to pay for itself in a few years." A Congregational minister, Jeremiah Platt, visiting in the mid-1880s, concluded, "I am more and more convinced that there is a Great Western Kansas which, in fifteen or twenty years from now will be as rich and productive and valuable as is the eastern part of the state, making Kansas the greatest and grandest agricultural state in the union." The Larned (Kansas) *Optic* claimed, "the largest immigration ever known in the history of the state is now steadily flowing into southwestern Kansas," and the Kinsley *Graphic* urged, "Come on! There is still plenty of room, land is cheap here yet, and thousands of acres for sale."[19] Between 1885 and 1887 the population of the western third of Kansas rose 370 percent, from 38,000 to 139,000 people, just as the rains inexplicably halted.

The boom ended more suddenly than it began, its collapse accelerated by the disastrous blizzards in early 1886 in which 80 percent of all range cattle died. Drought returned in the late summer of 1887. In the successive summers of 1889 and 1890, farmers produced only two and one-half bushels of wheat an acre in western Kansas, and an even less productive eight bushels of corn. Farm families that held some of the most fertile land in the world were living, they said, on "Andersonville fare," remembering the notorious Civil War prison in the South. Between 1890 and 1900, the number of farms in the twenty-four counties of western Kansas declined from 14,300 to 8,900. Across the Plains, 200,000 settlers felt fortunate to escape the region, now trailing a new slogan, "In God we trusted; in Kansas we busted." Cash-poor sodhouse farmers—"nine children and eleven cents"—could not cope with the 1889–1895 drought. Since large parts of the grassland remained in their native sod, dust storms did not blow, but without rain, settlers concluded that "there is no god west of Salina."

The Great Plains, at first reviled as the Great American Desert, then celebrated as the Great American Garden, became a 300-mile-wide near-empty swath ranging from Canada to Texas. By the mid-1890s, the central Plains had reverted to its virtually uninhabited prefrontier state. A failed farmer on the Nebraska Sand Hills left behind the sign, "God made this country right side up. Don't turn it over." Few people were ready to acknowledge that dry times were the norm rather than the exception, and most settlers (and bankers and businessmen) waited expectantly for the next rainy season and a return to "normal" weather.

The rains returned in 1891 and 1892, but a combination of more droughts and the nationwide financial collapse, the panic of 1893, once more created desperate conditions on the Great Plains. This was followed in 1894 by one of the driest years on record (only eight to nine inches of rain) and a particularly heavy plague of locusts (mutated grasshoppers). In 1901 U.S. Geological Survey official Willard D. Johnson called the rush to settle the Plains between 1870 and 1900 an "experiment in agriculture on a vast scale. It nevertheless ended in total failure, [resulting in] a class of people broken in spirit as well as in fortune."[20]

Despite warning signs that heavy rainfall was not the norm, Plains boosters reviled the renowned scientist and explorer John Wesley Powell as a doomsayer when he prefaced his 1878 government report with his view that realistically, in the American West, including the Great Plains, "the climate is so arid that agriculture is not successful." Since "practically all values inhere in the water," the only land that the government ought responsibly to offer settlers was parcels where "the water could be distributed over them."[21] Powell's argument was clear, direct, and precisely what potential settlers did not want to hear. He urged a sixteenfold expansion of the homesteading quarter section to a minimum of two to four sections

(1,280 to 2,560 acres, two to four square miles) to offer the best chance for success. At the very least, he concluded, the day of the independent farm family that prospered on the famous quarter section was long gone, and such families would never successfully settle the Great Plains. For his warnings, boosters and enemies drove Powell from his government post in the Geological Survey; he would receive more attention in the 1980s than in the 1880s.

Another government scientist, less aggressive than Powell, Frederick H. Newell, chief hydrographer of the Geological Survey, reported in 1896 that during a rare good year a Plains farm would bring "wonderful crops," but it would also encourage wasteful plow-ups of thousands of acres that were then prone to blow away. The "irregular and scanty rainfall" of the Plains meant that "total loss of crops and bitter disappointment inevitably follow, and the unfortunate settlers, if not driven from the country, alternate between short periods of prosperity and long intervals of depression. These misled, inept and intractable farmers have already damaged one-sixth of the nation's potential farmland." He added, "[The Plains farmer] is in a certain sense a gambler, staking everything upon luck, and with the chances against him." New homesteads should be cut off in order to return the Plains to pasture land. "Has the world not heard enough of droughts and crop losses, of famines and suffering, of abandoned farms and worthless Kansas mortgages? Why interpose to prevent the country from going back to its former conditions? It was, and can be, a magnificent grazing land."[22] Newell anticipated debates that followed the 1930s Dust Bowl.

For a time between 1900 and 1920, when grain prices went high, Plains farmers prospered. Not only did farm prices rise steadily, but also families on the Plains, for the first time, enjoyed bigger increases in income than the rest of the nation. They felt that at last they had left their frontier struggles behind them. The cost of the new technologies—from barbed wire to combines—finally paid off. The good life could be achieved on the farm, and most Americans still held to the belief that it was the best American way of life. American virtue paid off with hard work, thrift, saving, and investment in land.

America's "Golden Age of Agriculture" took hold particularly in 1910–1914, when commodity prices were high and stable. Farm exports of wheat and corn increased. Manifest Destiny had finally taken hold on America's last frontier region. World War I, despite its horrors, triggered sharp rises in farm prices in 1916. By the summer of 1920, with postwar famines, farmland prices had more than doubled since 1914. Plains farmers basked in the fruits of their extraordinary labors, only to have their prosperity collapse within months. Between the summer of 1920 and the summer of 1921, the price per bushel of wheat fell from more than $2 to under $1, and farmland prices fell by half.[23] Many Plains farmers could not meet payments on newly purchased sections. Thousands went bankrupt in the 1920s. Yet the Great Plains was now described as "The Breadbasket of the World."

The Dust Bowl and Plains Disaster

The Dust Bowl struck in the 1930s at the same time that the United States collapsed into its worst-ever depression. The federal index of farm prices fell from 148 in 1929 to 70 in 1933. Historian Paul Bonnifield described the Dust Bowl's effects:

On a small corner of the leeward side of a field, a particle of soil, broken loose by the wind, struck a cluster of soil particles like a cue ball striking the racked balls. The avalanching effect of soil erosion gathered force as it moved across the field. By the time the effects of one tiny wind-driven soil particle reached the opposite side of the field, a mighty force was assembled to assault the neighboring abandoned field. Soon a dirt storm was burning any living plant, while the soil around the plant's roots was joining the race across the stricken land.[24]

In July 1931, dryland farmers in southwestern Kansas harvested the biggest crop they had ever seen. Extensive fall rains and winter storms offered water-laden fields that farmers rushed to plant, cultivate, and harvest. But the price of wheat had fallen to only 25 cents a bushel, one tenth of its price at the end of World War I. In the middle of abundance, farmers were going broke. Then they experienced the second blow: a rainless August and September so severe that it burned next season's feed crop. The dry spell continued into the winter.

Reeling from this double stroke of misfortune, by the spring of 1932 many farmers abandoned fields that now went bare. March's strong winds built up into more than twenty dust storms that drifted blowing topsoil as high as fencerows. The farmers who tried to plant a spring crop averaged only five bushels per acre. Prices hovered between a low 30 and 36 cents a bushel. Whatever remained of wheat, alfalfa, and milo (an important drought-resistant spring sorghum for animal feed) went down to plagues of grasshoppers and rabbits. The year 1934 brought the poorest rainfall of the entire Dust Bowl. The land drifted into desertlike dirt dunes, the topsoil was gone, and the hardpan was exposed like a flayed skin laid open. New Year's Day of 1935 opened with a severe dust storm, followed by repeated blowings in February and damaging winds of hurricane force in March. Respiratory diseases became common, including "dust pneumonia." The emotional strain of months and years of wind and blowing dirt led to suicides, beatings, and murders.

The apocalyptic dust storm of April 14, 1935, darkened skies from Colorado to the East Coast and layered dirt on ships three hundred miles into the Atlantic Ocean. It was fixed in American popular culture by folk singer Woody Guthrie's new song from Pampa, Texas, "So Long, It's Been Good to Know Ya." The federal government offered to resettle farmers elsewhere, but this seemed too similar to the harsh Soviet farm collectivization that was going on at the same time. A locust invasion in 1937 and 1938 seemed a final blow, but was followed by plagues of army worms. Stretches of roads in the Oklahoma Panhandle and eastern Colorado ran slick from dead insects.

Half a million people did abandon the land, symbolized by the Okies who headed for California and were described in John Steinbeck's novel *The Grapes of Wrath* and John Ford's popular movie of the same name. Federal relief arrived belatedly, too late for thousands of farmers, in the spring and summer of 1934. President Franklin Delano Roosevelt's New Deal administration singled out the independent family farmer on the Plains as a national treasure. The New Deal offered assistance in the form of farm subsidies, credit programs, agricultural extension, and the Soil Conservation Service and spent more than $2 billion to keep the struggling Plains farmers on the land.

Rain and war, a strange mixture of good and evil, revived Plains life in the early

A wall of dust approaching a Kansas town. From "Effect of Dust Storms on Health," U.S. Public Health Service, Reprint No. 1707 from the *Public Health Reports*, Vol. 50, no. 40, October 4, 1935. Courtesy NOAA.

1940s. The revived Plains produced in 1942 a record wheat harvest that surpassed the bumper crop of 1931. Farmers patriotically set new records in 1943 and 1944 to offer more food for a war-ravaged globe. Farm income rose 165 percent in the war years 1939–1945. Nevertheless, Great Plains dependency upon federal subsidies hardly disappeared. Federal intervention continued to support farmers through the "little dust bowls"—as severe as that in the 1930s—of the 1950s, 1970s, and 1990s. Geographer John Borchert could write that there was "a widespread belief that, though there will be future droughts, there need be no future dust bowl."[25] The climate had not changed, but government and society had learned to compensate. Government policy to keep the people on the land continues today. Federal aid turned independent farmers into dependent clients.

IRRIGATION: THE TECHNOLOGICAL ANSWER TO THE PLAINS CLIMATE

Irrigation from underground water supplies became the climate beater of the Great Plains, but it did not start well. Where there was a town well, a common sight on the open prairie was a horse-drawn wagon or even a box on skids bumping along loaded with water barrels covered with burlap. Hundreds of wells were hand dug by the homesteaders themselves so that they could supply the family, but well water did not suffice for much more than a small garden patch and a few steers. Although farmers erected thousands of windmills on the Plains by 1880, they were oversold as the answer to the dry Plains because a windmill's wind-driven pumping suction could only reach down about thirty feet. Windmills could flood ten acres, but farmers needed at least sixteen times that in order to prosper. What was needed was an efficient deep-pumping technology.

The Ogallala Aquifer: Water for Irrigation

New settlers (and old-timers) took comfort in their almost mythic belief in a vast underground body of "sheet water" that was constantly replenished either from the Rocky Mountains or even from the remote Arctic. Farmers around Garden City, Kansas, insisted, for example, that a cavernous underground river existed with the advantage that it was inexhaustible. Did not artesian wells in the Dakotas already easily tap a strong underground flow? An unidentifiable flimflam man, "Captain" Livermore, claimed that underflow water was glacier water from the Arctic, although how it traveled thousands of miles and then fanned out widely "is a matter to be worked out." The Arctic theory remained a popular notion into the 1950s. An 1891 U.S. Geological Survey investigation acknowledged the "underflow" but found that it originated as runoff from the Rockies that flowed eastward, refreshed along the way by percolation from surface rain and snow.[26]

By the time of the Dust Bowl and depression in the 1930s, geologists had located the extent of the aquifer: it is groundwater trapped below 174,000 square miles of fertile but otherwise dry Plains farmland. This territory, most of the Great Plains, covers large parts of Texas, Oklahoma, Kansas, and Nebraska and extends into South Dakota, Wyoming, Colorado, and New Mexico. It is the largest underground body of water in the United States. Unlike most of the world's underground water supplies, Ogallala groundwater is mostly irreplaceable because its sources were cut off thousands of years ago. The Ogallala is essentially "fossil water" that descended onto the Plains 10,000 to 25,000 years ago from the glacier-laden Rocky Mountains to the west, before the melting ice and snow was diverted by geological forces to the Pecos and Rio Grande Rivers.

More than 3 billion acre feet (an acre

Irrigation Technology

After World War II, a synergy of old and new technologies allowed Plains farmers to reach the Ogallala to irrigate their crops. Efficient turbine impeller pumps that could pull water from deep levels began to appear in the 1930s, but they lacked cheap and efficient engines. After the war, farmers turned to used automobile engines, especially the durable low-revolution Ford V-8 and Chevrolet L-Head trademark six-cylinder gasoline power plants. Cheap fuels for irrigation engines lasted until the energy crisis of 1973. Gasoline sold for eleven cents a gallon in 1947 and did not top thirty-five cents a gallon until the early 1970s. Often irrigators could also depend upon free natural gas tapped from gas and oil wells on their own land, fortunately including the world's second-largest field of natural gas, the Guymon-Hugoton field. Farmers also took advantage of new materials, particularly the widespread postwar use of inexpensive aluminum piping.

Plains farmers, for the first time, could ignore the lack of rain by flooding their fields with pumped water. Irrigation on the Great Plains was not merely a response to climate, but its replacement. The other single most essential new technology was the center-pivot irrigator. Invented about 1950 by Colorado farmer Frank Zybach, the center pivot irrigator was called in a 1976 *Scientific American* article "the most significant mechanical innovation [worldwide] in agriculture since the replacement of draft animals by the tractor."[27] Irrigation, which is 10,000 years old, as old as agriculture itself, had always been synonymous with hard work for long hours. Traditional "flood irrigation" required constant tending of ditches that got overgrown with weeds, water gates that got stuck, and channels that collapsed. The self-regulating mechanical center-pivot sprinkler answered the Plains farmer's dream.

Aerial photo of center pivot irrigation. Courtesy John Opie.

foot is a foot of water across one square acre, or 325,851 gallons) were deposited under the Plains. Today the Ogallala trickles very slowly southeastward through sandy gravel beds, 500 feet a year, less than 2 feet a day. These vast water-saturated gravel beds are 150 to 300 feet thick but 50 to 300 feet below the surface. It was mostly impossible for early pioneers to dig a well that deep, nor could a windmill pump that deep. The Ogallala could have saved the Plains from the ravages of the Dust Bowl, but it could not be reached.

A Golden Age for the Ogallala Plains, 1960–2000

Beginning in the 1950s and 1960s, water was pumped from each of hundreds of wells at the rate of a thousand cubic feet a minute to water quarter sections of wheat, alfalfa, grain sorghum, and even corn. By the 1970s, farmers on the Great Plains had installed tens of thousands of wells, each pumping furiously. Once Plains farmers were committed to irrigation, they discovered that their work habits changed dramatically from classic farm life—pastoral and seasonal—to an industrial operation. Their physical labor was different, but not eased. The noisy motors ran day and night. They became full-time mechanics, as well as farmers dealing with pumps, gearboxes, motors, valves, and piping. Drilling and casing a basic well cost approximately $1,300, the pump and gearhead about $2,200, and a small used Ford V-8 or Chevrolet engine $500, for a total of $4,000. In 1950, Plains farmers had irrigated 3.5 million acres of farmland; in 1990, it was 15 million acres.[28]

Land values rose rapidly for productive irrigated land. In Lubbock, Texas, farmland was valued in 1990 at more than $400 an acre, compared to $20 an acre in 1935. After center-pivot sprinklers were installed on hundreds of quarter sections, even the barren Sandhills of southwestern Kansas produced corn, sorghum, and wheat yields that matched those of Iowa and Illinois. Corn demands the most water during the season, an astonishing 900,000 gallons laid on 130 acres of a 160-acre quarter section, wheat and sorghum half that amount.

By the year 2000, a center-pivot sprinkler system, from drilling the well to watering the milo, often cost a farmer $100,000 per 160 acres. Most irrigators need six to ten units for efficiencies of size. To pay for them, the irrigator needs good wheat or sorghum prices, which were in the late 1980s half of what they had been ten years before. By 2000, the value of these crops had fallen even further, forcing many farmers into

Modern day feedlot. Courtesy John Opie.

concentrated hog farming or cattle feed lots or, very often, out of farming entirely. Yet from any rational perspective, irrigation was a marvelous technology, and alternatives to irrigation are gloomy.

In some places on the Great Plains in 2000, irrigation had taken all but five or ten feet of usable Ogallala groundwater. In 1970, farmers around Sublette, Kansas, concluded that they had three hundred years of water left in the aquifer, based on current pumping and known supplies. By 1980, their estimate had fallen to seventy years as pumping rose dramatically, and by 1990 their estimate had dropped to less than thirty years. By 2000, using current techniques, many local irrigators said that they would be happy to hold on for another decade.[29]

More than one billion acre feet of Ogallala water were consumed by irrigation farmers between 1960 and 2000, mostly in southwestern Kansas, the Oklahoma Panhandle, and western Texas. (Western Nebraska, which is mostly cattle country, holds more than 60 percent of the remaining aquifer water.) Nothing can accelerate Ogallala flow, and artificial replacement remains unlikely in technological or financial terms.

GRASSLAND RENAISSANCE IN THE 21ST CENTURY

In 1981, farm economist Willard W. Cochrane described an emerging pattern on the Great Plains: the 1930s was a Dust Bowl and depression era of uncertainty and instability. Gradually, new irrigation technologies in the 1950s and 1960s rewarded farmers with an extraordinary fifty years of high-speed groundwater consumption. But these fifty years cannot be repeated because of the depletion of the aquifer. Cochrane sees two additional factors that will make the next fifty years more difficult. One is that many farmers stayed in business only because of large government subsidies. The other is that the smaller family farmer is uncompetitive with large industrial farming ("agribusiness"). A vertically integrated agribusiness in wheat or beef or pork needs copious water to serve its demand for corporate profits. The threat of the next drought (possibly intensified by the greenhouse effect) would triple water consumption.[30]

Beginning in the 1990s, Plains farmers also turned to confined animal farming operations (CAFOs) that promised not only survival but also high profitability. In the case of hogs, these were like crowded urban slums in which each hog was fattened on processed feeds and artificial nutrients to be speeded on its way to slaughter—"the new white meat." Efficiency was high, but costs included antibiotics to avoid the high risk of disease in crowded conditions. Environmental costs in pollution of land and water were at first played down, but quickly came under local and federal control as so-called lagoons of manure created "dead zones" uninhabitable by humans. More traditional are cattle feedlots that can cover an entire landscape, a form of vertical integration by enterprising farmers who could grow the feed that nourished the animals. Again, cattle growth was sped up by processed feeds and artificial nutrients. But in both hogs and cattle, much of the profitability does not remain on the Plains to rebuild the Plains. Instead, it is diverted to large national and international corporations.

Americans esteemed the Plains homestead as the place where patriotic virtues of rugged individualism, hardworking industriousness, and personal self-sufficiency were practiced best. Yet instead of achieving independence, when this farming encountered the environmental limits of the Plains, the independent farmer became a long-term government client. Government aid to farmers to compensate for low grain prices became part of their way of life during the difficult depression years of the 1930s and was not denied them until the gradual letdown scheduled by the 1995 Farm Bill. By 2000, Congress reverted to its subsidies. As a result, the American family farm has persisted for more than a hundred years on the Plains (and more than two hundred years nationally) as a decentralized "cottage industry" in an increasingly industrialized world.

"For a long time folks [on the Great Plains] have been trying to go down the road by looking into the rearview mirror," said U. S. Forest Service advisor Chris Wood. "Sometimes that sense of history, while important, may have prevented us from looking forward as much as we should have." The future of the Plains, he suggested, was not in grain or red meat. Up in North Dakota, rancher Ron Whited retorted, "[This land] wasn't bought for aesthetics and all these other values out there. Mother Nature never intended for this country to be pristine." Another Dakota rancher insisted that most ranchers practice "true ecosystem management," a model of agrarian self-government that encourages stewardship. But an alternative viewpoint says that an increasing number of local people see the Plains as more than range for cattle and a platform for oil derricks. Farmer Jim Oberfoell told a reporter, "Some people drive through the badlands and they say, 'There's nothing there—this is the most godforsaken place I've ever seen. But you spend some time out there, do a little camping, get up in the cool of the morning and listen to the sounds you don't hear outside the badlands, and it really grows on you." Another local person said, "It's the last best place." A North Dakota rancher, Scott Fitzwilliams, said, "There is change on the grasslands. People see new values out there. That's not a bad thing. Change can be positive if you give it a chance."[31] One hundred twenty-five years earlier, Theodore Roosevelt's experience as a young cowboy in badlands country turned into his presidential devotion to conservation.

FROM SODBUSTING TO CONSERVATION TO SUSTAINABILITY: ENVIRONMENTAL AND HISTORICAL PERSPECTIVE ON TODAY'S GREAT PLAINS

In the beginning, pioneer sodbusting with John Deere's plow opened a fertile dense sod that was 6,000 years in the making. This lasted well into the 1920s, encouraged by federal authorities. After a couple of years without rain, inches of it blew away in repeated dust storms. The famous Pare Lorentz documentary film *The Plow That Broke the Plains*, with its musical score by Virgil Thomson, had a double meaning of opening the soil for pioneer farmers and also destroying it during the Dust Bowl. Following the disastrous Dust Bowl of the 1930s, Plains farmers learned conservation techniques such as contour plowing and the growing of windbreaks. The modern Plains farmers of the late twentieth and early twenty-first centuries know the essential features of their personal ecosystem, although they may not call it exactly that.

The environmental history of the Great Plains is a series of crisis situations accelerated by repeated drought. As a result, the region became an inadvertent "experiment station" for crisis management on many levels, from local farmers to federal planners. Because of environmental conditions, when the Plains was settled after the Civil War as an agricultural region, it also went on permanent alert. Dust bowls after little or no rain roll through the region approximately every twenty years. The continuous crisis is particularly obvious if one sees today's costly irrigation from groundwater—the Ogallala Aquifer—as a form of dependency that is a mere brief blip in time—1960–2000—compared to long-term forces at work. It must be remembered that the groundwater was not part of the Plains' original environment, but was introduced to the surface only after it was discovered and then pumped with modern technologies. Historic environmental conditions do not disappear. The Plains environment sets limits on all human efforts.

By the 1960s and 1970s, Americans' thoughts about the Great Plains began to change. They began to learn more of its distinctive character through the new science of ecology and ecosystem analysis, rather than through scientific reductionism, which looks at increasingly smaller pieces of nature. The Plains can be considered an entire ecozone. This is a holistic and integrative approach that examines interlocking problems such as agricultural practices, soil erosion, groundwater consumption, and climate impacts and acknowledges that nature and humanity are profoundly connected to each other. It seeks multilevel and combined solutions to such apparently different, but interlocked problems as poverty, environmental degradation, and disintegration of rural communities.

Environmental science takes into account economics, politics, and social issues. According to one regional think tank, for example, at the level of the Plains as an ecozone, "communities are woven into the complex networks across diverse ecosystems, production, marketing and communication systems, and political administrative units."[32] Environmental science recognizes the complexity of the Plains environment, which is linked to human activity on the Plains. A small input, like a grain of soil at the beginning of a dust storm, can have an enormous outcome; a large input, like massive federal subsidies, can seem to disappear into the black hole of little rain.

Plains farmers were among the first environmentalists. One grizzled farmer, sitting on his harvester, when highly praised for the bushels of wheat he had produced per acre, looked at his fields and simply observed, "Yes, but look what it did to the soil." Today any Plains farmer who struggles to win over his thousand acres recognizes the complexity of his enterprise: soil types, water distribution and runoff, moisture depths, chemical and mineral conditions, application of pesticides and herbicides, tillage practices, crop types and crop soil consumption, pollution and waste, and, above all, the tension between soil consumption and profitable crop production.

Environmental science has been criticized on the Plains when it encourages the gradual suspension of farming in a difficult region. Environmental science has been praised by Plains farmers, both dryland farmers and irrigators, for its recognition of the complexity of their operations and the answers it has offered—land leveling, tailwater recovery, groundwater moisture analysis, and even cloud seeding. Americans are discovering the Great Plains as one of the nation's true wonders, both in its natural state and as one of the world's great agricultural regions.

The original Plains grasslands, sometimes parched, sometimes burned by natural fires, sometimes moistened into stunning green landscapes, would have prospered on their own indefinitely into the future. It was a vital, healthy, and dynamic region. Modern agribusiness, which now dominates the Plains, cares less about "what it did to the soil" than about the quarterly profit report to management and shareholders, sometimes as far away as New York City or Amsterdam. A few scattered remnants of the pre-European Plains are today preserved in federal and state grassland parks. But if the Plains were suddenly emptied of farmers and ranchers, it could not revert to its original condition because too many alien plants have been introduced.

One debate involves the expansion of the twenty national grasslands that stretch from the Little Missouri National Grassland through the Cimarron in the old Dust Bowl region of southwestern Kansas down to the Lyndon B. Johnson National Grassland in north central Texas. Larry Dawson, supervisor of the Dakota Prairie Grasslands near Bismarck, when in 2000 the Forest Service began to put severe limits on grazing rights for ranchers, said, "Our goal is no longer to maximize red meat production." These were fighting words, but perhaps only to those who were looking into the rearview mirror.

It is hard to argue against the productivity of the Plains, despite the price paid in depletion of water and soil. Industrial farming plays a major role in the ability of each American farmer today to feed a whopping eight dozen other people, compared to four others when the nation began. It is remarkable that less than 2 percent of Americans work on a farm, compared to 30 or 40 percent of a nation's population elsewhere in the world. This success story, perhaps the most important in all of modern history, does much to define all of America's prosperity. The Great Plains produces enormous surpluses of wheat, sorghums, soybeans, and even corn; no wonder it is still called "the Feedbag and Breadbasket of the World." The question remains, however, whether this bounty can continue, under what circumstances, and at what cost.

Even though the Plains grains and people have long been kept in place by taxpayer subsidies, they contain powerful historical and national symbols of rural and agricultural America. It is difficult to accept that the family farm has largely been swallowed up by industrial agriculture. As people leave, farm towns across the Plains are losing their last grocery store, gas station, bank, and even churches. The Plains still is wealthy in productive soil and water from the Ogallala. Farming, using the latest technologies, will continue on the Plains for an indefinite future.

But the memory of the Dust Bowl persists. The idea of the forced abandonment of the Plains to light grazing or empty grassland first came up in the 1930s, but a federal resettlement program was resented because it pushed failed farmers into "reservations" like Indians. Land-use planners Frank and Deborah Popper offered a radical proposal in late 1987. Let us finally admit, they argued, that more than a century of repeated farm abandonments, dust bowls, costly government interventions, and environmental destruction has resulted in the failure of the American ex-

Is the Future of the Plains in Its Cities?

The Great Plains are unlikely ever to have great metropolitan centers like Denver, Chicago, or Los Angeles. The Plains are challenged by extreme climate, lack of great scenery, and difficult access to water. With its high food production, agriculture will remain king, followed by regional manufacturing (such as aircraft in Wichita), with historical and environmental tourism as the king's eventual sidekick. Nevertheless, urban sprawl has touched the Plains. The 2000 census shows that Oklahoma City is edging toward 500,000 people, Tulsa toward 400,000, Amarillo in Texas has more than 165,000 people, and even Lubbock, situated in the heart of the blankest Plains, is growing toward 200,000 inhabitants. Further north, the two Kansas Cities facing each other on the Missouri River (more than 580,000), as well as Omaha (350,000) and Lincoln (more than 200,000), seek to prosper by nonagricultural means that include government agencies, universities, and defense, electronic, and trucking industries. Suburban tracts are common, as are downtown slums. Industrial expansion is also taking place in Topeka (almost 125,000) and Wichita (more than 310,000) in Kansas. Smaller cities are fighting for their existence. Their fortunes are still tied to agriculture: Liberal, Garden City, Colby, and Hays in Kansas. This is also true of places like Scottsbluff, North Platte, and Grand Island in Nebraska, Bismarck and Fargo in North Dakota, and Sioux Falls in South Dakota. Some cities are flourishing as seasonal tourist centers, such as the Black Hills center in Rapid City, South Dakota.

periment to live successfully on the Great Plains. Despite irrigation, between 1950 and 1970 half the people left the region, and between 1980 and 2000 it was expected that half again would have departed, leaving half a million farmers across the entire Great Plains, compared to two million in 1950.

More than a third of the Plains' counties (900,000 square miles) have fewer than six people per square mile, and half of those counties have fewer than two people per square mile. Seventy-two percent of the Great Plains counties lost population between 1960 and 1990. Kansas has more than 6,000 ghost towns, some very recent. One reporter wrote, "It's Manifest Destiny in Reverse." The Poppers identified a county-by-county wide swath of hopeless decline in 139,000 square miles across the Plains from Texas to North Dakota. By the standard of two people per square mile as a frontier region, Kansas has more frontier counties now than a hundred years ago, and thirty-five of North Dakota's fifty-three counties meet the frontier definition. Frank Popper said, "It doesn't take a rocket scientist to figure out this region will continue to de-populate, age, and face further economic declines." The Poppers concluded, "Over the next generation, the Plains will, as a result of the largest, longest-running agricultural and environmental miscalculation in American history, become almost totally depopulated."[33]

Buffalo grazing. Courtesy Oklahoma Tourism.

Frank Popper recommended a "Buffalo Commons" across the entire Great Plains from Canada through Texas. The Buffalo Commons would become open land and wildlife refuge, "the world's largest natural and historic preservation project." It would include public and private land, Native American properties, and land belonging to environmental organizations. Despite regional anger toward the Poppers, even loathing, in the late 1980s and into the 1990s, Deborah Popper noted in 2001, "People typically thanked us for giving them a wake-up call, even if they disagreed with everything else."[34] The Plains should be returned to their preagricultural condition, notably herds of bison, antelopes, and elk, with lurking wolves, coyotes, and birds of prey.

By 2003, more than 300,000 bison inhabited different preserves, if not the open range. In bison country, the ground is covered with a rainbow of flowers and the perennial plants of the short-grass and midgrass plains. Ecotourism is beginning to flourish. Bison products form an increasingly popular niche meat market. A processing plant in North Dakota turns 12,000 animals a year into sausages, burgers, and steaks. There are complaints, however, that bison herds can become feedlot animals ready only for processing. Among Native Americans, a tribal consortium in South Dakota herds 10,000 bison. The Nature Conservancy has more than 3,000 bison on 80,000 acres of its land.

The innovative Land Institute at Salina, Kansas, was founded by the visionary agriculturalist Wes Jackson. The institute is committed to keeping independent farmers on the Great Plains by returning them to the self-sustaining grassland ecosystem prior to settlement combined with ecologically sound food production. It is a vigorous opponent of the modern industrial agribusiness that has come to dominate the Plains economy. Its primary objective is "to develop an agroecosystem that reflects more the attributes of climax prairie than do conventional agricultural systems based on annual grain crops."[35]

The Land Institute and other alternative operations like the Kansas Rural Center advocate a broad environmental paradigm, biocentrism. Biocentric farming follows the natural patterns of the local ecosystem. This turns on its head the historic Western view that nature is humanity's raw material. In a biocentric viewpoint, farming cannot be like any other industry. North Dakota farmer-philosopher Fred Kirschenmann observed that "A farm is not a factory—it is an organism made up of numerous suborganisms, each alive and interdependent, each affected in numerous, complex ways" by outside forces—money, chemicals, technology, market prices—that are invariably disruptive.

The wild card in this poker game is global warming. The Great Plains is inescapably threatened by the world's changing climate due to greater quantities of industrial and automobile carbon dioxide, methane, and other substances pumped into the upper atmosphere. According to computerized global climate modeling at Princeton, New Jersey, and Boulder, Colorado, as well as in England and Switzerland, the U.S. Great Plains is one of several regions around the world that will turn into a major desert when the predicted CO_2-induced greenhouse effect gradually takes hold. Scientists and farmers have recently learned of the impact of global climate forces like El Niño from the south central Pacific Ocean. Farmers will have a harder time responding to "desertification" because they would need to take three times more water than today's rate to compensate for global warming. This would seriously harm most strategies for survival on the Great Plains. The low-rain climate of the Great Plains, deeply intensified by global warming, may once again have the direct impact it has not had for sixty years. For a time, the Great Plains emerged as the Great American Garden; the struggle will be to keep it from becoming the Great American Desert.

The Great Plains still has a long way to go in the American public eye. Families in their autos rush across on Interstates 70 or 80 or on U.S. Routes 6, 12, 20, or 30, for something less blisteringly hot or bitterly cold, for something less flat, for something "more scenic," and also to bypass a landscape that seems in Dust Bowl–like economic decline. They may see bunches of ugly grasshopper-like oil pumps or smelly cattle feed lots. What they may not see is America's last frontier, remnants of the famed Cattle Kingdom, the powerful shift from dryland farming to irrigation, and today's rise of corporate agribusiness that is swallowing up the historical family farmer. Instead, they only see a tedious two-day, 600-mile drive. The view from the air through the airliner's window is more attractive to the attentive sightseer: America's famous gridiron of mile-square sections, green and yellow in the summer, a black-and-white pattern in the winter, and across the central Plains, even beautiful circles inside squares where the center-pivot sprinklers spread their nourishing water across fields of wheat, sorghums, soybeans, and corn. Otherwise, the Plains do not resonate with most Americans who only see the boxed beef or pork, or the packaged bread or pasta, on the grocery shelves at their local store. In a more tragic vein, vast mounds of surplus wheat, sorghum, or corn pile up and never reach starving peoples in the Sudan because of bureaucratic confusion. Not the least, our entire American history contains a black hole from when the family farmer disappeared from our horizon. The Great Plains nevertheless persists as a reminder of the nation's iconic agricultural history, of its existence as a great world granary, and a future that embodies a combination of food abundance, restoration of grass and bison, and the rediscovery of one of America's great landscapes.

RESOURCE GUIDE

Printed Sources

The following are books that have become classic studies of the Great Plains, have made innovative contributions, or contain unique information. Several of them are collections of key essays. There are many broader environmental and historical studies that include the Great Plains, but the selections here focus primarily upon this specific region.

"At Home on the Planet: 21 Critical Ecoregions (Map)." *Sierra* 79, no. 2 (March/April 1994): 58–62.

Bailey, Robert G. *North American Ecoregions Map*. Miscellaneous Publication 1548. Washington, DC: U.S. Department of Agriculture, Forest Service, May 1998.

Blouet, Brian W., and Merlin P. Lawson, eds. *Images of the Plains: The Role of Human Nature in Settlement*. Lincoln: University of Nebraska Press, 1975.

Blouet, Brian W., and Frederick C. Luebke, eds. *The Great Plains: Environment and Culture*. Lincoln: Center for Great Plains Studies, University of Nebraska Press, 1979.

Bonnifield, Paul. *The Dust Bowl: Men, Dirt, and Depression*. Albuquerque: University of New Mexico Press, 1979.

Costello, David F. *The Prairie World: Plants and Animals of the Grassland Sea*. New York: Apollo Books/Thomas Y. Crowell Company, 1969, 1975.

Farb, Peter. *Living Earth*. New York: Harper Colophon Books, 1959.

Fiege, Mark. *Irrigated Eden: The Making of an Agricultural Landscape in the American West*. Seattle: University of Washington Press, 1999.

Fite, Gilbert C. *The Farmer's Frontier, 1865–1900*. New York: Holt, Rinehart and Winston, 1966.

Heat-Moon, William Least. *PrairyErth (a Deep Map)*. Boston: Houghton Mifflin, 1991.

Hillel, Daniel. *Out of the Earth: Civilization and the Life of the Soil*. Berkeley: University of California Press, 1991.

History of the Expedition under the Command of Lewis and Clark. Edited by Elliott Coues. 3 vols. New York: Dover Publications, 1965 reprint of 1893 Harper edition.

Hyams, Edward. *Soil and Civilization*. New York: Harper Colophon Books, 1976.

Knobloch, Frieda. *The Culture of Wilderness: Agriculture as Colonization in the American West*. Chapel Hill: University of North Carolina Press, 1996.

Land Resource Regions and Major Land Resource Areas of the United States. Agricultural Bulletin 296. Washington, DC: U.S. Department of Agriculture, Soil Conservation Service, December 1981.

Lawson, Merlin P. and Maurice E. Baker, eds. *The Great Plains: Perspectives and Prospects*. Lincoln: Center for Great Plains Studies, University of Nebraska Press, 1981.

Licht, Daniel S. *Ecology and Economics of the Great Plains*. Lincoln: University of Nebraska Press, 1997.

Malin, James C. *History and Ecology: Studies of the Grassland*. Lincoln: University of Nebraska Press, 1981.

Manning, Richard. *Grassland: The History, Biology, Politics, and Promise of the American Prairie*. New York: Penguin Books, 1995.

McIntosh, Charles Barron. *The Nebraska Sand Hills: The Human Landscape*. Lincoln: University of Nebraska Press, 1996.

Noss, Reed F., and Robert L. Peters. *Endangered Ecosystems: A Status Report on America's Vanishing Habitat and Wildlife*. Washington, DC: Defenders of Wildlife, 1995.

Opie, John. *Ogallala: Water for a Dry Land*. Lincoln: University of Nebraska Press, 1993, 2000.

Phillips Petroleum Company. *Pasture and Range Plants*. Bartlesville, OK: Phillips Petroleum Company, 1963.

Powell, John Wesley. *Report on the Lands of the Arid Region of the United States.* 1879. Rpt. Boston: Harvard Common Press, 1983.

Rabin, Jonathan. *Bad Land: An American Romance.* New York: Vintage Books/Random House, 1996.

Riney-Kehrberg, Pamela. *Rooted in Dust: Surviving Drought and Depression in Southwestern Kansas.* Lawrence: University Press of Kansas, 1994.

Sears, Paul B. *Deserts on the March.* 4th ed. Norman: University of Oklahoma Press, 1980.

Sherow, James Earl. *Watering the Valley: Development along the High Plains Arkansas River, 1870–1950.* Lawrence: University Press of Kansas, 1990.

The State of the Nation's Ecosystems: Measuring the Lands, Waters, and Living Resources of the United States. New York: Cambridge University Press, 2002.

Webb, Walter Prescott. *The Great Plains.* Boston: Ginn and Company, 1931.

Wessel, Thomas R. *Agriculture in the Great Plains, 1876–1936.* Washington, DC: Agricultural History Society, 1977.

Worster, Donald. *Dust Bowl: The Southern Plains in the 1930s.* New York: Oxford University Press, 1979.

Novels

Cather, Willa. *My Antonia.* Boston: Houghton Mifflin, 1918.

———. *The Professor's House.* New York: Alfred A. Knopf, 1925.

Michener, James. *Centennial.* New York: Fawcett, 1975.

Rølvaag, O. E. *Giants in the Earth.* New York: Harper and Brothers, 1929.

Sandoz, Mari. *Old Jules.* 1935. Rpt. Lincoln: University of Nebraska Press, Bison Books, 1962.

Web Sites

The Center for Applied Rural Innovation
http://ianrwww.unl.edu/ianr/csas/ (accessed July 23, 2003)

The center stresses sustainable agriculture as the best hope for the future of the Great Plains: "economically profitable, environmentally sound, and socially viable for the long term." Its Web site is particularly rich in other Web site links.

The Center for Great Plains Studies
http://www.unl.edu/plains (accessed July 23, 2003)

A research institute whose mission is to promote a greater understanding of the people, culture, history, and environment of the Great Plains.

The Conservation Alliance
http://www.conservationalliance.org/ (accessed July 23, 2003)

A nonprofit organization "guided in our work by science, particularly conservation biology, but we strive to be sensitive to the traditional knowledge of native people. Our hope is that one day the diversity of wildlife which once roamed Great Plains can be restored to a portion of its former range."

Environmental Protection Agency
http://www.epa.gov/surf/

EPA remapping of the United States in terms of watersheds rather than state or county lines.

The Grassland Heritage Foundation
http://www.grasslandheritage.org/ (accessed July 23, 2003)

A nonprofit membership organization devoted to prairie preservation and education.

The Great Plains Foundation
http://www.greatplainsfoundation.org/ (accessed July 23, 2003)

This foundation raises "awareness, appreciation, and knowledge of the Great Plains Ecosystem . . . that will work towards and encourage sustainable communities that recognize the interdependence of humans, cultures, natural resources, wildlife, and agriculture."

The Great Plains Institute for Sustainable Development
http://www.gpisd.net/ (accessed July 23, 2003)

The institute emphasizes the long-term viability of Great Plains communities, the productivity of its economic enterprises, the quality of its environment, and the prudent management of its resources.

The Great Plains Restoration Council
http://www.gprc.org/ (accessed July 23, 2003)

A "multicultural, multiracial non-profit organization building the Buffalo Commons step-by-step by bringing the wild buffalo back and restoring healthy, sustainable communities to the Great Plains."

Many state and federal agencies also have programs and information that focus on the Great Plains. See particularly the Web sites of the U.S. Department of Agriculture, the Environmental Protection Agency, the Fish and Wildlife Service, the Soil and Water Conservation Service, and the Geological Survey. There are parallel agencies in most of the Great Plains states. A small selection follows from a rich treasury of Web sites.

Greatplains.org
http://www.greatplains.org/ (accessed July 23, 2003)

One of this organization's key principles "is that economic and ecological interests can be compatible, even complementary, if thoughtful people apply good science and good sense."

The High Plains Regional Climate Center (HPRCC)
University of Nebraska
236 L. W. Chase Hall
Lincoln, NE 68583-0728
Phone: 402-472-6706; Fax: 402-472-6614
http://www.hprcc.unl.edu/index.html (accessed July 23, 2003)

A research center/think tank that offers scientific analysis of climate impacts on the Plains. Its Web site also includes access to federal resources from NOAA, USDA, USGS, and EPA. It is rich in historical materials and a large array of maps.

Kansas Geological Survey
http://www.kgs.ukans.edu/HighPlains/atlas/
Kansas atlas of High Plains aquifer.

The Kansas Rural Center (KRC)
http://www.kansasruralcenter.org (accessed July 23, 2003)

A nonprofit organization that emphasizes local action and strongly advocates family farming, stewardship of soil and water, agricultural sustainability, and the viability of local communities and rural culture.

The Land Institute
http://www.landinstitute.org (accessed July 23, 2003)

The Land Institute, founded by Wes Jackson, has its facilities just outside Salina, Kansas and has worked for more than twenty years on the problem of substituting sustainable agriculture that would properly mimic the grasslands of the Great Plains. The institute supports Plains writers and collaborates closely with scientists and other researchers, including ones from the National Academy of Sciences.

Prairies Forever
http://www.prairies.org/index.html (accessed July 23, 2003)

A nonprofit organization dedicated to promoting the ecological and cultural significance of the American prairie through education, outreach, and public engagement.

United States Department of Agriculture
http://www.usda.gov (then search Great Plains/High Plains/individual states)

United States Geological Survey
http://www.usgs.gov/
National Map Viewer with in-depth details.

Water Resources of Nebraska
http://ne.water.usgs.gov/highplains/hpactivities.html
Ogallala/High Plains aquifer.

Videos/Films

Dances with Wolves. Dir. Kevin Costner. Perf. Kevin Costner, Mary McDonnell, Graham Greene, Floyd Red Crow Westerman. Guild/Tig Productions, Jim Wilson. 1990.

Fargo. Dir. Joel Coen. Perf. Frances McDormand, William H. Macy, Peter Stormare. Polygram/Working Title. 1996.

High Plains Drifter. Dir. Clint Eastwood. Perf. Clint Eastwood, Verna Bloom, Marianna Hall. Universal/Malapaso. 1972.

The Last Picture Show. Dir. Peter Bogdanovich. Perf. Timothy Bottoms, Jeff Bridges, Cybill Shepherd. Columbia/LPS/BBS. 1971.

The Plow That Broke the Plains. Documentary. Dir. Pare Lorentz. Music, Virgil Thomson. Resettlement Administration, 1936.

Recordings

Guthrie, Woody. *Dust Bowl Ballads.* Folkways/Alan Lomax, Library of Congress (several versions). Recorded April 26, 1940. Released early July 1940. RCA Records.

ETHNICITY

A. Dudley Gardner

On the Plains, blue skies touch endless stretches of brown grass. Here vast open spaces seem to be the home for antelope and bison, not people. But the idea that the Plains is only wide open spaces with no people is far from reality. The Great Plains has always been home to people from numerous nations. For more than 12,000 years, Native Americans gathered wild plants and hunted and lived in the area. By the time Columbus reached the New World, Native farmers grew corn along the rivers that flowed through the future states of Kansas, Nebraska, Oklahoma, and North and South Dakota. On the eastern edge of the Plains, where grass gives way to trees, Native peoples long cultivated crops. By the time Europeans first reached the area in the 1500s, Caddo, Pawnee, Arikara, Mandan, and Hidatsa Indians hunted bison and grew corn and beans on the Plains. The people were as diverse as the land. When Europeans, Africans, and later Asians moved onto the Plains in the 1800s, they lived alongside Native Americans. Native peoples, whose ancestors had lived there for centuries, and newly arrived immigrants created a cultural landscape that matched the natural landscape: a place where diversity and contrast not only defined the land, but reflected the people who lived in the region.

For many Americans, the concepts of race and ethnicity have become blurred. Race, simply defined, is a gift given at birth. People are Chinese or French, however, based on cultural factors. A French child is trained (socialized) to use a fork and speak French; a Chinese toddler is trained to use chopsticks and speak Mandarin. Their identity as French or Chinese has little to do with what they look like and has more to do with how they are raised (socialized). It is in the raising of a child that a person gains his or her culture and, one might say, ethnicity. An ethnic group generally regards itself as distinct. This distinction is based on "social or cultural characteristics such as nationality, language and religion." Like race, "ethnicity tends to be passed from generation to generation and is ordinarily not an affiliation that one can freely drop."[1] There are complicating factors. Variations

Ukrainian dancers in North Dakota. Photo by Dawn Charging. Courtesy North Dakota Tourism.

exist within ethnic groups, and, as in the case of most groups, there are divisions that make generalizing about an ethnic group difficult. Here an ethnic group is defined as distinct based on "social or cultural characteristics such as nationality, language and religion."

What make America and the American West unique are the diverse races and ethnic groups that live there. The various races and ethnic groups who chose to live in the Plains will be described, with an examination of why people immigrated, where they came from, and when they first arrived. The approach here is to look at the people who lived on the Plains, the removal of eastern tribes to Oklahoma, the mixing of Native and European culture, and how this mixing shaped the region. The arrival of Europeans and Americans changed the way farming and building were done, but all who lived on the Plains faced the environmental extremes that wind and aridity or water and tornados can create. How did the Europeans get here, and in some cases, how did they live? Today there is a new wave of immigration from Asia and Mexico. All of these immigrant groups have brought with them a concept of cultural identity, and they have moved to a land where Native peoples have still held to their cultures, values, and traditions. Why and when and where did people from different cultures come together to live in the states of Kansas, Nebraska, Oklahoma, and North and South Dakota?

FIRST NATIONS

For at least 12,000 years, a variety of nations lived on the Plains.[2] Along the banks of the region's rivers, some nations lived for thousands of years. The Plains abounded in bison. Prehistoric hunters followed these bison out onto the Plains, ate their meat, slept in tipis made from their hides, and wore moccasins made from bison leather. The prairie offered food and shelter to those who knew what they were looking for. When people acquired knowledge of how to plant corn, they grew it along river bottoms and mixed hunting with farming. In so doing, they developed a culture unlike those anywhere else. In fact, the Plains Indian became the picture of what an "Indian" was. A rider racing across the Plains on a horse chasing bison and the family living together in a tipi came to be the picture of Native American life. The truth, as always, was more complex.

The Great Plains contained numerous nations when the Europeans arrived. The

Plains cultural concept includes the nations that occupied the grasslands and river bottoms of the Great Plains. Francisco de Coronado in 1541 called the Plains "nothing but cattle and sky." The cattle were bison; the sky was an allusion to the vast flat expanses where one sees more sky than land. But people lived on these vast expanses. In fact, the Plains could be divided into three types of people: those who hunted, those who farmed and traded, and those who did all three. This oversimplification points to the fact that farming has long been practiced on the Plains. As far north as present Bismarck, North Dakota, Mandan farmers planted corn. They traded corn to their neighbors for bison, obsidian, and any other thing of value. The Caddo in the southern Plains also grew corn and traded with their neighbors who roamed onto the Plains. The Pawnee in southern Nebraska farmed, hunted, and traded. The Platte River valley carried water past Pawnee fields. Their corn crops grew like weeds. The "Plains Indians" who lived in tipis lived like their ancestors, gathering seeds and hunting bison. They traveled onto the Plains using dog travois to carry their lodges and goods. Most Indian groups who lived in the area followed the big bison herds onto the Plains.

Farming on the Plains proved practical as long as water flowed or rains fell at the right time. Crop failures, unfortunately, proved common. If winds blew too strongly, the frost came too early, or the rains never fell at all, crops died. Bison, while sometimes hard to find, seemed always to be present. Pursuing bison on foot proved hard, but on a horse, the chase and hunt of bison provided a reliable source of food. Once the Plains Indians acquired the horse, many turned from just farming to hunting, and others turned to only chasing after the great bison herds. The American Plains Indian culture that Hollywood and Europe envisioned emerged only after the horse arrived. Coronado, the first to take the horse onto the Great Plains, initiated a revolution that gained strength as the horse herds grew. Following bison, setting up tipis, and living a life dictated by seasons were attractive to farmers.

In increasing numbers, Europeans came into contact with Plains Indians on both the northern and southern Plains in the 1700s. While no clean division of the Plains can be made, the northern Plains encompassed present Nebraska and North and South Dakota. The southern Plains included parts of Kansas and most of Oklahoma. Northern Plains Indians traded first with the French and later with the English. By the 1700s, the Mandan had established lucrative trade relations with French Canadian trappers and merchants in present-day Canada. On the southern Plains, Native Americans traded first with the Pueblo Indians and later with the Spaniards. By the 1600s, it appears that goods were exchanged with Spaniards following long-established prehistoric trade patterns. They traded bison hides and furs for corn. What the Native Americans came to want most from the Spaniards engaged in the trade networks were horses. In the 1700s, horses changed the region forever. A horse gave a hunter freedom to follow the game, and with the horse, the fabled Plains culture soon evolved.

While Spaniards could not control the trade of horses, they did prohibit the sale of guns to Native Americans. Guns found their way north from Spanish settlements, but rarely. To the north, however, guns moved freely across the Canadian and American Plains, carried by Indian and French traders. Unfortunately, the spread of guns, horses, and disease went hand in hand. On the positive side, the horse gave the Native peoples the mobility to hunt and travel freely over the Plains. The tribes became enriched through trading furs for metal and horses. But the improved standard of living came at a price. Diseases such as smallpox, measles, and chicken pox cut across the land and killed thousands of Native peoples, though exact death totals are not available. The Blackfeet legends and histories indicate that smallpox devastated their tribe, and the Mandan essentially vanished. Smallpox affected all tribes on the Plains before the United States acquired Louisiana in 1803.

The Louisiana Purchase directly or indirectly placed much of the northern Plains in the hands of Americans. Meriwether Lewis and William Clark's journals provide a clearer picture of the interaction of the Native peoples with French and Spanish entrepreneurs. Lewis and Clark's guide, Sacajawea, was a Shoshoni married to a Frenchman, and while Frenchmen lived on the northern Plains, Spaniards lived on the edges of the southern Plains. When Lewis and Clark headed north along the Missouri River, Spaniards moved across the plains from New Mexico through present-day Kansas and Nebraska in an attempt to intercept and arrest or kill the Americans. As they traveled north, the Spaniards were not met with a warm reception. While exchanges with Spanish traders proved profitable, Indians and Spaniards had mixed relationships. The Spaniards had long fought with Plains tribes. Spaniards fought with the Comanche on the southern Plains through much of the 1700s, but interactions went beyond battles. Native peoples and Spaniards, since their arrival in New Mexico in 1598, had lived and worked together. Spaniards traded with the Plains Indians. By the 1800s, at least minimal contact with most of the southern Plains Indians had been made. In many ways Spaniards and Indians got along well, especially since trade partners must cooperate. The Spanish could trade with a variety of tribes.[3]

Spaniards came onto the Plains in 1541 when Coronado headed east through Kansas in search of Quivira, a mythical city filled with gold. They never reached Quivira, but eventually claimed the southern Plains. The plains of Kansas did not offer fertile ground for settlement, but by the late 1700s Spanish explorers had knowledge of the region. The 1800s brought change to the Spanish empire. First, the southern Plains became a possession of France. In 1803, the southern Plains were sold to the United States. In 1821, Mexico essentially achieved its independence. This coincided with Mexico's interest in the northern frontier of the domain. The Arkansas River, which flows across southern Kansas, became the route to Mexico. With the U.S. Customs Office and steamboat landings in Independence, Missouri, American traders headed west along the Arkansas to Santa Fe. Along the Santa Fe Trail, Americans and Mexicans traded and lived. In 1848, following the Mexican-American War, the southern Plains became a permanent part of the United States, but the Hispanic influence continued. The watershed for most Native peoples came in 1803 when the United States obtained Louisiana. The Americans' interaction with First Nations forever altered the cultural landscape of the region. Americans came to occupy the region. They also looked to move Native Americans from the woodlands in the East to the West.

Shortly after acquiring the Louisiana Territory, the United States began to move toward resettling Indians from the East to the West. The United States decided to resettle groups from the eastern United States in an area already occupied by Native peoples. Indian Territory (present-day Oklahoma) became the destination of Shawnee, Miami, Sac, Fox, and other eastern tribes. The Seminole, Choctaw, Chickasaw, Creek, and Cherokee, the "Five Civilized Tribes," lost their lands in the East and traveled west via foot, wagon, horse, or steamboat to their new homes in Oklahoma.

The removal of eastern Indians west altered the cultural landscape of the southern Plains. The Cherokee provide a classic example of how the first civilized tribes were removed to Oklahoma. In the early 1800s, the United States increased pressure to remove the Cherokee from their homes to west of the Mississippi. As early as 1803, President Jefferson suggested to Congress the desirability of removing all eastern tribes to the West. In 1808, Secretary of War Henry Dearborn instructed Return J. Meigs to persuade a Cherokee delegation to exchange their present lands for territory west of the Mississippi. Since no funds were available for the removal, only two or three thousand migrated prior to 1817. In 1817, Andrew Jackson negotiated a treaty with the Cherokee that provided an equal amount of land west of the Mississippi, primarily in present-day Oklahoma, in exchange for land ceded in the East. The United States also promised transportation and compensation for any improvements made on the land to those who would migrate. Few Indians took advantage of the treaty of 1817. The Cherokee hoped that by becoming "civilized" they could avoid removal. The Cherokee became adamant in declaring their intentions not to remove to the West. In one debate, the Cherokee informed their acting agent that "The theory upon which you have founded the principle of taking private property for public good, we are not fully capable of comprehending . . . unless you mean that the public good requires the acquisition of this country, and that you are determined to seize it."[4] The Cherokee chiefs who delivered this speech had come to the crux of the matter: the Americans were determined to seize their land.

Georgia and the U.S. government soon resorted to coercive measures to drive the Cherokee westward. In 1828, Georgia extended the laws of the state over land owned by the Cherokee Indians. All Indians were disqualified as witnesses in court cases involving a white and a Cherokee in the state. In other words, the Cherokee were deprived of all their civil rights. In 1831, the Georgia legislature passed a law that prohibited the Cherokee from holding councils in the state and provided for the distribution of Cherokee lands among Georgia citizens. Further, the law stipulated that all white men within Georgia had to swear an oath of allegiance to the state.

Finally, in 1838, the U.S. government ordered General Winfield Scott to round up the 17,000 Cherokee in the Southeast for removal to the West. James Mooney, who obtained his information from actual participants or victims, gives the following account:

> To prevent escape the soldiers had been ordered to approach and surround each house, so far as possible, so as to come upon the occupants without warning. One old patriarch, when thus surprised, calmly called his children and grandchildren around him, and kneeling down, bid them pray with him in their own language, while the astonished soldiers looked on.[5]

The Cherokee, with the exception of a remnant in North Carolina, were forced to move west. They loaded their belongings in wagons or on horses or carried them and began the trek westward over what became known as the "Trail of Tears." Thirteen thousand people (including black slaves) walked west in the fall of 1838. They had only 645 wagons. It took six months to reach Oklahoma. The death toll was high. In the winter of 1838–1839, 1,600 of the 13,000 that headed for Oklahoma died. Ultimately the removal came at the cost of 4,000 Cherokee lives.[6] All southern tribes underwent a similar plight as women, children, and men suffered exposure to the elements and the danger of contracting cholera that they came into contact with as they moved west.

The Cherokee, like the other "Civilized Tribes," owned slaves. Cherokees had both Indian and African American slaves. They were not alone in owning slaves. The Chickasaw, Choctaw, Creek, and Seminole brought slaves with them from the East to the West. Indians first brought black slaves to Oklahoma. "By the eve of the Civil War, over four thousand slaves lived in the southern Indian nations west of the Mississippi." Percentagewise, the rate was not high. Only 2.3 percent of Native Americans in the area owned slaves. These slaveholders, however, dominated the political and economic life of the tribe. The Choctaw, Chickasaw, and Cherokee especially had tribal councils dominated by slaveholders.[7]

Enslaving African Americans had different effects on Native peoples. The Seminole, for example, did not regard African Americans as chattel. In fact, Seminoles freely intermarried with black slaves. Once the Seminole were removed to present-day Oklahoma from Florida, these Métis (from the French word meaning "mixed") formed a significant segment of Seminole society. Black Seminole slaves and Métis refused to be settled with Creeks in Oklahoma. A long-standing feud dating to the Creek Civil War of 1813–1814 led black Creek slaves to flee to the Seminole Nation. When the Creek were removed to Oklahoma, they wanted the slaves back. The Seminole took a stand to protect the blacks in their tribe. The Seminole viewed these individuals and their descendants as tribal members.[8] The feuds between Native peoples did not stem solely from slavery and ancient feuds. The federal government placed civilized tribes on land the Kickapoo, Kiowa, Osage, Comanche, Caddo, and Wichita had roamed over or claimed as their own. Oklahoma became a place where diverse cultures met, fought, cooperated, and changed.

War between Native nations deeply affected the tribes in Oklahoma. The Cherokee fought the Osage. Creek and Choctaw had their villages raided by Kickapoo, Kiowa, and Comanche. The Shawnee, newly settled in Oklahoma from Kentucky, fought the Creek. Not until the army built Fort Wichita in 1843 did many of the Choctaw settle on land given to them in Oklahoma. Native peoples often worked together, but in the 1830s and 1840s, battles between newly arrived eastern Indians and western tribes already living in the region created tensions that escalated to full-scale wars. From 1803 to 1865, the southern Plains provided a crucible for change. The diverse cultures that lived in Oklahoma forever affected the region's history. On the northern Plains, different dynamics were under way.

Assiniboine man. Courtesy Library of Congress.

Table 1. Select Native American groups living in the Plains states, 2000

Group	Kansas	Nebraska	North Dakota	Oklahoma	South Dakota
Cherokee	5,860	543	0	97,317	191
Cheyenne	358	127	0	3,335	372
Chippewa	298	191	13,345	521	608
Chickasaw	223	0	0	12,610	0
Choctaw	1,004	108	0	43,620	0
Creek	1,252	144	0	34,530	0
Delaware	616	0	0	3,676	0
Kiowa	246	0	0	5,903	0
Osage	318	0	0	3,946	0
Sioux	853	3,993	8,563	1,165	52,064

Source: United States Census, 2000.

THE NORTHERN PLAINS

The Sioux advanced onto the northern Plains in the late eighteenth and early nineteenth centuries and came into direct contact with settled Indian villagers strung from present-day Omaha to Bismarck. The Native peoples who farmed the Missouri River valley faced direct attacks from the Sioux who expanded westward, seeking bison. The Mandan, Hidatsa, Arikara, Omaha, and Pawnee faced serious threats from the Sioux between 1830 and 1840. The Sioux allied with the Assiniboine, Creek, and Northern Cheyenne in the attacks on the river tribes.[9] The Mandan, Hidatsa, and Arikara moved closer together to combat the invasion. Ultimately, they left the valley of the Missouri to hunt on the Plains. The invasion forced many river tribes to abandon their fields. When they returned to the river, smallpox struck. Only fifty Mandan survived the smallpox epidemics of the early 1800s. The remnant moved in with the Hidatsa. The Arikara continued to follow bison herds, but their diminished numbers made them no match for the Sioux. In fact, by the mid-1800s, the Sioux ruled the northern Plains.

Interaction among Native peoples reflected nations meeting nations. Proud nations competed for the Plains. The United States won the competition. This interaction between Native peoples, Europeans, and Americans played out in interesting ways, especially in terms of groups like the Métis.

The Métis

The Métis owed their existence to the meeting of Native peoples and French trappers and traders in the fur trade. Métis have come to mean a group that formed a common identity on the Plains of western Canada, North Dakota, and Montana. The group that formed the common identity proclaimed itself a "New Nation." They also stand as an example of how Native and European cultures mixed to form a distinct ethnic group. The Métis saw themselves as different from their Indian and European heritages, and indeed they were unique in many ways. French speaking and Catholic, they adhered to lifeways that had roots in Chippewa, Ojibwa, and Cree culture. This blended culture became the Métis of the Red River valley.

The Métis who settled in present-day Manitoba and North Dakota evolved out of marriages between French trappers and either Chippewa, Ojibwa, or Cree women. The French who were drawn westward by the lucrative fur trade moved deep into the North American interior by the 1700s. Moving west and north of the Great Lakes, they established stable unions with Native women. Both the Cree and Chippewa found the northern Plains attractive for hunting. Frenchmen's alliance with the Cree and Chippewa eventually brought them onto the Plains. The French and Indian families formed kinship ties that facilitated trade across the Plains. In this trade, Native wives proved invaluable. The women served as interpreters and trading partners. They also performed skilled "domestic tasks such as making moccasins and snow shoes, drying meat and dressing furs."[10] On the surface, it seemed that their principal skills lay in translating and preparing hides, but in reality they were the power brokers in trade negotiations. Often the women were the only bilingual negotiators in the trade process, and this fact gave them power.

By around 1800, the Métis had settled along the Red River that divides present-day North Dakota and Minnesota. The river flows north and finds its way eventually to Lake Winnipeg. "The 'classic' Métis culture emerged early in the nineteenth century on the Plains and along the Red River. Here, where rivers and woods meet the Plains, they hunted and provided food for the North-West Company." The Métis' lifestyle and freedom was based on hunting on the Plains. Every year, from settlements along the Red River the Métis moved onto the Plains. In the winter, they returned to fixed villages along this river. These Métis tended to have large families and soon dominated the area. The Métis "were bound by many ties of intermarriage and common participation in such activities as the communal bison hunt." Many French Métis spoke both French and English plus "Cree or Ojibwa from their mother's side. In time, a distinct composite language, usually termed Michif emerged based primarily on Cree and French." At Pembina, on the Red River just south of the Canadian-American border in present-day North Dakota, the Métis would meet to go out onto the Plains to hunt bison. Bison were the cornerstone of their economy. "Traveling in their distinctive two-wheeled Red River carts pulled by horses or oxen," they met and prepared to sally forth onto the Plains. "The carts, which were essential for transporting equipment and hauling meat, were made entirely of wood bound with rawhide." In time the hunts grew in size. One hunt in 1840 involved 1,600 people and 1,200 carts.

Women played an important role in the bison hunt on the Plains. The Métis women processed the meat. "They cut the meat into strips, dried it in the sun and over fires, pounded it into coarse powder, mixed it with melted fat and berries and sewed it into hide bags." Red River carts hauled back huge loads of pemmican, whose ultimate destination was distant trading posts. As the buffalo hunts went farther and farther onto the Plains, the Métis came into bitter conflict with the Dakota Sioux. The Sioux and Métis wanted the same thing. Not only were the Métis "depleting the bison herds in Dakota hunting grounds, but the Métis were closely associated by blood and marriage with the Cree and Ojibwa, the traditional enemies of the Dakota." The Métis and Sioux had a series of fights over hunting grounds. In a decisive battle, fought in 1851, the Sioux lost. This battle explains, in part, why the Dakota pressed westward to Montana and Wyoming in increasing numbers.[11]

French Influences

The first arrival of the French on the northern Plains came in the early 1700s. Between 1738 and 1743, the La Vérendrye brothers crossed the northern Plains. By the late 1700s, French and British trappers and traders knew much about the region. By the time the Americans arrived in the area in the early 1800s, Frenchmen and their "Indian" wives were living in the Mandan villages along the Missouri River. The world the Americans moved into had long witnessed interaction between Native peoples and Frenchmen. Like their Spanish counterparts in the southern Plains, Frenchmen had gained much from living, trading, and even battling with the Native Americans on the northern Plains.

Nations like the Mandan and Arikara who lived along the Missouri River came into contact with French and then English Canadian traders sometime in the eighteenth century. These European traders gave them guns and metal knives in exchange for bison and beaver furs. French Canadians along the upper Missouri River ultimately moved south along the river. While the French traveled south, they also traveled west from St. Louis along the Missouri River. While small in number, French entrepreneurs and explorers left a definite imprint on the region—names like Pierre, South Dakota, for instance, owe their origin to the French. The Métis who settled on the northern Plains established communities along the Red River that preceded towns like Grand Forks and Fargo, North Dakota. The French and the Métis became the forerunners of the great waves of immigration onto the northern Plains in the latter half of the nineteenth century.

THE AMERICAN PLAINS

In 1803, the United States purchased Louisiana, and the Plains became American property. What led to the establishment and growth of communities along the Missouri River was Americans' desire not to settle the Plains, but to cross them. First the explorers, then trappers, traders, and emigrants who were headed for Oregon, Salt Lake, Santa Fe, and California stopped in places like Independence, Missouri, and Leavenworth, Kansas. Fort Leavenworth (founded in 1827) became the reason for the town to emerge, but over time it became a jumping-off place for caravans headed west. Westport (in Kansas City) and Independence also served as supply centers for those who were crossing the Missouri and heading west. American emigrants, who first came in the late 1830s in diminutive numbers, surged west by the thousands in the 1840s. To Oregon in 1843, Salt Lake in 1847, and then to California gold fields in 1849, women and men from Europe and the eastern states headed across the Plains. Along the fringes of the eastern Plains, towns like Leavenworth, Kansas, Omaha, Nebraska, and Kansas City, Kansas, grew, and immigrants from Europe, slaves, and freemen from Africa came seeking work and opportunities. By the 1860s, the edges of the future Plains states contained people from around the world.

Irish immigrants began to settle on the Plains in the 1840s. The Potato Famine of 1845 destroyed the food the poor of Ireland lived on. Two years later, 106,000 Irish women and men sailed for America. During the next seven years, 1.1 million more made their way to the Atlantic shores.[12] Beginning in 1849, many came west to mine gold in California; others opted to settle in places like Fort Leavenworth

Table 2. Immigrants to the United States from Russia and the Baltic States, Germany, Ireland, Italy, and Scandinavia (single-year totals)

Year	Russia	Germany	Ireland	Italy	Scandinavia
1840	0	29,704	39,430	37	207
1850	31	78,896	164,004	431	1,589
1860	65	54,491	48,637	1,019	840
1870	907	118,225	56,996	2,891	30,742
1880	5,014	84,638	71,603	12,354	65,657
1890	35,598	92,427	53,024	52,003	50,368
1900	90,787	18,507	35,730	100,135	31,151
1910	186,792	31,283	29,855	215,537	48,267
1921	10,193	6,803	28,435	222,260	22,854

Source: *Historical Statistics of the United States from Colonial Times to 1970, Part 1* (Washington, DC: U.S. Government Printing Office, 1975), 105–106.

and Omaha. Some immigrated to Dakota Territory. In 1860, twenty-two Irish immigrants lived in present-day South Dakota. Most worked as either farmers or laborers. One particularly interesting situation is that of Margarette Coffee. In the 1860 census, her occupation was listed as farmer. Margarette, an Irish immigrant, was a single mother with three children under the age of seven at home. Other Irish families had homes on farms in the Dakotas in 1860. Some Irishmen worked as laborers.[13] Laborers were needed along the railroad in Nebraska after 1862, and Irishmen fit the bill.

At the end of the Civil War, the number of Irish in the West swelled. The building of the transcontinental railroad concentrated Irish railroad workers along a string of rails being laid between Omaha, Nebraska, and the Great Salt Lake in Utah. The construction of the railroad lines concentrated many Irish railroad workers in southern Nebraska. When the railroad was completed in 1869, Irish railroad workers sought jobs throughout the West. By 1900, 11,516 Irish lived in Kansas and 11,127 in Nebraska. Irish continued to work as laborers, but they also ran their own farms and businesses.

SCOTS

The Scots first entered the region in the 1700s. Trappers crossing the present Canadian border entered with their French counterparts in the employ of the

Table 3. Census totals for select groups in 1900

Group	Kansas	Nebraska	North Dakota	Oklahoma	South Dakota
Chinese	38	190	31	32	150
English	13,283	9,757	2,909	1,121	3,862
German	39,501	65,506	11,546	5,112	17,873
Norwegian	1,477	2,883	30,206	118	19,788
Russian	11,019	8,083	14,979	2,649	12,365

Source: *Abstract of the Twelfth Census of the United States, 1900* (Washington, DC: U.S. Government Printing Office, 1904), 58–62.

North-West Company and later the Hudson's Bay Company. The Hudson's Bay Company, like the North-West Company, ranged far and wide over the northern Plains and into the Rocky Mountains.[14] Canadian Scots came into contact with Scottish Americans moving up the Missouri River with the American fur companies. Scots settled throughout the northern tier of states. The arrival came early in the historic period and continued.

Scottish immigration to America spans almost the whole history of the nation. From 1750 to 1914, Scots for several reasons left their homeland to seek employment in the New World. Over time, 2 million left Scotland for distant shores. The 1860 Dakota census indicates that Scot farmers, traders, and lawyers lived in the territory.[15] By 1900, 4,219 Scots lived in Kansas, while Nebraska had 2,773, North Dakota, 1,800, Oklahoma, 333, and South Dakota, 1,153. Like other northern Europeans, some turned to farming, others to business. Scottish immigrants continued to settle on the Plains.

Massed pipe bands at Oklahoma Scottish Games & Gathering, Tulsa, Oklahoma. Photo by Fred W. Marve. Courtesy Oklahoma Tourism.

BLACKS

Black women and men entered the western frontier relatively early. Their arrival, in fact, predates the arrival of American and English settlers. In 1598, when Juan de Onate colonized New Mexico, he brought "three female Negro slaves, one mulatto slave, and other men and women servants."[16] Possibly the best-known entry of a black onto the Plains came in 1804. In that year, William Clark's slave York accompanied the fabled Lewis and Clark expedition up the Missouri. Six feet tall and more than two hundred pounds in weight, he attracted the attention of Plains Indians. The Gros Ventres considered him a great medicine man. He returned after the expedition ended, according to one legend, to live among the First Nations on the Plains.[17] Another legend has York returning east to St. Louis, where he ran a carting and "drayage" business. Either way, York is part of early American western history. Some blacks became fixtures in the fur trade that evolved after the Lewis and Clark expedition.

By the 1850s, blacks had begun to settle in Kansas. Some came to escape slavery in Missouri; others came to work in the "Free Territory." By 1865, 600 blacks lived in Kansas. Blacks living on the Plains before the Civil War worked at a variety of jobs. Some labored in the construction and maintenance of forts. Blacks worked at posts along the Santa Fe Trail, which crossed southern Kansas. At Fort Union, where the Yellowstone River meets the Missouri River in western North Dakota, one black named George worked as a brick maker. In 1862, three blacks served the fort, two as laborers and one as a cook.[18]

Nat Love's path from slavery to Kansas illustrates one African American's journey to the Plains. Nat wrote that he left his home near Nashville, Tennessee, in February 1869. At fifteen, he had already spent long years of hard work on a farm. He struck out for Kansas with little money to seek employment. "By walking and receiving occasional lifts from farmers," he reached Dodge City, Kansas. At the time, Dodge City was a cattle town. Here Nat Love began his career as a cowboy. Born a slave, Nat went far enough west to reach a place where he could get a free horse and $30 per month for his labor. Other African Americans also worked as cowboys on the Great Plains.[19] Some African Americans, like the Cherry County, Nebraska, settlers, homesteaded and prospered.

After the Civil War, many black Americans chose to take up homesteads on the Plains. In the mid-1870s, thousands of blacks chose to migrate to Kansas and either homestead or purchase land outright. Nicodemus, the first black town in Kansas, came into being to help black families and farmers. The services provided in the town helped farmers in the outlying areas get what they needed in the confines of less racially hostile villages. Kansas, particularly, proved a good place for blacks to homestead. Established in 1877, the Nicodemus Town Company gave blacks the freedom to establish their own form of self-government. Drawn by free land, blacks migrated in large numbers. Three hundred blacks moved to the southeast Kansas county of Cherokee. The blacks prospered, and their stories fed the rumors that circulated in eastern communities that blacks could succeed in Kansas. The mid-1870s move to Kansas predated the famous "Exoduster" exodus from the South to Kansas that dates from 1879 to 1880. In those two years, the numbers of blacks leaving for the Plains led Congress to hold hearings to determine why the flight from the South had reached the levels it did in the late 1870s. The rush continued.

Oklahoma witnessed an increase in black emigration in the early twentieth century. As already noted, black slaves entered Oklahoma with the Cherokee, Creek, and Seminole in the 1830s. Upon emancipation in the early 1860s, blacks had to

Table 4. Census Totals for Select Groups in 1930

Group	Kansas	Nebraska	North Dakota	Oklahoma	South Dakota
Mexican	11,012	3,411	333	3,496	294
Syrian	248	369	235	809	229
Japanese	30	285	48	264	9
Indian	7	4	264	25	57
Chinese	32	93	70	413	45
Russian	8,781	11,234	22,617	3,613	9,023
German	17,384	32,544	10,114	5,893	12,739
Norwegian	746	1,691	31,337	1,490	13,061
Swedish	7,315	14,335	8,470	4,017	6,540
Yugoslavian	2,781	762	336	162	223

Source: *Abstract of the Fifteenth Census of the United States, 1930* (Washington, DC: U.S. Government Printing Office, 1933), 131–135.

make a choice about what they would do with their newly gained freedom. Most often these newly freed slaves did not have the money to buy animals, seed, or equipment to begin farming. In 1907, when Oklahoma became a state, thirty towns had predominantly black populations. These towns had roots in an April 22, 1889, law that proclaimed that non-Indian settlers could homestead in Oklahoma. Black leaders in Kansas especially saw Oklahoma as an attractive place for former slaves to settle. In 1907, the special statehood census showed that the state contained 733,062 individuals, of whom 31,511 listed their ethnicity as black. Soon Oklahoma saw this number rise, partly because of an immigration of black homesteaders.[20]

JEWISH SETTLERS

Pioneer Jews lived in future Nebraska and Kansas by the mid-1800s. Jews and Muslims have a long history in the New World. Columbus' flotilla had an interpreter named Luis de Torres who greeted the "Indians" on the Caribbean islands in both Hebrew and Arabic.[21] In the present United States, the arrival of Jews usually is set in September 1654 when Jews who were fleeing persecution in Europe arrived in New Amsterdam (present-day New York). From the beginning, Jews settled in the English colonies. By 1776, 3,000 Jews lived in America. From the East Coast, the Jewish settlers moved inland with the expansion of the new nation. The gold rush that drew thousands to California in 1849 brought Jewish entrepreneurs onto the frontier. Some stayed in the Missouri River valley, choosing to earn a living selling goods to westward-bound pioneers.

Nebraska Territory came into existence in 1854. The territory gained statehood in 1867. During the territorial years, the first Jewish traders arrived. After Nebraska entered the Union, the number of Jewish families settling in the area increased. As was the case elsewhere in the West, the early decades of Jewish settlement drew only minor attention. By the 1870s and 1880s, however, members of the Jewish faith engaged in business in the larger eastern Nebraska towns. Omaha, which had the earliest Jewish entrepreneurs, and later Lincoln began to witness an increase in the number of the faithful. Prior to the 1880s, the believers held services in people's homes in Lincoln. In the 1880s, the numbers of Jewish families rose. In 1884, Congregation B'nai Jeshurun emerged in Lincoln, and in 1885 the Tifereth Israel Congregation was established.

The two congregations in Lincoln reflect the diverse nature of Jewish faith and culture. The B'nai Jeshurun, known as the South Street Temple today, came from Reform Judaism. As Jewish historian David Grodwohl notes, "Both B'nai Jeshurun, and South Street Temple are used today, and pretty much used synonymously, although B'nai Jeshurun, more properly is the congregation and South Street Temple is the building." The Tifereth Israel Congregation traced its roots to Orthodox Judaism and soon came to "incorporate conservative as well as Orthodox Judaism." Where the worshipers came from sheds light not only on the Jewish community's roots but also on the nature of nineteenth-century immigration. The first members of the B'nai Jeshurun primarily consisted of Western Ashkenazim and came mainly from Germany, Austria, Alsace-Lorraine, and France. The founders and early attendees of Tifereth Israel were Eastern Ashkenazim and immigrated from Russia, Poland, and Lithuania.[22] While both congregations held Jews from other countries, the homelands they came from illustrate how diverse the makeup of the Jewish immigration to the Plains was.

The Jewish immigrants who chose to homestead in North and South Dakota came from Russia, Poland, Romania, and Galicia. Many came because of oppression in Europe. Some had never farmed. The attraction of free land drew many people who had never tilled the soil. Claiming free land under the Homestead Act, they tilled the ground and tried like their neighbors to grow wheat, barley, or rye. Hard work made them successful.

One man, whom Sophie Trupin calls simply "father," left his family in Russia and at the turn of the twentieth century moved onto a quarter section of virgin land near Wilson, North Dakota. Sophie's father's name was Harry, and her mother's was Gittel. "Father" built a shack, dug a well, and constructed fences. In the winter, he worked in a coal mine to earn cash, a precious thing on the frontier. With the longer days of spring came a return to a job that required working from sunup to sundown and paid no cash. A lot of work and little money defined homesteading. Yet by 1909, this man on the prairie had saved enough to bring his family from Russia to his farm. Sophie remembers the land as treeless and the house as small. What North Dakota gave this man was a "piece of land, rock-strewn and stubborn," but it was his. In Russia, he could not, as a Jew, own land. In North and South Dakota, Jews with labor and perseverance could own land. The days of labor paid off. Norwegians, Danes, and Germans came to the Dakotas seeking the same thing that Sophie's family wanted, a chance to make a living and own something they could pass on to their children. Cultural anthropologist and Jewish historian David Gradwohl notes that Gittel Turnoy "insisted that her husband build a *mikvah* [ritual purification bath] for her so that she could maintain her Jewish identity and carry out the requirements of Orthodox Judaism. Years later, Sophie's younger brother went back to 'Nordakota' and found remains of the *mikvah* mostly obscured by the tall prairie grass."[23]

SCANDINAVIANS

As early as 1820, Scandinavians immigrated to the United States. In the decade between 1820 and 1830, 283 Scandinavians arrived in the United States. This soon changed. In 1832 alone, 334 sailed into eastern ports. It was not long before some of these immigrants headed into the interior, where land was cheap and readily available for farming. The 1860 census for Dakota Territory indicates that a Norwegian family headed by Caroline and Siebert Albertson lived in what would become South Dakota. They had six children, four of whom ranged in age from ten to fifteen. These older children had all been born in Norway. Halia, age ten, was born in Norway in 1850. Her younger brother Gather was born in Wisconsin in 1852. The youngest Albertson, Larsen, was born in Wisconsin in 1858. The census allows one to deduce certain things. Sometime around 1850 or 1851, the Albertsons immigrated to Wisconsin. From Wisconsin they emigrated to South Dakota, probably in 1859. The Anderson family followed a similar path to the Plains. The Amorson family took a somewhat different path. They went from Norway to Wisconsin, then to Nebraska, before settling in present-day South Dakota. In all, 127 Norwegians lived in South Dakota in 1860. Only 5 listed their occupation as laborers; the rest were farmers.[24] The 1862 Homestead Act, which

Table 5. Census Totals for Select Groups in 1940

Group	Kansas	Nebraska	North Dakota	Oklahoma	South Dakota
Mexican	5,122	1,773	56	1,425	76
Cuban	37	16	2	50	9
Central American	130	70	32	86	26
Spanish	53	25	4	41	0

Source: Statistical Abstract of the United States, 1942 (Washington, DC: U.S. Government Printing Office, 1943), 34–35.

gave land free to anyone willing to live and work on 160 acres, attracted even more Scandinavians.

In 1869, the first Norwegian family arrived in present-day North Dakota. The Red, Goose, and Sheyenne River valleys proved attractive to these settlers. The greatest number of Norwegian immigrants, however, came to the region between 1880 and 1905. Scandinavians made up 47 percent of the total immigration to the future state, and of that number 42 percent came from Norway. As late as 1965, of the 46,486 rural families in North Dakota, 13,879 had Norwegian roots. These roots extended to the farms of Norway.

In the 1800s, 900,000 individuals left Norway. Only Ireland exceeds Norway in the number of immigrants who crossed the Atlantic to seek homes in the New World. The immigrants from Norway came primarily from rural roots. Most who settled in North Dakota had much in common. First, they came from farming backgrounds. Second, they were relatively well educated and wanted to pass that legacy to their children. Third, Norwegian Americans, into the late twentieth century, tended to stay on their farms. Their Swedish counterparts had more of a tendency to move to more urban areas.

More than a million Swedes moved to the United States from the end of the Civil War to the beginning of World War I. These immigrants found the West a place where through labor and perseverance they might have a chance to own land and improve their plight. Like their Norwegian counterparts, Swedish settlers moved into the Red River valley in the late 1860s. Immigrants from Sweden found their way onto the Plains as early as 1870. Swedish homesteaders first came in small numbers, but soon they became the backbone of the immigrant farmer movement that settled the northern Plains. Homesteaders from Sweden and Norway did well in the northern Plains. Bringing a sense of hard work to their labors, they helped build communities in remote areas where few others would settle. Their descendants continue to dominate the upper Plains states. By 1890, 8,419 Swedes lived in North Dakota. By comparison, 44,698 Norwegians lived in the state. North Dakota's population had a distinctive ethnic makeup. Hardworking, literate, and generous, the Scandinavian homesteaders successfully turned the prairie into farms.

ICELANDIC SETTLERS

Icelanders reached North Dakota sometime in the 1870s. Settling in Pembina County, North Dakota, the settlers exhibited an ability to preserve their language and culture. The Icelanders held a strong love of their past that they handed down from generation to generation. One observer noted that they were poor and "insular" but dedicated to education and literature. Most Icelanders came to the New World because they could no longer eke out a living in Iceland. The community in North Dakota, while isolated, provided a chance to make a better living. In the 1880s, some of these early settlers moved to Manitoba and Alberta, Canada, but many remain today and continue a viable Icelandic community in northeastern North Dakota.[25]

GERMAN RUSSIAN AND GERMAN IMMIGRANTS

On December 4, 1762, Queen Catherine the Great put forth a manifesto that invited western Europeans to settle in Russia. This would have long-term implications not only for Russia but for the United States as well. The first call for immigrants did not have the desired effect, so on July 22, 1763, she issued a second manifesto that offered critical provisions. The edict provided for transportation to Russia, land, religious freedom, and political autonomy for any western European who chose to migrate to Russia. Soon, western Europeans, primarily Germans, immigrated to Russia. The first groups entered the Volga in 1764. By the latter half of the decade, immigrants began to settle in southern Russia. The Hutterites arrived in Russia in 1770, the Mennonites in 1789, but Germany provided the bulk of the settlers. By the mid-nineteenth century, Volga, Crimea, and the Caucasus had German immigrants. In the late nineteenth century and into the early 1900s, Germans moved into Siberia. In all, roughly 1.8 million Germans resided in Russia in 1900.[26] Political oppression ultimately brought many German Russians to the Great Plains states.

Many German Russians left Russia in the 1870s. Some chose to settle in Ellis and Rush Counties, Kansas. The out-migration from Russia to Kansas was a direct result of Russian politics. In 1871, the Russian government terminated the special privileges extended to German colonists. On January 13, 1874, the imperial Russian government under Alexander II issued a new decree that instituted compulsory military service for all male German colonists and their descendants. This decree caused thousands of German Russians to leave for North and South America. By February 1876, fourteen families had reached Hays, Kansas. From 1874 to the outbreak of World War I, colonists from western Europe, especially Germans, witnessed turmoil and oppression. The declaration of war on Germany by Russia in July 1914 brought to a head the problems the German Russians had witnessed for nearly three decades. The reason that so many chose the Plains lay firmly in the problems in Russia. The Plains still offered opportunities for farmers, and most of the Germans who left Russia had been farmers. States such as Kansas benefited from this migration. In 1900, Kansas had 11,019 individuals who had been born in Russia living in the state.

German-speaking farmers who left Russia in the 1870s formed the core of many Plains communities. German Russians settled from Oklahoma to North Dakota.[27] To Nebraska and Kansas came hardworking Mennonite immigrants. Like many immigrant farmers on the Plains, they chose to plant wheat on their homesteads. Using practices honed in Russia, the Mennonite farmers proved successful and prospered. The communities became nearly self-sufficient. The family provided the labor and nature the soils. The methods they used to farm proved profitable and viable. Mennonite communities provided models of efficiency in the Plains. These German Russians succeeded when many dryland farmers seemed to fail. Their success came from hard work and a community structure that fostered co-operation.[28]

Closely related to the German Russian Mennonites were the Pennsylvania Dutch immigrants who arrived in Kansas in the late 1870s. They also were Mennonites and had gone first to Switzerland, then to Holland, before immigrating to Pennsylvania. They settled on or near Susquehanna in the eighteenth century, and by the nineteenth century their numbers had increased to the point that they needed to find new areas to colonize. In the late 1800s, they established a well-organized colony near Abilene, Kansas. Kansas attracted Germans, Hungarians, Swiss Germans, Swiss French, and Bohemians in the 1880s who came to homestead.[29]

In the decades between 1880 and 1900, Germans settled throughout the region. Throughout much of the nation's history, Germany had provided large numbers of immigrants. As early as 1854, Germans could be found in Nebraska.[30] By 1856, towns such as Columbus, Nebraska, essentially contained only Germans or German Swiss immigrants. Grand Island and other towns in the future state also had deep-running German roots. In 1890, 72,000 Germans lived in Nebraska. In the nineteenth century, German-born immigrants made up 6 to 9 percent of the state's population.[31] Nebraska was not alone in this distinction. The Dakotas, Kansas, and, later, Oklahoma had large numbers of German-born citizens.

HUTTERITES

The Hutterites are a religious sect that emerged in Moravia in 1528. They adhered to a strict belief that "absolute authority comes from God" and that war was evil. They truly believed that men's and women's chief purpose in life was to serve God. In 1536, the Austrian government chose to make an example of their leader, Jakob Hutter, and burned him at the stake. This did not deter the faithful. Clinging to high German and historical patterns of dress and church structure, they chose to separate from mainstream cultures. Believing God's law superior to man's law, they refused to take allegiance to any earthly government. This fact and their separation from modern culture led to their persecution. Genocide and forced assimilation reduced their number to nineteen in 1750. In the late 1700s, the few remaining Hutterites, like Mennonites, fled to Russia to avoid persecution. In Russia, they further distinguished their faith by relying on self-sufficient communal villages. This would serve them well when political oppression drove many Hutterites to the New World in the 1870s.

Even before Alexander II's decree, Hutterites began to consider leaving Russia. In 1873, a Hutterite delegation selected South Dakota as an ideal place to settle. They would move the entire Hutterite population from Russia to the Plains. In South Dakota, Hutterites faced the same challenges that all homesteaders did. They also faced isolation, as well as the elements, but they desired this. Decades of repression and prejudice drove them to seek isolated spots to settle and then to work hard to cultivate the land they lived on. Their communal lifestyle and hard work enabled them to prosper.

The Hutterites who settled in the Dakotas purposefully chose demanding terrain. Between 1874 and 1877, the entire Hutterite population from Russia settled in South Dakota. Here they divided into three groups and established the groups' names of Lehrerleut, Schmiedeleut, and Dariusleut. "Each group or *leut* took its name from its first leader. *Lehrer* means 'teacher' in German, *Schmied* means 'blacksmith,' and *Darius* was the name of the minister who led the third group; *Leut* means 'people.'" Unlike the Puritans, they did not want to create a pure society. They simply wanted to be left alone. They chose a desolate, isolated location to ensure that no one bothered them, and through hard work and industry, they turned the land into productive farms. Their experiences in Russia had taught them how to cultivate the Plains. The Hutterites did well in South Dakota until the Spanish-American War erupted and threatened the Hutterite way of life. As pacifists, the Hutterites felt that they could not support the American government, and some chose to migrate to Canada. The outbreak of World War I found Canada engulfed in a deadly war. No longer could the Hutterites migrate to Canada to avoid the war since Canada had entered the war in 1914. The U.S. entry into the conflict in 1917 led to direct persecution of 2,000 Hutterites in the United States. "Their German language and their pacifism, as well as their wealth, made them targets." Some had their property seized. Others had to join the military. Four men went to prison, first to Alcatraz Island and then to Fort Leavenworth, Kansas, where due to brutal treatment, two died. After World War I, many Hutterites elected to emigrate to Canada. Nonetheless, a sizeable group remained in the Dakotas, Montana, Washington, and Minnesota. Including those living in Alberta, Saskatchewan, and Manitoba, there are now more than 36,000 Hutterites in 434 colonies. The majority live on the Great Plains of Canada or the United States.[32]

In the late 1940s, many Hutterites once again migrated to the United States. What brought Hutterites into Montana or the Dakotas was discrimination they received at the hands of the Canadian government. With a high birthrate of up to ten to twelve children, the Hutterite population grew in Alberta. Large families meant that they needed to acquire more and more land for their communal colonies. In 1942, the Canadian government passed a law that stated that enemy aliens and Hutterites could not be sold land in Canada. With nowhere else to turn, new colonies moved across the border into the United States. Here, not only could they buy land, they also received conscientious-objector status. In Montana they prospered.

The Hutterite colonies speak a dialect of German, share a common doctrine, and have a communal outlook toward life. The men dress in black, the women in dresses. Education ends at about the eighth grade, but because they work so hard, they own their farms outright and prosper due to working together. Pigs, horses, cows, chickens, wheat, vegetables, and a diverse agriculture system allow them to prosper in a region where many ranchers and farmers fail.

Currently, the Lehrerleut and Dariusleut groups live in Saskatchewan, Alberta, British Columbia, and Montana. The Schmiedeleut live in North and South Dakota and Minnesota. The Schmiedeleut split into two groups in 1992. These two groups, the Hutterian Brethren and the Committee Hutterites, center in Plains states, with colonies in Minnesota. In some areas of South Dakota, the Schmiedeleut groups show a great deal of resilience. Hutterites in Hanson County, South Dakota, make up 18.4 percent of the county. The 460 Hutterites there have roots that extend to the 1870s. They still live a life based on communal ownership and communal living and maintain a quiet prosperity.

CZECHS

Czechs have a relatively long history in America. In 1633, the first known Czech immigrant, Augustin Hermann (Herman), settled in New Amsterdam. In time he became one of the founders of the tobacco trade in Virginia. In 1647, another Czech, Frederick Philips, settled in New Amsterdam. He later became one of the wealthiest individuals in the American colonies. In the next century, Moravian missionaries, whose theological roots rested in the present-day Czech Republic, sailed to the colonies. In 1735, Moravian Brethren arrived in America. They were principally German speakers, but their faith grew from Moravian roots. Czech immigration to the United States came in a variety of forms, but in the 1800s thousands of women and men found their way to the New World.

Czechs migrated to the Plains from Bohemia and Moravia. In 1854, Joseph Francl passed through Nebraska bound for the California gold fields. Some credit him with being the first Czech-born traveler to cross the plains of present-day Nebraska. The first permanent Czech resident, Charles Culek (Karel Zulck), settled in Nebraska in 1856. Born in Bohemia on June 23, 1822, he reached Richardson County on August 27, 1856. Taking up a claim four miles from the tiny town of Humboldt, he foreshadowed a growing wave of immigration from the future Czechoslovakia. Czechs engaged in a variety of occupations, but most chose to farm. For example, Libor Alois Schlesinger, born in Bohemia on October 28, 1806, settled sixty miles north of Omaha. In 1860, he left his farm to freight across the Plains. After running freight wagons from Omaha to Denver until 1865, he turned once again to farming when he took up a homestead in Colorado. Czech immigrants on the Plains seemed to turn to farming in part because land could be had either at cheap prices or free. The Homestead Act of 1862 gave them access to free land, and Czechs from villages in Bohemia and Moravia took advantage of the opportunity.

By 1900, all Plains states had Czech immigrants within their borders. The number of Czechs (Bohemians) in Nebraska had climbed to 16,138 according to the 1900 census. Kansas, a distant second, had 3,039 "Bohemians" within its borders, while 2,320 lived in South Dakota, 1,445 in North Dakota, and 1,168 in Oklahoma. They came from an area ruled by outsiders. Prior to World War I, the Austro-Hungarian Empire governed the region. The eruption of war in Europe in 1914 gave hope to many Czechs that they would finally have an autonomous homeland. Various Czech organizations in the United States collected money to help free their country from Austrian control. Between 1914 and 1918, in Nebraska alone, these groups raised a total of $293,809.66. The ties to Central Europe ran deep. After World War I, Bohemia, Moravia, and Silesia formed Czechoslovakia. For the first time in centuries, Czechs had their own homeland.[33] Nonetheless, at the end of the war, Czechs continued to make up large segments of American communities. In 1920, the number of Czechs in Nebraska had diminished, but not by much. In the first census following World War I, Nebraska had 15,818 Czechs, Kansas 3,406, South Dakota 2,819, North Dakota 2,056, and Oklahoma 1,825. By 2000, 141,427 individuals in the five Plains states claimed Czech ancestors.

The Czech communities on the Plains currently exhibit a rich heritage. For example, the Yukon, Oklahoma, annual Czech Festival, held in October, coincides with the St. Havel Festival in Czechoslovakia. At this October festival, traditional foods are served, and folk musicians and traditional dancers perform. The Yukon festival is touted as the largest free party in Oklahoma. Places like Wilber, Nebraska, thirty-six miles southwest of Lincoln, hold annual Czech festivals. Declared the Czech capital of Nebraska, Wilber is only one of many towns that have active Czech societies. In northeast Nebraska, Clarkson, located in Colfax County, considers itself the "center of Czechland." Like Wilber, the community holds an annual Czech festival. In Omaha, the Czech Cultural Club sponsors the annual Folklore Festival. Singing, dancing, and cook-offs all center around Czech American traditions and help keep alive Old World cultural values. In 2000, 18,021 people in Kansas, 83,439 in Nebraska, 12,536 in North Dakota, 11,815 in Oklahoma, and 15,616 in South Dakota claimed Czech ancestry. The numbers of Czechs still living on the Plains reflect their tenacity; their festivals celebrate their heritage.

ASIAN IMMIGRANTS

The Chinese

Asians arrived on the Plains by the mid-1800s. Chinese arrived in California in large numbers after the discovery of gold in 1848, and it was only a matter of time before they began to move east. With the discovery of gold in South Dakota, Chinese moved into the region in larger numbers. The opening of the Black Hills gold field after 1877 led to one of the last great gold rushes in the nineteenth century. The Chinese, who had extensive experience in gold fields, moved to Deadwood, where a Chinatown emerged.

Chinese reside in every state from Canada to the Gulf of Mexico. Kansas has the largest Chinese population, while North Dakota has the smallest. Like Southeast Asians, Chinese reside in the area's cities, but there is also a tendency for the Chinese to live throughout the region. A look back helps explain this. In 1900, Kansas had 38 Chinese, Nebraska 190, North Dakota 31, South Dakota 150, and Oklahoma 32 residents from the "Middle Kingdom." By 1930, the number of Chinese on the northern Plains had decreased, but all states still had Chinese residents. Chinese ran restaurants and laundries, businesses that could succeed in a variety of environments, including the gold camps in the Black Hills and the towns along the Missouri River. In essence, the Chinese population dispersed, and when post–World War II immigration swelled their numbers, Chinese immigrants found fellow countrymen already in the region. By 2000, almost 20,000 Chinese lived in the Great Plains.

One of the overlooked ethnic groups on the Plains is the Japanese. The tugging factors that drew Japanese immigrants to the Great Plains of the United States differed little from the forces that drew European immigrants into the region in the latter half of the nineteenth century. On the New World's frontiers, perceived opportunity enticed immigrants eastward from Asia and westward from Europe.[34]

Japanese immigrants began to arrive in the Plains states in large numbers in the late 1890s. By the first decade of the twentieth century, Japanese railroad workers, coal miners, and farmers lived in remote communities stretching from Alberta to

Table 6. Census totals for select groups in 2000

Group	Kansas	Nebraska	North Dakota	Oklahoma	South Dakota
Arab	6,785	4,696	1,042	8,177	1,407
Egyptian	438	328	40	331	85
Iraqi	205	286	44	121	47
Jordanian	339	95	0	280	0
Lebanese	2,964	2,141	546	4,408	730
Palestinian	250	104	74	282	32
Syrian	730	782	199	608	294

Source: United States Census, 2000. http://www.census.gov/main/www/access.html (accessed February 1, 2004).

Nebraska. The immigrants adapted to the new environment and society but clearly retained elements of Japanese culture. The syncretism of two distinct cultures is clearly seen in their tombstones. In western Nebraska, Japanese graves reflect the view of two worlds and record the lives of people who left little in the written record.

In 2000, every state contained Japanese residents, but while the numbers are small in some of the Plains states, their contributions are significant. Nebraska illustrates the issue. In 2000, the state contained 1,582 Japanese. More Koreans (2,423) lived in Nebraska than residents whose ancestors came from the Land of the Rising Sun. In Omaha, 610 Japanese lived, in Lincoln, 254, and in Scotts Bluff County, 106. Scotts Bluff County only had 80 fewer Japanese residents than did the entire state of North Dakota. In fact, 6 percent of the state's Japanese population lived in the county. When Japanese settled in Scotts Bluff County is not known exactly. It is known that they came to work in the sugar-beet fields and soon owned farms. Japanese farmers proved capable. They worked hard and quickly adapted to the environmental conditions they found on the Plains. In the early twentieth century, Japanese farmers set the foundation for successful family operations. Growing a variety of crops, including sugar beets, they made enough money to weather the storms. Their legacy lay in succeeding on a high-elevation plain where wind, cold, and drought worked against growing crops.

Table 7. Comparison of groups in the Plains States, 2000

Group	Kansas	Nebraska	North Dakota	Oklahoma	South Dakota	Total
total	2,688,418	1,711,263	642,200	3,450,654	754,844	9,247,379
"White"	2,312,119	1,533,787	593,785	2,624,679	669,477	7,733,847
African American	150,584	67,435	3,673	258,532	4,518	484,742
Native American	20,256	13,071	28,778	248,037	57,134	367,276
Asian	44,772	21,126	3,342	45,546	4,729	119,515
Chinese	7,573	2,990	473	6,996	736	18,768
Hispanic	186,299	93,872	7,568	177,768	10,386	475,893
Mexican	146,912	70,525	4,447	133,124	6,096	361,104

Source: United States Census, 2000. http://www.census.gov/main/www/access.html (accessed February 1, 2004).

Asians in the Latter Half of the Twentieth Century

With the fall of Saigon in 1975, Southeast Asian refugees from Vietnam, Laos, and Cambodia fled to Thailand and safe havens in the region. The ultimate destination of many was the United States, and in the 1970s, Southeast Asians began to enter America in increasing numbers. Among those that came were hill tribes people from Laos, known as the Hmong. Unlike the Hmong, most of the Cambodian immigrants come from the lowlands. The Cambodians suffered greatly at the hands of Pol Pot, who ruled from 1975 to 1978. In these three years, out of 7 million Cambodians, 1 million died. One source put the number of deaths at between 500,000 and three million. Most sources feel that one in seven people were killed by the Cambodian Khmer Rouge.[35]

In many ways, lumping Cambodians, Hmong, Laotians, and Vietnamese into the category of Southeast Asians does a disservice to the individual sacrifices and tragedies that brought them to the Plains. As a group, they are one of the largest refugee communities ever to immigrate to America. Nearly all of them entered the United States as a result of the Vietnam War that ended in 1975. In April 1975, Khmer Rouge troops entered Phnom Penh. The Cambodian tragedy followed the fall of the capital. A few days later, on April 30, the South Vietnamese surrendered. In May of that same year, the Laotian government fell, and the Communist Pathet Lao came to power. These events not only changed Southeast Asia, but altered the lives of individuals forever. By 2000, 1,814,301 Southeast Asians lived in the United States.

Cambodians primarily immigrated to the West Coast but also moved into the interior. In 2000, 1,089 had settled in the Plains states. Seven hundred and thirty-two of these immigrants settled in Kansas. The majority settled in Wichita (454). Combined with the Laotians (5,553 persons) and Vietnamese (31,605 persons), Southeast Asians helped establish a sense of community in Kansas by attending New Year celebrations, establishing churches and temples, and setting up mutual-aid societies.

The Hmong supported the Americans throughout the Southeast Asian conflict. Today a small group lives in Kansas, most of them in Kansas City, which had 883 Hmong living in the city in 2000. Statewide, the 2000 census reported 1,004 Hmong. One hundred and one Hmong lived in Nebraska, and Oklahoma had 549. Their loyalty to their homeland and distaste for the Laotian Communist regime endeared them to the American government, but their road to the United States has been difficult.

The Hmong lived in the lush green hills of Laos. Some who went directly from Laos to Thailand and then to Kansas found the Plains too different from their homelands. One Hmong, Ge Lor, said that he left Laos for Thailand in 1979. "After one year of living in Kansas, my family—a wife and two sons—moved to Fresno, California. We moved mostly because there were no other Laotian [Hmong] in Kansas."[36] Other Hmong did stay. By 1995, Kansas had 10,085 Vietnamese, 2,338 Laotians, and 918 Cambodians. The meat-packing plants of the southeast part of the state recruited many of the immigrants.[37]

Most of the 101 Hmong in Nebraska lived in Omaha. Lormong Ho, a former city council member of Omaha, contended that the number was too low. He felt that the number of Hmong in Omaha ranged between 200 and 300 individuals.

Table 8. Select Asian Groups Living in the Plains States, 2000

Group	Kansas	Nebraska	North Dakota	Oklahoma	South Dakota	Total
Japanese	1,935	1,582	186	2,505	315	6,523
Asian Indian	8,153	3,273	822	8,502	611	21,361
Cambodian	732	107	0	250	0	1,089
Filipino	3,509	2,101	643	4,028	613	10,894
Laotian	3,361	902	0	1,036	254	5,553
Hmong	1,004	101	0	549	0	1,654
Vietnamese	11,623	6,364	478	12,566	574	31,605

Source: United States Census, 2000.

The majority of the Hmong held manufacturing jobs. They worked to help their children. Hmong immigrants "start low on the socio-economic pole, probably lower than any other Asian group." What they work for is to buy a home and put their children through school. In Omaha, "One of the four main annual Hmong social functions . . . is a spring celebration for all Hmong graduates. Students who have good grades receive awards." Hue Lo, a Hmong man who lived in Omaha for twenty-two years, said that the celebration encourages children to study hard.[38] Parents work hard, children study; their goal is to improve their situation in life.

On the Plains, Vietnamese live in every state. Kansas and Oklahoma have the largest populations, with the vast majority concentrated in Wichita and Oklahoma City. The cities on the Plains have the highest numbers of Vietnamese. Region-wide, most large cities have Vietnamese citizens. North Dakota and South Dakota are exceptions, but both states do have immigrants from Vietnam. In North Dakota, the vast majority live in Fargo. Fargo also contains a distinct Chinese minority.

Filipinos and Asian Indians

When the United States purchased the Philippines from Spain after the Spanish-American War in 1898, Filipinos immigrated legally to America. The Filipino immigration came in two waves: around 1900 to 1934, when the Philippines obtained conditional independence, and from 1965 to the present, after a 1965 immigration law abolished discriminatory national-origins quotas that had banned Asian immigration.

Filipinos were valued agricultural and railroad workers. After passage of the "Gentleman's Agreement" in 1907 curtailed Japanese immigration, Hawaiian plantation owners recruited Filipino "Manong" immigrants, who quickly headed for the Pacific coast. As U.S. nationals, they could immigrate freely to the United States. In 1920, 5,603 Manong were on the mainland. Ten years later there were 30,470 in California. Most Manong were young, single, uneducated men. Initially, Filipinos were not racially classified "Mongolian." Mongolians in California and elsewhere in the West had been barred from leasing and owning farmland. Later, some western states defined Filipinos as members of the Malayan race, forbade them to marry whites, and barred them from leasing and owning farmland. Although Filipinos were "Malay" and Christian, they experienced discrimination. Categorized as "little brown brothers" and stigmatized as violent and sexual predators, they worked as house servants, in restaurants and hotels, as railroad laborers, and in the fields. In 1934, Congress granted the Philippines transitional independence in order to end Filipino immigration and to eliminate the potential for naturalization. The next year, Congress allowed free transportation to Filipinos traveling to the Philippines on the condition that the repatriated person did not return. After the 1965 Immigration Act, thousands of Filipinos joined the military to gain entry into the United States. They were joined by family members. Other immigrants came from the medical profession, particularly doctors and nurses. The 1965 act led to an increase in the number of Filipinos who settled on the Plains.[39] By 2000, 10,894 Filipinos lived in the five Plains states. Many worked as nurses and professionals. Filipino laborers still worked in the fields, but recent immigration has brought a high number of professionals into the region.

In 1897, the first Asian Indians arrived in Canada. Two years later the first Sikhs landed in San Francisco. Coming from the Punjab, their numbers steadily climbed, but immigration from India slowed due to bans placed on Asian Indian immigration. Nonetheless, in 1930, all Plains states had at least a few residents from India. At the end of the twentieth century, the number of Asian immigrants who arrived and settled in the United States climbed significantly. In 2000, Kansas and Oklahoma each had more than 8,000 Asian Indians living within their borders. Many of the immigrants had come as professionals or as businessmen with money to invest in restaurants or motels. Like other immigrants, they brought their own faiths. Particularly, Hindus, Buddhists, and Janes (followers of Janism) could be found in many Asian Indian communities.

MIDDLE EASTERN IMMIGRANTS

The end of World War I in 1918 led to a new wave of immigrants who found their way west. Middle Easterners such as Syrians, Armenians, and Lebanese joined German, Portuguese, and Swiss immigrants who had arrived earlier. These new groups arrived in small enough numbers to not draw too much attention to their arrival. By 1930, Syrians could be found in every Plains state.

People from the Middle East lived in every state on the Great Plains in the year 2000. Kansas and Oklahoma had by far the largest number of Middle Easterners. The largest cities, such as Lincoln, Omaha, Oklahoma City, and Wichita, all had sizeable populations. In Oklahoma City, the Masjid an-Nasr Mosque serves the Muslim community. In Tulsa, the Islamic Society provides spiritual and social aid to Arabs and community members at large. In the Kansas City metroplex, which extends to Kansas City, Kansas, Masjid al-Huda, Masjid al-Inshirah, and Masjid Omar join the Islamic Center as mosques. The Islamic Center houses the masjid (prayer hall), an Islamic school, and a multipurpose area for social activities. Middle Easterners on the Plains, as elsewhere in the United States, adhere to a variety of faiths, but most are Muslims.

Lincoln, Nebraska, like Kansas City, has a thriving Muslim population. Lincoln is home to 122 Egyptians, 152 Iraqis, and 1,039 Lebanese. Many are Muslims. The federal government began resettling Iraqis in Lincoln in the aftermath of the Persian Gulf War in 1991. Here housing is safe and relatively affordable. On the basis of the Vietnamese refugees' experience in Lincoln, the government felt that the city would extend midwestern friendliness to the Iraqis. The city has two Middle Eastern grocery stores and two mosques.[40] There is also an Islamic Foundation in Lincoln that is Sunni. Like Islamic centers elsewhere, it offers social and religious services to the community. The Sunni Muslim center began serving the community in the early 1990s. Like all mosques, the one serving the Sunni is primarily dedicated to prayer, but it doubles as a community center. The primary function of the Islamic Foundation is to provide a strong support system.

HISPANICS

Spaniards were the first Europeans to see the Great Plains. For generations they controlled the Plains. Following the American acquisition of the Plains in 1803, the number of Spaniards dwindled. In 1900, 71 Mexicans lived in Kansas, one in North Dakota, 70 in Oklahoma, 13 in South Dakota, and 27 in Nebraska. Spanish residents numbered 39 in Kansas, 182 in Nebraska, 6 in North Dakota, 3 in South Dakota, and 16 in Oklahoma. One hundred years later, the Plains had changed. Hispanics (the term has come to mean all Spanish speakers in both the literature and popular culture) numbered 480,670 in the five Plains states, 5.1 percent of the area's total population. They live on the Plains because there are jobs.

The Hispanics come primarily from Mexico, and while the vast majority moved to cities, rural areas also saw an influx of immigrants. For example, West Point, Nebraska, located in the extreme northeastern part of the state, has 3,600 people. In the 1980s and 1990s, townspeople watched the youth graduate from high school and move away. For most of its history, the town consisted of the descendants of German, Czech, and Irish immigrants. One-hundred-year-old buildings mark the downtown. Brick-paved streets still can be seen in what might be considered a quiet midwestern town. As happened throughout the Plains, the exodus of youth left low-paid, low-skill jobs unfilled. The meat-packing plant in West Point needed help. Immigrants from Mexico fit the bill. Reina Bustamonte, a native of Honduras, came to West Point to work in the galvanizing plant. She earned nine dollars an hour and said: "When I was living in California, it was more hard . . . right here the salary is better. The people are more friendly." There are better schools for her children.[41] In all, 440 Hispanics live in West Point. Of this number, 366 are Mexican. In 2000, Hispanics made up 12 percent of the town's population. Similar situations are evident elsewhere on the Plains.

In the Panhandle of Oklahoma, huge hog corporations have drawn on Hispanic workers to fill positions. All northwestern Oklahoma counties have had an increase in the number of Hispanics. Guymon, Oklahoma, located in the center of the Panhandle, is a good example. Out of a population of 10,472 people, 4,018 are Hispanic, 38 percent of the city's population. Guymon reflects a changing ethnic matrix that is increasingly evident. Seaboard Farms employs 2,300 employees in its hog operation. The hog operators rely heavily on Hispanics to make the system work. In Guymon, 2,942 of these Hispanics come from Mexico. Families who often speak little English shop in grocery stores with three- and five-year-olds in their grocery baskets. Culturally, this is making a difference. It is best for good businessmen to know Spanish. Soon these toddlers will be headed to school, and already 15 percent of the city's 1,200 students are Hispanic.[42] Bilingual education

Hispanic girl in Kansas, Nebraska. Photo by M. Forsberg. Courtesy Nebraska DED.

is not a question, it is a fact. Teachers must teach, and that means instructing, at least sometimes, in Spanish.

While rural Plains communities have witnessed an influx of Hispanic immigrants, the cities have experienced the greatest change. As noted, 480,670 Hispanics live on the Plains. Of that number, 36 percent live in just six cities: Kansas City, Kansas, Topeka, Wichita, Omaha, Oklahoma City, and Tulsa. Kansas lost population in 57 of its 105 counties between 1990 and 2000. Yet in that same decade, the population of the state increased by 8.5 percent to 2,688,418. The change came in urban areas. In 1990, Hispanics made up 3.6 percent of the Kansas population; in 2000, 7 percent. The majority of these individuals went to urban areas. Metropolitan areas as a whole grew in the 1990s, but the Hispanic influx superheated the growth. On the Plains, essentially every city counted Hispanics among its numbers. What the official numbers for the 2000 census did not show was the number of Hispanics living illegally in the Plains states. Nationwide, the Immigration and Naturalization Service places the number of illegal aliens living in the United States at 6 million. It may be higher. In any case, Hispanics are now and will be a permanent part of the ethnic mix that makes the Great Plains culturally distinct.

Cinco de Mayo celebrations are now held throughout the Plains states from Oklahoma City to Dodge City and Topeka, Kansas. Cinco de Mayo commemorates the defeat of Emperor Napoleon III's army by a much smaller force on May 5, 1862. The battle at Puebla became a symbol of pride and is celebrated annually in many western states. In Oklahoma City, the festival has served as a means of bringing the community together to paint murals. In Dodge City, Kansas, Cinco de Mayo festivals bring the community together. In Topeka, Latino authors read

Table 9. Hispanics in the five Plains states in 2000

Group	Kansas	Nebraska	North Dakota	Oklahoma	South Dakota	Total
Total population of the state	2,688,418	1,711,263	642,200	3,450,654	754,844	9,247,379
Hispanic	188,252	94,425	7,786	179,304	10,903	480,670
Mexican	148,270	71,030	4,295	132,813	6,364	362,772
Central America	4,484	5,270	190	4,348	756	15,048
South America	2,627	1,197	240	3,212	227	7,503

Source: United States Census, 2000. http://www.census.gov/main/www/access.html (accessed February 1, 2004).

poetry and prose. In May 2003, the Cinco de Mayo parade in Omaha brought out 15,000 celebrants, including Maria Zavala, who noted that the celebration makes "her feel content." Magdalenia Garcia said that it made her proud. The Omaha celebration lasted for five days. In Hill City, South Dakota, in 2003, the event lasted one day, but like elsewhere, it emphasized music, food, and dancing. Hispanic culture is a part of the Plain's traditions.[43]

DIVERSITY

The diversity of the Native American population on the Plains, coupled with the rich immigrant traditions, in some ways makes the area one of the most ethnically diverse places in the United States. The Native nations that removed to Oklahoma in the 1830s remain. Changes took place, but the core culture remained in ways that reflect both their unique society and the process they endure to bring them to the twenty-first century. On the northern Plains, the Sioux culture not only recovered from the devastating Indian Wars, it flourished. One of the largest tribes in the county, the total Sioux Nation spans Montana, North Dakota, South Dakota, and Nebraska. The tenacity of the Sioux is mirrored in other tribes. Comanche, Cree, Seminole, and the other First Nations who call the Plains home reflect a continuity to the past that stretches back at least 12,000 years. Women and men endured to hold on not just to their beliefs but to their homeland. Now they live alongside Vietnamese, Muslims, and a wave of newcomers who are also trying to retain their culture while surviving on the Plains.

Since World War II, the Native American population in the United States has grown dramatically. By 2000, Oklahoma had the largest population of Native people in the country, 248,037. Only one out of five Native persons resided on reservations. On the Plains, however, one of the largest reservations exists. Second only to the Navajo Reservation (Arizona, New Mexico, Utah), the Pine Ridge Reservation in South Dakota was deemed the poorest place per capita in the United States. In 1990, 2.56 percent of South Dakota's population resided on the Pine Ridge Reservation. The Sioux who live on the Pine Ridge and Rosebud Reservations in South Dakota represent 4.4 percent of the state's population.[44] Nebraska, North Dakota, and Kansas Native populations, like those in South Dakota and Oklahoma, grew in 1990, but the 2000 statistics show how much.

In 2003, one South Dakota editorial claimed, "South Dakota's population is growing but mostly along the Interstate 29 corridor and on Indian Reservations." The fact is that regionwide, the Native populations are growing. Oklahoma and South Dakota have among the largest Native American populations in the United States, with 248,037 and 57,134, respectively. Few places are as diverse as Oklahoma. Here live Apache, Cherokee, Cheyenne, Chickasaw, Chippewa, Choctaw, Comanche, Cree, Creek, Crow, Delaware, Kiowa, Osage, Seminole, and Sioux. The Cherokee alone number 97,317.[45]

On the Plains, urban centers exhibit the greatest amount of diversity. Kansas City, Kansas, Topeka, Oklahoma City, Tulsa, Omaha, Rapid City, and Bismarck all reflect late-twentieth-century realities. Hispanics, Southeast Asians, and Europeans, along with Native peoples, live in these urban centers. The Native Peoples provide a window into the soul of the region. Indians have lived there for more than 12,000 years. They lasted because, like the Hutterite, German, Norwegian,

Resources on Plains Ethnicity

Several excellent general works about ethnic groups in the West deal with a variety of topics. One of the most significant is Sucheng Chan, Douglas Henny Daniels, Murio T. Garcia, and Terry P. Wilson, eds., *Peoples of Color in the American West* (Lexington, MA: D. C. Heath and Co., 1994). Another ethnic history of significance is Ronald T. Takaki, *Strangers from a Different Shore: A History of Asian Americans* (Boston: Little, Brown, 1989). Quintard Taylor, *In Search of the Racial Frontier: African Americans in the American West, 1990* (New York: W. W. Norton and Co., 1999), and Quintard Taylor and Shirley Ann Wilson Moore, eds., *African American Women Confront the West, 1600–2000* (Norman: University of Oklahoma Press, 2003), provide an excellent context for understanding blacks in the West.

Native Americans on the Plains

In terms of the Plains, W. Raymond Wood and Margot Liberty, eds., *Anthropology of the Great Plains* (Lincoln: University of Nebraska Press, 1980), provides one of the better overviews of Plains Indian history and culture. Theda Perdue, *Slavery and the Evolution of Cherokee Society, 1540–1866* (Knoxville: University of Tennessee Press, 1979), Annie Heloise Abel, *The American Indian as Slaveholder and Secessionist* (Lincoln: University of Nebraska Press, 1992), provide excellent information about Indians as slaveholders and also set the groundwork for understanding the complex nature of Oklahoma's cultural history. In Anthony McGinnis, *Counting Coup and Cutting Horses: Intertribal Warfare on the Northern Plains, 1738–1889* (Evergreen, CO: Cordillera Press, 1990), the author explains how tribal groups came to dominate certain sections of the Plains. Kenneth Marvin Hamilton, *Black Towns and Profit: Promotion and Development in the Trans-Appalachian West, 1877–1915* (Chicago: University of Illinois Press, 1991), provides a good outline of Blacks after the Civil War. Some of these are classics that have been reissued, for example, H. B. Cushman, *History of the Choctaw, Chickasaw, and Natchez Indians* (Norman: University of Oklahoma Press, 1999). Other good works are George E. Hyde, *The Pawnee Indians* (Norman: University of Oklahoma Press, 1988), and Hyde, *Red Cloud's Folk: A History of the Oglala Sioux Indians* (Norman: University of Oklahoma Press, 1979). An excellent work is Ernest Wallace and E. Adamson Hoebel, *The Comanches: Lords of the South Plains* (Norman: University of Oklahoma Press, 1987).

Religion and Non-Native Ethnic Heritage

Books dealing with ethnic groups on the Plains have added much to our understanding of the area's ethnic diversity. The Jewish experience on the Plains is represented in several works including Sophie Trupin, *Dakota Diaspora: Memoirs of a Jewish Homesteader* (Berkeley, CA: Alternative Press, 1984). Most states have good popular texts on ethnic history. D. Jerome Tweton and Theodore B. Jellif, *North Dakota: The Heritage of a People* (Fargo: North Dakota Institute for Regional Studies, 1976), Francie M. Berg, ed., *Ethnic Heritage in North Dakota* (Washington, DC: Attigeh Foundation, 1983), are good examples of this. Royden K. Loewen, *Family, Church, and Market: A Mennonite Community in the Old and New Worlds, 1850–1930* (Urbana: University of Illinois Press, 1993), takes a good look at Mennonite Communities. Frederick C. Luebke, *Immigrants and Politics: The Germans of Nebraska, 1880–1900* (Lincoln: University of Nebraska Press, 1969), provides good information about the German immigration to the Plains. Laura Wilson, *Hutterites of Montana* (New Haven, CT: Yale University Press, 2000), while dealing with Montana, devotes a great deal of effort to presenting the Hutterite experience on North America and therefore looks at South Dakota. For anyone wanting to know about the Hutterites this book is important.

The studies of ethnic groups in each state are invaluable. One of the premier works is Paul Olson, ed., *Broken Hoops and Plains People: A Catalogue of Ethnic Resources in the Humanities: Nebraska and Surrounding Areas* (Lincoln: University of Nebraska Press, 1976). Karel D. Bicha, *The Czechs in Oklahoma* (Norman: University of Oklahoma Press, 1980), provides details about Czechs' lives in Oklahoma. A good Bertha W. Calloway, and Alonzo Nelson Smith, *Visions of Freedom on the Great Plains: An Illustrated History of African Americans in Nebraska* (Virginia Beach, VA: Donning Publishers, 1998). There are numerous excellent works on Native peoples in each state.

In the text of this chapter, when a census statistic is given, we took the data from the census data, specifically, *Seventh Census of the United States, 1850* (Washington, DC: U.S. Government Printing Office, 1852); *Eighth Census of the United States, 1860* (Washington, DC: U.S. Government Printing Office, 1864); *Ninth Census of the United States, 1870* (Washington, DC: U.S. Government Printing Office, 1872); *Tenth Census of the United States, 1880* (Washington, DC: U.S. Government Printing Office, 1883); *Eleventh Census of the United States, 1890* (Washington, DC: U.S. Government Printing Office, 1892); and *Twelfth Census of the United States, 1900* (Washington, DC: U.S. Government Printing Office, 1901). For the twentieth century, the data cited in the text came from *Abstract of the Twelfth Census of the United States, 1900* (Washington, DC: U.S. Government Printing Office, 1904); *Department of Commerce Statistical Abstract of the Thirteenth Census of the United States, 1913* (Washington, DC: U.S. Government Printing Office, 1914); *Statistical Abstract of the United States, 1923* Washington, DC: U.S. Government Printing Office, 1924); *Abstract of the Fifteenth Census of the United States, 1930* (Washington, DC: U.S. Government Printing Office, 1933); and *Statistical Abstract of the United States, 1942* (Washington, DC: U.S. Government Printing Office, 1943). Statistical data also came from *Historical Statistics of the United States from Colonial Times to 1970, Part 1* (Washington, DC: U.S. Government Printing Office, 1975), and United States Census, 2000, http://www.census.gov/main/www/access.html. In this chapter, the source of the population figures comes either from the census or statistical summary for that year.

or Hmong immigrants, they "stuck it out." This "old western" phrase was a term applied to homesteaders with grit. It means that no matter what comes—wind, snow, or tornado—one takes what nature gives and remains on the land. One is not just a survivor, one is staying with something because one believes in the land and the people around him or her. On the Plains a person is measured by how hard he or she works. One is measured by whether he or she can stick it out. A person who works hard and stays with the land earns the grudging respect of the neighbors—whether those neighbors are in towns or on farms. The Native Americans have done just that—they still live on the land that their ancestors lived on, and their numbers are not diminishing, but increasing. Sioux Indians walking across the prairie today often are not rich and at times are still the object of prejudice, but because they remained on the land of their ancestors, they feel that there is a place where they belong—they belong on the Plains.

RESOURCE GUIDE

Printed Sources

Berg, Francie M., ed. *Ethnic Heritage in North Dakota*. Washington, DC: Attigeh Foundation, 1983.

Bicha, Karel D. *The Czechs in Oklahoma*. Norman: University of Oklahoma Press, 1980.

Chan, Sucheng. *Asian Americans: An Interpretive History*. Boston: Twayne, 1991.

Chan, Sucheng, Douglas Henny Daniels, Murio T. Garcia, and Terry P. Wilson, eds. *Peoples of Color in the American West*. Lexington, MA: D. C. Heath and Co., 1994.

Cottrol, Robert J., Raymond T. Diamond, and Leland B. Ware. *Brown v. Board of Education: Caste, Culture, and the Constitution*. Lawrence: University Press of Kansas, 2003.

Cushman, H. B. *History of the Choctaw, Chickasaw, and Natchez Indians*. Norman: University of Oklahoma Press, 1999.

Daniels, Roger. *Asian America: Chinese and Japanese in the United States since 1850*. Seattle: University of Washington Press, 1988.

Hamilton, Kenneth Marvin. *Black Towns and Profit: Promotion and Development in the Trans-Appalachian West, 1877–1915*. Urbana: University of Illinois Press, 1991.

Hyde, George E. *The Pawnee Indians*. Norman: University of Oklahoma Press, 1988.

———. *Red Cloud's Folk: A History of the Ogallala Sioux Indians*. Norman: University of Oklahoma Press, 1979.

Kelly, Gail Paradise. *From Vietnam to America: A Chronicle of the Vietnamese Immigration to the United States*. Boulder, CO: Westview Press, 1977.

Kim, Huang-chan, Dorothy Cordova, Stephen S. Fugita, Franklin Ng, and Singh, Jane, eds. *South Asians in North America: An Annotated and Selected Bibliography*. Berkeley: University of California, Center for South and Southeast Asian Studies, 1988.

Knoll, Tricia. *Becoming Americans: Asian Sojourners, Immigrants, and Refugees in the Western United States*. Portland, OR: Coast to Coast Books, 1982.

Kutz, William Loren. *The Black West*. 3rd ed., rev. and exp. Seattle: Open Hand Publishing, 1987.

Loewen, Royden K. *Family, Church, and Market: A Mennonite Community in the Old and New Worlds, 1850–1930*. Urbana: University of Illinois Press, 1993.

Luebke, Frederick C. *Immigrants and Politics: The Germans of Nebraska, 1880–1900*. Lincoln: University of Nebraska Press, 1969.

Melendy, H. Brett. *Asians in America: Filipinos, Koreans, and East Indians*. Boston: Twayne, 1977.

Muzny, Charles C. *The Vietnamese in Oklahoma City: A Study in Ethnic Change*. New York: AMS Press, 1989.

Sherman, William C., Timothy Kloberdanz, Theodore Pedeliski, and Playford V. Thorson. *Plains Folk: North Dakota's Ethnic History*. Fargo: North Dakota Institute for Regional Studies, 1988.

Singh, Jane, ed. *South Asians in North America: An Annotated and Selected Bibliography*. Berkeley: University of California, Center for South and Southeast Asian Studies, 1988.

Taylor, Quintard. *In Search of the Racial Frontier: African Americans in the American West, 1990*. New York: W. W. Norton and Co., 1999.

Taylor, Quintard, and Shirley Ann Wilson Moore, eds. *African American Women Confront the West, 1600–2000*. Norman: University of Oklahoma Press, 2003.

Trupin, Sophie. *Dakota Diaspora: Memoirs of a Jewish Homesteader*. Berkeley, CA: Alternative Press, 1984.

Tweton, D. Jerome, and Theodore B. Jellif. *North Dakota: The Heritage of a People*. Fargo: North Dakota Institute for Regional Studies, 1976.

Vo, Linda Trinh, ed. *Asian American Women: The "Frontiers" Reader*. Lincoln: University of Nebraska Press, 2004.

Wallace, Ernest, and E. Adamson Hoebel. *The Comanches: Lords of the South Plains.* Norman: University of Oklahoma Press, 1987.
Wilson, Laura. *Hutterites of Montana.* New Haven, CT: Yale University Press, 2000.

Web Sites

Caddo Nation Archives, 1998–2004
http://www.rootsweb.com/~usgenweb/ok/nations/caddo/caddo/

The Cherokee Nation, 1998–2002
http://www.cherokee.org/

Chickasaw Nation, n.d.
http://www.chickasaw.net/

Choctaw Nation, 2002
http://www.choctawnation.com/

The German American: An Ethnic Experience, 2002–2003
IPUPUI University Libraries
http://www-lib.iupui.edu/kade/adams/toc.html

The Golden Jubilee of the German-Russian Settlement Elis and Rush Counties, Kansas, 1999
http://skyways.lib.ks.us/genweb/archives/ethnic/german-russian/jubilee/index.html

The Hutterian Brethren: living in Community in North America, n.d.
http://www.hutterites.org/

Kansas: Emerging Asian American and Pacific Islander Communities, 1999
http://www.aapcho.org/draft/vs_draft.html

Kansas Advisory Committee on Hispanic Affairs, n.d.
http://www2.hr.state.ks.us/ha/html/enha.html

Mandan, Hidatsa, Arikara, 2004
http://www.mhanation.com/

Mardos Memorial Library online, Books and Maps,
http://www.rootsweb.com/~neethnic/czechs/czechs.html

Native American Times, 2004
http://nativetimes.com/

North Dakota Census Records, 2002–2004
http://www.censusfinder.com/north_dakota.htm

Northern Great Plains, 1880–1920, 1999
http://memory.loc.gov/ammem/award97/ndfahtml/hult_im.html

Oklahoma's History, 2001–2004
http://www.state.ok.us/osfdocs/stinfo2.html

Osage Nation, 2004
http://www.osagetribe.com/ho-way.htm

The Pawnee Nation, n.d.
http://www.pawneenation.org/

Pine Ridge Reservation, 2004
http://www.pineridgerez.net/index.php

The Seminole Nation, 2002
http://www.choctawnation.com/

Settlement of Volga Germans in America, 1999–2002
http://www.webbitt.com/volga/index.htm

The Shawnee Nation, n.d.
http://www.shawnee-tribe.org/Default.htm

Southeast Asia Resource Action Center, n.d.
http://www.searac.org/vietref.html

Spirit Lake Tribe, 2001–2003
http://www.spiritlakenation.com/

Turtle Mountain Chippewa Indian Heritage Center, n.d.
http://chippewa.utma.com/index2.html

Documentary Films

All My Relatives. Red Eye Video.

This hour-long documentary takes a look at the Spirit Lake Nation through the eyes of four generations who have lived at Devil's Lake Sioux Reservation in North Dakota.

Death of the Dream: Farmhouses In the Heartland. PBS, 1997.
http://www.pbs.org/ktca/farmhouses/index.html

This video is not a traditional ethnic study, but it does look at the changing nature of the Plains. It includes a look at where settlers came from in *Homes on the Prairie.*

The Germans from Russia: Children of the Steppe, Children of Prairie. Prairie Public Television, North Dakota State University, 1999.

This is a one-hour documentary produced by Prairie Public Television that looks at the Germans from Russia in North Dakota.

Homeland. PBS, 2000.
http://www.pbs.org/itvs/homeland/index.html

Four Lakota families are looked at in this portrait of reservation life.

Rural Communities: Legacy and Change (Episode 6). PBS, 1992.

"Think Globally." This film looks at Southeast Asians who moved to Kansas to work in a meat-packing factory.

Shaping America (Episode 20)*: Irrepressible Conflicts.* PBS ALS, 2001.
http://www.pbs.org/als/shaping_america/saamdescrip.htm

This film looks at the changing nature of slavery and its effects on blacks and whites. It also looks at the Kansas-Nebraska Act and the Dred Scott decision by the Supreme Court in 1857.

The West: Empire upon the Trails (Episode 2)*: The Trail of Tears.* PBS, 2001.

This series looks at the Trail of Tears and notes the impact the arrival of eastern Indians had on Native peoples living in Oklahoma.

The West: One Sky above Us (Episode 8)*: The Outcome of Our Earnest Endeavors.* PBS, 2001.

Congress passed the Dawes Act in 1887. Under this law, each head of an Indian family would be given 160 acres of farmland or 320 of grazing land. It led to the breakup of the reservations.

Recordings

Archive of Folk Culture
American Folklife Center
Thomas Jefferson Building, Room LJG49
Library of Congress
101 Independence Ave. SE
Washington, DC 20540-4610

The Archive of Folk Culture was created in 1928 and is housed in the Music Division of the Library of Congress. It houses American folk songs, some of which include music of a variety of origins. Twenty percent of the holdings include non-English-language traditions.

Dickinson County Historical Society
412 South Campbell Street
Abilene, KS 67410
http://www.aam-us.org/dickinson.htm

A collection of Kansas folk music and dance materials.

Kansas Folklore Archive
Forsyth Library
Fort Hays State University
600 Park Street
Hays, KS 67601-4099

This collection of recordings includes materials from various ethnic groups that settled in Kansas and consists of recordings of the beliefs, legends, poems, reminiscences, and recipes. Among the groups represented are Germans from Russia, Czechs, and Swedes. The collection contains 162 unpublished tape recordings.

The Plains Indian Music on the Internet
http://www.4thmoon.com/native/nativeindex.htm

Provides access to recorded Indian music online.

South Dakota Oral History Project
The American Indian Research Project (AIRP)
South Dakota Oral History Center
Institute of American Indian Studies
University of South Dakota
414 East Clark St.
Vermillion, SD 57069-2390
http://www.usd.edu/iais/oralhist/ohc.html

Contains more than 1,900 taped interviews.

Festivals or Events

Annual German-Russian Schmeckfest, Eureka, South Dakota, September (dates vary). The festival features food and entertainment along with a parade, a songfest, and bandstand performances.

Cherokee National Holiday, Tahlequah, Oklahoma, August 30–September 1. This annual event celebrates the signing of the Cherokee Constitution. The celebration includes a powwow at Tahlequah.

Chinese New Year, Deadwood, South Dakota. This annual event features Chinese lion dancers and a parade through this historic Old West town. Dates vary according to the Chinese calendar.

Cinco de Mayo in Omaha, Omaha Parade, May 5 every year. The Cinco de Mayo festival is a traditional celebration of Hispanic culture and includes eating, music, and politics.

Cinco de Mayo in the Greater Kansas City Area, May 5 each year.
http://www.fiestakc.org/AboutHCC.htm

Czech Days, Tabor, South Dakota, June (dates vary). This annual festival celebrates Czechoslovakian heritage and offers delicious Czech food, a parade, Beseda dancers, a craft fair, and free entertainment.

Festival of Cultures, Falls Park, Sioux Falls, South Dakota, June (date varies). This is a celebration of the many cultural traditions found in the Sioux Falls area and features exhibits, food, and entertainment in Falls Park.

German Fest, Hill City, South Dakota, September (dates vary). An Oktoberfest that features imported German beer, polka music, and activities, with the best of local German cooking, dancing, and entertainment. The event is held at the Three Forks Campground, three miles north of Hill City on Highway 385.

Høstfest, Minot, North Dakota, October of each year. This festival celebrates Scandinavian culture and features concerts and good food.

McPherson Scottish Festival and Highland Games, McPherson, Kansas, September (dates vary). This annual event has entertainment, demonstrations and exhibits, a pipe and drum competition, and traditional foods.
http://www.mcpherson.com/418/community/scot/festival.htm

Archives and Special Collections

Center for Western Studies
2201 S. Summit Avenue
Box 727
Augustana College
Sioux Falls, SD 57197
http://www.augie.edu/CWS/

Cherokee National Historical Society
Cherokee Heritage Center
PO Box 515
Tahlequah, OK 74464
http://www.powersource.com/heritage/museum.html

Forsyth Library
Archives and Special Collections
Fort Hays State University
600 Park Street
Hays, KS 67601-4099
http://www.fhsu.edu/forsyth_lib/arch.shtml

Germans from Russia
Germans from Russia Heritage Society
1125 W. Turnpike Avenue

Bismarck, ND 58501
http://www.grhs.com/

Institute for Regional Studies
North Dakota State University Libraries
PO Box 5599
Fargo, ND 58105-5599
http://www.lib.ndsu.nodak.edu/ndirs/

John and Mary Nichols Collection
University of Oklahoma Libraries
401 W. Brooks Street
Norman, OK 73019
http://www-lib.ou.edu/info/index.asp?id=23

Kansas State Historical Society
6425 SW Sixth Avenue
Topeka, KS 66615-1099
http://www.kshs.org/

Kenneth Spencer Research Library
The University of Kansas
1450 Poplar Lane
Lawrence, KS 66045-7616
http://spencer.lib.ku.edu/visit/

Nebraska State Historical Society
PO Box 82554
1500 R Street
Lincoln, NE 68501
http://www.nebraskahistory.org/index.htm

Oglala Lakota College Archives
Learning Resource Center Building
Woksape Tipi
PO Box 310
3 Mile Creek Road
Kyle, SD 57752
http://www.olc.edu/library/olcarchvs.htm

Oklahoma Historical Society
2100 N. Lincoln Boulevard
Oklahoma City, OK 73105
http://www.ok-history.mus.ok.us/

Omaha Public Library
215 S. 15th Street
Omaha, NE 68102
http://www.omaha.lib.ne.us/

Reinhart/Alumni Library
University Archives
Creighton University
2500 California Plaza
Omaha, NE 68178

Richard L. D. and Marjorie J. Morse Department of Special Collections
Hale Library
Kansas State University
Manhattan, KS 66506
http://www.lib.ksu.edu/depts/spec/index.html

South Dakota State Historical Society
900 Governors Drive
Pierre, SD 57501-2217
http://www.sdhistory.org/archives.htm

State Historical Society of North Dakota
612 East Boulevard Avenue
Bismarck, ND 58505-0830
http://www.state.nd.us/hist/index.html

Ukrainian Cultural Institute
1221 West Villard
Dickinson, ND 58601-4849
http://nd.scenariousa.com/stark/dickinson.html

Western History Collections
The University of Oklahoma Libraries
401 W. Brooks Street
Norman, OK 73019
http://www-lib.ou.edu/info/index.asp?id=22

Works Progress Administration
North Dakota Writers Project: Ethnic Group Files
Elwyn Robinson Department of Special Collections
Chester Fritz Library
University of North Dakota
Grand Forks, ND 58202
http://www.und.nodak.edu/dept/library/Collections/og1380.html

Organizations

Creek Indian Memorial Association
Creek Council House Museum
Town Square
Okmulgee, OK 74447

Croatian Cultural Society of Omaha
8711 S. 36th Street
Omaha, NE 68147
http://www.omahaculturefest.org/croatia/croatianlinks.html

Czech-Sokol Center
2021 U Street
Omaha, NE 68107
http://home.earthlink.net/~vbenak/sokol_south_omaha.htm

Five Civilized Tribes Foundation
c/o Chickasaw Nation
Bill Anoatubby, Governor
PO Box 1548
Ada, OK 74821

Islamic Foundation of Lincoln
3636 North 1st Street
Lincoln, NE 68521
http://www.ifol.org/articles.php?lng=en&pg=43

The Jewish Federation of Omaha
333 South 132nd Street
Omaha, NE 68154
http://www.jewishomaha.org/

Masjid an-Nasr
Islamic Society of Greater Oklahoma City
3815 N. St. Clair
Oklahoma City, OK 73112
http://www.okcislam.org/

Vietnamese American Association
Cuong Nguyen, Executive Director
919 N.W. 23rd Street
Oklahoma City, OK 73106

FASHION

Laurel E. Wilson

Clothing worn on the Great Plains was shaped by a number of factors, but climate was especially important since extremes in weather determined the kinds of dress needed for survival. Availability of materials such as skins and ornaments used to make clothing was vital before mass-manufactured fashions consisting of factory-made cloth and apparel were sold on the Great Plains by the 1850s. The culture of the various ethnic and racial groups that lived on the Great Plains was also significant in forming how clothing was created because religious practices and folk traditions led to a variety of styles. Finally, the variety of occupations and pastimes for recreation gave rise to specific clothing styles created for safety as well as function in the Great Plains environment. The word dress is used to refer to a universal, panhuman phenomenon, where the term fashion indicates shifting styles.

NATIVE AMERICAN DRESS

Native Americans first ventured onto the Great Plains many thousands of years ago. Unfortunately, virtually nothing related to dress of the earliest period has survived to be studied. Prehistoric burials in which articles of clothing have been found date to the 1300s, only about 250 years before Europeans recorded their observations about the people living on the Plains. The presence of Europeans in North America almost immediately affected dress worn by Native Americans, since European goods quickly traveled along already long-established trade routes. Once fur traders established trading posts by 1805 on the Plains, even more European goods changed the materials used for dress and even specific garments used by Native Americans. The dress of the Native American wives of Euro-American fur traders was affected even more than the dress of their relatives who maintained their traditional village life. When Native Americans were confined on reservations beginning in the 1870s, their way of life and their dress changed enormously since many of the materials once used to create clothing were no longer available. The

Ghost Dance clothing, in particular, shows the interaction of loss of traditional materials and beliefs about the supernatural in shaping style of clothing. The Ghost dance clothing, painted with visionary images, shows the interaction of loss of traditional materials and beliefs about the supernatural in shaping style of clothing. The clothing was worn for the Ghost dance that was performed to bring blessings that would return Native Americans to their old way of life. Although Native Americans now wear conventional clothing worn by most people on the Plains and in the rest of the United States, the dress they wear for powwows and other important ceremonies retains many characteristics seen in traditional Native American dress worn in the early nineteenth century.

Prehistoric Dress

A number of prehistoric cultural groups lived on the Great Plains from around 1000 to 1541, when Francisco de Coronado described the nomadic groups that roamed the southern Plains. While it is probable that they used dress in different ways, the absence of surviving garments for most of the groups leaves that aspect of their culture a mystery. There are very few remains of dress, but archaeological sites, particularly burials, provide information about the materials used to make and decorate clothing and accessories worn by these early people. The most common remains are the tools used to prepare the skins for use. Scrapers used to clean the hide and awls and needles used to sew clothing have been found in burials and in archaeological village sites. A variety of beads were used on clothing, including ones made of bone, which were probably made on site, and shells that were very likely traded to these inland people from groups who lived near the Pacific and Caribbean coasts. We know that prehistoric people decorated their clothing because quill flatteners for preparing porcupine quills to be sewn to leather were found in fourteenth-century burials of the Extended Middle Missouri traditions in North and South Dakota.[1] A wide variety of shells that were unaltered or ground smooth and perforated from both marine and freshwater mussels were also used to decorate clothing. Pendants, incised with markings of bird shapes or simple line patterns, were made of bone, shell, and the teeth and claws of animals, particularly bears and beavers. Tinklers that made sounds when the wearer moved were also fastened to clothing. Long, narrow pins used to fasten clothing were made of bone and antlers that were both plain and decorated. The archaeological evidence shows that people of all ages and both sexes wore pendants and clothing that was decorated. Pigments have also been found in burials and may have been used for funerary purposes or to decorate hair and skin. Since Native Americans still use face paints, it is likely that prehistoric people did so as well.

Although they used bone and shell beads, they made textiles from a variety of materials. Vegetable fiber cloth was used to make clothing, buffalo hair and rabbit fur were used to create mantles and blankets, and feathers were fashioned into mantles. They also used copper to make ear spools, a type of earring. Ear spools made of copper, shell, or bone show that people of the southern Plains had a sedentary life that permitted them to become highly skilled craftsmen.

Native American Dress, ca. 1541–1870s

Many Native American tribes have called the Great Plains home. Each tribe had its own style of dress that was created because of the materials used to make the clothing and accessories, the physical environment in which the dress was used, and the artistic influences that shaped the style and form of decorations. Information about Native American dress comes from some articles of dress worn there that are still extant and from early travelers who passed through the Great Plains and recorded their observations in words and pictures. Fourteenth century burials of the Southeastern Ceremonial Complex found in present-day Oklahoma show that people in the southern Plains dressed somewhat different than the people living on the northern Plains. However, by the early nineteenth century, when these travelers recorded their observations, Native Americans were already receiving manufactured trade goods from American, Canadian, and European trading companies. Even if they had no direct contact with European or American traders, they most likely traded for manufactured goods with other Native American tribes that had contact with these foreign traders. This means that the dress worn on the Great Plains, even in the early nineteenth century, often included elements that were mass manufactured in Europe or eastern America; however, these manufactured elements such as beads and ribbons were used completely differently from the way they were used by Europeans. The introduction of horses to southern Plains tribes in the sixteenth century, which then spread northward so that northern Plains tribes had horses by the beginning of the nineteenth century, meant that information and material culture moved among tribes more easily. Although traditional practices of each cultural group showed distinct regional or tribal characteristics, manufactured elements such as beads or metal tinklers were added to dress.

Among the first who recorded information about the dress of Native Americans who lived on the Great Plains was Patrick Gass (June 12, 1771–April 2, 1870), who was a sergeant in the Corps of Discovery headed by Lewis and Clark. Gass did not provide complete descriptions of the dress he observed, but he commented on things that were interesting to him, as in the entry of August 31, 1804, when he wrote, "Some of the [chiefs of the Sioux nation] had round their necks strings of the white bear's claws, some of the claws three inches long."[2] Artists Karl Bodmer (1809–1893) and George Catlin (1796–1872) were among the first to provide images of the Great Plains people. The paintings and drawings they created during the 1830s show that Native Americans still dressed in traditional clothing, with additions that were trade goods made in Europe or the East Coast of America.

Anthropologists have determined that the earliest men's dress consisted of leather breechclouts, plain and decorated, that were wrapped around the body and held in place with a belt. The breechclouts were worn with leggings that extended from crotch to ankle, and open-sided ponchos made of deerskin were worn over the torso when needed for cold weather. The earliest women's dress was a leather skirt that was wrapped around the body and held in place with a belt. They also wore ponchos that were open at the sides. Later women wore strap-and-sleeve dresses that were suspended from straps over the shoulders and extended from just under the arms to below the knees. Sleeves were sometimes tied over the strap dresses with thongs so the sleeves could be easily removed by slipping the thongs

Boy in the Water, Plains Indian. Courtesy Institute for Regional Studies, NDSU Libraries, Fargo.

over the head. The earliest dress for both men and women made economical use of skins that were available.

Hunting Technology and Dress

Once hunting technology changed so that people could kill more animals, more elaborately made clothing developed. Men's shirts that required two deerskins were among the developments. They were sewn so that the natural edges of the skins were left at the bottom, or the bottom edges were trimmed so they hung parallel to the ground. The loose edges could be left plain or cut into fringes at the sleeve and lower edges. Shirts were often trimmed with additional fringes, tails of ermine, and/or hair. The shirts were often further embellished with quillwork and paint. Anthropologists have determined that the earliest men's dress consisted of leather breechclouts, plain and decorated, that were wrapped around the body and held in place with a belt.[3] Women's dresses that required two or three skins show that hunting technologies improved markedly. The two-skin dresses were sewn in such a way that the hind legs of the skin formed the shoulders and sleeves of the dress, but the shoulder seam was sewn below the actual edges of the dress so the unsewn edges formed collarlike flaps at the top. If three skins were used, a separate skin was folded in the lengthwise direction to form a yoke to which the skirt skins were attached. Decorations of quillwork, beadwork, elk teeth, or shells usually followed the natural edges of the skins. Dresses also included additional fringes and dangles made of shells, bone, beads, and teeth. Painted buffalo robes, with the fur worn in, were used by both men and women as decoration and protection from the cold that was part of northern Great Plains life.

Moccasins that were designed for right and left feet were created in several ways. There were soft-soled moccasins that were made in one piece and hard-soled moccasins that had buffalo-hide soles and elk or deerskin uppers. The moccasins were often decorated with quillwork or beadwork designs over the top of the foot, but ceremonial moccasins even had quilled or beaded soles. Most Great Plains peoples wore ankle-high moccasins that had a short collar attached, but some wore knee-high or thigh-high moccasins that were combinations of moccasin and leggings, both parts decorated with quillwork.

Men and women also wore leggings made of leather. The men's leggings extended from ankle to crotch and were decorated with quillwork and paint. Breechcloths made of leather that was sometimes left plain or could be elaborately decorated were used with men's leggings. Women's leggings were usually knee length and decorated with quillwork or beads. Among the Kiowa of the southern Great Plains, women wore leg moccasins that extended to or above the knee with dresses made of leather. The legs of the moccasins were trimmed with paint and fringes and fastened with metal conchos, domed buttons with slots for leather ties. Kiowa men wore breechcloths and knee high moccasins and wrapped themselves in buffalo robes.

Decoration in Plains Peoples' Dress

Great Plains people wore a wide variety of necklaces, pendants, chokers, breast-plates, and earrings. These were made of the bones and claws of animals and birds, shells that came from the West Coast or Caribbean or that were found in local rivers, and beads that were manufactured of glass, clay, and metal in Europe and Africa. The men and women of the Comanche and Pawnee wore wrist cuffs and armbands. Headdresses in both the northern and southern Plains were made with leather, feathers, and furs. These were usually further embellished with quillwork or beading and tails or hair. Men and women used pigments, especially vermilion, a red pigment, to decorate their faces and bodies. Tattoos were also used by some tribes. Women used vermilion to paint the part in their hair.

Contrary to common belief, not all Indians dressed their hair in braids or wore feather war bonnets. Instead, they cut their hair in a variety of ways and decorated their hair with ornaments made of fur, metals, and feathers. Sometimes men and women plaited their hair for practical reasons, but they also wore it loose. George Catlin's paintings show the variety of hairstyles worn by the men and women in a number of northern and southern Great Plains tribes.

Beginning in 1808, tribes from north and south of the Ohio River were removed to Indian Territory in present-day Oklahoma and brought the dress used by the Five Civilized Tribes (the Cherokee, Choctaw, Creek, Seminole, and Chickasaw) to the Great Plains. Although they wore accessories that might be termed Native American, much of their dress was Euro-American, including cotton shirts, vests, coats, and trousers for the men and dresses for the women. Some of the men wore bandolier bags or sashes that were part of these tribes' traditional dress, and some covered their heads with head wraps that were made of European fabrics but were worn in a manner that was traditional within their Native cultures. Some forms of Euro-American dress were worn in styles that were uniquely Native American. Women of the Osage tribe of Oklahoma sewed amazing patterns with ribbons that were used to trim leggings and blankets. Osage ribbonwork is still done by a few skilled Osage craftswomen whose work is treasured by those who are fortunate to own clothing embellished with such cut and sewn ribbonwork.

These were the basic forms of dress found on the Great Plains when Euro-Americans began recording what they saw. The dress was made of materials available locally and through trade.

Observations of Great Plains Native Women

George Catlin, an American artist, was among the first people to record his observations about the appearance of Native Americans. His vivid descriptions provide details about the dress worn by Great Plains women. "The women in all these upper and western tribes are decently dressed and many of them with great beauty and taste; their dresses are all of deer or goat skins, extending from their chins quite down to the feet; these dresses are in many instances trimmed with ermine, and ornamented with porcupine quills and beads with exceeding ingenuity. . . . The Crow and Blackfeet women, like all others I ever saw in any Indian tribe, divide the hair on the forehead, and paint the separation or crease with vermilion or red earth. For what purpose this little, but universal, custom is observed, I never have been able to learn."[4]

Improved weapons that increased the amount of material available for clothing had already changed the styles of dress, as had the introduction of horses, which made hunting even more efficient. Mass-manufactured materials such as beads, ribbons, and metals had already made their way to Plains tribes, who quickly began to use them to create decorations based on traditional patterns long used on the Plains.

Fur-Trade Dress

The dress of Native Americans changed more rapidly as manufactured articles of clothing were shipped into the Great Plains. Some of these changes respected the traditions of the various tribes, while other changes departed very radically from traditions that were generations old. The changes in men's clothing were more rapid than in women's clothing since the men were in closer contact with the traders. There were exceptions. The women who married fur traders had access to the goods and influences of Euro-Americans and sometimes wore clothing that was more European than Native American.

Native Americans had technologies such as firearms and metal traps that enabled them to exploit the resources available to them on the Great Plains. They had weapons used to kill the buffalo that formed the core of their material culture since buffalo not only provided meat but hides and sinews used for housing and clothing. The hides were also valuable trade items, especially if they were well tanned. Beavers which were abundant along Great Plains streams, had been used by Plains tribes for food and clothing but were not trapped to the extent that the fur traders desired. The fur of beavers was needed to made fur-felt hats fashionable in Europe and America—the first instance of the influence of mass fashion on Great Plains people, albeit for people who did not live on the Plains. These valuable furs and hides were traded for goods manufactured with more sophisticated technologies then in use in Europe and the East Coast of America. Firearms were among the most desired trade goods since they could be used to further exploit the natural environment, but brass kettles, iron knives and axes, wool blankets, cloth shirts, and glass and clay beads were also among the goods traded to Native Americans.

Fur traders also influenced change in Great Plains dress by introducing Plains tribes to European styles of dress. Most of the kinds of dress traded could not be considered fashion since many of the garments were basics that had been in use in Europe for centuries. The shirts made of colored calicos were in a style very much like that worn in Europe since the end of the fifteenth century. Other kinds of trade goods were used by Native Americans in a manner consistent with their own cultural practices. Blankets were used in place of heavy buffalo robes, beads were used with quillwork and replaced the use of porcupine quills and vermilion, which was used in China as an artist's color but was used as a hair part and face paint by Native Americans. Fabrics were also used to replace leather goods. Breechclouts and leggings for both men and women were made of stroud, a woolen cloth made in Stroud in the county of Gloucester, England. Women sometimes wore dresses made of stroud cut much like the three-hide dresses with a length of fabric that extended across the body to form sleeves and yoke, both front and back, with two additional pieces of fabric sewn from the bottom of the yoke and extending below the knees. Native American women often adorned their stroud dresses with traditional trims such as dentalia shells or elk teeth or with metal and glass beads or bells. Because beads did not have to be picked, cleaned, and dyed the way that porcupine quills did, the amount of embellishment added to traditional clothing increased.

> ## Trade Goods Names
>
> Trade goods were often named for the place they were made. "These woolens may be so far out of the way of business as not to be fully known to thee by our names for them—They are 1st Strowd water a cloth about 4d broad about 4/p yd blue or red in purchasing wch a regard must be had not only to the Cloth & Colour but also to the list [selvedge] about which the Indians are Curious [i.e., exacting]. This is of the common breadth viz. about 3 fingers with a Stripe or two of white generally. Sometimes in black in ye blue psc. And always black in ye re. 2ndly. Duffels of near ye same breadth without any List for 20d to 2 sh or 2/2 (but that's too high) of the same Colours with the other. 3rdly Striped Blankets that are white like other Blankets only towds the ends they have generally for broad Stripes as each 2 red and 2 blue or black near—they are full 2 yds long or better and above 6/4d wide some near 7/4 they are sold by ye piece containing 15 blankets for about 3 lbs. 10/." From the letter book of James Logan in 1714.[6]

Euro-American Influence on Native American Dress

Euro-American clothing also became part of Native American dress as more trade goods were shipped into the Great Plains. Red or blue tail coats trimmed with braid called "chiefs' coats" were given as gifts to cement trading relations between Euro-American and Native American traders. Felt top hats appeared as Native American delegates to Washington, D.C., returned home with them as souvenirs. Some Native American men returned with complete outfits of Euro-American clothing. Thousands of cloth shirts made of printed calico were sold to Native Americans living on the Great Plains.

The dress of the Euro-American traders also was affected by interaction with Native Americans. Their Native American wives often made them clothing of buckskin that was decorated with beading and quillwork. The clothing was sometimes cut in the style of fashionable men's clothing worn in eastern America and Europe but was decorated in Native American style. The traders wore moccasins that were less costly and more comfortable than the shoes and boots that were made in the East and shipped up the Missouri River to the Great Plains. Some traders carried bandolier bags that were richly decorated with stroud, quills, and beads. Some of the Native American wives of the fur traders wore Euro-American clothing in the latest fashion. These women were the wives of the bourgeoisie who managed the affairs of the fur-trading companies in the West. Mrs. Denig, the Crow wife of Edwin Denig known as Deer Little Woman (1812–1858), a bourgeoise at Fort Union during the 1850s, dressed in the latest 1850s fashion from hairstyle to clothing. Mrs. Natawistacha (Medicine Snake Woman) Culbertson (1825–1893), wife of Alexander Culbertson (1809–1879), also a bourgeoise at Fort

Union and Fort Benton, preferred wearing moccasins and leggings with her Euro-American styled dresses. Unlike Mrs. Denig, who dressed her hair in Euro-American fashion, Mrs. Culbertson preferred wearing her hair plaited in braids in the style of her Blackfeet people. The clerks and laborers who also worked at the trading posts and their Native American wives wore clothing that was Native American in style but made of mass-manufactured cloth and ornaments since they did not have the income needed to clothe their wives and themselves in fine tailored suits and silken dresses.

Reservation Period Dress

Photographic evidence indicates that Native American men and women preferred to adopt some aspects of Euro-American dress but retained characteristics that had served them over the millennia. Men wore cloth shirts and pants and women wore cloth dresses, but both men and women wrapped themselves in blankets and wore traditional hair ornaments and other accessories. Hairpipes, long (3 to 5 inches) oval beads made with difficulty by hand from bone, were used to make breastplates that were a relatively new (1850s) addition to Native American dress. Once power tools were available, hairpipes were made in abundance from cow bones, but were still valued and used for necklaces and other ornaments.

During the 1890s, the Ghost Dance, which began about 1870 in Nevada, spread to the Great Plains. Native Americans believed that if they performed the traditional circle dance of the Great Basin, all white people would fall into a hole and

Settlers wore many-layered fashionable clothing, as seen in this typical Great Plains photograph, which demonstrates the Euro-American style of dress that was influential on Native Americans. Courtesy Stuhr Museum of the Prairie Pioneer.

be swallowed up and dead Native Americans would return to the earth with the buffalo. As part of this movement, they made ghost shirts from painted muslin decorated with sun, moon, and stars and eagles. They believed that the ghost shirt would protect them from bullets. The Ghost Dance movement came to a tragic end on the Pine Ridge Reservation when army troops killed nearly three hundred men, women, and children in a massacre at Wounded Knee in 1890.

Native American Dress in the Twenty-first Century

Native Americans have not abandoned traditional dress, but it has changed to make use of modern technology and to reflect changes in Native American culture. Traditional dress is time consuming to make, and leather garments are not as comfortable to wear in hot or very cold weather as clothing made of cloth. However, traditional leather garments decorated with beads and quills are still worn during Native American ceremonies and powwows. The feathered dance bustle and porcupine guard hair roach worn by men originated on the Great Plains. Fringed silken shawls are worn by leather- and cloth-clad women to dance the Fancy Dance, which is more flamboyant than traditional women's dances. Pendleton blankets are given as tribute to honored tribal members and as thanks for special favors granted to individuals. Jingle dresses that include tinklers that are often made of tobacco

American Indian powwow dancer. Photo by Clayton Wolt. Courtesy North Dakota Tourism.

can lids bent into a cone and hung from thongs long enough to cause them to jingle against one another are also part of modern Great Plains dance dress. Men's grass dance outfits are also a modern phenomenon. These consist of cotton shirts and trousers that are trimmed with brightly colored yarn fringes that sway with the dancer's movements.

Quillwork is still practiced by skilled craftswomen who work to pass this craft on to the younger generations. Beadwork has grown even more complex because Native Americans have leisure time to devote to creating beadwork masterpieces, including beaded vests, moccasins, leggings, dresses, shirts, and cradle boards. Although some traditional leather tanning still exists, most leathers used by Native Americans are purchased from leather suppliers who sell domestic and imported leathers.

U.S. ARMY ON THE PLAINS

The first army posts were established on the Great Plains during the period in which migrants were traveling the Oregon Trail to get to places farther west since the Plains was still considered inhospitable to farming. Some of the earlier military posts were actually fur-trading posts, such as Fort Laramie, which was built

Buffalo Soldiers

Among the most distinctive soldiers on the northern Plains were African Americans known as Buffalo Soldiers who made up the Ninth and Tenth Cavalries and the Twenty-fourth and Twenty-fifth Regiments of infantry organized just after the Civil War. They were known as Buffalo Soldiers because the Native Americans thought that their hair resembled the curly coats of buffalos. The men accepted the name as a badge of honor and even used the buffalo as part of their regimental insignia. Much of the Ninth and Tenth Cavalries' service took place on the northern Plains, where their charge was to guard stagecoaches and survey parties. Another important group was the Indian Scouts, who were Native Americans recruited to serve the army in the West and usually wore a combination of army dress and Native American dress.

in 1834 by fur traders and sold to the U.S. government in 1849 to serve as an army post to protect and assist migrants on the Oregon Trail. It is located in eastern present-day Wyoming, and the site is now a museum that shows how life was lived on army posts in the late nineteenth century. Fort Kearny was also established on the Oregon Trail south of the Platte River in present-day Nebraska in 1848. Two forts were built in present-day Kansas to protect the Santa Fe Trail, Fort Leavenworth in 1827 and Fort Larned in 1859. Once Euro-American settlers began to establish farms and ranches on the Great Plains, forts were established to keep the Native Americans on reservations, not an acceptable solution for tribes accustomed to following migrating herds of buffalo. Not surprisingly, there were many clashes between the army and Native American warriors who resisted this new order. Forts that were built on the northern Plains to control the "Indian problem" included Fort Rice, built in 1864 in present-day North Dakota, and Fort Robinson, built in 1874 in present-day Nebraska and still open to visitors, who can tour the buildings and grounds. Fort Sill was established on the southern Plains in present-day Oklahoma in 1869. These were the principal forts, although many others were built and eventually abandoned.

The soldiers who lived in the forts came from a variety of backgrounds. Some were recent immigrants to America and found that army life provided them with the opportunity to work and to see new country. Others were career army personnel who had fought in the Civil War. Still others joined the army as a means of making a living for themselves and their families.

Early Army Uniforms

In spite of the fact that Great Plains weather could reach 120 degrees during the summer and 60 degrees below zero during the winter, the War Department was loath to make changes in the uniform regulations since there were still stores of uniforms after the Civil War even though the standard uniform was not suited for these extreme conditions. In addition, contractors often cut corners during the Civil War, and the quality of fabrics, cut, and construction were not suited to the rigors of frontier use. To compound the problem, supplies were harder to get because of poor supply routes and distance from suppliers. The hats that had been developed for the cavalry were despised because they blew off easily and got in the way of the men's rifles. Forage caps were preferred since they were easier to wear on the windy Plains. The heavy-skirted frock coats that were regulation dress were put aside for loose fatigue sack coats since they accommodated physical motion and were cooler to wear in the heat of the Plains summer than the frock coats.

Blouses made of lightweight wool (what would be called shirts today) were even more practical for the work done at forts on the Great Plains. Soldiers wore flannel shirts and drawers under their blue uniforms. Most soldiers modified clothing to make it more comfortable—the drawers in particular were often cut to knee length. During very cold weather, men wore as many layers as they could and still move, and many men bought their own nonregulation buffalo-hide coats to keep as warm as possible. The army did not provide special winter headgear, so soldiers devised a number of ways to keep their heads warm, including tying the overcoat cape over their heads as a hood. Unfortunately, this reduced the needed layers over the body, but it prevented the ears from freezing. Often men bought their own fur or woolen caps with earflaps or made their own earflaps to be worn with forage caps. The quartermaster general did not include gloves as part of winter wear for troops stationed on the Plains, so frostbitten fingers were often a reality of Great Plains service. Soldiers pulled their cuffs over their hands or bought or made their own mittens. The best mittens were made of fur, buffalo hide being the most common, and had wide gauntlets to accommodate the bottom of the coat sleeves.

Soldiers wore regulation uniforms at the fort but were free to adapt their clothing for the conditions they found in the field. Consequently, they sometimes wore cotton shirts with their wool campaign blouses that could be easily removed during the summer months

Uniform and Dress of the Army of the United States.

(G.O. No. 31 G.G.O. 1851.)

Coat for Commission Officers.

1. All officers shall wear a frock-coat of dark blue cloth, the skirt to extend from two-thirds to three fourths of the distance from the top of the hip to the bend of the knee; single-breasted for Captains and Lieutenants; double-breasted for all other grades.
2. FOR A MAJOR GENERAL—two rows of buttons on the breast, nine in each row, placed by threes; the distance between each row, five and one-half inches at top, and three and one-half inches at bottom; stand-up collar, to rise no higher than to permit the chin to turn freely over it, to hook in front at the bottom, and slope thence up and backward at an angle of thirty degrees on each side, making the total opening in front an angle of sixty degrees; cuffs two and one-half inches deep, to go around the sleeves parallel with the lower edge, and to button with three small buttons at the under seam; pockets in the folds of the skirts; with one button at the hip, and one at the end of each pocket, making four buttons on the back and skirts of the coat, the hip button to range with the lowest buttons on the breast; collar and cuffs to be of dark blue velvet; lining of the coat black.
3. FOR A BRIGADIER GENERAL—the same as for a Major General (par. 2.) except that there will be only eight buttons in each row on the breast, placed in pairs.

For Enlisted Men.

11. The uniform coat for all enlisted men shall be a single-breasted frock of dark blue cloth, with a skirt extending one-half the distance from the top of the hip to the bend of the knee.[7]

when temperatures often were above one hundred degrees during the day but could drop into the forties at night. Since soldiers carried only one blanket into the field, the woolen blouse provided an extra layer of warmth when needed.

Description of the Cold

Dr. Henry R. Tilton, an Army doctor, described the clothing he wore as protection against temperatures of forty degrees below zero: "I wore two pair of woolen socks, buffalo moccasins and leggings, and buffalo overshoes; 2 pr drawers, one of them buckskins; 2 pr pants, one made out of blankets; 5 shirts, one of them buckskin and one made out of blanket; a coat and buffalo overcoat; blanket cap, which would cover the face when necessary; a comforter; and buckskin gloves inside of blanket line buckskin mittens—and yet, on two days when marching in the face of a snow and wind storm, I felt as if there were no blood in my body."[8]

Redesigned Uniforms and New Problems

Finally, in 1872, new uniforms were authorized and distributed to the army, at least to enlisted men, since officers had to purchase their own uniforms. In most ways the uniforms resembled earlier ones, but there were some additions. One was the folding campaign hat that had been designed specifically for Great Plains use. It had a wide brim that was cut in an oval shape so it could be folded and fastened up at the sides or worn down to provide protection from the sun. Unfortunately, it was black, so it absorbed the sun's rays, and it had no ventilation holes to dissipate heat, contrary to recommendations. Furthermore, the hat did not stand up to frontier wear and became useless after a matter of weeks in the field. The fatigue blouse was of a completely new design since it had a pleated front and skirt designed to go over two to three layers of underclothing or to be worn alone. Bag pockets were concealed within the pleats, one at the breast and two in the skirt. The blouse was available in lined and unlined versions. The only change made to pants was to add a saddle piece in the seat and the inside legs to provide another layer of fabric for wear and comfort. The pleated blouse was a failure since the pleat flapped in the wind and snagged easily, so men often stitched down the pleats, changing its function back to a blouse with no pleats. Unfortunately, underwear designed for conditions in the West was not a part of the new uniform regulations.

In 1873, the army considered the need for warm footgear when it issued overshoes made of buffalo hide with the hairy side in. These worked just fine for foot soldiers during very cold, dry conditions but became soggy in wet conditions. Furthermore, they did not fit into stirrups and thus were useless for mounted men. It was not until the winter of 1876 that below-the-knee buffalo coats made double breasted with high collars were authorized for northern Plains use. In 1878, additional outer clothing was developed for Great Plains conditions. The most important was a blanket-lined overcoat, but it was sent only to soldiers posted north of forty-two degrees latitude, including most of Wyoming, Nebraska, and the Dakotas but not southern Wyoming, Southern Nebraska, and all of Kansas and Oklahoma, which still had temperatures below zero and high winds during the winter months. A way that the quartermaster general devised to reduce costs was to add a second cape to the caped overcoat already in use by the army. Even these coats did not adequately protect men from the bitterly cold conditions on the Great Plains, and they were still forced to invent other ways of keeping themselves warm. Soldiers who could afford it bought their own buffalo-hide coats; those who lacked money but had sewing skills made their own. The army provided knitted wool gloves, but these fell far short of keeping hands warm. Again, men bought or made warm fur or wool mittens and headgear.

Plenty Horses, an Ogallala man, and two U.S. soldiers standing in front of a cannon in a military camp near Pine Ridge, South Dakota, 1891. Courtesy of the Library of Congress.

Uniforms Finally Adapted to Climate

New garments were added after numerous complaints were made by soldiers who served on the frontier. One of the first was a new campaign hat that was made of XXX (triple-X) wool (better quality wool than that used for the folding hat) and had a ventilated crown but was still the same sun-absorbing black. A new blouse that had no waistline seam or pleats and was available lined or unlined replaced the hated pleated blouse. Shirts with a breast placket were made in two weights to serve the needs of troops in cold as well as hot weather. All-wool stockings made fourteen inches tall helped to keep northern Plains troops a little warmer, but the best thing to happen was that special winter outerwear was developed for use on the Great Plains. The first such outerwear consisted of sealskin hats with earflaps, back cape, and visor and gloves that had gauntlets at least five inches tall to accommodate the sleeves of the coat. Muskrat caps designed like the sealskin caps and muskrat gloves lined in lamb's fleece and with gauntlets lined in flannel were authorized in 1878.

Cavalry service uniforms changed from blue to olive drab in 1898, a color that was more comfortable for soldiers on the Great Plains since the lighter olive drab color did not absorb heat as readily as dark blue. During World War II, Fort Robinson, located in western Nebraska, became the nation's largest K-9 training center where dogs were trained as guards, sentries, scouts, and messengers. Heavily padded garments were used as protection from the bites that were part of the training regimen. German prisoners of war were also sent to Fort Robinson during World War II. They wore cotton pants and sack coats marked with P.W. and the prisoners' names painted on the front and a large P.W. painted on the back. These uniforms can be seen in museums at Fort Robinson and at Fort Riley near Junction City, Kansas.

IMMIGRANTS

Although the immigrants who traveled through the Great Plains on the Oregon and Santa Fe Trails did not remain there, they had to consider conditions on the Plains as they planned what kinds of things to take with them. Clothing was certainly important for such comfort as was possible on hot, dusty or cold, muddy drives. In addition, clothing was sometimes important for survival as people crossed the Plains, where the weather was often very changeable. Most of the wagon trains left St. Joseph or Independence, Missouri, in April, about when grass began to green on the Plains but also when winter had not necessarily loosened its grip. Travelers had to be prepared with clothing to handle the tail end of winter and the heat of summer encountered before they left the Plains. Handbooks listed the kinds of clothing needed for the journey, including underwear, outerwear, and overcoats. Men were advised to have flannel shirts, woolen trousers, woolen undershirts, thick drawers, woolen and cotton stockings, and stout shoes. Rainproof ponchos, broad-brimmed hats, and lined coats were among the clothing recommended. Less advice was available for women, so many of them relied on the conventions in dress of more settled places. At the beginning of the trip, some women wore "traveling dress" that consisted of styles that were made of dark-colored woolen or worsted fabrics and were cut somewhat more simply than "at-home" dresses. However, they were floor length, designed to be worn on smooth floors or paved sidewalks, and not suited for walking on Great Plains bunch-grass prairies or dusty trails. Most women soon abandoned this confining costume and wore cotton work dresses that provided ease of movement. Nearly all the women began the trip in long skirts that soon were worn to ankle length or shorter by friction on the ground or by being caught in cactus and sagebrush. Some women shortened their skirts to above the ankle so they could walk over uneven ground without lifting their skirts to keep from tripping. A very few women decided to wear the new bloomer costume consisting of knee-length skirts and pantalets of matching fabric. Although this would seem to be very practical clothing for the arduous journey, propriety nearly always reigned supreme, and even women who had bloomer costumes with them wore them only when their other clothing was not fit to wear. Since pale skin was valued as a symbol of upper-class status, women and girls wore sunbonnets with very deep brims and long capes in the back to protect them from the sun's rays. Shawls were the most common form of outer wrap for women during the 1850s, but they also had lined coats to protect them from the cold. Sturdy shoes were necessary in a place that had plenty of hazards for bare feet, especially low-growing cactus found on the Plains.

Children who traveled the trails west wore cotton clothing that in another place might have been considered play clothing. Although illustrators whose work appeared in *Frank Leslie's Monthly* and *Harper's Weekly* often pictured children bare-footed, the photographic record shows that children, like their parents, wore sturdy shoes or boots to protect them from Great Plains hazards. Boys wore hats and girls wore bonnets to protect them from the relentless sun of the Great Plains.

SETTLERS

Settlers began to establish homes on the eastern edges and along some rivers in the Great Plains before the Civil War, but settlement increased because of the Homestead Act, enacted in 1862, which made it possible for citizens or intended citizens to select 160 acres of surveyed but unsettled land and gain title to it after five years of residence. Settlement increased after the war since Civil War veterans could count their service toward the residence requirement. Great Plains conditions soon proved that 160 acres were not sufficient, and the Timber Culture Act of 1873 made 480 acres available. In 1904, 640-acre homesteads were permitted in the Sand Hills of Nebraska, and finally, in 1916, full sections were opened for homesteaders on the Great Plains. The free land available on the Great Plains brought people from all over the world, but principally Europeans and Americans from the East and Midwest, to build new homes. A few immigrants brought their own traditions of dress with them, but since most were anxious to become truly American, they soon abandoned their traditional clothing and wore clothing that was fashionable. There is no doubt that functional dress was important, but since the ability to buy and wear clothing in the latest styles has long been an indicator of economic success, the fashionable clothing seen in many photographs of Great Plains families was very common.

Women

Fashionable clothing changed in style during the last half of the nineteenth century when settlers made their way into the Great Plains, but some of the characteristics of dress remained constant. The clothing for both men and women consisted of many layers, perhaps appropriate for the winter months but not for hot, dry summers. Women were dressed, from the skin out, in calf-length drawers in cotton or linen and loose-fitting, cap-sleeved chemises slightly longer than the drawers. Next were stockings that were supported by garters that were fastened above the knee. A corset, considered necessary for propriety, was worn over a chemise and drawers and drawn tight. Then at least two nearly floor-length petticoats were worn over corsets, along with corset covers that covered the top of chemises and corsets. Over all this went the garments meant to be seen, one- or two-piece dresses and shoes and other accessories that changed according to the dictates of fashion. Underclothing that supported the other clothing came and went. For a time, from the 1850s through the 1860s, women wore wide artificial crinolines, which are called hoopskirts today. During the 1870s and 1880s, a variety of different-shaped bustles rose and fell. Even corsets changed, forcing the body into a variety of shapes, but throughout this period, women who followed the dictates of fashion and propriety were encumbered by many layers of fabric.

Men

Men, too, suffered under confining layers, but they had more freedom of movement than women. Men wore drawers of cotton or wool that extended from waist to ankle with collarless, long-sleeved undershirts. Their stockings were calf or knee length and made of cotton or wool. Over that they wore collarless shirts that were usually cut quite full across the shoulders. Stiffly starched, removable collars were buttoned to the collar band. Sometimes removable cuffs were used as well. Woolen trousers were held up by braces that fit over the shoulders and were buttoned to the waistband at front and back. Matching vests buttoned over trousers and shirts and matching wool coats in skirted frock styles or looser sack styles were worn as top layers. Finally, men wore neckties, shoes, and hats to finish their fashionable appearance. Their clothing changed more slowly than the clothing worn by women, but fashion was still an influence.

Children

Children were not as encumbered as their parents were. They still wore layers, but the layers tended to be looser. Both boys and girls wore stockings held in place by suspenders that fit over their shoulders. Then they put on drawers that buttoned to sleeveless undershirts. Petticoats usually extended from the shoulder to below the knees, and dresses were worn over them. Little boys wore dresses until they were four or five years old, when they began to wear knee pants and shirts that were buttoned onto the pants. Little girls began to wear corsets by the time they were twelve, but corsets for even younger children were available and sometimes used. Children's fashions changed at about the same rate as those of clothes worn by their parents, girls' fashions changed more rapidly than boys' fashions.

Work Clothing

Functional clothing, within the limits of propriety, was also available. Women often wore cotton house dresses called Mother Hubbards that were made with no waistline seam and were gathered from a yoke at the shoulder. They usually came with matching belts that could be adjusted in size. These dresses were considered appropriate to be seen by family members or close friends, but were not to be worn in public places. Since they were loose in the waist, a woman could loosen her corset to more comfortably do the heavy housework that was the norm during that time. It is possible that some women did not wear corsets and the many layers of underclothing when they were doing heavy farm work, but proper women did not write of such things in their diaries or letters, so only speculation is possible about what they actually did.

Photographs of men wearing shirts and trousers held up by braces show that they discarded heavy layers when they needed ease of movement. There are even a very few pictures of men wearing trousers and knitted undershirts as they did heavy work. Men too had specialized work clothing. Levi Strauss developed riveted, canvas pants that were eventually made of more comfortable denim. Work shirts made of sturdy fabrics had sewn-on collars that were soft instead of stiffly starched. Men on the Great Plains probably imitated the soldiers who cut their drawers to knee length for use during the summer months, but again, this was not mentioned in letters, diaries, or reminiscences.

SPECIFIC RACIAL, ETHNIC, AND RELIGIOUS GROUPS

Exodusters

Among the first to settle the plains of Kansas after the Civil War were the Exodusters, who were former slaves headed by Benjamin Singleton (1809–1892). They bought part of the Cherokee reservation that was still part of Indian Territory and began the all Afro-American communities of Dunlap and Nicodemus. While they carried some traditions such as head wraps with them, these styles were soon abandoned as they dressed according to the fashions of the day, including corsets that were hot and uncomfortable and made it difficult to breathe. Some photographs of farm families show that older women wore work dresses and aprons and were uncorseted, but the younger women paid more attention to the styles dictated to women during the nineteenth century, even while going about their work on the farm. Although the men wore work shirts and trousers with braces or bib overalls to do their work, they wore frock coats, vests, and trousers with stiff-collared shirts when attending community functions. As with all people who strive to improve their economic status, dressing in fashionable clothing showed themselves and the world that they were successful.

Russian Germans

Many of the settlers who homesteaded on the Great Plains came from eastern Europe where economic hardship and changing political conditions caused them to seek new country. Among them were the Russian Germans, sometimes referred to as Volga Germans since so many of them had settled along the Volga River in southern Russia. During the eighteenth and early nineteenth centuries, many Germans from the northern part of Germany immigrated to Russia because Catherine the Great promised them land and was willing to allow them to practice their traditional culture. This meant that children learned German in school, young men could avoid military service, and they could practice their own religion. These promises were broken at the end of the nineteenth century, so many of these ethnic Germans decided to leave Russia. Since Germany was not really "home" anymore and there was free land available in the United States, many decided to immigrate to America. They brought little in the way of personal belongings since transporting goods by sea was very expensive, but they did bring trunks full of bedding and clothing as well as Bibles and some books. Their clothing marked them as new immigrants since the women wore head scarves called babushkas and the men wore jackets with straight fronts and high collars that were distinctly Russian in style. Young men and women chose fashionable dress fairly quickly, but older men and women tended to retain the dress of their adopted Russian homeland where they had been living for four or five generations. Some older women of Russian German ancestry who live in Nebraska still wear babushkas when they appear in public places.

Norwegians

Another large ethnic group that settled the Great Plains consisted of subsistence farm families from Norway. They brought immigrant trunks full of things, including their folk dress as well as fashionable clothing they wore in their home country. They often wore a combination of the two, as shown by this 1880 description of a woman donning her clothing:

> Mother's dressing would go like this: first, next to the skin went a long bandage, wrapped tightly about the abdomen, cotton in summer, wool in winter. This was her corset, and she was never without it. Over that would go a clean white shift of sturdy cloth. Then a full tan cotton petticoat with a border of many colors around the bottom, red and green and brown. This was topped by a pretty white cotton petticoat with lace or embroidery at the bottom, about two or three yards around. Her dress of black alpaca with a tight-fitting waist and full skirt, tight-fitting sleeves, and a little black collar around the high neck, fastened with a black bone pin in the shape of a four-leaf clover. Black jet buttons closed the front and the sleeves.[9]

There were a few things that identified them as Norwegian. The practice of wearing aprons for dress occasions as well as for work remained part of Norwegian American culture when most women used them only for functional reasons. These aprons often included openwork embroidery or colorful embroidered patterns, but woven or printed aprons were used as well. Patterned neck scarves for women called "fortune scarves" were also a part of traditional Norwegian dress that was carried to the Great Plains. Some women continued to wear caps reminiscent of those they had worn in Norway long after they had gone out of fashion in America. Women wore brooches called sølje that were made of silver and had small dangles that sparkled with movement with their fashionable dress as well as chains presented to brides as part of traditional wedding dress. Although virtually all the photographs of Norwegian immigrants show them wearing fashionable dress, older women wore theirs without the body-shaping corsets considered necessary for decency by most women.

Men, too, retained some of the fashion of Norway. The most important feature was a style of beard worn long and without mustaches. They sometimes retained the standing collars that were part of traditional style on coats, vests, and jackets. Their vests often retained silver, brass, or pewter buttons that buttoned from waist to nearly chin height. Many men preferred wearing silk neck scarves without the stiffly starched collars that were part of American men's fashion during the nineteenth and early twentieth centuries. Men also continued to wear work smocks that were long, loose shirts with the lower part gathered to a deep yoke at both front and back. Some men wore soft, brimless caps typical of traditional Norwegian dress. Wooden shoes were sometimes retained by both men and women for dirty farm work, and hand-knitted stockings continued to be a tradition among Norwegians in America.

Children's clothing tended to be typical of the dress of American children, with the exception of colorful woven braids that were worn as neckties. Sometimes traditional clothing was used for baptisms or for important events like confirmations and holidays.

People of Norwegian descent began wearing their folk dress for festivals during the 1890s, when Norway struggled for freedom from Sweden that was finally won in 1905. This movement toward use of traditional Norwegian dress began in Norway, but it was soon adopted by those of Norwegian descent in America. The American interpretation of Norwegian traditional dress for women consisted of a red vest, white blouse with full leg-of-mutton sleeves, a long dark skirt with colorful ribbons sewn horizontally near the hem, and a white apron. Men wore white shirts and colored vests buttoned with bright metal buttons, knee pants, and knitted stockings. Children's clothing was similar to adult clothing, but little girls' skirts were below knee length rather than floor length. This form of festival dress has continued to change in Norway but has become fossilized in America; that is, the original clothing worn around 1900 in both Norway and America has remained static with little change into the present in America, while it has continued to change in Norway.

Swedes

Large numbers of Swedes settled the area around Lindsborg, Kansas, but they did not wear the folk dress that represented each parish once worn by their ancestors, but dress then in the fashion in Sweden as well as in the rest of Europe. Unlike their Norwegian neighbors, most of the Swedish immigrants were of the middle class rather than subsistence farmers. Although some customs such as a wedding crown made of brass, silver, or gold wire fashioned into beautiful shapes continued to be worn by Swedish brides, other forms of Swedish folk dress disappeared. However, during the twentieth century, people of Swedish descent from Lindsborg began to investigate their cultural past and reinstated their connection with Sweden with a midsummer celebration that falls on the summer solstice in June, the Svensk Hyllningsfest in October, and crowning Santa Lucia on the second Saturday of December.

Dancers wearing the folk dress of Sweden are part of the June and October events. Since folk dress had once marked the wearer as coming from a particular parish in Sweden, the residents of Lindsborg now go to great trouble to find out where their ancestors came from so they can wear appropriate traditional dress. In general, the dress for women consists of full-sleeved white blouses, full skirts that are midcalf to ankle length, vests, and aprons. There are variations in the styles of each of the garments and the headdresses that mark the wearers as coming from particular provinces in Sweden. Men's clothing generally consists of shirts and knee breeches worn with vests and gartered knee-length stockings, again with regional details. Most of the clothing worn on the Great Plains is not an exact copy of the clothing that represents the various provinces in Sweden today, for the folk dress of Sweden has changed with the times, whereas the costume worn in Lindsborg is a fossilized version that was worn in Sweden 150 years ago, even earlier than emigration to America.

Dress is also part of the Santa Lucia recognition in December, when fourth-graders in the elementary schools celebrate with white robes and artificial candles on a crown of holly. On the second Saturday of December, a high-school senior, selected from the Swedish dancers group at the high school, is crowned with a wreath having real candles that are lighted as part of a community celebration. This is a hybrid practice that resembles the crowning of beauty queens and prom queens in America, as well as reinterpreting the practice followed in Sweden where the youngest daughter wears the wreath on December 13 as she carries saffron-flavored buns to sleeping family members.

Hutterites

Groups of people who sought to practice their own religion in their own ways also settled the Great Plains. Among them were the Mennonites and a sect of Mennonites called Hutterites that believed in communality of property, which differentiated them from the Amish and the General Conference Mennonites. The Hutterites, named for Jakob Hutter (d. 1536), a Mennonite leader, immigrated from Europe to found three colonies in South Dakota during the 1870s. There are now many colonies of Hutterites on the Great Plains of the Dakotas and Montana. The communal nature of their belief system affected not only how they owned property but how they lived and dressed. Each member of the community was allotted a set amount of yardage from which to make clothing. This has resulted in styles of clothing, especially for women, that have remained nearly unchanged for generations. The women and girls wear polka-dotted scarves that are stiffly starched and dresses made of colorful flower prints, stripes, and plaids. The dresses consist of skirted jumpers worn over blouses with collars and short or long sleeves and nearly ever-present aprons. Although the fabric garments have changed very little for women, the shoes they wear today vary in style from running shoes to loafers. Slatted bonnets like those worn by pioneer women in the ninteenth century are still used when women spend time working in the sun.

While at one time men's shirts and pants were probably made at home, now men and boys wear ready-made plaid or printed shirts with black pants held up by braces, jackets, and hats that are black broad-brimmed cowboy hats except during the summer when light-colored straw cowboy hats are used. Boys sometimes wear caps with stiff, straight-sided crowns, much like those their ancestors wore in Russia. Expand-a-back, gimme caps often given as gifts to tractor-buying farmers are worn by boys in some Hutterite colonies. Men and boys wear loafers and laced work boots, and boys also wear running shoes. All married men have beards.

The fabrics used to make Hutterite clothing have changed over time. Women no longer wear fabrics made of natural fibers but purchase ready-made fabrics made of combinations of synthetic and natural fibers since Hutterite women, like most women, prefer easy-care clothing that requires little or no ironing. Men's shirts are purchased rather than made at home, and their

Hutterite Rules for Dress

Communalistic societies often have written regulations to make sure that everyone in the community is treated equally. This was certainly true for the Hutterites.

"The rule book specifies to the inch how much yardage each person shall have on the basis of his age. Ten-year-old boys shall have material for a jacket annually at the rate of 3 yards and 6 inches. Eleven-year-old boys shall be allotted 3 yards and 12 inches, and men over fourteen shall receive 4 yards. When someone is over-weight he shall have 9 additional inches. Clothing allotments change most dramatically when boys and girls become adults (fourteen years old in *Lehrerhof*). The rule book allows 9 yards of material for a girl's dress. It takes only about 5 yards to make a modern dress, but the traditional allotment is still passed out." (This was true in 1967, but the rules may have changed since then.)[10]

hats and caps are like their non-Hutterite neighbors' headgear—cowboy hats made of felt or synthetic straw and gimme caps. Shoes, particularly those worn by children, are flat-soled practical styles but are the same as those worn all over the Great Plains.

Other Immigrant Groups

Most of the immigrant groups who took up residence on the Great Plains could not be distinguished from those who had lived in America for generations. There may have been some subtle clues that showed their ethnic identity, but most dressed in fashionable clothing for community events and in functional work dress at home. It was not until the 1960s, when the struggle for civil rights by African Americans and Native Americans brought ethnic identity to the forefront, that people of European ancestry also began to search for their roots. Since dress is the most visible indicator of culture, folk dress was adopted by Americans who wanted to honor their cultural heritage as they reestablished their connections to their ancestors in folk celebrations. These groups include Scandinavians as well as Scots and Irish who also dress in their folk costumes, which consist of pleated plaid skirts, gillies (soft-soled laced shoes), and bonnets.

AMERICAN IMMIGRANTS

Along with settlers who came from Europe were people whose ancestors had lived in America for many generations. Many of them moved west to take advantage of free land not available to them in the East or Midwest. They came with the expectation that they would better their own lives and the lives of their children by establishing homes as farmers on the vast open country of the Great Plains. Some moved to establish businesses in the towns that grew on the Plains. These were storekeepers, bankers, and craftsmen who believed that they could make a better living in the West than they could in the places they left behind.

The farm women in the photographs of Great Plains settlers were usually wearing washable cotton dresses, practical for the Great Plains environment. They were often shown in aprons, as though they were interrupted in their work, but they did not let their standards of propriety fall—all were wearing corsets. The farm men were usually dressed in printed or striped shirts, since soil was less visible on patterned cloth, and in trousers supported by braces. Their pale foreheads and tanned cheeks and jaws show that they usually wore hats as they worked under the relentless sun but left their hats off for the photographs so their faces would be visible. Children were dressed in simple clothing. Little girls wore printed dresses and pinafores that covered all but the sleeves and collars of their dresses. Little boys wore shirts and trousers. It is interesting to note that the women are often dressed in more fashionable clothing than the men. It is as though they dressed up and called the men, both young and old, from the field so they could all have their pictures taken. Furthermore, young women wore more fashionable clothing than their mothers or grandmothers. Some families had time to put on their very best clothing to show the folks back home that they were indeed successful in their endeavors, but the pale foreheads of the men wearing their best clothing show that they too spent most of their days in the sun.

TOWN SETTLERS' DRESS TO THE 1960s

The settlers who lived in towns wore clothing that resembled the clothing worn by men in the same professions in eastern America and Europe that indicated their professions. Business clothing for bankers, lawyers, and doctors consisted of coats and trousers, vests and shirts with stiffly starched collars, and ties. Barbers, butchers, and storekeepers shed their coats but wore white aprons that could be easily washed. Men who worked as laborers wore clothing that resembled the farmers' dress, including hats—judging by pale foreheads and tanned cheeks in photographs taken of men who worked on the railroad. City marshals wore silver stars on their blue wool uniforms. Prostitutes were also part of Great Plains town life, and a remarkable feature of their dress is that they did not wear corsets over the chemises they wore in the photographs. They did wear their hair dressed very elaborately and wore shoes and stockings. Nearly every town on the Great Plains, even very small ones, had bands, and all the men wore uniforms. Baseball teams were also common, and they too wore uniforms to distinguish them from their rivals.

There are some important reasons why Great Plains settlers, even those who lived in remote areas, could dress in fashionable clothing. Perhaps the most important factor was rural free delivery by the postal service, since people could receive mail that included letters detailing the latest styles from their relatives back home and, even more important, magazines like *Godey's Lady's Magazine, Peterson's Magazine, Harper's Bazaar,* and the *Delineator,* a magazine put out by the Butterick publishing company that also produced sewing patterns. All included patterns so women could sew their own fashionable clothing. Secondly, *Montgomery Ward Catalog* after 1872 and *Sears, Roebuck Catalog* after 1886 brought information, as well as products, to Great Plains families. Both catalogs included practical clothing as well as some more fashionable clothing in addition to fabrics and findings such as buttons, thread, and trims needed for the most elaborate garments. Packages containing all the necessities for making functional as well as fashionable clothing were also carried to people on the railroads that crisscrossed the Great Plains and were delivered by the postal service.

Bib overalls were among the goods sold through the Montgomery Ward and Sears, Roebuck catalogs. They were first sold as carpenters' pants, but farmers appreciated their comfort and practicality and adopted them for farm use. By 1900, the photographs show more farmers wearing them since they were looser and more comfortable to wear in the summer heat of the Great Plains. Bib overalls became the preferred style for farm use by the 1930s, when several companies specializing in men's work clothing produced them. Classic bib overalls have bibs with specialized pockets for holding watches and pencils, as well as cigarette makings, including a pouch of tobacco and cigarette papers that were a common part of men's culture until manufactured cigarettes were less expensive and more available. Bib overalls are still in use in America's farming communities.

As times and culture changed in America as a whole, dress was altered to reflect these changes. In particular, the dress of women became looser and more comfortable in the 1910s and 1920s. Women were still expected to wear dresses that were modest, but skirts no longer dragged in the dirt as they went about their farm chores, and tight corsets were no longer part of women's dress. Some farm girls even wore boys' trousers and shirts even though it was still considered indecent for a girl to dress this way. During the Dust Bowl years of the Great Depression when families on the Great Plains suffered through terrible droughts as well as economic hardship, food came ahead of clothing. Luckily, flour, salt, and chicken feed came in cloth bags that were used for making some of the clothing needed by family members.

After World War II, many women adopted trousers as they did the physical work required of farm women, but

> ## Unwritten Rules for Girls
>
> Ann Marie Low had to follow the unwritten rules concerning dress, even during times of scarcity that happened during the Great Depression.
>
> "I wanted to wear my boy's shirt, pants, and boots I wore on the farm. Dad would not let me, saying it was bad enough that I wore boy's clothes at home; to go to town I must put on a dress and look respectable. I grumbled in my diary. 'When I grow up I'll wear pants all I want to!'"[11]

traditions die hard, and other women retained dress they considered "proper" female dress. They wore house dresses that were constructed more simply than the fashionable clothing they wore for public view. By the end of the 1960s, most Great Plains women wore trousers made of new, easy-to-care-for polyester for dress occasions and comfortable blue denim for functional purposes.

OCCUPATIONAL DRESS

Occupation affects dress. There are many specialized garments that have been created for specific occupations. Cowboys wear spurs, miners use hard hats, nurses wear clothing that can be easily washed. Some of the clothing was created for the sake of safety while others have practical purpose. Much of the clothing worn for occupational reasons was created because of a specific function. Other kinds of dress are made to make it easy to identify the position a person holds—like the uniform worn by a law enforcement officer.

Cowboys

The first cowboys on the Great Plains were not permanent inhabitants but drovers who were herding Texas cattle to railheads, first in Missouri, then, as the railroads were built farther west, to Kansas. Native Americans knew that the Plains had fertile grasslands, but farmers accustomed to the rich, green lands of the Midwest still considered them desert. It was not until the buffalo had been killed by hunters who used the hides for trade or who killed them to feed railroad builders that cattlemen began to realize that the Plains provided excellent grazing for cattle as well. Because cattle were simply turned loose to roam on the Plains, the occupation of cattle herder, or cowboy, as it is known today, developed. The first cowboys to live on the Great Plains were Texans who followed great herds north, but soon young men, mostly from the Midwest, saw the possibilities of adventure and joined them.

The dress of cowboys originated in the Southwest, where the environment required protective clothing. Chaps or chaparejos were the most distinctive garments added to protect cowboys from the thorny brush found there. Broad-brimmed hats and bandanas worn around the neck prevented sunburn, and high-heeled boots prevented a cowboy's foot from catching in the stirrup and trapping him to be dragged if he were thrown. Spurs were needed to goad his horse into action. This form of gear was set in tradition by the time cowboys occupied the Great Plains and was modified as the occupation spread north. During the period when great herds of longhorn cattle were driven to railheads, bandanas became essential for pulling over the nose and mouth to keep from breathing the dust churned up by the cattle. Firearms were needed to protect the herds from predators that often followed the herds and to turn stampeding cattle. Chaps were less necessary since the Plains did not have thorny brush, but they were used instead as windbreaks on cold, windy days, common on the Plains. Hats were modified since hats that were very broad brimmed blew off too easily. Cowboys preferred wearing woolen pants since they were more comfortable than stiff canvas or denim trousers available at the time and provided warmth needed much of the day. The shirts they wore were sturdy work shirts made to withstand the physical labor that was part of cowboy life. They usually added vests to provide another layer of warmth that could be easily removed as the temperature rose during the day. Vests also had pockets handy for holding cigarette papers and tobacco smoked by nearly every cowboy. Long underwear made of cotton flannel prevented chafing from the woolen trousers. Some cowboys wore leather wrist cuffs that protected their arms from rope burns.

Most of the drovers ended their work once the cattle were driven to the railheads, but when ranching became part of the Great Plains economy, cowboys were hired to keep track of the herds that wandered the unfenced grasslands. Cowboys were hired during the spring, when cattle were rounded up to castrate bull calves and brand the new calves, and in the fall, when all the cattle were rounded up so steers could be sent to market. Most returned home during the bitterly cold winter months, but those who stayed to open water holes and keep an eye on the cattle needed winter gear. Much of the winter clothing worn by cowboys resembled that worn by the army. They wore fur hats with earflaps and a back cape and wrist-length fur gloves and mitts, some of which were designed so that the right hand was a glove for handling reins and the left was a mitt that kept hands warmer. Buffalo coats were certainly desired, but if they were not available, blanket- and quilt-lined canvas coats were used instead. Wooly chaps were heavy, but the angora goatskin with hair left on provided a good layer to cut the wind and insulate the skin. Union suits that were combination long-sleeved tops and long-underwear bottoms were used along with heavy socks, and leather boots were worn under felt-lined overshoes. Knitted mufflers were sometimes added to keep cowboys warm.

After cowboy culture changed with the advent of barbed-wire fencing to keep cattle from roaming, there were new problems to contend with. During the winter, cattle no longer foraged for grass but were fed hay cut during the summer months. This meant that men had to venture out into the cold to pitch hay from haystack to wagon and from wagon to the ground where the cattle could reach it. This was heavy work that required some changes in winter clothing since it was dangerous to work up a sweat while pitching hay and then to ride back to the bunkhouse on an open hay wagon. A person could freeze on the way. The very heavy clothing was

Clothes from Sacks

Ann Marie Low also noted, "Purchases were usually only tea, coffee, yeast, baking soda, spices and flavoring, baking powder, fresh fruit if it could be afforded, gasoline and kerosene in barrels, and flour and sugar in hundred-pound sacks. Those sacks were useful. From them we made dishtowels, aprons, underwear, pillowcases, and even sheets."[12]

Two riders experience the best of cowboy life, sitting in the saddle, riding through the tall grass under a big, clear sky. Courtesy South Dakota Tourism.

replaced with flannel shirts and woolen thigh-length jackets that sometimes had quilted linings. Wool caps with earflaps and a cape that could be turned up for ventilation or worn down for warmth replaced fur caps. Cloth gloves replaced heavy fur gloves, but leather gloves or mittens were kept handy to put over the cloth ones once the hay was delivered. Felt overshoes remained to keep vulnerable feet from freezing.

Now ranchers feed their cattle huge round bails unrolled from a truck or tractor. Although they spend less time in the cold and the wind that are part of Great Plains winters, they still wear clothing to protect themselves. Down- or polyester batting-lined jackets are worn with synthetic-fleece-lined caps and gloves. Their feet are protected by batting-lined boots. They still wear long underwear, but it is likely to be made of silk or recycled plastic synthetic fibers, far beyond the imagination of nineteenth-century cowboys.

Cowgirls

There were very few "cowgirls" who rode the Great Plains, but they made an important mark on the history of women in the region. One of the first to document the work of cowgirls was Eve Cameron (1868–1928), who photographed women working cattle in western Montana during the 1890s and early twentieth century. Among these women were the Buckley sisters. Cameron's photographs show that they wore fringed leather skirts with shirts, coats, hats, boots, and gloves. This form of dress was common for cowgirls, along with divided skirts that had a modesty panel that buttoned over the front when bifurcation was not needed.

Two young women wearing trousers on a farm located near Casselton, North Dakota, circa 1935. Courtesy Institute for Regional Studies, NDSU Libraries, Fargo (457.1).

By the 1910s, more women were wearing trousers, but they were considered quite scandalous. Rodeo cowgirls began wearing trousers in the arena by the end of the 1920s, and by the 1930s, when movie stars were seen in trousers, more ranch women began wearing trousers as they rode on horseback and did their ranch chores.

Miners

There were some gold miners in the Black Hills that rise above the western borders of South Dakota and coal miners who mined the coal in underground and strip mines on the Plains. During the nineteenth century, their dress was typical of sturdy work clothing worn all over the United States. Those who were working placer mines that required the use of water added rubber boots and slickers to their store of clothing. Although mining activities slowed during the winter months, most men who dreamed of big strikes did not stop their work altogether. Miners who worked in underground mines often wore canvas overalls, made more durable by Levi Strauss when it added rivets to the stress points on what have become classic blue jeans. Because underground mines are warm, miners shed coats and shirts to long-sleeved underwear as their work dress. The first lighting for underground miners used candles inserted into candle holders with horizontal points that were shoved into the wall of the mine. These primitive lighting devices were used even after better forms of lighting became available. Safety lamps were developed in 1815 that were enclosed lanterns carried into the mine. By 1886, portable electric safety lamps were in use in underground mines, and, finally, electric cap lamps were developed in Scotland in 1909. This lamp had a bulb inside a casing that was attached to the cap and a wiring cord attached to an acid battery suspended by a belt. By the 1920s, hard hats with built-in lanterns came into being. Now coal miners working the open strip mines wear hard hats and hard-toed work boots, along with warm batting-lined coats, pants, and gloves during the winter months.

Oil

Oklahoma once was the center of oil production for the United States. The dress worn for oil exploration and development was not very different from the dress worn by other blue-collar workers. Oil workers wore work shirts, trousers or bib overalls or coveralls, broad-brimmed hats, and work boots. However, some safety gear was added. As early as the 1920s, gas masks were used in areas where gas settled in gullies. By World War II, hard hats were used by drillers and the men who worked near the drill rigs. Aluminized suits and hoods protected workers who put out petroleum fires. Familiar sights at gas stations from the 1920s through the 1960s were uniformed gas station attendants who dressed in khaki trousers and shirts and wore military-style hats with hard bills and soft, full crowns.

MODERN TIMES

Dress on the Great Plains today is not very different from the dress worn in the rest of the United States because Great Plains residents see the same programs on television and read the same magazines as people elsewhere and commonly travel outside the Plains. It is true that trends in fashion are accepted more slowly in some Great Plains communities than on the east and west coasts, but in spite of that, dress is influenced by the larger American culture that is immediately available through mass communication, mass marketing, and mass delivery systems. The Internet and numerous specialty catalogs make fashion available to all Americans at about the same time. An article of dress that originates in the Black Hills, located in South Dakota within the Great Plains, is jewelry made of Black Hills gold that is characterized by its pinkish color and is usually paired with gold that has its usual gold appearance. Black Hills gold jewelry is often fashioned into natural designs, including roses and leaves, that display the contrast in the two colors of the naturally occurring mineral.

Some Great Plains dress has been reinterpreted as popular fashions, such as bib overalls worn by hippies during the 1960s and 1970s. Cowboy chic is now a common element in American high fashion. Bankers and lawyers wear cowboy boots and western Stetson hats with their more conventional business suits. Full-skirted "broomstick" skirts characterized by tiers of wrinkled pleats are worn with blue chambray shirts, Navaho jewelry, and cowboy boots by women who have never stepped into a saddle. Gingham dresses styled with long sleeves and full skirts that also occasionally appear on fashion pages are reminiscent of the dresses worn by immigrants as they crossed the Great Plains on the Oregon Trail.

Sports, especially football, are often the most important form of entertainment on the Great Plains. The crowd and the football players at the nationally competitive University of Nebraska and the University of Oklahoma are dressed in a sea of red, the color of both schools. Rodeo, still important on the Plains, brings out contestants and viewers who wear tight blue jeans and western-cut shirts, big trophy buckles, high-heeled boots, and broad-brimmed cowboy hats. Gun sports are also important, and special clothing has been developed for hunting that not only is suited for the severe weather encountered on the Plains but also has special camouflage patterns for hunting waterfowl, birds, and deer in the Plains environments. Camouflage patterns such as "Shadow Grass," "Wetlands Camo," and "Snow Shadow" used for parkas, insulated bib overalls, and coveralls were developed for hunting wild animals and birds in a number of natural environments. Some gear is even named in a way that indicates its use for the Great Plains environment. One camouflage pattern is called "Open Country," and *Cabela's Catalog* from the Cabela's sporting goods company, headquartered in Sidney, Nebraska, includes a line of hunting gear called "Northern Flight."

RESOURCE GUIDE

Printed Sources

General References

Beck, Warren A., and Ynez D. Haase. *Historical Atlas of the American West*. Norman: University of Oklahoma Press, 1989.

Cole, George S. *Dictionary of Dry Goods*. Chicago: J. B. Herring Publishing Co., 1894.

Grafton, John. *The American West in the Nineteenth Century: 255 Illustrations from "Harper's Weekly" and Other Contemporary Sources*. New York: Dover Publications, 1992.

Lamar, Howard R., ed. *The New Encyclopedia of the American West*. New Haven, CT: Yale University Press, 1998.

Montgomery, Florence M. *Textiles in America, 1650–1870*. New York: W. W. Norton and Co., 1984.

Schlissel, Lillian. *Black Frontiers: A History of African American Heroes in the Old West*. New York: Aladdin Paperbacks, 1995.

Truettner, William H., ed. *The West as America: Reinterpreting Images of the Frontier, 1820–1920*. Washington, DC: Smithsonian Institution Press, 1991.

Dress and Culture

Hamilton, Jean. "Dress as a Cultural Sub-system: A Unifying Metatheory for Clothing and Textiles." *Clothing and Textiles Research Journal* 6, no. 1 (1987): 1–7.

McCracken, Grant. *Culture and Consumption: New Approaches to the Symbolic Character of Consumer Goods and Activities*. Bloomington: Indiana University Press, 1988.

Roach-Higgins, Mary Ellen, and Joanne Eicher. "Dress and Identity." *Clothing and Textiles Research Journal* 10, no. 4 (1992): 1–8.

Native American

Brown, Mark H., and W. R. Felton. *L. A. Huffman Photographer of the Plains: The Frontier Years*. New York: Bramhall House, 1955.

Catlin, George. *Letter and Notes on the Manners, Customs, and Conditions of North American Indians, Volumes 1 and 2*. 1844. Rpt. New York: Dover Publications, 1973.

Conn, Richard. *Circles of the World: Traditional Art of the Plains Indians*. Denver, CO: Denver Art Museum, 1982.

DeVore, Steven Leroy. *Beads of the Bison Robe Trade: The Fort Union Trading Post Collection*. Williston, ND: Friends of Fort Union Trading Post, 1992.

Ewers, John C. *Plains Indian History and Culture*. Norman: University of Oklahoma Press, 1997.

Hail, Barbara A. *Hau, Ko'la!* Bristol, RI: Haffenreffer Museum of Anthropology, 1980.

Horse Capture, George P. *Powwow*. Cody, WY: Buffalo Bill Historical Center, 1989.

MacGregor, Carol Lynn, ed. *The Journals of Patrick Gass*. Missoula, MT: Mountain Press Publishing Company, 1997.

Meade, Dorothy Cook. *Heart Bags and Hand Shakes: The Story of the Cook Collection*. Ann Lake, MI: National Woodland Publishing Company, 1994.

Neuman, Robert W. *The Sonota Complex and Associated Sites on the Northern Great Plains*. Lincoln: Nebraska State Historical Society, 1975.

Paterek, Josephine. *Encyclopedia of American Indian Costume*. New York: W. W. Norton and Co., 1993.

Penney, David W. *Art of the American Indian Frontier*. Seattle: University of Washington Press, 1992.

Schlesier, Karl H., ed. *Plains Indians, A.D. 500–1500*. Norman: University of Oklahoma Press, 1994.

Strickland, Rennard. *The Indians in Oklahoma*. Norman: University of Oklahoma Press, 1980.

Taylor, Colin F., and William C. Sturtevant. *The Native Americans: The Indigenous People of North America*. New York: Smithmark Publishers, 1996.

Walton, Ann T., John C. Ewers, and Royal B. Hassrick. *After the Buffalo Were Gone*. St. Paul, MN: Northwest Area Foundation, 1985.

Army

Billings, John D. *Hardtack and Coffee: The Unwritten Story of Army Life*. Lincoln: University of Nebraska Press, 1993.

Langellier, John P. *Sound the Charge: The U.S. Cavalry in the American West, 1866–1916*. Mechanicsburg, PA: Stackpole Books, 1998.

Leckie, Shirley Ann, ed. *The Colonel's Lady on the Western Frontier: The Correspondence of Alice Kirk Grierson*. Lincoln: University of Nebraska Press, 1989.

McChristian, Douglas C. *The U.S. Army in the West, 1870–1880: Uniforms, Weapons, and Equipment*. Norman: University of Oklahoma Press, 1995.

Quartermaster General of the Army. *U.S. Army Uniforms and Equipment, 1889, Specifications for Clothing, Camp, and Garrison Equipage, and Clothing and Equipage Materials*. Lincoln: University of Nebraska Press, 1986.

Steffen, Randy. *The Horse Soldier, 1776–1943*. Vol. 2, *The Frontier, the Mexican War, the Civil War, the Indian Wars, 1851–1880*. Norman: University of Oklahoma Press, 1978.

Migrants

Butruille, Susan G. *Women's Voices from the Western Frontier*. Boise, ID: Tamarack Books, 1995.

Jeffrey, Julie Roy. *Frontier Women: The Trans-Mississippi West, 1840–1880.* New York: Hill and Wang, 1979.

Marcy, Randolph B. *The Prairie Traveler.* Bedford, MA: Applewood Books, 1859/1993.

Peavy, Linda, and Ursula Smith. *Frontier Children.* Norman: University of Oklahoma Press, 1999.

Piekarski, Vicki, ed. *Westward the Women: An Anthology of Western Stories by Women.* Albuquerque: University of New Mexico Press, 1984.

Settlers

Budde, Gene, and Kathy Woitaszewski, eds. *Trails into Time: Images of Hall County [Nebraska].* Marceline, MO: D-Books Publishing, 1997.

Colburn, Carol Huset. "Norwegian Folk Dress in America." In *Norwegian Folk Art: The Migration of a Tradition*, ed. Marion John Nelson, 156–169. New York: Abbeville Press, 1995.

———. "'Well, I Wondered When I Saw You, What All Those New Clothes Meant': Interpreting the Dress of Norwegian-American Immigrants." In *Material Culture and People's Art among the Norwegians in America*, ed. Marion John Nelson, 118–155. Northfield, MN: Norwegian-American Historical Association, 1994.

Colburn, Carol Huset, and Laurann Gilbertson. "'Is the Old Shoemaker Still with You?' The Impact of Immigration on Footwear." Unpublished abstract.

———. "Worn with an Accent: Norwegian and Norwegian-American Clothing for Work." Parts 1 and 2, *Avisen* (February 2001): 39–41; (May 2001): 6–10.

Emmet, Boris, and John E. Jeuck. *Catalogues and Counters: A History of Sears, Roebuck and Company.* Chicago: University of Chicago Press, 1950.

Gibson, Arrell Morgan. *Oklahoma: A History of Five Centuries.* Norman: University of Oklahoma Press, 1980.

Gilbertson, Laurann. "To Ward off Evil: Metal on Norwegian Folk Dress." In *Folk Dress in Europe and Anatolia: Beliefs about Protection and Fertility*, ed. Linda Welters, 199–210. New York: Berg, 1999.

Hoobler, Dorothy, and Thomas Hoobler. *The Scandinavian American Family Album.* New York: Oxford University Press, 1996.

Hostetler, John A., and Gertrude Enders Huntington. *The Hutterites in North America.* New York: Holt, Rinehart and Winston, 1967.

Low, Ann Marie. *Dust Bowl Diary.* Lincoln: University of Nebraska Press, 1984.

Nelson, David T., ed. *The Diary of Elizabeth Koren.* New York: Arno Press, 1979.

Prewitt, Terry J. *German-American Settlement in an Oklahoma Town: Ecologic, Ethnic, and Cultural Change.* New York: AMS Press, 1989.

Redekop, Calvin. *Mennonite Society.* Baltimore, MD: Johns Hopkins University Press, 1989.

Shortridge, James R. *Our Town on the Plains: J. J. Pennell's Photographs of Junction City, Kansas, 1893–1922.* Lawrence: University Press of Kansas, 2000.

Wilkins, Robert P., and Wynona Huchette Wilkins. *North Dakota: A Bicentennial History.* New York: W. W. Norton and Co., 1977.

Williams, Patricia. "New World Bride." *Viking* 90, no.6 (June 1993): 20–21, 36, 37.

Wilson, Laura. *Hutterites of Montana.* New Haven, CT: Yale University Press, 2000.

Zempel, Solveig. *In Their Own Words: Letters from Norwegian Immigrants.* Minneapolis: University of Minnesota Press, 1991.

Cowboys

Beard, Tyler. *100 Years of Western Wear*. Salt Lake City, UT: Gibbs-Smith Publisher, 1993.

Dary, David. *Cowboy Culture*. Lawrence: University Press of Kansas, 1981.

Fletcher, Robert H. *Free Grass to Fences: The Montana Cattle Range Story*. New York: University Publishers, 1960.

Green, Donald E. *Panhandle Pioneer: Henry C. Hitch, His Ranch, and His Family*. Norman: University of Oklahoma Press, 1979.

Hoy, Jim. "The Coffeyville Boot." *Persimmon Hill* (Spring 1991): 15–19.

Rickey, Don. *$10 Horse, $40 Saddle: Cowboy Clothing, Arms, Tools, and Horse Gear of the 1880s*. Ft. Collins, CO: Old Army Press, 1976.

Rollinson, John K. *Pony Trails in Wyoming*. 1941. Rpt. Lincoln: University of Nebraska Press, 1988.

Turner, Patrick T. *Riding the High Country*. 1933. Rpt. Seattle, WA: Fjord Press, 1983.

Wilson, Laurel E. "'I Was a Pretty Proud Kid': An Interpretation of Differences in Posed and Unposed Photographs of Montana Cowboys." *Clothing and Textiles Research Journal* 9, no. 3 (1991): 49–58.

Cowgirls

Cleaveland, Agnes Morley. *No Life for a Lady*. 1941. Rpt. Lincoln: University of Nebraska Press, 1977.

Jordan, Teresa. *Cowgirls: Women of the American West*. Garden City, NY: Doubleday, 1984.

LeCompte, Mary Lou. *Cowgirls of the Rodeo*. Urbana: University of Illinois Press, 1993.

Lucey, Donna M. *Photographing Montana, 1894–1928: The Life and Work of Evelyn Cameron*. New York: Alfred A. Knopf, 1990.

Poirier, Thelma, ed. *Cowgirls: 100 Years of Writing the Range*. Edmonton, Alberta, Canada: Lone Pine Publishing, 1997.

Shirley, Gayle C. *More than Petticoats: Remarkable Montana Women*. Helena, MT: Falcon Publishing, 1995.

Van Cleve, Barbara. *Hard Twist: Western Ranch Women*. Santa Fe: Museum of New Mexico Press, 1995.

Miners

Gardner, A. Dudley, and Verla R. Flores. *Forgotten Frontier: A History of Wyoming Coal Mining*. Boulder, CO: Westview Press, 1989.

Statham, I.C.F. *Coal Mining*. New York: Philosophical Library, 1956.

Young, Otis E., Jr. *Western Mining*. Norman: University of Oklahoma Press, 1970.

Oil

Conoco Oil Company. *Conoco: The First One Hundred Years*. New York: Dell Publishing Co., 1975.

Knowles, Ruth Sheldon. *The First Pictorial History of the American Oil and Gas Industry, 1859–1983*. Athens: Ohio University Press, 1983.

Phillips Petroleum Company. *Phillips: The First 66 Years*. Bartlesville, OK: Phillips Petroleum Company, 1983.

Organizations and Web Sites

Buffalo Bill Historical Center
720 Sheridan Avenue
Cody, WY 82414
Phone: 307-587-4771
www.bbhc.org (accessed July 2003)

National Cowboy and Western Heritage Museum
1700 Northeast 63rd Street
Oklahoma City, OK 73111
Phone: 405-478-2250
www.nationalcowboymuseum.org (accessed July 2003)

National Park Service
www.nps.gov/index.htm (accessed July 2003)

Includes information about its activities and exhibits as well as an index to the holdings of the Donald C. and Elizabeth M. Dickinson Research Center.

Kansas

Kansas State Historical Society
6425 SW Sixth Avenue
Topeka, KA 66615
Phone: 785-272-8681
www.kshs.org/ (accessed July 2003)

The emphasis is on the Kansas State Historical Society Museum in Topeka, but links are provided to the Web pages of related organizations. Provides information about current and upcoming exhibitions and research resources.

Lindsborg, Kansas
www.lindsborg.org (accessed July 2003)

Celebrates its Swedish heritage through Midsummer's Day on the third Saturday in June, Svensk Hyllningsfest on the third weekend in October in odd-numbered years, and Lucia Fest on the second Saturday in December.

McPherson, Kansas
www.mcphersonks.org (accessed July 2003)

Scottish Festival takes place at the end of September each year.

Nebraska

American Historical Society of Germans from Russia
631 D Street
Lincoln, NE 68502-1199
www.ahsgr.org (accessed July 2003)

This society has an archive research center that includes photographs and printed sources, a museum of buildings built by Germans from Russia, and an exhibition of some costumes.

Museum of the Fur Trade
6321 Highway 20
Chadron, NE 69337

Phone: 308-432-3843
E-mail: museum@furtrade.org
www.furtrade.org (accessed July 2003)

This museum, erected on the site of the Bordeaux trading post, exhibits artifacts that represent the history of the fur trade in North America.

Nebraska State Historical Society
PO Box 82554
1500 R Street
Lincoln, NE 68501
www.nebraskahistory.org (accessed July 2003)

The easy-to-use Web site provides a comprehensive listing of state historical sites and research resources.

Sturr Museum of the Prairie Pioneer
3133 West Highway 34
Grand Island, NE 68801
Phone: 308-385-5316
www.stuhrmuseum.org (accessed July 2003)

The museum has exhibitions that show the material culture of the various ethnic groups that settled Grand Island and the nearby countryside.

North Dakota

Fort Union
Buford Route
Williston, ND 58801
Phone: 701-572-9083
www.nps.gov/fous/ (accessed July 2003)

An authentically reconstructed trading post of the American Fur Company, 1829–c. 1867, that includes a trading room and museum.

North Dakota State Historic Sites
612 East Boulevard Avenue
Bismarck, ND 58505-0830
Phone: 701-328-2666
www.state.nd.us/hist/sitelist.htm (accessed July 2003)

The Web site lists the fifty-six historic sites administered by the State Historical Society of North Dakota. The sites include archeological sites such as the Knife River Villages as well as a reconstruction of Fort Buford, a nineteenth-century army post. Links are provided for historic sites that have Web pages.

Oklahoma

Oklahoma Historical Society, *The Encyclopedia of Oklahoma History and Culture*
www.ok-history.mus.ok.us/enc/ENCINDEX2.htm (accessed July 2003)

This Web site links to other Web sites about Oklahoma history and culture. It is easy to use since logical categories such as "American Indian" and "Military" are used to help users find information.

South Dakota

South Dakota State Historical Society
900 Governors Drive
Pierre, SD 57501-2217
Phone: 605-773-3458
www.sdhistory.org/ (accessed July 2003)

The Web site provides information about exhibits at the State Museum and links to other historic sites and museums in South Dakota.

FILM AND THEATER

Ronald W. Wilson

"Toto, I don't think we're in Kansas anymore." From the viewer's perspective Dorothy's observation in *The Wizard of Oz* (Victor Fleming, 1939) seems to be an unnecessary statement of the obvious. The film's sepia-toned opening sequence clearly sets it apart spatially from the vibrant Technicolor landscape of the fantasy world of Oz itself. Along with the color scheme, additional visual codes—the farmhouse, the flat landscape, and the tornado—let the viewer recognize the cultural geography as that of a Plains state. At the end of the film, Dorothy's wish to go home, "There's no place like home," provides an even larger perspective for the spectator who has been drawn into the narrative and whose "home" may be in any region within or without the United States. Granted, *The Wizard of Oz* only superficially involves Kansas, but this film has become a cultural icon associated, for better or worse, with the state of Kansas. Likewise, when the phrase "America's Heartland" is used, it can stand for either the Great Plains or the Midwest region of the United States, depending on where it is used. At different times in history the Great Plains has been referred to as "The Great Desert," "The Great American Desert," and "Indian Territory." In film, the image is closely associated with many westerns that depict the settlement of the region, and the barrenness of the landscape is used metaphorically in many contemporary films.

Frederick C. Luebke, in an article titled "Regionalism and the Great Plains: Problems of Concept and Method," suggests a means for studying regionalism that can be applied to film. Luebke states that "Regions are therefore best conceptualized in terms of the interplay between environment and culture; they are best described and analyzed through appropriate comparisons in time, space, and culture." "Fruitful studies of the Great Plains (or any other region), he adds, "can emerge from analyses that are based on the interaction between environment and culture; regional studies should be found on the complex interrelationships between the people and the land they live on." The proposed method is based on a tripartite grouping: temporal, spatial, and cultural. According to Luebke, temporal refers to time or the history of the region, which is the study of change over time. Geography concerns the spatial relationships of the region. Culture integrates these into a sociohistorical concept of the region and its inhabitants.[1]

Though Luebke does not refer to film in his article his concept is applicable to this medium. A study of the temporal relationship to a particular region would address the way the region's history has been represented in film. In many respects, this seems to be the simplest approach. Yet it is also necessary to look at how that temporal relationship has been depicted over time. For instance, from *Dark Command* (1940) to *Ride with the Devil* (1999), the filmed history of the raid on Lawrence, Kansas, in 1863 has represented the figure of William Quantrill in differing aspects. Likewise, the depiction of the Plains Indians has changed considerably during the one hundred years of filmed history. Any temporal study of the films of a region must take this into account. Various important figures who were born in the region and whose lives have provided film biographies include Will Rogers (*The Story of Will Rogers*, Michael Curtiz, 1952) and Buster Keaton (*The Buster Keaton Story*, Sidney Sheldon, 1957). These films likewise provide a temporal context for showing how the region of the Great Plains was interpreted because of its historical significance.

In analyzing the spatial relationship to the region, films that utilize the landscape and geographic landmarks for specific purposes should be taken into account. The change in spatial relationships can also be accounted for in film. For example, in *North by Northwest* (1959), Alfred Hitchcock uses the location of Mount Rushmore, South Dakota, for a specific purpose in the film's narrative and also in the film's artistic concept. That choice was a specific one, but it also is in keeping with other thrillers by the director that utilize unique landmarks, such as the Statue of Liberty in *Saboteur*, the Royal Albert Hall in *The Man Who Knew Too Much*, and the British Museum in *Blackmail*. The directors of films such as *Badlands* and *Paper Moon* use on-location photography for specific creative reasons. The flat landscape of Kansas was a choice that was made in order to represent character relationships to the landscape in *Paper Moon*. Likewise, the bleak deterministic landscape in *Badlands* adds considerably to the mood and tone of Terence Malick's film in its depiction of the Starkweather-Fugate murder spree. A region is a geographic fact; the way a filmmaker uses the landscape of that region is determined by creative choices in order to produce a desired visual effect. At the beginning of his article, Luebke states, "American scholars have used the concept of regionalism to organize their thinking about certain aspects of national experience for many decades."[2] This can also apply equally to filmmakers who have "organized their thinking/filming" around regionalism when it concerns the creative process of cinematic art.

The use of cultural relationships comes into play when a filmmaker draws on more culturally shared conventions and norms of a particular region. Often this involves connotative (implied) rather than denotative (explicit) meanings. Alexander Payne's *About Schmidt* (2002), for instance, is located and filmed in Nebraska. Louis Begley's novel of the same name is set in New York. Payne, a native Nebraskan himself, relocated the narrative in order to take advantage of certain cultural expectations and meanings that he wanted to convey. The musical *Oklahoma!* (Fred Zinnemann, 1955) by Richard Rodgers and Oscar Hammerstein II, set in the Oklahoma Territory in 1907, is a portrait of the culture of settlers in that territory on the eve of statehood. The narrative and music play with cultural meanings specific to the region, for example, with songs such as "Everythin's up to Date in Kansas City" and the title song, "Oklahoma!" which was adopted from the musical to become the state song. An additional example of the use of cultural meaning in a film is in the apocalyptic made-for-television film *The Day After* (Nicholas Meyer, 1983), which details the effects of a nuclear bombing of Lawrence, Kansas. The heartland of America, rather than a major metropolitan center such as New York or Washington, D.C., is chosen as a target site in order to convey a stronger sense of the idea of "Americanness" and the threat to the nation as a whole. If an attack can occur in the "heart" of America, it can occur anywhere at any time.

Film will be discussed in the context of three primary areas: temporal, spatial, and cultural, with an examination of how each has been utilized in films about the Great Plains region. The temporal section will examine the history of the region as it has been depicted in film and the historical context for films set in the Great Plains from the Plains Indian Wars to the Great Depression. Filmmakers have concerned themselves with the history of the region in different ways. Historical events and persons from Quantrill to Will Rogers have enriched the celluloid history of the Plains region. The films will be examined chronologically within their respective historical time frame. How the geographic space of the region has been explored in film will be examined as well. Film examples will include *North by Northwest* (1959), *Badlands* (1973), and *Paper Moon* (1973). The cultural relationship to the region will be analyzed with regard to such films as *Paper Moon*, *Oklahoma*, and *About Schmidt*. Theater within the region and how the region is reflected in its dramatic literature will also be considered. The work of William Inge, both plays and film (*Bus Stop*, *Picnic*, *Splendor in the Grass*) will constitute the major focus. Both theater and film festivals in the region will be briefly discussed, and their importance to the culture of the area of the Great Plains will be detailed. Many filmmakers and performers were born in the Great Plains, and the region can be seen to have influenced their work. These too will be considered.

In defending his use of the terms "myth" and "symbol" in the preface to his seminal work *Virgin Land: The American West as Symbol and Myth*, Henry Nash Smith stated, "I use the words to designate larger or smaller units of the same thing, namely an intellectual construction that fuses concept and emotion into an image. The myths and symbols with which I deal have the further characteristic of being collective representations rather than the work of a single mind. I do not mean to raise the question whether such products of the imagination accurately reflect empirical fact. They exist on a different plane. But as I have tried to show, they sometimes exert a decided influence on practical affairs."[3] The historical and cultural significance of the Great Plains has exerted a "decided influence" on how the region has been represented in film and theater. Whether it is in a film such as *The Doolins of Oklahoma* (1949) or even *The Wizard of Oz* (1939), the region of the Plains states has become empowered with a significance that has been accumulated from numerous "myths" and "symbols" inherent to it.[4] These myths are reiterated time and again for specific purposes in order to designate something of importance to the creative work at hand. The historical, geographic, and cultural relationships between the inhabitants and the region of the Great Plains are evidenced in the ways both film and theater have utilized them.

HISTORY OF THE GREAT PLAINS ON SCREEN

The history of the Great Plains region has contributed to the rich film history of the area. After the Louisiana Purchase of 1803, a major portion of which consisted of the future Plains states (Oklahoma, Kansas, Nebraska, and North and South Dakota), the land mass between the one hundredth meridian and the Rocky Mountains became the starting point for settlement trails westward. It was also the land crisscrossed by cattle drives as well as transcontinental railroads. The Great Plains in film is greatly influenced by its historical heritage and its association with the hardships endured by its inhabitants. This history covers the period between the American Civil War and the Oklahoma land rush. As Peter Stanfield states, "The frontier myth is formed through an understanding of American history predicated on the idea of westward migration as the defining principle of American exceptionalism."[5] The concept gained acceptance through Frederick Jackson Turner's seminal work "The Significance of the Frontier in American History," first delivered as a lecture in Chicago in 1893. According to Turner, the various phases of frontier expansion contributed to the development of American democracy, as well as the American character. Turner viewed the frontier areas as regions that witnessed different phases of historical change, which contributed to sectional characteristics.[6] The frontier theory, as it is popularly known, has influenced the representation of historical events in film. Many of the films that depict the settlement of the West and the western expansion of the territory of the United States do so as if, to borrow Woodrow Wilson's assessment of the film *The Birth of a Nation* (1915), it were "history written in lightning." Significant persons and phases of Great Plains history are selected and utilized time and again for narrative purposes that highlight the benefits of the "progress of civilization" through the wilderness. Therefore, the western film should not be judged through its lack of historical accuracy. It has a more cultural narrative thread within its patchwork. As Scott Simmon has observed, "The films offer up arguments through narrative about America and its history, and if we must judge them, it would be less for accuracy than coherency."[7] The history, geography, and culture of the area help to contribute a narrative framework that filmmakers have utilized in different ways. This metanarrative of western expansion and the pioneer spirit is found in many films concerning the Great Plains from *The Covered Wagon* (James Cruze, 1923) to *About Schmidt* (Alexander Payne, 2002).

American Indians and Film

The Plains Indians, though consisting of more than fifteen separate tribes, have often been generically reduced to one tribe in films that depict their way of life. The Sioux (themselves comprising four tribes, Teton, Yankton, Santee, and Yanktonai) are the Native American tribe most often associated with the Great Plains on film. One of the earliest films that featured the Sioux was *The Indian Wars* (1914). This film is of interest primarily because it attempted to reenact four military engagements between the U.S. Cavalry and the Plains Indians in a semidocumentary fashion. Directors Theodore Wharton and Vernon Day reconstructed the Battle of Summit Springs (1869), the Battle of Warbonnet Creek (1876), the Battle of the Mission (1890), and the Battle of Wounded Knee (1890). The concluding footage of the film showed contemporary Native American children attending modern schools and Native American farmers at work, thereby justifying the military engagements that brought the Native Americans the "benefits of civilization."

Other films concerning the Sioux are "revisionist" in that they are somewhat more sympathetic in their treatment of these Native Americans. Their narratives address the cultural clash between Anglos and the tribes and the assimilation of tribal culture by whites who "go native." In 1970, two films were released that address this issue. In *A Man Called Horse* (Elliot Silverstein, director), an English nobleman, Lord John Morgan (Richard Harris) is captured by the Lakota Sioux. Lord Morgan, dubbed "Man Called Horse" by the tribe, gradually becomes a warrior himself. Much of the dialogue in the film was spoken in the Sioux language, but further attempts at historical accuracy proved ineffectual because of its use of several white actors (e.g., Dame Judith Anderson) as Sioux Indians. Arthur Penn's *Little Big Man* (1970), based on the novel by Thomas Berger, also concerned an Anglo captured and raised by the Sioux. *Dances with Wolves* (Kevin Costner, 1990) concerns a Civil War soldier, Lt. John W. Dunbar, who, after becoming an unintentional hero, is posted to a remote area of South Dakota. Here he encounters and becomes intrigued by the Sioux lifestyle. Though all three films were far more sympathetic in their treatment of the Plains Indians than previous depictions on the screen (*Dances with Wolves* even employed English subtitles for the Native American language spoken), their central focus remained their nonnative characters.

Another Plains tribe was featured in film director John Ford's attempt to reconcile his past transgressions to Native Americans in his western films. According to writer George Macdonald Fraser, "Even more than the Sioux, the Cheyenne ('The People', as they called themselves) were the aristocrats of the Plains."[8] *Cheyenne Autumn* (1964) recounts the defiant migration of three hundred Cheyenne from their Oklahoma (then known as Indian Territory) reservation to their native lands in Wyoming. This migration was instigated by the neglect and suffering the tribe experienced at the reservation. The migration occurred in 1878 and was known as "Dull Knife's Outbreak." The U.S. Cavalry is led by Captain Thomas Archer (Richard Widmark) in pursuit of the tribe. Based on the novel by Mari Sandoz, this film was Ford's elegy to the Native Americans and his last western film. Though it may have been more sympathetic to their plight, in typical Hollywood fashion the main Native American characters in the film, Little Wolf and Dull Knife, were portrayed by non–Native American actors, Ricardo Montalban and Gilbert Roland, respectively. Since *Dances with Wolves* (which did employ Native Americans as Native Americans), several films have been made that redress this casting issue from the past. Regrettably, most of these have been in the form of made-for-television films.

GREAT PLAINS PIONEERS IN FILM

The pioneer experience has also been the subject of many films set in the Great Plains region. Since the starting point for many of the trails, railroads, and wagon trains was on the western bank of the Missouri River, the Great Plains (often called "the Great American Desert" and "Indian Country") was the first natural obstacle that was encountered in the transcontinental journey to California or Oregon. The settlement of the region occurred only when the West was tamed through techno-

Oscar Micheaux (1884–1951)

African American filmmaker, Oscar Micheaux, produced and directed forty-four independent feature-length films during his prolific career. He was the first African American to direct, write, and produce a feature film, *The Homesteaders* (1919). That film was based on his novel, which in turn was based on his own homesteading experience in South Dakota. Born in Chicago, Illinois, the fifth child of a family of thirteen, Micheaux moved to South Dakota in his early twenties. He bought a farm in Gregory, South Dakota, and began his writing career. The popularity of one of these novels, the aforementioned *The Homesteader*, prompted the Lincoln Motion Picture Company to acquire the rights. During the negotiations, Micheaux's interest was piqued and he formed the Micheaux Film and Book Company and in 1918 filmed his semiautobiographical novel. Micheaux's second film, *Within Our Gates* (1920), was filmed in response to D. W. Griffith's *Birth of a Nation* (1915) and was just as controversial. The film depicts the racist attitudes of whites over blacks and the lynching of a black couple. Micheaux's subsequent films also explored controversial themes: domestic violence in *The Brute* (1920), the Ku Klux Klan in *The Symbol of the Unconquered* (1920), and lynching again in *The Gunsaulus Mystery* (1921). In 1928, Micheaux declared bankruptcy and with new capital formed the Micheaux Film Corporation in 1929. His sound films include *The Exile* (1931), *Darktown Revue* (1931), *Harlem after Midnight* (1934), *Temptation* (1936), and *God's Step Children* (1937). Although his film career ended with the coming of World War II, Oscar Micheaux has received critical acclaim and rediscovery in recent years. Two film festivals are devoted to critical assessment of his oeuvre, the Oscar Micheaux Film Festival, held in Gregory, South Dakota, and one in Great Bend, Kansas. There is also a Web site posted by the Oscar Micheaux Society: http://www.duke.edu/web/film/micheaux/.

logical and cultural "advances." The gradual settlement of the region is marked by significant events: the pony express (1860), the first transcontinental railroad (1869), the invention of barbed wire, which helped homesteaders (1873), the numerous cattle drives that established cattle towns such as Dodge City and Abilene, and the discovery of gold in the Black Hills. These in turn gave rise to notable individuals who became a part of the mythologizing of the West: Buffalo Bill Cody, Bat Masterson, Wyatt Earp, Doc Holliday, George Armstrong Custer, and the Dalton Gang. Films concerning the history of the Great Plains region often utilized these myths and the historical events that produced them within their narrative framework. To paraphrase the concluding line of John Ford's *The Man Who Shot Liberty Valance* (1962), "When the legend becomes fact, film the legend."

Two silent epic westerns took as their subject matter significant events in western American history, *The Covered Wagon* (James Cruze, 1923) and *The Iron Horse* (John Ford, 1924). Both located much of their action on the Great Plains (though they were filmed in other locations). *The Covered Wagon* deals with the trek of emigrants from Westport Landing, Missouri, to California. Westport Landing was an important jumping-off point for the overland trails used by settlers; Independence and St. Joseph were two others. Cruze utilized long shots that emphasized the landscape and the assemblage of covered wagons to great effect. The film is considered very influential, especially on John Ford. Prior to this, westerns were the domain of William S. Hart and Tom Mix and were concerned with the exploits of their respective heroes rather than monumental historical events. *The Covered Wagon* contained several episodes that have been associated with the history of the Great Plains region: the panorama of covered wagons trekking across the Plains, the hardships of nature (snow and mud) encountered by the pioneers, a buffalo hunt, and an Indian attack. All of these would become synonymous with the settling of the region and would be utilized again and again by filmmakers. John Ford's *The Iron Horse*, another western epic, recounts the events of the building of the first transcontinental railroad. Both films were shot almost entirely on location (albeit in the Nevada desert), and both were noted for their action sequences. John Ford considered *The Iron Horse* his best film in a 1953 interview.

During the 1930s, several films centered on the technology that helped conquer the American West and were set on the Great Plains. A renewed interest in the "A" western as historical spectacle was generated by the popularity of such escapist films as *The Adventures of Robin Hood* (Michael Curtiz, 1938) and *Captain Blood* (Michael Curtiz, 1935). According to Peter Stanfield, "A-feature Westerns also sought to distance themselves from the negative connotations of series Westerns and their implied audience of lower-class men and boys. They did this through higher production values, and also the marketing of Westerns as both a more authentic *and* romantic vision of American history."[9] Cecil B. DeMille directed two of these, *The Plainsman* (1937) and *Union Pacific* (1939). The pony express and scouting were the subject matter of *The Plainsman*, which starred Gary Cooper as Wild Bill Hickok and James Ellison as Buffalo Bill Cody. The legendary and short-lived pony express was the focus of other films as well, primarily *Pony Express* (1953), which starred Charlton Heston as Buffalo Bill Cody. *Union Pacific* again told the story of the transcontinental railroad. The film, which starred Barbara Stanwyck, Joel McCrea, and Robert Preston, was highlighted by action sequences that depicted a spectacular train wreck and an Indian attack. *Wells Fargo* (Frank Lloyd, 1937), *Stagecoach* (John Ford, 1939), and *Western Union* (Fritz Lang, 1941) likewise couched their romantic narratives within the framework of historical progress. *How the West Was Won* (Henry Hathaway, John Ford, and George Marshall, 1963) was another western of epic scope and was considered at the time the "ultimate western." It told the story of the Prescott family and their adventures as they trekked across the Plains to settle the new frontier. The film is episodic and

James Stewart in *How the West Was Won* (1963), the story of three generations of a family that settled on the Plains. Courtesy Photofest.

is highlighted by segments titled "The Rivers," "The Plains," "The Outlaws" (directed by Henry Hathaway), "The Civil War" (directed by John Ford), and "The Railroad" (directed by George Marshall). *How the West Was Won* was photographed in the Cinerama process (one of the few narrative films to use it; most were travelogues such as *Cinerama Holiday*) and utilized spectacular action sequences to engage its audience. Much like the earlier silent epics, these included an attack by Plains Indians, a buffalo hunt, and the building of the transcontinental railroad. As its title implies, the film depicted the conquering and settlement of the American West, and if this was not made clear visually to its audience, it contained a voice-over narration by Spencer Tracy, who assured the viewer that this wilderness had to be "won from Nature and primitive man." The conclusion of the film cross-fades from the frontier landscape to a modern urban city, complete with automobiles and skyscrapers, thereby codifying the film's title and the epic transition from the wilderness to "civilization."

Another milestone event in the history of the settlement of the Great Plains region was the opening of the "Indian Territory" of present-day Oklahoma. Oklahoma (a combination of the Choctaw words "okla," meaning people, and "humma," red) was part of the Louisiana Purchase of 1803. Early settlers felt that the land was unsuited for white colonization but perfectly suited for the Indians. The territory became the "permanent" residence of the Five Civilized Tribes, who received the land in exchange for their lands east of the Mississippi. The Trail of Tears was the forced removal by the U.S. government of tribes that were not willing to commit to the terms of the Indian Removal Act of 1830. After the Civil War, the land came under closer scrutiny by white settlers as the railroad and cattle drives increased interest in the region. In 1889, President Benjamin Harrison initiated what would become a series of land rushes that opened certain sections of Indian Territory for white settlement. Oklahoma eventually entered the Union in 1907, the last of the Great Plains states to do so. Many Hollywood films have centered on the various land rushes and the dramatic conflict created by "Sooners," those individuals who grabbed land allotments before the prescribed rush. *Tumbleweeds* (King Baggott, 1925) marked William S. Hart's first western epic, and its sequence of the land rush of the Cherokee Strip is perhaps its most potent one. The sequence is brilliantly edited and was reused time and again in other films. The 1931 Academy Award winner for best picture, *Cimarron*, starring Richard Dix and Irene Dunne, also centered on the land rush and the subsequent statehood of Oklahoma. Based on the novel by Edna Ferber, it concerns the fortunes of the Cravat family in the settlement of Oklahoma, focusing on Sabra Cravat (Irene Dunne) and her visionary husband Yancey (Richard Dix). Warner Brothers' *Oklahoma Kid* (Lloyd Bacon, 1939), starring James Cagney and Humphrey Bogart, was yet another story that revolved around the historical event of the land rush and the greed and corruption associated with the settlement of the region. This time the visionary words of a would-be settler express the sentiments of the American spirit (à la Hollywood): "All around are thousands of acres of the richest land in Oklahoma and it will all be peopled by this time tomorrow, by folks that'll need doctors, lawyers, merchants. It's a new start for all of us. But it's gonna mean a lot of hard work and it's gonna mean sticking together for the common good." This sense of "sticking together for the common good" is nowhere more apparent than in the one film that best exemplifies it. Rodgers and Hammerstein's 1955 musical

Oklahoma! remains the best celebratory film concerning the state. Though it does not specifically center on a historical event, the film, nonetheless, is important not only for its depiction of Oklahoma but also because the title song itself was adopted from the musical as the state song on May 11, 1953. Other films that concern different aspects of Oklahoma's history and the region include *Tulsa* (Stuart Heisler, 1949) and *Oklahoma Crude* (Stanley Kramer, 1973), both of which deal with the oil boom in 1918–1922, *The Oklahoman* (Francis D. Lyon, 1957), *Oklahoma Territory* (Edward L. Cahn, 1960), and *The Story of Will Rogers* (Michael Curtiz, 1952) and *The Boy from Oklahoma* (Michael Curtiz, 1954), both of which star Will Rogers Jr.

The violent history associated with the settlement of Kansas and Nebraska has also been the source for numerous films dealing with this historical conflict between proslavery and abolitionist ("free state") causes. The twin territory of Kansas and Nebraska was created by the Kansas-Nebraska Act of 1854. The decisive issue of slavery was to be left not to Congress, but to the settlers of the regions to decide. This sectional issue helped widen the breach between the North and the South in the years leading up to the American Civil War (1861–1865). The most violent and notorious incident associated with "Bleeding Kansas" was the raid on the abolitionist center of Lawrence, Kansas, by the Confederate guerrilla leader William Clarke Quantrill on August 21, 1863. In the attack, 150 male civilians were killed, and much of the town burned. The legacy of Quantrill's Raiders gave rise to a number of outlaws who claimed to be members and adopted the guerrilla leader's tactics in their exploits, namely, Frank and Jesse James, the Younger brothers, the Dalton and Doolin Gangs, and Belle Starr. The Lawrence massacre and the personage of Quantrill achieved celluloid status in numerous films, including *Quantrill's Son* (1914), *Dark Command* (1940), *Kansas Raiders* (1950), *Quantrill and His Raiders* (1954), *Quantrill's Raiders* (1958), *The Jayhawkers* (1959), *The Outlaw Josey Wales* (1976), and *Ride with the Devil* (1999). According to John C. Tibbetts, "Significantly, these films find consensus in their interpretation of Quantrill as a megalomaniac who attempted to forge a Confederate empire in the West, with Kansas as his seat of power. To what degree the man was motivated by selfish greed, blood lust, revenge, or driven by genuine patriotism, depends on the particular film."[10] Ang Lee's *Ride with the Devil*, based on the novel *Woe to Live On*, by Daniel Woodrell, was the only film to deal with the political and social issues relating to Quantrill's raid. The other films, because of limitations imposed by the Motion Picture Code, severely sanitized their subject matter and consequently melodramatized the character of Quantrill. "Thus, like other films of that time, the Quantrill films had to avoid radical political discussion; sidestep controversies in religion, race and gender; and minimize graphic sex and violence."[11] *Ride with the Devil* told the story of Jack Bull Chiles (Skeet Ulrich) and his best friend, Jake Roedel (Tobey Maguire), who join the Bushwhackers, a group of renegade Southerners who support the Confederate cause and become involved in the Kansas/Missouri border wars. The film helps depict the controversial issues that instigated the conflict and the raid on Lawrence, Kansas, more than the Hollywood "A" and "B" Quantrill films before it.

Cattle Towns, the Law, and Gunslingers

Similar in their concern with the violent history of the frontier are the many films that deal with the notorious cattle towns that were a part of the Great Plains and the infamous lawmen and gunslingers associated with them. The massive cattle drives from Texas gave birth to cattle towns on the Great Plains. Since railroad lines at the end of the Civil War only reached as far as Kansas, that state became the region for cattlemen and buyers to meet. Cattle towns such as Abilene, Dodge City, and Wichita were centers for trade and business in the cattle industry. The increased settlement of the area also gave rise to the conflict between "free-range" cattlemen and homesteaders. These frontier towns became notorious for gambling, prostitution, and lawlessness. Lawmen and gunfighters such as Wild Bill Hickok, Wyatt Earp, and Bat Masterson contributed to the myth of the American West with their exploits.

The most famous of the cattle towns was Dodge City, Kansas. Originally founded in 1872, five miles west of Fort Dodge, the town was a resting place for buffalo hunters and traders along the Santa Fe Trail. With the coming of the Atchison, Topeka, and Santa Fe Railroad and the disappearance of the vast buffalo herds, Dodge City became a cattle town. From 1875 to 1885, more than five million head of cattle were driven up the Chisholm Trail to Dodge City. The most famous of the lawmen to keep the peace in Dodge City were Bat Masterson, Wyatt Earp, Bill Tilghman, and Charlie Bassett. The town's most famous fictional lawman was Matt Dillon, sheriff of Dodge City in the television western series *Gunsmoke* (CBS, 1955–1975). With the closing of Fort Dodge in 1882 and the end of the cattle drives by 1886, Dodge City's frontier history passed into legendary status. That legend has provided the subject matter for numerous westerns whose titles alone invoke the "Queen of the Cowtowns." Films such as *Dodge City Trail* (1937), *Dodge City* (1939), *King of Dodge City* (1941), *Vigilantes of Dodge City* (1944), *West of Dodge City* (1947), *Desperadoes of Dodge City* (1948), and *Gunfight at Dodge City* (1959), as their titles suggest, recount the violent past of the town. The many motion pictures that tell and retell the exploits of the lawmen are too numerous to mention. A few of them are *Wild Bill Hickok* (1923, 1938), *Wild Bill* (1995), and Lawrence Kasdan's epic-length *Wyatt Earp* (1994), starring Kevin Costner. Other cow towns lent their names to the titles of films, for example, *Abilene Town* (1946) and *Wichita* (1955). The mere mention of the town's name invokes a host of associations (historical, cultural, geographic) for the intended audience, and these associations are reinforced when they are accompanied by historical characters. The same is true for the host of films concerning the exploits of the western outlaws associated with Great Plains history: *When the Daltons Rode* (1940), *The Daltons Ride Again* (1945), *The Dalton Gang* (1949), *The Doolins of Oklahoma* (1949), *The Daltons' Women* (1950), and *The Last Ride of the Dalton Gang* (1979). The region and its historical heritage help codify names, places, and events in the cultural imagination so that the mere mention of the name will bring forth associations with its nomenclature, whether real or imaginary. The same is true of another historical event that is synonymous with the Great Plains historical experience, the Dust Bowl.

The Dust Bowl in Films

The severe drought conditions of the 1930s, coupled with poor agricultural practices, brought on "the Dust Bowl" in the southern Great Plains states of Kansas and Oklahoma. The term was first used by an Associated Press reporter on April 14, 1935, when he saw a large dust storm cover a wide area of the region, darkening the sky and "raining" dirt. The dust storms covered a large area and left drifts of soil everywhere, almost burying homes, as well as killing cattle. The effects of the conditions of the Dust Bowl during the economic hard times of the depression caused the migration of families and communities to California, where they felt that farming conditions would be better and allow for more work. These migrant workers were known as "Okies" since about 20 percent were from Oklahoma. Because of the great number of migrants to California, work not only became scarce but wages decreased significantly. The plight of the migrants and the cause of their calamity, the Dust Bowl itself, are the subjects of two classic film accounts of the times, one a documentary and the other an adaptation of one of the great works of American literature.

Filmmaker Pare Lorentz made *The Plow That Broke the Plains*, his first film, for the U.S. Resettlement Administration, one of President Franklin Roosevelt's New Deal agencies, in 1936. The documentary detailed the causes of the Dust Bowl conditions and its effects on farmers and families in the southern Plains. The conclusion of the film showed the Resettlement Administration in action helping the dispossessed farmers find work and its efforts to prevent another such dust bowl from occurring in the region. According to Richard Barsam, the combination of the film's editing and music made a "persuasive argument for the conservation of human and natural resources." "Much of the film's strength lies in its often ironic juxtaposition of images and sound (such as the counterpoint image of tractors and tanks against the sound of threshing machines and bullets)."[12] Lorentz was very much a champion of the Roosevelt administration and also believed in the close association of music with film. The dramatic score to *The Plow That Broke the Plains* was written by American composer Virgil Thomson. The film encountered distribution problems primarily because many motion-picture theater owners considered it to be nothing more than propaganda in support of the Roosevelt administration. Today it is considered one of the classic documentaries of the 1930s because of its superb editing style and its dramatic effect.

A more traditional narrative approach to the plight of the migrant workers was made by John Ford in 1940. *The Grapes of Wrath*, starring Henry Fonda and Jane Darnell, was adapted from John Steinbeck's Pulitzer Prize–winning novel, first published in 1939. Steinbeck had written two other books that chronicled the plight of the migrant workers, *In Dubious Battle* and *Harvest Gypsies* in 1936, but *The Grapes of Wrath*, with its focus on one family's hardships, is his most enduring work. The film follows the novel closely in recounting the odyssey of the Joad family, who travel from their Oklahoma farm to California in search of a new home. The sharecroppers have been evicted from their forty acres of land in Oklahoma and migrate to the "promised land" of California. Tom Joad, played by Henry Fonda, has recently been released from prison and returns home to find the family in dire straits. The film ends with a speech from "Ma" Joad (Jane Darwell) that places the theme and focus of Ford's film clearly on the ability to endure: "For a while it looked as though we was beat. Looked like we didn't have nobody in the whole wide world but enemies. Like we was lost and nobody cared. Rich fellas come up an' they die, an' their kids ain't no good, an' they die out. But we keep a-comin'. We're the people that live. They can't wipe us out. They can't lick us. We'll go on forever, Pa, cause we're the people." This speech, which is underscored by the classic song "Red River Valley," is emblematic of the pioneer spirit itself and the endurance of those who settled the Great Plains region.

THE GREAT PLAINS ENVIRONMENT ON FILM

As can be seen, the depiction of the history of the Great Plains on film is vast, but the majority of these films were not actually filmed on the Plains themselves but on studio backlots or in other locales. The spatial depiction of the region emphasizes the relationship to the landscape itself. As Plains writer Willa Cather stated in her novel *O Pioneers!*, "The great fact is the land itself."[13] The imaginative use of the landscape by filmmakers dramatizes its barrenness, isolation, and inner beauty. Jane Tompkins claims that the landscape has a rhetorical effect in western stories and films:

> It is an environment inimical to human beings, where a person is exposed, the sun beats down, and there is no place to hide. But the negations of the physical setting—no shelter, no water, no rest, no comfort—are also its siren song. Be brave, be strong enough to endure this, and you will become like this—hard, austere, sublime. This code of asceticism founds our experience of Western stories (and film). The landscape challenges the body to endure hardship—that is its fundamental message at the physical level. It says, "This is a hard place to be; you will have to do without here. Its spiritual message is the same: come, and suffer."[14]

One interesting film that equates the physical hardship of the region with a spiritual hardship is *Leap of Faith* (1992), directed by Richard Pearce. The film concerns a pseudo–faith healer, Jonas Nightingale (Steve Martin), and his menagerie of acolytes and fellow con artists who are stranded in the small, drought-stricken town of Rustwater, Kansas. There he decides to set up camp and provide the gullible citizens with an old-fashioned revival. When two real "miracles" occur during his stay, the evangelist leaves both the town and his traveling caravan of spiritual swindlers. The cinema has long been fascinated with the exploits of faith healers and traveling evangelists from Frank Capra's *The Miracle Woman* (1931) to *Elmer Gantry* (1960) and the documentary film *Marjoe* (1972). *Leap of Faith* was the first film to actually show the barnstorming theatrical means by which the would-be evangelists conned their misunderstanding congregations. The use of the plains of Kansas as the setting of the film seems to imply that Kansans are a simple, gullible people, especially given the fact that the film was shot entirely in Texas locations—a miracle of landscape, perhaps.

Whenever a filmmaker consciously utilizes the landscape of the Great Plains region, it is a deliberate choice that invokes the cultural heritage of the landscape. Its effect on the viewer likewise invokes that heritage, as well as symbols of regional and national identity. Two films by Terence Malick, *Badlands* (1973) and

Days of Heaven (1978), utilize the Great Plains landscape in different ways. *Badlands* was based on the Starkweather-Fugate killing spree that took place in Nebraska in 1957–1958. The young couple in the film, played by Martin Sheen and Sissy Spacek, travel across a barren and desolate Dakota landscape that reflects their own alienation. This sense of dissonance and isolation in the film is accompanied by Holly's voice-over narration, an example of which occurs after their eighth murder, "At this moment I didn't feel shame or fear, but just kinda blah, like when you're sitting there and the water's run out of the bathtub." Kit Carruthers (Martin Sheen) drives a large black '49 Monarch and is often compared to a cultural icon of the fifties, James Dean. But Malick uses the landscape to mirror the isolation of his main characters in a world that no longer has meaning for them. Similarly, *Days of Heaven*'s title refers to a nostalgic, pastoral ideal that the characters now have only in their collective memory. The movie is set on the plains of the Texas Panhandle in 1916 and concerns migrant wheat harvesters and their relationship with the land. The film follows the couple Bill (Richard Gere) and Abby (Brooke Adams) as they flee Chicago to the Texas plains. There they work the wheat fields of a wealthy rancher (Sam Shepard) who falls in love with Abby. The film, whose lackluster love-triangle plot machinations are its severest weakness, is greatly enhanced by its use of wide-screen cinematography by cinematographer Nestor Almendros, which effectively captures the vastness of the landscape and people's relation to it.

Peter Bogdanovich's film adaptation of Joe David Brown's novel *Addie Pray* (1971) illustrates another way in which the geography of the Great Plains region was used to great effect. *Paper Moon* (1973) features Ryan and Tatum O'Neal as con artists in depression-era Kansas. The source novel is set in Alabama, but when the screenplay was being developed, screenwriter Pollie Platt recalled a trip that she and Bogdanovich had made across Kansas in 1964. It took three days traveling in a 1952 Ford convertible whose top would not go up, and they nearly baked to death in the Kansas heat. Platt recalled concerning her adaptation that "I didn't want to do the Depression with the food lines and all those stupid signs, and I thought, how can I make it clear that life is tough and that it's o.k. that Ryan steals? And I remembered Kansas and how small and insignificant I felt in that car with Peter—a lot of sky, little horizon—and I thought that was all that was necessary to convey their neediness—the fact that they were stuck together in this car traveling this great distance, uncertain about where their next meal was coming from."[15] The flat, barren Kansas horizon is used to great effect as the background image when the two con artists are on the road. The desolate landscape of the Kansas countryside effectively highlights the neediness of the depression in the Great Plains.

Richard Brook's 1967 film adaptation of Truman Capote's award-winning "nonfiction novel" *In Cold Blood* is yet another example of the use of a realistic landscape as a representational environment. The cold, barren Kansas landscape becomes an objective correlative for the emotional emptiness of the two killers, who are the central characters of the film, which was filmed almost entirely in Holcomb, Kansas (where the actual murders occurred). Cinematographer Conrad Hall's stark black-and-white photography effectively captures the barrenness of the region with a documentary-like aspect. Perry Smith (Robert Blake) and Dick Hickock (Scott Wilson) are two ex-cons who plan the robbery of the home of the Clut-

Paper Moon (1973) with Ryan and Tatum O'Neal traveling by car through Kansas. Courtesy Photofest.

ters who they suspect have $10,000 hidden in a safe. The Clutters are roused from their sleep and murdered. Alvin Dewey (John Forsythe) leads the police in tracking down the killers. Director Richard Brooks allows the audience to get into the minds of the killers with his effectively detailed adaptation of Capote's novel.

In his espionage thriller *North by Northwest* (1959), Alfred Hitchcock used South Dakota's monumental "Shrine of Democracy" Mount Rushmore for the climactic chase sequence that concludes the film. The landmark statue as a symbol of America is in keeping with other chase sequences in Hitchcock films such as those at the British Museum in *Blackmail* (1929), the Royal Albert Hall in *The Man Who Knew Too Much* (1934 and 1956), and the Statue of Liberty in *Saboteur* (1942). In both *Saboteur* and *North by Northwest*, the chases are given an almost iconic significance because in both the very idea of America is being attacked from within by enemy agents. In *North by Northwest*, Cary Grant plays Richard Thorndike, an advertising executive who is mistaken for a fictitious CIA agent by Communist spies. The film is one continuous chase from beginning to end as Thornhill attempts to get away from both the police and the Communist spies in a cross-country flight that eventually leads to Mount Rushmore. The mountain-monument has become a symbol of the Cold War struggle, just as the Statue of Liberty was a symbol in *Saboteur* of the fight between fascism and democracy. Hitchcock

Motion-Picture Industry Personnel from the Great Plains

Robert Altman (b. 1925). Director. Born on February 20, 1925, in Kansas City, Missouri. Altman is a maverick film director who has consistently worked outside the Hollywood system. His distinguished body of work includes such films as *M*A*S*H* (1970), *McCabe and Mrs. Miller* (1971), *The Long Goodbye* (1973), *Nashville* (1975), *The Player* (1992), and *Gosford Park* (2002).

Roscoe "Fatty" Arbuckle (1887–1933). Silent film comedian, director, and screenwriter. Born on March 24, 1887, in Smith Center, Kansas. An original member of Mack Sennett's Keystone Cops, Arbuckle became a comic star who wrote and directed his own short comedies. In 1917, he formed the motion picture company Comique and gave another native Kansan, Buster Keaton, his start in films. At the height of his popularity, Arbuckle's career was cut short by an infamous scandal in 1921. Notable films include *Mabel and Fatty's Wash Day* (1915), *The Butcher Boy* (1917), *The Garage* (1920), and *The Hayseed* (1920).

Burt Bacharach (b. 1928). Composer and songwriter. Born on May 12, 1928, in Kansas City, Missouri. Bacharach received two Oscars in 1969 for the musical score and best song, "Raindrops Keep Fallin' on My Head," for the film *Butch Cassidy and the Sundance Kid*. Additional film scores include *Lost Horizon* (1973), *Arthur* (1981), and *Night Shift* (1982). Hit songs from films include ones from *What's New Pussycat?* (1965, title song), *Alfie* (1966, title song), *Casino Royale* (1966, score and songs), *Bob & Carol & Ted & Alice* (1969, song, "What the World Needs Now"), and *The Boys in the Band* (1970, song, "The Look of Love").

Stan Brakhage (1933–2003). Experimental and avant-garde filmmaker. Born on January 14, 1933, in Kansas City, Missouri. Brakhage's filmmaking is noted for its formal elements as opposed to any narrative ones. His theories on film, particularly his idea of "hypnagogic vision," were published in the journal *Film Culture* in 1963. His films include the monumental *Dog Star Man* (1961, 1964), *Sirius Remembered* (1958), and *Mothlight* (1963).

Marlon Brando (1924–2004). Actor. Born on April 3, 1924, in Omaha, Nebraska. Perhaps the chief exponent of the "Method" style of acting in the 1950s, Brando began his acting career with the Dramatic Workshop in New York and then with the famous Actors Studio. He made his film debut in 1950 in Stanley Kramer's *The Men*. His films include *A Streetcar Named Desire* (1951), *Julius Caesar* (1953), *On the Waterfront* (1954), *The Godfather* (1972), and *Apocalypse Now* (1979).

Walt Disney (1901–1966). Animator and producer. Born in Chicago, Walt Disney's early career as an animator was spent in Kansas City, Missouri, where he and fellow artist and collaborator Ub Iwerks developed a series title, *Laugh-O-Grams*. His production company, also called Laugh-O-Grams, soon went bankrupt, and Disney and Iwerks moved to Hollywood, California, where his career as an animator and producer became more distinguished.

Richard Edlund (b. 1940). Motion-picture special-effects technician. Born in Fargo, North Dakota, on December 6, 1940. Edlund was a pivotal figure in the visual-effects renaissance brought on by the critical and commercial success of *Star Wars* (1977). He shared an Academy Award for the film and stayed with George Lucas' Industrial Light and Magic to work on the special effects for such films as *The Empire Strikes Back* (1980), *Raiders of the Lost Ark* (1981), and *Return of the Jedi* (1983).

Henry Fonda (1905–1982). Actor. Born on May 16, 1905 in Grand Island, Nebraska. Distinguished American actor whose film career included such work as *You Only Live Once* (1937), *Young Mr. Lincoln* (1939), *The Grapes of Wrath* (1940), *The Lady Eve* (1941),

The Ox-Bow Incident (1943), *My Darling Clementine* (1946), *Mister Roberts* (1955), *Once upon a Time in the West* (1969), and *On Golden Pond* (1981).

Ron Howard (b. 1953). Actor, director, producer. Born on March, 1, 1953, in Duncan, Oklahoma. A former child actor (*The Andy Griffith Show*, 1960–1968), he has become a significant director in Hollywood. In 1977, he directed his first film, *Grand Theft Auto*. His list of successful films includes *Splash* (1984), *Cocoon* (1985), *Parenthood* (1989), and *Apollo 13* (1995).

Ub Iwerks (1901–1971). Animator. Born on March 24, 1901, in Kansas City, Missouri. While working at an ad agency in Kansas City, Iwerks befriended fellow artist Walt Disney. In Kansas City, they developed several cartoon series before moving to Los Angeles, California. Iwerks was instrumental in developing the cartoon character of Mickey Mouse and the *Silly Symphony* cartoons in the late 1920s. After a brief stint away from Disney, Iwerks returned as a supervisor of special effects on many of the studio's major productions.

Buster Keaton (1895–1966). Silent-film comedian, film director, and producer. Born on October 4, 1895, in Piqua, Kansas, of a theatrical family of vaudevillians. Keaton, along with Charlie Chaplin and Harold Lloyd, was a significant comic artist during the silent era. His films include *Our Hospitality* (1923), *The General* (1926), *Steamboat Bill, Jr.* (1928), and *The Cameraman* (1929). An Annual Keaton Festival is held in Iola, Kansas, near his birthplace during the last weekend in September, where scholars and fans screen and discuss his work.

Carol Littleton (b. 1948). Film editor. Born in Oklahoma in 1948, Littleton attended the University of Oklahoma. After working as an editor of television commercials, she became a distinguished film cutter (particularly with the films of Lawrence Kasdan) in the 1980s. Some of the films she has edited include *Body Heat* (1981), *E. T.—The Extraterrestrial* (1982), *The Big Chill* (1983), *Places in the Heart* (1984), *Silverado* (1985), *The Accidental Tourist* (1988), and *Grand Canyon* (1991).

Harold Lloyd (1893–1971). Silent-film comedian, born on April 20, 1893, in Burchard, Nebraska. Lloyd's career as a silent-film comedian began with producer Hal Roach in 1914. After some undistinguishable comic characters such as Willie "will he" Work and Lonesome Luke, he found a character that created his most popular comic screen persona, using simply a pair of horn-rimmed glasses. Throughout the 1920s, Lloyd consistently outdrew his fellow comedians, Charlie Chaplin and Buster Keaton, at the box office. His comedies include *Grandma's Boy* (1922), *Safety Last* (1923), *Why Worry?* (1923), *Girl Shy* (1924), *The Freshman* (1925), *Speedy* (1928), and *Feet First* (1930).

Fred Niblo (1874–1948). Director. Born on January 6, 1874, in York, Nebraska. Prolific silent-film director of such actors as Rudolph Valentino, *Blood and Sand* (1922), Douglas Fairbanks, *The Mark of Zorro* (1920) and *Three Musketeers* (1921), and Greta Garbo, *The Mysterious Lady* (1928). He also directed the first Hollywood blockbuster, *Ben-Hur* (1926).

Gordon Parks (b. 1912). Novelist, photographer, director. Born on November 30, 1912, in Fort Scott, Kansas. Parks, an African American, regarded the camera as a weapon against poverty and racism. He was the first black photographer for the Farm Security Administration in 1942. In 1949, he joined the staff of *Life* magazine as a photojournalist. As a filmmaker, he directed the film version of his novel about small-town racism, *The Learning Tree* (1968), thereby becoming one of the first black artists to direct a mainstream Hollywood feature. It was filmed in his hometown of Fort Scott, Kansas. Parks then directed two features that are part of the "blaxploitation" cycle of the early 1970s, *Shaft* (1971) and *Shaft's Big Score* (1972). In addition, he filmed a biopic of an African American blues artist, *Leadbelly* (1976).

ZaSu Pitts (1898–1963). Actress. Born on January 3, 1898, in Parsons, Kansas. After a distinguished career in the silent cinema, in both dramatic and comic roles, she was one of Erich von Stroheim's favorite actors (*Greed* 1925, *The Wedding March* 1927). With the coming of sound, she turned almost exclusively to comedy. She appeared in a series of comic two-reelers with Thelma Todd in the 1930s. Her befuddled, impish character became a staple for supporting roles in several films, particularly *Mrs. Wiggs of the Cabbage Patch* (1933), *Ruggles of Red Gap* (1935), *Life with Father* (1947) and *It's a Mad, Mad, Mad, Mad World* (1963). Her unusual first name came from combining the names of two of her father's sisters, Eliza and Susan.

Charles "Buddy" Rogers (1904–1999). Actor. Born on August 13, 1904, in Olathe, Kansas. A leading man in the silent era, Rogers appeared in the following films: *My Best Girl* (1927), *Wings* (1927), *Abie's Irish Rose* (1928), *Varsity* (1928), *This Reckless Age* (1932), and *Take a Chance* (1933). In 1937, he married Mary Pickford, his leading lady in *My Best Girl*.

Will Rogers (1879–1935). Humorist, actor, and essayist. Born on November 4, 1879, in Colagah, Indian Territory (now Oklahoma). Rogers had an extensive film career dating from the silent era. His films capitalized on his stage persona (developed in vaudeville) of the homespun, common-sense philosopher and folk hero. In the 1930s, he made three films for director John Ford that are considered classics of Americana: *Dr. Bull* (1933), *Judge Priest* (1934), and *Steamboat round the Bend* (1935). Rogers' films include *A Poor Relation* (1921), *The Headless Horseman* (1922), *A Connecticut Yankee* (1931), *Ambassador Bill* (1931), *State Fair* (1933), *The Country Chairman* (1935), and *Doubting Thomas* (1935).

Virgil Thomson (1896–1989). Composer. Born on November 25, 1896, in Kansas City, Missouri. Thomson's musical scoring for films include several key documentaries of the 1930s and 1940s. His most notable film scores include *The Plow That Broke the Plains* (1936), *The River* (1937), *The Spanish Earth* (1937), and *Louisiana Story* (1948).

Darryl F. Zanuck (1902–1979). Studio executive and producer. Born on September 5, 1902, in Wahoo, Nebraska. He was a noted film producer for Twentieth Century–Fox, a studio he founded as Twentieth Century Pictures in 1933. Zanuck led the company as a major studio through several prestigious productions such as *The Grapes of Wrath* (1940), *How Green Was My Valley* (1941), *Gentleman's Agreement* (1947), *All About Eve* (1950), *Viva Zapata!* (1952), *The Man in the Grey Flannel Suit* (1956), and *The Longest Day* (1962).

deliberately chose a landmark within the heartland of America to convey this ideological struggle in what T. S. Eliot would term an "objective correlative."

GREAT PLAINS CULTURE IN FILM

Both the history and geography of the Great Plains region have been utilized by filmmakers in different ways.

Filmmaker Alexander Payne (b. 1961) a native of Omaha, Nebraska, has utilized the region for many of his film projects. Payne studied history and Spanish literature at Stanford University before going to UCLA's film school, where his sixty-minute thesis film *The Passion of Martin* landed him a position at Universal Pictures. Working in close association with screenwriter Jim Taylor, Payne has developed a penchant for satirical examinations of American mores and cultural values via the Great Plains region. Payne's so-called Omaha Trilogy uses the city as the setting for *Citizen Ruth* (1996), *Election* (1999), and *About Schmidt* (2002). Nicknamed the "Bard of Omaha" in a *New York Times Magazine* article concerning his work, Payne is viewed by many critics as a regionalist. Novelist Tom Perrotta commented on Payne's adaptation of his novel *Election* and the relocation of the novel's setting from New Jersey to Omaha, Nebraska: "It's a very literary decision, in a way, to bring the films to Omaha. He's claiming a kind of prerogative to be a regionalist—which is unusual for a filmmaker, but for an American writer to do that is nothing at all. It puts him in the company of Sherwood Anderson, William Faulkner, William Kennedy."[16] This cinematic regionalism is best evidenced in *About Schmidt* (2002), starring Jack Nicholson and Kathy Bates. The film is a bittersweet comic examination of a "life without any singular accomplishment."

Based on the novel *About Schmidt* by Louis Begley, Payne's film transposes the setting from Manhattan, New York, to Omaha, Nebraska. By doing so, he is able to cultivate a keener satirical viewpoint than if he had simply done a straight adaptation. The film concerns Warren R. Schmidt, the recently retired assistant vice president and actuary of the Woodmen of the World Insurance Company. Schmidt is opposed to his daughter's upcoming marriage. When his wife dies suddenly from heart failure, Schmidt decides to visit his daughter in Denver. He ends up traveling by recreational vehicle to various locales in Nebraska and Kansas in an attempt to rediscover his roots or, as he puts it, "clear a few cobwebs from my memory." Payne uses Schmidt's road trip not only to satirize Midwestern mores but to comment on the cultural heritage of the Great Plains. His recreational vehicle, a thirty-five-foot Adventurer, is a modern-day Conestoga wagon traversing the same landscape as the pioneers who made their way across the region. Schmidt visits

About Schmidt (2002) with Jack Nicholson (far left) and Kathy Bates (far right). Courtesy Photofest.

such places as the arrowhead collection in Broken Bow, Nebraska, and Buffalo Bill's home in North Platte. In an ironic sequence, Schmidt is seen talking to a Native American, "as they liked to be called nowadays," he recalls in his letter to his foster child, Ndugu. "Those people really got a raw deal." Payne then immediately follows this with Schmidt's visit to Buffalo Bill Cody's home: "What a remarkable man!" he informs Ndugu. In addition to the on-site locations, Payne uses other cultural icons of the western heritage of the region. Beef is prevalent throughout the film, from Schmidt's retirement dinner at Johnny's Cafe, "Home of Two 1969 Ak Sar Ben Championship Steers," to shots of cattle throughout Schmidt's road trip. The beef references in the film recall the frontier experience and the vast cattle drives that crossed the region in the nineteenth century. When Schmidt returns from his daughter's wedding in Denver, he visits the arch over the interstate in Kearney, Nebraska. This arch commemorates the pioneers who made their way west. Schmidt looks at a plaque that reads: "The Cowards Never Started / The Weak Died on the Way / Only the Strong Arrived / They Were the Pioneers." Schmidt's self-reflection in this scene, again in a letter to Ndugu, contrasts his own experience with those of the pioneers. Although Payne's satire may be strong, it is also nostalgic and bittersweet. Schmidt comes to realize that his may be an imperfect life, but it is not a hopeless one. As he is told by his best friend at his retirement dinner at the beginning of the film, "What really matters is that you devoted your life to something meaningful." That accomplishment is finally arrived at in his communication to his foster child, Ndugu.

Science Fiction and Horror on the Great Plains

Vivian Sobchack in her classic study of the science-fiction genre, *Screening Space: The American Science Fiction Film*, argues that the use of familiar landscapes in many science fiction films contributes to the "subversion of the landscape" itself.[17] The use of familiar terrain in an "alien" way causes the viewer to become defamiliarized with it. Two motion pictures utilize Lawrence, Kansas, in just such a fashion. Nicholas Meyer's postapocalyptic nuclear holocaust made-for-television film *The Day After* (1985) graphically depicts the aftermath of a nuclear attack in America's heartland. Made at the height of the Reagan-era Cold War with the Soviet Union, the film effectively contrasts the pastoral green landscape before the attack with the cold grayness of the nuclear fallout. According to William J. Palmer, these postapocalyptic films "present a future so bleak, a wasteland so arid, that it makes T. S. Eliot's vision of the twentieth century seem almost utopian."[18] *The Day After*, originally shown on ABC became the most widely watched television program of all time, as well as one of the most controversial.

Herk Harvey's 1962 low-budget horror film *Carnival of Souls* was filmed in and around Lawrence, Kansas. With budget of a mere $30,000, Harvey, working with a skeletal cast and crew, made a film that can be best described as a combination of William Inge and Ambrose Bierce. The film concerns the lone survivor of a car crash, Marie Henry (Candace Hilligoss), who is constantly haunted by a ghastly apparition. Accepting a job as a church organist, she moves to Utah, where the apparition leads her to a deserted amusement park. There she makes a startling discovery. Herk Harvey had made more than 400 industrial and educational films for Centron Studios in Lawrence, Kansas, and took three weeks' vacation to make the feature film, written by fellow Centron employee John Clifford. The film was released in 1962 as part of a drive-in double feature by Herts-Lion Corporation. It was virtually forgotten until 1989, when it was rereleased to critical acclaim. It has now enjoyed cult-movie status and garnished critical praise as an independent film that stresses mood and atmosphere over special effects.

The depiction of the Great Plains region in film has offered filmmakers and cinematographers the opportunity to explore aspects of the history, environment, and culture of the region. Films have utilized the narrative history of the Great Plains in ways that have emphasized the hardships and perseverance of its inhabitants and settlers. The harsh landscape of the area has provided a visual metaphor for the endurance of its inhabitants as well. Coming out of both of these areas, the cultural heritage of the Great Plains continues to provide creative artists a rich palette with which to work. Films have both championed and criticized the region as representative of "Americanness." Filmmakers such as John Ford have viewed the region as a representation of the nation as a whole, whereas some filmmakers, particularly Alexander Payne, have looked at the region more satirically. The region itself was a mixing ground for Northern and Southern settlers, as well as immigrants, so in that respect it truly seems to be a melting pot of American ideals and values. The numerous films that depict, historically, geographically, or culturally, the rich heritage of the region display its transformation from "the Great American Desert" into "America's Heartland."

THEATER ON THE GREAT PLAINS

William Inge

The foremost dramatist associated with the Great Plains is the playwright William Inge (1913–1973). Born in Independence, Kansas, Inge attended the University of Kansas from 1927 to 1930. After a number of jobs, including working on a road gang, as a news announcer, and as a high-school English teacher, he completed his M.A. in English from George Peabody School for Teachers in Nashville, Tennessee in 1943, and taught composition and drama at Stephens College, in Columbia, Missouri. He also served as the dramatic critic for the *St. Louis Star-Times*. Inge's first dramatic triumph was the drama *Come Back, Little Sheba*, which was produced on Broadway in 1950. He wrote the play while teaching at Washington University from 1946 to 1949. His other plays include *Picnic* (1953), *Bus Stop* (1955), *The Dark at the Top of the Stairs* (1957), and *A Loss of Roses* (1959). In addition, he wrote an original screenplay, *Splendor in the Grass* (1961), for which he received an Academy Award. Following a number of critical and commercial failures, *Natural Affection* (1963), *Where's Daddy?* (1966), and *The Last Pad* (1970), Inge fell into a deep depression and committed suicide in his home in the Hollywood Hills on June 10, 1973.

Inge's dramatic work is influenced considerably by his small-town origins in the Great Plains. Almost all of his work reflects his midwestern roots, especially his sensitivity to the frustrations, sexual repressions, and thwarted opportunities of small-town people. Most of his major plays are set in the region and in small-town environments. *Picnic* and *Bus Stop* are specifically set in small Kansas towns, according to Inge's stage directions, *The Dark at the Top of the Stairs* is placed in a small Oklahoma town, and *Come Back, Little Sheba* is located "in one of those respectable neighborhoods in a Midwestern city." This is not necessarily a nostalgic look (as, say, Eugene O'Neill's *Ah, Wilderness!* is); on the contrary, Inge uses the landscapes to examine the longings and desires of his characters, who seem to be stifled by their drab small-town existence. Inge himself once commented on the relationship of the environment to its people. In an introduction to *The Plains States* in the Time-Life Library of America series, he observed that "Nowhere can we find a closer correlation of landscape and character than in the Plains States. The people there are, for the most part, as plain and level and unadorned as the

Scene from the stage production of *Picnic*. Courtesy Photofest.

scenery."[19] Much of Inge's work concerns loss among his characters—the loss of innocence, the loss of promise, and the loss of love. The characters in his plays seem to be landlocked by their frustrated desires as well as by their loneliness. In *Picnic*, for instance, this loneliness is voiced by the schoolteacher, Rosemary, who pleads with her friend Howard to marry her: "Come back here, Howard. I'm no spring chicken either. Maybe I'm a little older than you think *I* am. I've formed my ways too. But they can be changed. They *gotta* be changed. It's no good livin' like this, in rented rooms, meetin' a bunch of old maids for supper every night, then comin' back home alone. . . . Each year, I keep tellin' myself, is the last. Something'll happen. Then nothing ever does—except I get a little crazier all the time."[20] Inge's work is exceptional in that he was the first playwright to look at small-town life and its frustrations in a dramatic fashion. Inge's biographer Ralph F. Voss states that "Even an isolated prairie village can produce a killer or an artist, a thief or a saint, a dreamer or a builder: whatever possibilities human beings have anywhere else, they have also in the midwestern village. That such an environment is uniformly wholesome and unerringly beneficent was a myth that had been well exposed by such Inge predecessors as Sinclair Lewis, Sherwood Anderson, and Edgar Lee Masters, who was also a native of southeastern Kansas. William Inge, however, was the first American writer to expose the myth in the dramatic genre."[21]

Inge's original screenplay for *Splendor in the Grass* focuses on love and frustrated desire in a small Kansas town during the 1920s prior to the stock market crash. The film, directed by Elia Kazan and starring Warren Beatty (his feature-film debut) and Natalie Wood, was filmed entirely in New York (unlike the movie version of *Picnic*, which was filmed on location in Kansas), primarily because Kazan's father was ill at the time and the director wanted to be close to home. Inge's dramatic themes deal with the conflict between the youths' frustrated desires for one another and moral codes and parental domination, all within the small-town setting. The film itself, because of its subject matter, was a cause célèbre among critics and censors alike. Inge also worked on a series of dramas concerning small-town life to be telecast by CBS on *Chrysler Theatre*. Inge and the series' producer, David Susskind, disagreed, however, on the themes and characters to be explored, and the series was not completed. However, a script was developed that reached production on NBC in 1964. "On the Outskirts of Town," was telecast on NBC on November 6, 1964, with Anne Bancroft and Jack Warden. As its title implies, it too was set in a small town in the Midwest.

William Inge Theatre Festival

The William Inge Theatre Festival, held every April in Independence, Kansas, honors the author and his work, as well as that of other American playwrights. Established in 1982, the Inge Theatre Festival includes numerous performances, readings, workshops, panel discussions, retrospectives, and awards ceremonies conducted over a four-day period. The festival not only honors the life and work of William Inge but also playwriting itself. A Professional Playwrights-in-Residence program stimulates the craft by allowing a playwright to teach and write at Independence Community College while residing in Inge's boyhood home. The Margo Jones Medal is named for the pioneer in regional theater, Margo Jones, and honors the spirit of its namesake and her commitment to new work. Past recipients include Margaret Goheen, Richard Coe, Otis L. Guernsey Jr., Abbot Van Nostrand, Henry Hewes, Jane Alexander, Robert Whitehead, Al Hirschfeld, George C. White, and Eileen Heckart. The Distinguished Achievement in Theatre Award honors a playwright whose body of work has had a significant impact on the American theater. Past recipients include Arthur Laurents, John Kander and Fred Ebb, Lanford Wilson, A. R. Gurney, John Guare, Stephen Sondheim, Neil Simon, August Wilson, Arthur Miller, Betty Comden and Adolph Green, Wendy Wasserstein, Peter Shaffer, Edward Albee, Horton Foote, Sidney Kingsley, Garson Kanin, John Patrick, Robert Anderson, William Gibson, Robert E. Lee and Jerome Lawrence, and William Inge.

The festival also honors new and coming playwrights with its New Voices award, now called the Otis after its originator, Otis Guernsey, who initiated it in 1992. A nominated playwright submits a work to be read by a selection committee, which in turn picks the playwright to receive the award. The award includes a trip to the Inge Festival, a reading of the new work by the playwright, and an honorarium. The William Inge Theatre Festival has become a nationally recognized event that truly honors the playwright and playwriting in the American Theatre.

Other Great Plains Playwrights

Recently other playwrights have been exploring the Great Plains historical heritage in their works. Delbert Unruh, a University of Kansas theater professor, adapted a nonfiction work, *Ogallala: Water for a Dry Land*, by John Opie, for the stage in 1996. His play, *To the Last Drop: The Ogallala Aquifer and the High Plains of Kansas*, explores the history, present state, and future of the Ogallala Aquifer in western Kansas. This aquifer of groundwater extends from the Panhandle of Texas through Nebraska and into South Dakota, covering some 174,000 square miles. Opie's book is a regional history that discusses the origin and development of the aquifer through the Great Plains. Opie's environmental history describes "the geography, hydrology, soils, and plants of the region, then relates them to human settlement, technology, and civilization. Environmental history reminds us, often in painful ways, that humanity, no matter how technologically sophisticated it is, is still embedded in nature."[22] Similarly, Unruh's four-part play examines the environmental history from prehistoric

The William Inge Collection

The William Inge Collection, located in the Independence Community College Library in Independence, Kansas, is a repository and resource of more than four hundred manuscript documents pertaining to Inge and his work. The collection, begun in 1965, contains primary documents, as well as critical and biographical works. In November 1969, Inge contributed to the collection the original manuscripts of four of his dramas: *Picnic, Come Back, Little Sheba, Natural Affection*, and *Splendor in the Grass*. Inge's sister Helene Inge Connell donated his private book collection in 1976. In 1980, she contributed the author's private record collection. The collection was officially dedicated in 1981. The collection also maintains an extensive amount of materials relating to the films based on Inge's plays. These include lobby cards, posters, publicity stills, and pressbooks. Also represented are the original editions of many of Inge's published works.

times through the pioneer settlement of the region and into the present. A narrator ties the numerous historical incidents and characters together. According to Unruh, adapting such material was challenging: "It was difficult to find the glue that holds it all together, so the narrator evolved. I didn't want to write exposition. I just wanted to get to the heart of the event and tell what happened. So the narrator provides the background information the audience needs to have for the right perspective on the rest of the action."[23]

In a similar fashion, John Gronbeck-Tedesco's tetralogy *Prairie Fire* examines a portion of the history of Kansas through the lives of some of its unremembered settlers. The four plays in the cycle (*Lift Off, Flight and Denouement, The Four Horsemen*, and *Prairie Cabaret*) relate the story of the Fultons, a family of Irish immigrants who come to the northeastern Kansas Territory in 1854. The plays present a contemporary astronaut, the future progeny of the Fultons, who continually chides the family to get on with their lives in order to produce him. Thus the historical past is represented by the Fultons and the future history of the region by the astronaut. In this way Gronbeck-Tedesco effectively links the historical heritage of the region to the present without being particularly didactic. Gronbeck-Tedesco based the play on reminiscences, memoirs, diaries, and oral histories that focused on life in Kansas during and just after the settlement period, 1854–1876. While researching these, the playwright found that the large historical events are not the only ones that contribute to the present. "Private sufferings and personal achievements and failures also contribute to the larger scheme in which we live." The four plays that comprise the cycle utilize masks, doubling of actors, puppets, and choruses to achieve their dramatic effects.

Both of these works are considerably more theatrical than William Inge's naturalistic dramas, but their theatricalism is important in relating the historical heritage of the region for a specific effect. Yet all of these plays contribute to a depiction of the hardship the inhabitants faced and the perseverance they exhibited in the settlement of the Great Plains. Whereas Inge's dramas are intimate in their depiction of familial dramas, Unruh and Gronbeck-Tedesco both paint a larger canvas; in fact, they use an almost Brechtian approach to the region's history, culture, and geography. For instance, the second play of the *Prairie Fire* tetralogy, *Flight and Denouement*, uses a chorus composed of four pony express riders and four ponies. Delbert Unruh's use of a narrator helps to fill in the information the audience needs in its understanding of the environmental history of the Ogallala Aquifer and its effect on the region's history and future. Above all, these playwrights have contributed significantly to an artistic understanding of the Great Plains region through its historical and cultural record. In so doing, they lead the way for additional contributions from theater artists across the region.

RESOURCE GUIDE

Printed Sources

Barsam, Richard M. *Nonfiction Film: A Critical History*. Bloomington: Indiana University Press, 1992.

Bonnefeld, Matthew Paul. *The Dust Bowl: Men, Dirt, and Depression*. Albuquerque: University of New Mexico Press, 1979.

Fenin, George N., and William K. Everson. *The Western: From Silents to the Seventies*. Harmondsworth: Penguin Books, 1973.

Fraser, George MacDonald. *A Hollywood History of the World*. New York: Fawcett Columbine, 1988.

French, Warren G. *Filmguide to The Grapes of Wrath*. Bloomington: Indiana University Press, 1973.

Gregory, James N. *American Exodus: The Dust Bowl Migration and Okie Culture in California*. New York: Oxford University Press, 1989.

Harris, Thomas J. *Bogdanovich's Picture Shows*. Metuchen, NJ: Scarecrow Press, 1990.

Hodgman, J. "The Bard of Omaha." *New York Times Magazine*, December 8, 2002, 88–91.

Lamar, Howard R., ed. *The New Encyclopedia of the American West*. New Haven, CT: Yale University Press, 1998.

Luebke, Frederick C. "Regionalism and the Great Plains: Problems of Concept and Method." *Western Historical Quarterly* 15 (January 1984): 19–38.

McClure, Arthur F. *Memories of Splendor: The Midwestern World of William Inge*. Topeka: Kansas State Historical Society, 1989.

Odum, Howard W., and Harry Estill Moore. *American Regionalism: A Cultural-Historical Approach to National Integration*. New York: Henry Holt and Co., 1938.

Opie, John. *Ogallala: Water for a Dry Land*. Lincoln: University of Nebraska Press, 1993.

Palmer, William J. *The Films of the Eighties: A Social History*. Carbondale: Southern Illinois University Press, 1993.

Rainey, Buck. *Western Gunslingers in Fact and Film*. Jefferson, NC: McFarland and Co., 1998.

Shortridge, James R. *The Middle West: Its Meaning in American Culture*. Lawrence: University Press of Kansas, 1989.

Simmon, Scott. *The Invention of the Western Film*. New York: Cambridge University Press, 2003.

Smith, Henry Nash. *Virgin Land: The American West as Symbol and Myth*. Cambridge, MA: Harvard University Press, 1950.

Sobchack, Vivian C. "The *Grapes of Wrath* (1940): Thematic Emphasis through Visual Style." *American Quarterly* 31 (1979): 596–615.

Stanfield, Peter. *Hollywood, Westerns, and the 1930s: The Lost Trail*. Exeter: University of Exeter Press, 2001.

Stott, William. *Documentary Expression and Thirties America*. New York: Oxford University Press, 1973.

Thacker, Robert. *The Great Plains: Fact and Literary Imagination*. Albuquerque: University of New Mexico Press, 1989.

Tibbetts, John C., "Riding with the Devil: The Movie Adventures of William Clarke Quantrill." *Kansas History: A Journal of the Central Plains* 22, no. 3 (autumn 1999): 182–199.

Tibbetts, John C., and James M. Welsh. *The Encyclopedia of Stage Plays into Film*. New York: Facts on File, 2001.

Tompkins, Jane. *West of Everything*. New York: Oxford University Press, 1992.

Turner, Frederick Jackson. *The Frontier in American History*. New York: H. Holt, 1920.

Voss, Ralph F. *A Life of William Inge: The Strains of Triumph*. Lawrence: University Press of Kansas, 1989.

Worster, Donald. *Dust Bowl: The Southern Plains in the 1930s*. New York: Oxford University Press, 1979.

Web Sites

Duke University Program in Film and Video, The Oscar Micheaux Society Home Page
http://www.duke.edu/web/film/Micheaux/

Emporia State University, Uber Inge: A William Inge Reference Site
http://emporia.edu/cw/Inge/uberinge.html

Shorock, Don, The Oscar Micheaux Home Page
http://www.micheaux.org/

William Inge Theatre Festival Web Page
http://www.ingefestival.org/

Videos/Films

About Schmidt. Dir. Alexander Payne. Perf. Jack Nicholson, Hope Davis, Kathy Bates. New Line Cinema. 2002.

Badlands. Dir. Terence Malick. Perf. Martin Sheen, Sissy Spacek, Warren Oates. Pressman-Williams/Warner Brothers. 1973.

Bus Stop. Dir. Joshua Logan. Perf. Marilyn Monroe, Don Murray, Arthur O'Connell. 20th Century Fox. 1956.

Carnival of Souls. Dir. Herk Harvey. Perf. Candace Hilligoss, Sidney Berger. Harcourt Productions/Hearts-Lion International. 1962.

Cheyenne Autumn. Dir. John Ford. Perf. Richard Widmark, Carroll Baker, Karl Malden. Warner Brothers. 1964.

Cimarron. Dir. Wesley Ruggles. Perf. Richard Dix, Irene Dunne, Estelle Taylor. RKO Radio Pictures. 1931.

Come Back, Little Sheba. Dir. Daniel Mann. Perf. Burt Lancaster, Shirley Booth. Paramount. 1949.

The Covered Wagon. Dir. James Cruze. Perf. J. Warren Kerrigan, Lois Wilson, Alan Hale. Famous Players/Paramount. 1923.

Dances with Wolves. Dir. Kevin Costner. Perf. Kevin Costner, Mary McDonnell, Graham Greene. Orion. 1990.

The Day After. Dir. Nicholas Meyer. Perf. Jason Robards, Steve Guttenberg, JoBeth Williams. ABC Circle. 1983.

Days of Heaven. Dir. Terence Malick. Perf. Richard Gere, Brooke Adams. O.P. Productions/Paramount. 1978.

Dodge City. Dir. Michael Curtiz. Perf. Errol Flynn, Olivia DeHavilland. Warner Brothers. 1939.

The Grapes of Wrath. Dir. John Ford. Perf. Henry Fonda, Jane Darwell, Charley Grapewin. 20th Century Fox. 1940.

How the West Was Won. Dir. Henry Hathaway, John Ford, George Marshall. Perf. Gregory Peck, Karl Malden, Debbie Reynolds. MGM/Cinerama. 1962.

In Cold Blood. Dir. Richard Brooks. Perf. Robert Blake, Scott Wilson, John Forsythe. Columbia Pictures. 1967.

The Indian Wars. Dir. Theodore White, Vernon Day. Col. William F. Cody Historical Picture Co. 1914.

The Iron Horse. Dir. John Ford. Perf. George O'Brien, Madge Bellamy, Fred Kohler. Fox. 1924.

Leap of Faith. Dir. Richard Pearce. Perf. Steve Martin, Debra Winger, Lolita Davidovich, Liam Neeson. Paramount. 1992.

Little Big Man. Dir. Arthur Penn. Perf. Dustin Hoffman, Faye Dunaway. Cinema Center 100 Productions/National General Pictures. 1970.

A Man Called Horse. Dir. Elliot Silverstein. Perf. Richard Harris. National General Pictures. 1970.

North by Northwest. Dir. Alfred Hitchcock. Perf. Cary Grant, Eva Marie Saint, James Mason. MGM. 1959.

Oklahoma! Dir. Fred Zinnemann. Perf. Gordon MacRae, Shirley Jones, Rod Steiger. Magna/Rodgers and Hammerstein. 1955.

Oklahoma Kid. Dir. Lloyd Bacon. Perf. James Cagney, Humphrey Bogart. Warner Brothers. 1939.

Paper Moon. Dir. Peter Bogdanovich. Perf. Ryan O'Neal, Tatum O'Neal, Madeline Kahn. Paramount. 1973.

Picnic. Dir. Joshua Logan. Perf. William Holden, Rosalind Russell, Arthur O'Connell. Columbia Pictures. 1955.

The Plow That Broke the Plains. Dir. Pare Lorentz. Resettlement Administration, a U.S. Documentary Film. 1936.

Return of a Man Called Horse. Dir. Irvin Kershner. Perf. Richard Harris. National General Pictures. 1976.

Ride with the Devil. Dir. Ang Lee. Perf. Skeet Ulrich, Tobey Maguire, Jewel. USA Films. 1999.

The Sea of Grass. Dir. Elia Kazan. Perf. Spencer Tracy, Katharine Hepburn, Robert Walker, Melvyn Douglas. MGM. 1947.

Splendor in the Grass. Dir. Elia Kazan. Perf. Natalie Wood, Warren Beatty, Pat Hingle. Warner Brothers. 1961.

Tumbleweeds. Dir. King Baggott. Perf. William S. Hart, Barbara Bedford. United Artists. 1925.

The Wizard of Oz. Dir. Victor Fleming. Perf. Judy Garland, Bert Lahr, Ray Bolger, Margaret Hamilton. MGM. 1939.

Organizations

Center for Great Plains Studies
1155 Q Street, 306 Hewit Place
Lincoln, NE 68588-0214
http://www.unl.edu/plains/index.html

Martin and Osa Johnson Safari Museum
111 North Lincoln Avenue
Chanute, KS 66720
http://safarimuseum.com

The museum houses the film footage/photographic archives and personal memorabilia of wildlife and ethnographic documentarists Martin and Osa Johnson.

Museum of the Great Plains
601 NW Ferris Avenue
Lawton, OK 73507
http://www.museumgreatplains.org

The Museum of the Great Plains includes archives, photographic collections, and a research library pertaining to the ethnology, natural history, and cultural history of the region.

National Cowboy Hall of Fame and Western Heritage Center
1700 NE 63rd Street
Oklahoma City, OK 73111
http://www.cowboyhalloffame.org

The Western Performers Gallery celebrates more than one hundred years of western movies and examines the role of fiction in the perception of the American West.

FOLKLORE

Amanda Rees

Folklore is made up of the common and everyday rather than the extraordinary, it is the informal rather than the formal or institutional, and it is the marginal, the personal, and traditional. Everyone, no matter how urbanized and modernized, participates in folk culture of some sort. Folklorist Elliott Oring argues that the study of folklore is part of a larger study of folklife that embraces material, social, and spiritual aspects that shape both the everyday and special days of people's lives. It includes the contemporary traditions people live with, traditions rooted in their ethnicities, their religions, their communities, their occupations, and their regions. It is a dynamic part of culture, but it is also a conserving force that works to retain tradition.[1]

Folklore offers a wonderfully idiosyncratic and always intriguing window on Great Plains culture. At first glance, folklore suggests both the incorrect, fantastic, and distorted and traditional costumes and dance performances. But the work of folklorists offers a much broader sense of regional folklife, including vernacular (local, communal, and informal) traditions. Folklorists argue that those who make individual folkloric expressions, whether they are songs, poems, stories, or roadside attractions, are working within a larger historical and regional context of traditions. Indeed, folklore is a process at work in the Great Plains region, a process that shifts over time, but one that is constant in its work to fill the needs of the region's inhabitants. These needs are often based in specific historical moments, and so the themes and issues discussed here fulfill the particular needs of a particular period in time, but also, in a number of cases, have a way of meeting future needs of the region.

The Great Plains is a sometimes incomprehensible and often forgotten landscape. Many regional visitors are overwhelmed by the prospect of driving through the region and drive quickly, sometimes at night, or if they are too overwhelmed, they fly. This region is often labeled as having nothing there. Others develop a profound feeling of being overwhelmed by the immense sky and extensive rolling landscape that offers few moments of visual relief. But in moving quickly through the region, travelers miss a rich folklife that can be uncovered by a slower pace and a more languorous exploration of place.

Two of the most important concepts in understanding Great Plains folklore are the environment and migration. Though evidence of early Native American life can be found on the Plains going back at least 12,000 years, Plains Indians are known to have moved on and off the Plains according to its environmental cycles. Some historical moments were wet and hospitable to habitation; others were too dry and unforgiving. Indeed, the region went through a period of arid summers and large dust storms during the 1400s C.E. that led to the abandonment of large areas of the region by Native peoples. Many of the contemporary Plains tribes were either migrants or were forcibly removed from the East due to intolerable pressures from European migration. They found a region dramatically unlike either the South or the Midwest from which they had come.

Europeans and Euro-Americans either moved from further east or moved directly from Europe to the region. African Americans, especially after emancipation, also moved to the region. More recently the region has seen growth in Southeast Asian populations, particularly Vietnamese and Laotians, who came to work in the meat-packing plants that dot the Plains states, as well as Hispanics who work in these same plants and as migrant agricultural workers. The dominant experience that has shaped Plains folklore has been the movement into a region that was very often dramatically different from those Plains folks had left. Being a part of that regional environment, imagining new possibilities for it, and living within its very powerful limitations profoundly influenced people in the Dakotas, Nebraska, Kansas, and Oklahoma.

In addition to the importance of migration and the environment, it is necessary to understand the concept of folklife and how it relates to folklore. Folklorist Barre Toelken identifies three major distinctions in folklife study: verbal folklore, material folklore, and customary folklore. These three distinctions will be drawn upon to understand Plains folklore. Verbal folklore includes stories and myths (stories of universal import that peoples, cultures, religions, and nations believe in), ballads and lyrical songs, legends (stories of local import that people believe actually happened but that they learned from someone else), memorates (culturally based first-person accounts and interpretations of striking incidents), and folktales and jokes, those fictional narratives that hold cultural values. Material folklore includes the study of vernacular structures such as houses and barns, roadside attractions, tombstones, food, costumes, needlework, decorations, and culturally based musical instruments. Finally, customary folklore includes those shared popular beliefs that are not transmitted through formal systems of science or religion and are sometimes referred to as superstition, vernacular or traditional medical practices that fall outside formal medical systems, dances, music, gestures, occupational folkways, and celebrations. Folklife includes the study of foodways, folk art, architecture, recreation, music, dance, and costume, all areas covered in other chapters. This chapter will explore the folklife of oral traditions, material cultural traditions, and occupational folklore.[2]

Historically, folklore has been studied from the perspective of the antiquarian or collector. The antiquarian collects, records, and studies vestiges of older cultures. Today some folklorists still practice this method of study, while others explore the ways in which folklore is celebrated, performed, and reiterated in contemporary culture through folk festivals or the everyday lives of individuals. Here evidence is drawn from the collection perspective and the performative aspects of folklore research.

A rich variety of ethnic folklife exists in the Great Plains. Ethnic folklife is defined when members of an ethnic group claim and share a historically derived cultural tradition or style. This can include certain attitudes, behaviors, ideas, and values. There is also a perception outside that group that there is a collection of individuals who share a common bond within the larger population. As Toelken suggests, these groups can only exist if they are recognized and a claim for their existence is made. Folk groups located on the Great Plains that are commonly recognized ethnic groups include those of American Indian, European, Asian, African, and South and Central American traditions. It should be noted that an ethnic group can often be indistinguishable from a religious affiliation such as the Amish or German Catholics, as religion can comprise the central core of the tradition or style that creates a sense of ethnicity identification. Immigration is probably the most profound force in creating ethnic groups and identities on the Great Plains. The ethnic groups that are recognized in the region are made up of foreign immigrants and their descendants. Among the Native American groups recognized on the Plains are descendants of some who were moved from the Midwest and South. African Americans, forcibly moved from numerous locations along the West African coast, had only their skin color to distinguish them. Thus, peoples originating from the African continent can be understood to have formed an ethnic identity of African American in the Americas, with the almost universal common experience of slavery.

Dolina Polish Dancers from Minnesota at the Polish Center in Ashton, Nebraska. Courtesy The Polish Heritage Center Inc.

Dancer at Red Earth Festival in Oklahoma City. Courtesy Oklahoma Tourism.

The Great Plains landscape has had a similar all-encompassing effect on ethnic groups, at least in the study of oral traditions. Folklorists have argued that the extremes of the continental climate that shape the region's landscape were so severe that the celebration of ethnic oral traditions was overshadowed by the need to come to grips with this new space. This new landscape required new folklore stories that dealt with settlement and learning to live in it. Indeed, the literature offers small evidence of strong ethnic folklore oral traditions in the region, and it raises the question of whether folklorists have focused less on collecting ethnic stories and more on the ways the various groups worked to engage their new landscape.

Ethnic folk traditions can be seen to be alive, well, growing, and evolving on the Great Plains in the incredible and increasing number of folk festivals, as the Resource Guide shows. This region's ethnic celebrations range from those that celebrate various Native American traditions, often revolving around powwows and art fairs, to European immigrant traditions, as well as the celebration of New World Mexican ethnic traditions. Ethnic festivals are very strongly a twentieth-century phenomenon, and more specifically a predominantly post–World War II development on the Plains. A few festivals began in the prewar years, such as the Swedish Festival in Lindsborg, Kansas, begun in 1941. The Moorhead-Fargo, Minnesota/North Dakota, festival, more of a pan–Northern European festival, did not begin until 1977. This festival promotes itself as a celebration of both Old World and Scandinavian American traditions. Northwestern European festivals that celebrate German culture can be found in Bismarck, North Dakota, and Tulsa, Oklahoma. Eastern European festivals that celebrate Czech ethnicity can be found in Oklahoma and especially in Nebraska. Three such ethnic festivals, in Prague, Oklahoma, Wilber, Nebraska, and Yukon, Oklahoma, were begun in 1959, 1961, and 1965, respectively. This closely associated establishment of Czech festivals suggests an important moment in Czech folklife during this period. In an interesting contrast, the Polish festival in Ashton, Nebraska, began only in 1992. In addition, there is a growing collection of Scottish games and festivals in South Dakota in Scotland, Sturgis, and Rapid City, begun in 1998, 1999, and 2003, respectively, again suggesting, like the Czech example, a sudden and infectious interest in the celebration of Scottish folk traditions. There are fewer southern European ethnic festivals on the Plains, but an Italian Festival, established in 1971, is held in McAlester, Oklahoma. Examples of New World folk traditions are the Mexican and Mexican American ethnic festivals such as the Fiesta Mexicana, in Topeka, Kansas, begun in 1933, and the Cinco de Mayo celebration, in Omaha, Nebraska, begun in 1985. Ethnic celebrations and the performance of ethnic identity in eating, drinking, dancing, singing, playing ethnic instruments, and taking part in sports traditions all reveal a rich celebration of ethnic folkways in the region.

Finally, in considering the workings of folklore, it is important to be aware of the concept of time. Though folklore seems to be timeless in nature, it is indeed highly time sensitive. Early Euro-American folklore traditions were fastened closely to the extremes of the Great Plains environment, as will be seen in the stories outlined later. In the mid-twentieth century, these stories were still being told and were shaping some of the car-focused folk traditions that were arising in the region, from giant men to giant grasshoppers. More recently, the Plains, like many other places, has turned its attention to urban legends. Some folklorists have suggested that the power of both old and new media has reduced regional variation in Plains folklore narratives. However, this does not mean that folk stories are not continuing to be told. But the oral tradition may be giving way to other, perhaps less obviously narrative traditions such as narrative painting and the family stories associated with material cultural objects, including quilts or charm chains.

GREAT PLAINS ORAL TRADITIONS

In the study of oral folklife, the narratives that people tell among themselves are divided into three categories: myth, folktale, and legend. Myths are sacred beliefs held by people, and they tell about the formation of the world. These myths are located before or outside time. Though there are a number of myths held by Native peoples in the Great Plains, beyond Native traditions there are no specific myths about the region. Folktales are defined as those stories that are understood, both by the people who tell them and by those who listen to them, to be fictional accounts. Finally, legends are told and generally believed as true even though they might contain supernatural events. They tell stories about the world people actually inhabit. These stories are often humorous, sometimes informative, and always entertaining.

The Great Plains oral folklife is nothing if not humorous and full of larger-than-life imaginings, whether it is about the potential of the region itself or the enormous grasshoppers and cornstalks that populate the region. Beginning with the art of storytelling on the Plains, folktales seem to fall into three distinct categories: regional myths in the national imagination, environmental extremes, and the rise of urban legends.

The art of storytelling on the Plains is quite distinctive, for example, tall tales. Tall tales, as a form of folktale genre, rely on the creation of a highly improbable fictional account and are a way of "codding" or kidding newcomers or more naïve Plains residents. These humorous stories begin seemingly openly with a series of events that appear believable and that the storytellers say they have witnessed. The weather is a common folktale subject, as in the tale of the storytellers' house blowing away in a tornado or twister that goes on to tell that "the cookstove was left undisturbed with fire going and the teakettle steaming. All of his listeners who are aware of what is going on pretend to be not at all interested. The conclusion of the story may be that a sack of meal had been hanging on a neighbor's porch and the wind blew the sack away, leaving the meal hanging there!"[3] This humor is also found in contemporary folk stories and is thoughtfully captured in folklorists

Tom Isern and Jim Hoy's *Plains Folk* syndicated column. The folklorists tell the story of receiving, via electronic mail, a list cataloging North Dakotan distinctive traits titled "You Might Be a North Dakotan If . . .":

> If you define summer as "three months of bad sledding," or,
>
> If your definition of a small town is one that doesn't have a bar . . .
>
> If you can identify a Minnesota accent . . .
>
> If "down south" to you means Aberdeen . . .
>
> If you have no problem spelling "Wahpeton" . . .
>
> If you have an ICBM in your back yard . . .
>
> If you have as many Canadian coins in your pockets as American ones . . .
>
> If your kids' baseball and softball games have ever been snowed out . . .
>
> If you drive 70 mph on the highway and pass on the right . . .
>
> If at least 50% of your relatives smell like beets . . .
>
> If you don't understand what the big deal about Moorhead is . . .
>
> If people borrow things to you . . . [4]

This column drew so many responses adding to the "You might be a North Dakotan" list that Isern has collected and categorized them according to topical content. These categorized representations can be found at Isern's Web site and include weather, landscape and nature, regional culture, fine cuisine, "how we talk," and community and neighbors.[5]

The discussion of Plains oral traditions will begin with an overview of Native American traditions and then move to a discussion of regional myths, larger-than-life heroes, and the environment. It concludes with some rural and urban ghoulishness, and regional folk songs.

Native American Stories

Oral traditions have been and remain an essential element of Native American folklife on the Plains because this was the primary medium for communicating philosophies, literatures, religions, or a whole culture's belief system, as Native peoples did not use the written word. One of the most challenging aspects of exploring Native American folklore is the relationship between the narrative and religious traditions, because many narratives weave story and religious traditions together. In the past, anthropologists have tried to untangle this complex relationship, but contemporary folklorists both acknowledge and embrace the complexity. In addition to the folklore/religion relationship, another challenge in discussing Native American folklore in the Plains is the risk of conflating the rich variety of tribal groups into one ethnic and regional identity, namely, the Plains Indian. With these two caveats in mind, Native American tribes on the Plains are worthy of attention within an examination of Plains folk traditions.

Both myth and folktale as a form of oral folklife among Native American tribes in the Great Plains will be explored. Anthropologist Keith Basso categorizes myth and historical tale, his term for folktale. These distinctions, which he originally posed for a group from the Southwest, are a useful way of approaching such oral traditions because they identify narratives with different time scales and different roles in society. For example, mythic stories are often set in "the beginning" and focus on the time when the universe was in the midst of realizing its present form and place. Myths offer the listener enlightenment and instruction. In contrast, historical tales tell of "long ago" when the tribe was forming characteristic ways and customs. Historical tales are set mostly before the white man came, though not always, and are frequently designed to alarm and criticize those among the listeners who are socially delinquent and indicate to them that their behavior is undesirable, and that if they do not change their ways, there will be disciplinary consequences.[6]

Locating the story and its role in Native oral tradition is one aspect of making sense of Native folk traditions. Another aspect is understanding the themes within the narrative. Three themes are explored here that shape Native Plains folk traditions: stories of sustenance, stories about particular regional animals, and the role of central characters like the Trickster, the Hero, or Grandmother Spider. Stories collected and recorded are discussed, but the performance of these oral traditions is not explored.

The story of the importance of a particular source of sustenance in a tribe's spiritual and material culture is a crucial aspect of many Plains tribes and often is classified in the "myth" category described earlier. Stories about essential food sources might focus on the role of corn in the Southwest or salmon in the Northwest, while on the Plains the buffalo is understood to be central to several tribes. The Blackfeet called the buffalo Ni-ái, "my shelter and my protection," whereas the Sioux thought that everything required for life, material and spiritual, was contained symbolically in the buffalo. Each tribe understood and interpreted the role of animals in different ways. Indeed, if an animal were strong, agile, numerous, or even an important source of food, it would often take on the characteristics of a divine messenger. "The End of the World: The Buffalo Go," a Kiowan story, reveals the importance of the buffalo as well as the impact of its demise.

> Everything the Kiowas had came from the buffalo. Their tipis were made of buffalo hides, so were their clothes and moccasins. They ate buffalo meat. Their containers were made of hide, or of bladders or stomachs. The buffalo were the life of the Kiowas.
>
> Most of all, the buffalo were part of the Kiowa religion. A white buffalo calf must be sacrificed in the Sun Dance. The priests used parts of the buffalo to make their prayers when they healed people or when they sang to the powers above.
>
> So, when the white men wanted to build railroads, or when they wanted to farm or raise cattle, the buffalo still protected the Kiowas. They tore up the railroad tracks and the gardens. They chased the cattle off the ranges. The buffalo loved their people as much as the Kiowas loved them.
>
> There was war between the buffalo and the white men. The white men built forts in the Kiowa country, and the woolly-headed buffalo soldiers [the Tenth Cavalry, made up of Negro troops] shot the buffalo as fast as they

could, but the buffalo kept coming on, coming on, even in the post ceme-tery at Fort Sill. Soldiers were not enough to hold them back.

Then the white men hired hunters to do nothing but kill the buffalo. Up and down the plains those men ranged, shooting sometimes as many as a hundred buffalo a day.[7]

Thus the buffalo story articulates not only the role of this creature in the spiritual and material lives of the Kiowa, but the impact of various stages of white settle-ment on the destruction of the buffalo. Not long after the white hunters decimated the buffalo herds, the Kiowa were forced to give up their nomadic lifestyle and re-main on the Fort Sill reservation.

The primary powerful being in Native American religious tradition is the Cre-ator, and under him are a variety of other supernatural beings, including the Sun (father) and the Earth (mother). The Sun and Earth communicate with each other and to humans through the weather (winds, clouds, rain, thunder). In addition, the physical geography, including mountains, deserts, rivers, and stones, as well as ani-mals and plants, has protective power. Believing that nature is bound within a re-ligious philosophy, Plains tribes have a distinct respect for and communion with the natural world. Animals such as the bear or eagle characterize various attributes that Native peoples admire and wish to emulate. However, this does not mean that tribes share the same attitude to these animals, as the example of the bear shows.

In Cheyenne and Arapaho folk traditions, the bear is an ancestor, and thus to eat a bear is understood to be cannibalism. The Kiowa feared that the bear was so great that they would not speak its name. However, the Comanche did not fear or respect the bear and found it good to eat. The Comanche story that follows is an origin myth, starting with the "beginning days" and explaining "How and Why: Why the Bear Waddles When He Walks." In the beginning days, creatures did not know what to do with the sun. It would rise and shine for a long while, and then it would go away for a long while and leave everyone in the dark. The animals who were active in the day wanted the sun to shine all the time; this way they could live without being interrupted by the darkness. Conversely, the animals of the night-time wanted the sun to go away completely so they could do what they wanted to do without interruption. Finally, they met to talk about the problem. The Coyote argued that one or the other side should have it. The Flycatcher believed that the sun could not be told what to do. The Bear suggested playing a game, and the win-ning side could keep it or throw it away. The animals decided to play the game, with Coyote umpiring for the day side and the Owl umpiring for the night side. The Bear was playing for the night side and was getting tired. He had a cramp in his legs, and they began to ache, so he removed his moccasins to give his feet a rest. Finally, the sun wanted to know what was happening, and as it came up, it frightened the night animals. The Bear jumped up quickly, put the wrong feet in his moccasins and waddled away with the wrong moccasins on crying, "Wait for me." As no one won the game between the day and night animals, day and night continued to take turns, and everyone had the same amount of time to live their lives as they wanted.[8] Not only does this story tell its listener about the character-istic of the bear, but it also propels the value of equality among all things.

There are a number of primary characters in Native American folk culture that should be acknowledged, in particular the Hero, who represents wisdom, strength, and the understanding of men, the Trickster, who is utilized to explain natural phenomena, especially when a moral can be drawn from the story, the Trickster Hero (a combination), Grandmother Spider, who represents all women, and the Twin Gods of War, Spider's grandsons, who represent humanity and are very much action oriented. These characters take a greater or lesser role in different Plains tribes for example, Grandmother Spider is common in Lakota (Sioux) folklore, but not as common in Caddoan tradition.

The role of smallpox, which was brought from the Old World with the conquest of the Americas, in the decimation of Native peoples was dramatic. Historians have argued that in some regions 90 percent or more of the population was killed. Thus it should come as no surprise that this deadly disease occurs in folktales on the Plains. In the following story about the Trickster Hero, Saynday, and Smallpox, Saynday works to save the Kiowa people from Smallpox, and at the same time instructs the listener in the disease's pathology.

Saynday finds himself in a world that has changed: cows have replaced buffalo, the once clear river is now muddy, there are no deer or antelope to hunt, settler soddies have replaced white tipis, and fences contain the Kiowas. Saynday decides that he needs to go away from this new world, but before he leaves, he suddenly sees a dark spot traveling from the east and moving very slowly. He is puzzled, as things from the east are known to move quickly, as they are alive and fast. As he moves toward the spot, it materializes into a man on a horse. The horse is black with red dust spots, the man's clothes are black with red dust, and his face is pitted with appalling scars. The stranger stops and asks:

> "Who are you?"
> "I am Saynday, Old Uncle Saynday of the Kiowas."
> "I haven't heard of you or the Kiowas."
> Saynday then asks who the stranger is.
> "I am Smallpox."

Saynday tells Smallpox that he has never heard of him or where he came from. Smallpox reveals that he came from across the eastern ocean and was at one with the white man and that he brought death. He then tells Saynday that he will spare his life if he tells him where the Kiowas live. Concerned about the Kiowas, Saynday tells Smallpox that they are very few and poor, whereas the Pawnees have large villages where every house is full of people. Smallpox becomes interested in the Pawnees, telling Saynday that he does his best work when people are crowded together. Saynday goes on to describe the Pawnees, saying that they cannot run away because they are very rich with piles of rugs, cooking pots, and bedding. Smallpox asks where the Pawnees live and mentions that he will visit the Pawnees first and get to the Kiowas later. Smallpox then makes a special request of Saynday, asking him to tell the Kiowas to put out their fires, as fire is the only thing he is afraid of because it destroys him. As Smallpox moves off to find the Pawnees, Saynday takes out a flint and steel and makes a fire in the grass. The wind picks up the fire and carries it to make a ring around the Kiowas' camp. Saynday then concludes that he probably can be of use to his people after all. Thus the Trickster outwits Smallpox and becomes central to survival stories of the Plains Indian in the time after the white man comes.[9]

Thus in exploring Native American folklore, it is interesting to consider the type of story: whether, for example, it is mythic in its focus on beginning stories, or historical, discussing the establishment of tribal beliefs and customs. The role of nature, in particular, important Plains animals, is also a feature of regional folk tradition, as well as the role of central characters such as the Trickster or Hero.

Regional Myths

Though the Great Plains narratives outlined here may not fall fully into the definition of myths as sacred beliefs that explain how the world came to be, for example, the Christian Creation story, they are close enough to the formation of the Great Plains that they might be called mythic. In particular, the focus will be on three Great Plains myths that can be understood as central to Euro-American Plains experience: the garden, the desert, and the rain follows the plow.

In the early to middle part of the nineteenth century, there were two competing myths about the Great Plains. The myth propelled by the likes of Thomas Jefferson and his East Coast supporters was that the region, known as the Great Interior Valley, was a vast and productive area, a garden that would offer never-ending land to Americans so that they could engage in the only truly virtuous occupation, agriculture. With this great valley, Jefferson assumed that Americans need never engage in an industrial revolution, an inhuman revolution that placed people in an enclosed factory environment away from the democratic influences of working the land as a yeoman farmer.

This grand vision of the region ran in direct opposition to another, perhaps more powerful regional myth, that the Plains was no more than a Great American Desert, a place unfit for Euro-American civilization, though an excellent dumping ground for Eastern Native American tribal groups whose land was being increasingly inhabited by Euro-Americans. This myth perpetuated itself in the minds and school textbooks of generations of Americans.

By the 1870s, this myth was being tested by new homesteaders and railroad developers, and a new myth evolved to counter the Great Desert vision of the region. The simplistic and optimistic belief that the rain follows the plow was promoted by railroad land agents, community boosters, the U.S. Geological Survey, and the University of Nebraska. They argued that breaking the sod increased air humidity and would change the climate to be more humid and favorable for agriculture. This myth was then elaborated on with the introduction of trees. It was argued that the presence of trees would also increase precipitation because the trees stopped wind and prevented moisture from evaporating from the soil, and their foliage diverted water vapor upward through transpiration that then accumulated and fell to earth as rain. In the nineteenth century, it was thought that using explosives would loosen rain from the clouds, and so traveling cannons were often encouraged to visit communities in the hope that rainfall would be stimulated.

Of course, there were a number of popular folk methods of creating rain, including "killing a snake and hanging it belly side up on the fence." In the great drought of the 1890s, an all-but-despairing Bohemian farmer ruefully told a passerby: "I've killed three snakes and hung them on the fence, and each time we got a sprinkle of rain. If I could find enough snakes we'd get plenty of rain."[10]

In the twentieth century, enormous plans were created to relieve the problems of water in the region. Great lasers located in space, it was proposed, would help in the construction of canals to bring water from Canada and Alaska to the Plains. The tensions of drought are always on the minds of Plains folk, and this was thoughtfully articulated in Steve Martin's movie *Leap of Faith* (1992), which told the story of a huckster who through a religious tent revival conned Plains folk to give up their money in hopes of cures from physical ailments as well as much-needed rain. At the end of the film, as the fraudulent faith healer leaves town, rain does indeed fall on the community.

Larger-than-Life Heroes, Cowboys, and Outlaws

Along with these large regional myths go stories about larger-than-life heroes, cowboys, and outlaws. These were an important characteristic of Plains folklore during the late nineteenth and early twentieth centuries, whether they were of Paul Bunyan, Febold Feboldson, John Henry, or the many regional cowboys and outlaws. Stories of Paul Bunyan were an important part of the Oklahoma Oil Patch. Bunyan had a great gray wolf who was often described in terms of Oil-Patch lore as "derrick-high and slushpit wide," an animal that Bunyan meets in the middle of the ocean while swimming, and that he hitches to a buckboard to create the first mail line to Oklahoma.

It should be stated at the outset that including Paul Bunyan, Febold Feboldson, and even John Henry as folklore raises some interesting folkloric issues. A number of these characters might more realistically be called fakelore rather than folklore. For example, the Bunyan character has been traced back to a logging company that not only created a Paul Bunyan logo to sell its products but also created the story around the Bunyan character, which might more properly be called a product of popular culture.[11] However, this brings up another point about folklore and popular culture. It can also be argued that though Bunyan began his life as a pop-culture icon, he can also be understood to be appropriated from popular culture by local folks and made into folklore. This is a point of debate among folklorists, but offers another way to understand the fluid nature of folklife.

Another example of this move from pop culture to folk culture, is the stories of Febold Feboldson, which seem to have originated in Nebraska and provide yet another example of a humorously exaggerated mythical figure. Feboldson tales were originally published by Nebraskans Wayne Carroll and Don Holmes. These tales were then popularized through the work of Paul R. Beath.[12] Febold, like his larger-than-life counterparts, liked big jobs, whether they were killing pests like grasshoppers and coyotes or killing droughts. Febold, it was said, laid the boundary between Nebraska and Kansas after Paul Bunyan's futile attempt to plow a twisted furrow that was to become the Republican River. It was said that Febold, in his ingenuity and inventiveness, patiently spent fifteen years in breeding eagles with bees until he had a hive of bees as big as eagles.

African Americans in Oklahoma often told both Paul Bunyan and John Henry stories. The John Henry character appears to have come from a distinctive southern folk ballad tradition. The story that follows was recorded and published as part of the WPA guides to all the states created in the 1930s. These guides were apparently not always reliable in distinguishing authentic folk traditions from liter-

A Wild Bill Hickock reenactor stands guard over Deadwood's historic Main Street. The real Hickock was gunned down in a saloon here, forever connecting him with the mining camp. Gaming and historic preservation are the town's main draws now. Courtesy South Dakota Tourism.

ary or quasi-literary fabrications, which may account for the John Henry ballad/song tradition being turned into the story that echoes the move to Oklahoma of former slaves in the post–Civil War period.

Old John Henry drifted into Oklahoma without either cottonseed or planting tools and found that none of the Indians would sell him any land. But he wasn't discouraged; he just up and drank all the water out of the Canadian River, then took and put his two hands together and drug'em along the sandy bed of the river, plowing it up with his fingers. Then he reached into the sky to get him cotton plants from the big patches up there that some folks call clouds. . . . Was this John Henry a big man? Well, I never seen him till he was four hundred and sixty years old, and by then he was kind of shriveled, not more than seventeen hoe-handles between his eyes.[13]

From Bunyan to Febold to Henry, all these stories, whether folklore, fakelore, or fakelore appropriated as folklore, reveal a heroic, ingenious, and inventive pioneer mythology mixed with a humorous, tall-tale account of frontier and settler life. It should not be forgotten that in the age of the comic-book heroes, Superman landed in Kansas and was brought up by Kansas natives.

The cowboy, although perhaps not quite of the stature of Bunyan, Henry, or Superman, was still an important larger-than-life figure in Great Plains folklore.

The cowboy was a man in full, a rootin' tootin' son-of-a-gun, tougher than the leather of this saddle. Had he met a "big wind," he would have galloped dead against it; had he encountered a giant grasshopper, he would have peppered the insect with his six-shooter. Indeed, the ordinary activities of the cowboy out-fictioned the farmer's folk fiction. The puncher rode hard, shot fast, drank copiously, and, as verified by subsequent exhumations, often died with his boots on. In his midst moved "Bat" Masterson, "Wild Bill" Hickock, "Doc" Holliday, "Big Nose Kate," and other incredible persons.[14]

A number of stories are characterized by exaggeration in relation to outlaws. For example, there was the tale of the Panhandle cowboy who was caught by outlaws about 1870.

The hard hearted villains cooped the cowboy up in a barrel and rolled him out on the prairie to die of thirst and starvation. Several hours later a herd of buffaloes passed that way and one came close to sniff curiously at the barrel. As it turned away, its tail slipped through the bunghole and the cowboy seized it. The frightened animal began to run and, the cowboy guiding him by instinct, they reached a town where the barrel was opened and the man released.[15]

Stories abound about all those who came into contact with various regional outlaws such as Jesse James or the Dalton Gang, sometimes portrayed in Robin Hood style, sometimes as evildoers. Jim Hoy tells two stories handed down in his family of meetings with both James and the Daltons.

It seems that a stranger came by one evening (this was before Grandpa Russell's birth) riding a spirited, beautiful black stallion. He asked for supper, a stall for his horse, and permission to sleep in the barn. All were granted, except the stranger was denied the barn; the family insisted that he sleep in the house—and that he eat breakfast with them as well.

Next morning as they were finishing breakfast, a group of men rode up and the stranger met them at the door, talked softly with their leader, then went to saddle his horse. As the men were galloping out of the farmyard, the family heard one of the band call out, "Let's go, Jess," just as their late guest turned in his saddle on his rearing horse to wave good-bye. Under his plate at the breakfast table was a twenty-dollar gold piece, tribute to the legendary generosity of Jesse James.[16]

Hoy also mentions that there are stories of James dressing up as a woman who stays the night and then gives to the female of the house a big bag of flour and a gold coin at the base of that sack.

Not to be outdone with stories of James and his gang, Hoy also tells the story of a family member, Uncle Frank Goodnight, meeting the Dalton Gang:

Uncle Frank spent his youth near Dexter, Kansas, in the southern Flint Hills. While in his late teens he and another boy made money one fall by custom-shelling corn. Good money. In fact, one autumn Saturday when some of their customers met the boys in town to settle up, Uncle Frank had over eight hundred dollars in his pocket. His partner told him that he'd better get the money in a safe place because Grat Dalton had been seen on the streets of Dexter earlier that day. So Uncle Frank put the money in the bank (which wouldn't seem to me to have been the safest place, considering the attitude of the Daltons towards banks, but it turned out that Uncle Frank knew what he was doing), then later that evening got into his wagon and started the drive to the family ranch.

The trail home led through a grove of trees in an unpopulated area, and in the darkness of the grove a voice rang out, ordering him to stop and give over the money—or whatever it is that outlaws yell. For some reason (bravery, or perhaps dread because he had no money to give over) the boy slapped the reins and the horses took off at a run, shots and yells ringing out. The outlaws soon quit the chase, but Uncle Frank kept running the horses—until one of them fell dead in the traces as they neared the house, victim of a gunshot wound. Once inside, Uncle Frank discovered that the middle finger of his left hand was hanging by a shred. He hadn't felt any pain from the bullet because of all the excitement, but he did feel it when the doctor amputated what was left.

I'm told that Uncle Frank usually wore buckskin gloves, and that the empty little finger of the left glove always stuck out, a reminder for the rest of his life of this close call with the notorious Dalton Gang.[17]

Environment

The natural world played a central role in Plains life and folklife. Stories about the weather and about the environment, in particular, its flora and fauna, form a central thread in Plains folklore. The weather is harsh and extreme in the Great Plains. Unlike other regions whose climate is modified by the influences of large bodies of water, the Great Plains is located at the center of the country, away from maritime influences, and thus has extremes of hot and cold, as well as the drama of the tornado. This harsh climate inspires a generous amount of folklore with a strong dose of improbability to test the uninitiated, as is demonstrated by the stories of testing the wind before leaving home.

Almost every dwelling will have some opening that can be pointed out as a "crowbar hole." The town innocent, inquiring into the purpose of the opening, will learn that it is to test the wind velocity. If the crowbar merely bends when thrust through the hole, it is safe to go out. However, if the bar is broken off, it is better to stay in the house.[18]

The antics of the wind were also a source of humor for Plains storytellers, as is indicated by this story from Kansas:

The winds that swept across the big farms often reached hurricane velocity. The ducks' feathers were invariably blown onto the ducks. Frequently the wind scooped the cellar from beneath the house but left the house intact, hoisted the well from under the pump but left the pump intact, and carried the whole farm away but left the mortgage intact.[19]

Weather is always a topic of conversation on the Plains, as in this folk meditation on Oklahoma weather:

To say that the weather in Oklahoma is subject to extremes is an understatement. Instead of rain storms, we get dust storms. On the same day, one man can die of sunstroke at noon while his neighbor freezes to death that night.

Now, as you may well suspect, this finicky weather has an adverse effect upon our frogs. I've known the temperature to drop so fast that our frogs are stuck with their heads above the ice. One bull frog I seen musta been caught in the middle of a leap, because he was sprawled across the ice with the tip of one foot caught inside![20]

Drought is a fear at the back of most Great Plains residents' minds, as the drought buster story shows. However, one must remember the caveat about Feboldson as either fakelore or folklore.

> Back in the early days, the Plains folk were often in need of a good drought buster during the hot summer months. The sun would shine and shine, and the clouds would scuttle right quick over the Plains without dropping rain. One year, it got so bad that Febold Feboldson, that legendary Swede who could bust the driest drought in a day, got annoyed. He liked his fishin', right enough, and there was no fishin' to be had in that drought. So he sat down and thought up a way to bust that there drought.
>
> Febold Feboldson decided to build huge bonfires around all the lakes in the region. If he kept the fires real hot, the lake water would evaporate and form clouds. Febold set to work at once hauling wood and building bonfires. Soon, there were so many clouds in the sky on account of all the vaporizing water that they bumped into one another and made rain.
>
> Once the pump was primed, so to speak, the rains came regularly again. But were the settlers happy? No sir. Now they had no place to swim![21]

The Great Plains is dominated by agriculture and ranching activities. Thus an engagement with the world of nature forms an important part of Great Plains folklore, whether it be in folk stories that represent the environmental region as a whole or the many ways to combat the pests that threatened Plains life. Plains fauna offers a rich set of regional stories and folk activities in the Plains. Whereas insects and animals could be a scourge of regional life, the racing of turtles gave pleasure to both young and old.

A number of insects and animals have been and are a scourge to agricultural life in the region and are an important part of understanding Plains life, such as the grasshopper, the Hessian fly, the chinch-bug and the jackrabbit. In the 1950s and 1960s, schools and farming organizations would assign points to various pests such as sparrows and starlings or rats, crows, mice, skunks, and coyotes, and teams would collect points to win. The grasshopper and the jackrabbit exemplify various folk traditions developed to address large infestations of these creatures.

Grasshoppers

Grasshoppers have given birth to numerous stories of their great size, power, and disdain, as the following story from Kansas gives notice. It tells of grasshoppers as

> large as mules. Champing huge mandibles and lashing great antennae, the monster insects deliberately bullied the hogs, cows, and sheep. Nothing escaped their voracious appetites. Wagons and well platforms were favored tidbits. Armed with axe handles, buggywhips, and pitchforks, the gargantuan

hoppers fought viciously in fence corners for the last ear of corn. After devouring the crops they would insolently pick their teeth on the bars of the barbed wire fence.[22]

In a collection of folktales for children compiled by the South Dakota state government, children are told the following grasshopper story that mingles giant insects and the power of God:

> They tormented the cattle and horses and ate the leaves off vegetables, the wood off pitchforks, rakes and hoes. They flew in swarms thick enough to choke a man. Beginning in 1874, an infestation of the worst kind plagued the plains of eastern South Dakota. Fighting the swarms of grasshoppers was beginning to look like an effort in futility when Father Pierre Boucher decided to appeal to a Higher Authority to help save the crops. The pastor led a pilgrimage on an 11-mile trek from field to field. In each field a giant cross was erected to ward off the grasshoppers, and the people prayed for divine intervention to stop the horrible plague. Miraculously, their prayers were answered. The grasshoppers disappeared that very same day.[23]

Grasshoppers, as Great Plains folklorists James Hoy and Tom Isern point out, find a perfect habitat in the mix of both crop production and livestock production on the Plains.[24] Thus the region has historically seen great infestations in the 1870s, 1890s, and 1930s, which led to some rather dramatic folk inventions often called hopperdozers. These various folk responses often revolved around designing a sled maneuvered by a team of horses. Grasshoppers would jump up in front of the sled, bound off a barrier at the front, die, and then fall into a reservoir of oil. Though some tried to submit patents on these various inventions, the designs sprang up so frequently at particular historical moments around the region that patents were rarely granted. Because of the application of pesticides, it is much rarer to see large infestations of grasshoppers today, but one can still walk through fields and pastures and watch them rise up before you. Grasshoppers are still an important, recognizable regional animal, as the example of the roadside attraction that claims to have the largest grasshopper in the world suggests.

Jackrabbit Culls

One remarkable folk tradition arose around the jackrabbit in the latter part of the nineteenth century and especially during drought years such as the 1930s. Jackrabbit drives were created to cull explosive numbers. These events were social in nature and were often sponsored by fraternal organizations such as the Lions or by chapters of the Farm Bureau and chambers of commerce. At the center of a rabbit-drive area was a large pen shaped like a V. Hundreds and occasionally thousands of people would encircle an area waving their arms, making loud noises, and carrying implements. In doing so, they would move toward the center of the drive, propelling frightened rabbits into the pen. Hoy reports that one of the most successful drives occurred in Dighton, Kansas, when 35,000 rabbits were killed.[25]

Turtle Diversions

According to Hoy, turtles are often raced in the Plains during the summer to provide local diversion for children who might win a free pass to swimming pools or other summer activities.[26] However, in the 1930s, prizes were more substantial when a number of rodeo promoters offered turtle racing as a prominent side attraction. The 101 Ranch in Ponca City, Oklahoma, had a National Terrapin Derby at the same time as its annual rodeo. Indeed, turtle racing was such a large event that the National Terrapin Derby saw thousands of turtles placed on the racing circuit, with prize money running from the hundreds to the thousands of dollars.

Fauna on the Highway

Plains people think nothing of driving tens or sometimes hundreds of miles just to visit with friends or relatives or to do marketing or business. Several folk stories relate to taking long road trips and bumping into the enormous armadillos or giant blacksnakes sunning themselves on the road (as they are wont to do). A collision between these great animals and a car often leaves the humans in worse shape and frequently lands the car in the ditch.

Larger-than-Life Flora

The mythology around Plains farming arose at a time when farming was seen as creating an incredible, sometimes unbelievable, abundance of larger-than-life crops.

> The story goes that Lem Blanchard went forth one afternoon in mid-July to inspect his cornfield in the Republican Valley. He scaled a young stalk to overlook the forest-like field and from its top was able to see into the next county. When he turned to descend he was horrified to find that the stalk was growing upward faster than he could scramble down. For ten days he made back-breaking efforts to reach the ground. At last, to keep himself from starving to death, kind neighbors who had tracked him down to the foot of the towering stalk shot Lem dead.[27]

Another version of the story suggests that Lem was rescued by a balloonist, and of course these large cornstalks grew in gigantic Kansas fields "so wide that by the time the mortgage was recorded on the west side, the mortgage on the east side had come due."[28] Instead of Jack and the bean stalk, Jack on the cornstalk was also a favorite of Kansas storytellers:

> Once, a Kansas farmer sent his son Jack to check on the growth of the corn in the field. Now Jack was not a tall lad, so he decided to take a ladder with him. When he found a nice big stalk of corn, he leaned the ladder against it and climbed up until he could reach the first joint. From there, he proceeded to the top of the cornstalk, and looked out over the field. There was enough corn there for a rich harvest.
> Excited by his discovery, Jack started back down the corn stalk. He real-

ized suddenly that it had kept growing while he was at the top. He stepped from joint to joint, but it grew so fast he never reached the ground. Meanwhile, Jack's father wondered what was taking the boy so long. He knew there was no use in hunting for him in the forest of corn, so he climbed to the top of the windmill. He saw Jack's predicament soon enough, and gathered the neighborhood men. They tried to chop down the cornstalk, but the cornstalk was growing so fast there were eighteen inches separating every chop. Finally, they gave up, and Jack was forced to stay on the cornstalk until a drought came and it finally stopped growing.[29]

Rural and Urban Ghoulishness

Many of the stories previously related were recorded and published beginning in the 1930s under the Works Progress Administration Project, one of Franklin Roosevelt's programs to give work to writers and researchers in the Great Depression. Other stories have come from Plains folklorists who were reflecting back on their youth. There is yet another type of story that should be included, namely, the ghost story. WPA Project workers reported rural legends such as the Greeley County, Kansas, ghost of White Woman Creek. This is a white-clad woman who drowned herself in the river after she found her lover lying dead on its banks. There was also said to be a giant panther whose fiery eyes and hideous screech occasionally revive themselves. More recently there have been numerous rural legends, often told by teenagers, of men traveling the countryside looking for romantic youths in parked cars and killing one or both occupants. However, in the latter part of the twentieth century, there was apparently a move to tell stories of urban legend rather than rural. For example, there is the story of the Hamburger Man of Hutchinson, who was so disfigured by an accident that his face was like a hamburger. According to Hoy and Isern, he lives either in a shack in the sandhills or close to the state reformatory, among other sinister locations, and roams the Hutchinson area, in particular, Hamburger Hill. "What he does to teenagers found parked in the country is too horrible to relate. In his spare time he also steals children and mutilates livestock. Sometimes he carries an ax with which to dispatch his victims. Other times he has a hook in place of his right hand."[30]

Another powerful folk legend involves the Albino Lady near Rochester Cemetery in Topeka, Kansas. She also has physical oddity as an albino and dresses in white with a white poodle. Teenagers look for her; younger children are afraid because she is said to steal children from schoolyards if they stay too late in the evening. The Caney River (Kansas) Wildman, the Ponca City (Oklahoma) Deer Woman, and the McLaughlin (South Dakota) Bigfoot are other examples of such characters.

Folklorist Jennie Chin has argued that though there are very strong ethnic traditions in the state represented in food, folk arts, and folk performance (music, song, and dance), there are few ethnic oral traditions in the Great Plains.[31] This is not to say that narrative traditions are not passed on, but that these traditions are now wrapped in the transfer of material folk possessions within families.

Folk Songs

Just as folktales can be modified in each generation and within a region, so songs can be transformed. Folklorists argue that in each generation, some aspects of a song are transformed while others remain stable. They also argue that songs can be considered as recomposed in each generation. There are, of course, folklore practitioners who like to identify the original song and perform that, whereas others enjoy watching how the needs of the culture at any particular historical moment will be met by modifications in tradition.

A song usually begins as an expression of someone's personal experiences and feelings. It transforms into a folk song when it is passed along, rephrased, and used by others who find that it also articulates their feelings. It remains a folk song as long as people sing it in their own way, adding various styles or nuances in performance so that it is a dynamic, living tradition. A folk song is not usually memorized word for word, but instead is recomposed each time it is performed. Great Plains folk songs revolve primarily around the landscape itself, echoing the importance of landscape in regional identity, as well as farming and ranching. The most famous example of a song that has changed across the region is the song originally called "My Western Home."

"My Western Home," Dr. Brewster Higley (?–1911)

Oh, give me a home where the Buffalo roam,
Where the Deer and the Antelope play;
Where never is heard a discouraging word,
And the sky is not clouded all day.

CHORUS
A home! A home!
Where the Deer and the Antelope play,
Where seldom is heard a discouraging word,
And the sky is not clouded all day.

Oh! give me a land where the bright diamond sand
Throws its light from the glittering streams,
Where glideth along the graceful white swan,
Like the maid in her heavenly dreams.

Oh! give me a gale of the Solomon vale,
Where the life streams with buoyancy flow;
On the banks of the Beaver, where seldom if ever,
Any poisonous herbage doth grow.

How often at night, when the heavens were bright,
With the light of the twinkling stars
Have I stood here amazed, and asked as I gazed,
If their glory exceed that of ours.

I love the wild flowers in this bright land of ours,
I love the wild curlew's shrill scream;
The bluffs and white rocks, and antelope flocks
That graze on the mountains so green.

The air is so pure and the breezes so fine,
The zephyrs so balmy and light,
That I would not exchange my home here to range
Forever in azures so bright.[32]

"My Western Home," better known as "Home on the Range," was adopted as the
state song of Kansas, but it is a song familiar to people all over the Plains. Created
by an obscure folk poet, Dr. Brewster Higley, a country doctor, it was written as a
poem known as "Western Home." It was put to music by local musician Dan Kelley
and called "My Western Home." At this point the song is not folklore. It becomes
folklore when it is transformed, moving about the region in true folk tradition and
becoming variously "My Texas Home," "My Colorado Home," and, further afield,
"My Arizona Home." A wonderful sense of how this folk song has been richly interpreted and reinterpreted can be gained from visiting National Public Radio's Web
site and listening to artists such as Gene Autry in the early 1940s, Frank Sinatra, and
the Central Heights Elementary Chorus, Richmond, Kansas (2002), sing this song.[33]
The role of landscape in regional folk songs cannot be overestimated. Numerous
American anthems celebrate the nation in terms of its landscape, for example, "America the Beautiful"'s "amber waves of grain" and "for purple mountain majesties." Just
as landscape profoundly shapes national identity, so it shapes regional identity.

There are also regional songs that celebrate the agricultural abundance of the
region, as seen in the Methodist hymn "Beulah Land" that was transformed to reflect the Kansas experience.

"Beulah Land"

I've reached the land of corn and wheat,
Of pumpkin pies and potatoes sweet.
I bought my farm from Uncle Sam,
And now I'm happy as a clam.
Oh, Kansas Land, sweet Kansas Land.

As on the highest hill I stand,
I look the pleasant landscape o'er,
For acres broad I'll sigh no more,
Till Gabriel's trump, in loud command,
Says I must leave my Kansas Land.

My chickens, they are Plymouth Rock,
My horses, Clydesdale Norman stock,
My cattle, Durham, very fine,
And Poland China are my swine.
Dakota Land, Dakota Land,

As on the highest hill I stand,
I look the pleasant landscape o'er,
For acres broad I'll sigh no more,
Till Gabriel's trump, in loud command,
Says I must leave Dakota Land.

Saskatchewan, the land of snow,
Where winds are always on the blow,
Where people sit with frozen toes—

And why we stay here, no one knows.
Saskatchewan, Saskatchewan,

There's no place like Saskatchewan.
We sit and gaze across the plains,
And wonder why it never rains,
Till Gabriel doth his trumpet sound,
And says the rain has gone around.[34]

"Beulah Land" was then metamorphosed through folkloric means into numerous Plains variants such as "Kansas Land," or "Dakota Land." Not only does the song have regional variations, but the various songs often reflect the prevailing Plains environment, from the land of "corn and wheat" to the land of "drought and heat."

Ranching or, more specifically, cowboy songs and ballads display some interesting themes. For example, they often deal with meeting an untimely end and exhibit a powerful preoccupation with death and the afterlife.

"The Dim Narrow Trail"

Last night I lay on the prairie
Looking up at the stars in the sky
I wondered if ever a cowboy
Would go to that sweet by and by.

The trail to that far mystic region
Is narrow and dim all the way,
While the road that leads to perdition
Is posted and blazed all the way.

They say there will be a grand round-up,
Where cowboys like cattle must stand,
To be cut by the riders of judgement
Who are posted and know every brand.

Perhaps there will be a stray cowboy
Unbranded by anyone nigh
Who'll be cut by the riders of judgement
And shipped to the sweet by and by.[35]

Cowboy songs can also indicate a lighthearted disregard for life and death, as in this song:

A friend of mine once stole a horse,
   'Twas a place out West.
The horse just left his owner
   Cause he liked my friend the best.
My friend had lots of trouble
   When the owner came on deck,
When he found the horse had had
   A string around his neck.

Chorus:
   A little piece of string it seems a tiny thing,
   But strong enough to keep the horse in check

When my friend I last did see, he was hanging from a tree
With a little piece of string around his neck.[36]

Folk songs often reveal the working life of cowboys and the desire to be back on the range after a hard winter, as this song suggests:

"Come alive you fellers," hear the foreman shout.
  "Drop your books and banjos, fetch your saddles out. . . .
"Shake that squeaky fiddle, Red, go and get your hoss,
  "Dutch, ain't you got duties, as the chuck-wagon boss?
"Range is gettin' grassy, winter draws its claws,
  "Calves are fat an' sassy, teasin' of their maws,
"Loafin' days are over, dreamin' time is gone,
  "No more life in clover, for the round-up's on."[37]

Cowboy poetry is alive and well on the Great Plains, and poets get together regularly across the American West to celebrate and perform their craft. These get-togethers can range from the large-scale National Cowboy Poetry Gathering in Elko, Nevada, to small-scale meetings such as the Lawrence (Kansas) Cowboy Winter Gathering.[38] Whether they are stories of pests and weather or songs celebrating the beauty of the landscape and the hard work done in that space, folk stories and folk songs reveal a fascinating preoccupation with the regional environment.

GREAT PLAINS MATERIAL FOLKLORE AND ITS PRACTICE

Though folk stories and songs had a strong tradition in nineteenth- and twentieth-century life, the harshness of the environment in which Plains folk live has been at least somewhat modified by various agricultural and domestic technologies, from pesticides to the air-conditioned cab of a combine harvester and to homes with double glazing and satellite television. Some folklorists have argued that tales of the environment have diminished in importance as people have developed ways of limiting its effects on Plains folk. If that is the case, and this is a big if, then it is necessary to look to other places to establish Plains folklore. These places can include, but should not be limited to, familial folklore that surrounds material culture, the material culture of the automobile age, namely, the roadside attraction, and the cemetery.

Familial folklore is often associated with material culture, family keepsakes such as jewelry, quilts, and the like. This familial folklore can also be a place where the stories of women's lives are revealed and social relations become more apparent. The desire for luck has always been an important force in folklife, and one particular association can be found with the little-known folk tradition of charm strings. Folklorists have identified charm strings as being made of very small items, such as buttons, that were traded among girls who attended social events in the late nineteenth and early twentieth centuries. These charms were seen as giving good luck. They also work as an aid to memory. As a person moves his or her hands down a charm string, the individual items can both catalog past events and create good feelings from remembering good times and people. Folklorist Jay Bailey suggests that family stories surrounding and inhabiting charm strings can provide information about a region's folklore, in particular, the social relations that shape regional life. A string that belonged to Bailey's maternal grandmother, who lived on the Plains, spanned a sixty-year period from 1888 to 1950 and holds 271 items threaded on a four-foot length of string. The string contains a few unusual mementoes, including an inch-long pair of beaded moccasins that, according to Bailey, were given meaning by the story his mother told. The shoes were

given to grandmother by a Potawatomi Indian family which had made them. This was near Earlsboro, Oklahoma. At that time not everyone was friendly with the Indian population, but this family had been befriended by my great-grandmother. They, in turn, gave this little token to grandmother as a kind of goodwill gesture. Grandmother was nine at the time, so the year would have been 1897.[39]

Another rich folkloric tradition was connected to a rain slicker (raincoat) button on the charm string. Bailey recounts a story located in Nebraska that his mother recalled her mother telling her about this button.

Auntie was alone in the farmhouse when a man rode up one rainy day asking for food and some hot water. This raised suspicions, but she complied with the request. She excused herself briefly on the pretext of securing meat. While in the kitchen, she put out a distress flag. Apparently neighbors in the area had mutually prearranged to summon help for one another at this signal. Auntie took her time preparing the meal; she even packed other food for the man to take along with the hot water. In the meantime, a neighbor had seen the flag and had gone to summon the sheriff. He arrived in time to track the man's horse in spite of the rain. As the story goes, he was a member of the Dalton gang. He needed the hot water to dress the wound of a gang member who had been shot during a holdup. As he turned his horse to leave, the button caught on the gate. Auntie kept it as a memento. It so happened that there was a reward for the capture of the gang, so Auntie was able to collect the money. It must have been a substantial amount, for the tale ends with the money being used by the family to move to Oklahoma and buy a land relinquishment. The story is almost too romantic to be true. But who am I to question a good family tale![40]

In Bailey's case, his family strings reveal much about the relationships between Indian and Euro-American settlers and between the community and nefarious interlopers.

These material culture possessions, whether they be lucky charms, a rain slicker button, quilts, handmade toys, or even recipes or songs, are handed down attached to the folklore of the Plains. However, there are a number of larger-scale folk traditions that are visible beyond the family context that also reflect folk concerns on the regional landscape.

Roadside attractions are a profound material representation of both historical and contemporary Great Plains folklore. However, as with the Feboldson, Bunyan, and Henry examples, the situation is a little more complex. These often eccentric landscapes offer the viewer a fascinating display of how at least some Plains folk see themselves and their region and how they seek to both portray it and sometimes play on its stereotypical image. Great Plains roadside attractions vary from the more official landscapes of Mount Rushmore and its evolving neighbor the Crazy Horse Memorial, both in South Dakota, to the quirky Carhenge in Alliance, Nebraska. Folklorist John Dorst suggests that these are all places to which the tourist might be drawn on the spur of the moment to explore various, often radical landscapes.[41] Roadside attractions are about the strange, the wondrous, the bizarre, and the kitschy. This strangeness distinguishes them from other landscape locations such as historical markers and scenic overlooks and includes both commercial and vernacular folk spaces because the wondrous, strange, bizarre, and kitschy know no boundaries. The roadside attractions mentioned here are both what folklorists call true folk tradition and popular culture. For example, the Garden of Eden and the Biggest Ball of Twine (both in Kansas) can truly be called folk, while some of the pieces of large statuary are used to promote commercial ventures, such as the world's largest pheasant on a liquor store in South Dakota. While these distinctions are important, it seems that all of these material creations have some folkloric aspects, for example, when pop culture appropriates the folkloric traditions of the biggest and tallest local fauna to sell alcohol.

Great Plains roadside attractions are rich and various and reveal several prominent themes that often echo regional folklore narratives, such as the abundant and oversized flora and fauna and big men. Additional themes that echo unique aspects of the region include the celebration of conserving materials and the modification of urban spaces.

Great Plains Flora and Fauna

Creating roadside attractions out of vegetative matter has long been a tradition on the Plains. One of the best places to find information on roadside attractions is the Web site http://www.roadsideamerica.com/, which offers a mix of folklore and commercial material culture and often keeps a running commentary from different travelers who tell if the attraction is still there, has been modified, or has been moved to another location. For example, the Corn Palace in Mitchell, South Dakota, was constructed as a monument to South Dakota's fertility with a rich mix of onion domes and minarets. Built out of reinforced concrete, it is covered every spring by large murals made from thousands of bushels of native South Dakota corn, grain, and grasses. The world's largest peanut can be found in Durant, Oklahoma, in front of the city hall. For a number of years at the end of the 1990s and early into the 2000s, there was a hay-bale family waving at the road beside a hay-bale tractor made of large round hay bales located in Beulah, North Dakota, a landscape that comes and goes at the whim of its creators.

There are three giant buffaloes to be found in Chamberlain, South Dakota, outside Al's Oasis, a twelve-foot cow outside Dickinson, North Dakota, and a large bull outside the cattle stockyards in Napoleon, North Dakota. A giant whooping crane stands just off I-90, and the world's largest pheasant is placed atop a liquor store in Huron, South Dakota (twenty feet tall and forty feet long), while a diminutive version graces Redfield, a city that calls itself the Pheasant Capital of the World. Prairie dogs seem to be perhaps the most repeated representation of Plains fauna. At Cactus Flats, South Dakota, is a concrete prairie dog outside a store created in the 1950s, while Oakley, Kansas, features the "biggest prairie dog in the world," made from 8,000 pounds of concrete. Perhaps most unlikely is the Blue Whale in Catoosa, Oklahoma, where Hugh Davis, in true folkloric tradition, created a sandy beach, picnic tables, and a snack stand for his wife's birthday. It is now owned and operated by the city of Catoosa as a unique feature of the community's cultural landscape.

Taking the fauna theme further than its mid-twentieth-century tradition, local artists have been creating large animals en masse. In Montrose, South Dakota, the Porter Sculpture Park displays a giant bullhead, a jumping fish from a cracked bowl, vultures, and various dragons. Not to be outdone, a group has raised money to create a large animal highway between Regent and Gladstone, North Dakota, including a group of large pheasants, a sixty-foot rooster and fifty-foot hen with three twelve-foot chicks, together with the world's largest grasshopper, flying geese and jumping deer, and a seventy-foot buffalo, strung along what is now called the Enchanted Highway, a thirty-two-mile paved country road that leads from Interstate 94. Is this folklore, fakelore, or an economic development effort to encourage passing tourists to stop in a community to spend a little money? Perhaps it has aspects of all three.

The Biggest

Claims for the biggest bird, prairie dog, or grasshopper are rife on the Plains, along with the world's largest sandhill crane in Steel, North Dakota, which is close to the world's largest holstein in New Salem, North Dakota. The world's largest pheasant in Huron, South Dakota, has already been mentioned. But it is not only the fauna that are flaunted with the "biggest" claims. Grandiose claims include the deepest hand-dug well in Greensburg, Kansas (completed in 1888 at a depth of 109 feet), and the largest ball of twine (also in Kansas), or the "World's Largest Ball of Stamps" in Omaha, Nebraska. Why might this region enjoy making such grand claims? In many ways, this region was shaped by very grand and ultimately unrealizable claims of generous rainfall, "the rain will follow the plow." When these claims were not

Steel and fiberglass have been molded to create a 28-foot-tall, 22-ton pheasant in Huron. From its beak to the tip of its feathered tail, the world's largest pheasant affirms Huron as a premier pheasant hunting spot. Courtesy South Dakota Tourism.

Biggest ball of stamps created in Omaha, Nebraska, is a solid ball weighing 600 pounds, and pasted by the Boys Town stamp-collecting club in the 1950s. © Girls and Boys Town.

realized, equally grandiose plans were made to meet the limitations of the land, including channeling water from Alaska and diverting water from one watershed to another to meet the Plains' agricultural needs. Perhaps these grandiose claims are part of a much larger tradition of imagining great possibilities. Others might argue that in a landscape where everything is made so small by an infinite sky, things need to be built big to be recognized in a landscape that can flatten human-constructed spaces.

Indeed, another important subset of roadside attractions is made up of those that work to locate the individual in this large space. For example, the geographic center of the forty-eight states is celebrated in Lebanon, Kansas, with a stone podium, flagpole, and a "Chapel at the Center." In contrast, the geographic center of North America is celebrated in the town of Rugby, North Dakota, with a fifteen-foot-tall rock obelisk flanked by Canadian and U.S. flags. The first person to map North Dakota, David Thompson, is celebrated with a globe that sits in a field west of the town formally known as Verendrye.

Big Men of the Great Plains

Matching the rich variety of giant fauna are a remarkable number of large men who populate the Great Plains landscape. These large-scale figures advertise a local merchant or organization created in the mid-twentieth century and then handed down to new commercial vendors whose products may not bear much connection to these tall figures. It should be noted that many of these types of roadside sculptures are more booster-inspired commercial objects than strict folklore, though they often appropriate folkloric and sometimes fakeloric images to do their work. Remarkably, there are few if any large women. In Carrington, North Dakota, there is a Muffler Man outside a hotel; in Auburn, Nebraska, Hamburger Man can be found outside the small café of Dairy Sweet. The giant oil man or roustabout in Tulsa, Oklahoma, also called the "Golden Boy" or "Golden Driller," has been located on the top of the International Petroleum Exhibition building in the Tulsa Fair Grounds since 1966. In a play on the roustabout icon, the Golden Boy was recently joined by "Roustabird," an oil-drilling penguin with overalls and hard hat, part of a local project to raise funds for Tulsa's new penguin habitat. Native American men are also featured on the Plains, including a fifteen-foot fiberglass Indian in front of a car dealership in Clinton, Oklahoma,

The Golden Driller, located in Tulsa, was built in 1966 for the International Petroleum Exposition. This 76-foot-tall symbol of an oil field worker represents a major part of the region's history. Courtesy Oklahoma Tourism.

and an Indian chief approximately twenty-five feet tall outside a tobacco shop in Big Cabin, Oklahoma.

In New Town, North Dakota, Earl Bunyan, supposed brother to Paul Bunyan, was dreamed up and built to the height of twenty feet by Fred La Rocque. Ironically, this regional theme of large men was then caricatured in the movie *Fargo* by a statue of Paul Bunyan created by the moviemakers and placed outside Bathgate, North Dakota. These monumental roadside sculptures of big male figures, utilizing both folklore and fakelore, are perhaps an example of masculine boosterish desire to promote community in the region.

The Celebration of Recycling

In honor of the conservative tendencies of agricultural communities, recycling materials is a popular theme. Agricultural practitioners and agricultural communities have traditionally been labeled as conservative, promoting the desire to conserve items that may be needed at some point in the future. During the 1920s, rural America experienced great economic difficulty, which was then compounded in the 1930s as the Great Depression continued to reshape folklives and promoted values of preservation, just in case things might have a future use. In an interesting example of conservation, Arthur, Nebraska is home to a hay-bale church with stucco coating (1928). These types of collections include Casselton, North Dakota's "largest stack of empty oil cans." Reportedly built in 1933, it stands forty-five feet wide and eighteen feet high. Individuals born during or just after the depression may have maintained a particularly strong desire to conserve possibly useful items, or at least things they could not bear to throw away. The biggest ball of stamps, created in Omaha, Nebraska, is a solid ball weighing six hundred pounds, that was pasted by the Boys Town stamp-collecting club in the 1950s. Yet another case of celebrating conservation is the 16,828-pound ball made of six million feet of sisal twine, with a forty-foot circumference, located in Cawker City, Kansas, also begun in the 1950s. This tradition was taken a step further in the 1980s in Nebraska when Carhenge was constructed by six local families during a reunion in 1987. Whether it be string, old stamps, old cars, or oil cans, the marking of their preservation is an important part of the region's folklore, revealing a strong desire to conserve materials.

Small Town Landscape

Finally, the landscape of small Plains towns has not gone untouched by those who seek to reshape the uniform architecture that simply heralds the name of the community. From the decoration of water towers to city cemeteries, these landscapes reveal the diverse and often humorous folklife of the region. Worthing, South Dakota's metal water tank has been painted as a Pepsi can, whereas Ogallala, Nebraska, has reenvisioned its tower as a giant spaceship with green aliens peeking out of the windows, and Axtell, Nebraska's water tower offers a Smiley Face.

Deathscapes are another important and revealing part of Great Plains folklore, and this region has a number of unique and interesting cemeteries that give a visual indication of regional distinction. In the town of Eli, Nebraska, a number of grave markers are made of petrified wood. In the town of Hugo, Oklahoma, there is an intriguing community celebrated through grave markers, a community of circus people. In Leedey, Oklahoma, the town has created a sculpture that commemorates six fatalities in the tornado that hit the community in 1947. This monument presents a twisted metal representation of a twister (tornado), including elements such as a cow skull, a rusty tricycle, and a cowboy boot.

Ethnic traditions also show themselves in the Plains cemetery landscape. In both North Dakota and Kansas, there is a small tradition of wrought-iron grave markers that is still practiced today and forms an important part of the cemetery landscape. In central North Dakota, Russian German traditions still practiced today have created a fascinating landscape of hand-crafted crosses, bringing Old World folk traditions to the Plains. This tradition can also be found in Victoria, Kansas. Founded originally as an English settlement, Victoria saw itself being claimed by Russian Germans whose cemetery folk landscape was also shaped by a strong wrought-iron tradition. Finally, in the east central part of Oklahoma, areas that were settled by the Seminole and Creek, traditional aboveground cemetery decorations are handmade wooden and sometimes stone structures made to look like small houses, working to cover graves, and many have lasted for decades.

OCCUPATIONAL FOLKLORE

Occupational folklore on the Great Plains includes the study primarily of agriculture (ranching and farming) and resource extraction (oil-patch workers or miners). It includes verbal aspects such as the specific occupational language or jargon, skills and techniques learned informally, codes of behavior, and the customs designed to mark a worker's move through his career. The study of occupational folklore on the Plains has been focused primarily on men's rather than women's occupational work.

Most of the Plains occupations just mentioned were learned through informal methods rather than by formalized training or through a handbook. Thus to understand the folklife of the region, these informal aspects need to be explored. Indeed, most Plains occupations were learned by listening, watching, and participating. For example, cowboys had to learn to anticipate the other workers when herding cattle, rather than to wait for verbal prompts. Oil pipeline fitters learned what their peers were doing outside the line of sight by listening to the specific rhythmic tapping of a wrench to indicate the next plan of action.

Agriculture

There is a rich mix of ethnic groups who were involved in Plains farming in the nineteenth and twentieth centuries. Native Americans such as those members of the Five Civilized Tribes located in Oklahoma brought cotton culture to the southern Plains at the turn of the twentieth century. Former black slaves freed after the Civil War farmed in Oklahoma and to a lesser extent in Kansas. European American settlers from Germany, Czechoslovakia, and Scandinavia, as well as Russian Germans, brought new crops and traditional farming practices. One of the most transformative traditions brought to the region was the introduction of winter wheat, a specific type of wheat bred and grown on the harsh Russian steppes, by the Germans from the Volga region of Russia, a move that dramatically reshaped the region's agricultural economy.

Cowboy and Cowgirl, Farmer, and Miner Occupational Folklore

Great Plains farming, ranching, and mining occupational traditions offer another sense of folklife in the region that complements the larger-than-life folk stories outlined earlier. The work songs, jargon, and skills developed in this landscape offer a unique reaction to life on the Plains frontier. Environmental concerns pervade a number of Plains occupational folk traditions. For example, agricultural folklore suggested that a tipped new moon is an indication of frost. The farmers' folklore goes on to suggest that surface crops, such as grain, should be planted in the light of the moon, and underground root crops must be planted in the dark of the moon.

Environmental factors that change within the Plains also lead to subregional variations in agricultural activity. A useful example of this can be found in the ways in which Plains farmers preserve hay. Hay in the more humid eastern parts of the Plains, where mold can be a problem, is stacked more carefully. In Kansas, for example, it is stored in round, loaf-shaped stacks or in small round bales. Further north and west, as in the western Dakotas and the Nebraska Sand Hills, where the humidity and the resulting mold are not an issue, round metal frames that buckle together act as a dumping ground for a rough stack. Folklorist Jim Hoy points out that this stacking base can be easily unbolted and moved to another location.[42] Though new technology has brought the big round baler to the landscape, not all farmers have invested in such capital-intensive machinery.

Lingering in Great Plains folklore is the concern that agricultural practices may not be good for this region, as the following story about a North Dakota farmer suggests:

> One spring in the early 1880s, a North Dakota pioneer was plowing his land. As he broke through the long prairie grass and turned it under in preparation for planting a crop of wheat, he noticed an old Dakota man watching him. When the pioneer stopped to rest, the old man approached him. The old man examined the plowed ground and finally picked up a clod of prairie grass which had been turned over by the plow. "Wrong side up," he said, and put it down with the grass on top. Then he walked away.
>
> The pioneer thought it a great joke at the time. But the old man was right. North Dakota lost millions of acres of good soil, blown away by the wind, because the settlers had turned the prairie grass wrong side up.[43]

Thus folklore traditions can also work to query the agricultural norms of Plains life.

In the realm of ranching occupational folklore, counting cattle is an activity that dominates cowboy life. Making sure that they are all under surveillance and that the new spring cattle are part of the herd in the fall is essential to a successful ranching operation. Hoy says that every cowboy thinks he can count cattle. "But cattle counting transcends the pragmatic, goes beyond the purely practical consideration of having to pay for missing steers at the end of the pasture season. It's one of those benchmarks of cowboying, a rite of passage that separates the kid from the hand."[44] Counting needs to go on when cattle are delivered in the spring, about once a week during the summer, and then in the fall. Counting usually occurs early in the morning before the cattle start to move toward water for their first drink of the day, or in the evening when the cattle wander off to cool down after a hot Plains day. Counting has its own techniques and protocol. Counting by twos rather than singularly is common, some count higher, in fives, and when cattle are coming by very fast, it is best, according to Hoy to keep counting so at least one can form a good estimate. Cowboys count up to one hundred and mark that figure by holding out a finger, so that counters talk in terms of three fingers and 48, meaning 348 head, or by transferring a rock from one pocket to another.[45]

The role of the cowgirl in Great Plains folklore has received somewhat more belated acknowledgment. Hoy argues that the cowgirl did not become established until a generation after the cowboy, as is highlighted in the story of Willie Mathews, a woman who disguised herself as a man. Mathews' father was an early cattleman, and she was inspired to become a cowgirl from his stories. Mathews, who worked on the cattle trail, apparently told her fellow cowboys her gender just before returning home.

> My papa is an old-time trail driver from Southern Texas. He drove from Texas to Caldwell, Kansas, in the '70s. He liked the country around Caldwell very much, so the last trip he made he went to work on a ranch up there and never returned to Texas any more. . . . I used to hear papa talk so much about the old cow trail and I made up my mind that . . . I was going up the trail if I had to run off. I had a pony of my own and read in the paper of the big herd passing Clayton, so I said, now is my chance. . . . I saddled my pony

and told brother I was going out in the country, and I might be gone for a week, but for him to tell papa not to worry about me, I would be back. I had on a suit of brother's clothes and a pair of his boots. In three or four days I was in Clayton looking for a job and I found one. . . . . Mr. Houston, I am glad I found you to make the trip with, for I have enjoyed it. I am going just as straight home as I can and that old train can't run too fast for me, when I get on it.[46]

Mining

Resource extraction in the form of mining is not extensive on the Plains, but most Plains states have some sort of present or former mining history associated with coal. Mining in Oklahoma was recorded in the Choctaw Nation in the early 1870s, and the state has seen both underground and surface activities. Underground shaft mining was the primary extractive method used until World War II, and miners often worked in pairs, as friends or sometimes family members who shared the same language. Early miners often traveled from the east coast and were British in origin. In the Oklahoma coalfields, the second-largest ethnic group was Italian. Other groups included Germans, Bulgarians, Lithuanians, Poles, and Mexicans. Italians also shaped coal mining in Kansas, for example, in the community of Pittsburg. However, Welsh miners inhabited the town of Emporia, Kansas, and townspeople still celebrate St. David's Day (the patron saint of Wales) on March 1st. Coal miners were often isolated in company towns; mining families took a long time to assimilate into the larger culture. Miners and their families often lived in ethnic neighborhoods that offered services run by other migrants, and thus these groups retained their languages, customs, and folk traditions, including neighborhood social gatherings where they could eat, sing, and dance and celebrate their ethnic folk cultures.

CONCLUSION

The Great Plains is a dramatic and often harsh landscape that has inspired a rich set of folklore traditions. The study of regional folklore offers a wonderfully idiosyncratic and always intriguing window on Great Plains culture. The themes and issues discussed here reveal a number of historical trends in Great Plains folklife. Native American folk traditions focus on the lifeways of Plains tribes, their attitudes to their environment, stories about their beginnings, the establishment of tribal cultures, and their interaction with Euro-American migrants. Native American traditions speak of the central role of the buffalo in Plains life and reveal the impact of European Americans on their way of life. Conquest by white settlers brought biological threats such as smallpox, and folklore traditions also speak about the ways in which Native groups worked to avoid infection.

From the beginning of European interest in the Plains, this region seemed to generate grand, regionwide stories such as that of the seven cities of gold. Early explorers in the nineteenth century offered often contrasting stories about the region, as a desert and a garden. In the post–Civil War period, when whites and blacks began to migrate into the region en masse, folklore traditions revealed some of the frustrations and limitations of the region. Folklore was filled with the drama of a new environment, from gigantic grasshoppers chomping their way through the wheat fields of Kansas to bounteous, enormous ears of corn. Stories of larger-than-life heroes taming the wilderness and creating an agricultural life in the region were prevalent, whether Bunyan, Feboldson, or Henry was the central character. With the rise of the automobile culture in the twentieth century, these folklore characters made their way into the region's material culture representations, from giant gophers to immense corn palaces on the Plains. In the oral folklore of settlers, the differences in religious or ethnic background were less important than the struggles with the region's natural limitations. This "environmental" folklore still lives in contemporary Plains society for several reasons. Plains agriculture remains at the mercy of extreme climatic conditions. In addition, the small farmer and rancher, the backbone of much of the Plains rural life, is disappearing as large agrobusinesses buy up bankrupted properties. The stories of heroic struggle against seemingly impossible odds still have resonance in the region. However, there are other sources of folklore that must be included in the understanding of the region's folklife, stories attached to objects and landscapes. Items such as small charm strings and quilts, occupational folklore, and the study of material culture landscapes of cemeteries should be incorporated to gain a rich sense of the region. In addition, as the Plains rural landscape is depopulated and residents either leave or move to larger communities, the shift from rural to urban legends becomes an increasingly important part of the understanding of the Great Plains.

RESOURCE GUIDE

Printed Sources

Basso, Keith H. "'Stalking with Stories': Names, Places, and Moral Narratives among the Western Apache." In *On Nature: Nature, Landscape, and Natural History*, ed. Daniel Halpern. San Francisco: North Point Press, 1987.

Dorson, Richard M. "Folklore and Fake Lore." *American Mercury* 70 (1950): 335–343.

Dorst, John. "Roadside Attractions." In *Encyclopedia of the Great Plains*, ed. David J. Wishart. Lincoln: University of Nebraska Press, forthcoming 2004.

Hoy, Jim. *Cowboys and Kansas*. Norman: University of Oklahoma Press, 1995.

Hoy, Jim, and Tom Isern. *Plains Folk: A Commonplace of the Great Plains*. Norman: University of Oklahoma Press, 1987.

Marriott, Alice Lee, and Carol K. Rachlin. *American Indian Mythology*. New York: Thomas Crowell, 1968.

Nebraska: A WPA Guide to the Cornhusker State. Lincoln: University of Nebraska Press, 1979.

Oring, Elliott. *Folk Groups and Folklore Genres: An Introduction*. Logan: Utah State University Press, 1986.

Toelken, Barre. *The Dynamics of Folklore*. Boston: Houghton Mifflin, 1979.

WPA Guide to 1930s Kansas. Lawrence: University Press of Kansas, 1984.

WPA Guide to 1930s North Dakota. Bismarck: State Historical Society of North Dakota, 1990.

WPA Guide to 1930s Oklahoma. Lawrence: University Press of Kansas, 1986.

Web Sites

General Sites

American Folklife Center at the Library of Congress
http://lcweb.loc.gov/folklife/afc.html

American Folklore
http://www.americanfolklore.net/folktales/nd.html

American Folklore Society
http://afsnet.org/

Founded in 1888, the society is an association of people who discuss folklore throughout the world.

Center for Folklife and American Heritage at the Smithsonian Institution
http://www.folklife.si.edu/

National Storytelling Network
http://www.storynet.org/

Roadside America
http://www.roadsideamerica.com

A rich and comprehensive roadside attraction Web guide that includes some history.

Urban Legends Research Center
http://www.ulrc.com.au/index.asp

Regional Sites

International Quilt Study Center, University of Nebraska, Lincoln
http://www.quiltstudy.org/

Oklahoma History Museum
http://www.ok-history,mus.ok.us/folk/charm_strings.html (accessed January 8, 2004)

The Web site has some excellent essays on Oklahoma folklife as part of the *Oklahoma Folks* online journal of Oklahoma folklife.

Plains Folk
http://www.plainsfolk.com/songs/song6.htm (accessed January 15, 2004)

Plains Folk is a self-syndicated newspaper column written by Jim Hoy (Emporia, Kansas) and Tom Isern (West Fargo, North Dakota) and devoted to life on the Great Plains of North America.

South Dakota's Governor's Office
http://www.state.sd.us/governor/Kids/legends.htm (accessed January 9, 2000)

Includes a section about legends for kids.

Videos/Films

Some of the best documentaries made about Plains folklife can be found in state public television organizations. A search of their sometimes extensive libraries offers a rich sense of Plains folk traditions. The documentary series are listed here.

Kansas Public Television, *Sunflower Journeys*
http://ktwu.wuacc.edu/journeys/

Nebraska Public Television, *Next Exit*
http://mynptv.org/nextexit/nex_food01.html

Oklahoma Educational Television Authority, *Stateline* and *Gallery*
http://www.oeta.onenet.net/

Prairie Public Television in North Dakota, *Plainstalk*
http://www.prairiepublic.org/

South Dakota Public Broadcasting, *Dakota Life*
http://www.sdpb.org/

Festivals

Kansas

Fiesta Mexicana, Topeka, mid July, begun in 1933 and organized by Our Lady of
Guadalupe Parish
http://www.olg-parish.org/fiesta.htm

Flint Hills Folklife Festival, mid-June, begun in 1998
http://www.flinthillsfolklifefestival.com/default.htm

Svensk Hyllningsfest Lindsborg, begun in 1941
http://www.svenskhyllningsfest.org/

Lindsborg is a small town that boasts that it is "more Swedish than Sweden." The bi-
ennial festival features Scandinavian music, cuisine, and folk dancing.

Nebraska

Buffalo Commons Storytelling Festival, McCook, begun in 1997
http://www.buffalocommons.org

Cinco de Mayo, Omaha, May 5 for five days, begun in 1985
http://www.theindependent.com/stories/050403/new_parade04.shtml
Celebrates with food and music.

Czech Festival, Wilber, August, begun in 1961
http://www.ci.wilber.ne.us/festival_events.htm
Polka bands and dancing.

Polish Festival, Ashton, September, begun in 1992
http://www.polishheritagecenter.org
The festival features food, dance, and music.

North Dakota

Bismarck Folkfest, one week in mid-September
http://www.ndmotorcoach.com/events.html
This Bavarian-style annual citywide celebration includes parades, dances, ethnic foods,
and arts and crafts.

Dakota Cowboy Poetry Gathering, Medora, May, begun in 1987
http://www.ndmotorcoach.com/events.html

Local and national cowboy poets, arts, and crafts.

Norsk Høstfest, Minot, October, begun in 1978
http://www.hostfest.com/

Scandinavian culture, particularly Norway's, with food, music, dancing.

North Dakota Ukrainian Festival, Dickinson, July
http://www.ukrainiannd.org/

Organized by the Ukrainian Institute.

Northern Plains Heritage Festival, Dickinson, September
http://www.ndmotorcoach.com/events.html

This ethnic celebration on the campus of Dickinson State University includes food, music, dance, crafts, and traditional dress of the various ethnic groups of North Dakota.

Northern Plains Indian Culture Fest, Stanton, July
http://www.ndmotorcoach.com/events.html

Encompasses a wide range of activities that exemplify the Northern Plains tribes who frequented the Knife River area from several thousand years ago to the present and includes programs and demonstrations.

Scandinavian Hjemkomst Festival, Moorhead, Minnesota and Fargo, North Dakota, last full weekend of June, begun in 1977
http://www.scandinavianhjemkomstfestival.org/home/main.htm

Celebrates the historical and contemporary arts and ethnic traditions of five Scandinavian countries, Denmark, Finland, Iceland, Norway, and Sweden, as well as Scandinavian America.

Tatanka Festival, Jamestown, July
http://www.ndmotorcoach.com/events.html

Citywide festival that celebrates White Cloud's birthday. White Cloud, the albino buffalo, is a part of the small buffalo herd at the National Buffalo Museum.

United Tribes International Pow Wow, Bismarck, second week in September
http://www.ndmotorcoach.com/events.html

This event draws singers and dancers for the competition. Indian foods and artifacts add to the festivities. Native American foods, arts, and crafts are sold on the grounds.

Oklahoma

Czech Festival, Yukon, begun in 1965
http://www.americaslibrary.gov/cgi-bin/page.cgi/es/ok/czech_1

Czech food, costumes, and dances.

Italian Festival, McAlester, May, begun in 1971
http://www.italianfestival.org/

Arts, crafts, and food.

Kolache Festival, Prague, May, begun in 1959
http://www.pragueok.org/even_kola.html

Arts and crafts, parades, dancing, and costumes.

Oklahoma Scottish Games and Gathering, Tulsa and Oklahoma City begun in 1979
http://www.tulsascottishgames.com/

Piping, dances, games, and demonstrations.

Oktoberfest, Tulsa, October, begun in 1980
http://www.tulsaoktoberfest.org/ofest2003/thanks2003.html

Red Earth Native American Cultural Festival, Oklahoma City, begun in 1986
http://www.okccvb.org/special/native_am.htm

Art market and competition, dance competition.

South Dakota

Black Hills Highland Festival and Scottish Games, Sturgis, mid-September, begun in 1999
http://www.maclachlans.org/internet/sd.htm

Corn Palace Polka Festival, Mitchell, mid-September
http://www.cornpalacefestival.com/

Dakota Celtic Festivals and Highland Games, Rapid City, early September, begun in 2003
http://www.blackhillscelticshop.com/area_event.htm

German-Russian Schmeckfest, Eureka, third week in September
http://www.sdglaciallakes.com/eurekacity.htm

Parade, pioneer demonstrations, kids' shows, variety acts, and food.

South Dakota Highland Festival, Scotland, September, begun in 1998
http://www.scotlandsd.org/HighlandFest.htm

Regional Studies Centers on the Plains

Center for Great Plains Studies at Emporia State University, Emporia, Kansas
http://www.emporia.edu/cgps/center.htm

Center for Great Plains Studies, University of Nebraska, Lincoln
http://www.unl.edu/plains/

Institute for Regional Studies, North Dakota State University, Fargo
http://www.lib.ndsu.nodak.edu/ndirs/

FOOD

Barbara Shortridge

"Beef, it's what's for dinner" is a slogan taken seriously in the Great Plains. In a recent survey, 70 percent of residents said that this meat would be the core of any representative meal from their region.[1] Beef production also is the highest-value agricultural enterprise in the Plains and is therefore important to local economies. Residents are accustomed to seeing cattle at pasture and in feedlots, and these images also dominate on calendars, postcards, and promotional tourist materials. The rest of a typical meal in this region is more varied. Pies that use nuts and fruits from local sources are important to many, however, with apple, cherry, pecan, and rhubarb among the favorites. Other consumer choices are determined by cultural heritage, the influence of adjoining regions, and, frankly, by what tastes good.

Despite the stereotype implied by its name, the Great Plains is not homogeneous culturally or physically. Outsiders who traverse these states only on east-west interstate highways see mostly the high, flat divides between river basins and often eat generic road food. This view does an injustice to the physical geography of these states and to the diverse food habits of their people. Although the signature foods of the Great Plains may be plain, as some residents modestly note, cooks strongly support both the local agricultural base and its ethnic heritage. Bountiful home tables traditionally existed to satisfy the caloric needs of hardworking farmers and ranchers. Some of these habits carry over to the present day.

PHYSICAL ENVIRONMENT AND AGRICULTURE

The treeless Great Plains was a formidable challenge to early settlers. Magnificent soils (mollisols) promised farming success, but since trees grew only on riparian sites, people worried about the climate. Everything worked well in years of sufficient precipitation, but droughts could destroy the faith of a farmer. So could a grasshopper infestation or hail that beat down the ripe wheat. Because of variable precipitation and other factors, farmers in the Plains have more of a gambler mentality than people elsewhere. "Next year will be better" was (and is) the motto of the optimists who elect to stay. Dry-farming techniques in the early twentieth century, and more recently, irrigation, federal aid, and improved seed varieties have greatly lessened the traditional risk.

The imagery of dryness applies mainly west of the one hundredth meridian. Wheat is the major cultivated crop there, and irrigation produces corn and alfalfa. East of this point, agriculture is more traditionally midwestern. Alfalfa, corn, milo, and soybeans are the leading agricultural products of the eastern half, with sunflowers and canola added in the north and cotton in the south.

Cattle, another major agricultural source of income in the Great Plains, have traditionally been confined to pastures on rougher terrain. The Flint Hills of Kansas and the Sand Hills of Nebraska have long associations with grazing economies. Relocations of beef-packing plants from Chicago, Kansas City, and similar settings to western counties in the 1970s now have added complexity to this pattern. In their wake, large feedlots and irrigated grain fields also have come to these same High Plains locations. Major agribusiness agglomerations now exist, especially in the valleys of the Arkansas and Platte Rivers.

The wheat-growing and cattle-ranching people in the Great Plains do eat lots of bread and beef, but connections between other leading agricultural products and food on the table are not as clear. Crops such as alfalfa, field corn, and milo are used for animal feed or as ingredients in highly processed foods. The relationship between sugar beets grown in North Dakota and the sugar in frostings on cakes is not immediate either. Still, seasonal produce from home gardens and orchards and from small-scale farmers who market directly through CSAs (community-supported agriculture such as subscription arrangements between consumers and small-scale farmers), farm stands, farmers' markets, or pick-your-own arrangements provides the basis for many regional dishes. In addition, other Great Plains foods are gathered, hunted, or fished in the wild.

CULINARY INFLUENCES OF NEIGHBORING REGIONS

The Great Plains was settled largely via east-to-west migration paths that followed well-established transportation routes. Settlers from northern states populated most of the Dakotas, while North Midland peoples (Illinois, Indiana, and Ohio) came to Kansas, Nebraska, and northwestern Oklahoma. The southern and eastern areas of Oklahoma were settled by people from Arkansas, Kentucky, Tennessee, and other southern states. Ethnic enclaves formed by nineteenth-century Europeans and Native Americans interrupt this model, of course, especially in North Dakota and Oklahoma, as does Hispanic settlement in parts of Kansas and Oklahoma.

Historical origins of the various settlers are reflected in food preferences. Dinner plates in the "southern" parts of Oklahoma include many fried foods, for example, along with biscuits, black-eyed peas, greens, okra, and pork. Tables in the "northern" Dakotas, in contrast, are calorie laden, with many dishes per meal, abundant baked goods, and a variety of dairy products. Ethnic influence is even more obvious. Migrants who have brought tacos, enchiladas, and sopapillas are partially responsible for the growing preference for Mexican food in the western Plains and in metropolitan areas almost everywhere.

HISTORICAL FOODS

Native Americans and Pioneers

Native American subsistence in the Great Plains traditionally relied heavily upon bison, wild fruits and vegetables, and the cultivated crops of beans, corn, and squash. Jerky (dried meat preserved with salt) and pemmican (dried bricks of buffalo suet and fruit later reconstituted as soups or stews) were important ways of preservation for leaner times of the year. An inventory from Lewis and Clark in 1804, for example, lists buffalo, deer, ducks, geese, grouse, elk, plover, turkeys, and white catfish as important edible resources of this area. They also refer to wild cherries, gooseberries, grapes, and plums.

Beyond the foodstuffs available in the wild, early settlers also brought with them some staples: flour, a sweetener (coarse brown sugar or molasses made from sorghum), and coffee (green and thus needing to be roasted and ground before consumption). Some people had a cow and a few hogs and chickens, but many migrants did not have ready access to butter, eggs, lard, or milk. As people settled in, cornmeal often replaced wheat flour for several years because corn was an easier crop to grow on partially turned prairie and cobs were useful for heating as well. Coffee usually became scarce in these years as well, and many stories exist about ways to stretch a dwindling supply by adding field beans and other ingredients. In the sod-house period, cooking stoves were often called "hayburners" because of the fuel source. Dried buffalo and cow chips were better sources because they burned longer. Early stoves required constant stoking and lacked the heat regulation necessary for quality baking.

The slaughtering of several hogs was an autumn ritual once farmers became established because ham, bacon, and sausage could be salt cured or smoked and thereby preserved for future use. This process also produced lard for shortening and soap. Chickens were killed as needed for immediate consumption. Fried chicken was a custom when company called and was often called "parson food" because it was often fed to visiting ministers on Sunday. On less-than-prosperous farms, diets were simple and not nutritious by modern standards. Cornmeal mush and sowbelly (salted side pork) constituted a common meal. Homestead wives, who had to contend with limited food supplies, exchanged recipes and looked for new ones printed in the local newspaper.

Cowboy fare during the open-range period of the cattle industry in the 1870s is often viewed nostalgically, but chuck-wagon cooking actually was monotonous. Space was scarce for the cook's supplies, and so beans, coffee, and sourdoughs formed the core items, with dried fruits, rice, and canned corn and tomatoes as additions. Cooking over a campfire led to innovative methods such as baking biscuits in a Dutch oven that was buried in coals. Frying was a common preparation style, along with the making of stews. The famous son-of-a-bitch stew, for example, used every part of a recently slaughtered animal, a necessity without refrigeration.

Most people who lived in Kansas City or Omaha during the 1880s and 1890s had running water and electricity in their homes. Cooking, however, was still done from scratch because few processed foods were available. National cookbooks were beginning to be published in quantity, and women's church groups and aid societies compiled and sold their own versions of recipes and household hints. Gen-

Chuck wagon, circa 1889. Courtesy Kansas State Historical Society.

teel turn-of-the-century households probably had a well-stocked pantry and possibly servants. The mistress of the house did not hesitate to have seven-course dinner parties, for which the menus were heavy and rich.

Reconstructing food habits from the past is a difficult process because not much information exists. Few recipes remain from the territorial years of Great Plains settlement, for example, and cultural biases distort what has been preserved. Often the only remaining cookbook for a time and place may come from a wealthy family that was not typical of the population at large. The most accurate information available uses multiple sources such as diaries, fiction, housekeeping books, inventories, and locally produced charitable cookbooks. The fictional work and essays of Bess Streeter Aldrich, Willa Cather (especially *My Antonia*), Mari Sandoz, and Carrie Young contain many engaging stories about foodways in an earlier Great Plains.

Harvey House Restaurants

Fred H. Harvey (1835–1901) changed travelers' eating habits when he opened the first Harvey House Restaurant at the station of the Atchison, Topeka, and Santa Fe Railroad in Topeka, Kansas. Harvey was an Englishman and a former ticket and freight agent for the Chicago, Burlington, and Quincy line. His experience had told him that meals for train passengers were deplorable. Restaurant service at depots was unreliable because of low quality and not enough time to eat the meal. As a result, travelers sometimes bought from vendors on the train or brought along their own food. Food-borne illnesses were a frequent consequence. In 1876, Harvey leased a lunch counter at the Topeka depot and impressed officers of the Santa Fe line with the cleanliness, good food, and service of his enterprise. Soon he was granted control over all food service on that railway. Harvey House Restaurants inside stations throughout Kansas and Oklahoma (plus states to the west) were later supplemented by Harvey House Hotels and "Meals by Fred Harvey" in dining cars.

When he died in 1901, forty-seven restaurants, fifteen hotels, and thirty dining cars were under his care.

Harvey can be considered the inventor of one form of "fast food" through his plans for how meals could be served efficiently:

> There are still men and women in Topeka who remember the scene at the depot when the train came in. A white-aproned waiter, beating a brass gong with a wooden mallet, brought the passengers quickly to the dining room door. The first course was on the table and as soon as the diner was seated, the waitress went down the table asking, "Tea, iced tea, coffee, or milk," and at the same time positioning the coffee cup at each place accordingly, so that the girl coming behind to pour the drinks knew just what to pour. The service in the dining room was table d'hote with two choices for the main course. The plates already served in the kitchen with meat and vegetables, were quickly placed on the tables.[2]

Much of the success was based on well-trained Harvey Girls (waitresses) who followed a strict dress code and rules of decorum. Writers have often referred to these women as a civilizing force for the American Southwest.

Although reasonable in cost, the meals served in these depots were elegant in several respects. Lobster salad, capon, asparagus, mince pie, and a variety of cheeses appeared on menus from the 1880s, for example. The company arranged for shipments of fresh produce and meat by trains that used refrigerated and ice cars.

Most of the old Harvey House depots and restaurants between Kansas City and California have been torn down or converted to other uses. One in Florence, Kansas, however, remains in service as a Harvey House Museum, where volunteers serve a meal that mimics the elegant ones from the past. The station and restaurant in Guthrie, Oklahoma, is now the Railroad House Bed and Breakfast.

PEOPLE AND PLACES

People

The majority of Plains residents are Anglo in background and represent past migration streams from various eastern locations in the United States. To this base came significant numbers of European migrants during the late nineteenth and early twentieth centuries. People with British Canadian, Czech, Danish, German, German Russian, Norwegian, and Swedish ancestry are common in the Plains today, particularly in its northern half. Even a small Icelandic community exists in North Dakota. The power of food to maintain and reinforce ethnic ties in this area is important. Bierocks, kolaches, lefse, and lutefisk are still common in private homes and are shared with the public through annual festivals and church suppers. Such traditional foodways are easy to perpetuate because of modest expense, small time investment, and ease of transferability from one generation to the next.

Native Americans were the first inhabitants of the Plains. Their food is also a component of Great Plains contemporary cuisine, although usually not in public venues. Today the most populous groups of American Indians living in the Great

Plains include the Cherokee, the Sioux, the Chippewa, and the Choctaw. Within-group use of food for identity occurs at powwows and other tribal celebrations. Sharing of foodways with outsiders is done through festivals and moneymaking Indian taco sales.

Finally, several more newly arrived ethnic groups influence the regional food scene as well. Many Central American, Mexican, and Vietnamese people continue to come to the Plains as agricultural workers and packing-plant employees. With them are entrepreneurs who have established ethnic grocery stores and home-owned restaurants that now are adopted by the resident population. Garden City, Kansas (one of the packing centers), now has a Salvadoran restaurant, along with several Mexican and Vietnamese ones. The residents of this city of 30,000 are delighted with their new culinary choices.

Density of Population

One of the distinguishing characteristics of the Plains is its sparse population, especially in western locations. In Kansas, for example, the overall population density is less than half of the U.S. average, with numbers as low as 1.9 persons per square mile in Wallace County along the border with Colorado. States to the north have even lower densities: Arthur and McPherson Counties in the Sand Hills of Nebraska report .6 persons per square mile, while Harding County in far northwest South Dakota has only .5. Time and distance have different meanings in such settings. Bus rides to consolidated schools can be thirty miles one way (some districts even have in-town boarding facilities), a lack of near neighbors prompts farmers to move to town and commute back to fields or pastures, and people do not hesitate to drive two hours to see a movie.

What effect does low population density have on household food choices and eating out? Individual restaurants obviously must serve much larger geographic areas to capture the patrons needed to survive. Often only one exists per county, and it typically serves as a gathering place for residents to chat over a cup of coffee and a piece of pie. Because of the social importance of such cafés, towns use extraordinary measures to retain them. The impending retirement of a longtime café cook becomes a crisis. Cooperative, town-owned restaurants also exist where a different set of residents is responsible for preparing the noon meal each day.

Most towns in the Plains are too small to attract a franchise restaurant. Because residents crave fast food as much as people in the rest of the nation, however, several companies have worked out innovative solutions. Sonic Drive-Ins are popular, for example, especially in Oklahoma, because this regionally based corporation has purposefully targeted a population base smaller than that of its competitors. Even more innovatively, traveling Pizza Hut wagons serve several communities, with a set schedule of days and hours in each.

A grocery store in a small town is also a chancy operation. In order to survive, many of these businesses must keep small stocks of given items on the shelf and accept the risk that they will sell out before the next wholesale shipment. Demand for fresh produce is especially difficult to anticipate, and as a result, these sections are often either sparse or the items for sale are of questionable quality. The trials of procuring fresh fruits and vegetables in isolated places can be considerable. Residents often compromise by using local stores for limited food items and then traveling long distances to do monthly bulk shopping at larger supermarkets. They also keep an ice chest in their vehicle to transport frozen items. Other people place special orders with shop owners or purchase unusual items online.

A low density of people combined with consistent out-migration and failing small towns prompted Deborah and Frank Popper in 1987 to suggest that the western Plains perhaps should return to a Buffalo Commons where native animals might roam without fences as they did in the past. This proposal, predictably, was rejected by local residents. After all, the Poppers were outsiders from New Jersey who were telling long-

Diner in Iola, Kansas, 1930s. Courtesy Kansas State Historical Society.

established residents what to do. They also had created their argument by using census numbers, not by talking to people who had a strong attachment to the land. Still, as the population continues to decline, school and even county consolidations are discussed openly, and ranchers are beginning to raise buffalo.

Larger Metropolitan Areas

The major cities of the Plains—Fargo, Kansas City, Lincoln, Oklahoma City, Omaha, Sioux Falls, Topeka, Tulsa, and Wichita—are all located in the region's eastern half. These communities are abundantly served by grocery stores, have active restaurant scenes, sponsor a wide variety of festivals with local foods at the concession stands, and otherwise operate in a metropolitan food realm little different from the rest of urban America. Some of these cities even have signature foods for which they claim exclusive bragging rights.

College towns also stand out as distinctive food centers within the region. They have a relatively large variety of restaurant types, including more franchises and pizza joints to satisfy young, poverty-stricken students. These towns have more countercultural vegetarian and ethnic restaurants as well, plus at least one long-time establishment that has become a sentimental, almost iconic spot. A short list would include Nick's Hamburger Shop in Brookings, South Dakota; Bison Turf in Fargo, North Dakota; Bronze Boot Steak House and Lounge, Frenchy's, and Red Pepper in Grand Forks, North Dakota; Free State Brewing Company, Joe's Bakery, and Wheatfields Bakery and Cafe in Lawrence, Kansas; Crane River Brewpub and Cafe, Lazlo's Brewery and Grill, and Valentino's in Lincoln, Nebraska; Hibachi Hut, Kite's Bar and Grill, Rusty's Last Chance Restaurant and Saloon, and Texas Star Cafe in Manhattan, Kansas; Brothers Eatery and Pub, Legends Restaurant, The Mont, and O'Connells Irish Pub and Grill in Norman, Oklahoma; Eskimo Joe's and The Hideaway in Stillwater, Oklahoma; and Jerry's Place in Tahlequah, Oklahoma. These businesses all are enthusiastically patronized by students, alumni, and town residents alike.

Regional Identity through Food

Group distinctiveness, a fundamental component of a person's identity, has been undermined in recent years as rapid cultural change has placed stress on family structure, gender roles, and other traditional means of pegging who people are in a postmodern world. As one way to counter this process, citizens increasingly have embraced, reaffirmed, and even reinvented aspects of regional food and other local culture. "Eating the local" is an inexpensive way to evoke such pride in place. It does not involve a major time commitment and is an activity that easily can be shared. In addition, because regional foods are tangible reminders of the past, they can be especially effective in establishing heritage. Participatory activities such as attendance at farmers' markets, cooperative gardening plots, pick-your-own berry patches, food festivals, and church suppers are effective ways to celebrate one's roots. So is contributing a recipe to the grade-school fund-raising cookbook, going to a local restaurant to see friends, and having a July neighborhood cookout focused on fresh corn on the cob.

What function does the food people consume play in establishing their identity? Daily food choices (where often food is viewed as fuel) do not necessarily involve much thought along the lines set out earlier, but symbolic dishes are prominent on the menu for special occasions. Some of these dishes appear only for birthdays, Thanksgiving, and other holidays. Other occasions such as entertaining guests from out of state require the host to consider which foods are representative of his or her region. For the Great Plains as a whole, the symbolic foods are steak and pies, plus a set of place-specific signature dishes that will be itemized later.

Garfield's—Oklahoma City. Courtesy Garfield's.

INFLUENCE OF ENVIRONMENT ON FOOD PRODUCTION

Climate

Twenty inches of rainfall per year is the amount needed for agriculture without additional water being supplied through irrigation or the implementation of fallowing and other dryland-farming techniques. Annual precipitation in the Plains is under this magic number throughout North Dakota and the western two-thirds of South Dakota (except for the higher elevations of the Black Hills), the western half of Nebraska, the western quarter of Kansas, and two Panhandle counties of Oklahoma. Higher evapotranspiration rates (evaporation of soil moisture plus transpiration through plant leaves, both of which are accelerated by heat and wind) in the warmer temperature regimes of the southern Plains serve to offset, to some degree, the higher precipitation there. Because of this, some agricultural pursuits are possible in North Dakota with a lower rainfall than at places in the southern Plains.

In general, precipitation amounts increase from northwest to southeast, with the highest values for each state being found in their southeast corners. This high value is nineteen inches for North Dakota and increases progressively southward until it exceeds fifty-six inches in Oklahoma. Crop yield is strongly affected by water deficiencies that modify plant growth. Climatologists also often talk about clusters of years with drought conditions as the deciding factor that determines changes in agricultural practices or out-migration of people. Lack of consistent rainfall in some parts of the Plains, therefore, severely restricts the kind of agriculture that is practiced for economic reasons. Corn is preferred over wheat because of its higher market value, but wheat needs less moisture to grow. Without irrigation, this small grain is one of the few possibilities for a crop in western locations.

Another critical variable that affects agricultural patterns is the length of the frost-free season. In Nebraska, the median spring freeze date varies from April 21 in the far southeastern corner to May 21 in the far northwestern corner. Similarly, the median autumn freeze date is September 21 in the far northwest and October 9 in the southeast. In general, the length of the growing season increases from north to south in the Plains, with slightly longer seasons in the eastern half of these states. Since weather is unpredictable, however, yearly exceptions to these long-term averages abound, and the potential for crop failure from frost damage in the spring is always present. No wonder farmers talk about the weather.

Fruit trees, especially at the budding stage, are often hit by a late frost, and the crop is destroyed for that year. Home gardeners with orchards can tolerate such failures, but people who depend upon fruit trees for a living have anxious moments. Annual crops hit by a late frost, in contrast, often can be salvaged for the year by reseeding (although usually for a smaller yield). Plants resistant to a light frost, such as wheat, sunflowers, and sugar beets, are especially suitable for northern locations within the Great Plains. Rice, peanuts, and other species that cannot survive even brief freezing temperatures grow successfully only in southern locales.

Rolling harvest dates from south to north are part of the Plains agricultural scenario. The wheat harvest occurs first in Oklahoma around mid-June and finishes in the Dakotas in late July. This process is symbolized by the regular appearance of custom cutting crews that haul their combines northward as the region's wheat comes to maturity. Similarly, strawberry picking usually begins about June 11 in the far southeastern corner of Oklahoma and July 1 in the northeastern corner of South Dakota. This spread throughout the summer theoretically could make fresh strawberry fanciers happy for a month, but few berries are commercially distributed through a regional system these days. Instead, red berries displayed in grocery stores, even at the peak of the local harvesting season, are still coming from California and Mexico.

Irrigation

Much crop agriculture in the western Great Plains depends on irrigation. Streams, associated sand deposits, and surface reservoirs are important sources for the needed water, but an extensive underground layer of unconsolidated rock and gravel known as the Ogallala or High Plains Aquifer is the real treasure of the Great Plains. Capped top and bottom by impermeable rock, this water-saturated zone is thickest in western and central Nebraska, where it reaches 1,200 feet in some places, but is also present in far western Kansas and the Panhandle of Oklahoma. Its water is recharged by precipitation in the Rocky Mountains, where these sediments appear at the ground surface, but the recharge rate is very slow. Real concerns about drawing down this aquifer (it essentially is a nonrenewable resource) recently have led to water conservation measures. The integrated agribusiness economy of irrigated crops, feedlots, and beef-processing plants is especially at risk.

Irrigation before the 1970s usually involved a ditch system that ran between the rows and was fed by a larger ditch at one end. Gravity distributed the water as needed. More recent techniques involve center-pivot sprinkler systems that are attached to a well-pumping mechanism in the center of a large field. Water is then distributed along an arm that slowly rotates in an arc. Before concerns about water conservation, the heads on these sprinklers were oriented upward, and the water spray provided a sign of abundance in an otherwise parched landscape. Now the heads are mounted lower and oriented toward the ground to reduce evaporative losses. Aerial views of this irrigation process reveal huge circles of lush green growth that contrast strikingly with interstitial barren areas.

In Kansas, major irrigated crops include corn (the largest water user in the Plains), soybeans, and wheat for grain; in Nebraska and South Dakota the leaders are alfalfa, corn, and soybeans. These crops are supplemented in Oklahoma by minor acreages devoted to orchards, peanuts, and vegetables.

Landscape

Most outsiders have agricultural images of the Great Plains that involve flat fields of golden wheat extending to the horizon and herds of cattle grazing contentedly in pastures. This symbolism of wheat and cattle on a featureless plain does not accurately reflect the entire region. To begin with the flat stereotype, it is important to realize that the Great Plains are, in fact, tilted upward toward the west, with elevations as high as 3,506 feet above sea level in White Butte, North Dakota, 4,039 feet at Mount Sunflower in Kansas, 4,973 feet at Black Mesa in the Panhandle of Oklahoma, and 5,424 feet in Kimball County, Nebraska. These higher elevations of the west provide relatively lower summer nighttime temperatures because of adiabatic cooling and allow dryland farming (mostly wheat) to prosper in most years.

Beyond variations in elevation, the dominant horizontal physiography of the Great Plains is also broken by an extensive series of local hills and cuestas that have been exposed by eons of river erosion. Large rivers that drain the region include the Arkansas, Canadian, James, Kansas, Missouri, Platte, Red, and Republican, all with paths that generally flow from west to east. Because of their length, with headwaters in the mountains, the Arkansas and Platte are highly utilized for irrigation purposes. A 1995 ruling in favor of Kansas in a lawsuit initiated by Kansas over water withdrawals from the Arkansas River by Colorado indicates how important this issue is.

The extent of past glaciations in the Great Plains partially determines which areas are suitable for plow agriculture. The line of glacial extent follows a southeastern diagonal from midway on the western border of North Dakota toward the northeastern corner of Kansas. North of this line, till plains (unsorted debris carried by the glaciers) form a deep, fertile cover. Americans should thank Canada for the soil materials that were "bulldozed" into these north central states and deposited as the glaciers retreated. South of the glacial line, no such deposits exist except for thin surfaces of windblown loess. In the Dakotas, the Missouri River (marking the extent of glaciation) forms a distinct boundary line between farming and ranching. "East River," including the exceptionally rich Red River valley, has been glaciated and consists of low hills, glacial lakes, and excellent soil, all suitable for alfalfa, canola, corn, sugar beets, sunflowers, and wheat. In contrast, "West River" consists of rolling plains, buttes, and deep canyons. This rougher terrain and poorer-quality soil preclude extensive plow agriculture and make ranching a more suitable activity. In the states to the south, the glacial division is not as apparent. None of Oklahoma, for example, was ever glaciated.

The most extreme terrain in the Great Plains can be found in the Arbuckle Mountains of Oklahoma, the Badlands of North and South Dakota, the Black Hills of South Dakota, the Flint Hills of Kansas, and the Sand Hills of Nebraska. The last two of these are regionally famous grazing areas. Each summer a million cattle are fattened on 4.5 million acres of nutritious grasses in the Flint Hills. Greenwood County, Kansas, ranchers, for example, run 75,000 head each year.[3] This is almost a ten-to-one ratio of animals over people. Equally impressive are the Sand Hills, which are vegetated, relict sand dunes in the west central portion of Nebraska supported by a high water table. Rangeland grasses there continue to grow throughout the spring, summer, and fall and are supplemented in the winter by locally cut hay. An estimated 1.2 million head of cattle graze this expansive pasture that stretches for 250 miles across western Nebraska.[4] The majority of ranchers in both locales run "cow-calf operations," meaning that the calves are usually marketed in the fall after weaning. Some remain on rangeland for a second grazing season before they are sent off to be finished in a feedlot.

The traditional imagery of the Flint and Sand Hills is important to the ranching industry even in these modern times. Grazing cattle, windmills and stock (water) tanks, corrals and cattle pens, livestock trailers, and working cowboys on horseback maintain the older symbols of ranching life at a time when the beef industry at large is under scrutiny. Cattle today are fattened in contained feedlots, eating grain and other by-products that are enhanced with hormones and antibiotics. These extensive feedlots are located near a new generation of industrial packing plants and are, in turn, surrounded by irrigated fields that produce corn for animal feed. In Kansas, for example, Dodge City, Garden City, and Liberal in the southwestern corner of the state form a triangle where the beef industry dominates the economy. Such facilities have changed the way of raising cattle for large-scale consumption—no more long cattle drives of Texas longhorns to railheads in Kansas; no more trucking of cattle to local slaughterhouses by individual ranchers. Many residents of the Plains naturally are reluctant to dismiss the imagery of the past and the high-quality meat product that went with it. Some choose to fight the trend by patronizing ranchers who produce grass-fed cattle and local, small-scale packing houses.

The geography of agriculture on the Plains has both an east-west and a north-south component based on environmental conditions. In general, beef operations and wheat growing take place in the western half of the region, where rougher terrain or periodic drought prohibit other agricultural pursuits. More intensive farming of corn and soybeans takes place in the east, where precipitation is more reliable. Variations in this general pattern occur when water is available for irrigation. More changes have come with the deregulation of crops by the federal government. Farmers are growing cotton in southern Kansas, for example, and similar experimentation is going on elsewhere. Some of this is market driven, and some occurs because of climatic variation. Several wet years in a row, for example, may encourage a farmer to abandon his or her traditional crop rotation and instead plant another crop with higher potential value.

LEADING CROPS AND LIVESTOCK

Agricultural specializations state by state provide a basic context for food choice. This is based partly on economics, but also on the premise that what consumers are exposed to in their environmental surroundings becomes part of their food preference decisions. The preferences also may be influenced by wanting to support the local economy, to eat farm-fresh products, and to reinforce regional identity by consuming and preparing locally popular dishes.

Beef

The importance of cattle to the Plains region is overwhelming. National rankings by state for animals on hand in 1997 were second for Nebraska (6,732,637 head), third for Kansas (6,506,089), fourth for Oklahoma (5,321,161), seventh for South Dakota (3,723,271), and sixteenth for North Dakota (1,810,409). Cherry County, in the northern part of Nebraska's Sand Hills, is the tenth-leading county in the United States in inventory. In all states, cattle outnumber people, and the ratio reaches as high as five to one in South Dakota.

The cultural landscape associated with ranching is well known. Cowboy hats and jeans, corrals, lariats, and rodeos have been adopted by popular culture as symbols of an independent lifestyle. They appear prominently on calendars and postcards. Within the region, one also sees additional icons of this business. One is a collection of old cowboy boots placed on fenceposts along a road. No practical reason exists for putting them there, but they suggest personal satisfaction in doing a job well and over a long period of time.

Wheat

Wheat is the second economic mainstay of the Plains states. In 1997, using bushels of wheat harvested for grain as the measure, Kansas ranked first in the nation (407,515,802 bushels), followed in second place by North Dakota (260,522,260), fifth for Oklahoma (141,302,977), eighth for South Dakota (89,470,811), and eleventh for Nebraska (61,578,806). Sumner County, Kansas (south of Wichita) was the sixth-leading county in the country. In these states, the number of bushels per acre at harvest time becomes front-page news because even the most sophisticated urban resident knows that as the wheat harvest goes, so goes the overall economy.

The grain elevators associated with wheat culture are often the subjects of photography. Mills used to be similarly noticed and appreciated, but these are now much less common in the region because of a change in freight-rate structure. Mills are larger now and clustered in Kansas City, Minneapolis, and other cities outside the core areas of grain production. With the return to artisan-style bread baking, however, a renewed interest in the production of custom flours can be seen. Stafford County Flour Mills Company (Kansas) produces a successful premium product called Hudson Cream Flour, for example. Shawnee Milling Company in Shawnee, Oklahoma (southeast of Oklahoma City), and North Dakota Mill in Grand Forks are other small commercial operations. As the only state-owned milling facility in the United States, the latter was created in 1922 as an alternative destination to the large mills in Minneapolis. Unless consumers read flour labels carefully for source and consciously support smaller operations, they have difficulty eating locally.

The most vivid agricultural imagery from wheat harvesting comes when custom combine crews and trucks full of wheat clog the back roads, creating dust and excitement. Harvest time is when scattered family members return home to contribute their labor. An occasion of great bustle and long days of work, the wheat harvest now is much different than it was in the past when entire communities helped each other through the hard days of cutting and threshing (removing grain from straw). Large meals were needed to satisfy big hungers and thirsts, and local women were at least as busy as the men, either bringing food to workers in the fields at noontime or serving similar portions at the farmstead, with everything prepared ahead of time. Carrie Young in *Nothing to Do but Stay* remembers the experience in North Dakota during the 1930s as follows:

> I see my mother in the kitchen. She is lining a large dishpan with a snowy floursack dish towel and heaping it high with butter sandwiches and doughnuts. . . . I tag along, barefoot, for the pure joy of it as they walk out to the threshing rig to serve the men their nine a.m. coffee break. Only we don't call it a coffee break. We call it "forenoon lunch." . . . We make a similar trip at four p.m., and we call this "afternoon lunch." There are, of course, also breakfast, dinner, and supper—which the men eat in the kitchen.[5]

Combines (single machines that do cutting and threshing done by a single machine) appeared in the Great Plains around 1917, but were not common until much later because of their expense. Harvesting with this new equipment required less labor, and so the task of feeding neighbors was drastically cut. Still, twelve-hour workdays continue to require sustenance, and tailgate picnics out of pickup trucks are common. Some cooks claim that the best invention for harvest time is Tupperware (plastic bowls with lids). Because farm wives often are drafted as truck drivers, who shuttle between field and grain elevator, harvest crews now often head for the nearest small-town restaurant for their noontime meal. Since many of these crews start in Texas in late spring and end up in Canada late in the summer, the participants have a well-developed restaurant guide.

In some parts of the Plains, especially western North Dakota, folk monuments have evolved using abandoned or obsolete threshing (or separating) equipment. These machines are placed on the tops of hills or ridges where they are visible for long distances. One prominent display along Highway 52 southeast of Velva, North Dakota, is known as "Thresherman's Heaven." A local poet, Shadd Piehl, says about these displays:

> These wrecks are Dakotan lamentations
> Mourning the stubble of necessary past—
> Harvesting time, threshing the years.[6]

Two major kinds of wheat are grown in the Plains, each with a specific geographic distribution. Winter wheat in Kansas, Nebraska, and Oklahoma is sown in the late fall, overwinters as a seedling, starts growing again early in the spring, and is harvested in early summer. Crimean varieties of this hard red wheat were first popularized in the 1870s by Mennonite immigrants in Kansas. By avoiding having plants in the ground during the dry summer heat, this crop is an ecologically sound response to local conditions. In North and South Dakota, however, winter wheat cannot survive the January temperatures. As a result, spring wheat (which is sown in the spring and harvested in late summer) is the crop of choice.

The harder the wheat, the higher the protein content in the flour, and therefore the more suitable it is for use in breads. Softer, low-protein wheats are used in cakes, cookies, crackers, and pastries. In a golden triangle that focuses on the eastern Dakotas, durum wheat is grown for semolina flour that is used to make couscous, egg noodles, and pasta. Durum is the hardest of all wheats, and its density, high protein content, and gluten strength make it perfect for pasta products that require consistent cooking quality. Dakota Growers Pasta Company in Carrington, North Dakota, is a grower-owned milling and manufacturing cooperative that represents 1,080 farmers. This modern facility with imported Italian machinery markets under its own label and through other store brands. The company advertises its fourth-generation work ethic and pride.

Other Crops and Livestock

Wheat and cattle's domination of the agricultural economy in the Plains shrouds other crops and livestock there that are important to human food supply. Many of the region's high-count products such as corn or alfalfa are grown as feed or silage for animals; others such as soybeans or canola lose their identity when they enter the mammoth food-processing industry. Some crops and livestock that especially influence consumer food choices are discussed here.

Hogs are important in Nebraska (ranking sixth among states in 2000), Oklahoma (eighth), and Kansas (ninth). For the most part, this hog inventory is scattered throughout the eastern half of these states and functions as a continuation of the classic midwestern corn-hog belt of Illinois, Indiana, and Iowa. In Oklahoma, however, a newer focus of hog production is centered on Guymon in the state's Panhandle. Intensive operations there support a large (and controversial) Seaboard Farms production facility. Ham, pork chops, and sausage appear on menus throughout the Plains, but they are not nearly as important as beef.

North Dakota ranks number one in production of all dry edible beans, followed by Nebraska (third), Kansas (twelfth), and South Dakota (thirteenth). The emphasis is upon navy and pinto beans. Production is concentrated in eastern parts of these states except in Nebraska, where it is in the Panhandle. Menus collected from these states regularly include bean soup and baked beans, but not at especially high levels. More curious are the rankings for honey: North Dakota is first in the country, South Dakota third, and Nebraska thirteenth. White wooden boxes of apiaries dot the landscape throughout these states, especially in small groves of trees or broken lands adjacent to cultivated fields.

Oklahoma demonstrates its southern food attachments and more temperate climate through several items in its agricultural rankings—seventh for peanuts, tenth for pecans, thirteenth for watermelons, and fifteenth for peaches. Pecans are commercially grown and harvested in a swath that goes north to south through the middle of the state, while the other three crops are concentrated in the southern half. Peaches and pecans are important ingredients in Oklahoma desserts. Rush Springs (southwest of Oklahoma City) is home to a watermelon festival on the second Saturday in August. This event attracts 20,000 people who eat 50,000 pounds of free melon.

Individual food choices are not strictly related to large-scale, commercial agriculture, except in a few cases. The long process from wheat to flour to bread and then from grocery-store shelf to peanut-butter sandwich negates the sense of a wheat farmer "eating local," for example. Produce grown in home gardens, berry patches, and orchards provides a more immediate feel for this process. Since home food production is but a fraction of what it was fifty to seventy-five years ago, however, most of this market is served by small-scale entrepreneurial farmers who work outside the formal distribution system. In Oklahoma, blackberries, cucumbers, okra, squash, strawberries, sweet corn, tomatoes, and watermelon are the most popular products sold through farmers' markets, roadside stands, and pick-your-own arrangements. In Nebraska, this list is led by beans, cucumbers, onions, peppers, pumpkins, squash, sweet corn, and tomatoes, while in North Dakota the leaders are beets, carrots, cucumbers, green beans, potatoes, squash, sweet corn, and tomatoes. Horseradish is a notable product for North Dakota, although it is not a high-count item.

Sustainable Meals

Every year on the third Tuesday in September, the small town of Ulysses, Kansas, serves a special dinner to 2,000 guests. The Grant County Home Products Dinner has been around since 1941. By tradition, every item on the menu is grown or raised in the county: barbecued beef, scalloped potatoes, sweet corn, pinto beans, candied squash, cherry tomatoes, coleslaw, wheat rolls, strawberry jam, watermelon, caramel popcorn, and milo doughnuts. Only the drinks (tea and coffee) are exceptions. Mostly the seven hundred volunteers cook for community members, but occasionally special guests attend, such as the governor and other state politicians in 2000.

Although this Grant County celebration of local foods has existed for a long time and is intended primarily as a community-building activity, other meals based on locally grown foods are now appearing throughout the Plains as interest in sustainable foodsheds increases. One major group is even sponsored by the W. K. Kellogg Foundation through the University of Nebraska. The purpose of such meals is to get people thinking about what they eat, and how their choices affect the economy, society, and environment. Theoretically, with careful attention to seasonality, a region could eat locally and be completely sustainable. Producers and consumers potentially benefit from this arrangement because transportation costs are less and freshness of product is increased.

SIGNATURE FOODS

Dishes throughout the Great Plains

Two dishes dominate in menus throughout the Plains—steak and pie. Although these items are both eaten elsewhere in the country, their consumption is not as high in other regions and does not involve as much pride and sense of place. Steak and pie are highlights on menus from fancy restaurants and ordinary hometown spots alike. They are a part of meals in venues as diverse as country clubs, outdoor cookouts, state dinners, sports banquets, wedding rehearsal dinners, and home backyards. Preferences for these foods also cross lines of gender and class.

Steak

Advertisements created for the national checkoff program sponsored by the Cattlemen's Beef Promotion and Research Board remind people, "No one ever left a cookout wishing there'd been more macaroni salad." Such advertising is probably not needed to prompt local consumption, however, because beef has long been a favorite regional main dish. Of the possible variations, steak always ranks at the top for residents, exceeding hamburgers and roasts in popularity. Steaks are viewed as the tenderest cuts of the animal and therefore the ones that best demonstrate quality of product and palatability. These slabs of meat, varying in thickness, are cut across the muscle grain and cooked using a high-heat method such as broiling, grilling, or frying.

In both eating-out and at-home situations, much thought goes into the selection and cooking of a steak. Favorite cuts in the Plains are ribeye, sirloin, and T-bone. Omaha Steaks, a regional purveyor, has built an international shipping business based upon quality of product. Promotional materials for the city of Omaha also capitalize upon the beef connection by using the phrase "Omaha. Rare. Well done." as a logo. Other steak consumers patronize specific ranchers, local slaughterhouses, meat shops, or simply the meat department of their favorite grocery store. Rubs, sauces, source of heat for grilling (gas or charcoal), and degree of doneness are all important calculations in producing a superior product in the backyard. Male cooks collect secret tricks as part of informal steak lore for outside grilling.

Pie

Pies, because they came to America with its early settlers and have been anticipated, consumed, and bragged about ever since, do not belong strictly to the Plains. Making this a regional signature dish is therefore suspect. Eating pie is so deeply engrained in regional culture, however, that the dessert plays a special role in the performance of identity. "Homemade" is the first critical defining characteristic for Great Plains pie. The word is obligatory on special-of-the-day menu boards in cafés, and most sellers who claim this distinction are telling the truth. In some restaurants, a special employee comes in early in the morning to make the day's batch of pies and then leaves before the rest of the kitchen gears up for the day. Running out of a particular variety is a cause for dismay and careful timing for daily customers.

The second pie characteristic for the region is a higher percentage of fruit, nut, and vegetable fillings that reflect local gardens and orchards. A two-crust fruit pie is more popular than any chiffon, cream, ice cream, or mousse version, and the emphasis is upon flakiness of crust as a measure of quality. Pie-baking contests are important components of county and state fairs and indirectly at community potlucks. Many favorites exist and often are accompanied by heritage statements such as "like my mother used to make." Recipes are shared only grudgingly in some communities. Apple pie is the preferred filling in the Plains, just as it is in the rest of the country. Secondary choices reflect local food sources: rhubarb in the Dakotas, cherries in Nebraska and Kansas, and pecans in Oklahoma.

Entrepreneurs have taken advantage of the Plains love affair with pie (and the decline of pie baking as the population gets busier or forgets how to make them) by producing products that can be passed off as homemade. One such operation is MarCon Pies (the name combines the first syllables from Marilyn and Connie), located in Washington, Kansas. Started in a garage, the operation has grown over the years to produce four hundred pies daily. Fresh pies are distributed to grocery stores and restaurants over a wide territory in Kansas and Nebraska. Similar operations exist in other states.

Place-Specific Dishes

Bierocks

Bierocks, referred to as "sandwiches" and "savory pies" in regional cookbooks, are made with a filling of ground beef, cabbage, and onions that is encased in a sweet yeast dough. This square or oblong product is then baked and eaten without utensils. Brought to America by German Russian Mennonite immigrants in the 1880s, the food has persisted in central Kansas and Nebraska where these groups are still active. A portable food, bierocks were used for a noontime meal in the wheat fields (similar in purpose to the pasty of Michigan's Upper Peninsula that was part of a miner's lunch). Most bierocks today are still made in home kitchens, but select restaurants have them on the menu. They are served at lunchtime in school cafeterias in the western half of Kansas and also (under the alternate name of runsa) have become the signature dish of a fast-food restaurant chain. The story goes that Sally Everett of Lincoln, Nebraska, converted her homemade bierock/runsa from a picnic food into a commercial product in 1949 by trademarking it as a "Runza®" and serving it at a drive-in restaurant of the same name. As with most ethnic foods that have made it big-time, some corruption of the authentic dish inevitably occurs—now the franchise also sells an Italian Runza.

Bison

Bison are returning to the Great Plains. They were hunted almost to the point of extinction, but large herds have now been reestablished to supply a new culinary interest in "buffalo" meat. An estimated 250,000 head currently exist in the region, and the number is increasing rapidly. Bison feed on low-quality grasses, give birth unassisted, and shun shelter in winter. Ranchers essentially leave their animals alone.

Bison is an alternative red meat that is healthy because of low fat and cholesterol counts. The meat has a darker color than beef because it does not marble; this lack of fat means faster cooking. The taste is sweeter and richer than that of beef and is sought after by chefs outside the Plains who are looking for a novelty item. Bison dishes (usually burgers) are prominently positioned on menus in North Dakota. Farther south, Governor Kathleen Sebelius of Kansas selected bison meat for her inauguration dinner in 2003. All five Plains states have ranches, local processing facilities, retail outlets, producer associations, and restaurant sales of the meat. One prominent organization is the Intertribal Bison Cooperative in South Dakota.

The first packing plant devoted solely to bison is the North American Bison Cooperative in New Rockford, North Dakota. A modest facility that kills approximately 12,000 bison a year, it serves an international customer base of consumers looking for alternatives to beef. Weekly shipments go to Brussels, for example, and the group has an aggressive marketing staff whose activities are supported by a checkoff program for advertising.

Chicken-fried Steak

Chicken-fried steak (CFS) is the meat entrée of choice in Oklahoma and is revered in southern parts of Kansas as well. Made from beef round steak that has been tenderized, soaked in buttermilk, and "fried like a chicken," this dish has as many preparation methods as there are cooks. Among the variations are dredging the meat in seasoned flour, buttermilk (or beaten eggs), and then flour again; frying in a large cast-iron skillet with hot oil; and turning the meat only once. CFS is always served with mashed potatoes, white, pepper-flecked cream gravy, and a green vegetable such as beans. In the Little Dixie of southeastern Oklahoma, black-eyed peas or cooked greens may replace the green beans. Claims by Oklahomans that some people eat this meal at least two times a day are likely exaggerated but not outside the realm of possibility. CFS is everywhere, including the menus of fast-food restaurants such as Braum's, a regional franchise headquartered in Oklahoma City. It is the true comfort food for the southern Plains.

Hot Dishes

Hot dishes, a popular one-dish regional cooking method in the northern Plains, are almost a mirror to pot roast dinners (discussed later). In both cases, the completed dish is brought to the table and supplemented by perhaps a salad, dessert, and beverage. They are not prepared at the frequency that they once were in these postmodern times when fresh foods appear on tables everywhere and slow cooking has lost its appeal, but the historic role of hot dishes in Dakota culture is too important to be ignored. Church suppers and hot dishes in this region used to go hand in hand.

The basic hot dish, also called a casserole or covered dish, uses ground beef, a condensed cream soup, and Tater Tot brand frozen potatoes. Tuna or chicken, tomato sauce, and rice or noodles are common substitutions. It is no surprise that such a convenient format would be popular at potlucks and similar social occasions that involve shared food. Such community events are enjoyed by all, but still produce an undercurrent of competition among cooks. Popular first in the 1950s because of advances in oven cookware, extensive brand advertising, and recipes in women's magazines, hot dishes have faded nationally. But with the current nostalgic move back to comfort foods, the old recipes may ascend again. A North Dakota bumper sticker claims that one "Can't get into heaven without a covered dish."

Indian Fry Bread

Indian fry bread has evolved as a pan–Native American food for the Great Plains and the one that is presented most often to outsiders. Fry bread is found wherever peoples of Native American ancestry are concentrated, especially for ceremonial events such as church socials, funerals, giveaways, and weddings. The students at Haskell Indian Nations University in Lawrence, Kansas, also serve it regularly at public powwows and Indian taco sales.

This flat bread made from wheat flour is not an indigenous food despite its current symbolic status. Starving northern Plains tribes, whose migrations were restricted following resettlement in the nineteenth century, were issued wheat flour by the federal government as a supplement to their usual food supplies. Although this ingredient was not part of their diet, cooks used it to create fry bread. Today the dough (made of flour, baking powder, salt, and water) is flattened to the thickness of a pancake and deep fried in cooking oil or sometimes lard. Served with a variety of toppings such as ground beef or beans, it is a main dish. Alternatively, with honey, it becomes a snack or dessert.

As with other Native American foods, attempts are being made to market fry bread to the general public, often through the Internet. Woodenknife ("Your Native American Foods Company") from Interior, South Dakota, sells an Indian Fry Bread Mix made from an original Sioux recipe. The last item on its ingredient list is timpsula (also known as prairie turnip or *Psoralea esculenta*), a traditionally gathered food that also has symbolic value as a poverty food. Difficult to find in prairie settings in modern times, the plant was important to diets in the past, when roots were dried and reconstituted in soups and stews.

Jams and Jellies

Jams and jellies are accompaniments to bread products especially popular in the northern Plains. Although store-bought versions are acceptable on the table, homemade preserves give cooks an opportunity to utilize regionally grown products and make a meal distinctive. Standard strawberry and raspberry products exist, but wild fruit jams and jellies are common too. Kansans prefer sandhill plum preserves made from the fruit of *Prunus americana* Marsh, which grows wild along fencerows and in river bottoms and ditches. This treat, a regional favorite since pioneer days, is pleasingly tart, with an apricot-like flavor.

People from the Dakotas and Nebraska choose chokecherry jelly (*Prunus virginiana L.*). These tiny, reddish-black fruits, harvested in midsummer, have a sweet-tart-bitter flavor even when sugar is added during cooking. North Dakotans claim that chokecherries can best be found in isolated coulees and that everyone has his or her secret gathering spot. Commercial jams and jellies using these fruits (with pseudohandmade labels) are available in specialty gift stores throughout the region, but at a premium price.

Jell-O

Jell-O is still a part of many meals on the Plains. Highly constructed, molded gelatin salads appear regularly on special-occasion tables such as at Thanksgiving, at church suppers, and in restaurant buffets. Even the cafeteria at the state office capitol complex in Bismarck, North Dakota, serves Jell-O. In general, however, these dishes have lost an importance that they once had in these states. Kathleen Norris explains the history in this way:

> It's hard to talk about western Dakota without mentioning Jell-O. A salad, in local parlance, is a dish made with Jell-O. . . . It wasn't until the advent of electric refrigeration that Jell-O became a staple of the potluck supper or the women's club luncheon, and that meant town women could serve Jell-O long before country women. Jell-O remained elusive for the most remote rural women until well into the 1950s. Statistics can give some perspective on this. In 1925, when 53.2 percent of American homes had electricity, the figure for eastern North Dakota was 38.8 percent and for western North Dakota, 2.9 percent.[7]

There are similar tales for other states in the Plains. In addition to the lack of electricity, the cost of a refrigerator was substantial for many rural residents. Beyond these obstacles, even transporting a Jell-O dish many miles over bumpy roads in the summertime heat as a contribution to a picnic probably was foolhardy. With modernization, this dish has lost its initial symbolic value.

Ingenuity in Jell-O salads, the subject of contests and informal competitions among local cooks, was infamous. Cookbooks from the 1950s and 1960s contain countless recipes for highly constructed concoctions, and antique stores now display the elaborate molds. Many versions feature a layering of colors and inclusions of whipped cream, fruits, or marshmallows. People have said with great seriousness that in their judgment, Jell-O is not Jell-O without marshmallows. Others say that adding fruit, often canned, makes this product into a salad, while adding whipped cream makes it a dessert.

Kolaches

Kolaches (kolace) are pastries of renown in Wilson, Kansas, Wilber, Nebraska, Tabor, South Dakota, and other Czech centers of the Great Plains. At the Wilson Czech Fest every July, St. Wenceslaus Catholic Church always sells out of the 4,000 kolaches made by fifty women in the preceding month. The Nebraska Czech Festival at Wilber includes a kolache-eating contest and kolache stands downtown. This treat has now spread beyond its ethnic affiliation and is available in other Plains locations through commercial bakeries.

Kolaches are yeast-leavened buns topped with fruit that is inserted into a hole made by a thumb imprint of the cook. Prunes and apricots are common fillings, but apples, cherries, cottage cheese, peaches, and poppy seeds are also favorites. The coordinator of the annual Kolache Shoot-out in Elba, Nebraska (a competitive baking event), claims, "It's a lost art, making kolaches." Her comment echoes those of many who are concerned about the demise of ethnic baking.

Peach Cobbler

Peach cobbler, a specialty throughout Texas and the South beyond, is also extremely popular in southern Oklahoma. Orchards of this fuzzy yellow-orange fruit are common in this region and a source of considerable pride. During the harvest season, roadside stands proliferate, and community residents without trees of their own are able to purchase fresh peaches.

Cobbler is a form of deep-dish pie with either a biscuit or pastry topping. Served warm with ice cream, whipped cream, or just cream, it is a simple dish but often a family standard. Other fruit and dough desserts in the Plains include crisps and crunches. They are more easily assembled and casual in presentation than a pie. Recipes are simple and often exchanged orally because the ingredients are few.

Pheasant

Pheasant is one of several grassland game birds that appear often on tables in the Great Plains. Unlike grouse, prairie chicken, quail, and wild turkey, however, the pheasant is especially symbolic to the people of South Dakota, where it is the state bird. In the fall, hunters in camouflage gear and their dogs walk through prairies and fields hoping to startle a colorfully plumed male bird into flight. Hunters who do not live in the area often belong to clubs that lease land for the sport of their members. Pheasants were introduced to America in 1881 when a diplomat brought Shanghai birds home to his Oregon farm, and they multiplied throughout much of the northern half of the country.

Cooking a pheasant entails much the same rules as for domestic poultry, although heavy cream or some other moisture-giving ingredient is usually added to a roasting pan to counter the dryness of the flesh. Wild pheasant has a gamier flavor than a farm-raised bird and is much leaner than chicken. Extra pheasants from hunting season usually end up in home freezers to be brought out for special occasions.

Pickles

Pickles are found on many tables in North Dakota and the eastern half of Nebraska and South Dakota, where the making of dill, sweet, and beet varieties is especially common. The role of pickles in a meal is unclear. Perhaps they are a way to promote the concept of bounty by adding extra dishes to the table (the custom is to put each variety in a fancy dish and then set it in the middle of the table). Occasionally pickles become part of an elaborate tray of raw vegetables or are accompanied by relishes made from vegetables such as corn. With a strong vinegar component, they also provide a taste counterpoint to the rest of the meal. Certainly in the past, when a woman's job was the management of a household and kitchen garden, pickles and preserves were important ways to utilize an over-abundance of vegetables and fruits, always with pride in the number of jars "put up" for the coming year.

Pot Roasts

Pot roasts may be the ultimate in home-cooked food. In the northern Plains, this is a common way to prepare beef for a family meal. A cut from the chuck or rump is used. The meat is browned, raw vegetables are added along with some form of liquid, and then everything is braised until the meat is fork tender. Variations exist, but carrots, celery, onions, and potatoes are the most common vegetable additions. The simplicity of preparation, the aroma of the gently cooking meat, and the agreeability of the completed dish have made this a favorite for Sunday family dinners. Pot roasts rarely come out of restaurant kitchens, however.

Red Beer

Red beer ("a red one") is a beverage distinctive to Nebraska. Some people claim that because it mimics the color of the University of Nebraska, the drink was invented as a way to show allegiance to the school. To prepare one the bartender adds a healthy proportion of tomato juice to whatever beer is on tap, plus a dash of Worcestershire sauce, some Tabasco, celery salt, and pepper. Roger Welsch claims that it "is the standard morning-after drink out here on the Plains and is very popular with the ladies at all hours, but it is not considered a breach of tavern etiquette to drink a red beer anytime of the night or day."[8] Although red beer also can be found in western Kansas and other locations outside Nebraska, the tale seems especially appropriate for the Cornhusker State.

Rhubarb

Rhubarb is a popular ingredient in desserts on the northern Great Plains. Also known as "pie plant" because of its use for this purpose, rhubarb is botanically a vegetable. Its reddish-green stalks are a regional symbol of spring and, as such, provide one of the first fresh ingredients available for a pie filling. Rhubarb is quite tart and needs a lot of sugar to make the stalks edible in pies, crisps, and cakes or simply stewed in a sauce. Since it is similar to zucchini in that home production often exceeds possible daily consumption within a family unit, novel ways of using rhubarb abound, preservation is necessary (canning or freezing), and an extensive giveaway procedure exists within neighborhoods.

Rhubarb lovers are especially common in the Dakotas. Rhubarb pie is available there in many restaurants, with no duplications in recipe. Rhubarb custard is best. A cookbook from Litchville, North Dakota (population 210), is entirely devoted to rhubarb.[9] Although more rhubarb is grown commercially in Oregon and Washington than in the Dakotas, regional enthusiasm is strongest in the northern Plains, where the perennial plant provides a major treat after a long winter.

Rocky Mountain Oysters

Rocky Mountain oysters (also known as prairie oysters, calf fries, or bull fries) are calf testicles, and their consumption is an important part of ranching culture. People outside this way of life, including many city dwellers in the Great Plains, have never heard of them, and so they remain a cult dish. When calves are castrated or "worked," the excised testicles are thrown in a bucket and later peeled, breaded, and fried in a skillet. They end up on home tables and in steak restaurants and private clubs. Jim Hoy, a Kansas folklorist and rancher, says: "I remember mountain oysters as the main course for informal community gatherings. These were usually stag affairs (no pun intended) at which area ranchers and cowboys would celebrate the end of the calf-working season with a party that would include oysters, beer, and poker." Wilson, Kansas, hosts a "testicle festival" every June as another way to celebrate this food. Although some residents consider eating them a male rite of passage, others view these "oysters" as a delicacy. Truly they are one of the remaining folk foods in the Plains.

AT-HOME EATING IN THE GREAT PLAINS

For an ongoing project that seeks to determine regional foods for various sections of the United States, a 1996 to 2001 survey asked Great Plains residents to provide hypothetical menus for a meal representative of their part of the state that they would serve to out-of-state guests. Using a set of 463 menus collected in this way, common and symbolic dishes and meals were identified. Although great variability undoubtedly exists from household to household in choices of foods for daily replenishment and pleasure, the choices for a special occasion are more restricted and tend toward the traditional.

The most common meal expressed by the sample group provides context for the discussion that follows. Beef is the main dish, chosen by 70 percent of respondents, with a grilled steak as the preferred method of preparation. Potatoes and some form of bread also would be in the meal, with corn the preferred vegetable except in Oklahoma, where green beans would take precedence. Pie is the most common dessert, and apples are the leading choice for a filling. Finally, coffee is the most popular beverage, closely followed by iced tea.

Main Dish

Admonitions to "Eat Beef" posted on pickup trucks and along roadsides across the Great Plains are reflected by survey respondents, who select beef at an exceptional rate, with numbers as high as 80 percent for Kansas. Roast as a preparation method is preferred at the highest rate by people in North Dakota (38 percent of all responses in that state), steak by Nebraskans (40 percent), and chicken-fried steak (20 percent) and barbecued brisket (16 percent) by Oklahomans. In general, beef roasts dominate in the Dakotas and steaks in the middle states. Pork (9 percent) and chicken (11 percent) dishes are minor in comparison to beef, both being highest in Oklahoma. Fish is mentioned by only 4 percent of respondents.

Starch

Potatoes are the preferred starch source overall (84 percent of responses), with an almost equal preference between mashed and baked. A baked bread product (biscuits, bread, cornbread, or rolls/buns) is the second choice (67 percent), with the numbers highest in Kansas, where many respondents refer to homemade bread. Biscuits and cornbread are selected at the highest rate by Oklahomans. Such high percentages, of course, suggest the presence of both potatoes and bread on some tables. Other carbohydrate dishes that perform similar functions in a meal are present only in very low counts. Rice is selected by 3 percent of respondents, pasta by only 2 percent.

(Cooked) Vegetable

Corn and beans are the dominant vegetables in the Great Plains, with a persistent theme of "garden fresh" running throughout the responses. People select sweet corn as their favorite vegetable (48 percent of all responses), with corn on the cob being the primary serving style. The second choice is beans (41 percent), with green beans dominating in the northern states and pintos in Oklahoma. Carrots are a distant next choice (9 percent), with Dakotans specifying these most frequently. Oklahomans indicate a special preference for fried okra. Not all people in the Plains eat cooked vegetables—12 percent of respondents do not list one on their menu.

Salad

A generic lettuce salad is the preferred form for this food category (chosen by 43 percent), with higher numbers in Kansas and Nebraska. Respondents sometimes indicate specific raw vegetable ingredients for this dish and often include tomatoes. Coleslaw and potato salad are popular in Oklahoma and Jell-O (as a salad) in North Dakota. Again, some respondents (especially in Oklahoma) do not include a salad with their menu (17 percent).

Dessert

Pie is by far the most common dessert, constituting 59 percent of all responses, led by Nebraska and South Dakota. Cake is a weak second at 14 percent. No other fruit or nut filling matches the importance of apple in the Great Plains as a whole, but smaller preference pockets are related to local horticultural conditions. Secondary pie areas exist in eastern portions of three regions: pecan in Oklahoma,

The fruit- or cheese-filled yeast-raised cake known as kuchen is usually served for breakfast, but it is also enjoyed as a dessert. The word kaffeekuchen is German for "coffee cake." Courtesy South Dakota Tourism.

cherry in Kansas and Nebraska, and rhubarb in the Dakotas. Peach cobbler, also based on a locally grown fruit, is popular in Oklahoma. In the drier western counties, people tend to select cakes and other desserts constructed from generic ingredients. Chocolate cake is the most popular of these.

Beverage

Most respondents in the survey would offer more than one beverage to their guests. Coffee (54 percent) and iced tea (50 percent) lead the preferences, but surprising geographic differences exist. Iced tea appears on menus north all the way to a line that runs through the middle of the Dakotas. Coffee, in contrast, extends south to northern Oklahoma. These patterns create a broad transition zone in the middle of the Plains where both beverages are served in nearly equal amounts. Milk in the survey is highly concentrated in the Dakotas. As for beer and carbonated drinks, Great Plains people are nonenthusiasts (6 percent and 4 percent, respectively), at least for this special-occasion meal.

EATING OUT IN THE GREAT PLAINS

Franchise Restaurants

Arby's, Burger King, Hardees, KFC, McDonald's, Steak 'n Shake, Subway, Taco Bell, and Wendy's—the Great Plains has them all and more. Some residents fear that fast-food units such as these are replacing local restaurants, and a way of life is disappearing. They have a point—seasoned waitresses are indeed giving way to teenagers who work behind the counter, the cook's special of the day to standardized menus, and regional dishes to bland and anonymous foods. Instead of a discussion of the standard assortment of franchise restaurants that are in the Plains, the focus here is on several that originated in the region. Many of these, surprisingly, sell pizza.

Braum's Ice Cream and Dairy Stores, started in 1968 by Bill Braum in Oklahoma, combine fast-food restaurants with limited-product food stores (their buildings are literally divided in half) and now number 280 throughout Arkansas, Kansas, Missouri, Oklahoma, and Texas. All locations are within a day's delivery distance of the company's ice cream plant in Tuttle, Oklahoma (southwest of Oklahoma City). Unique in the dairy industry because of its vertical integration, Braum's milks 10,000 cows a day and has seven farms and ranches.

Godfather's Pizza has been in business since 1973. Starting with one restaurant in Omaha, the franchise now operates in thirty states.

Mazzio's Pizza was started in 1961 in Tulsa as The Pizza Parlor. It changed to the current name in 1975 and began expansion to locations throughout the central part of the country.

Pizza Hut, begun in Wichita in 1958 by two college-age brothers, Frank and Daniel Carney, has grown to become the largest pizza restaurant chain in the world. Despite (or perhaps because of) several mergers, including one with the PepsiCo corporate family, it remains a giant in the food-service industry.

Runza®, headquartered in Lincoln, is a fast-food establishment with a twist. In addition to burgers and soft drinks, it features a sandwich called a Runza®. Made of ground beef, cabbage, and potatoes encased in dough, this product is similar to a bierock. Runza restaurants began franchising in 1979 and had expanded by 2000 to sixty-three locations in Colorado, Iowa, Kansas, Nebraska, and South Dakota.

Sirloin Stockade is now headquartered in Hutchinson, Kansas, but opened its first restaurant in Oklahoma City in 1966. With a buffet format, it sets itself apart from classic steakhouses with a family atmosphere and lower cost. In some locations, the concept also is marketed under the names Montana Mike's Steakhouse and Coyote Canyon.

Sonic Drive-In first opened in Shawnee, Oklahoma, in 1953 as a root-beer stand. Now it is the nation's largest chain of drive-ins, with 2,600 locations in thirty states. It differs from other burger places by having carhops, curbside speakers, and cooked-to-order service. The name comes from an early advertising slogan, "Sonic, Service with the Speed of Sound."

Valentino's opened as a pizza business in Lincoln in 1957. Today it has fifty-two restaurant locations across the northern Plains. Promotional materials tout their home region's work ethic: "Valentino's approach is a lot like our way of life here in Nebraska. It's striving to always do the best job you can. It's part of what they call the good life in Nebraska."

White Castle, the first of the hamburger chains, opened in Wichita in 1916. After a partnership was established in 1921, the company expanded and was the model for other hamburger franchises, including one started by Ray Kroc. Small one-inch-square burgers on a bun for five cents each were advertised using the "buy 'em by the sack" slogan. White uniforms of workers and standardized white

Kansas State Fair circa 1950s. Crops "Raised by J.W. Gilman, Leavenworth, KS."
Courtesy Kansas State Fair, Hutchinson, KS.

buildings contributed to an image of efficiency and sanitariness that eventually influenced the rest of the industry. White Castles are still around.

Ethnic Food Venues

Ethnic foods are available in the Plains, but sometimes the consumer has to be inventive in finding public venues where he or she can participate as an outsider. Because most ethnic groups do not support restaurants devoted exclusively to their cuisine, festivals and other celebrations are often the best places to find their foods in large quantities. Fund-raising events such as church suppers are another possibility. The three activities discussed here are typical of ethnic gatherings in the Great Plains.

Mennonite Relief Sales

Mennonite food (German with several twists deriving from the group's residence in Russia and elsewhere) is accessible to outsiders through thirty-two annual fund-raising events throughout the United States and Canada. Events for the Plains region include the Kansas MCC (Mennonite Central Committee) Sale at the Kansas State Fair Grounds in Hutchinson; the Nebraska MCC Sale at the Hamilton County Fairgrounds in Aurora; the Upper Midwest Relief Sale at Minot, North Dakota; the Oklahoma MCC Relief Sale at Enid; and Minn-Kota Mennonite Sale at Sioux Falls, South Dakota. At these events, the auctioning of hand-stitched quilts and other handmade crafts draws many visitors, but the main attraction is food. The lines are long, but the eating is good. Preparation work starts months ahead of time, and the German Buffet in Kansas, for example, typically serves between 6,000 and 10,000 people.

The foods for sale at the dinners and food booths for these events are largely German Russian. Verenika, a dumpling filled with cottage cheese and sometimes served with ham gravy, is the most common single item. Bona beroggi (buns filled with mashed sweetened pinto beans served with a sweet cream sauce), New Year's cookies (portzilka or raisin fritters rolled in granulated sugar), and pluma mos (fruit soup with prunes in cream sauce) are other popular foods.

Native American Powwows

Authentic Native American food is difficult to sample outside of private homes since these groups believe more in sharing food than in selling it. A public venue that provides access is a powwow, a tribal gathering that, while devoted primarily to dancing, also offers food vendors. Powwows are held widely throughout the Plains, especially in Oklahoma and South Dakota. The most common dish is fry bread, discussed earlier.

Many traditional dishes such as wild game, the Cherokee canuche (a soup made with hickory nuts), and northern Plains specialties of bison stew and wojapi (a thick pudding of wild berries boiled with bison suet) are inaccessible at powwows. Foods such as these normally are eaten only for within-group special occasions. Contemporary Native American diets are, in fact, quite Americanized: game is rarely eaten, wheat replaces corn, and sweet things along with butter and vegetable oils are common, as are coffee, tea, and soft drinks. The Kickapoo tribe's Golden Eagle Casino in Horton, Kansas, however, does offer a Native American Day when older foods are served buffet style. These include fry bread, corn soup, baked quail, smoked buffalo baron, and wild rice.

Scandinavian Festivals

Høstfest in Minot, North Dakota, is a celebration of heritage intended to recognize all Scandinavian groups. Held every October in this city of 37,000, the four-day event is attended by 70,000 people from the United States, Canada, and Scandinavia and is known for its live entertainment, craft demonstrations, and unbelievably good food. Repeat guests (sometimes representing three generations) are common. Høstfest is modeled after the pleasures and memories of a small town on a Saturday night, when farmers and townspeople would socialize and enjoy each other's tales of the past week.

Food plays a dominant role in this celebration. The Dining Hall of the Nordic Chefs features fine cuisine prepared by master chefs imported from Europe. Exotic foodstuffs such as Arctic reindeer and Icelandic cod appear at these venues, but so does the much more common lefse (a thinly rolled potato pancake served with butter, jam, or sugar), rømmegrøt (cooked sour cream drizzled with butter, brown sugar, and cinnamon), and Swedish rice pudding. Also popular are nightly lutefisk and Norwegian meatball dinners. Lutefisk is made from dried cod that has been soaked in lye. As the fish is reconstituted during cooking, it begins to "stink" and for this reason has been banned in many households. Instead, enthusiasts visit rotating weekly fall lutefisk dinners in the area. "Annual Church Suppers in North Dakota" gives a wonderful description of a 1947 dinner.[10]

Emblematic Restaurants

Barbecue, chicken, and European ethnic restaurants, along with steak houses, dominate the nonfranchise eating establishment in the Plains. A polling of local experts provided the following list of restaurants that were, in their opinion, symbolic for their states. Such selections, of course, are dependent upon individual tastes, but my results correspond well to listings in available restaurant guides.

Barbecue

Bob's Bar-B-Q, Ada, Oklahoma
Bricks Restaurant, Sulphur, Oklahoma
   Known for all-you-can-eat ribs.
Budros Rib Joint, Ardmore, Oklahoma
Earl's Rib Palace, Oklahoma City, Oklahoma
   A roadside diner almost as famous for its Elvis memorabilia as for its beef and
   pork.
Guy and Mae's Tavern, Williamsburg, Kansas
Hayward's Pit Bar-B-Que, Overland Park, Kansas
King's Pit Bar Bq, Liberal, Kansas
Slick's Bar-b-que, Muskogee, Oklahoma
   The house specialty is pork ribs.

Chicken

Barto's Idle Hour and Steak House, Frontenac, Kansas
   Despite the name, Barto's specialty is chicken.
Brookville Hotel, Abilene, Kansas
   In business since the 1870s and well known to the vast majority of Kansans. The
   owners serve only family-style chicken dinners.
Chicken Annie's, Yale, Kansas
Chicken Mary's, Yale, Kansas
   Equally popular and dividing the loyalty of southeast Kansans, these two restaurants are adjacent to each other in an old coal-mining camp. Both were started
   by wives of miners who had to support their families after injuries to their husbands.

European Ethnic

Bohemian Cafe, Omaha, Nebraska
   This restaurant accurately describes itself as "Omaha's European connection
   since 1924." Roast duck and liver dumpling soup are specialties.
Kroll's Kitchen (German Russian), Bismarck, North Dakota
   Borscht, knoephla (soup with dumplings), and pierogies (dough filled with
   mashed potatoes).

Olde Towne Restaurant (German Russian), Hillsboro, Kansas
 The main attraction is a Saturday-night Low German buffet that includes
 verenika (cheese-filled dumpling) and cherry moos (stewed fruit).

Steak Houses

Anthony's Restaurant and Cocktail Lounge, Omaha, Nebraska
 Known for certified Angus beef and Italian specialties, this establishment is easily
 identifiable by a brown-and-white cow perched on its roof.
Caniglia's, Omaha, Nebraska
 Steaks with Italian side dishes since 1940.
Cattleman's Steak House, Oklahoma City, Oklahoma
 Built in 1920 in the stockyards, Cattleman's is the "granddaddy" of Oklahoma
 steak palaces. Locals go there for breakfast too.
Georgia's and the Owl, Amidon, North Dakota
Grain Bin Supper Club, Garden City, Kansas
Johnny's Cafe, Omaha, Nebraska
 Advertised as Omaha's original steak house, it was started by Polish immigrant
 Frank Kawa and appears in the film *About Schmidt*.
Minerva's Restaurant and Bar, Sioux Falls, South Dakota
 A downtown eatery that features ribeyes and pasta.
Scotch and Sirloin, Wichita, Kansas
 Known for its well-marbled meats, this restaurant is owned by the butcher shop
 next door.
Tea Steak House, Tea, South Dakota
 Voted as serving the "best steak dinner" in South Dakota, it specializes in sir-
 loins.

General

Al's Oasis, Oacoma, South Dakota
 This expansive truck stop on I-90 advertises, "We Have It All." Its menu in-
 cludes buffalo burgers, five-cent cups of coffee, and excellent pie.
The Cassoday Cafe, Cassoday, Kansas
 A small restaurant in a Flint Hills town of ninety-five residents. The owners pro-
 vide a breakfast buffet for motorcyclists the first Sunday of the month from
 March to November.
Chieftain Restaurant and Sports Bar, Carrington, North Dakota
 A central meeting place for North Dakotans, it advertises, "Cooking the good
 old fashioned way."
Dreisbach's, Grand Island, Nebraska
 Until it closed in 2002, Dreisbach's served family-style meals that featured rab-
 bit, steak, and biscuits with honey.
Hays House Restaurant, Council Grove, Kansas
 In business since 1857, this is said to be the oldest continuously operating
 restaurant west of the Mississippi.
Tower City Cafe, Tower City, North Dakota
 Known as a pie place; "sour cream raisin pie is a must."

RESOURCE GUIDE

Printed Sources

"Annual Church Suppers in North Dakota." http://www.webfamilytree.com/ annual_church_suppers_in_north_dakota.htm (accessed July 8, 2003). (Originally published: *Hannaford Enterprise*, November 1947, 1.)

Fertig, Judith M. *Prairie Home Cooking: 400 Recipes That Celebrate the Bountiful Harvests, Creative Cooks, and Comforting Foods of the American Heartland.* Boston: Harvard Common Press, 1999.

Graber, Kay. *Nebraska Pioneer Cookbook.* Lincoln: University of Nebraska Press, 1974.

Haber, Barbara. "The Harvey Girls: Good Women and Good Food Civilize the American West." In *From Hardtack to Home Fries: An Uncommon History of American Cooks and Meals*, 87–106. New York: Free Press, 2002.

"Harvey House Gong." http://www.kshs.org/cool3/harveygong.htm. (Originally published: Millbrook, Minnie Dubbs. "Fred Harvey and the Santa Fe." In *The Santa Fe in Topeka*. Shawnee County Historical Society Bulletin 56 [Topeka: Shawnee County Historical Society, 1979].)

Hoy, Jim, and Tom Isern. *Plains Folk: A Commonplace of the Great Plains.* Norman: University of Oklahoma Press, 1987.

———. *Plains Folk II: The Romance of the Landscape.* Norman: University of Oklahoma Press, 1990.

Ireland, Lynne. "Great Plains." In *Smithsonian Folklife Cookbook*, ed. Katherine S. Kirlin and Thomas M. Kirlin, 212–233. Washington, DC: Smithsonian Institution Press, 1991.

Isern, Tom. *Dakota Circle: Excursions on the True Plains.* Fargo: Institute for Regional Studies, North Dakota State University, 2000.

Jakle, John A., and Keith A. Sculle. *Fast Food: Roadside Restaurants in the Automobile Age.* Baltimore: Johns Hopkins University Press, 1999.

Martin, Rebecca. "We're Just Wheat People." *Kansas Heritage* 7, no. 4 (winter 1999): 4–8.

Norris, Kathleen. *Dakota: A Spiritual Geography.* New York: Ticknor and Fields, 1993.

Stratton, Joanna L. *Pioneer Women: Voices from the Kansas Frontier.* New York: Simon and Schuster, 1981.

Welsch, Roger. *It's Not the End of the Earth, but You Can See It from Here: Tales of the Great Plains.* New York: Villard Books, 1990.

Welsch, Roger L., and Linda K. Welsch. *Cather's Kitchens: Foodways in Literature and Life.* Lincoln: University of Nebraska Press, 1987.

Winge, Jane. *Ritzy Rhubarb Secrets Cookbook.* Litchville, ND: Litchville Committee, 2000.

Young, Carrie. *Nothing to Do but Stay: My Pioneer Mother.* Iowa City: University of Iowa Press, 1991.

Young, Carrie, and Felicia Young. *Prairie Cooks: Glorified Rice, Three-Day Buns, and Other Recipes and Reminiscences.* Iowa City: University of Iowa Press, 1993.

Young, Kay. *Wild Seasons: Gathering and Cooking Wild Plants of the Great Plains.* Lincoln: University of Nebraska Press, 1993.

WEB SITE

Isern, Tom. Plains Folk Web site
http://www.plainsfolk.com/oases/ (accessed July 17, 2003)

Food Festivals

Kansas

Beef Empire Days, Garden City, June
http://www.beefempiredays.com/

Beefiesta, Scott City, August
http://www.scottcity.com/index.asp?DocumentID=228

Chili Challenge, Lenexa, October
http://www.ci.lenexa.ks.us/parks/chilichallenge.html

Chili Cookoff, Hutchinson, September

Grant County Home Products Dinner, Ulysses, September
http://www.ulysseschamber.com/index.php?loc=4

Spinach Festival, Lenexa, September
http://www.lenexaartscouncil.org/Spinachfestival.html

Watermelon Feed, Oxford, September
http://www.oxfordks.org/contact.htm

Watermelon Festival, Clyde, September
http://www.clydekansas.org/watermelonfestival.htm

Watermelon Festival, DeSoto, August

Nebraska

Applefest, Orleans, October
http://www.megavision.net/hctour/Special%20Events.html

Applejack Festival, Nebraska City, September
http://www.nebraskacity.com/events.html

Honey Fest, Randolph, June

Kool-Aid Days, Hastings, August
http://www.kool-aiddays.com/

Popcorn Days, North Loup, August
http://www.mormacpopcorn.com/popcorndays.htm

Pork Day, Stamford, September
http://www.megavision.net/hctour/Special%20Events.html

Watermelon Festival, Norfolk, August
http://www.norfolk.ne.us/Chamber/?Page=Watermelon%20Festival

North Dakota

Goosefest, Kenmare, October
http://www.kenmarend.org/goose.htm

Sunflower Festival, Enderlin, September
http://www.tour-nd.com/membership/cityofenderlin.html

Oklahoma

Blackberry Festival, McLoud, July

Blackeyed Pea Festival, Hollis, August
http://www.pe.net/~rksnow/okcountyholliscev.htm

Green Corn Festival, Bixby, June

Huckleberry Festival, Jay, July

Ice Cream Festival, Tuttle, July
http://www.travelok.com/ourevents/eventsdetail.asp?id=1+60+82

Kolache Festival, Prague, May
http://www.uncommondays.com/states/ok/events/kolache.htm

Okrafest, Checotah, September
http://www.uncommondays.com/states/ok/events/okrafest.htm

Peach Festival, Porter, July
http://www.porterpeachfestival.com

Peach Festival, Stratford, July
http://www.unitedcountry.com/stratfordok/events.htm

Pecan Festival, Okmulgee, June
http:www.lasr.net/leisure/oklahoma/okmulgee/okmulgee/att11.html

Sorghum Festival, Wewoka, October
http://www.sorghum.org/

State Chili Championship, Midwest City, July

Strawberry Festival, Stilwell, April
http://www.lasr.net/leisure/oklahoma/adair/stilwell/att8.html

Watermelon Festival, Rush Springs, August
http://home.flash.net/~mvincent/Festival.htm

Watermelon Festival, Valliant, August

South Dakota

Buffalo Roundup Chili Cookoff, Custer, September
http://www.custerstatepark.info/round.htm

Center of Nation Chili Cookoff, Belle Fourche, September
http://www.bellefourche.org/Cook-Off.html

Honey Days, Bruce, July
http://www.svschool.org/yellow%20pages/bruce/bruce.html

International Vinegar Festival, Roslyn, August
http://www.vinegarman.com/VinegarFestival.html

Potato Day, Clark, July
http://www.clarksd.com/potato.htm

LANGUAGE

Pamela Innes

The Great Plains region is commonly perceived as having little linguistic variation or accent. The style of speaking associated with the Great Plains has been the model for news broadcasters, politicians seeking national office, business leaders, and others needing a cultured, but rather generic, speech pattern. However, a number of languages and varieties of English are spoken by people in the Great Plains region, though many of these languages and dialects apparently have gone unnoticed by the general public, according to the common view of language in the Great Plains.

Linguists, on the other hand, have long noted and been interested in the variation in language patterns on the Great Plains. This has led to a great deal of study of language spread and variation across the states that constitute the Great Plains. In pursuing research in these states, linguists have tended to divide them into different geographic groupings or have considered other states to be part of the Great Plains region.

For instance, in the influential *Linguistic Atlas of the Upper Midwest*, a three-volume work that covers many aspects of variation in the English used in the Upper Midwest, one can see that the Upper Midwest includes North Dakota, South Dakota, and Nebraska, all of which are included in this volume's definition of the Great Plains. Speakers were interviewed throughout these states, and each speaker was identified by a number for identification purposes.[1]

In the *Atlas*, the forms of English present in the Dakotas and Nebraska are compared with English forms used in Minnesota and Iowa and are not compared with English forms from the states of Kansas and Oklahoma. In essence, only slightly more than half of the states in the Great Plains region are included in the Upper Midwest as formulated in the *Atlas*. The focus on the states included in the Upper Midwest was based upon the known movement into those states of speakers of forms of English that differentiated them from more southerly states, such as Kansas and Oklahoma.

The *Handbook of North American Indians: Plains* is an important reference for information about the Native American groups in the Plains, including states that border the five states identified in this text and some Canadian provinces. References to other states and provinces will be made when languages or forms of English cross the regional border. Indeed, several of the linguistic varieties discussed here can be found among speakers who live in states outside of the region because linguistic variation here, as in other regions of the world, rarely coincides exactly with political boundaries (such as state lines). For this reason, if a reader consults some of the works cited, he or she may find that the regional definition or the states considered to be part of the region differ from those considered here.[2]

LINGUISTIC TERMS

There are a number of terms that are useful in discussing the similarities and differences of Plains languages and dialects. When people think of the various languages spoken in the region, they need to think of them as members of language families. Language families are collections of languages considered to have descended from a common ancestor, much as one draws one's genealogy or family tree by finding common ancestors. Languages are thought to have common ancestors when the sounds, ways of forming words and sentences, and vocabulary items found within the languages have similar forms or structures. Languages from several families, and often multiple members of these families, are spoken by people who live in the Great Plains.

When linguists speak of different languages, they are referring to a means of communicating that has distinctive sounds and ways of organizing those sounds in words (called phonology in linguistic literature), ways of creating words and organizing units of meaning (morphology), rules governing the order of words in sentences (syntax or grammar), and kinds of words (lexicon). Linguists differentiate between two languages when speakers of the two are unable to understand each other, even after spending a good deal of time listening to each other. The languages discussed here are widely recognized by linguists as separate entities, even though some related languages may sound very similar to one who does not speak either of the languages.

Even when people are speaking the same language, such as English, listeners may discern differences in pronunciation, word use, or grammar in the speech of people from different geographic areas, socioeconomic classes, or ethnic groups. These different forms of the same language are called dialects in linguistic literature. Some dialects may be so divergent that it takes the speakers quite some time to get used to the different grammatical forms, pronunciation patterns, and word choices. Yet because speakers can pick out much of what a speaker who is using a different dialect of the same language is saying, linguists do not consider these to be two distinct languages.

Linguists discern dialect differences by analyzing the pronunciation, vocabulary, and syntax of the speech of a number of people across a geographic region. When a number of distinct differences in vocabulary (the use of different terms for the same object or action), pronunciation, or syntax can be documented in the speech of people in a region, linguists feel confident that they have discerned the boundaries of dialects of a language. Often, however, the lines that separate the use of different words, pronunciations, or grammatical constructions do not overlap absolutely. Instead, it is common for linguists to draw several isoglosses (lines showing the dividing line between dialectal forms) in a region and look for places where these are closest together. It is where the isoglosses tend to overlap most closely that linguists are comfortable talking about distinct dialect boundaries.

In some areas, however, as in the Great Plains states of Nebraska and Kansas, the isoglosses range across a fairly wide area and do not indicate clear dialect boundaries. In these regions, linguists note that two dialects are in contact and both are influencing the speech of people in the region, but they cannot draw clear dialect areas because of the geographic range covered by the distinct isoglosses. Often, as in the case of Nebraska and Kansas, linguists will find it necessary to consider these areas of mixture as being influenced by a "dialect layer" or a hybrid of two dialects, which is distinctive in its own right. Thus when discussing the

Native American Language Families

Languages from a number of different Native American language families are spoken by residents of the Plains. The following is a list of the language family names with languages within each family that were or still are spoken in the Plains region. Those language families that are present on the Plains due to forced relocation of speakers by governmental agents are indicated by "(recent arrival)" following the language family's name.

Siouan: Assiniboine, Crow, Hidatsa, Mandan, Teton, Yankton, Omaha, Ponca, Otoe, Iowa, Quapaw, Kansa, and Osage

Algonquian: Plains Ojibwa (Chippewa), Cheyenne, Arapaho, Delaware, Kickapoo, Potawatomi, Sauk-Fox, Shawnee

Caddoan: Arikara, Pawnee, Wichita, Caddo

Athabaskan: Ná'isha, Chiricahua

Kiowa-Tanoan: Kiowa

Uto-Aztecan: Comanche

Muskogean (recent arrival): Muskogee/Creek, Seminole, Choctaw, Chickasaw

Iroquoian (recent arrival): Seneca, Cayuga, Cherokee

Yuchi (A language isolate—unconnected to any other languages and thus not part of a language family: a recent arrival to the Plains region.)

variety of English spoken by people in Nebraska and Kansas, they talk about the Midland dialect layer, which is a combination of forms from the South and North dialects of English.

The number of dialects of English is a legacy of settlement by speakers of many languages in the Great Plains. The number of dialects of English has also been affected by the migration patterns of speakers of English onto the Great Plains, for some dialect differences on the Plains are based on even stronger dialect distinctions in the eastern United States. Rather than being a land of homogeneous speech, the Great Plains region is quite varied in language.

NATIVE AMERICAN LANGUAGES

The earliest speakers of any languages to settle in the Great Plains were speakers of Native American languages.[3] Languages from a number of different language families have been, and continue to be, spoken in the Great Plains. There were a handful of language families represented on the Plains shortly after European contact. Several other language families are now present in the region due to relocation of speakers after European colonization had taken place. Thus throughout the past three centuries there have been a large number of Native American languages spoken on the Plains.

Classes of Language Extinction

Languages are considered to be at greater or lesser danger of becoming extinct based on the numbers of speakers and their ages. Linguists tend to assign languages to different levels of maintenance status based on these criteria, with Class 1 languages having the least likelihood of dying out and those classified as Class 3 having the greatest likelihood of dying out within this generation.[4] The following is a list of the various levels of maintenance status, with the criteria that cause linguists to put a language in each level. In this list, the levels are arranged from least likely to die out soon (the best position for any given language) to most likely to die out soon (the worst position for any given language).

Not Endangered: Several thousand speakers, with many children learning the language as their first language.

Class 1: Several thousand speakers, with good numbers of children learning the language as their first language.

Class 2: A few thousand speakers to hundreds of speakers, primarily adults, though a few children may learn the language as their first language.

Class 3: Spoken by fewer than one hundred speakers, all of whom are late-middle-aged or elderly.

Extinct: The language is no longer spoken by anyone.

Because of relocation and placement on reservations, a number of the Native American languages of the Plains are now found outside of the original areas where they were spoken. Also, as a result of governmental and educational policies, population decline, and economic factors, many Native American languages are being spoken by fewer and fewer people. The outlook for many of the Native American languages varies, depending upon their maintenance status, but each is facing some decline in use. Many of the tribes have recognized the danger of losing their languages and are now working to maintain or revitalize them.

In the following discussion of Native American languages on the Plains, language families and their constituent languages found on the Plains at early European contact are presented first, then language families found on the Plains as a result of forced relocation are discussed. Within these divisions, the language families are examined in an order based on the number of languages from each family found in the region. After each language family has been explored individually, the overall impact of Native American languages on the Plains is examined.

Siouan Languages

The language family with the highest number of languages spoken in the Plains region is the Siouan family. Member languages of this family spoken by indigenous inhabitants of the Plains are Assiniboine, Crow, Hidatsa, Mandan, Teton, Yankton, Omaha, Ponca, Otoe, Kansa, and Osage. The family gets its name from the group of tribes commonly known as the Sioux, among whom are included speakers of Teton and Yankton.

Speakers of Siouan languages inhabited the Plains region at the time of the earliest contact with Europeans. In actuality, languages from the Siouan language family were spoken outside of the Great Plains region into the Midwest, the Rocky Mountain region, and the South. In the Great Plains region itself, the Assiniboine, Crow, Hidatsa, Mandan, and Yankton occupied parts of North Dakota. Of these, the Assiniboine, Crow, and Yankton also migrated into other regions, generally the Rocky Mountain region, throughout the year. The Teton, Ponca, and Yankton occupied areas of North and South Dakota, and each of these groups pursued game outside of these states toward the Rocky Mountain region. The Omaha, Ponca,

Iowa, and Otoe occupied parts of Nebraska, with the Otoe and Iowa occasionally moving into parts of Iowa and Missouri. The Kansa were located primarily in Kansas, and the Osage occupied territory in southeastern Kansas and northeastern Oklahoma.

The majority of Siouan languages are now spoken by residents of reservations, some of which are located outside of the Plains states. The greatest concentrations of the Ponca, Iowa, Otoe, and Kansa populations are currently located on land in Oklahoma that is not considered reserved land. These tribes, along with many others located in Oklahoma, underwent a process called "allotment" as a result of the Dawes Severalty Act of 1887. As a result of that act, tracts of land were allotted to tribal members, and the remainder of the unallotted land was opened for sale to non-Indians. Thus while these tribes have maintained population concentrations in the regions in which their reservations had originally been located, they are no longer residents of a reservation. The languages spoken by tribes that no longer live on reservation lands are presented later because the discussion of Siouan languages here progresses from north to south.

The Assiniboine language is spoken by previous inhabitants of northern North Dakota who were removed to reservations in Montana and Saskatchewan. There are two dialects of Assiniboine. One is used by speakers who live on Fort Belknap Reservation in Montana and on Mosquito–Grizzly Bear's Head and Carry the Kettle Reserves in Saskatchewan. The other dialect is used by speakers from Fort Peck Reservation in Montana and Ocean Man, Pheasant Rump, and White Bear Reserves in Saskatchewan. The language is of Class 3 status at this time, as only a few speakers on the Montana reservations, most of whom are elderly, still have some knowledge of the language.

The Crow and Hidatsa languages, spoken by people who originally inhabited the central and western sections of North Dakota, but are now located on reservations in Montana and central North Dakota, are very closely related. These languages are so similar that speakers of one can easily learn the other. The majority of Crow people are currently located on Crow Reservation in Montana, and the Hidatsa are located on Fort Berthold Reservation in North Dakota.

Of these two languages, Crow is in a much better position for preservation than is Hidatsa. In the mid-1990s, it was estimated that 85 percent of those aged forty or older were fluent in the language and that nearly a quarter of young children and teens learned the language as their mother tongue. Crow would thus be considered in the Class 2 category, endangered but still a viable language. Hidatsa, on the other hand, has an estimated 451 speakers, a handful of whom are monolingual, and nearly all of whom are elderly. The outlook for maintenance of Hidatsa is dubious even though its status is Class 2, though a concentrated, sustained attempt to revitalize the language might result in increased numbers of speakers.

The Mandan also are currently located on Fort Berthold Reservation, North Dakota, which is near their original territory. Mandan's maintenance status is that of a Class 3 language. It was spoken by only eight speakers, two of whom were not completely fluent in the language, in the early 1990s. Each of the six completely fluent speakers was an elder of the tribe. For languages in this situation, immediate action is necessary for retention of the language, and even when immediate action is taken, it may not be possible to record all aspects of the language or create new fluent speakers before the last fluent speakers pass away.

Yankton and Yanktonai, who speak a single dialect of the Sioux language, once inhabited southern North Dakota and northern South Dakota. Today the Yankton-Yanktonai have been dispersed to several different reservations, including Yankton Reservation, South Dakota; Crow Creek Reservation, South Dakota; Sisseton Reservation, South Dakota; Standing Rock Reservation, South and North Dakota; Spirit Lake Reservation, North Dakota; and Fort Peck Reservation, Montana. According to the Ethnologue database maintained by the Summer Institute of Linguistics, there are 15,355 speakers of the language, including 31 monolinguals. This Siouan language is in relatively good shape for maintenance, as some children are being raised in the language, and some communities are vigorously pursuing language maintenance.

The Teton division of the Sioux is often divided into three different groups, though these are all related: the Oglala, the Brule, and the Saone. Of these, the Saone is a collection of five tribes: the Minneconjou, Hunkpapa, Sans Arc, Blackfeet, and Two Kettles. At the time of European contact on the Plains, these groups inhabited southwestern North Dakota, western and central South Dakota, northwestern Nebraska, and eastern portions of the Rocky Mountain region. These groups are currently located on the Standing Rock Reservation in North and South Dakota and the Cheyenne River, Pine Ridge, Lower Brule, and Rosebud Reservations in South Dakota. Teton is spoken by approximately 6,000 speakers, most of whom are residents of these reservations, though some speakers were relocated to major cities (Los Angeles, Minneapolis, Chicago, and others) in the late 1960s. Some children are being raised in the language, primarily on the reservations, which is a hopeful sign for future maintenance of this language.

The Ponca and Omaha languages, spoken by groups that originally inhabited northeastern Nebraska, are closely related, though some linguistic differences are noted. The Ponca are split between a small reservation in northern Nebraska and allotted lands in north central Oklahoma. The Omaha are currently located on the Omaha Reservation in Nebraska, though many live in the metropolitan areas of Omaha and Lincoln, Nebraska. Neither of these languages is in very good shape, as Southern Ponca is still fully commanded by only about twenty-five elderly speakers and Omaha is spoken fluently by only an estimated seventy elderly speakers.

The Iowa originally inhabited areas of Iowa, northern Missouri, Illinois, Wisconsin, Minnesota, eastern Nebraska, eastern Kansas, and eastern South Dakota. Initially, the Iowa were resettled in northeastern Kansas and southeastern Nebraska. In 1881, many moved to an area in north central Oklahoma and have remained in that region since that time. The Otoe, who are closely related linguistically and culturally to the Iowa, formerly resided in southern Minnesota and later moved to the south near the mouth of the Platte River. From 1880 to 1882, the Otoe were moved to a reservation in north central Oklahoma. Both the Otoe and Iowa were Siouan groups affected by the allotment process and are not residents of a reservation today. Perhaps as a result of the small population of these tribes and the dissolution of a corporate land base, their languages have become extinct. The last speakers of Iowa and Otoe died in 1996, though some older adults can remember bits of the languages, but not to the point where they are able to hold conversations.

The Quapaw, another Siouan group that had originally inhabited lands outside of the Plains region, were moved from the Ohio valley to areas of Arkansas and from there to northeastern and north central Oklahoma in 1833. Today the majority of the tribe still lives in the region of Quapaw, Oklahoma. The Quapaw language is in the Class 3 category in regard to maintenance. According to a census conducted in 1990, there were still 34 speakers left, most of whom were elderly. Each of the remaining speakers was fully bilingual in English.

The Kansa, also called the Kaw, used to inhabit portions of central and southern Kansas. Currently, the Kansa have their tribal headquarters in Kaw City, Oklahoma, which provides a centralizing point for the residents of the allotted lands in the surrounding area. Kansa is a Class 3 language, as there are only nineteen remaining speakers. Language classes are provided at the tribal headquarters. These classes are necessary for some amount of language maintenance, given the low number of remaining speakers.

The Osage used to occupy lands in central and western Kansas at the time of European contact with the Plains tribes. The majority of Osage speakers are currently located in Osage Indian Reservation in north central Oklahoma. Like many of the Siouan languages, Osage is a Class 3 language, with only a few dozen elderly speakers in the community. Unless immediate steps are taken, the language will become extinct in the near future.

Algonquian Languages

Languages from the Algonquian family are some of the most northerly languages in the Great Plains. The Plains Ojibwa (Chippewa), who are culturally and linguistically related to the Ojibwa located near the Great Lakes region in Canada, roamed the area from northern North Dakota to southern Saskatchewan and Alberta. Originally, the Cheyenne and Arapaho were both located in northern reaches of the Great Plains, occasionally migrating into western South Dakota and Nebraska. During and after the period of the Indian Wars, however, some groups that spoke these languages formed alliances and located themselves with more southerly groups that did not speak Algonquian languages. Today the Southern Cheyenne and Southern Arapaho are located in Oklahoma, while their northern counterparts are located in Wyoming (the Northern Arapaho) and Montana (the Northern Cheyenne).

These Algonquian languages are related to several languages located in the Midwest, New England, and Mid-Atlantic regions in the United States and in Saskatchewan, Alberta, and Quebec in Canada. It appears that speakers of the northern Algonquian languages in the Great Plains are rather recent immigrants who perhaps moved onto the Great Plains by the early 1700s. Despite their recent arrival on the Plains, speakers of the Plains Algonquian languages have a rich vocabulary for the activities and items found in this region.

Speakers of the Algonquian languages found on the southern Plains also are new residents in the region. Speakers of Kickapoo, Delaware, Potawatomi, Sauk-Fox, and Shawnee had previously lived near the Great Lakes, primarily in Michigan (Kickapoo, Potawatomi, Sauk-Fox) and the Ohio River valley (Delaware and Shawnee). Speakers of these languages were moved into areas of Kansas and Oklahoma between 1820 and 1835.

The Plains Ojibwa, also known as the Chippewa, are currently located on the Rocky Boy's, Fort Belknap, and Fort Peck Reservations in Montana and the Turtle Mountain and Spirit Lake Reservations in North Dakota. Those who are located on reservations in North Dakota are teaching classes in schools and utilizing other means of retaining the language in their communities. In all of the communities, both in the United States and Canada, almost all speakers are middle-aged or older, and this language is in the Class 3 category for maintenance.

Both the Cheyenne and Arapaho tribes have been divided into two separate entities, based upon the location of their settlement areas. At the time of European contact, both the Cheyenne and Arapaho lived on the northwestern reaches of the Plains region, traversing western South Dakota and Nebraska and also inhabiting the Rocky Mountain states of Wyoming and Colorado. At present, the Northern Cheyenne live on the Northern Cheyenne Reservation in Montana, and the Northern Arapaho are located on the Wind River Reservation in Wyoming. The Southern Cheyenne and Southern Arapaho live in close association with each other in western Oklahoma.

There are approximately 1,721 speakers of Cheyenne spread across both the northern and southern groups. The majority of Cheyenne speakers in both communities are either middle-aged or elderly, which puts this language in jeopardy of extinction within the next two generations. Speakers of Arapaho number approximately 1,038, including speakers from both the northern and southern communities. Some children in the Northern Arapaho community hear the language in the home, but very few develop fluency from childhood. Programs have been instituted to teach Arapaho in the public schools on the Wind River Reservation, and a number of middle-aged people still command the language. Thus the Northern Arapaho tribe has begun steps to maintain its language.

Kickapoo, Shawnee, Delaware, Sauk-Fox, and Potawatomi are all spoken in the southern Plains region. The Kickapoo are located in both northeastern Kansas and central Oklahoma on the Plains, with other settlements in southern Texas and northern Mexico. The language is in relatively good shape from a maintenance perspective, as there are speakers in all age groups, about 540 in the United States and approximately 300 in Mexico. Shawnee and Sauk-Fox, located in central and northeastern Oklahoma, respectively, are not as well off in terms of maintaining the language in the future. Few children are learning Shawnee and Sauk-Fox at this time, as most young speakers have begun to use English almost exclusively. Delaware and Potawatomi, whose speakers are located in northeastern Oklahoma, are in the worst category (Class 3) from a maintenance perspective, as only a few older speakers know these languages.

There are materials available in each of these languages, though the numbers and qualities of the materials vary. A dictionary and some language-teaching materials are available in Kickapoo. Bible portions are available in Sauk-Fox. Potawatomi has a grammar and some Bible passages in translation. Shawnee has a dictionary and some Bible passages in translation. Language-revitalization programs have been developed for both the Shawnee and Kickapoo languages, so there is hope that these languages will be retained by future generations.

Caddoan Languages

Caddoan languages are named for speakers of Caddo, one of the languages in this family. The Caddoan languages originally spoken on the Great Plains are

Arikara, Pawnee, and Wichita. Speakers of Caddo, who originally lived in the South, primarily along watersheds in the states of Missouri and Louisiana, were moved to Oklahoma in 1859. The Arikara ranged in an area extending from southwestern Nebraska to north central Kansas. The Pawnee lived in the region from south central Nebraska to northwestern Oklahoma. The Wichita lived in a smaller region located in central Oklahoma.

All Caddoan groups, including the Caddo proper, pursued agriculture to some extent. Their vocabularies for farming activities and plant names are quite extensive. Caddoan terms of importance to English speakers generally have to do with place names, however. For instance, the name of Anadarko, Oklahoma, is derived from a Caddoan word, as is the name of the state of Texas, which was derived from teša (TAY-sha), the word for "friend."

Each of the Caddoan languages is endangered. The language with the largest numbers of speakers is Caddo, which has an estimated 141 speakers, 6 of whom are monolingual in Caddo. Most speakers of Caddo live near Binger in western Oklahoma. Arikara has the next-largest number of speakers, with approximately 90 who live on the Fort Berthold Reservation in North Dakota, which they inhabit jointly with the Mandan and Hidatsa. Both Pawnee and Wichita are in danger of becoming extinct in the near future, as both have 10 or fewer elderly speakers, Pawnee with 4 and Wichita with an estimated 10. The Pawnee speakers live in north central Oklahoma, the Wichita speakers near Anadarko in west central Oklahoma.

The Caddo and Arikara tribes have been creating teaching materials and offering language classes at their tribal headquarters since the early and mid-1990s. Despite the fact that there are few young children learning these languages as their first languages, both Caddo and Arikara are considered Class 2 languages because of the number of adult speakers. With attention to the languages growing among tribal members and the production of language-teaching materials, there is a chance that these languages will persist beyond the next two generations. Wichita and Pawnee, however, will become extinct at the end of this generation due to the small number of speakers and their advanced ages.

Athabaskan Languages

The only Athabaskan language originally located on the Plains is Ná'isha (NA-ee-sha), which is spoken by very few members of the Apache Tribe of Oklahoma. Speakers of Chiricahua Apache were not indigenous inhabitants of the Plains, but were moved to the Fort Sill Reservation in 1894, at which point the language was spoken in this region. Chiricahua is no longer spoken on the Plains, however, as the last speaker of Fort Sill Chiricahua died in the mid-1990s. There are still speakers in Arizona and New Mexico, however. The majority of Athabaskan languages to which Ná'isha and Chiricahua are most closely related are found in the Southwest. Navajo, Jicarilla, and Western Apache are some of the southwestern languages related to Ná'isha and Chiricahua. The greatest number of Athabaskan languages, however, are found in the northwestern region of Canada and central and southern Alaska.

Ná'isha speakers were located in North and South Dakota in the late prehistoric period. Increased pressure from Siouan and Algonquian language speakers drove them southward to northwestern Kansas and western Oklahoma. The Ná'isha, who have always had a small population, allied themselves with larger groups on the southern Plains, eventually coming to share a reservation with the Kiowa and Comanche. Now the few remaining Ná'isha speakers live on allotted lands west of Anadarko, Oklahoma. It is estimated that there are only two or three speakers of this language, and each of the remaining speakers is quite elderly. The tribe has taken steps to educate younger members about the language and has compiled an extensive documentary and audio collection of language materials. However, given the low number of speakers and their ages, the language is likely to become extinct within the next twenty years.

Chiricahua Apache, as spoken by members of the Fort Sill Tribe, is extinct. The language is still spoken by members of the Chiricahua Apache Tribe of New Mexico, the community of speakers from which the members of the Fort Sill Tribe were taken in 1894. The loss of the language is still mourned by members of the tribe, and some individuals have begun to work with speakers from New Mexico to bring back their language.

Kiowa-Tanoan Languages

The only Kiowa-Tanoan language located on the Plains is Kiowa. In the late prehistoric period, the Kiowa roamed western South Dakota and North Dakota. As pressure for land increased from the Siouan groups, the Kiowa migrated south to Oklahoma, where they were located by early travelers. The Kiowa entered onto a reservation with the Apache Tribe of Oklahoma and the Comanche in the late 1800s, then took lands in western Oklahoma, south and west of the town of Anadarko, Oklahoma, at allotment. The Kiowa language is related to languages spoken in the Southwest, particularly by inhabitants of the Tanoan pueblos, such as Taos, Isleta, Sandia, and Jemez.

Today Kiowa is spoken by approximately 1,092 speakers, the majority of whom are elderly individuals. Language materials have been developed in the language, and Kiowa is taught in the local public schools and preschool programs. The language has remained relatively strong, given the number of speakers and the tribe's focus on educating children at a young age. The outlook for maintenance of Kiowa at this time is fairly good.

Uto-Aztecan Languages

Like Algonquian and Athabaskan, the Uto-Aztecan family reaches well beyond the Great Plains region. Languages of this family are found in the Pacific, Rocky Mountain, and Southwest regions of the United States and into Mexico. Comanche is the only Uto-Aztecan language found in the Great Plains region.

Comanche speakers roamed across western and central Oklahoma, all of central Texas, and into northern Mexico. The Comanche are now located near Lawton, Oklahoma. The Comanche have actively pursued language-preservation projects for several years and continue to develop materials and methods for maintaining their language. It is estimated that there are 854 speakers of Comanche, 7 of whom are monolingual, with a good number of speakers in the younger generations.

Muskogean Languages

Speakers of Muskogean languages were moved into the Plains region in the 1820s and 1830s. European pressure to remove speakers of these languages from their indigenous region, the Southeast, grew as large numbers of European and American settlers entered the southern states. As a result of this pressure, the U.S. government began removing Creek, Seminole, Choctaw, and Chickasaw speakers to Indian Territory, which later became the state of Oklahoma. These southeastern tribes were granted lands in the eastern half of Oklahoma, where most remained even after allotment.

Of the four Muskogean languages found in the Plains region, Choctaw and Creek are in the best shape for language maintenance as a Class 1 language, while the others are in the Class 2 category. What defines these classes are the number of speakers, as well as the number of children learning it as their natural language. Choctaw is spoken by a large number of people, approximately 11,140 in Oklahoma and another 6,750 in Mississippi. A number of children still hear and speak the language in Mississippi, but speakers in Oklahoma are beginning to include very few children. Creek and Seminole are spoken by about 6,200 speakers in Oklahoma and Florida, and some children learn them as their first languages. There are 1,000 or fewer speakers of Chickasaw today, and almost no children speaking this as their first language at this time.

The Seminole, Creek, and Choctaw have taken decisive steps in instituting language programs aimed at all age ranges and fluencies. Head Start classes are taught in these languages, which allow children to hear and use the languages at the point when they have the most facility to learn any language. Written, audio, and video materials and some formal language classes are available for older students. Hopefully, through these actions, the tribes will be able to preserve their languages far into the future.

Iroquoian Languages

Speakers of Iroquoian languages were moved onto the Plains in the 1830s. Prior to this, there were no speakers of Iroquoian languages living on the Plains, as all were located in the northeastern and southeastern United States. While only Seneca, Cayuga, and Cherokee are still spoken on the Plains today, several other Iroquoian languages were spoken at the time when Iroquoian speakers were moved onto the Plains. Several different Iroquoian groups who spoke other Iroquoian languages, including Erie, Conestoga, Oneida, Mohawk, Onondaga, Tuscarora, and Wyandot, had been placed together with the Seneca and Cayuga as the Seneca of Sandusky, Ohio. In the years since removal to Oklahoma, the majority of these languages have not been maintained and are no longer spoken by residents of Oklahoma.

Unfortunately, like the other Iroquoian languages spoken by those who made up the number spoken by members of the Sandusky Seneca, neither Seneca nor Cayuga are doing very well from a maintenance perspective. Both are Class 3 languages on the Plains, though there are a good number of both Seneca and Cayuga in Canada. When the speakers from all communities are combined, Seneca has 200 primarily elderly speakers in the United States and Cayuga has 370 (though only about 10 in the United States). It is highly likely that these languages will become extinct within the next generation on the Plains. However, some members of the Seneca community have been seeking help with language maintenance from the Seneca of New York, and this may enable the language to remain in use for a longer period of time.

Cherokee, on the other hand, has a very large number of speakers, and children are learning this language as their mother tongue, placing Cherokee in Class 1. The Cherokee community has a long history of interest in its language and its maintenance. A large body of material is available in Cherokee, thanks in part to the creation of the Cherokee syllabary by Sequoyah in the early 1800s. The syllabary is a collection of eighty-five characters, each of which represents either a consonant-vowel combination or a vowel alone. Thus it is possible to write Cherokee words,

Cherokee Alphabet. Courtesy Library of Congress.

syllable by syllable, with the syllabary. The first newspaper printed in Indian Territory (later Oklahoma) was the *Cherokee Advocate*, which printed columns in both English and the Cherokee syllabary. Today many members of the Cherokee communities of both Oklahoma and North Carolina are literate in the syllabary.

Yuchi, a Language Isolate

Yuchi speakers originally inhabited the southeastern United States and were moved to Oklahoma with the Muskogee. They currently inhabit an area near Tulsa and Sapulpa, Oklahoma. The Yuchi are culturally and linguistically distinct from the Muskogee, but they have never been recognized as a separate tribe from the Muskogee.

Yuchi is a language isolate. This means that there are no other languages similar to Yuchi in sound system, grammar, and means of constructing words. Thus Yuchi stands alone and is not part of another language family, though some linguists have suggested that it has some affinity to Siouan languages. However, the majority of linguists who work with Native American languages are so far not convinced of this connection and keep Yuchi separate from the other Siouan languages.

Yuchi is a Class 3 language with only a few elderly speakers left. However, the Yuchi have been holding language classes since the 1980s, and some younger members of the community are gaining knowledge of the language. The tribe also has put effort into documenting the language and has amassed a large number of video and audiotapes, as well as written materials. Materials such as these are useful for future generations who desire to learn the language but have only limited time with speakers themselves. They also provide the tribe with a wealth of information about cultural issues.

Loan Words from Native American Languages

Expansion into and exploration of the Great Plains region brought speakers of several nonindigenous languages into contact with speakers of the Native American languages discussed earlier. In some cases, English speakers began to use words for items, locations, or activities taken from the Native American languages. Words incorporated into a language by this means are called "loan words" and are often incorporated so fully that speakers are unaware of their foreign origin.

One of the clearest areas of Native American linguistic influence on the Great Plains is that of place names. The names of each of the Great Plains states are based on Native American terms. The Dakotas are named for one division of the Sioux, Nebraska is derived from an Otoe term for "flat water," perhaps a reference to the Platte River, Kansas is derived from the name of the Kansa, and Oklahoma is derived from a Choctaw construction meaning "red people (Indians)." Many town and county names in each of these states also are derived from Native American words, though these have sometimes been altered by English speakers. For instance, Oglala, the term for one band of the Lakota (Sioux) Indians, was altered to Ogalala, with an extra /a/ inserted between the g-l cluster, when settlers chose it as the name for the Nebraska settlement. Likewise, Anadarko, Oklahoma, has been modified from its original pronunciation in Caddo. In the Caddo pronunciation, the word is *nada'ko*, with a slight break signified by the apostrophe between the second /a/ and the following /k/ (rather like the break between the uh and oh of uh-oh). As this sound does not occur very frequently in English, English speakers began to insert an /r/ sound for the break, and that has carried over into the current pronunciation of the town name.

Native American languages have been the sources for words for items as well. A widely known loan word is "tipi" from the Siouan languages. In Teton, this word refers to a family lodge. Both its pronunciation and the item to which it commonly refers were kept intact upon its incorporation into English. Another term used by people in western Oklahoma is "bote," the Kiowa term for cow entrails. These are eaten by both Indian and non-Indian people in western Oklahoma, and the term is now widely used in that region to refer to this part of the cow.

Outlook for Native American Languages on the Plains

The majority of the Native American languages on the Plains either have already become extinct or are on their way to extinction. Those languages classified as Class 3 are likely to be no longer spoken by anyone within the next two generations. Those languages labeled Class 2 have a better chance of remaining in use, though it is highly likely that within three generations several of these will no longer be spoken. Even languages within the Class 1 category, which still have some young speakers and are used or known by a few thousand people, are in danger of decreasing in usage and becoming extinct if the trend toward decreasing numbers of speakers continues.

As more and more of the Native American languages spoken in the Plains region lose speakers and/or die out altogether, people lose opportunities to hear the distinctive history of the region. The many languages on the Plains, including those spoken by European settlers, provide a glimpse into the migrations of people and cultures into the region. Language loss also plays a role in loss of some aspects of cultural practice and knowledge, so the loss of languages threatens the vitality and distinctiveness of some of the Native American and European cultures of the Plains.

Many Native American tribes and local communities are acutely aware of the status of their languages and have begun to take steps to preserve or revitalize them. The Teton, Cherokee, and Comanche, among others, have established school programs to teach the language to children as young as four years old. The Lakota, Northern Arapaho, and others also have established language programs for older members, with classes ranging from the elementary to college levels. Tribes also have begun promoting the use of their languages in daily and governmental activities, for example the Seminole, who have a translator who speaks Seminole at governmental meetings where the primary language is English.

The increased interest among younger members of the tribes in learning their Native American languages is promising for the retention of some of these languages into the future. Increased pride in a Native American identity, the recognition of the richness and beauty of these languages, and the depth of cultural expression provided by proficient use of the languages may be enough to drive some tribal members to keep their languages alive. While the outlook is rather bleak for most of the Native American languages still spoken on the Plains, there is some hope that a few in the Class 2 and 3 categories will persist and still be spoken in the future.

LANGUAGES FROM THE OLD WORLD

European and non-European migrants onto the Great Plains brought their languages with them. While English was the language of the majority of settlers in the Great Plains region, many non-English-speaking groups also migrated into the region. Each of these languages has left some mark on the history and culture of the Great Plains because each has influenced some aspect of use, pronunciation, or word choice in the linguistic variation found upon the Plains.

While the language spoken by the majority of inhabitants on the Plains today is English, many languages besides English were brought onto the Plains by early and current immigrants to the region. The diversity of the languages other than English that are still spoken or were spoken by inhabitants of the region is examined here. Languages within the family to which English belongs will be explored first; then languages that are not related to English will be discussed.

This order will be observed because the majority of the earliest non-English speakers on the Plains spoke languages related to English, which is part of the Indo-European language family. Languages that are not part of the Indo-European family, such as Mandarin Chinese, a member of the Sinitic language family, have also been spoken on the Plains for a long time. For instance, Mandarin Chinese was spoken by workers on railroad teams and is still spoken by residents in some of the larger Plains cities. Finnish, which belongs to the Finno-Ugric family, was spoken by early settlers in parts of Nebraska and South Dakota. Japanese and Korean (members of the Korean-Japanese-Okinawan family), Laotian (a member of the Tai-Kadai family), and Vietnamese (a member of the Austroasiatic family) are spoken by more recent inhabitants of the Plains states.

Entries begin with a general discussion of the languages heard on the Plains that are included under each family as each is discussed. The migrational movements and the settlement areas that came to be occupied by speakers of the language(s) under discussion are then explored. Finally, the numbers of speakers of each language still to be heard on the Plains are presented.[5]

Indo-European Languages

French, Spanish, Swedish, Icelandic, Danish, German, Norwegian, Czech, Polish, Russian, and Greek, all of which are members of the Indo-European language family, were spoken by people who explored or settled in the Great Plains.

French and Spanish

French explorers entered the Great Plains region from the southeastern and eastern edges in the early to mid-1700s. Their interest in trade and furs brought them into contact with Native American groups in the area from eastern South Dakota to the middle of Oklahoma. Spanish explorers (conquistadors) entered the Great Plains from the southern and southwestern edges, with the majority of their influence centered on the southwest of Oklahoma.

Census Information on Languages

Information on languages spoken by people in all regions of the United States has changed through time. As described in the narrative presented in the 1970 census volume concerned with "mother tongue" data for the country, the kinds of groups for which such data was presented have changed, as have the ways in which such data was collected.[6] For instance, in the 1910 and 1920 censuses, informants were asked about the language spoken in the home when they were children. This information was only analyzed for those who were designated as "foreign white stock," meaning that either they or their parents were foreign born, had not become naturalized citizens, and were white. In 1930, these data were presented for the "foreign-born white stock," which included those who had become naturalized citizens. In 1940, census takers asked informants to name the language spoken in the home during their earliest childhood.[7] These data were presented for all white people.

By the 1970s, census takers asked, "What language, other than English, was spoken in this person's home when he was a child?" Five possibilities were listed: Spanish; French; German; Other—specify; None, English only. The respondent was to fill in only one of these options. Language data from the 1970 census were presented for all persons and according to different subgroups. From the 1980 census on, the language questions have become more specific and inclusive and give greater detail about the languages spoken in the United States. On the 1980, 1990, and 2000 censuses, people were allowed to write in any and all languages spoken in the home, so information about all languages is gained, even for those with very few speakers or that are not well known. However, specific numbers of speakers of all languages still are not presented in the census tables that resulted from these questions. The three questions that collect language data in the 1980, 1990, and 2000 censuses are the following:

A. Does this person speak a language other than English at home?
B. [For those who speak another language] What is this language? [Respondents could write in the name(s) of the language(s)]
C. How well does this person speak English?—very well, well, not well, not at all

There are no real concentrations of French speakers on the Great Plains today, though 21,333 people claimed French as their mother tongue on the 2000 census. Spanish speakers, however, are becoming more numerous. The number of people claiming to speak Spanish in the region climbed from 160,505 in the 1990 census to 374,277 in the 2000 census.

Germanic Languages

German, Swedish, Norwegian, Danish, Dutch, and Icelandic are all members of the Germanic branch of Indo-European (as is English). Speakers of these languages tended to settle in the more northerly states in this region: North and South Dakota and Nebraska. For the most part, speakers of these languages remained on the Plains as homesteaders, farmers, and ranchers.

While there are no absolute divisions between the settlement areas chosen by speakers of these languages, there were some differences in areas that had the densest concentrations of speakers of the languages. German speakers entered Nebraska along the Platte River in the 1850s. The largest concentrations of German speakers in Nebraska were located in the communities of Columbus and Grand Island. In South Dakota, German speakers settled primarily in the eastern part of the state, around the current communities of Sioux Falls and Watertown. In North Dakota, communities of German-language speakers are concentrated in the southeastern corner of the state, around Minot in north central North Dakota, and in the counties between Dickinson and Bismarck. According to the 2000 census, there were 67,484 speakers of German in the Great Plains.

Swedish speakers moved into Nebraska along the railroad and formed dispersed communities off this route into the state. In South Dakota, Swedish-speaking communities were established in Dewey, Harding, Stanley, and Lawrence Counties west and north of Pierre. North Dakota did not attract a large number of Swedish-speaking settlers, except in the counties north of Fargo and north of Bismarck.

Norwegian speakers are the largest non-English-language group in both North and South Dakota. Relatively few Norwegian speakers settled in Nebraska. Norwegian speakers spread throughout the eastern part of North Dakota and throughout the entire state of South Dakota.

Speakers of Danish established early colonies in Nebraska in Dannebrog in Howard County and throughout Lancaster County. Danish-speaking communities also were located in the far southeastern portion of South Dakota, in Yankton, Clay, and Turner counties. In North Dakota, settlements where Danish was the primary language were to be found near Jamestown, north of Fargo in Cass County, and in the far northeastern corner of the state.

The states of Nebraska, South Dakota, and North Dakota attracted relatively large numbers of Dutch speakers. In Nebraska, Dutch speakers spread throughout the state and did not form any large colonies of speakers. In South Dakota, their settlement pattern was concentrated in the eastern part of the state from Grant County south to Charles Mix County. As in Nebraska, Dutch speakers in North Dakota spread throughout the state and did not aggregate in any areas of concentration.

The majority of Icelandic speakers migrated into the Great Plains states from Canada. The most concentrated settlements of Icelandic speakers were established in Pembina County, North Dakota. Traces of the influence of Icelandic pronunciation can still be heard in the English spoken by some individuals in this county.

Unfortunately, the 2000 census does not list separately the numbers of people who speak Swedish, Norwegian, Danish, Dutch, and Icelandic in the home. Speakers of these languages are grouped together in a tabulation listed for "Scandinavian languages." The number of people who stated that they speak these Scandinavian languages in the home was 6,580 in all of the Great Plains states in the 2000 census.

Slavic Languages

Russian, Czech, and Polish are members of the Slavic branch of the Indo-European language family. They are more closely related to one another than any of them are to English. However, English and each of these languages arose from the same ancestral language thousands of years ago.

People who spoke Russian formed communities along the James River from Yankton County in South Dakota to Dickey County in North Dakota. Russian speakers also pushed westward into both South and North Dakota, where they set up dispersed settlements. A relatively large concentration of Russian speakers also settled in Lancaster County, Nebraska. Currently, there are 5,546 Russian speakers still located on the Great Plains.

Czech speakers settled more thickly in the more southerly states of the Great Plains. Czech speakers were to be found in mid-central Oklahoma, central Kansas, and Douglas County, Nebraska. Small numbers of Czech speakers also established communities in southeastern South Dakota and in three counties in North Dakota:

Richland, Walsh, and Stark. In the 2000 census, the number of Czech speakers in the Great Plains states is included in a grouping that includes other Slavic languages. The total number of "other Slavic language" speakers located on the Great Plains is 8,481, some of whom are Czech speakers.

Polish also was to be heard in some Great Plains communities, with the fewest of these located in North Dakota. Just to the south, however, a large concentration of Polish speakers settled in Day County, South Dakota. In the remaining Great Plains states, Polish speakers formed more dispersed communities, such that they comprised only a small proportion of language speakers in the area. According to the 2000 census, there are still 3,313 Polish speakers living in the Great Plains region.

Finno-Ugric Languages

The only language belonging to the Finno-Ugric family that has many speakers in the Great Plains region is Finnish. Finnish speakers settled in the states of South and North Dakota and did not establish large populations in the more southerly states in the region. In South Dakota, Finnish speaking communities were established in the eastern counties of Hamlin and Brown and in the far western counties of Harding, Butte, and Lawrence. In North Dakota, Finnish-speaking populations were highest in the southern and western portions of the state, though they were spread across the counties in these areas. The number of Finnish speakers in the Great Plains region is not specified in the 2000 census results, though the 714 Hungarian speakers, another Finno-Ugric language, is listed.

Korean-Japanese-Okinawan Languages

Speakers of Japanese, a member of the Japanese-Okinawan language family, have settled in some of the larger metropolitan areas of the southern Great Plains. There are populations of Japanese speakers in Omaha, Nebraska, Kansas City, on the Missouri-Kansas border, and Oklahoma City, Oklahoma. The number of speakers in the region is not large, but speakers of the language do inhabit some areas of the Great Plains. The total number of Japanese speakers living in the Great Plains states, according to the 2000 census, is 6,061.

Korean also is spoken by residents of the Plains states. Most speakers of Korean inhabit the larger metropolitan regions in the southerly states of the Great Plains (Oklahoma, Kansas, and Nebraska). According to the 2000 census, there were 9,341 people who spoke Korean in the home.

Sinitic Languages

Mandarin Chinese was spoken by some of the workers on railroad construction gangs in the late 1800s. Although they worked in several regions of the Great Plains states, there are few remaining effects of Mandarin Chinese speakers in most of the Plains states. However, concentrations of Mandarin Chinese speakers can still be found in the larger metropolitan areas of the Great Plains. Omaha and Lincoln, Nebraska, have relatively high numbers of Mandarin speakers, as does Oklahoma City, Oklahoma. The number of Chinese speakers, not necessarily only of Mandarin but of all Chinese languages, was 16,301 in the 2000 census count.

Recent Languages on the Great Plains

Speakers of languages discussed here have been the most recent to enter the Great Plains in any large numbers. The numbers of speakers in each state have been added together to reach the totals presented here (U.S. Bureau of the Census, 2003). The numbers of speakers of each of these languages increases as one moves from the northern Plains states to the Southern Plains states.

The languages are presented in order based on the total number of speakers in the region. In each case, the language family to which the language belongs is presented in parentheses between the name of the language and the number of people who speak that language in their homes. The numbers of speakers for all languages given here are aggregates from the 2000 census figures.

- Vietnamese (Austroasiatic language family) is spoken by 28,525 people.
- Arabic (Afro-Asiatic language family) is spoken by 8,372 people.
- African languages (unspecified languages, language families unknown) are spoken by 7,468 people.
- Laotian (Tai-Kadai language family) is spoken by 5,360 people.
- Persian (Indo-European language family) is spoken by 4,462 people.
- Hindi (Indo-European language family) is spoken by 3,996 people.
- Urdu (Indo-European language family) is spoken by 3,015 people.
- Gujarathi (Indo-European language family) is spoken by 2,052 people.
- Hebrew (Afro-Asiatic language family) is spoken by 1,000 people.

The numbers of people in the Plains states who speak each of these languages, and many others, are likely to grow as people continue to move into the region. Thus the outlook for these languages, along with the languages of longer standing on the Plains, is very good. Despite the fact that almost all but Vietnamese have lower numbers of speakers than some of the Native American languages like Lakota and Cherokee, it is more likely that these languages will be maintained and actually flourish while the Native American languages decrease in usage. Arrivals of more speakers and continued contact with communities in the country of origin (both for the speakers and their languages) will act to increase the likelihood that these languages will continue to be spoken in the Plains region.

ENGLISH ON THE GREAT PLAINS

English has by far the largest number of speakers of any language on the Plains. While speakers of other Indo-European languages were early settlers on the Plains, speakers of English outnumbered those who used other languages from the earliest period of settlement. There is a common perception that the English spoken throughout the Plains is homogeneous and lacking in variety. However, residents of one area of the Plains can identify differences in pronunciation, vocabulary, and grammar in the English spoken by someone from a different area. These perceived differences are not figments of the residents' imagination, but are the result of actual dialect differences.

Dialects of English in the Great Plains

Contrary to popular belief, there are several dialects of English found in the Great Plains region. In part, this arises because of the varying sources of migrations of English speakers into the Great Plains region. In the eastern United States, linguists have determined that there are three rather distinct dialects, each generally associated with a geographic portion of the east. The Upper North dialect, which includes the speech traits of speakers from New England and central Pennsylvania, extends from Maine south to western Massachusetts and west through New York and northern Pennsylvania to the southern border of Iowa. The Upper Midwest dialect is generally applied to the speech of people in Wisconsin, Minnesota, Nebraska, the Dakotas, northern Illinois, northern Iowa, and eastern Wyoming and Montana. Speakers in Virginia, West Virginia, the Carolinas, Georgia, Florida, Mississippi, Alabama, Tennessee, Kentucky, Louisiana, Arkansas, the southern portions of Indiana and Illinois, and the eastern sections of Oklahoma and Texas generally exhibit the most pronounced South dialect.[8]

Each of these dialects is represented to some degree on the Great Plains. People who spoke the Upper North dialect moved into parts of North Dakota, South Dakota, Nebraska, and Kansas. Speakers who used the Upper Midwest dialect settled in the states of North Dakota, South Dakota, and Nebraska. Traces of the South dialect may still be heard in the speech of people from areas in Kansas and Oklahoma. The differences in pronunciation, syntax (grammar), and vocabulary among speakers from different areas within the Great Plains region will be explored from north to south through the Great Plains states.

North Dakota

English speakers from eastern North Dakota use a dialect similar to that found in northern Minnesota (the Upper Midwest dialect). This speech has been influenced by several features of the Scandinavian languages of early settlers in the region, both in North Dakota and in Minnesota. For instance, most speakers of English pronounce the sound of the /o/ in "so" as though there was a /w/ following the vowel. This kind of movement of the mouth after a vowel sound has begun causes linguists to designate this sound as a diphthong. Many speakers of English in eastern North Dakota, however, tend to pronounce vowels like this as "pure vowels," meaning that they do not move their mouth once they have begun producing the vowel sound (they do not have a /w/ quality to the vowels in "so" or "go"). This is a quality found in Norwegian, Danish, and Swedish, which were the languages, besides English, spoken by the majority of early settlers in the eastern part of the state.

Farther west in North Dakota, the dialect used is more like the dialect of the western Plains and northern Rocky Mountain region (a switch to a variant of the Upper North dialect). Vowels are pronounced with /w/ and /y/ qualities, which is common for English speakers pronouncing words such as "so" and "weigh." The same vowel-pronunciation pattern also is common among speakers of English in South Dakota and western Nebraska.

Distinctive terms for items are shared by many speakers of the North Dakota dialects. In North Dakota, a bluff refers to a stand of trees, as well as a steep hillside. This may be the result of the relatively smooth terrain (which lacks many true steep hillsides) of the state, so that stands of trees became notable features on the landscape, similar to bluffs in other regions. North Dakota is called "the flickertail state" in reference to a ground squirrel (Richardson's ground squirrel) that is common in the state. In other regions, a flickertail is generally regarded as a type of bird. A North Dakotan who says that he or she has been "snow-stayed," means that he or she has been delayed due to snow or blizzard conditions.[9]

The Scandinavian languages also have left their mark on North Dakota English. Lutefisk (LOO-tuh-fisk), a term for skinned and deboned cod or whitefish soaked in a lye solution before cooking, is commonly prepared in the winter. Another food known to North Dakotans is lefse (LEF-suh), a crepelike item made from potatoes, common among Scandinavian cuisines. While these terms are commonly recognized in North Dakota, they also are known and used by English speakers in South Dakota and parts of Nebraska, where Scandinavian influence also has been strong.

South Dakota

The majority of English speakers in South Dakota share their dialect of English with speakers in Wisconsin, Illinois, Iowa, Nebraska, and eastern Montana and Wyoming. This is not surprising, given that many early settlers in the 1850s came into the state from Nebraska and the Mississippi valley states and were already speaking the North dialect. In the eastern portion of the state, however, the dialect is more closely related to the Scandinavian-influenced speech of Minnesota and North Dakota, also known as the Upper Midwest dialect. The pronunciation differences between these dialects, the Upper Midwest and North, described in the section on North Dakota dialects, are maintained in the English spoken by South Dakotans in the eastern and western portions of the state, respectively.

In the eastern third of the state, for instance, a /y/ seems to occur before a /u/. Thus the word "humor" ends up sounding like /hyu-mer/, and the word "fuse" sounds more like /fyuz/. In the western two-thirds of the state, the /y/ quality before a /u/ is much less pronounced, so that little /y/ sound occurs between the transition from the first sound to the /u/. In South Dakota, one also finds that unstressed vowels (vowels that are not in a stressed syllable within a word) are pronounced differently by speakers of the North and Upper Midwest dialects. For instance, the word "appendicitis" will be pronounced as "a-pen-dah-sie-tis," /'schwa'pend'schwa'saitis/, by an Upper Midwest dialect speaker, and as "a-pen-di-sigh-tis," /'schwa'pendisaitis/, by a North dialect speaker.

South Dakota English has its share of distinctive words and grammatical forms. In South Dakota, a speaker will use the term "badlands" to refer to any barren, arid spaces, as well as to refer to the well-known geological formation in the western portion of the state, "the Badlands." An insect known as a "Canadian soldier" in other parts of the country, a common bug with red markings on its predominantly black-gray body, is known as a "box elder bug" in South Dakota due to its preference for feeding on box elder trees. This term also is commonly used by North Dakotans, Nebraskans, and Kansans to refer to this insect.

Nebraska

The English spoken by people in Nebraska has been influenced by the confluence of speakers of the North dialect with a smaller number of speakers of the Midland-South dialect in the southern portion of the state. The influence of Slavic and Germanic languages on the vocabulary and pronunciation of English in some areas also may still be heard in the speech of Nebraska natives. Despite this mixing of dialect and linguistic styles, the North dialect has had the greatest impact on the form and pronunciation of English used by most speakers in the state.

Nebraska vocabulary has some distinctive terms for items that set it apart from dialects used in other states. "Pickles" or "pickle cards" is the term used to refer to lottery cards, called "pull-tabs" in other states. It has been suggested that this name comes from the practice of storing these cards in pickle jars, which could be hidden under bar and store counters when selling these cards was illegal. This etymology shows that the cards themselves became known by the type of jar in which they were commonly stored.[10]

Distinctive geographic terms used in Nebraska speech include "chop hills," "chops," or "choppies" for low, bare hills that look as though they have been chopped apart. A "blowout," as used by a Nebraskan, does not mean a tire bursting or an exhaling contest, but a bare hollow place on the side of a hill or in the ground created by wind that has blown out the sand or dirt from the space. The term "blowout" is used by geologists to refer to this kind of formation throughout the world, as is the term deflation basin.

Evidence of the effect of the South dialect on Nebraska English can be found in the terms "armload" (an armful), "blinds" (rolled window shades), "woolly worm" (a large, hairy caterpillar), and "mud daubers" (a variety of wasp that builds a mud nest). Many of these terms appear to have been derived from forms used by persons who spoke a Scotch dialect of English. This Scotch dialect was brought into the United States by people who eventually settled in southeastern Pennsylvania and tidewater Virginia, hence its connection to the South dialect.

Slavic and Germanic languages also have had an effect on the vocabulary of Nebraskans. The terms for two food items, runza (RUN-zuh) and kolache (koe-LAH-chee or koe-LACH-kee), are derived from German and Czech, respectively. A runza is a baked pastry containing ground meat, spices, and onions, available through a commercial food chain in Nebraska. This form of baked meat pastry is made by many eastern European and German people and usually contains cabbage when it is not made commercially.

A kolache is a sweet pastry of Czech origin, a ring of sweet dough that surrounds a sweet fruit, seed, or cheese filling. Kolache is a common word in other Great Plains states where concentrations of Czech speakers are found, so it is not unheard of outside of Nebraska.

Kansas

Like English spoken in Nebraska, English speakers in Kansas have been influenced by both the Upper Midwest and South dialects. The South dialect has been most influential on Kansas English in the southern and eastern parts of the state, while the Upper Midwest dialect clearly influences the English of speakers from the northern and western parts of the state. Thus in the southern portion of the state, one can find speakers who pronounce "pen" and "pin" with the same vowel sound and pronounce "I" with a vowel sounding somewhat like "ah," both of which are general South dialect traits. In the northern portion of the state, speakers will evidence differing pronunciations of "pen" and "pin" and will pronounce "I" as a diphthong (the vowel sound changes during its production). These are traits common to the Upper Midwest dialect.

Two authorities on dialect mapping and differentiation, Craig Carver and Hans Kurath, have designated the dialect variety in Kansas and Nebraska as the Midlands form because both the Upper Midwest and South dialects influence the speech in both states, and there are no clear-cut boundaries between the regions where one dialect is predominant over the other.[11] Carver prefers to speak of the Midlands not as a distinct dialect in its own right, but as an amalgamation of the two (South and Upper Midwest), technically termed a dialect layer. Kurath initially (1939–1943) proposed Midland as a distinct dialect of its own.[12] He later (1949) suggested that his initial designation might have overstated the position of the Midland data and began to question whether the Midland dialect was truly separate from either the North or South dialects.[13] In the end, linguists are still debating how to categorize the dialect(s) of English found in the central Plains states. Perhaps future work in dialectology will illuminate the answer to this question.

There are a number of vocabulary items used in Kansas English that arise from both the South and Upper Midwest dialects. From the Upper Midwest/Midland dialect layer come the terms "scoot," "house shoes," "hay frame," "hay rick"/"rick" "hedge apple," and "hull." To scoot something is to move it along by sliding, as when a person makes space for another person to sit down on a bench by "scooting over." As one would expect, "house shoes" are slippers worn around the house, though these may be worn outside occasionally, as when picking up the paper or retrieving the mail. Both "hay frame" and "hay rick" or "rick" are terms relating to the agricultural heritage of Kansas. When hay is gathered, it will be picked up and formed in the hay frame (the hay wagon), and its final form will be as a hay rick or rick (the term for a stack of hay). "Hedge apple" is another name for an Osage orange tree, often used to form hedges or windbreaks around farms.

Terms in Kansas English that arise from the South dialect include "whetrock" "hands," "cowlot," "light bread," and "cold drink." A "whetrock" is a honing stone, used to sharpen and polish cutting blades. "Hands" and "cowlot" are terms derived from Kansas's (and the South's) agricultural production. "Hands" is a term used to refer to the workers on a farm or ranch and has become widely used in the West. A cowlot is the holding pen for cattle, generally near the barn. Both "light bread" and "cold drink" have to do with food. Light bread is white bread and generally, though not always, refers to store-bought bread. A cold drink is a carbonated soft drink.

Kansas English also has terms that are not as widely shared with speakers who use the South or Upper Midwest dialects. The term for state backers and the name of the University of Kansas sports teams is "Jayhawk." Shortly after the Civil War, this term was used to refer to an outlaw or a criminal. In Kansas, however, the term has come to refer to someone who is from the state or who supports the university athletic teams. "Post rock" is another term that is specific to the central and west region of the state. This term refers to a kind of rock found in the region that can be mined in rectangular pieces and was used to form fence supports in the late 1800s and early 1900s. As one drives on Interstate 70 west from Russell or east from Wakeeney, signs made from this rock advertising the area as "post rock country" are visible.

Oklahoma

It is probably not surprising that in Oklahoma, the southernmost state in the Great Plains region, speakers utilize a high number of constructions, pronunciation rules, and vocabulary found in the South dialect of English. Many of the settlers of Oklahoma came from the South and brought along with them the dialectal usages already in place before their migration. South dialect is most prominent in the speech of Oklahomans from the eastern portion of the state and generally fades into the style associated with the Midland dialect layer in the central and western parts of the state.

Oklahoma pronunciation of vowels tends to follow the South dialect to some degree. Throughout most of the state, but particularly in the southeastern portion of the state, vowels are pronounced with the characteristic diphthong quality of the South (e.g., the "ah" pronunciation of "I" and pronouncing "can't" as "cayint"). The /r/ sound following a vowel, called postvocalic /r/ in the linguistic literature, is dropped by some speakers, as when the word "where" is pronounced as "wheya." A pattern of dropping postvocalic /r/ is most common in the speech of speakers from the southern third of Oklahoma and does not reach much farther north in the state.

Further examples of the effect of the South dialect on Oklahoma speech patterns are found in the use of "y'all" or "you all" as a reference to the second-person plural ("you" referring to more than one person), as in "Do y'all want gravy with that?" Some speakers, particularly in the southeastern portion of the state, will use double negatives in a sentence, such as "He didn't want no more." Yet another form found in South dialect that is used by some Oklahoma speakers involves using two modal (helping) verbs in a sentence. For instance, a speaker might show some uncertainty about an action by saying, "I might could do that," in which the sentence contains both "might" and "could." In other English dialects, only one of these modal verbs is used at a time. However, in some versions of the South dialect, this is a common construction.

Some of the distinctive vocabulary of Oklahoma, compared with the other Great Plains states, also exhibits the effects of the South dialect. Soured milk or buttermilk is called "clabber milk" in Oklahoma and other parts of the South. The depression running alongside a roadway is referred to as a "bar ditch" in Oklahoma, which is a term used in other southern states. In common with other speakers of the South dialect, Oklahoma speakers may refer to an inexperienced or incompetent laborer as a "boll weevil."

Speakers of Oklahoma English also use terms that are more localized. When something is very exciting or funny, it may be called "a hoot" by an Oklahoma speaker. A term that is common to the English speech of Texans and southern Oklahomans is "blue whistler," which refers to a cold wind from the north. Central and southern Oklahomans may speak about "Rush Springs melons" during the late summer. These are watermelons grown in Rush Springs, Oklahoma, which is locally famous for the sweetness and juiciness of its melons. Unlike speakers from most other states, an Oklahoman will pronounce Miami as "my-AM-ah" when referring to the city in northeastern Oklahoma. When speaking about the city in Florida, however, an Oklahoman will use the more common "my-AM-ee" pronunciation.

Black English Vernacular

Black English Vernacular (BEV), also called African American Vernacular English (AAVE), is the dialect of English associated with African American English speakers. BEV is the result of the mixing of African languages and the South and North dialects of English. The pronunciation, vocabulary, and syntax of BEV distinguish it from other dialects of English.

BEV is used by some speakers in the metropolitan areas of the Great Plains states. It is more commonly heard in the southern states, Oklahoma, Kansas, and Nebraska, than in the northern states, primarily because of the differences in population densities of African American residents. In Nebraska, the form of BEV used in the larger cities, Omaha and Lincoln, most closely resembles the form used in Midwestern cities like Chicago and cities of the mid-South, such as St. Louis. The form of BEV used in cities in Kansas and Oklahoma more closely resembles the BEV forms used by speakers from more southerly cities, such as Dallas and Houston, Texas, as well as St. Louis.

CONCLUSION

The amount of linguistic variation across the Great Plains states is greater than most people might imagine. The languages discussed here and the English dialects have had an effect on the ways in which speakers from the Plains talk. Indeed, the linguistic forms utilized by speakers throughout the Great Plains are anything but homogeneous when one becomes aware of the differences in pronunciation, word choice, and syntax.

The many migrations of speakers of different dialects of English and of non-English languages onto the Great Plains have left their mark. English spoken by residents of the northern states, North and South Dakota in particular, are marked by sound qualities and word choices strongly influenced by the Scandinavian language communities that formed dense settlements in these states. The North dialect forms of the early English-speaking settlers also are still found in the speech of residents of these states, particularly in the northern portion of North Dakota and the eastern and northern parts of South Dakota.

Nebraska and Kansas are marked by transitions and mixing between speakers of the North, Midland layer, and South dialects. These English dialects also have been strongly influenced by the Germanic and Slavic languages in Nebraska. The effect of the South dialect is noticeable in the speech of people in central and southern Kansas. The dialects merge into one another throughout these states, however, so there are no clear-cut boundaries between them in this region. Still, differences in pronunciation, vocabulary, and syntax are apparent in the speech of people from various areas in these states.

The South dialect and Midland dialect layer have had the greatest influence on the speech of people from Oklahoma. The vocabulary, pronunciation styles, and syntax of Oklahoma English retain several facets of South and Midland layer speech. This is a result of the migration patterns of English speakers into Oklahoma, with most coming from southern states. In the northwestern part of the state, however, the effect of the Midland dialect layer becomes more prominent, and speakers in this region tend to use fewer of the South dialect forms. Thus the speech patterns of people from Oklahoma vary as one travels from north to south and east to west in the state.

The speech of the people on the Great Plains is thus far from homogeneous and unvarying. The many languages spoken in this region besides English also provide some interesting linguistic variation, and their distribution across the Plains is telling. The histories of settlement and migration have left their mark on the speech of the inhabitants of the Plains and provide one means of tracing the movement of people in this region. Continuing human movement across this region will leave further linguistic evidence in the speech patterns of speakers in each of the states of the Great Plains.

RESOURCE GUIDE

Printed Sources

Allen, Harold B., ed. *The Linguistic Atlas of the Upper Midwest.* 3 vols. Minneapolis: University of Minnesota Press, 1973–1976.

Bailey, Garrick A. "Osage." In *Handbook of North American Indians: Plains,* ed. Raymond J. DeMallie, 476–496. Washington, DC: Smithsonian Institution, 2001.

Bailey, Garrick A., and Gloria A. Young. "Kansa." In *Handbook of North American Indians: Plains,* ed. Raymond J. DeMallie, 462–475. Washington, DC: Smithsonian Institution, 2001.

Bailey, Guy, Tom Wikle, Jan Tillery, and Lori Sand. "Some Patterns of Linguistic Diffusion." *Language Variation and Change* 5 (1993): 359–390.

Bates, Robert L., and Julia A. Jackson, eds. *Glossary of Geology.* 2nd ed. Falls Church, VA: American Geological Institute, 1980.

Brown, Donald N., and Lee Irwin. "Ponca." In *Handbook of North American Indians: Plains,* ed. Raymond J. DeMallie, 416–431. Washington, DC: Smithsonian Institution, 2001.

Campbell, Lyle. *American Indian Languages: The Historical Linguistics of Native America.* Oxford: Oxford University Press, 1997.

Carver, Craig M. *American Regional Dialects: A Word Geography.* Ann Arbor: University of Michigan Press, 1987.

Cassidy, Frederic G., ed. *Dictionary of American Regional English.* 4 vols. Cambridge, MA: Harvard University Press, 1985–2002.

DeMallie, Raymond J. "Teton." In *Handbook of North American Indians: Plains*, ed. Raymond J. DeMallie, 794–820. Washington, DC: Smithsonian Institution, 2001.

———. "Yankton and Yanktonai." In *Handbook of North American Indians: Plains*, ed. Raymond J. DeMallie, 777–793. Washington, DC: Smithsonian Institution, 2001.

———, ed. *Handbook of North American Indians: Plains*. Washington, DC: Smithsonian Institution, 2001.

DeMallie, Raymond J., and David Reed Miller. "Assiniboine." In *Handbook of North American Indians: Plains*, ed. Raymond J. DeMallie, 572–595. Washington, DC: Smithsonian Institution, 2001.

Fowler, Loretta. "Arapaho." In *Handbook of North American Indians: Plains*, ed. Raymond J. DeMallie, 840–862. Washington, DC: Smithsonian Institution, 2001.

Goddard, Ives, ed. *Handbook of North American Indians: Languages*. Washington, DC: Smithsonian Institution, 1996.

Krauss, Michael. "The World's Languages in Crisis." *Language* 68, no. 1 (1992): 4–10.

Kurath, Hans. *Linguistic Atlas of New England*. 3 vols. Providence, RI: Brown University, 1939–1943.

———. *Word Geography of the Eastern United States*. Ann Arbor: University of Michigan Press, 1949.

Liberty, Margot P., W. Raymond Wood, and Lee Irwin. "Omaha." In *Handbook of North American Indians: Plains*, ed. Raymond J. DeMallie, 399–415. Washington, DC: Smithsonian Institution, 2001.

Lowie, Robert H. *The Crow Indians*. New York: Farrar and Rinehart, 1935.

Metcalf, Allan. *How We Talk: American Regional English Today*. Boston: Houghton Mifflin, 2000.

Schweitzer, Marjorie M. "Otoe and Missouria." In *Handbook of North American Indians: Plains*, ed. Raymond J. DeMallie, 447–461. Washington, DC: Smithsonian Institution, 2001.

U.S. Bureau of the Census. Sixteenth Census of the Population, 1940. *Population*. Vol. 4, *Characteristics by Age, Part 1: U.S. Summary*. Washington, DC: U.S. Government Printing Office, 1943.

———. Sixteenth Census of the Population, 1940. *Population*. Vol. 5, *Special Reports, Part 8: Nativity and Parentage of the White Population*. Washington, DC: U.S. Government Printing Office, 1943.

———. Census of Population, 1970. *Subject Reports: Final Report PC(2)-1A, National Origin and Language*. Washington, DC: U.S. Government Printing Office, 1973.

Voget, Fred W. "Crow." In *Handbook of North American Indians: Plains*, ed. Raymond J. DeMallie, 695–717. Washington, DC: Smithsonian Institution, 2001.

Wolfram, Walt. *Dialects and American English*. Englewood Cliffs, NJ: Prentice Hall, 1991.

Wolfram, Walt, and Natalie Schilling-Estes. *American English: Dialects and Variation*. Oxford: Blackwell, 1998.

Web Sites

Cassidy, Frederic. Dictionary of American Regional English. March 23, 2004. http://polyglot.lss.wisc.edu/dare/dare.html

The Dictionary of American Regional English is a reference work presenting dialectal forms found across the country. The rationale for such work and the methodology followed to collect the information is presented on the Web site. Audio clips of speakers from different areas of the country, as well as queries concerning words for inclusion in the dictionary, also are available on this site.

http://www.comanchelanguage.org/

Provides a great deal of information about both Comanche language and tribal history.

http://www.elexion.com/lakota/iyapi/index2.html

Presents both written and audio examples of Lakota, a Siouan language.

Labov, William. TELSUR. The Atlas of North American English. March 23, 2004.
http://www.ling.upenn.edu/phonoatlas/

Through the Web site, one can access the TELSUR project, a survey of linguistic changes now under way in North America, which seeks to systematically describe the phonology of the U.S. and Canada. It contains an article by William Labov titled "The Organization of Dialect Diversity in North America," as well as maps.

http://raven.cc.ukans.edu/~pyersqr/kuds/

A link to the Kansas Dialect Survey Form, a short version of a dialect survey instrument, similar to the kind of forms that dialectologists working on large studies use to gather their data. Visitors may fill out the form, which asks respondents about their pronunciation, vocabulary, and grammatical structures.

The Summer Institute of Linguistics
http://www.ethnologue.com/show_country.asp?name=USA

The Summer Institute of Linguistics provides lists of all languages spoken in the United States, as well as data regarding numbers of speakers, some history, and outlook for continued use.

Varieties of English
http://www.ic.arizona.edu/

This dialect site has a good overview of general linguistics (phonology, International Phonetic Alphabet (IPA) and so on) and features information on: African American English, American Indian English, British English, Canadian English, Chicano English, Northeast U.S. English, and Southern English, with sound samples.

Organization

American Dialect Society
http://www.americandialect.org

LITERATURE

Stacy Coyle

From James Fenimore Cooper to Willa Cather to Louise Erdrich, writers of the Great Plains have conveyed a strong theme of a powerful cycle of forces that Plains inhabitants barely transcend. They offer a sense of endless potential wasted as both the natural and human-made environments eclipse and condition the individual. But against these forces emerges a romantic belief that the community, not the individual, despite his or her intense labor and effort, can overcome these obstacles. The romantic strain arises largely in response to the seemingly unending beauty and potential of the grassy landscape. The landscape of the Plains, however, can also quickly annihilate the individual. The young male narrator of Cather's *My Antonia* soon observes, "Everywhere, as far as the eye could reach, there was nothing but rough, shaggy, red grass, most of it as tall as I."[1] He says that against the sky and grass, he feels erased and blotted out. Thus unlike the literature of the West, in which the primary obsession concerns what it means to be a man,[2] the literature of the Great Plains is more concerned with the survival of the community, whether that be a loosely knit group of farmers on a prairie in Nebraska, a drought-plagued cooperative in Kansas, a band of motley cowboys in Saskatchewan, or a decaying reservation in Oklahoma.

LITERARY DEFINITIONS OF THE GREAT PLAINS

The image of the seas of grass, and especially the windswept seas of grass, is the most prominent and pervasive image in the literature of the Great Plains. Naturalist writers and others also often distinguish between the short-grass and tallgrass prairies created by the division of the one hundredth meridian, a rough demarcation that suggests more than twenty inches of annual rainfall to the east and less than twenty inches of rainfall to the west. Finally, the effort to describe not only the vistas of the short- and tallgrass prairies but the protuberances that interrupt these vistas comprises another traditional natural image in Plains literature.

Early journals of exploration and emigration reveal strongly contrasting pictures of the Plains. One source of these differing perceptions obviously lies in the different geographies and smaller ecosystems that comprise the Plains. Meriwether Lewis (1774–1809) and William Clark's (1770–1838) relatively peaceful passage as they traced a northern river route through the Plains and the West and their success in cataloging the abundant flora and fauna of the region in 1804–1806 helped perpetuate the notion of the plenitude and potential of the prairie: "From the top of this Mound we beheld a most butifull landscape. Numberous herd of buffalow were seen feeding in various directions; the plain to north N.W. & N.E. extends without interuption as far as can be seen."[3] During the fourteen-month period in which they were on the Great Plains, they discovered and described more than twenty new species of plants, at least seven new species of mammals, and at least five new species of birds of the Great Plains, including at least three species of sagebrush, the Plains cottonwood, black-tailed prairie dogs, the greater sage grouse, and the western meadowlark.

At the other extreme, explorers like Zebulon Pike (1779–1813) and Stephen Long (1784–1864), who traveled more southerly routes in drier years, found the prairies far less consistently inhabitable, as described by naturalist Edwin James in the *Account of an Expedition from Pittsburg to the Rocky Mountains; Performed in the Years 1819 and '20 . . . under the Command of Major Stephen H. Long:* "Extensive tracts of loose sand, so destitute of plants and so fine as to be driven by the winds, occur in every part of the saline sandstone formation southwest of the Arkansa. . . . These fields of sand have most frequently an undulated surface, occasioned, probably, not less by the operation of winds than by the currents of water."[4] Zebulon Pike's record of his experiences traveling through the sandhills region of the Plains was published in 1810. Perhaps his most infamous comments concerned his description of the "sandy deserts," which some argue retarded the movement of people onto the Great Plains:

> I would not think I had done my country justice, did I not give birth to what few lights my examination of those internal deserts have enabled me to acquire. In that vast country of which we speak, we find the soil generally dry and sandy, with gravel, and discover that the moment we approach a stream, the land becomes more humid with small timber. . . . These vast plains of the Western Hemisphere may become in time equally celebrated as the sandy deserts of Africa; for I saw in my route, in various places, tracts of many leagues, where the wind had thrown up the sand, in all the fanciful forms of the ocean's rolling wave, and on which not a speck of vegetable matter exhibited.[5]

Images like this led Pike to describe thousands of square miles of prairie as "a barrier to prevent too great an extension of our population westward."[6] Ironically and perhaps quite knowingly, Pike employs the metaphor of the "ocean's rolling wave" to describe these barren lands, a comparison used relentlessly in later journals of exploration, diaries, and literature more typically to describe the grasses of the prairies rather than the sand.

Never having traveled to the Plains, James Fenimore Cooper (1789–1851) was heavily influenced by the early journals of exploration and anxious over the implications of the opening of so much new territory as a result of the Louisiana Purchase (1803). Cooper's *The Prairie* (1827), the third of the *Leatherstocking Tales* and the first literary work about the Plains, emphasizes the immensity of the landscape through the familiar trope of the sea: "From the summits of the swells, the eye became fatigued with the sameness and chilling dreariness of the landscape. The earth was not unlike the ocean, when its restless waters are heaving heavily. . . . There was the same waving and regular surface, the same absence of foreign objects, and the same boundless extent to the view."[7] Notably, Cooper's use of the sea comparison is not strictly romantic; the landscape is "chilling," "heaving," and "boundless." At the other end of the nineteenth century, in 1891, Hamlin Garland (1860–1940) describes the Dakota prairie in his short story "Among the Corn Rows": "The scene was characteristically, wonderfully beautiful. . . . the level plain was green and yellow, and infinite in reach as a sea; the lowering sun was casting over its distant swells a faint impalpable mist."[8] At the end of the twentieth century, Kathleen Norris (b. 1947) in her "spiritual geography" *Dakota* describes the way in which the sea that had stretched out before her in Maili in Oahu is transformed to the Plains of North Dakota: "wind-lines, restless as waves," she writes, "flash like the ocean in the sunlight."[9]

Early emigrant accounts, such as Sarah Raymond Herndon's (1840–1914) *Days on the Road: Crossing the Plains in 1865*, acknowledge the common perception of the Plains as oceans of endless green and provide a corrective. "Here we are on the Platte with about two hundred wagons in sight," she wrote. "We are now on what is known as 'The Plains.' My idea of the Plains has been very erroneous, for I thought they were one continuous level or plain as far as the eye could reach, no hills nor hollows, but it is nothing else than the Platte River Valley with high bluffs on either side. There is some timber on the banks, but the timber of any consequence is on the islands in the middle of the river, out of reach of the axe of the emigrant."[10] Her diary, like many others, also describes the violent storms, relentless mosquitoes, fine dust, and "very disappointing" "Noble Red Men." Many other accounts, like Catherine Haun's (1829–1908) describe the day-to-day difficulties in finding firewood, ample grazing, and water for the stock and company. She describes the "desolate, rough country" at the edge of the Badlands, "entirely destitute of vegetation, the unsightly barren sandstone hills . . . with ravines and gulches between and mighty full of crowching, treacherous Indians."[11]

Washington Irving (1783–1859) was invited to accompany the new Indian commissioner, Henry L. Ellsworth, on an expedition through the present-day prairies of Oklahoma in 1832. He used the experience to write *A Tour on the Prairies* (1835). Describing a buffalo hunt in his elevated romantic style, he finds that he too must correct the common idea of the open, level plains through realistic detail. He notes the unevenness of the terrain, cut up not so much by "hill and dale" as by ravines formed by heavy erratic rain, large and numerous animal burrows, and hollows made by the buffalo to cool themselves. Notably, the image of the buffalo, much like the gradual transformation of the grasses, provides a sort of historical marker for the Great Plains: massive buffalo herds appear in the Lewis and Clark journals as well as in these early romantic texts by Cooper and Irving; the image of buffalo herds is transformed to images of buffalo hides and bones (shipped to eastern markets); finally, these buffalo remnants are replaced entirely by images of longhorn and other cattle as the buffalo are eradicated and the Plains are domesticated. Ian Frazier (b. 1951) in *The Great Plains* describes the massive deaths of both cattle and buffalo on the prairies as a result of the blizzards of 1886–1887; as a result, hundreds of trainloads of buffalo bones were shipped to factories in the East, where they were made into fertilizer and china.

The image of large buffalo herds has been resurrected in recent years in environmental studies like Anne Matthews' (b. 1957) *Where the Buffalo Roam: Restoring America's Great Plains* (1992, 2002) and Ernest Callenbach's (b. 1929) *Bring Back the Buffalo: A Sustainable Future for America's Great Plains* (1996) as an economic solution to depopulation, deaquification, and continued dependence of Plains agriculture on federal subsidies. The image, however, remains highly romantic because the promotion of these buffalo commons recalls the boosterism that led to the rapid population growth of the Plains and the continued belief that humans can—in some communal fashion—still overcome the environment they have so radically altered. Other writers, like Linda Hasselstrom (b. 1943), describe less communal responses to repopulating the Plains with buffalo—ranchers who raise herds for hunters rather than the restaurant market. In her piece "Black Powder Smoke and Buffalo" (2002), Hasselstrom describes an outing to a buffalo ranch in Nebraska where the owner entertains her group with stories of the dangerous buffalo hunt mishaps he has observed. In conclusion, all he can tell them is not to kneecap the buffalo, and definitely not to shoot for the head, since the hide and skull are almost impossible to penetrate.[12]

Despite the many realistic depictions of the varied topography, harsh weather, and uneven rainfall of the prairies, several theories persisted through the end of the nineteenth century that resulted in a steady onslaught of homesteaders: the view that settlement itself and the planting of trees and cultivation would alter the climate (rain will follow the plow); the view that irrigation (a well and a windmill) would minimize drought; and the view that the entire continent was "divinely intended for white man's occupancy" (Manifest Destiny). Between 1840 and 1870, a quarter of a million Americans crossed the continental United States to claim free land or strike it rich by mining gold and silver. According to Lillian Schlissel, most had moved to free land at least once before and thus formed a class of "peasant proprietors."[13] More than eight hundred diaries were published or archived, written by men, women, and children; unlike the journals of exploration, the journals of emigration reflect more immediate needs: keeping the family together and finding good trails, friendly natives, adequate water, food, and shelter from bad weather and pests.

Literature of the Great Plains, from the explorers and diarists to present-day accounts, depicts not only the vistas of grass, whether it be the tallgrass prairies to the east or the shorter grass to the west of the one hundredth meridian, but also the very ecology of grasses. Sharon Butala relates her education, or "apprenticeship," on the grasses of the Great Plains. As a hay farmer, she learned to identify a number of grasses: "timothy, bromegrass, foxtail—and legumes—clover, alfalfa—which I saw every day, some of which were imported species, crested wheat grass, Russian wild rye, and many of which, like reed canary grass, were very beautiful."[14] She attended three-day-long range schools in order to learn to identify the native species of grass, including needle-and-thread, June, blue grama, and buffalo grass. Paul Gruchow (b. 1947) in his *Journal of a Prairie Year* (1985), addresses not only the geologic era (the final ice age of the Pleistocene) and the process of glaciations that formed the grasslands but the various botanical components of grass that have enabled it to survive the wind and uneven precipitation of the prairies. Gruchow discusses the way in which grass grows from the roots up, spending most of its energy in the first three years in developing a root system like an underground forest or thicket. The thicket of roots can reach for water in the subsoils in times of drought and catch more water and nutrients near the surface in times of rain. Because grass grows from the base rather than the tips, it can also withstand the abuse of wind or even hail. He explains the functional ecology of the grass mat or sod, stems, leaves, flowers, and seeds. Even in the most marginal environment, grass, Gruchow reveals, is not just a survivor but a colonizer, an army that "embraced, beginning 25 million years ago, the wide spaces of the American Plains."[15]

John Madson (1923–1995), also a naturalist, looks both horizontally, like Gruchow, and vertically at the grasses that form the different geographies of the prairies in *Where the Sky Began: Land of the Tallgrass Prairie* (1982). Like Gruchow, he notes the special structures prairie grasses have for adjusting to wind, drought, and grazing: an outer rind reinforced by an oxide of silicon, hinge cells that cause the leaves to roll into tubes, light seeds designed to float on the wind, and barbed seeds designed for transport by animals. He moves through the distinct communities of grasses graded by drainage and elevation: from the hydric sloughgrass and rigput of the sloughs to the mesic midland grasses that extend up the gentle slopes to the xeric or dry-loving grasses of the well-drained upper parts of the prairie. He points out the confusion created by early settlers who referred to "low prairie" and "high prairie." The settlers were referring to elevation, not grass height, as "generally, low prairie has high grasses and high prairie has low grasses." Madson gives special attention to the dominant, authentic, and most universal grass of the prairie, the big bluestem. The big bluestem is the stuff of stories, reaching the pommels of horses, hiding herds of cattle, and magnificent for hay and pasture (early in the season) and soddies. He turns upslope from the big bluestem to the shorter, finer, and more delicate little bluestem, "the master of its upland realm." To see both bluestems in late summer with their shifting waves of color, revealed by the wind, he writes, "is to see prairie." Madson also notes that grasses of the prairie are as much a product of longitude as latitude because they are classified as either "cool-season" or "warm-season" types, terms that refer to the time of year when they ripen and seed.

Ultimately, Madson aims to reveal the process by which the tallgrass prairie has been eliminated through overuse: the manner in which plowing, mowing, and overgrazing have weakened these hardy native species to the point that they have been overtaken by an unlikely invader, bluegrass. Today what people often perceive to be prairies are not; they are simply neglected pastures with a long history of use. True tallgrass prairies are small "scraps," "edges," and "remnants" in a tame landscape, remnants, however, truly worth seeking and saving.[16] Larger stands might take more than one hundred years to reemerge. While he is not as plaintive in his cry and is far more specific about what exactly needs to be saved, Madson's call for salvation is a familiar one in literature of the Great Plains.

As Gruchow's and Madson's analyses of grass's unique adaptation to and dependence on the wind testifies, the Plains would literally not be plains if they were not windswept. Certainly, the familiar image of the Plains as rolling waves of grass created by the wind is poetic and comforting. Mari Sandoz (1896–1966), in *Love*

Mari Sandoz. Courtesy Sandoz Society Collection at the Mari Sandoz High Plains Heritage Center, Chadron, Nebraska.

Song to the Plains (1961), describes in a single breath the great rivers, far horizons, open skies, and winds "that could sweep in great bloomings across the prairies, yellow, blue and purple-red, or white as summer snow."[17] However, the image of wind in literature of the Plains is just as frequently a negative and realistic one. Mildred Walker (1905–1998) opens her novel *Winter Wheat* (1944) by comparing the month of September to a quiet day after an entire week of wind. "I mean real wind that blows dirt into your eyes and hair and between your teeth and roars in your ears after you've gone inside," she clarifies.[18] Lewis and Clark note the common ailment among the men of sore eyes, arising, they discern, from the wind blowing fine grit and dust. Katherine Wood in her poem "Plains Preponderance" (1997), describes the way in which the wind obliterates the idyllic scene of her farm as viewed from the road: a red and yellow barn, new ranch house, three silos, livestock pens, and the John Deere tractors. "Then the dry spring wind comes up," she writes, "billowing across the farm-perfect view, / swirling dirt against the Jeep. . . . She pulls forward / through a rolling sea of thick brown air."[19]

The wind is more than simply a companion image to the seas of grass that populate Great Plains literature. Its more serious incarnations in the form of blizzards and tornadoes and as an aggravator of drought provide a common naturalist element the inhabitants of the Plains must often battle. John Steinbeck (1902–1968) famously describes the relationship between wind and drought that created the Dust Bowl in *The Grapes of Wrath* (1939): "During a night the wind raced faster over the land, dug cunningly among the rootlets of the corn, and the corn fought the wind with its weakened leaves until the roots were freed by the prying wind and then each stalk settled wearily sideways toward the earth and pointed the direction of the wind."[20] In the novel, the wind not only "cunningly" digs and pries but then cries and whimpers through the night until the men and women must tie handkerchiefs over their noses and wear goggles to protect their eyes; it lifts the dust so that it blackens the skies both day and night. When it vanishes, it leaves the dust hanging like fog and the men and women perplexed and then angry, but not yet broken.

In *PrairyErth* (1991), William Least Heat-Moon (b. 1939) examines the origins of the name "Kansas." He notes that he has found more than 140 ways to spell the word and a number of meanings, but most of these meanings refer to wind. "Kansa" and its variants, he notes, have been translated as "wind, windy, wind-people, south wind people, those-who-come-like-wind-across-the-prairie, swift, swift wind."[21] He also notes that the six surviving full-blood Kansa natives accept "People of the South Wind" or "Wind People" as a fair definition. Heat-Moon, however, finds it more likely that this meaning has been hardened over time to fit perceptions of the Kansas plains. Ironically, he notes that Kansa may at one time have called themselves Hutanga, which meant "big fish" or "big water-dweller," which better explains the Kansa's most sacred item, the conch shell.

In *PrairyErth*, William Least Heat-Moon also observes that he, like all western travelers before him, was drawn to the lone protuberances of the prairie and, in this case, Jacobs' Mound in Kansas. Also like these other travel writers, he endeavors to refute the popular perception of Kansas and the Plains as "that place you have to get through, that purgatory of mileage."[22] Thus the effort to describe not only the vistas of the short- and tall-grass prairies but the protuberances that interrupt these vistas comprises another traditional image in Plains literature. William Clark describes Spirit Mound eight miles north of Vermillion, South Dakota, in his August 24, 1804, entry: "in an imence Plain a high Hill is Situated, and appears of a Conic form and by the different nations of Indians in this quarter is Suppose to be the residence of Deavels . . . they are Said to Kill all persons who are so hardy as to attempt to approach the hill."[23] Lewis and Clark describe a number of other protuberances that break up the Plains, including McCormack Loess Mounds in Missouri, the Cupola north of Lynch, Nebraska, and Pompeys Pillar east of Billings, Montana. In "Crow Butte" (1930), Luther Standing Bear (1868–1939) tells the story of the lone rocky butte, a longtime landmark for the Sioux, in southeastern South Dakota.[24] Mildred Walker discusses another butte on the Plains of Montana "that thrust up out of the ground like

Scene from *The Grapes of Wrath* with Henry Fonda. Courtesy Photofest.

some earthwork made by children" in her novel *Winter Wheat* (1944).[25] Wallace Stegner (1909–1993) writes of the aberrant feature of the Cypress Hills on the Montana-Saskatchewan border in *Wolf Willow: A History, a Story, and a Memory of the Last Plains Frontier* (1955). These hills, jutting fifteen hundred feet above the Plains, he argues, preserved all stages of the frontier's history well past its time.[26] Pulitzer Prize–winning author N. Scott Momaday (b. 1934), who is viewed as the keystone of the Native American literature renaissance, focuses on the image of a single knoll that sprouts from the Plains in Oklahoma in his effort to define the cultural and spiritual history of the Kiowas of the region in *The Way to Rainy Mountain* (1969).[27]

The image of the one hundredth meridian, unlike grass, wind, and geographic protuberances, or even the images of man's presence in the familiar forms of windmills, railroads, silos, plows, and barbed wire, is an abstract but equally common thread in literature of the Plains. In *The Great Plains*, Ian Frazier, a transplant to the Plains of Montana, reminds the novitiate of the Plains that the Rocky Mountains form the western border of the Plains; then he turns to the more problematic issue of the eastern border and the role of the one hundredth meridian. He writes, "Many geographers and botanists have said that the Great Plains begins at the hundredth meridian, because that is the approximate limit of twenty-inch annual rainfall. Before Europeans came, it was more or less where the tall grasses of the East stopped and the Western short grasses started. Since the same amount of rain never falls two years in a row, this eastern boundary always changes."[28]

Kenneth Porter (1905–1981), a poet born in central Kansas, also treats the image of the one hundredth meridian with some skepticism in his poem "Land of the Crippled Snake."

> The geographers have thrown a loop
> north and south across the Great Plains,
> a crippled snake—
> . . .
> or maybe a length of discarded lariat,
> dropped carelessly in the dust of a vast corral;
> the geographers call it
> "The Line of Semi-Aridity"—
> which means that east there's usually enough rain for a crop
> and west there usually isn't.
> But you can't depend on either.
> Let a thrill of awakening life
> run through the snake's broken body,
> let someone twitch idly at the frayed rope-end—
> and farms west of the line are east;
> again—
> and farms that were east are west—.[29]

Suggesting the precariousness of this imaginary meridian through language like "broken," "frayed," and "twitch," Porter also reinforces the associated precariousness of livelihoods dependent on these lines, livelihoods implied in the cattle and agricultural imagery of "lariat," "corral," "crop," and "farms." The poem continues to describe the precarious nature of all life on the prairies as seen in the progressive disappearance of buffalo, hunters, "close curling grass," Native tribes, longhorn cattle, and eventually the immigrants themselves.

This arbitrary element of the one hundredth meridian is connected to a general sense of impermanence and transience due to an agricultural economy dependent on the unpredictability of nature and the vagaries of the market. Kansas poet William Stafford (1913–1993) imagines the phone call he will make to "The Farm on the Great Plains" (1993). Finally, he reaches someone, but that someone is the last tenant, and then "the line will be gone / because both ends will be home: no space, no birds, no farm."[30] Linda Hogan (b. 1947, Chickasaw) also writes of a literal and figurative return home in "Calling Myself Home" (1991). Referring to the repeated dispossessions of Oklahoma Indians, she notes that her people are an old and plodding people whose faces come back "with the new grass." Yet she comes back "to say goodbye / to the turtle / to those bones / to the shells locked together / on his back."[31] In a slightly later poem, "Crossings" (1993), Hogan overlaps the history of the ancient transformation of the Plains from water to land with the history of Native peoples born of wetter climates and transplanted to the dry prairie. The transformation and displacement, she suggests, remain incomplete, and so she tells the member of the clan of crossings to go. This poem, too, ends in an image of absence: "Dark was the water, / darker still the horses, / and then they were gone."[32] Nebraska poet, Marjorie Saiser (b. 1943) also creates a poem whose movement is from inhabitation to departure. She opens her dramatic monologue "Adios, Goodbye" (2003) by exalting the writing possibilities: "I can write anything today." She delineates a number of Plains images she might write of— railroad tracks, sandhills, trees, a deer, a "trace of a breeze," "crickets, synchronizing," perhaps, the coneflower centers of the addressee's eyes. The poem concludes, however, "I'll write a road . . . I'll write / gone."[33]

In a more modern depiction of transience, Ian Frazier describes the array of hitchhikers he encounters as he drives through the Plains: Darryl, a recently fired irrigator from Wyoming, a stranded trucker driver in North Dakota, a German anthropology student in Kansas, a family from the Wind River Reservation in Wyoming, and a Sioux Indian in South Dakota who leads him to the site of Sitting Bull's cabin.[34] In a related image of modern transience, Wallace Stegner describes the principal invention of western American culture as the motel: "Whatever it might want to be, the West is still primarily a series of brief visitations or a trail to somewhere else."[35]

A more historical image of transience on the Plains is that of the railroad. In his landmark study *The Great Plains*, William Prescott Webb (1888–1963) compares the transforming role of the railroads to the role of the horse in the life of the Plains Indians. Webb discusses the dramatic difference between the development of the railroads in the East and the railroads in the West. In the East, the massive grids of railway reveal that the rails followed the population or trailed behind it; in the Plains, the railroads preceded the population. As a result, the railroads shot across the Plains and mountains as directly as topography would allow. Moreover, given the absence of population, the development of the railroads on the Plains was a losing financial battle—the fever of railroad construction was often considered a cause of the panic of 1873.[36]

Louise Erdrich (b. 1954) opens her novel *The Beet Queen* by noting that "Long before they planted beets in Argus, and built highways, there was a railroad."[37]

Watercolor *Street in Elko* by Thomas Kennet-Were, 1868. Courtesy American Heritage Center, University of Wyoming.

Everything that made the town and diminished the town, the narrator says, came on those rails. The young brother, Karl Adare, in fact, breaks both his feet jumping from the train, landing in "tall dead grass."[38] Willa Cather's (1873–1947) *My Antonia* opens in a train car where Jim Burden begins to recall Antonia while the train flashes by fields of corn and wheat, pastures, and oak groves, and the dust and the wind lead the men to recollect their childhoods growing up in the prairie towns of Nebraska. Jim Burden, we learn, quite appropriately, is now legal counsel for one of the great Western railways.[39]

The romantic image of the railroads on the Plains, like those of the grasses and the buffalo, has also undergone a dramatic transformation. William Least Heat-Moon describes the town of Matfield Green, named by a settler who recalled a big green common in Matfield, England, where he played cricket. Matfield Green, in Kansas, however, is neither green nor a "common" in the English sense, as the un-mowed grasses extend for miles beyond it. The town's life and perceived prosperity, he explains, like those of a number of Plains towns, were connected to the railroad. He quotes a newspaper headline from 1923: "Matfield Green, the last great cattle town without a railroad, after waiting half a century, has realized her dreams and has a railroad and will celebrate the event by a rousing OLD TIME PICNIC."[40] The railroad, Least Heat-Moon admits, did bring some short-term economic progress, but by midcentury highways and truck transport displaced them, and all the people of Matfield Green could expect from the Santa Fe was a whistle blast. Today this holds true for many of the cities of the Plains that have less to transport out and fewer to transport in. In situations where the towns have not declined, but actually grown around the railroad tracks, the tracks are seen as a dangerous, unattractive, and time-consuming impediment to growth and city travel. Several answers emerge: constructing costly overpasses and moving miles of tracks further onto the undeveloped Plains.

As the cycle of these Plains images reveals, the romantic belief in the vastness of the prairies and the accompanying sense of their vast economic potential has from the outset been tempered by a double fatalism: the belief that these pristine plains would quickly fall prey to wagon trains, farm plows, fences, and railroads, and the belief that even these technological innovations and the people themselves would eventually become part of that annihilation, that nature would, in the end, win out.

THE NATURALIST TRADITION

When people speak formally of naturalism in literature, they refer to a literary movement in American letters that developed in the last decade of the nineteenth century. The movement had a great deal in common with the larger realism movement, but grafted onto it a Darwinist or deterministic philosophy. In George J. Becker's seminal article "Realism: An Essay in Definition," published in the *Modern Language Quarterly* (June 1949), he gives three criteria of Realism: (1) the verisimilitude of detail derived from observation and documentation; (2) the representation of the norm or representative experience rather than the exceptional (in plot, setting, and character); and (3) the "objective" view of human nature and experience.[41] Huck Finn's description of his dad provides a quintessential example of the use of objectively observed detail:

> He was most fifty, and he looked it. His hair was long and tangled and greasy, and hung down, and you could see his eyes shining through like he was behind vines. It was all black, no gray; so was his long, mixed-up whiskers. There warn't no color in his face, where his face showed; it was white; not like another man's white, but a white to make a body sick, a white to make a body's flesh crawl—tree-toad white, a fish-belly white. As for his clothes— just rags, that was all. He had one ankle resting on t'other knee; the boot on that foot was busted, and two of his toes stuck through, and he worked them now and then. His hat was laying on the floor; an old black slouch with the top caved in, like a lid.[42]

In similarly realist fashion, Nebraska native Wright Morris (1910–1998) has his protagonist describe Aunt Clara in *The Home Place:* "My Aunt Clara is a raw-boned woman, a little over six feet tall, flat as a lath, and with the stalking gait of a whooping crane. In the early morning she wears a bright green stocking cap . . . the tassel dangling over the ear that once troubled her."[43]

As one means of representing the normal experience, the Realist and Naturalist texts often employ the local dialects or a simulation of the vernacular speech natural to their characters. Twain's "Explanatory" to *Huck Finn*, for example, both prepares his reader and defuses his critics: "In this book a number of dialects are used, to wit: the Missouri negro dialect; the extremest form of the backwoods South-Western dialect, the ordinary 'Pike-County' dialect, and four modified varieties of this last." He notes that these "shadings" have been created "painstakingly" from his "personal familiarity."[44] North Dakota poet Roland Flint (1934–2001), in "Are You in Town Too?" provides a Great Plains example of capturing dialect. Describing a scene at the Luxury Ice Cream Store and Creamery where he bought sundaes with Indian-head pennies stolen from his mother, he relates the dialogue of two Norwegian farmers: " 'Are you in town today, too, then?' 'No,' / said the other, 'I just come in with the cream.' / As if to be in town you had to be in town to be there, rather like being 'at home.' "[45] What Flint also captures here is the almost clichéd stoicism that suggests that the Plains dialect is as much a product of immigrant cultures as it is a response to the sparseness and parchedness of the landscape. In her work *The Solace of Open Spaces*, Gretel Ehrlich (b. 1946) argues that "Cowboys have learned not to waste words from not having wasted water, as if verbosity would create a thirst too extreme to bear. If voices are raspy, it's because vocal cords are coated with dust."[46] Writing about the North Platte River valley on the Nebraska frontier of the 1870s, Mari Sandoz, in *Miss Morissa: Doctor of the Gold Trail*, similarly describes cattleman Tris Polk's "Westerner's reluctance": "Tris Polk made no inquiries of Morissa but kept up a little talk about the last few weeks here, while he waited to cross with his beef herd, overdue for meat at Deadwood. He spoke quietly with long silences."[47]

In addition to these realist traits, the naturalist text examines human experience in terms of the biological and environmental factors that have conditioned it. Becker summarizes naturalism as "social realism laced with determinism."[48] Naturalists emphasize the smallness of humanity against the immensity of nature. In his introduction to *Maggie, a Girl of the Streets*, Stephen Crane (1871–1900) writes, "Environment is a tremendous thing in the world and frequently shapes lives regardless."[49] Notably, however, the environment Crane and other naturalists refer to is not strictly nature and its elements, but also the binding institutions, laws, and codes designed by man, the "iron laws of tradition and law."[50]

In Plains literature, the tragedies that face the citizens of the Plains are often environmental, but even early romantic prairie literature exhibits a clear sense that these tragedies are often human conditioned as well. The fact that Cooper depicts the death of Leatherstocking on the Plains in the final chapter of the final book of the series suggests, as Donald Ringe argues, that the human ideal that Leatherstocking represents in humility, self-control, reverence for God, and respect for nature likewise dies on the prairie.[51] Recent legislative attempts to revive Plains towns by turning the prairies into windmill farms, nature preserves, and buffalo commons or by creating a New Homestead Act suggest the painful persistence of this theme in plains life: "Someone dies in this town," says Matt Kroke of eastern North Dakota, "and it affects our bottom line."[52]

Willa Cather's *O Pioneers!* and *My Antonia* provide quintessential examples of the Plains brand of naturalism. *O Pioneers!* opens with images that convey the struggle between humans and nature. The howling wind blows both over and under the huddled and straggling houses and buildings, none of

Willa Sibert Cather

Born in 1873 in Virginia, Cather moved at the age of ten to Webster County, Nebraska, where she lived on a farm for two years before moving to the town of Red Cloud. Cather was a highly regarded managing editor at *McClure's Magazine* in New York from 1906 to 1912. It was during this time that she met the New England regionalist writer Sara Orne Jewett, who inspired Cather to write about the region she knew best, Nebraska. Cather returned to Nebraska to receive a doctorate of letters in 1917. In addition to novels, Cather wrote poetry, short stories, and essays. In 1922, she won the Pulitzer Prize for her novel *One of Ours* about a Nebraska farm boy who goes to World War I. In additon to her Nebraska novels, Cather wrote *Death Comes for the Archbishop* (1927), *My Moral Enemy* (1926), and *The Professor's House* (1925). Cather's presence in Red Cloud is still strong. The Willa Cather Pioneer Memorial and Educational Foundation at Red Cloud preserved her childhood home and other buildings associated with her writings. These buildings are now adminstered as the Willa Cather Historical Center by the Nebraska State Historical Society. In addition, the Nature Conservancy purchased 210 acres of native grassland south of Red Cloud and dedicated it as the Willa Cather Memorial Prairie.

Willa Cather and Edna St. Vincent Millay, February 2, 1933. Courtesy Photofest.

which, Cather writes, "had any appearance of permanence."[53] In case the images do not convey the implied struggle and victor, Cather delineates that the "great fact" is "the land itself, which seemed to overwhelm the little beginnings of human society that struggled in its sombre wastes."[54] O.E. Rølvaag's (1876–1931) *Peder Victorious* opens similarly with images of sod houses ready to do battle with the elements. He describes the structure as a "bulwark," the heaped sod in the corners like "stores of ammunition for defence of the stronghold."[55]

In the second chapter of *O Pioneers!*, Cather describes the emblematic life of John Bergson, who spent his first five years of farming getting into debt and the last six getting out. Cather compares the land to a wild horse that no one knows how to break and who leaves only destruction in his wake. Alexandra Bergson, John's daughter, will be the one to tame the wild horse. Her farm prospers for two reasons. One, she has imagination. Two, she creates a community. Alexandra puts up the first silo and plants the first alfalfa and wheat instead of corn on the Divide. She takes in Crazy Ivar, buys her niece a piano, serves as an intermediary between her brother Emil and friend Marie, and works to get a pardon for her brother's murderer. When Frank Shabata complains about his neighbor's hogs getting into his wheat field, Alexandra tells him that it sometimes pays to mend other people's fences. Cather also makes it clear that Alexandra's struggle is against a human environment, as well as a natural one. It is her fate, Carl Linstrum says, to be surrounded by little men. Cather also makes it clear that like the huddled windswept buildings that open the book, Alexandra's conquest is impermanent. "We come and go," she tells Carl, "but the land is always here."[56]

Cather's *My Antonia* provides a similar epic narrative of an immigrant woman's conquest of the Plains, but is more complicated in both structure and substance. Antonia Shimerda is a successful breeder and farmer; in addition to cattle and rye fields, she has two orchards, where she grows cherries, gooseberries, currants, and grapes. She tells Jim that there wasn't a single tree there when they came. Like Alexandra, Antonia must battle with the human environment, as well as the natural one: she is reprimanded by her employer for dancing in town with the young men. But it is the young hired girls, with Jim as an odd adjunct, who create their own community, rising above the criticism and supporting each other's strengths and eventual professions. Tiny Soderball moves west, starts her own sailors' lodging house in Seattle, and sells it to go to the Klondike Fields, where she sees the fifteen hundred homeless miners in camp and starts a new hotel. She eventually sells her hotel and invests the money in building lots and buying up claims from discouraged miners. She returns to San Francisco, not surprisingly, with a considerable fortune. Lena Lingard, another hired girl from the small town in Nebraska, also leaves to start her own business, a dressmaking enterprise in Lincoln. With Tiny's encouragement, she moves her business to San Francisco. When Lena thinks that Tiny needs a new dress, she simply makes her one and sends it with a bill.

Although Antonia is the novel's protagonist, the story is recollected by Jim Burden, who writes it over the course of a few months and delivers it to his friend, the unnamed narrator of the introduction. Despite Antonia's hard-won victory over the landscape, the elements, and the stubborn values of the Plains' immigrants, Jim's ownership of the story suggests Antonia's physical impermanence. Even her immigrant husband, Anton Cuzak, is only tethered to the landscape and his wife by her ability to create some semblance of culture and community for him. When Jim asks Cuzak if he misses the company he had been used to, Cuzak replies that at first, he almost went crazy with loneliness, but Antonia is so warm and good, not to mention the addition of all their boys, that it is livable. Perhaps the most complicated image of man's battle with nature on the Plains is Mr. Shimerda's grave. Years later, when open grazing days are gone, when the fields are all fenced and the roads are straightened to follow surveyed section lines, his grave remains with a sagging wire fence and weathered wooden cross, covered in unmowed grass, "like a little island."[57] The unmowed grass suggests that he has been absorbed by the Plains, not by civilization. Linda Hasselstrom ends her work *Feels like Far* by recounting a more intentional effort to do the same. She puts in metal markers with the Latin names of the native perennials and leaves a sign near her families' graves: "Please Do Not Mow Hasselstrom or Snell."[58]

The struggle against the environment and the victory of the community pervades the literature of the Plains. Wallace Stegner's "Genesis" from *Wolf Willow* relates the story of a motley group of cowboys who are working to bring home cattle in the blizzard of 1906 on the western Plains. Young Rusty, also fighting for acceptance into the group of seasoned cowhands, contemplates the way nature has obliterated all those who came before him:

> The voices of all the lost, all the Indians, *metis*, hunters, Mounted Police, wolfers, cowboys, all the bundled bodies the spring uncovered and the warming sun released into the sting of final decay; all the starving, freezing, gaunt, and haunted men who had challenged this country and failed; all the ghosts from smallpox-stilled Indian camps, the wandering spirits of warriors killed in their sleep on the borders of the deadly hills, all the skeleton women and children of the starving winters, all the cackling, maddened cannibals, every terrified, lonely, crazed and pitiful outcry these plains had ever wrung from human lips, went wailing and moaning over him.[59]

The men who are walking before Rusty are obliterated in this instance, not by

Wallace Stegner

Wallace Stegner, born February 18, 1909 in Lake Mills, Iowa is considered one of the most distinguished and accomplished writers in American letters. Although he is often considered the father of western literature, a great deal of his work deals with living in the environment west of the one hundredth meridian. He was not only an accomplished writer, but an environmentalist and teacher of creative writing. Some of his former students include Wendell Berry, Edward Abbey, and Robert Haas. His first four novels received little attention, but his fifth novel, *The Big Rock Candy Mountain* (1943), was widely hailed. He won the Pulitzer Prize for *Angle of Repose* (1971) and the National Book Award for *The Spectator Bird* (1976). Stegner wrote more than thirty books, including *Beyond the Hundredth Meridian* (1954), which chronicles the life of John Wesley Powell, the explorer and naturalist, a collection of essays reflecting on what it means to live in a dry land, *Where the Bluebird Sings to the Lemonade Springs* (1992), and his famous *Wilderness Essay*, written in 1960 to David Pesonen at the University of California's Wildland Research Center. In the essay, Stegner speaks of the "geography of hope," a phrase incorporated into the opening of the Wilderness Act of 1964. Stegner died on April 13, 1993.

the sky and high grasses, but by the snow. He makes out Spurlock as the only "hooded, blanketed, moving stoop, not human, not anything" that he can follow. The river, wind, and snow shape all the men. The wider the river swings, the more the wind plucks at them until they are reduced to animals, tied to the wagon and each other by a rope and mindlessly plodding one foot after another. In typical naturalist fashion, nature not only reduces the men to animals, but reduces them to subanimals until they have only the consciousness of an angleworm, only the sideways movements of crabs. Yet the group, frostbitten, weary, and full of pain, survives the battle against this arctic prairie, forming a mystical brotherhood. Rusty learns in the end that he would never "want to do anything alone again, not in this country."[60]

Blizzards serve as a strong adversary in humans' battle against nature on the Plains. Joy Harjo (b. 1951), a Native Plains poet born in Tulsa, Oklahoma, opens her poem "Grace" by observing that they still talk about the winter when "the cold froze imaginary buffalo on the stuffed horizon of snowbanks." Like Stegner, she describes the way the blizzard brings the beaten ghosts of the past: "the haunting voices of the starved and mutilated." Like Stegner, she also implies that survival or grace comes through community and the promise of balance, "with coffee and pancakes in a truck stop along Highway 80."[61] The victory through community in these blizzard tales poses a sharp contrast to more traditional naturalist texts like Jack London's (1876–1916) "To Build a Fire" or "The Law of Life," where the protagonists inevitably succumb to the Alaskan tundra.

William Least Heat-Moon identifies several other natural forces that he labels

Joy Harjo. Photo by Hulleah Tsinhnahjinnie.

the four horsemen of the Plains: tornado, locust, drought, and fire.[62] The stark images of the drought and Dust Bowl of the 1930s illustrated in Steinbeck's *Grapes of Wrath* and hardened by the powerful film adaptation and the government's corollary documentary *The Plow That Broke the Plains* have been difficult to shake. William Allen White (1868–1944) describes the equally devastating but less written-about drought of the 1890s on the Kansas plains that not even the "prevailing spirits of the community" could survive.[63] The narrator describes the successive caravans away from Kansas: first the men going east looking for work, then entire families in dust-covered wagons, and finally just the skeleton of a serpent twisting through the treeless landscape.

Leaning into the Wind: Women Write from the Heart of the West, edited by three active ranchwomen, Linda Hasselstrom, Gaydell Collier, and Nancy Curtis, provides a more contemporary collection of almost two hundred women's personal experiences living on the high Plains. Not surprisingly, the work is comprised of stories of calving, herding, planting, canning, cooking, haying, riding, and surviving: surviving bankruptcy, drought, dust storms, hail, floods, blizzards, grasshoppers, army worms, and a hundred forms of death. Like Mrs. Burkholder in White's tale, who mourns for the loss of the cottonwood saplings on the front eighty, these women are parents to everything—saplings, seedlings, goats, lambs, piglets, foals, and children. They are amazingly practical. The narratives reveal, for example, that one can run four elk to one beef cow on pasture, that one can catch a wolverine on a number three Victor trap on a toggle, that in a twelve-foot-wide trailer in a windstorm in Laramie in January, "at fifty-five m.p.h., only the table and chairs moved. At sixty, the couch slid. Anything higher propelled the refrigerator." It is best to schedule weddings "after brandings but before haying, or after fencing but before weaning."[64] One of the entries even explains step-by-step how to put up and mud drywall on those winter days when one is snowed in. To help elucidate that the survival of these women is not simply a matter of individual perseverance, the second collection by the editors, *Woven on the Wind* (2001), focuses on the friendships of women in the sagebrush West, and the third, *Crazy Woman Creek* (2004), looks at accounts of women and community.[65]

As the quintessential texts by Cather, Rølvaag, and Stegner reveal, the Great Plains brand of naturalism, despite its depiction of the daunting power of the environment, is optimistic in that it conveys a faith in the Plains people's survival through community. Linda Hasselstrom's poem "Coffee Cup Cafe," like Harjo's poem "Grace," finds soothing conversation and communion in a cup of coffee.[66] In their stories of the drought of the 1930s, the snow of last winter, and the hail of last summer, they find encouragement from knowing that someone has had it worse and that people like themselves can take it. Hasselstrom's poem thus also shares a key trait of Native American storytelling in that bad stories are as valuable as the good. Even the notion of community in Plains writing, however, is not overly romantic. One of William Stafford's best-known poems, "The Darkness Around Us Is Deep," ends by warning against a kind of mindless community in which people parade through their mutual life like elephants at the circus, tail to trunk; they must be aware and awake, giving clear signals.[67] Kathleen Norris's *Dakota: A Spiritual Geography* also reveals the complex sociology of the Plains community: while community is critical to its economic and social survival, the Plains community can be incredibly insular and resistant to change. She talks about a Lutheran minister, G. Keith Gunderson, who understands "the deep resistance to change that is embedded in the prairie consciousness." She quotes from his letter that encapsulates the vicious cycle: "And hidden in their rejection [of newcomers, professionals, and especially ministers] . . . is a seed by which they set themselves up to be exploited and then abandoned, over and over again."[68] Wes Jackson (b. 1936), in his essay from the collection *Rooted in the Land: Essays on Community and Place*, advocates a completely new type of community based on a better understanding of humans' role in the ecology. Like William Least Heat-Moon, he uses the community—and the grasslands—of Matfield Green in Kansas as a starting point, arguing for new industries and lifestyles based in renewability and sustainability, including photovoltaic cells, wind machines, bison herds, and polycultures of native and cereal grasses.[69]

To emphasize that survival is dependent on community, many Plains writers show the harsh correlative: madness as a result of isolation. Crazy Ivar in *O Pioneers!* provides an easy example. Until he goes to live with Alexandra, Crazy Ivar lives "in the rough country across the county line, where no one lived but some Russians."[70] Even the grasses around his home are different, the draws deeper. In many ways, Ivar is the perfect romantic, living on the prairie for years without disturbing nature, his sod home almost invisible. As a romantic, Ivar enjoys his solitude, holds disdain for the material litter of humans, and is a grossly misunderstood thinker. Other isolated characters in Plains literature fare less well. Frank Shabata, emotionally isolated and maddened with jealousy, kills his wife and ends up in a prison in Lincoln. In her study of Great Plains fiction, Diane Quantic examines the variants of isolation and madness in Mari Sandoz' *Old Jules* as well as other works, noting that most often it is the women who are victims, driven to killing their children as well as themselves.[71]

Thus certain character types are best suited to surviving or adapting to the Plains environment. As revealed by the trials of the Shimerdas in *My Antonia*, the ranchers in "Genesis," or the Joads in *The Grapes of Wrath*, survival on the Plains requires hard labor, self-denial, and extreme perseverence, even though one knows that the hard labor may still result in failed crops or stranded cattle. The Plains people also exhibit a willingness to help out but a respect for boundaries. Linda Hasselstrom observes a cardinal rule of respecting boundaries in "Red Glow in the

Western Sky": country neighbors never call each other after ten at night, but when fire approaches the foohills, they wait by the phone all night and answer on the first ring.[72] Finally, a true Plains person is born from a lifetime's understanding of the relationship between humans and the land. Speaking of her husband, a "true rural person," Sharon Butala observes that he "had formed his attitude to the prairie and his understanding of its weather, its growth patterns and its animals by a lifetime of immersion in it."[73]

A lifetime's immersion in the landscape is nowhere more evident than in the poetry of Nebraska writer Ted Kooser (b. 1939). Even the titles of Kooser's books—*Weather Central* (1994), *Winter Morning Walks: One Hundred Postcards to Jim Harrison* (2000), *Local Wonders: Seasons in the Bohemian Alps* (a low range of hills in eastern Nebraska) (2002), and *Braided Creek: A Conversation in Poetry* (2003)—reflect his immersion in the landscape of Nebraska. His proximity to the land connects him to its very history. In the poem "Site" in *Weather Central*, he opens by describing a "fenced-in square of sand and yellow grass" that was the site of the County Poor Farm in 1900. In "Lincoln, Nebraska," an oasis of landscape also brings him to the past: a clump of prairie grass next to the train rails stands like "the last scalp-lock / of the last Pawnee, / like the last black cough of the bison." In the poem "In Late Spring," he observes that even though he has forgotten his place in the world, the world knows his place "here on these acres near Garland, Nebraska."[74] In *Winter Morning Walks*, Kooser brings a sense of variety to the bitter winter weather of Nebraska that only a Nebraskan could. While "clear," "still," and "cold" appear regularly in the elliptical one-line opening reports, the poems that follow show the movement and warmth beneath the cold: hundreds of starlings, a good-sized deer, five noisy crows, a weeping willow turning in the breeze, and cedars with black limbs bleeding into the light.[75] Kooser's personal essays in *Local Wonders: Seasons in the Bohemian Alps* likewise look at the particulars of the landscape and find constant links to his community. Observing a slew of ladybugs bumping against his window—perhaps a migration—he contemplates that while many creatures are restless nomads, some settle in.[76]

ETHNIC VOICES

Survival through community is perhaps an even more urgent and pervasive tradition in ethnic literature of the Plains, particularly Native American. Historian Walter Prescott Webb discusses the revolutionary impact of the introduction of the horse on the lives of the Plains Indians, which enabled them to be far more efficient and secure nomadic hunters. The role of the horse was so important, he notes, that anthropologists label the period from 1540 to 1880 as the horse-culture period.[77] The importance of the horse and buffalo in the lives of Plains Indians is clear from their earliest recorded writings. In "When the Buffalo Herd Went West," Zitkala-Ša (Gertrude Simmons Bonnin) (1876–1938) tells one of the many Native stories about the origins of the buffalo of the Plains. In her story, a Dakota woman is gathering rose berries from a thorny bush (her husband has been crippled in a buffalo chase) when she encounters a man on a snowy white pony chasing a roaring buffalo. The hunter kills the buffalo, loads up his bounty of meat, and shares with her only the tripe. As a result of his selfishness, the woman and her crippled husband are able to wrest away his magical powers over the horse and buffalo. They live well until the Mischief Maker, Iktomi, opens the sacred bag and releases the entire herd, whose hooves shake the earth as they head west, leaving the Plains.[78] In the classic work *Black Elk Speaks* (1932), John Neihardt (1881–1973) relates Black Elk's narrative, which covers key events in the history of the Plains Indians. Black Elk notes that even though the Wasichus had created an iron road that cut the buffalo herd in two, there were still many buffalo on their lands.[79] Luther Standing Bear relates in his story "The Holy Dog" (1930) that the horse was first encountered when the buffalo were bountiful, feeding close on the green grass that grew around their tipis. His story shows the buffalo and horse as part of the community, not just a means to survival.[80]

More contemporary Native voices continue to address the issue of community. Louise Erdrich's (Ojibwa) first

Louise Erdrich

Louise Erdrich was born in Little Falls, Minnesota, in 1954 and grew up in Wahpeton, North Dakota, where her parents taught school for the Bureau of Indian Affairs. Her parents encouraged her writing at a young age, her father paying her a nickel a story and her mother designing covers for her books. Erdrich graduated in 1976 from Dartmouth and received her M.A. in writing from Johns Hopkins University in 1979. Erdrich returned as a writer-in-residence in the Native American Studies Program at Dartmouth, where she was reunited with the director of the program, Michael Dorris. They were married in 1981, and their partnership was both domestic and literary. They collaborated on several books, and Dorris persuaded Henry Holt and Company to publish her book of poetry, *Jacklight*. He also persuaded her to to compete for the Nelson Algren Fiction Award. Erdrich won the $5,000 award for "The World's Best Fisherman," the story that became the opening chapter to *Love Medicine*. *Love Medicine* was Erdrich's first and most acclaimed novel, originally published in 1984 and republished in an expanded form in 1993. It received the National Book Critics Circle Award for Best Fiction.

novel, *Love Medicine* (1984), which received the National Book Critics Circle Award, is structured around interwoven genealogies and stories. The novel ends with Lipsha Morrisey acknowledging that their problems are not as easily solved today as they were when the Dakotas had been covered in water. Yet the tone is realistic and positive. "It was easy to imagine us beneath them vast unreasonable waves," Lipsha says, "but the truth is we live on dry land."[81] The acknowledgment and affirmation stem from the recognition that he is a Nanapush man—they all have an odd thing within their hearts. The characters and events in *Love Medicine* are interwoven with three other novels that comprise Erdrich's quartet: *Beet Queen* (1986), *Tracks* (1988), and *Bingo Palace* (1994).

The community examined by Linda Hogan, a descendant of Nebraska pioneers and the Chickasaw Nation, is an even more historical one because she looks at the repeated dispossession of Oklahoma Indians and concludes in *Mean Spirit* (1990) that their continued survival is now dependent solely on the community, not the land.[82] In her poem "What I Think," the speaker cuts vegetables for soup while listening to the woman upstairs singing and the woman downstairs, drunk, hitting the dog. She decides not to call the landlord to complain, for tomorrow, the drunk woman will be planting tulips, petting her dog, and cooking meat on the stove. Their connection is reinforced with the final image of the poem of the black coal in the basement, beneath them all, "with its inner light."[83] Clearly it is the shared stories, poems, and songs that form the "savings" of the book's title. Other poetry and prose by Hogan include *Calling Myself Home* (1978), *Eclipse* (1983), *Book of Medicines: Poems* (1993), and *Dwellings* (1995).

Even the texts of different Native American writers create a kind of interwoven text and communal history. Ella Cara Deloria (1889–1971) in *Dakota Texts* (1932) and her novel *Waterlily* (1998) examines her Sioux heritage with the precedents of Luther Standing Bear and Black Elk (1863–1950) before her. *Black Elk Speaks* covers a period of history that includes the establishment of reservations, the Battle of the Little Big Horn, the massacre at Wounded Knee, and even Black Elk's participation in Buffalo Bill's Wild West Show. James Welch's (b. 1940, Blackfeet) novel *The Heartsong of Charging Elk* (2000) incorporates this history in his fictional account of a Sioux Indian performing in Buffalo Bill's Wild West Show who gets left behind in Europe.

THE POSTMODERN THREAD

Recent literature of the Plains reveals a darker thread, a striking reincarnation of the work of the French Decadents of the nineteenth century who chose subject matter that was ugly, perverse, neurasthenic, and pathological but found in it a deeper beauty; the Decadent texts also revealed an intense self-consciousness, a restless curiosity, and a sense of moral and spiritual perversity. Overlapping and sharply juxtaposed imagery, often verging on the grotesque, is a key trait of the Decadents. In Baudelaire's *Les Fleurs du Mal*, for example, desire of an icy woman is described as "A choir of wormlets pressing towards a corpse," and "beauties unknown to ancient peoples" are equated to "visages gnawed by sores of syphilis."[84] The ranch home of sisters Renti and Roany in Annie Proulx's story "The Governors of Wyoming" is nearly as ugly and perverse as Baudelaire's women but similarly reflects sexual desire: "Now, two sisters in the house, a knife clotted with orange jam as though used to crush some monstrous insect, dead flies on the bathtub surround, a window streaked with bird excreta seemed squalid evidence of his [Shy Hamp's] private longings."[85] The description occurs just a few paragraphs beyond the boiled Chihuahua dream of Renti, a dream stimulated by the breakup with her boyfriend and the announcement that she is going to Wyoming. Louise Erdrich's *Beet Queen* also reveals moral perversity. The abandoned daughter, Mary, sends her mother a postcard, "Aerial View of Argus, North Dakota," on which she writes, "All three of your children starved dead."[86] This act becomes even more perverse for the reader, who is immediately made aware of the mother's bizarre plane accident at the county fair.

The dark thread is equally evident in Plains poetry. Nebraska poet laureate William Kloefkorn in his poem "Free Cheese" juxtaposes the image of small gray bodies in mousetraps to the image of his grandfather using ballpeen hammers to tap in tin cans to cover the holes in the granary.[87] Henry Taylor (b. 1942), in "Landscape with a Tractor," describes mowing a field with a bushhog to keep the weeds down and discovering a corpse, "some four days dead, and ripening," and the damp dent and swarming bluebottle flies left in the tall grass.[88] E. I. Pruitt in her poem "Corn," interlaces images of fields in full tassel with images of a one-armed man on the tractor and "lost farm cats and the skeletons of dogs / churning up in the combine teeth." In Decadent fashion, the final sensual image is juxtaposed with a decadent one: a man lieing in bed at night, touching his wife's body, is sharply contrasted with the degenerators of corn: "corn earworm, cotton bollworm, corn borer, corn rootworm. / Corn smut, smut galls, maize dwarf mosaic, stunt. / Leaf hoppers, locust, hail."[89]

The source of these perverse associations, in addition to reflecting general post-modern tendencies, may rest in an increasing pessimism about the survival of the Plains community despite plans of buffalo commons, windmill farms, and ecological communities, despite physical-plant, labor, and tax inducements to attract outside industries. A headline in the *Denver Post* reads, "Great Plains Ailing As Livelihoods Dry Up, Poverty Soars." According to a University of Nebraska poll of rural attitudes, Plains residents feel more powerless to control their lives and more pessimistic about their futures. The general feeling, according to a nonprofit research group, the Center for Rural Affairs, is that this is the last generation to inhabit the Great Plains.[90] If the literature of the Great Plains, however, is any indication, the communities—though in sparer form—will indeed survive.

JOURNALISM ON THE GREAT PLAINS

The rise of literary magazines at the end of the nineteenth century helped establish writers like Mark Twain, Stephen Crane, and Harriet Beecher Stowe and also provided a venue for local-color writers who were trying to bring to life the people and landscapes of regions like New England, Mexico, and the far West. The literary journals, magazines, and newspapers of the Great Plains have likewise played a significant role in supporting the literature and culture of the Plains region. Newspapers in the major cities like the *Omaha World-Herald*, the *Bismarck Tribune*, the *Forum* (Fargo), the *Capitol Journal-Pierre*, the *Huron Plainsman* (South Dakota), the *Kansas City Star*, the *Topeka Capitol-Journal*, the *Kansas City Kansan*, the *Oklahoman* (Oklahoma City), and the *Tulsa World* are recognized for their national news coverage and local reporting. More specialized papers like the *Oklahoma Indian Times*, which serves the federally recognized Indian Nations of Oklahoma, clearly address the concerns of a more specific audience. In addition to newspapers, most states produce their own regional magazines, providing updated event guides and descriptions of cultural and historical attractions. These include *Nebraska Life*, *North Dakota Horizons*, and *Oklahoma Today*. *Oklahoma Today*, for example, recently ran this announcement: "*Oklahoma Today* is seeking Oklahoma-flavored fiction, nonfiction, and personal essays by up-and-coming authors for our inaugural amateur writing contest. From N. Scott Momaday to S. E. Hinton, Oklahoma writers have long been inspired by the state's sweeping landscapes, warm people, rural charms, and thriving urban environments. Now it's time to have your best work recognized."[91]

The literary journals of the Great Plains, though not strictly devoted to publishing Plains literature, do publish a great deal of western and Plains-focused writing and often devote particular issues to Plains writers or themes. The winter 1998 issue of *South Dakota Review*, for example, opens with five poems by Nathan Whiting, including "The Prairie." Editor Brian Bedard titles his introductory article "Still Life, with Cows." Other notable literary journals of the Great Plains include *North Dakota Quarterly*, the *Nebraska Review*, *Cottonwood* (Kansas), and *Nimrod* (Oklahoma). *Prairie Schooner*, published by the University of Nebraska at Lincoln, is one of the oldest literary journals in continuous publication and offers annual prizes in poetry, fiction, and nonfiction, including the Faulkner Award for Excellence in Writing ($1,000) and the Larry Levis Prize for Poetry ($1,000).

In addition to producing high-quality literary journals, the universities and colleges of the Great Plains make significant efforts to collect and archive literature, historical documents, art, and photography of the Plains. The Institute for Regional Studies at North Dakota State University in Fargo, for example, holds two collections that contain more than nine hundred photographs of rural and small-town life at the turn of the twentieth century. The institute also compiles its own bibliography of publications that provide historical, economic, and cultural information about the northern Great Plains, particularly covering the period between 1880 and 1920. The University of Nebraska at Lincoln (UNL) Center for Great Plains Studies supports both ongoing endeavors and long-term research programs. The center publishes both the *Great Plains Quarterly* and *Great Plains Research*, multidisciplinary journals that promote research and creative scholarship on Plains topics. The *Encyclopedia of the Great Plains* and the *Journals of Lewis and Clark* are long-term projects unique to the Center for Great Plains Studies. In 2002, the center has also published a chapbook of poems portraying images of bison and the prairie, *Bison Poems: Of Bison and the Great Plains*. The book originated from a juried reading at the Center's conference on bison in April 2000 in Lincoln at the Cornhusker Hotel. The center also publishes *Plains Song Review*, whose mission is to explore the culture of Nebraska, including its landscape and people. The *Journals of Lewis and Clark* project, under the editorial direction of Gary E. Moulton, professor of history at UNL and associate director of the center, consists of a thirteen-volume edition of the diaries of Meriwether Lewis and William Clark, the division of four enlisted men, an atlas, a botanical volume, and a comprehensive index.

The Center for Great Plains Studies at Emporia State University in Kansas emphasizes the study of the grasslands as one of its primary responsibilities to Kansas and the region. According to its Web site, "Academic programs, public service activities, and research projects are intended to inform, interest and promote appreciation of the sprawling mid-continental grasslands."[92] The center publishes several journals, including *Heritage of the Great Plains*, that promote scholarship on the life and culture of the Great Plains region. Articles in the fall/winter 2003 issue, for example, include "The Economic Survival of Louisville, Nebraska, in the Great Depression," "The Desiccated Plain: Comanche and Non-Indian Settler Responses to Drought in the Southern Plains," "McPherson County, Kansas, Conscientious Objectors during World War II," and "The Savage Dance of Death: The Omaha Newspapers' Coverage of the Ghost Dance, 1890–1891." The center at Emporia State also publishes *Tales out of School*, a newsletter geared toward teachers of Kansas history.

RESOURCE GUIDE

Printed Sources

Bair, Julene. *One Degree West: Reflections of a Plainsdaughter.* Minneapolis: Mid-List Press, 2000.

Butala, Sharon. *The Perfection of the Morning: A Woman's Awakening in Nature.* St. Paul, MN: Hungry Mind Press, 1994.

Cooper, James Fenimore. *The Prairie.* New York: Oxford University Press, 1989.

Flint, Roland. *Stubborn.* Urbana: University of Illinois Press, 1990.

Frazier, Ian. *The Great Plains.* New York: Farrar, 1989.

Garland, Hamlin. *Main-Travelled Roads.* 1891. Rpt. Lincoln: University of Nebraska Press, 1993.

Gruchow, Paul. *Journal of a Prairie Year.* Minneapolis: University of Minnesota Press, 1985.

Hansen, Ron. *Nebraska.* New York: Atlantic Monthly Press, 1989.

Harjo, Joy. *Mad Love and War.* Middletown, CT: Wesleyan University Press, 1990.

Haruf, Kent. *Plainsong.* New York: Vintage Books, 1999.

Hasselstrom, Linda. *Between Grass and Sky: Where I Live and Work.* Reno: University of Nevada Press, 2002.

Hasselstrom, Linda, Gaydell Collier, and Nancy Curtis, eds. *Leaning into the Wind: Women Write from the Heart of the West.* Boston: Houghton Mifflin, 1997.

Haun, Catherine. "A Woman's Trip across the Plains in 1849." In *Women's Diaries of the Westward Journey,* ed. Lillian Schlissel. New York: Schocken Books, 1982, 1992.

Heat-Moon, William Least. *PrairyErth.* Boston: Houghton Mifflin, 1991.

Herndon, Sarah Raymond. *Days on the Road: Crossing the Plains in 1865.* Guilford, CT: Globe Pequot Press, 2003.

Hogan, Linda. *Book of Medicines.* Minneapolis: Coffee House Press, 1993.

———. *Red Clay.* Greenfield Center, NY: Greenfield Review Press, 1991.

Kloefkorn, William. *This Death by Drowning.* Lincoln: University of Nebraska Press, 1995.

———. *Treehouse: New and Selected Poems.* Fredonia, NY: White Wine Press, 1996.

Kooser, Ted. *Weather Central.* Pittsburgh: University of Pittsburgh Press, 1994.

———. *Winter Morning Walks.* Pittsburgh: Carnegie Mellon University Press, 2000.

Low, Denise. *Starwater.* Lawrence, KS: Cottonwood Press, 1988.

Madson, John. *Where the Sky Began: Land of the Tallgrass Prairie.* San Francisco: Sierra Club Books, 1982.

Manfred, Frederick. *Apples of Paradise.* New York: Trident Press, 1965.

Momaday, N. Scott. *The Names: A Memoir.* Tucson: University of Arizona Press, 1976.

———. *The Way to Rainy Mountain.* Albuquerque: University of New Mexico Press, 1976.

Neihardt, John. *Black Elk Speaks.* 1932. Rpt. Lincoln: University of Nebraska Press, 1988.

Norris, Kathleen. *Dakota.* Boston: Houghton Mifflin, 1993, 2001.

Porter, Kenneth. *No Rain in These Clouds: Poems, 1927–1945.* New York: John Day and Company, 1946.

Rølvaag, O. E. *Peder Victorious: A Tale of the Pioneers Twenty Years Later.* New York: Harper and Brothers, 1929, 1956.

Sandoz, Mari. *Love Song to the Plains.* Lincoln: University of Nebraska Press, 1961.

———. *Miss Morissa: Doctor of the Gold Trail.* Lincoln: University of Nebraska Press, 1955, 1980.

Stafford, William. *The Darkness around Us Is Deep: Selected Poems.* New York: Harper-Perennial, 1993.

———. *Kansas Poems.* Topeka, KS: Woodley Memorial Press, 1990.

Steinbeck, John. *The Grapes of Wrath.* New York: Penguin Books, 1939, 1992.

Unger, Douglas. *Leaving the Land.* 1984. Rpt. Lincoln: University of Nebraska Press, 1988.

Vitek, William, and Wes Jackson, eds. *Rooted in the Land: Essays on Community and Place.* New Haven, CT: Yale University Press, 1996.

Walker, Mildred. *Winter Wheat.* Lincoln: University of Nebraska Press, 1992.

Wright, Morris. *The Home Place.* Lincoln: University of Nebraska Press, 1948, 1998.

Regionalism and the Great Plains

Fink, Deborah. *Agrarian Women: Wives and Mothers in Rural Nebraska, 1880–1940.* Chapel Hill: University of North Carolina Press, 1992.

Jensen, Merrill, ed. *Regionalism in America*. Madison: University of Wisconsin Press, 1951.

Luebke, Frederick C. "Regionalism and the Great Plains: Problems of Concept and Method." *Western Historical Quarterly* 15 (January 1984): 19–38.

Quantic, Diane Dufva. *The Nature of the Place: A Study of Great Plains Fiction*. Lincoln: University of Nebraska Press, 1995.

Smith, Henry Nash. *Virgin Land: The American West as Symbol and Myth*. Cambridge, MA: Harvard University Press, 1950.

Stauffer, Helen Winter, and Susan J. Rosowski. *Women and Western American Literature*. Troy, NY: Whitson Publishing Company, 1982.

Thacker, Robert. *The Great Prairie: Fact and Literary Imagination*. Albuquerque: University of New Mexico Press, 1989.

Turner, Frederick Jackson. *The Frontier in American History*. New York: H. Holt, 1920.

Turner is basic to understanding the historical thought of both William Prescott Webb and Wallace Stegner.

Webb, W. P. *The Great Plains*. Lincoln: University of Nebraska Press, 1931, 1959.

Willa Cather

Bennett, Mildred R. *The World of Willa Cather*. New York: Dodd, Mead & Co., 1951. 2nd ed. Lincoln: University of Nebraska Press, 1962.

———, ed. *Antonia*. New York: Chelsea House, 1991.

———, ed. *Willa Cather's* My Antonia. New York: Chelsea House, 1987.

Cather, Willa Sibert. "Nebraska: The End of the First Cycle." *Nation* 117 (September 5, 1923): 236–238.

———. *On Writing: Critical Studies on Writing as an Art*. New York: Knopf, 1949.

Gustafson, Neil. "Getting Back to Cather's Text: The Shared Dream in *O Pioneers!*" *Western American Literature* 30 (August 1995): 151–162.

Murphy, David. "Jejich Antonie: Czechs, the Land, Cather, and the Pavelka Farmstead." *Great Plains Quarterly* 14 (spring 1994): 85–106.

Murphy, John J. "Nebraska Naturalism in Jamesian Frames." *Great Plains Quarterly* 4 (fall 1984): 231–237.

Olson, Paul A. "The Epic and Great Plains Literature: Rolvaag, Cather, and Neihardt." *Prairie Schooner* 55 (spring/summer 1981): 263–285.

Rosowski, Susan J. *The Voyage Perilous: Willa Cather's Romanticism*. Lincoln: University of Nebraska Press, 1986.

———, ed. *Approaches to Teaching Cather's* My Antonia. New York: Modern Language Association of America, 1989.

Woodress, James. *Willa Cather: A Literary Life*. Lincoln: University of Nebraska Press, 1987.

Wallace Stegner

Benson, Jackson J. *Wallace Stegner: His Life and Work*. New York: Viking, 1996.

Isern, Thomas D. "The Sensuous Savage in All of Us: Wallace Stegner in Review." *North Dakota History* 66 (winter 1999): 16–20.

Isle, Walter. "History and Nature: Representations of the Great Plains in the Work of Sharon Butala and Wallace Stegner." *Great Plains Quarterly* 19 (spring 1999): 89–95.

Lojek, Helen. "Wallace Stegner, Herodotus of the Cypress Hills." *Prairie Forum* 24 (spring 1999): 41–50.

Stegner, Wallace. *Marking the Sparrow's Fall: Wallace Stegner's American West*. Ed. Page Stegner. New York: Henry Holt, 1998.

Web Sites

Center for Great Plains Studies, Emporia State University
http://www.emporia.edu/cgps/gpgb.htm

Center for Great Plains Studies, University of Nebraska at Lincoln
http://www.unl.edu/plains/

Lindhard, Anne, Willa Cather Page
http://fp.image.dk/fpemarxlind/

A developing, comprehensive site with biography, bibliographies, and other background materials.

[Newstrom, Scott], Willa Cather Home Page
http://www.gustavus.edu/oncampus/academics/english/cather/

Wallace Stegner Environmental Center, Wallace Stegner
http://206.14.7.53/gic/stegner/wallace.html

Willa Cather Pioneer Memorial
http://www.willacather.org/

Videos/Films

Fargo. Dir. Joel Coen Polygram/Working Title. 1996.
The Grapes of Wrath. Dir. John Ford. Twentieth Century–Fox. 1940.
My Antonia. Dir. Joseph Sargent. Gideon Productions. 1995.
The Plow That Broke the Plains. Dir. Pare Lorentz. Resettlement Administration. 1936.
Wallace Stegner: A Writer's Life. Stephen Fisher Productions and KCET Television, Los Angeles. 1997.

Organizations

Kansas Center for the Book
Topeka/Shawnee County Public Library
1515 SW 10th Ave.
Topeka, KS 66604-1374
Phone: 785-231-0588; Fax: 785-231-0519
http://kcftb.tscpl.org

Nebraska Center for the Book
Nebraska Library Commission
The Atrium
1200 N Street, Ste. 120
Lincoln, NE 68508-2023
Phone: 402-471-2045 or 800-307-2665; Fax:402-471-2083
www.unl.edu/NCB

North Dakota Center for the Book
North Dakota State Library
604 E. Blvd. Ave.—Dept. 250
Bismarck, ND 58505-0800
Phone: 701-328-1303; Fax: 701-328-2040
http://ndsl.lib.state.nd.us

Oklahoma Center for the Book
Oklahoma Department of Libraries
200 NE 18th St.
Oklahoma City, OK 73105-3298
Phone: 405-521-2502; Fax: 405-525-7804
http://www.odl.state.ok.us/ocb/

South Dakota Center for the Book
PO Box 7050
University Station
Brookings, SD 57007
Phone: 605-688-6113; Fax: 605-688-4531
E-mail: SDSU_SDHC@sdstate.edu
http://web.sdstate.edu/humanities/center.html

MUSIC

*Paula Conlon,
Addie deHilster, and
T. Chris Aplin*

The music and dance of the Great Plains run the gamut from classical to polka to popular, in addition to the music and dance of the Native peoples of this area. Just as the forced removal to Indian Territory brought tribes that had originally been far apart into interaction with one another at intertribal powwows, so music and dance such as the polka provided an outlet for settlers to visit and meet new people. The result is a fascinating mix of expressions of creativity in music and dance that offered entertainment and pleasure to countless settlers from the old country, alongside the music and dance of the Native peoples of this country. These diverse traditions have been handed down and have undergone transformations over the centuries. The various facets of these music cultures and how they reflect the Great Plains identity are examined here, including classical, polka, jazz, country and western, folk, bluegrass, popular, rock, and Native American music. Hybridity is a feature of numerous subgroups of these genres.

NATIVE AMERICAN MUSIC

Music and dance were integral parts of both ceremonial and everyday life in traditional Native American culture, enabling the elders to express pride in their heritage and hand down this knowledge to the young people of their tribe. In the Plains area, and especially in Oklahoma, a variety of traditional ceremonies continue to provide a venue for keeping Native American culture alive through song and dance. Lullabies and love songs, whether sung or played on the Native American flute, provide a vehicle for individual expression that can be used for relaxation and personal fulfillment, as well as for entertaining others in both private and public settings.

Grand Island, Nebraska's 1892 Mandolin and Guitar Club. Courtesy Stuhr Museum of the Prairie Pioneer.

Native American Powwows

Powwows are a celebration of being Indian and inspire cultural and personal pride in Indians' heritage. The term "powwow" derives from the Algonquian word "pau wau," meaning "he dreams," referring to a spiritual leader in a curing ceremony. While the origins of the word reveal personal and sacred traditions, the contemporary Native American powwow is a group-oriented event that is open to the public. Social dances such as powwows are times for relaxation, getting together with relatives and friends from other tribes and nations, and enjoying intertribal songs and dances.

The concept of the powwow as an intertribal dance originated among the tribes who inhabited the Great Plains. In the prereservation era, many Plains tribes formed intertribal alliances and exchanged songs, dances, and ceremonies, laying the historical foundation for the modern-day powwow. The first intertribal powwow was held in 1889 in Ponca, Oklahoma, then called Indian Territory. The forced removal of numerous tribes from the eastern United States to Indian Territory in the nineteenth century settled sixty-seven different tribes in what was to become Oklahoma. Tribes that participated at the first Ponca Powwow included the Omaha, Ponca, Kaw, Osage, Pawnee, and Oto-Missouria. Many of the dancers had traveled more than a hundred miles by horse, some from neighboring states, to participate. Tribes across the Plains began to adopt the emerging intertribal powwow to express their Native heritage through song and dance, and the powwow spread across North America. After World War II, there was a dramatic increase in the number of powwows as tribes welcomed returning veterans back home, and the powwow has continued to thrive up to the present day.

Individual dances are categorized by the dance steps along with specific regalia worn by the dancer, which is *not* referred to as a costume. The Men's Northern Traditional outfit is identified primarily by the large bustle worn on the dancer's back; the dancers portray tracking an enemy. The Men's Southern Straight, sometimes referred to as Southern Traditional, also represents a warrior scouting the enemy. The Southern Straight regalia's main feature is an otter-skin trailer that hangs down the dancer's back.

The Men's Grass Dance, which originated in the Plains area, is considered to be the oldest style of the powwow dances. There are several stories as to how the Grass Dance began. The version from the Ponca tribe tells of how, long ago, the people went to an isolated spot on the prairie to give thanks, and some of the men stomped down the

American Indian powwow at Fort Union, Williston, North Dakota. Photo by Clayton Wolt. Courtesy North Dakota Tourism.

grass to make way for dancing. Grass Dancers use many sways, dips, and sliding steps that portray these movements. The distinguishing feature of their regalia is the rows of brightly colored yarn (originally grass) that adorn their outfits. The Men's Fancy Dance originated in Oklahoma and provides the opportunity for each dancer to demonstrate his athletic ability and originality. What sets the Fancy Dancer's outfit apart is the set of double bustles worn on his back, usually trimmed with brightly dyed hackle feathers. Fancy Dancers are expected to dance to both Northern and Southern drum groups, adjusting their style of dance to complement the style of music that accompanies them.

Women's Northern Traditional dancers wear two types of regalia, fully beaded buckskin and cloth dresses; both styles carry a shawl folded over an arm. This dance requires much skill to stay in perfect rhythm, stepping lightly, slightly bobbing up and down, and allowing the fringe on their dresses and shawls to sway gracefully. Women's Southern Traditional dancers also carry a shawl over the arm; their outfits generally have less beadwork on both buckskin and cloth dresses than those of their Northern counterparts. The beat of the dance is slower on Southern songs, and the dancer sways gracefully as she steps.

The Jingle Dress Dance originated with the Ojibway Nation in the 1920s and gradually made its way west across the country into the Plains. Jingle dresses are decorated with rolled snuff-can lids (other types of metal lids may also be used) that hit each other when the dancer moves, creating a pleasing "jingle" sound. The Women's Fancy Shawl, originating from the northern Plains area in the 1950s, is the counterpart to the Men's Fancy Dance. Dancers use spins and freestyle footwork to demonstrate their originality. To allow freedom of movement, women wear calf-length skirts and drape their shawls across their shoulders; the dance represents the transition of a cocoon to a butterfly.

Many contemporary powwows have competitions in which dancers are grouped by dance style and age and compete for cash prizes. They are judged on creativity of their dance and outfit, staying with the beat, and stopping on time (i.e., knowing the song). Powwows originally were less structured and consisted mainly of informal intertribal dancing, with lots of visiting time.

Intertribal dances are still very much a part of contemporary powwows. In these social (as opposed to a competitive) dances, everyone (both Native Americans and non–Native Americans) is welcome to come and join in the circle. In the Plains area, dancers generally move clockwise in a large circle to a straight drumbeat (strong, weak). For the Intertribal Dance, a basic toe-heel step is used by the men, and a variation of the basic step with flat foot and bent knee is used by the women. For the Round Dance, another social dance that occurs at powwows throughout the Plains area, dancers face inward in a circle and move sideways in a clockwise direction. The drumbeat has a distinctive "strong, rest, weak" accent. In the Round Dance, dancers step sideways onto the left foot on the downbeat, then bring the right foot over on the upbeat (weak accent).

Powwow singing styles are differentiated as being "Northern," originating in the central and northern Great Plains, Canada, and the Great Lakes regions and characterized by a high pitch and hard drumbeat, and "Southern," synonymous with Oklahoma and characterized by a lower pitch and less strident drumbeat. Dancers use a Northern drum group if their dance originated in the northern Plains, such as the Men's Northern Traditional and Grass Dance and the Women's Northern Buckskin/Cloth, Jingle Dress, and Fancy Shawl. They dance to a Southern drum group if their dance originated in the southern Plains, such as the Men's Southern Straight and Southern Fancy Dance and the Women's Southern Buckskin/Cloth. Male Fancy Dancers, the showpiece of the contemporary powwow, dance to both Northern and Southern drums.

Powwow Fancy Shawl (Dancer Leslie Deere). Photo by Dr. Paula Conlon.

Northern and Southern powwow styles have a basic song structure of "lead" (the first line of the song sung by the head singer), "second" (a repeat of the first line by the entire group of male singers/drummers), "first chorus" (the first half of the song), "honor beats" (strong beats on the drum that both honor the drum and help cue the dancers; in southern Plains songs, these are usually three sets of strong/weak beats), "second chorus" (the second half of the song), a series of repetitions of the basic structure (each repetition is often called a "push-up"), "tail" (a repeat of the second chorus without the first half, which signifies the end of the song), and a series of strong drumbeats to close the song (in southern Plains songs usually five strong beats in succession).

Numerous tribes across the Plains host intertribal powwows that include drum groups from both Northern and Southern styles, not restricting themselves to the drum style of their particular tribe. A typical drum group consists of eight to twelve male drummers/singers, with female singers, seated behind the men, joining in partway through the song at a higher pitch. Dancers acknowledge the honor beats in different ways according to their style of dance. For example, the dignified Southern Cloth dancer bows her head at this time, while the energetic Jingle Dress dancer raises and waves her fan.

Although older powwow songs frequently had translatable text interspersed throughout the song, contemporary songs often consist mainly of syllables without dictionary definition that are related to the language sounds. The use of syllables enables singers from various tribes to join in the song. They are not arbitrary or improvised; syllables are sung roughly the same way each time the song is sung, much as one would sing translatable text transmitted by oral tradition as opposed to a written score.

Drum contests have become a feature of contemporary powwows, and drum groups often travel the same circuit as the competitive dancers. In Oklahoma City in June of each year, the Red Earth Festival is host to hundreds of dancers and singers/drummers, and spectators of all ages are welcome. Award-winning Northern drum groups from the Plains area include Badland Singers, Black Lodge, Eagle Tail, Iron Wood, Mandaree, Porcupine Singers, and Rocky Boys. Award-winning Southern drum groups from the Plains area include Bad Medicine, Cozad, Rose Hill, Sizzortail, Southern Thunder, and Yellowhammer.

Every weekend all summer long throughout the Plains, someone is hosting a powwow. For a number of tribes, the intertribal powwow has replaced the ceremonial dances that were outlawed by the government in the late 1800s, and people travel great distances to meet friends and relatives at these annual reunions. Powwows are accessible to the public and are a good place to start to learn about Native American people who are very much a part of the heritage of the United States.

The book *Native American Dance: Ceremonies and Social Traditions* (1993), edited by Charlotte Heth, provides an excellent overview of Native music in both the Northern and Southern Plains, with additional inserts on traditional ceremonial music of this area such as the Kiowa Black Leggings, the Sun Dance, the Apache Fire Dance, and the Stomp Dance. The juxtaposition of these sacred events along-

Gourd Dancing

Gourd Dancing is now a familiar feature at powwows throughout the Plains, especially in Oklahoma, although the dance did not originate in the powwow arena. Several tribes historically held Gourd Dances, including the Ponca, Kiowa, Comanche, and Cheyenne. The musical accompaniment for Gourd Dance songs is a large powwow-style drum, along with gourd or metal rattles shaken by the male dancers. Seated males drum and sing; female singers sit behind the drummers and join in partway through the song. Gourd Dance songs consist of two main parts, with softer drumbeats while the male dancers move around the arena, changing to sections with loud, strongly accented drumbeats during which the men stand stationary while moving up and down to the rhythm of the drum. In the Kiowa tribe, the origin story tells of a red wolf that appeared to a young warrior in a vision, singing and dancing on his hind legs, shifting his weight from side to side while shaking a gourd rattle, and emitting a howl at the end of the song. These actions are depicted by the men as they perform the Gourd Dance. Women wearing shawls dance on the outskirts of the circle facing inward, mirroring the steps of the men as they dance in place.

side the primarily social dancing that occurs at a powwow is particularly well depicted with quotes from Native writers who have lived the tradition, such as the extract from Linda Hogan's poem about elderly female shell-shakers at a Stomp Dance: "Their dark hands laced the shells of turtles together, pebbles inside and they danced with rattles strong on their legs."[1]

Native American Flute

The Native American Plains flute is an aerophone (the sound is produced by vibrating air) that is similar to a European recorder, but with an external block instead of an interior whistle mouthpiece. This block is often carved to reflect the origin story of the flute, in which the flute and its music were gifted by a spirit to aid young men in courtship rituals.

With the advent of the boarding-school era in the late nineteenth and early twentieth centuries, coupled with the simultaneous suppression of Native culture in an attempt to assimilate Native people into the dominant White culture, the flute was in danger of dying out. Comanche artist and flute player Doc Tate Nevaquaya (1932–1996) was instrumental in the rejuvenation of traditional Native American flute playing in the 1960s, which has continued to the present day. Doc Tate recognized the need to resurrect the old songs, formerly handed down by example and imitation, before the flute players who knew the songs passed away. He took it upon himself to approach these players, win their confidence, and learn their songs. From his home in Apache, Oklahoma, Doc Tate traveled to various museums, such as the Smithsonian Institution and the Library of Congress, to examine their flute collections and listen to tapes of flute melodies. Doc Tate dedicated himself to preserving traditional Native American flute music, giving lecture-recitals to both Native American and non–Native American audiences across the United States and overseas. The Smithsonian Institution commissioned him to perform on the flute on a Goodwill Tour of England (1970), play the flute at the National Folk Festival (1973), and record *Comanche Flute Music* for Folkways Records (1979). He received numerous awards, including the National Endowment for the Arts (1986), Living Legend (1990), and Oklahoma Treasure (1995). Doc Tate Nevaquaya inspired a whole generation of Native American musicians. He taught four of his sons to play the flute and to make flutes by hand. Sonny, Edmond, Timothy, and Calvert Tate Nevaquaya all continue to carry on their father's legacy.

Tom Mauchahty Ware (1949) is a descendant of Belo Cozad, a well-known Kiowa flute player of the older generation, and lives just outside Anadarko, Oklahoma. Ware's repertoire consists of adaptations of various southern Plains social dance songs, hymns, and his own compositions. Ware has performed at powwows, rodeos, and various expositions that feature Native American music and dance traditions, as well as folk festivals in Europe.

Kevin Locke (b. 1954, Tokeya Inajin is his Lakota name, meaning "the first to

A Flute Collector and Maker

Dr. Richard W. Payne (1918) of Oklahoma City is an avid flute collector and maker who has amassed the largest privately owned collection of aerophones of the Americas in the world. Payne has been studying the Native American flute since before World War II and has visited with very nearly all of the major Native flute players over the years. Although non-Native, Payne is very respected in the Native flute world, and his flutes are highly prized.

arise") is acknowledged to be a driving force in the now-powerful revival of the Native American flute tradition. In 1990, Locke was awarded a National Heritage Fellowship by the National Endowment for the Arts. During the past two decades, Locke has performed and lectured in more than eighty countries and has served as a cultural ambassador for the U.S. Information Agency (USIA) since 1980. Locke has recorded twelve albums of music and stories, most recently *The First Flute*, *Open Circle*, *Keepers of the Dream*, and *Dream Catcher*. Locke's repertoire includes melodies that were once played by older-generation Sioux flute players, like Richard Fool Bull and John Coloff, to supplement his repertoire, and he has performed on flutes that were made by Richard Fool Bull and Dan Red Buffalo, two well-known Sioux flute makers of the older generation.

In the last decade of the twentieth century, there was an explosion of interest in the Native American flute, and the instrument and its music have been experiencing a renaissance, promoted by both Indian and non-Indian players, makers, and scholars. Although this renaissance has not restored the flute's

Doc Tate Nevaquaya with flute. Photo by Dr. Paula Conlon.

traditional role in private courtship ritual, it has been instrumental in creating new avenues for the exploration of the Native American flute.

Contemporary flute players frequently perform a combination of styles of playing, moving back and forth between traditional melodies and their own compositions. They often take advantage of modern technology to create an echo effect with digital delay, first advocated by Navajo/Ute flutist R. Carlos Nakai (1946). Up-and-coming Native flutist Terry Tsotigh (1956), of the Kiowa tribe, is a proponent of this blending and mixing of styles, as is Doc Tate's oldest son, Sonny Nevaquaya. All of these men are active in their local communities, as well as touring. Flute circles, with both Native and non-Native participants, have sprung up all over the country, headed by the International Native American Flute Association (INAFA), whose goal is to foster the preservation, appreciation, and advancement of the Native American flute.

POLKA

Polka is one of the most widespread music and dance practices in the Great Plains. Variations on this genre can be found among the descendants of European immi-

Native Hip-Hop

The rhythms, attitudes, and styles of hip-hop are typically attributed to innovations in major economic centers such as Los Angeles and New York and to the African American artists who brought the style to national awareness. Within the state of Oklahoma, however, hip-hop is Indian Territory. The multicultural hip-hop crew Culture Shock Camp is a performance group that is strongly influenced by its Native American members and proud of its Oklahoma roots and promotes a message of empowerment to its audiences. Pawnee/Seminole actor, motivational speaker, entrepreneur, and Culture Shock Camp deejay Brian Frejo created the guiding message behind the group when he envisioned the concept for C4G productions. C4G is an abbreviation for Created for Greatness, a phrase that acts as the mission statement for the group's goals.

Emphasizing the importance of a positive outlook in a post-9/11 America, Frejo states that "the message is to anybody—black, white, yellow, green, [or] purple." While the themes of empowerment can be seen as universal in message, other lyrical elements give their music a distinctive Oklahoma/southern Plains character, exploring what it means to be an Oklahoman by discussing life within the state, the stereotypes outsiders have of the state, and the stereotypes non-Natives have of Native Americans. They make reference to prominent Oklahomans such as Woody Guthrie and speak of their religious beliefs and tribal heritage. Culture Shock Camp remains in step with national trends in hip-hop through creating a music that seeks to effect a positive change in its audience, Native culture, and the broader Oklahoman and American society.

grants in the Dakotas, Nebraska, Kansas, and Oklahoma. These states form part of the so-called polka belt, a region that extends from Connecticut around the Great Lakes in the Midwest and down the Plains into Texas, connected by polka music and the paths of traveling bands. A lively couple dance in 2/4 time, the polka is generally believed to have originated in the province of Bohemia in what is today the Czech Republic. There are four main types of polka music: German, Polish, Slovenian, and Czech, all of which have a presence in the Great Plains region.

German

The German polka is the brassy "oompah" style that most people imagine when they think of polka. Present throughout the Great Plains region, German American bands have been active in maintaining and popularizing polka in America. In Russian German bands, the violin was most often used as the lead instrument in a string-dominated ensemble, and clarinets often led the wind bands. After World War II, brass instruments such as trumpet and trombone became commonplace, along with an occasional guitar or banjo.

Polish

A number of Polish communities were established in the Great Plains region during the nineteenth century. In North Dakota, Polish settlers arrived from Minnesota and Wisconsin as early as 1873, but the majority immigrated to the Plains directly from Poland. The Polish American polka has evolved to include not only influences from Polish folk song, but also elements of pan-European polka and American styles popular in the heyday of dance music.

Slovenian

The Slovenian style is up-tempo polka music made popular by Cleveland-based Frank Yankovic and his band, the Yanks. The Slovenian community of Kansas City, Kansas, has had a marked influence on the area's local ethnic musics.

Czech Polka: Ethnic Identity and the Mainstream

Many of the Czech immigrants to the United States chose to settle in the Midwest and Plains regions because of the similarities to the rural areas that they had left behind, and Czech bands have been active in the Plains region since the nineteenth century. In the 1890s, a Czech band in Omaha performed for composer Antonín Dvořák of Czechoslovakia during his famous tour of the United States. Czech polka bands have a wind-dominated instrumentation like German bands, usually including trumpet, trombone, tuba, accordion, and drums, with saxophonists doubling on clarinet. Czech groups, however, tend to have a more traditional style, relying more on Czech polkas, waltzes, and schottisches, with other types of numbers interspersed during sets.

One of the vehicles for the transmission of Czech music and culture in America has been the community halls established as mutual-aid societies for immigrants. Active Czech community centers are located throughout the Plains states, but the Czech Hall in Yukon, Oklahoma, is one of the few that hosts a dance with a live Czech band every Saturday night, continuing a tradition that it has maintained since 1930. One of the Yukon Czech Hall's two house bands, the Masopust Polka Band, was organized by the Masopust family in the 1890s and is now in its fifth generation, with members of the family performing alongside the other musicians whom they have recruited.

The Mark Vhylidal Orchestra of Fremont, Nebraska, is another example of a family band, as Mark Vhylidal represents the younger generation of polka musicians in his family. In May 1993, his band performed for more than a million listeners on Garrison Keillor's *Prairie Home Companion* radio show, and it was later selected by the Smithsonian Institution to be included in the 2001 Folkways recording *Deeper Polka*. The Mark Vhylidal Orchestra travels throughout the polka belt, performing in Nebraska, Kansas, Oklahoma, Texas, North and South Dakota, Minnesota, Wisconsin, Michigan, Iowa, and Canada, often traveling by van with an entourage of fans following to dance their way through the tour. These are established destinations for touring polka bands; even polka royalty like Al Grebnick, the "Nebraska Polka King," have performed their way down this musical pipeline through the Plains.

The Button Accordion

In recent years, a revival of the button accordion has been led in Kansas City by Don Lipovac (1935). The button accordion is considered more traditional than the common keyboard accordion. Lipovac was born in 1935 in the Slovenian part of Kansas City, Kansas, and his grandfather began teaching him about his musical heritage when he was still a toddler. By age ten or eleven, Lipovac was playing Slovenian polkas and waltzes at weddings and parties in the community. He earned degrees in music theory and music education from the Kansas City Conservatory (now part of the University of Missouri at Kansas City) and, in the 1950s, competed in accordion competitions playing classical music, winning the national accordion competition in 1958. As he continued with the instrument, Lipovac's interest in the traditional music of his heritage became stronger, and in 1958, he performed Slovenian polkas on *The Lawrence Welk Show*. Eventually, his performances gained the attention of Croatian tamburitza musicians in Kansas City who asked him to join their group. (A tamburitza is an ensemble of folk string instruments that began its development in countries across Europe during the 1840s.) The result of this collaboration has been a mixing of Croatian and Slovenian traditional musics that some refer to as the "Kansas City style" of South Slavic music. Lipovac's career in traditional music in Kansas City has spanned several decades, and his more than five hundred compositions and arrangements, as well as more than four hundred students, contribute to a legacy that will continue to impact the ethnic music scene in the region.[2]

The lyrics of Czech songs often invoke pastoral images of the landscape, water, snow, and birds, as well as nostalgia for elements of Czech culture such as prunes and kolache, key ingredients in the national cuisine. Many other songs are named for women or for features of women's clothing, as in the "Blue Skirt Waltz," with lyrics about love newly found or long lost. "Pisnièka Èeska" speaks about music's role in maintaining Czech culture:

> This song will always remain in my heart
> That is our song
> It is so beautiful
> It is just like a meadow with flowers
> This song is like that
> Our song grew just like that flower in the meadow
> And if we lose this song
> Then we would not have anything.[3]

Czech polka is a symbol of ethnic identity for the descendants of Czech immigrants, but this does not mean that non-Czechs are excluded from participation. Saturday-night dances at Czech Hall in Yukon are always open to the public, and in Nebraska, people in small towns with a Czech population expect that wedding receptions will be open to the entire community for dinner and dancing. This inclusiveness extends to the repertoire of Czech bands as well; polkas, waltzes, schottisches, and folk songs are the staples of their performances, but transcriptions of swing and country and western tunes arranged for polka ensembles by their members have a significant presence. Sometimes termed "modrens" (a corruption of "moderns"), these types of songs were initially implemented to help bands appeal to the younger generations and to more diverse crowds. Songs like "Alley Cat" and "Your Cheating Heart" are typical, remaining "modrens" in the Czech repertoire despite their age. Czech music's connection with the American mainstream has not been a one-way exchange of influences. Musical activities like fiddling held in common by Czech and Anglo groups alike made the transfer of ideas natural, and early in the twentieth century, many of the same musicians who were developing the style known as western swing were also playing Czech polkas.

Radio Shows and the International Polka Hall of Fame

Along with live music at dances, the continued life of polka is maintained through radio shows, mostly on AM stations. Oklahoma and South Dakota each have at least one weekly polka show, heard on stations KCRC in Enid, Oklahoma, and WNAX in Yankton, South Dakota, respectively. In North Dakota, *Bob Becker's Old Tyme Variety Show* plays on Saturday mornings on KQKX in Lisbon, and *Uncle Sig's Old Time Show* is broadcast from October through April on KXPO in Grafton. Nebraska airwaves host no fewer than half a dozen different radio shows, such as the *Mark Vyhildal Show* on KJSK in Columbus, the *Moustache Joe Show* on KHUB in Fremont, and the daily broadcasts of *Willie Skala's Early Morning Show* and *Willie Skala's Mid-Morning Show* on KMMJ in Grand Island.

A seventeen-year veteran of daily radio broadcasts on KTTT in Colombus, Nebraska, Al Grebnick (b. 1919) was inducted into the Pioneer Category of the International Polka Association's Polka Music Hall of Fame in 1988. The Polka Music Hall of Fame and Museum was organized in Chicago in 1968 to memorialize performers like Grebnick, who provided music for more than 5,000 dances in his career of more than fifty years.

Polka as a Multiethnic Movement

Participation in the polka movement of the twentieth century was not restricted to European Americans. Mexicans and Mexican Americans encountered the accordion in the nineteenth century when Czech and German immigrants arrived in Texas and northern Mexico. *Conjunto*, an original Tejano style, was developed when musicians fused Mexican instruments and aesthetics with the accordion and German and Czech songs. Subsequently, this style has moved into the Plains region with the growing Mexican American populations in these states. The word *conjunto* means "group" in Spanish, and the current ensemble has evolved over the past century to include accordion, *bajo sexto* (a guitar-related instrument with twelve strings), bass, and drums. The accordion is the lead instrument and is used not only for melodies, but for two- and three-part harmony, introductions, obbligatos, and solos. Polkas, schottisches, waltzes, mazurkas, and the *redowa* were staples of the repertoire for early groups, but in the 1940s and 1950s these dances began to disappear in favor of *rancheras*, duple-

Lawrence Welk

Lawrence Welk (1903–1992) is a famous example of how polka can serve as an emblem of ethnic identity and at the same time can be a vehicle for joining and influencing the mainstream. Welk was born near Strasburg, North Dakota, to German parents who had emigrated to the United States from the Ukraine in 1892. He grew up on an isolated farm with little formal education and as a result did not learn to speak English fluently until he was an adult. His father played the accordion, and as a child, Welk began learning to play. In 1925, Welk formed his first band, and in 1927 he moved to Yankton, South Dakota, where his four-piece ensemble, Welk's Novelty Orchestra, was featured on the local WNAX radio station. Welk built a strong following during his nine-year stay in Yankton, and owing to the radio station's strong signal, he began to attract bookings all over the Upper Midwest. From these early years in his career as a bandleader, Welk aspired to compete with the swing bands of the 1920s and 1930s, and in order to do so, he incorporated the popular standards of the day into the band's repertoire, playing as many foxtrots and marches as he did German waltzes and polkas.

Welk's approach and visibility made polka part of the mainstream dance repertoire, not just in areas familiar with polka, but on a national level. By the late 1930s, Welk had developed his ensemble into an American dance band that sprinkled a few ethnic numbers into a performance. The band's image matched its "Champagne Music" repertoire since he had the players wear tuxedos rather than *lederhosen*. In 1951, Welk's regular radio show was made into a local television show, and in 1955, the show moved to national broadcasting on ABC. *The Lawrence Welk Show* aired on ABC from 1955 to 1971, when it was canceled; however, Welk continued to broadcast his shows on a syndicated network of his own creation and was actually able to reach more stations than before. The show's finale was in 1982 when Welk retired from show business, but episodes may often still be seen on public television stations. His success was confirmed by the popularity of his recordings: forty-two of his albums hit the best-seller charts between 1956 and 1972.

meter forms similar enough to be frequently confused with polkas. Some Mexican Americans also enjoy attending European American polka dances. As a growing part of the population in Nebraska, Mexican Americans have begun to be represented at public tea dances as participants in Czech polka.

Dances

The *schottische* is a dance in 2/4 time performed following a circular path like a polka, but at a slower tempo. The name *schottische* is from the German word for "Scottish."

The *mazurka* is a Polish folk dance from the region of Mazovia, played in triple meter with accents on the weak beats.

The *redowa* is a Czech folk dance in two parts: the first part is danced in a moderate triple meter, followed by the second half, which is a sped-up version of the melody in duple meter.

TERRITORY JAZZ

Territory Jazz is jazz played within the central Plains states (and states immediately adjacent) as part of an interrelated network of venues, audiences, bands, and musicians whose musical exchange and innovation expanded upon the earlier forms of New Orleans jazz and paved the way for the emergence of swing jazz as a national phenomenon. Jazz within the territories was at its height circa the late 1920s to 1940.

Complex jazz touring networks emerged throughout the central Plains in the late 1910s and early 1920s, uniting its citizens—African Americans, Scots-Irish, Scandinavians, Czechs, and Germans—through diverse sounds based on dance and musical improvisation. Jazz history typically portrays Kansas City, Missouri, as the influential center of this regional phenomenon, but secondary cities within the Plains region often also supported their own local scene. Highway 77 was the major north-south artery in the region connecting Texas, Oklahoma, Kansas, Nebraska, and Iowa. Route 66 was another artery of significant impact within the region at the time.

Omaha, Nebraska, another tributary of Plains jazz performance during the 1920s and 1930s, was located in proximity to secondary transportation corridors and the regional hub, Kansas City. The Kansas City metro area was centrally located within the central Plains (separated from Kansas City, Kansas, by minimal distance and an abstracted border) and served as a hub for interstate rail, commercial, and musical traffic. Its geographic location lay at the crossroads between the major cities of Chicago, Dallas/Fort Worth, Des Moines, Minneapolis, Omaha, Oklahoma City, and St. Louis. Rural towns within the Plains were also an important support base for jazz music in the 1920s and 1930s. Small-town working musicians were drawn toward the economic centers for employment and acted as the raw materials for the prominent big bands in the region. Rural Plains audiences from North Dakota to Oklahoma also frequently booked touring jazz groups to serve their social needs. Audiences crowded into the local social clubs, dance halls, and bars that dotted the Plains landscape. Bandleader Jay McShann (b. 1916) recalls his experiences playing at dance halls throughout the region in the thirties:

> Some of them were out in the country, especially when you got further north, like in the Dakotas, Nebraska, and Iowa. I played some places where it wasn't but three buildings there. The biggest building was the dance hall. We used to wonder, "Who in the world is going to come out here?" . . . But people didn't think anything about going 150–200 miles to dance, back in those times.[4]

Jazz groups within the Central Plains "territories," as this region and interconnected touring network are often called, were at their height during the 1920s. Scores of territory bands played weekly, if not nightly, for both urban and distant rural dances in the years leading up to World War II. Regionally famous groups abounded within the central Plains, including bands such as Oklahoma City's Blue Devils and Andy Kirk and the Twelve Clouds of Joy, Art Bronson's Bostonians of Salina, Kansas, the Topeka- and Kansas City–based Tommy Duncan Orchestra, Bennie Moten's Kansas City Orchestra; and its famed splinter group, the Count Basie Orchestra, and two Omaha-based groups: Nat Towles' Orchestra and Lloyd Hunter's Serenaders. Prominent musicians who performed as members of these groups are significant not only in their association with a musically rich region and time, but also because of the national prominence guaranteed by the contribution they made to jazz history as a whole. The names of performers associated with territory groups are of considerable influence, both nationally and regionally, including Leroy "Stuff" Smith and Claude Williams (violin); Freddie Green and Charlie Christian (guitar); Snub Mosely, Eddie Durham, Thamon Hayes, Druie Bess, Jack Teagarden, and Dickie Wells (trombone); Buddy Tate, Herschel Evans, Lester Young, Harlan

Musician Jay McShann. Courtesy Library of Congress.

Leonard, and Charlie Parker (saxophone); Mary Lou Williams, Jay McShann, Bill "Count" Basie, and Bennie Moten (piano); Walter Page, Andy Kirk, and Eppie Jackson (tuba/bass); Willie Hall, Jo Jones, and Gus Johnson (drums); Peggy Lee, Joe Turner, and Jimmy Rushing (vocalists); and Terence T. Holder, Herbert "Peanuts" Holland, and Oran "Hot Lips" Page (trumpet), among others.

Bennie Moten's Kansas City Orchestra in many ways epitomizes Kansas City jazz. Moten was born, raised, and received his musical education in Kansas City. Songs such as "Kansas City Shuffle," "Vine Street Blues," and "18th Street Strut" attest to his fondness for his native home. Bennie Moten was reliant upon the Oklahoma Blue Devils and other territory acts for musicians. The territory bands were in some way similar to minor league ball clubs—Moten and Kansas City representing the major leagues for the region at that time. It was within the "territories" that instrumentation moved from a horn bass section to the stand-up bass (often attributed to Walter Page, of *Oklahoma Blue Devil* fame) section from which Kansas City received its characteristic ensemble sound. Moten's orchestra, with its strong swing based on a 4/4 rhythm, the use of "riffs" (short, repetitive melodic phrases that serve as the compositional foundation of a song), heavy blues influence, and lyrical, improvised solos, also helped to solidify the musical sound identified with Kansas City. Moten, like Count Basie and Jay McShann after him, bolstered the prestige of the Kansas City jazz scene through frequent tours in the East, including substantial stints in New York City. His was the first big Kansas City jazz act to expand territory jazz to national prominence through commercial recording. Because he was Kansas City's premier band leader from the mid-1920s until his untimely death in 1935, his band became the training ground for the who's who of the city's jazz, ensuring the continuation of his legacy locally. At the same time, Moten also laid the foundation for future Kansas bands to move forward and spread the Kansas City sound further to New York and Chicago, where jazz evolved from its dance roots to the later concert format known as bebop.

Saxophonist Charlie Parker (1920–1955) was the bridge that linked Kansas City's musical legacy with the future of American jazz performance. Parker's mother, a woman of Oklahoma origins and African American/Choctaw heritage, gave birth to Charlie in Kansas City, Kansas/Missouri, where he was raised during his early childhood. His family later relocated to the Missouri side of Kansas City, near the famous Twelfth and Vine district that was the heart of Kansas City jazz. Charlie Parker was a product of the Lincoln High School music program in Kansas City, shaped his musical chops through improvisation with local and visiting jazz musicians, and was a performer with Tommy Douglas and Jay McShann, among others. His playing style, shaped as it was by territory musicians and characterized by its melodic sensibility within a solid harmonic framework and rhythmic drive, was at its roots a product of the territory jazz scene. Parker eventually relocated to New York in the early 1940s, where, despite his groundbreaking improvisatory innovations, his Plains-derived playing style remained a constant undertone. His musical innovations in the American Northeast set a new standard for jazz performance in the 1940s and 1950s and later proved highly influential in the creation of bebop.

Popular Kansas City band leaders often sought out fresh talent for their own groups among nearby territorial bands, particularly in the late 1920s and 1930s at the height of Kansas City's musical influence. Territory jazz bands such as the Oklahoma Blue Devils were not only an important element of local social life, but a training ground for Kansas City musicians. Bennie Moten raided the Blue Devils for personnel on several occasions. Through these raids, he harvested the talents of prominent performers such as Count Basie, Jimmy Rushing, Hot Lips Page, and Jay McShann. Later a Kansas City band leader himself, McShann looked toward Nebraska musicians when he was assembling the first band under his leadership: "I knew to go to Omaha and get musicians. . . . I knew I was probably going to have to go there to get the first men [lead soloists] that I wanted, because there were more bands there than here [in Kansas City]."[5]

A range of distinctive forms emerged even within the greater central Plains context. Hot jazz, a form characterized by driving rhythms and energetic improvisation, was the preferred jazz form of African American Kansas City musicians, as well as many territory bands from Nebraska south through Oklahoma. However, "sweet jazz," which emphasized a smoother musical ensemble, softer timbral shadings and dynamics, less dense arrangements, and a more measured approach to improvisation, held stronger interest for northern Plains consumers of Euro-Scandinavian descent, particularly through the Dakotas. The extensive appeal of this musical form is perhaps epitomized by the popularity of the Lawrence Welk Orchestra, Guy Lombardo, and Jan Garber throughout the northern Plains area.

Singer Peggy Lee (1920–2002) really made it big with Glen Miller *outside* of the central Plains. But, as with M. Sweet and Paul Revere, regional identity isn't necessarily always assumed actively on the part of the performer, but on the part of the region and neighbors who claim their allegiance to the artist. She did form her early musical and performance abilities within the state—at various venues and on the radio—and youthful experience often has long lasting implications for the artist.

Though clear marking of boundary lines is difficult when discussing individual musicians and bands within the central Plains territories, one commonality of Plains jazz emerges—performers were but a component part of an interrelated network of venues, bands, and musicians whose interactions, innovations, and exchange advanced jazz performance both within the region and the nation.

COUNTRY AND WESTERN MUSIC

The term *country and western music* denotes a form of commercial music that emerged in the first half of the twentieth century. Its origins rest in older styles of folk music in southern Appalachia and the American South. Appalachian culture spread westward with the expansion of the United States, with the result that the Great Plains region has been a significant contributor to the advancement of this musical style. Performers who are identified with the region include Garth Brooks, Vince Gill, Reba McIntire, Hoyt Axton, Ronnie Dunn, Toby Keith, Roy Clarke, Dwight Twilley, and Don King.

Country and western music in the hands of Great Plains musicians took on a very distinctive flavor that was often based around the lifestyle of Plains ranching. The American cowboy was therefore a prevalent image within Great Plains music making. One early brass band was the Dodge City Cowboy Band from Kansas, organized in the late 1870s–1880s. Donning cowboy hats and dressed in chaps, spurs, and pearl handled pistols, the group traveled the nation promoting the romantic cowboy heritage of the Plains. In the 1920s, Otto Gray and his Oklahoma Cowboys string band capitalized on the western cowboy image through nationwide tours and radio performances.

Another Oklahoman, Gene Autry (1907–1998), was perhaps most responsible for popularizing the cowboy mystique through song. In a chance encounter, Autry was

Western Swing in the Great Plains

Bob Wills (1905–1975) was born and raised in Kosse, Texas, where ranch dances and fiddle contests were important stimuli to the young Texas fiddler. Wills became the most visible promoter of western swing, a style representative of its south central Plains roots. Wills' most famous and longest-running band, the Texas Playboys, was dominated by guitar, string bass, and, as the main melody instrument, the fiddle. Schottisches and waltzes appeared in the band's repertory, courtesy of the heavy Czech-German influences in Texas, as did hints of the Latino musical culture common in the state. The melodic language and improvisatory spirit taken by the Playboys were heavily indebted, however, to the African American blues and jazz players of the region. Wills and his Texas Playboys took up residence in Tulsa, Oklahoma, in 1934 and became an integral part of Oklahoma social life through their radio show on KVOO and frequent live performances throughout the area. Wills' string-based jazz transferred easily to its new environment with a few adaptations. The song "Take Me Back to Texas" was given lyrics and renamed "Take Me Back to Tulsa." The novelty song "Cherokee Maiden" played on Tulsa's location within the Cherokee lands of northeastern Oklahoma, while the instrumental "Osage Stomp" alludes to Tulsa's close proximity to Osage Indian territory. The instrumental "Big Beaver" takes its name from a dance hall located in Osage territory and frequented by the Playboys. These songs and the more generalized "Oklahoma Rag" reached out to the band's adopted audience and attested to its connection with its new home.

The South Dakota–based country/rock/western swing Red Willow Band continued into the 1970s to promote the sounds of Wills and his Texas Playboys within its state and nationally through tours of the upper United States. Sioux Falls, South Dakota, also produced a western swing festival during this period. More recently, Kansan Elana Fremerman (fiddle) and Tulsa, Oklahoma, native Jake Erwin (bass) and their national touring group, the Hot Club of Cowtown, have mixed western swing and the French hot jazz of Django Reinhardt.

On a larger scale, Wills and his Texas Playboys were among the first to popularize the use of drums, electric guitars, and Hawaiian/pedal steel guitars in country music. In recognition of these accomplishments, Wills was inducted into the Country Music Hall of Fame in 1968.

encouraged by Oklahoma comedian Will Rogers (1879–1935) to perform his cowboy songs on the radio. Autry followed his advice and went on to find fame as a star of radio, the recording industry, film, and television. The music and image of the old West continues to fascinate much of the Great Plains. North Dakota, South Dakota, Nebraska, Kansas, and Oklahoma each support performers and a state Western Music Association that continues to perpetuate the music of the American West and the cowboy. The influence of Gene Autry and his cowboy persona is still evident in the music of many prominent songwriters, including Marty Robbins, who collaborated with Nebraska musician/song writer Joe Babcock for many years.

Woody Guthrie (1912–1967) was born in Okemah, Oklahoma, into a family of Scots-Irish descent. Although he is often labeled simply a "folk" singer, his music is indebted to the traditions that formed the basis of country music and bluegrass. While the label "folk singer" emphasizes Guthrie's link to a historical past, his music was at the time of its creation very contemporary. Guthrie's music can best be understood within the cultural context of the geography and politics of Oklahoma, the depression and the Dust Bowl of the 1930s, the growing power of the Communist message during the 1930s and 1940s, the horrors of World War II, and many other news events that marked the landscape of Guthrie's tumultuous lifetime.

Guthrie wrote songs about the American experience, both good and bad. His song "This Land Is Your Land," originally titled "God Blessed America" at the time of its penning, exemplifies this approach clearly. The song was written on February 23, 1940, as a counterpoint to Irving Berlin's "God Bless America," which Guthrie believed too transparent in its patriotism. Regardless, Guthrie's national-

Sioux Falls JazzFest includes two stages and two days of free music and fun each July. Top-name entertainment, a children's area, rides, games, arts and crafts, fireworks, and more than twenty food vendors fill Yankton Trails Park. Courtesy South Dakota Tourism.

istic love of his country is apparent in his lyrics: "I saw below me that golden valley. . . . This land was made for you and me."

"This Land Is Your Land" is considered by many as an unofficial national anthem, and it continues to be popularly taught, in truncated form, to young children in public schools as a result of the tune's simplicity and optimism. Yet within the same song, Guthrie recognized the need to continue efforts to improve life within his own country: "As they stood there hungry / I stood there wondering if / This land was made for you and me."

While Guthrie's optimism and pride in his homeland are infectious, his keen eye for critique and political associations with the Communist left remain problematic. The unease between the state of Oklahoma and one of its greatest champions remains. A movement

Folk musician Woody Guthrie. Courtesy Library of Congress.

was mounted as late as 1999, in part a reaction against Guthrie's politics, to have "Home of Woody Guthrie" struck from the Okemah water tower. At the same time, 1998 was the inaugural year for the local Okemah Woody Guthrie Folk Festival.

Regardless, the music of Guthrie remains a portrait of America during some of its most difficult times in the twentieth century. Guthrie's skills as a musician, lyricist, documenter, commentator, artist, and personality continue to influence musicians such as his son Arlo Guthrie, Bob Dylan, Bruce Springsteen, Ani DiFranco, Billy Bragg, and Wilco. Wilco's 1998 "Mermaid Avenue" collaboration with Billy Bragg was a popular hit and brought Woody Guthrie's name to a new generation.

New bands and music scenes continue to pop up throughout the region. Localized bands such as Jimmy Crew (Yankton, South Dakota), Cactus Hill (Lincoln, Nebraska), Wildfire (Omaha, Nebraska), and No Justice (Stillwater, Oklahoma) ensure the vitality of country and western music.

Most recently, the sound of the Red Dirt movement, named for the red-clay earth of the Oklahoma landscape, has been dominating new country and western music in Oklahoma. Bands include Cross Canadian Ragweed, Jimmy LaFave, the Burtschi Brothers, Red Dirt Rangers, Jason Bolan and the Stragglers, Bob Childers, and Stony Larue and the Organic Boogie Band. Clubs such as the Red Dirt Café (Norman), the Wormy Dog Saloon (Stillwater), and the legendary Cain's Ballroom (Tulsa) provide venues for performance. Radio stations KVOO (Tulsa) and KMMZ ("The Bull," Oklahoma City) promote the sound to larger audiences than can typically make it to a bar show. Evident as early as the musical fusions of South Dakota's Red Willow Band, the phenomenon of "alternative country" musical creation is still prevalent throughout the Great Plains states and is perpetuated today in the continued innovations of music artists such as those associated with the Oklahoma Red Dirt movement and Kansas City's Rex Hobart and the Misery Boys.

BLUEGRASS

Unlike contemporary country music, bluegrass remains relatively fixed in instrumentation. It is usually rendered with harmonies emphasizing high, nasalized vocals (called the "high lonesome sound") accompanied by bass, with solo instrumentalists on banjo, fiddle or resophonic guitar, and mandolin. While bluegrass is based on older "traditional" forms, it emerged as a distinct substyle of country music in the late 1940s and 1950s, and its origins are typically attributed to the music of Kentuckian Bill Monroe (1911–1996) and his band, the Blue Grass Boys. Radio performances by Bill Monroe from Omaha, Nebraska, or nearby Shenandoah, Iowa, in the early 1930s are responsible in part for the popularity of the bluegrass style within the Great Plains region. These AM signals, with the benefit of a good, clear night, could be received nationwide. Bluegrass and country music are rooted in ideas of past, tradition, and often rural philosophical and religious values. Due to economic change following the depression years, both musical forms accompanied their supporters into new regions and urban locales. For this reason, the bluegrass sound is often inflected with elements of jazz improvisation and blues, as well as older "folk" forms.

Oklahoma maintains one of the more robust bluegrass communities within the region, with the greatest concentration of performers, bands, and festivals occupying the eastern half of the state. Events are promoted by the Oklahoma Bluegrass Club, the Green Country Bluegrass Club, and the Greater Oklahoma Bluegrass Music Society. The state is home to several renowned performers. Billy Joe Foster toured with Bill Monroe and played fiddle for country artist Ricky Skaggs. Guthrie, Oklahoma, resident and regional fiddle guru Byron Berline played with Bill Monroe and his Bluegrass Boys, as well as with artists Graham Parsons, James Taylor, Bob Dylan, the Byrds, and the Rolling Stones. Berline is claimed by Kansans as well, since he grew up and shaped his musical chops in Caldwell, Kansas.

Bluegrass performance in Kansas is centered in the southern part of the state around Wichita, and secondarily around the Kansas City metropolitan area. Kansan Jack Theobald introduced the bluegrass style to Kansas in the late 1960s. With his son Mike Theobald on banjo and fiddle, he formed the band Jack Theobald and the Bluegrass Country Boys. The Kansas Bluegrass Association was founded in the early 1970s. In combination with the Kansas Prairie Pickers Association, the current number of registered bluegrass enthusiasts within the state is more than four hundred. Out-of-state excursions are common for Kansas enthusiasts, who often travel to Missouri, northeastern Oklahoma, or nearby Iowa to attend festivals.

In Nebraska, most bluegrass activity occurs outside of any formal organizations. Nebraska has its share of local bluegrass bands, including the Kenaston Family (Weston), Golden Harvest (Omaha), and the Bald Mountain Rounders (Chadron). Deejay Al Weekley broadcasts a radio show that highlights bluegrass, gospel, and other forms of traditional music in Lexington, Nebraska, every weekend, as he has done since 1998.

The Friends of Traditional Music in South Dakota provides a forum for blue-grass musicians to meet, learn, and promote traditional performances in the state. The Black Hills Bluegrass Festival has been an annual venue for performance in southwestern South Dakota since its inception in 1980. Though the local group Black Hills Bluegrass Band was highlighted during the early years of this festival, the majority of the bluegrass performers were imported from outside the state.

North Dakota's bluegrass community is smaller than its southern Plains counterparts. Performers tend to live and practice the bluegrass style within their state, though residents near the eastern border frequent festivals in Minnesota. Because radio signals from southern radio stations once reached into North Dakota, blue-grass has been present in the state since the 1940s.

A recent resurgent interest in the bluegrass style has been noted by many Great Plains performers. As younger audiences become aware of roots music through alternative country formats, many are guided to the sounds that originally inspired these new musical trends. The renewed appeal of this genre to younger audiences may be encouraged by the greater accessibility of bluegrass music through MP3 Internet file sharing, and the Great Plains along with the world at large was recently reminded of the flavor and energy inherent in the bluegrass sound through the popular soundtrack to the Coen brothers' movie *O Brother, Where Art Thou?* (2000).

PLAINS INDEPENDENT POP/ROCK MUSIC

Rock and pop music forms have permeated the central Plains region since the earliest formative days of the rock-and-roll style. The basic instrumental foundation for Plains rock may include vocals (often multipart), guitar (sometimes with lead and rhythm parts), bass guitar, and drums. This instrumentation is flexible, and parts are frequently omitted or expanded. Other elaborating voices, such as keyboards, violin, cello, pedal steel guitar, or horns and reeds, may be used to supplement the instrumentation.

The strongest regional music scenes are typically situated around the major state economic centers or in university towns. The dense populations in regional centers allow for a larger base of musicians for collaborative band efforts and also, because of greater audience demand and venue choice, optimize the potential for economic success. Major university towns throughout America have long provided a foundation for rock and pop musical creativity. Other university music scenes have nurtured local music talent, producing national stars from small town college bands such as R.E.M., Pavement, and the Squirrel Nut Zippers. The university-band phenomenon is common throughout the Central Plains as well, with active rock/pop communities present in Norman, Oklahoma (the University of Oklahoma), Lincoln and Omaha Nebraska (University of Nebraska), and Lawrence, Kansas (University of Kansas).

Movement away from the region may indicate a shifting of regional allegiance, but if the artists were raised within the Plains and spent their formative, musical chop-building days in Nebraska, it is likely that this young experience was instrumental in shaping their musical perspective.

The university-band phenomenon is common throughout the Central Plains, with active rock/pop communities present in Norman, Oklahoma (the University

Great Plains Identity in Rock and Pop Lyrics

Central Plains musicians are products of their surrounding environment and culture, and the lyrical content is the most concrete vehicle for the expression of identity within their music. Among rock communities within the region, lyrics reflect individual, local community, or broader Plains identities in diverse ways. Local musician and University of Oklahoma student John Whitaker, for example, seizes upon the lighter, humorous aspects of Plains life in his university town, Norman, Oklahoma, in the composition "College Girl Love Song":

> I know you're thinking
> About our futures
> And it's wonderful to know that you are looking ahead
> But maybe instead
> Of staying in bed
> You'll blow off your dumb homework and just give it a rest
>
> And please don't write your paper
> It's just too many pages to write
> So please don't write your paper
> And just go out with me tonight
>
> I know of a fire out by Dan Pringle's
> And we could buy a dozen beers
> And fraternize with our friends
> But with the moonlight and starlight sparkles
> Well, we could also sneak away and just mug down for a bit

Whitaker's song is rendered with a single vocal line and guitar, bass, and drum accompaniment (with live drumming and campy, pre-programmed Casio keyboard rhythms). The lyrics are wryly humorous and, even though laced with some degree of personal sympathy, perhaps more absurd than earnest in its pleas: "And please don't write your paper / It's just too many pages to write." Sung in a Lou Reed–style monologue, the lyrics are spoken by a supportive boyfriend trying to subtly—perhaps sweetly, perhaps deviously—steer his girl away from what she *should* be doing, to what he *wants* her to do.

The composer, himself, finds little appealing about the song, noting that he was simply amused by the lyrical use of the word "fraternize" and that he liked the reference to his good friend in the second stanza. This makes the song interesting in several ways. The fact that this song has meaning to its writer simply because of the invocation of his friend's name—despite its context in humorous song—is revealing as a personal document of their longstanding friendship. Its lyrics are equally revealing of the relationship of the local university to Norman residents and musicians, as well as the unique sense of dead-pan humor held by some local musicians. Further, it indicates the impromptu and informal approach to independent recording sometimes taken by Plains musicians: the song was written and recorded on a four-track home recorder within minutes of composition, while the writer was trying to amuse himself.

This song is only one of many that represent some specific aspect of central Plains life. The lyrical material is diverse in character, covering sentiments from reflection, to frustration, to sarcasm. Plains performers have documented a spectrum of human sentiment in song and sung many stories about the places in their lives—the towns, the state, the geography, the history, or the weather. In the end, musicians are musicians because playing music is often a central element of their person. But, some of these musicians become *central* plains musicians through exploring the meanings of their time, place, and heritage, simply because a Plains identity is an equally important element of their personality.

of Oklahoma), Stillwater, Oklahoma (Oklahoma State University), Lincoln and Omaha, Nebraska (University of Nebraska) and Lawrence, Kansas (the University of Kansas).

Rapid City, South Dakota, is home to a folk-influenced singer/songwriter scene that is supported by local audiences, coffeehouses, and bars, a community group called Backroom Productions, an annual Black Hills Songwriters Invitational that promotes local performers through live shows, and airplay on the local radio program *House Blend*. Prominent performers include Steve Thorpe, Willy Grigg, and Andrea Potts.

Despite the fact that most Great Plains groups enjoy little or no support from the major-label recording industry, the production of studio recordings is a substantial component of band life. Access to recording equipment and technicians knowledgeable in their use are, therefore, also very important among musician communities. Musicians often record their own music in their home, using skills passed orally through the community, by intuition, or via Internet and literary research. Such efforts yield informal studios such as Alien Studios or Rock, Paper, Scissors (Norman, Oklahoma) that are usually promoted only through word of mouth, modest in technical means, and often affordable for local musicians. While many bands exercise this ability to record themselves, a group will sometimes enlist one of the numerous professional studios prevalent throughout the Plains, such as Bell Labs Recording (Norman, Oklahoma), Black Lodge Recording (Eudora, Kansas), or Presto! (Lincoln, Nebraska).

The Plains is also home to a number of independent recording labels. Though funding for band support, record distribution, and promotion is often limited in comparison to the major industry labels, smaller regional labels offer more exposure than the performer could otherwise expect by marketing their albums on their own. Most Plains states offer band support through labels such as Little Mafia Records in Oklahoma City, Noisome Records in Lawrence, Kansas, or Saddle Creek Records in Omaha, Nebraska.

Support communities are necessary for the continuation of these localized music scenes, so local clubs, bars, and coffeeshops, audiences, organizations, Internet communities, music stores, recording studios, record stores, and festival organizers create the infrastructure necessary to perpetuate local music production. Because of geographic isolation from the national recording industry, Plains performers of yesterday and today—in a tradition as apparent during the time of Kansas City jazz performer Bennie Moten as now—have relied on their own resources and independent record production to create music modest in distribution, but considerable in diversity and innovation.

CLASSICAL MUSIC

The Great Plains region is home to an active classical music scene. Professional symphony orchestras can be found in each of the major cities in these states, and several important composers and performers in American classical music have called this region home. The world of classical music in these states also extends to the areas of world-class instrument making and dance. Innovations involving classical music have taken place here as well, with the popular group Mannheim Steamroller of Omaha, Nebraska, experimenting with combinations of musical styles.

Composition

The composers of the Great Plains are a diverse group, representing several ethnic groups and several different avenues of the classical music field in their compositional careers. Between them, the musical genres covered range from military band music to opera to television soundtracks.

Roy Harris (1898–1979) was born near Chandler, Oklahoma Territory, in 1898, and until 1903, he was raised on land his father had claimed in one of the last land rushes in the Panhandle. Harris became one of the most important figures in establishing American symphonic music as a rival to the European tradition. In the 1940s, Harris was regarded as an equal candidate with Aaron Copland for the mantle of the "great American symphonist." His nationalistic style was developed in his studies with fellow Americanist Arthur Farwell and in France with the famous pedagogue Nadia Boulanger. Harris composed more than two hundred works, including choral music, a ballet, and a film score, but his symphonies and his chamber music have received the most acclaim. Harris used folk tunes in his works, calling upon American images in programmatic works that were often centered on patriotic occasions, folk legends, and American idealists such as Walt Whitman and Abraham Lincoln. His promotion of American composers through organizations like the Composers' Forum-Laboratory in New York and through international festivals is a significant contribution to the cause of American classical music.

Louis Ballard (b. 1931) was born in Miami, Oklahoma, and grew up with the traditional music of his Quapaw and Cherokee heritage. In addition, Ballard has studied the music and dance traditions of many tribes. His mother learned to play the piano at a Baptist mission school and gave Ballard his first music lessons, teaching him to play her own compositions, which were arrangements of Quapaw songs. Truly a bimusical student, Ballard studied composition at the University of Tulsa and in 1962 became the first Native American to earn a graduate degree in composition. He then pursued private lessons with Darius Milhaud and other famous composers. Ballard's compositional style involves creating a syncretic music in which Western elements combine with Native American musical aesthetics. His music employs Native American instruments in combination with Western instruments and uses forms, rhythms, scales, and phrasings from indigenous musical traditions. Ballard's works contrast with those of composers who have used Native melodies simply as novel sources for tunes and have forced them to conform to the Western musical rules without much of an interchange between the two aesthetic worlds. Ballard has published several books on the educational uses

Thurlow Lieurance sitting with Native American musicians. Courtesy Library of Congress.

of Native American musics, and in 1984, he was nominated for a Pulitzer Prize for his *Fantasy Aborigine IV.*[6]

Thurlow Lieurance (1878–1963) was born in Iowa, but spent the majority of his life in Kansas, where his first music instruction was from his bandmaster uncle, who taught him to play cornet. Lieurance began composing at a very early age, and his first work, written at age eleven, was still in print as late as 1940. In 1903, Lieurance visited the Crow Reservation in Montana. This experience sparked his lifelong interest in Native American music and cultures. The first of his many field recordings of Native American music from thirty-three different tribes dates from 1911, and the collection now resides in the Archive of Folk Culture at the Library of Congress. Lieurance also collected Native American flutes, and around half of his compositions use flute songs as their basic material. The majority of Lieurance's works were composed for piano and voice, but he often featured the Native American flutes in his collection in combination with the European orchestral flute. Among his other compositions are five large-scale orchestral works, an oratorio, vocal octavo arrangements, and piano-violin-flute-clarinet ensembles. *Minisa*, one of his large-scale works, won a Presser award, but his most famous piece is *By the Waters of Minnetonka.*

N. Clark Smith (1877–1933) was born in Fort Leavenworth, Kansas, and had a distinguished career as a conductor, composer, and music educator. In 1898, he was appointed conductor of the Eighth Illinois Regiment Band on the basis of his experience conducting amateur bands and teaching music in Wichita. The next year he traveled to the Pacific and to London on tour with the M. B. Curtis All-Star Afro-American Minstrels. During his stay in London, Smith studied at the Guildhall School of Music, and he continued his education at the Chicago Musical College when he returned to the United States in 1901. In Chicago, Smith was very active in the city's music scene, organizing three new ensembles himself: Smith's Mandolin and String Instruments Club, the N. Clark Smith Ladies' Orchestra, and a symphony orchestra for African American musicians, possibly the first ensemble of this kind in the nation. His compositions include works for piano, arrangements of spirituals, and the *Negro Choral Symphony*, which was written for the 1933 Chicago World's Fair. Following his accomplishments outside of the Plains, Smith returned to Kansas, and his musical legacy was carried on by his students, Bennie Moten and Walter Page, among others.

Howard Hanson (1896–1981) is perhaps the most famous classical composer to come from the Great Plains region. Born in Wahoo, Nebraska, Hanson was of Swedish ancestry, and he studied at Luther College in Wahoo before going on to the Institute of Musical Art and Northwestern University. In 1921, Hanson won the prestigious Prix de Rome for his composition *California Forest Play 1920* and was the first American composer to go to Rome on this prize. In Rome, he studied with Ottorino Respighi, whom Hanson credited for developing his skills in orchestration. Hanson was a neo-romantic composer, and during the mid-twentieth century, he was considered America's best composer of large-scale, sweeping, romantic works. According to Hanson, his major influences were Sibelius and Grieg, whose compositions inspired his lyrical and harmonic style. Hanson's conducting career is notable; he directed major symphony orchestras, including the Boston Symphony and the New York Symphony Orchestra, frequently composing works specifically for these occasions. Hanson won a Pulitzer Prize for his Symphony No. 4 and was awarded thirty-six honorary degrees from American institutions.

Hanson's connection to his Scandinavian heritage and to his home in the Plains is demonstrated through his preference for Scandinavian composers such as Sibelius and Grieg. He was inducted into the Royal Swedish Academy of Music, and his hometown of Wahoo still bears a large sign by the road, proudly claiming Hanson for the town and the region.[7]

Felix Vinatieri (1834–1891) was born not in the Great Plains, but in Turin, Italy. By the age of ten, he was a skilled violinist, and he graduated from the Conservatorio di Musica San Pietro a Majella in Naples in 1853. In 1859, Vinatieri immigrated to the United States, and enlisted with American military bands in Boston and New York, serving during the Civil War before being discharged out west in 1870. He settled in Yankton, South Dakota, during the same period that General George Custer's Seventh Regiment of Cavalry was arriving to explore the Black Hills. Vinatieri led the music at a ball that was given in Custer's honor, and Custer, a music lover, was impressed with Vinatieri and offered him the job of chief musician with the regiment. Vinatieri accepted the position, not knowing that he would witness Custer's famous "last stand" at Little Big Horn on June 26, 1876. The musicians had to act as an emergency medical crew during the battle because they had been left behind on the boat and ordered not to join the fighting. As a composer, Vinatieri wrote the typical band fare of marches, waltzes, and mazurkas, but he also has the distinction of having composed the earliest American operas written west of the Mississippi. *The American Volunteer* and *The Barber of the Regiment* were patriotic light operas for which Vinatieri wrote not only the music, but also the complete libretto and stage directions. *The American Volunteer* received good reviews from the local press and was set to be presented by the composer at the Columbian World's Fair in Chicago in 1893, but unfortunately, Vinatieri died of pneumonia before this performance could take place.

Performers

The Plains region has been home to several acclaimed performers, particularly opera singers. Important Great Plains classical performers include distinguished opera singers Joseph Benton (1898–1975) from Oklahoma; Samuel Ramey (b. 1942), of Colby, Kansas, a bass and bass-baritone opera superstar; and Jess Thomas (1927–1993), born in Hot Springs, South Dakota, who became a well-known Wagnerian tenor. Phyllis Bryn-Julson (b. 1945), originally from Bowdon, North Dakota, is one of the leading performers of twentieth-century vocal music. Other notables include Richard Stoltzman (b. 1942), a highly regarded American clarinetist from Omaha, and David Wiebe, of David City, Nebraska, a world-class maker of stringed instruments, with a list of prominent clients, including Yehudi Menuhin and the Winton and Branford Marsalis Bands.

Tsianina Redfeather Blackstone (1882–1985), a mezzo-soprano of Cherokee/Creek heritage, was born in Indian Territory. By 1915, she had joined Indianist composer Charles Wakefield Cadman on a fourteen-year series of successful concert tours. Cadman's opera *Shanewis* was loosely based on Blackstone's life. It was unusual because it pre-

Classical Crossovers

Mannheim Steamroller, an ensemble based in Omaha, Nebraska, is world famous for its eclectic style. Often labeled "New Age," the music of Mannheim Steamroller defies categorization, but nonetheless is performed by classical musicians—often by members of the Chicago and London Symphonies—and combines elements from the Renaissance to jazz, rock, and electronic music. Composer and creator Chip Davis refers to the music as "18th century rock 'n' roll," and his albums often feature previously unrelated classical works united by a theme, as in *Yellowstone: The Music of Nature*, which contains works by Respighi, Debussy, and Vivaldi interspersed with those by Davis. *Yellowstone* was made in response to the 1988 fires that ravaged the national park, and the album's sales raised more than half a million dollars to help the rebuilding process. *Mannheim Steamroller Christmas*, an "updating" of traditional holiday songs, was released in 1984 and sold more than four million copies. Davis's composition career began when he began writing advertising jingles for an advertising agency in Omaha after the completion of his classical training in bassoon and composition. Failing to convince any record labels that his unique Mannheim Steamroller sound was marketable, Davis founded his own label, American Gramaphone. He received the Grammy for Best New Age Recording in 1990 for *Fresh Aire VII*.

Alf Clausen (b. 1941), composer, arranger, and conductor of music for television, spent his early years in North Dakota. After graduating from North Dakota State University, Clausen studied composition at Berklee College of Music in Boston. He went to Los Angeles to find work in show business. Clausen's interest in jazz and rock music had prepared him well for television work, and he landed a job as music director of the *Donny and Marie Show*. This job was followed by music director duties on the *Mary Tylor Moore Comedy Hour*, the Emmy Awards show, *Charlie's Angels*, and *Moonlighting* with Bruce Willis. His current job is on *The Simpsons*, an animated show in which music plays a key role. Clausen credits his hardworking North Dakota values for his ability to deal with the intense schedule of composing and recording music for twenty-four to twenty-eight prime-time episodes a year. Clausen's success has been recognized with twenty-two Emmy nominations, two of which he won, as well as a plethora of awards from ASCAP and other organizations.

sented a story about the current realities of Native American life, departing from the usual Indianist idealizations of an imagined Indian past. Blackstone performed the lead role in *Shanewis* at the Hollywood Bowl, but declined the opportunity to sing it at the Metropolitan Opera in New York, working instead as an advisor. After her retirement from the stage, Blackstone became an advocate for Indian rights, dedicating herself to improving education for American Indians.[8]

Arts Related to Musical Performance

Other natives of the Great Plains have made their mark on music and dance, including important instrument maker David Wiebe and Native American ballerinas. The extrodinary careers of Yvonne Chouteau (Shawnee/Creek/French, b. 1929), Rosella Hightower (Choctaw/Irish, b. 1920), Moscelyne Larkin (Shawnee/Peoria/Russian, b. 1926), Maria Tallchief (Osage/Scottish/Irish, b. 1925), and Marjorie Tallchief (Osage/Scottish/Irish, b. 1927), five ballerinas from Oklahoma, did much to establish the art of dance in the Great Plains. Each woman in this group is of Native American heritage, and they were all exposed to ballet through the midwestern tour of Les Ballets Russes de Monte Carlo. All except Marjorie Tallchief eventually joined this company; Marjorie declined the invitation to join because she would be competing with her sister Maria, already a member, for roles. Instead, Marjorie became the first American *première danseuse étoile* of the Paris Opera Ballet and was the first American to dance with the Paris Opera Ballet at the Bolshoi Theater in Moscow. In 1991, the five ballerinas were designated "Oklahoma Treasures" by the Oklahoma Arts Council.

CONCLUSION

The relative isolation of the Plains area in contrast to more urban centers in the United States has allowed musicians in this region to enjoy the freedom to musically define and develop their own identities. In the area of popular music, many bands face a choice of relocating to a more commercial center where they may achieve more popularity, but they then risk giving up their independence. In the realm of classical music, Americanist composers often draw images of their country's heroes, such as Roy Harris' Symphony No. 10, "Abraham Lincoln."

Polka bands from this region have found several ways of preserving their ethnic identity while simultaneously influencing and being influenced by mainstream music. Popular performers such as Lawrence Welk were primarily involved in dance bands that brought an awareness of polka music to an audience that would otherwise not have been exposed to this folk tradition.

A number of composers found inspiration in the music of Native American tribes, such as Thurlow Lieurance, whose composition *By the Waters of Minnetonka* was inspired by a Sioux love song he recorded in 1911 at a Crow reservation in Montana. Similarly, Bob Wills utilized Native American and Oklahoman themes in a number of his songs, such as "Cherokee Maiden." A list of Native American flute players from the Great Plains area includes the strictly traditional player Doc Tate Nevaquaya and contemporary musician Tom Mauchahty Ware, who negotiates the boundaries of the older traditional style of

Native flute playing and the crossover to the syncretic music of his band, Blues Nation.

The blending of elements from the many different cultures that settled in the Plains area alongside the Native population has resulted in a musical mosaic. The Great Plains region, once the frontier of this country, is now and has historically been receptive to freedom of expression and individual creativity, which is readily apparent in the variety of music that characterizes this area.

RESOURCE GUIDE

Printed Sources

Andersen, Mark, and Mark Jenkins. *Dance of Days: Two Decades of Punk in the Nation's Capital.* New York: Soft Skull Press, 2001.

Babcock, C. Merton. "Czech Songs in Nebraska." *Western Folklore* 8 (1949): 320–327.

Benton, Joseph. *Oklahoma Tenor: Musical Memories of Giuseppe Bentonelli.* Norman: University of Oklahoma Press, 1973.

Boyd, Jean A. *The Jazz of the Southwest: An Oral History of Western Swing.* Austin: University of Texas Press, 1998.

Browner, Tara. *Heartbeat of the People: Music and Dance of the Northern Pow-wow.* Urbana: University of Illinois Press, 2002.

———. "Transposing Cultures: The Appropriation of Native North American Musics, 1890–1990." Ph.D. diss., University of Michigan, 1995; Ann Arbor: Michigan University Microfilms, 1997.

Burton, Bryan. *Moving within the Circle.* Danbury: World Music Press, 1993.

Cantwell, Robert. *Bluegrass Breakdown: The Making of the Old Southern Sound.* New York: Da Capo Press, 1992.

———. *When We Were Good: The Folk Revival.* Cambridge, MA: Harvard University Press, 1996.

Carney, George O. *The Sounds of People and Places: A Geography of American Music from Country to Classical and Blues to Bop.* 4th ed. Lanham, MD: Rowman and Littlefield, 2003.

Chinn, Jennie A., and Carl R. Magnuson. "Don Lipovac: Button Box Accordian." In *American Musical Traditions,* ed. Jeff Todd Titon and Bob Carlin, 86–90. New York: Schirmer Reference, 2002.

Conlon, Paula. *Doc Tate Nevaquaya: Master Comanche Artist and Flute Player.* Norman: University of Oklahoma Press, in press.

———. "The Flute of the Canadian Amerindian: An Analysis of the Vertical Whistle Flute with External Block and Its Music." M.A. thesis, Carleton University, 1983.

———. "The Native American Flute: Convergence and Collaboration as Exemplified by R. Carlos Nakai." *World of Music* 44, no 1 (2002): 61–74.

Gann, Kyle. *American Music in the Twentieth Century.* New York: Schirmer Books, 1997.

Garofalo, Reebee. *Rockin' Out: Popular Music in the USA.* Upper Saddle River, NJ: Prentice Hall, 2002.

Ginell, Cary. *Milton Brown and the Founding of Western Swing.* Urbana: University of Illinois Press, 1994.

Greene, Victor. *A Passion for Polka: Old-Time Ethnic Music in America.* Berkeley: University of California Press, 1992.

Grover, Barbara. "Bluegrass in the Black Hills." *Bluegrass Unlimited* 23 (June 1989): 73–75.

Hensley, Betty Austin. *Thurlow Lieurance Indian Flutes.* Vida, OR: Oregon Flute Store, 2002.

Hesmondhalgh, David. "Post-Punk's Attempt to Democratise the Music Industry: The Successes and Failure of Rough Trade." *Popular Music* 16, no. 3 (October 1997): 255–274.

Heth, Charlotte, ed. *Native American Dance: Ceremonies and Social Traditions.* Golden, CO: Fulcrum Publishing, 1992.

Hitchcock, H. Wiley, and Stanley Sadie, eds. *The New Grove Dictionary of American Music.* London: Macmillan, 1986.

Kansas City Museum. *Kansas City . . . and All That's Jazz.* Kansas City, MO: Andrews McNeel, 1999.

Keeling, Richard. *North American Indian Music: A Guide to Published Sources and Selected Recordings.* New York: Garland Publishing, 1997.

Keil, Charles, and Angeliki V. Keil. *Polka Happiness.* Philadelphia: Temple University Press, 1992.

Klein, Joe. *Woody Guthrie: A Life.* New York: Dell Publishing, 1980.

Koskoff, Ellen, ed. *The Garland Encyclopedia of World Music: The United States and Canada.* New York: Garland Publishing, 2001.

Kuhn, Laura. *Baker's Dictionary of Opera.* New York: Schirmer Books, 2000. S.v. "Bentonelli (real name Benton), Joseph (Horace)."

Larkin, Colin. *The Encyclopedia of Popular Music.* 3rd ed. London: MUZE UK, 1998. S.v. "Mannheim Steamroller."

———, ed. *The Guinness Encyclopedia of Popular Music.* London: Guinness Publishing, 1995. S.v. "Welk, Lawrence."

Lassiter, Luke E. *The Power of Kiowa Song.* Tucson: University of Arizona Press, 1998.

Laubin, Reginald, and Gladys Laubin. *Indian Dances of North America.* Norman: University of Oklahoma Press, 1977.

Leary, James P. "Czech Polka Styles in the U.S.: From America's Dairyland to the Lone Star State." In *Czech Music in Texas: A Sesquicentennial Symposium*, ed. Clinton Machann, 79–95. College Station, TX: Komensky Press, 1988.

Levinson, David, and Melvin Ember, eds. *American Immigrant Cultures: Builders of a Nation.* New York: Macmillan Reference USA, 1997.

Livingston, Lili Cockerille. *American Indian Ballerinas.* Norman: University of Oklahoma Press, 1997.

Machann, Clinton. "Country-Western Music and the 'Now' Sound in Texas-Czech Polka Music." *JEMF Quarterly* 19, no. 69 (1983): 3–7.

Macy, L. *The New Grove Dictionary of Music Online.* http://www.grovemusic.com (accessed July 9, 2003).

McDaniel, Laura. "D'oh!-re-mi: North Dakota Makes Music for 'The Simpsons.'" *North Dakota State University Magazine.* http://www.ndsu.edu/ndsu/news/magazine/vol03_issue02/doh_re_mi.shtml (accessed July 29, 2003).

Nakai, R. Carlos, and James De Mars. *The Art of the Native American Flute.* With additional material by David P. McAllester, Ph.D., and flute maker Ken Light. Phoenix, AZ: Canyon Records Productions, 1996.

Partridge, Elizabeth. *This Land Was Made for You and Me: The Life and Songs of Woody Guthrie.* New York: Viking Publishing, 2002.

Payne, Richard W. *The Native American Plains Flute.* Oklahoma City: Toubat Trails Publishing Company, 1999.

Pearson, Nathan W. *Goin' to Kansas City.* Urbana: University of Illinois Press, 1987.

Pedeliski, Theodore. "The Poles in North Dakota: A Brief History." In *Festival of Ethnic Musical Traditions in North Dakota, University of North Dakota, June 17–19, 1983*, ed. Tamar C. Read. Grand Forks: University of North Dakota, 1983.

Reid, Brian Holden, and John White. *American Studies: Essays in Honour of Marcus Cunliffe.* New York: St. Martin's Press, 1991.

Roberts, Chris. *Powwow Country.* Helena, MT: American and World Geographic Publishing, 1992.

———. *Powwow Country: People of the Circle*. Missoula, MT: Meadowlark Publishing Company, 1998.

Russell, Ross. *Jazz Style in Kansas City and the Southwest*. Berkeley: University of California Press, 1971.

Sabin, Roger, ed. *Punk Rock: So What?* London: Routledge Press, 1999.

Savage, William W., Jr. *Singing Cowboys and All That Jazz: A Short History of Popular Music in Oklahoma*. Norman: University of Oklahoma Press, 1983.

Sheldon, Ruth. *Bob Wills: Hubbin' It*. Nashville: Country Music Foundation Press, 1995.

Slonimsky, Nicolas, and Laura Kuhn, eds. *Baker's Biographical Dictionary of Musicians*. Centennial [9th] ed. New York: Schirmer Books, 2001. S.v. "Welk, Lawrence (LeRoy)," by William Ruhlmann.

Spotted Eagle, Douglas. *Voices of Native America: Instruments and Music*. Liberty, UT: Eagle's View Publishing, 1997.

Titon, Jeff Todd, and Bob Carlin, eds. *American Musical Traditions*. Vol. 1, *Native American Music*. New York: Schirmer, 2002.

Townsend, Charles R. *San Antonio Rose: The Life and Music of Bob Wills*. Urbana: University of Illinois Press, 1976.

Wapp, Edward Wahpeconiah. "The Sioux Courting Flute: Its Tradition, Construction, and Music." M.A. thesis, University of Washington, 1984.

Welk, Lawrence, and Bernice McGeehan. *Wunnerful, Wunnerful: The Autobiography of Lawrence Welk*. Englewood Cliffs, NJ: Prentice-Hall, 1971.

Westermeier, Clifford P. "The Dodge City Cowboy Band." *Kansas Historical Quarterly*. http://www.kshs.org/publicat/khq/1951/51_1_westermeier.htm (accessed August 31, 2003).

White, Julia. *The Powwow Trail: Understanding and Enjoying the Native American Powwow*. Summertown, TN: Book Publishing Company, 1996.

Wiebe, David. *David Wiebe: Violinmaker*. http://www.violoncello.com/index.htm (accessed July 29, 2003).

Wills, Rosetta. *The King of Western Swing: Bob Wills Remembered*. New York: Billboard Books, 1998.

Wolfe, Charles. *The Devil's Box*. Nashville: Vanderbilt University Press, 1997.

Wright, Muriel H. *A Guide to the Indian Tribes of Oklahoma*. Norman: University of Oklahoma Press, 1951, 1986.

Zotigh, Dennis W. *Moving History: The Evolution of the Powwow*. Available at http://www.ok-history.mus.ok.us/folk/movinghistory.html (accessed August 1, 2003).

Web Sites
Native American Music

Cunningham, Don, "An Art within a Craft"
http://justuskids.com/Wiebe.htm (accessed August 9, 2003)

http://www.powersource.com/gallery/powwow/ (accessed June 4, 2004)
Information on Julia White's book *The Pow Wow Trail*.

International Native American Flute Association
http://www.worldflutes.org/ (accessed June 4, 2004)
Information on the Native American flute.

National Music Museum Vinatieri Archive
http://www.usd.edu/smm/vinatieri.html (accessed July 29, 2003)

Nativeculture.com
http://www.nativeculture.com (accessed June 4, 2004)
Links to a variety of information sites about Native American culture.

PowWows.com
http://www.powwows.com/ (accessed June 4, 2004)
Information on powwow dances and background material.

Wapp, Edward Wahpeconiah, Comanche/Sac and Fox, *The American Indian Courting Flute: Revitalization and Change*
http://www.msstate.edu/Fineart_Online/Gallery/Trophies/wapp.htm (accessed July 11, 2003)

Polka

International Polka Association
http://www.internationalpolka.com/ (accessed August 31, 2003)

National Polka Festival: Mark Vhylidal Band
http://nationalpolkafestival.com/vyhlidalband.htm (accessed July 21, 2003)

Jazz

Kansas City Jazz Museum
http://www.americanjazzmuseum.com/ (accessed June 4, 2004)

Saddle Creek (Independent Pop)
http://www.saddlecreekrecords.com (accessed June 4, 2004)

Vagrant (Independent Pop)
http://www.vagrant.com (accessed June 4, 2004)

Western Music Association
http://www.westernmusic.org (accessed June 4, 2004)

Other

Mannheim Steamroller
http://www.amgram.com/html/home.html (accessed July 31, 2003)

Samuel Ramey
http://www.samuelramey.com/biography.html (accessed July 31, 2003)

Woody Guthrie Foundation and Archives
http://woodyguthrie.org (accessed June 4, 2004)

Videos/Films

Into the Circle: An Introduction to Native American Powwows. Full Circle Videos. 1992.
Native American Men's and Women's Dance Styles. Volumes 1 and 2. Powwow, Gourd Dance, Hoop Dance. Full Circle Videos. 1993 and 1995.
Songkeepers. Native American flute, including Kevin Locke and Sonny Nevaquaya. Lake Forest, IL. International Native American Flute Association. 1999.

Recordings

Bennie Moten's Kansas City Orchestra, 1923–27. Melodie Jazz Classic, 1996.
Deeper Polka: More Dance Music from the Midwest. Smithsonian Folkways 40140, 2002.
The Get Up Kids. *On a Wire.* Vagrant Records, 2002.
Guthrie, Woody. *This Land Is Your Land: The Asch Recordings.* Vol. 1. Smithsonian/Folkways Records, 1997.
Kiowa Gourd Dance: Volume 1. Indian House Records IH 2503, 1974.
Love Songs of the Lakota. Kevin Locke, Native American flute. Indian House Records IH 4315, 1982.
Mannheim Steamroller. *Yellowstone: The Music of Nature.* American Gramaphone Records, 1989.
McCall, C. W. *Black Bear Road.* MGM Records, 1975.
Monroe, Bill, and the Bluegrass Boys. *Off the Record.* Vol. 1, *Live Recordings, 1956–69.* Smithsonian/Folkways Records, 1993.
Yellowhammer—Live at Hollywood, Florida. Southern Plains powwow. Indian House Records IH-2016, 1995.

Music Festivals

Kansas

Country Stampede
Tuttle Creek State Park
2319 Tuttle Creek Blvd.
Manhattan, KS 66502
http://www.countrystampede.com/manhattan/about.html

Fiesta Mexicana
Our Lady of Guadelupe Church
1008 NE Atchison
Topeka, KS
http://www.olg-parish.org/Pages/fiesta.HTM

Walnut Valley Festival
P.O. Box 245
918 Main
Winfield, KS 67156
http://wvfest.com/index.html

Nebraska

Annual National Country Music Festival
Ainsworth Area Chamber of Commerce
335 North Main
Ainsworth, NE 69210
http://www.loc.gov/bicentennial/propage/NE/ne_s_hagel2.html

Wilber Czech Festival
Wilber, NE
Phone: 1-888-4-WILBER
http://www.ci.wilber.ne.us/festival_events.htm

Winnebago Powwow Annual Homecoming Celebration
Veterans' Memorial Park

Highway 75
Winnebago, NE 68071
http://www.winnebagotribe.com/powwow2.htm

North Dakota

International Old-Time Fiddlers Contest
International Peace Garden
1725 11th Street SW
Minot, ND 58701
Phone: 701-838-8472

Norsk Høstfest
Box 1347
Minot, ND 58702
http://www.hostfest.com/index.html

United Tribes Powwow
United Tribes Technical College
3315 University Drive
Bismarck, ND 58504
http://www.unitedtribespowwow.com/

Oklahoma

OK Mozart Festival
PO Box 2344
Bartlesville, OK 74005
http://www.okmozart.com/default.asp

Oklahoma Czech Festival
205 N. Czech Hall Rd.
Yukon, OK 73099
http://www.czechhall.com

Oklahoma's International Bluegrass Festival
PO Box 1585
Guthrie, OK 73044
http://oibf.com/

Red Earth
Oklahoma State Fair Park
State Fair Arena
333 Gordon Cooper Boulevard
Oklahoma City, OK 73107
http://www.redearth.org/RE.htm

Woody Guthrie Folk Festival
Pastures of Plenty, Okemah, OK
The Woody Guthrie Coalition, Inc.
PO Box 661
Okemah, OK 74859
http://www.woodyguthrie.com/main2.htm

South Dakota

Corn Palace Festival
World's Only Corn Palace
Main Street
Mitchell, SD 57301
http://www.cornpalacefestival.com/index.html

Deadwood Jam
Deadwood Chamber of Commerce and Visitors Bureau
735 Main Street
Deadwood, SD 57762
http://www.deadwoodjam.com/default.htm

Sioux Falls Jazz and Blues Festival
Sioux Falls Convention and Visitors Bureau
200 N. Phillips Avenue, Ste. 102
Sioux Falls, SD 57104
http://www.sfjb.org/

Research Collections and Museums

Kansas

Lawrence

University of Kansas
Department of Music and Dance
1530 Naismith Drive, Rm. 460
Lawrence, KS 66045-3102
Phone: 785-864-3436
http://www.ku.edu/~sfa/mad/facilities.html#archive

University of Kansas Libraries
Department of Special Collections
Kenneth Spencer Research Library
1450 Poplar Lane
Lawrence, KS 66045-7616
Phone: 785-864-5803
http://spencer.lib.ku.edu/sc/

The Kenneth Spencer Research Library has a collection of music from radio programs in 1933–34 that featured Gershwin presenting his own music. This library also holds music books of the early nineteenth century, as well as the papers, including songs and lyrics, of vaudeville performer Roger Imhof. Early editions of music by George Gershwin, Irving Berlin, and Jerome Kern are held in the Henry M. Katzman Collection.

Manhattan

Kansas State University Libraries
Manhattan, KS 66506
Phone: 785-532-3014
http://www.lib.ksu.edu/depts/spec/rarebooks/stratton.html

Topeka

Kansas State Historical Society
6425 SW Sixth Ave.
Topeka, KS 66615
Phone: 785-272-8681
http://www.kshs.org/

Wichita

Wichita State University Libraries
1845 Fairmount
Wichita, KS 67260-0068
Phone: 316-978-3590
http://specialcollections.wichita.edu/collections/index.html

Nebraska

Lincoln

Nebraska State Historical Society
1500 R Street
Lincoln, NE 68501
Phone: 402-471-4751
http://www.nebraskahistory.org/

Plains Humanities Alliance
1221 Seaton Hall
University of Nebraska–Lincoln
Lincoln, NE 68588-0692
Phone: 402-472-9478
http://www.unl.edu/rcplains/index.html

University of Nebraska–Lincoln Library
13th and R Streets
Lincoln, NE 68588-4100
Phone: 402-472-2531
http://www.unl.edu/libr/libs/spec/botkin.html

Red Cloud

Nebraska State Historical Society Willa Cather Historical Center
Box 326
Red Cloud, NE 68970
Phone: 402-746-2653
http://www.casde.unl.edu/history/counties/webster/redcloud/redcloud.htm

Wilber

Dvoracek Memorial Library
419 W. Third Street
Wilber, NE 68465
Phone: 402-821-2832
http://saline.unl.edu/library.htm

North Dakota

Bismarck

North Dakota State Historical Society
612 E. Boulevard Ave.
Bismarck, ND 58505-0830
Phone: 701-328-2091
http://www.state.nd.us/hist/index.html

Fargo

Institute for Regional Studies
Skills and Technology Training Center, Rm. 117
1305 19th Avenue North
Fargo, ND 58105-5599
Phone: 701-231-8914
http://www.lib.ndsu.nodak.edu/ndirs/collections/manuscripts/lit&music/index.html

Grand Forks

University of North Dakota Chester Fritz Library
Department of Special Collections
University Ave. and Centennial Drive
Grand Forks, ND 58202
Phone: 701-777-4625
http://www.und.edu/dept/library/Collections/music.html

Oklahoma

Lawton

Percussive Arts Society Museum
701 N. Ferris Ave.
Lawton, OK 73507
Phone: 580-353-1455
http://www.pas.org/Museum/index.cfm

Norman

Jacobson House Native Art Center
609 Chautauqua Ave.
Norman, OK 73069
Phone: 405-366-1667
http://www.jacobsonhouse.com/kiowa.html

University of Oklahoma Western History Collections
630 Parrington Oval
Norman, OK 73019
Phone: 405-325-3641
http://libraries.ou.edu/info/index.asp?id=22

Oklahoma City

National Cowboy and Western Heritage Museum
1700 NE 63rd Street
Oklahoma City, OK 73111

Phone: 405-478-2250
http://www.nationalcowboymuseum.org

Oklahoma Historical Society
2100 N. Lincoln Blvd.
Oklahoma City, OK 73105
Phone: 405-521-2481
http://www.ok-history.mus.ok.us/

Tulsa

University of Tulsa McFarlin Library
2933 East 6th Street
Tulsa, OK 74104-3123
Phone: 918-631-2873
http://www.lib.utulsa.edu/

South Dakota

Pierre

South Dakota State Historical Society
900 Governors Drive
Pierre, SD 57501-2217
Phone: 605-773-3458
http://www.sdhistory.org/Default.asp

Sioux Falls

Center for Western Studies
2201 S. Summit Ave.
Augustana College
Sioux Falls, SD 57197
Phone: 605-274-4007
http://www.augie.edu/CWS/collections.html

Vermillion

National Music Museum and Center for the Study of the History of Musical Instruments
University of South Dakota
414 East Clark Street
Vermillion, SD 57069
Phone: 605-677-5306
http://www.usd.edu/smm/

University of South Dakota I. D. Weeks Library
Special Collections, Rm. 305
414 East Clark Street
Vermillion, SD 57069
Phone: 605-677-5450
http://www.usd.edu/library/special/

W.H. Over Museum of Natural History
1110 Ratingen St.
Vermillion, SD 57069
Phone: 605-677-5228
http://www.usd.edu/whover/index.html

RELIGION

Steve Foulke

The twin spires of St. Anthony of Padua Catholic Church in tiny Hoven, South Dakota, are part of a magnificent structure that has been a focal point in north central South Dakota since 1921. Dubbed the "Cathedral on the Prairie," it was built for approximately a quarter of a million dollars and required a decade to complete. When St. Anthony's needed restoration in the early 1970s, locals donated more than 20,000 volunteer hours to the task. The church was placed on the National Register of Historic Places in 1980 and is a source of pride for parishioners, townspeople, and local historians. However, St. Anthony's needs a new roof, a large and expensive project, likely to cost more than $750,000. Compounding this financial challenge is the steady population decline in the region throughout most of the last century. Hoven is home to just over five hundred residents, and the parish rolls have dwindled to a few hundred families.

The challenge faced by parishioners of St. Anthony's is repeated time and again across the Great Plains. Massive changes in agriculture and population patterns are taking place across the region, from North Dakota to western Oklahoma. If the population of and optimism about the Great Plains peaked at the beginning of the twentieth century, it could be said that much of the region has been in an economic and demographic free fall for a century. Yet some communities endure. At least some of the credit for the survival of small communities goes to the continuing importance of religion in virtually every hamlet on the Plains. More than a set of symbols and practices expressing adoration for the divine, religion forms a large part of the basis for a sense of place.

The Great Plains stands apart from the rest of the country in terms of religiosity. Outside of the intermountain West, Texas, and portions of the Upper Midwest, the Great Plains is the most "churched" portion of the United States. Unlike the intermountain West, where a single faith group, the Church of Jesus Christ of Latter-Day Saints (also known as the Mormon Church), accounts for the vast majority of the churched population, in the heartland diversity is the rule, albeit mainly variations of Christianity.

Aside from Native American religious traditions, the churched population in the region adheres overwhelmingly to faiths of European (Christian) origin. Non-Christian and non-European faiths are virtually nonexistent on the Great Plains. In part, this remains a function of the enduring rural and small-town character of this region. Non-Christian faith expression is linked to metropolitan areas with more diverse populations. Urban settings, in which religious diversity other than Christianity can flourish, such as Denver, Kansas City, Dallas, and Minneapolis, are at the periphery of the Plains. While Jews, Muslims, Hindus, Jains, Sikhs, Baha'is, Unitarian Universalists, and Buddhists are found in substantial numbers in other areas of the country, they exist almost exclusively in the major cities on the Great Plains. For example, data indicate that the Islamic population of the United States is estimated to be approaching 1.75 million, yet fewer than 15,000 Muslims live on the Great Plains, and fewer than 100 reside in all of South Dakota.[1]

There were some historical exceptions to this. For example, the Jewish Agriculturists' Aid Society of America assisted a handful of Jewish farmers in resettling in Kansas during the late nineteenth century, but they remained only a few years. Non-Christian followers in the region today exist in isolated pockets of labor-intensive economic development. For example, dramatic expansion in the meat-packing industry in southwestern Kansas and in the Oklahoma Panhandle has lured thousands of migrants from Southeast Asia, especially Vietnam, since the 1980s. This has created a small but distinctive Buddhist presence in and around Garden City, Kansas, where Buddhists transformed a former convenience store into a tem-

Interior of St. Anthony's of Padua, South Dakota. Courtesy Kathy Gorecki.

ple. Likewise, a small colony of Syrian-Lebanese Muslims made its way to North Dakota at the end of the nineteenth century and built a small mosque in the farm town of Ross in the late 1920s.[2] Some believe that this was the first mosque constructed in America. These exceptions, however, help prove the rule on the Plains.

Another modest measure of non-Christian diversity can be found in the larger university communities and towns near military bases that dot the Plains. Viewed from outside the region, university communities, such as Lincoln, Manhattan, Lawrence, Stillwater, Norman, Vermillion, Brookings, Fargo and Grand Forks, and cities adjacent to military bases, such as Junction City and Minot, would not likely be perceived as diverse communities. However, within the context of the Great Plains, such communities have a fairly robust mix of religious and ethnic diversity. Minot, for example, has both a Jewish synagogue and a Baha'i fellowship.

While today the Plains is likely the most religiously homogeneous region of the country, in the nineteenth century it may have seemed more like a hodgepodge of northern European traditions. When the region was "settled" in the late nineteenth and early twentieth centuries, the vast majority of the European settlers were Christian. As these settlers pushed onto the Plains, most brought a faith along with them. Some denominations rushed to the Great Plains in order to meet the needs of adherents, while others established churches and related faith-based institutions such as colleges, seminaries, and hospitals to lure members to the Plains. Countless European tongues were spoken on main streets, across farm fences, and inside churches. Children dressed in ethnic attire, and women cooked Old World dishes. In part because of geographic isolation and the patterns of agricultural settlement within the region, these traits lingered for decades. Although distinctive ethnic qualities such as language, dress, housing types, and occupational patterns have all but vanished, religious orientation remains as evidence of settlement patterns and ethnic origin. Many religious followers today are mindful of their faith's history on the Plains and the way in which their faith bonds with an ethnic past.

The figures about religion used here are drawn from the work of the Glenmary Research Center during the past four decades.[3] Glenmary assembles data from statistics reported by denominational headquarters. It is important to put the reliability of these statistics into context. While a person may claim to belong to a church, that says little about his or her commitment or regular participation. For example, a survey conducted by George Gallup in the late 1990s suggested that nearly 70 percent of Americans "claim membership in a church, synagogue, or other religious body."[4] It is one thing for an individual to answer a few unsolicited questions about his or her religious preferences quickly over the phone. A statistician at a denominational headquarters, on the other hand, is likely a more reliable source of information. Nevertheless, it is impossible to be completely precise about church membership numbers. The figures used here encompass the broadest notion of adherence to a religious group. Denominational membership numbers include people who are formal members of the church, children, and those who participate in the denomination but have not yet formally joined. Rather than being paralyzed by the inexactness of religious data, it is perhaps more appropriate to acknowledge that just as religion is a complex and challenging cultural expression that defies easy description and explanation, statistics about religion and religiosity are at once meaningful and imperfect.

The most recent survey work in the year 2000 of the Glenmary Research Center indicates that slightly more than 50 percent of the population of the United States claims membership in a religious group and attends church regularly. However, this figure rises to 60 percent on the Great Plains and climbs to more than 70 percent in North Dakota. A century ago, Lincoln, Nebraska, was named the "Holy City." Faith was as central to its identity as politics, as this state capital boasted of having a ratio of one church for every seven hundred residents.[5] Data from the U.S. Census Bureau suggest that the ratio for the entire Great Plains is even higher today, approximately one church for every six hundred people. Those familiar with the region joke that there is a church on every other corner. There is more than a little truth to this.

PROMINENT FAITHS OF THE PLAINS

On the outskirts of many small communities on the Great Plains stands a "welcome" sign. Likely funded by the local ministerial alliance (the group of area ministers who collaborate on community projects of common interest), the sign includes the logos, addresses, and times of worship for the churches in the community. Amazingly, even the smallest towns (e.g., population of a few hundred) have multiple churches. For example, in Kansas alone, Glenmary established the existence of more than seventy different Protestant groups. However, what makes one religious group "different" from another can often be traced to a seemingly innocuous moment in their history.

As in the rest of the country, the Catholic Church represents the largest group of religious adherents. In the aggregate, Protestant membership on the Great Plains outnumbers that of Catholics. The Protestant mosaic is quite complex, however, and requires closer examination of the many groups that comprise this major portion of religious life on the Plains.

In a region of substantial uniformity (e.g., climate, landscape, settlement patterns, and agricultural output), Protestantism represents an area of considerable variety. For example, Lexington, Nebraska, a community of approximately 10,000, is home to twenty-three congregations, twenty-one of which are Protestant. Baptists, Disciples of Christ, Lutherans, Methodists, Nazarenes, Presbyterians, and many others live and worship across the region in considerable numbers. Throughout these five states are scores of Protestant dominations, a dozen of which, according to Glenmary data, have at least 50,000 constituents. It is important to note, however, that Catholicism is a viable presence in what many likely consider a largely Protestant part of the country.

While Jews, Muslims, Hindus, Jains, Eastern Orthodox adherents, Sikhs, Baha'ists, Unitarian-Universalists and Buddhists are found in substantial numbers in other areas of the country, they exist almost exclusively in the major cities on the Great Plains. For example, there are fewer than ten Greek Orthodox parishes in this vast region, and these are located in the larger towns on the Plains, such as Wichita, Tulsa, and Omaha. In addition, Glenmary data indicates that the Islamic population of the United States is estimated to be approaching 1.75 million, yet less than 15,000 Muslims live on the Great Plains, and fewer than 100 reside in all of South Dakota.

Native American Spirituality

Seared by contact with Anglo settlers, it is difficult to articulate the extent to which the culture of indigenous peoples was altered. Nevertheless, they persevered, and many of their sacred traditions have endured as well. Of the scores of indigenous peoples that lived on the Great Plains prior to contact with Europeans, only a handful of nations are mentioned here.

In general terms, the northern Plains were inhabited by the Mandan, Arikara, Hidatsa, and Lakota. The Ponca, Omaha, Pawnee, and Kansa were found in the lands later known as Nebraska and Kansas. The southern Plains was home to the Wichita, Comanche, Kiowa, and Osage. The nineteenth century brought formalized federal intervention into Native life. The Indian Removal Act of 1830 mandated the resettlement of First Nation peoples who lived in the southeastern United States to Indian Territory, later known as Oklahoma. Specifically, the Cherokee, Chickasaw, Choctaw, Creek, and Seminole nations were forced to migrate on the "Trail of Tears" to the southern Plains, where they were labeled the "Five Civilized Tribes" because of their perceived adoption of Anglo culture. Later, the Dawes Act allowed the redistribution of reservation land, such that large tracts of land throughout the Plains fell into the hands of Anglo settlers. In the early twentieth century, Indian Territory was brought into the Union, but not before even more land was seized by Anglo settlers during organized land rushes. Consequently, with the exception of South Dakota, large reservation tracts do not exist on the Great Plains, despite the sizeable number of Native nations that live in the region today and the fact that many nations can point to the region as their ancestral home.

By the early 1880s, most of the best land on the more humid areas of the Plains had been or was in the process of being claimed by Anglo settlers. Across the region, Natives were reeling, having just finished a decade of terrible military battles with the federal government, on top of the government's removal policies. The way of life that Natives had long known seemed lost. It was in this context of despair that the Ghost Dance emerged among Natives on the Plains in the late 1880s. Originated by a Paiute prophet named Wovoka (1856–1932), the ritual encouraged Natives to acquiesce to the demands of Euro-Americans; in exchange, Natives would be reconnected with loved ones and familiar culture in an afterlife. Authorities, worried about the culture of personality that surrounded this prophet and the popularity of this ritual, worked to eliminate the Ghost Dance and succeeded. Following the massacre at Wounded Knee Creek in 1890, the life of the Ghost Dance movement was largely snuffed out.[6]

Despite its relatively short existence, the Ghost Dance remains an essential image of indigenous spirituality on the Plains. In the wake of practices such as the Ghost Dance, European faiths have established a solid foothold in the lives of Native Americans here on the Plains. However, this is not without controversy. Few elements of Native American life have generated as much pain and debate as has religious expression, because it was one of many aspects of indigenous life specifically attacked by the federal government and some religious leaders. Virtually all of the major Christian faiths in the nineteenth and early twentieth centuries participated in missionary-style outreach with Native groups, often against the will of Native leaders.

Organized faith made early and lasting connections with indigenous peoples on the Plains. For example, Catholic priests accompanied trappers as they pushed up the Missouri and Platte Rivers in the late eighteenth century. However, the Catholic presence among the Native peoples of the northern Plains was not institutionalized until 1874, when the Bureau of Catholic Indian Missions was formed to help the church coordinate its missionary efforts with the federal government. In addition to the Catholic Church, many other denominations had a foothold in the region by the mid-nineteenth century.

While each strain of organized faith had a different approach to working with indigenous peoples, the differences were subtle. In general terms, faith groups wanted to bring Christianity and Western culture to the Native Americans. Whether through the construction of missions, boarding schools, or the journey of a lone missionary into the field, reconstructing the spiritual and cultural direction of Natives was the goal. Churches found a willing partner in the federal government. For example, many church mission projects used revenue supplied by the government, and missionaries and the government's Indian agents often worked together. The government frequently gave a denomination sole access to a tribe. For example, for a time the Quakers had "exclusive" access to the Kaw, Shawnee, Kickapoo, Osage, Wichita, and Kiowa living in Kansas and Indian Territory,[7] and the Catholic Church had exclusive dominion over the Devil's Lake and Standing Rock Agencies in the Dakota Territory. At other periods, different religious groups worked to convert the same Native group. Even Catholic and Protestant groups could find themselves trying to bring the same sheep into their respective folds.

Religious groups, however, did not shrink from the "challenge" of bringing Christianity to Natives. They lent their support to the government's policy of Indian removal from land and, eventually, consolidation of Native reservation holdings. Scholar Robert Keller Jr. described the participation of Anglo faith groups in dismantling indigenous culture in the 1870s as a period of "gentle genocide."[8] Nomadic tribes were constrained on small landholdings. Agriculture was taught to nonagrarian Natives, even where the soil was poor and the climate dry. In addition to faith, Christian missionaries tried to alter Native diet, clothing, and language. Cultural relativism was not en vogue.

Spurring on the zeal of Christian groups to change Native culture was the aura of success that surrounded Carlisle Indian Industrial School. Founded in 1879 in a series of abandoned military barracks in Pennsylvania, the school became a model for faith groups. Carlisle, led by Lt. Richard Henry Pratt (1840–1924), a former military officer who had spent several years in Indian Territory, was a nominally secular institution that took Native youth from the West and consciously transformed them into non-Natives through a regimen of educational instruction in English and vocational training. The first step for all students was to have their hair cut by a Carlisle official, an act of grave cultural significance for many Natives.

Christian principles were incorporated into Carlisle's curriculum, but because the students were not in the hands of missionaries, the Carlisle school was considered "secular." While Carlisle was not wholly original and modeled its program on those promoted by missionaries, the school became the standard by which other schools for Indians, whether religious or secular, were measured. During the 1880s on the Great Plains, the government opened "secular" schools in Chilocco, Oklahoma, Lawrence, Kansas, and Genoa, Nebraska. Today Haskell Indian Nations University stands in place of the Kansas boarding school.

Using federal funds, religious groups such as Quakers, Methodists, Baptists, Episcopalians, and Catholics opened scores of mission schools on reservation lands for Indian youth during the late nineteenth century, many of them on the Great Plains. Attendance was compulsory, and the instruction was in English. The type of cultural reeducation that was attempted in such schools was hindered by the fact that Native youth were near enough to cultural traditions to make immersion difficult. Consequently, denominations threw their weight behind off-reservation schools, such as Carlisle.

The heavy-handed methods used at these boarding schools began to be questioned only after the results were evident. By the 1920s, the government and many observers perceived graduates of these schools to be poorly trained to enter the economy of the larger culture and traumatized by their reeducation process. Boarding schools, it seemed, produced people who were caught between two cultures, unable to integrate into either. Still, religious groups expressed some reluctance toward the Indian Reorganization Act, which was enacted in 1934 and effectively put an end to federal support of the onerous boarding-school era. The enormous control Anglo Christianity had held over Native culture was dramatically weakened. While the results of this act were mixed for Natives during this desperate economic time, it did help establish the right of Natives to define their own spiritual course.

Apart from the Ghost Dance saga and its connection to the Wounded Knee massacre in the late nineteenth century and the appropriation of scattered elements of Native spirituality in so-called New Age religions, the faith systems and practices of Native peoples are not particularly well known to the general public. It is a well-worn mantra, but worth repeating, that the extraordinary diversity of Native culture makes a detailed rendering of indigenous faith impossible in any brief account. However, a number of indigenous practices emerge as iconic and should be noted in any discussion of significant faith traditions and practices on the Great Plains.

Although it is perhaps not immediately recognizable as a religious ritual with large cultural significance, film buffs may well recall the scene from the 1970 film *A Man Called Horse* that showed the British actor Richard Harris (1930–2002) undergoing a painful ritual in which hooks attached to a bent pole appeared to be placed in his chest. As the pole was straightened, Harris's character was lifted off the ground, the skin on his chest apparently stretching and tearing, a symbolic moment of Native initiation and personal rebirth for the character. The scene in this film appropriates elements of the Sun Dance practiced by the Lakota and other nations on the Great Plains.

Historically, when word of a planned Sun Dance spread, many were drawn to it. The ritual was believed to deliver good to all who participated. Large crowds, often from a variety of bands, gathered. Thus the Sun Dance was used to integrate new people into a group, as well as to celebrate the creation story. The ceremony lasts several days and involves several dancers who abstain from food and water during the event, a major sacrifice during a series of scorching summer days in the Black Hills.

The Lakota, in particular, emphasized the torture aspect highlighted by Hollywood. Young men attached themselves by a cord or strand to a center pole, remaining tethered, in excruciating pain, until their flesh tore and set them free. By the late nineteenth century, the Sun Dance was a powerful feature of Native life on the plains. Particularly for the Lakota, the dance was a dominant symbol and gave strength in the face of withering defeats against federal troops and encroaching Anglo settlers. The U.S. government banned the ritual in 1883, but it was still covertly practiced for decades by a variety of Native clans. Following World War II, the ceremony was publicly revived in a less bloody form.

At about the same time as the Sun Dance was being restricted, another ritual dance was gaining favor among the Omaha, Lakota, and other Plains nations. The Grass Dance incorporated extravagant costumes, tricks, and illusions in order to demonstrate prestige. While little religious meaning was attached to the ritual by the early twentieth century, its popularity increased because of the creation of dance competitions. In a sense, the dance became commercialized, as anyone could learn the steps and mimic the costume, thus completely stripping the ritual of any spirituality. Today the Comanche and Kiowa perform a similar ritual they named the "Gourd Dance." Grass and Gourd Dances are performed at powwows across the Plains. The Sun Dance, similarly, is still performed at powwows and cultural festivals, but there is little agreement among Natives and those who study them about the cultural significance of the dance today, apart from honoring the cultural legacy of Native ancestors.

A native "War Dance" (yet another name for the Grass Dance) can be performed for a rapt audience of non-Natives without the audience feeling threatened. However, controversy shadows many sacred Native rituals, particularly because such ceremonies were perceived by the wider (non-Native) culture as somehow threatening or countercultural. When a ceremony is connected to a hallucinogen, the response from the dominant culture is swift. Such is the case with peyote, a small cactus that grows in northern Mexico and the southwestern part of the United States. Derisively called the "Big Chief," when dried and ingested, the plant produces a mild hallucinogenic effect. The plant has played a role in Native spirituality for centuries, but from 1974 until 1994 the federal government deemed it a controlled substance and made its possession a federal crime. However, because peyote's cultural context is complex, the U.S. Justice Department, along with state judiciaries in Oklahoma, Kansas, and South Dakota, eventually made allowances for its use by members of the Native American Church.

The Native American Church, also referred to as the "Peyote Church," dates back to 1918 when anthropologists helped adherents legally incorporate the church. Fusing Christianity with peyote-fueled visions, each congregation uses lay leadership and consumes peyote during lengthy rituals. The institutional character of the Native American Church is not comparable to that of other formal denominations, as local congregations have considerable autonomy. Buttressed by the American Indian Religious Freedom Act of 1994, which guarantees Native Americans the right to use peyote for religious purposes, at least one congregation of the Native American Church can be found on each Native reservation, and others are located in communities with large Native populations across the region.

Today Native Americans remain dispersed across the Plains. Oklahoma has the largest number of Native Americans within its borders, although every Plains state has at least one Native reservation. In large part due to the work of missionaries in the nineteenth century, Lutheran, Catholic, and, Anglican bodies have been the most "successful" in terms of church plantings on reservation land. For example, on the western half of the Pine Ridge Indian Reservation in southwestern South Dakota, the site of the Ghost Dance confrontation of 1890, Glenmary's most recent study notes that two-thirds of the congregations are either Catholic or Episcopal. In the end, like many elements of Native life, spirituality among First Nation peoples is a tragic and complex story.

The Roman Catholic Church

The Catholic Church is by far the largest religious group in the United States. Nearly half of all Americans with a religious affiliation claim a Catholic identity. This number shrinks to around one-third of religious adherents (approximately 1.3 million) on the Great Plains, clustered primarily in the Dakotas and large portions of Nebraska and Kansas. As mentioned earlier, in raw numbers Catholics are the largest religious group in the region.

Catholicism has enormous cultural, political, and economic influence in many parts of the country, including areas on the Great Plains where its numbers are the largest. However, outside of the Deep South and the intermountain western states (such as Utah), nowhere in the United States is Catholicism less prominent than in large portions of the Great Plains. This is most dramatically expressed throughout Oklahoma and southern Kansas. In Oklahoma, for example, Catholics make up less than 10 percent of all religious followers, and only one county in the entire state (Texas County in the western Panhandle) has a preponderance of Catholics.

Nebraska, on the other hand, is robustly Catholic and has been since its inception. As was often the case in the central part of the United States, waterways facilitated the distribution of Catholicism. For Nebraska, the Missouri and Platte Rivers were important thoroughfares for Catholic missionaries. Irish and German Catholic pioneers flowed into Nebraska in the late nineteenth century, particularly into the central part of the state. The legacy of these settlers can be seen in many aspects of the cultural landscape, including, for example, the large parochial school network in the state. Hispanic Catholics have long been present in the railroad towns along the length of the Platte River. Although Catholic schools are relatively rare on the Great Plains, parochial instruction is a long-standing part of the educational network of Nebraska. More than one hundred Catholic primary and secondary schools are located in the state, primarily in Omaha and central Nebraska.

Omaha, while famous around the country for livestock markets, the annual college baseball championship tournament, and its wealthiest favorite son, tycoon Warren Buffet (b. 1930), is also well known in the region for its Catholicism. The first mass was held in the city in 1855. In its infancy, the city attracted many Catholic immigrants, including uncommon migrants such as several thousand deeply religious Bohemian immigrants. Jesuits founded Creighton University in the city in 1878, and today the school is the largest private university on the Great Plains. Also, in 1917, Father Edward Joseph Flanagan (1886–1948) opened a mission in the city aimed at wayward boys. A few years later Flanagan moved his mission a few miles outside Omaha, and Boys Town was born. Boys Town today works with

Hoven, South Dakota, is known as "the little town with the big church." St. Anthony's Church was built in stages, with final touches put on the main level in 1920. The Cathedral on the Prairie is listed as a National Historic Landmark. Courtesy South Dakota Tourism.

troubled girls and boys, aids parents, and maintains outreach centers in other parts of the country.

Catholics are also found throughout Kansas. Apart from the cities of Topeka and Wichita, a considerable percentage of the 400,000 adherents reside in the northeastern and west central part of the state. In the late 1860s, Benedictine leaders eyed Kansas, particularly the new cities on the Missouri River, for community planting. St. Benedict's Abbey of Atchison is one of the oldest Benedictine communities in the United States and helped spawn a number of faith-based institutions in the area, including Benedictine College. Jesuits also founded St. Mary University in nearby Leavenworth.

The prevalence of this religion in western Kansas can be attributed to a mass migration of German Catholics who had been living in Russia and who moved to the Plains in the 1870s. Descendants of these so-called Volga Germans are found throughout western Kansas. The most noteworthy community in the cluster of small Catholic farm towns in the area is Victoria, where the towering St. Fidelis Church (better known as the Cathedral of the Plains) is a landmark visible for many miles. In addition, the Hispanic presence in southwestern Kansas and in the major communities along railroads, including Newton and Topeka, helped solidify the faith. This Hispanic influx intensified in the western part of the state as more jobs in the meat-packing sector became available in the 1980s and 1990s.

The first Catholic presence in what later became South and North Dakota was in the form of a spate of missionaries, most of whom traveled up the Missouri River beginning in the late eighteenth century, but large-scale Anglo settlement was still decades away. Czech, German, and Polish Catholic immigrants streamed into the Dakotas, and today, many of the counties and communities near the Missouri River still retain an ethnic flavor. This faith tradition in North and South Dakota is deeply connected to ethnicity, and adjacent communities can have vastly different ethnic traditions, despite sharing the same faith. German Russian identity remains a potent cultural force in North Dakota, and a pocket of Catholicism in extreme north central North Dakota, encircling the community of Rugby, is in place today because of the German Russians who moved to the region from the Black Sea region of czarist Russia in the late nineteenth century.

Catholicism is the shared faith of a large patchwork of ethnic groups that flooded onto the Great Plains. The church also brought thousands of Great Plains Native Americans into the fold through mission efforts, often using brutal techniques. However, as is the case with many Protestant denominations, an exploration of Catholicism in this region is largely an exploration of European ethnicity.

Lutheranism and the Evangelical Lutheran Church in America (ELCA)

Strongly tied to Scandinavian and (northern) German ethnicity, the Lutheran presence dominates the northern Great Plains. The major Lutheran assembly, the Evangelical Lutheran Church in America (ELCA), was created through a merger of several smaller Lutheran groups in 1982. Lutheranism has nearly 500,000 adherents throughout the region, and the faith is a ubiquitous part of life in the northern half of the Plains. For example, as the largest Protestant denomination in North Dakota, the ELCA is divided into two governing synods that together monitor nearly 450 active ELCA congregations in the Peace Garden State alone.[9] In Nelson County, located in eastern North Dakota, it is estimated that nearly 85 percent of the residents who maintain ties with a church belong to an ELCA congregation. Although the northern Plains hosts more Lutherans than the southern Plains, the faith is represented throughout the Great Plains, with large pockets of Lutherans as far south as central Kansas.

Emerging from the religious protests of Martin Luther (1483–1546) in the sixteenth century against the state church in Germany, Lutheranism eventually diffused across northern Europe and Scandinavia. The faith was introduced to North America in the early eighteenth century. When settlers pushed onto the Plains in large numbers a century later, some Lutherans migrated to the region from the established religious communities in the upper Midwest, but most early Lutherans came to the Plains en masse from Scandinavia, and immigrants continued to trickle into the region well into the 1920s. More than a century removed from the initial nineteenth-century wave of immigration, Danish, Swedish, and Norwegian culture on the plains is most often associated with Lutheranism.

A large part of the faith's influence comes from the decision in the nineteenth century to create a broad network of parochial schools and colleges. Four of the twenty-eight ELCA-related colleges in North America are on the Great Plains. These institutions deeply shape their home communities. Lindsborg, Kansas, is home to the ELCA-affiliated Bethany College and a number of Swedish and Lutheran cultural festivals. Since 1881, Bethany College has presented George Frideric Handel's *Messiah* annually. Held every other year, Lindsborg's Svensk Hyllningsfest honors the area's Swedish Lutheran pioneers. In east central Nebraska, the farming town of Blair retains a strong Danish Lutheran flavor. For many decades, Dana College, the local ELCA-affiliated college, has joined with the community to put on a holiday festival in mid-December, highlighting Lutheran hymns and Danish food such as *frikadeller* (meatballs) and *medisterpølse* (sausage). Augustana College of Sioux Falls, South Dakota, called several communities home before it settled along the banks of the Missouri

Lutheran Culture

During the past half century, the Lutheran faith has received a publicity boost from, first, the literary work of Ole Rølvaag (1876–1931) and, later, Garrison Keillor (b. 1942). Rølvaag's noteworthy *Giants in the Earth* details the struggles of Norwegian pioneers on the unbroken and fearsome prairie. Keillor's depictions of small-town life in the novel *Lake Wobegon Days* and on his popular long-running radio show *A Prairie Home Companion* frequently use the Lutheran faith as a springboard for humor. Today, while those outside the faith may know little about Lutheran theology, they readily recognize "Sven and Ole" jokes[10] and the Lutheran passion for casseroles (called a "hot dish" in the Northern Plains and Northern Midwest), sweet soups, and lutefisk.

River in 1918. Its Center for Western Studies is a major repository for material related to the northern Plains. Last, in the early 1960s, Luther Junior College of Wahoo, Nebraska, moved to nearby Fremont, Nebraska, and merged with the existing Midland College to become Midland Lutheran College.

Another sizeable Lutheran group in the region is the Lutheran Church–Missouri Synod (LCMS), whose members are found in sizeable numbers in Kansas, Nebraska, and Oklahoma. In these three states, according to Glenmary data, around 200,000 individuals adhere to this form of Lutheranism. Founded in 1847 and formally separating from other Lutheran groups in 1976, the LCMS has less of an ethnic flavor than the ELCA. The LCMS is more theologically conservative than the ELCA and has emphasized the inerrancy of the Bible, a tenet that frequently puts it at odds with the ELCA and other more moderate denominations. However, like other denominations on the Great Plains, it too invests in higher education. Founded in 1894, Concordia University of Seward, Nebraska, is the only Great Plains member of the ten-member LCMS Concordia University system.

Anabaptism and Mennonites

Like other faiths, Anabaptism came to the Great Plains as part of the cultural heritage of European immigrants. Organized around a belief in baptizing only adult followers, Anabaptists emerged in western Europe in the sixteenth century because of disputes with state religion authorities over issues such as infant baptism and conscription. Anabaptists defined themselves by virtue of baptizing practices, separating themselves from the larger culture, practicing simple living, and, most controversially, believing in pacifism. Rather than a name for a denomination, the term Anabaptist refers to those religious groups that incorporate Anabaptist principles. These groups include the Amish, Brethren, Hutterites, and Mennonites.

Mennonites, the largest of the Anabaptist groups, have lived in the Plains since the 1880s, after thousands immigrated to the region from many points in Europe. At the encouragement of state officials and fledgling railroads, such as the Santa Fe, entire Mennonite villages often migrated from Europe en masse to the Great Plains to flee state-sponsored persecution. A considerable number of Mennonite congregations and towns founded by adherents across the Great Plains retain their European place names of origin. For example, Elbing, Kansas, is named for Elblag (German Elbing), Poland.

In the twentieth century, pacifism for Anabaptists took the form of conscientious objection to conscription and public protest of war and militarism. Mennonites, in particular, suffered during World War I for their German ethnicity. This persecution lingered into the era of World War II. However, the period between the wars proved significant for Anabaptists as they laid the institutional foundations for providing religious support for pacifism. Anabaptists vigorously denounced World War II, the Korean War, and, in particular, the Vietnam War. All were conflicts in which thousands of young Anabaptist men took part in alternative service rather than take up arms for the military. Striving for peace is still a fundamental topic for this faith tradition. Today support for community-based nonviolence campaigns, such as those that target domestic abuse, and development of conflict-mediation agencies have become the primary outlets for these pacifist beliefs. While struggles with the federal government over conscription are no longer common, when war is waged, Anabaptist groups are among those who show their displeasure publicly.

By the late nineteenth century, Anabaptists had accumulated in the Great Plains in considerable numbers, primarily in Kansas, Nebraska, Oklahoma, and South Dakota. The mass migrations helped Mennonites create several distinctive population hearths in this region. Mennonite immigrants found land and a climate that encouraged settlement near Beatrice and Henderson in south central Nebraska. They also congregated in southeastern South Dakota, near present-day Freeman. U.S. Highway 81, which runs north-south through the eastern part of the Great Plains, was dubbed the "Mennonite Highway" by followers because the road linked important Mennonite settlements on the Great Plains, as well as population clusters all the way from Manitoba in Canada to Latin America.

The vast majority of the 30,000 Mennonite followers in the Sunflower State live in south central Kansas and today continue to make this area a major Mennonite cultural hearth. The roots of this core date back a century, in large part to the construction of three liberal arts colleges. Mennonites constructed Hesston College in Hesston, Tabor College in Hillsboro, and Bethel College in North Newton. Despite the fact that these schools stand only a few miles from each other, each embraces a unique Mennonite tradition and continues to thrive despite the intense competition among them, as well among more than half a dozen faith-based colleges in the immediate vicinity.

In addition to the Mennonite colleges, several hospitals and senior-care facilities and a number of other Mennonite-related agencies are found in Kansas. Perhaps it is in the business sector that Anabaptists have left their biggest mark in Kansas. Anabaptists have long been known as skilled farmers, but by the latter half of the twentieth century a number of factors, including the agricultural economy and trends toward increasing urbanization, combined to make a strictly agrarian lifestyle difficult to achieve. Thus Anabaptists made economic contributions in farm-related activities. The most noteworthy of these achievements is the Mennonite-founded Hesston Corporation (today known as Hay and Forage, Incorporated) in Hesston, Kansas. The enterprise became one of the world's leading agricultural machinery manufacturers. The company's best-selling product has long been its swathing equipment, implements that allow farmers to cut hay efficiently. The legacy of this important piece of production machinery was embraced by the local high school, which uses "Swathers" as the mascot for its athletic teams.

The Brethren offshoot of Anabaptism is also represented in pockets of adherents around the region, most of whom belong to the Church of the Brethren sect. Like all Anabaptists, the Brethren came to the region seeking land, but during the last century they have become increasingly integrated into communities across the region. Approximately 10,000 Brethren reside in the region, the majority in Kansas. McPherson College, built in McPherson, Kansas, during the late 1880s both to anchor the Brethren presence on the Plains and to lure other Brethren settlers from hearths in Pennsylvania and the Midwest, continues to thrive. However, Church of the Brethren numbers on the Great Plains have dropped precipitously in recent years, mirroring the pattern in the denomination overall.

When Anabaptists came to the region in the late nineteenth century, Germanic dialects, wearing distinctive, simple garb, and living in isolated rural enclaves defined all Anabaptist groups. Today, most Brethren and Mennonites have largely acculturated. However, two Anabaptist strains, Hutterites and Amish, retain many distinctive characteristics. Anabaptists have long believed that their faith was incompatible with urban life, and currently around 7,000 Hutterites in the Dakotas still live this ethos. They prosper on the northern Plains, living in isolated, homogeneous settlements in the countryside. Wearing distinctive garb and speaking a version of German, they still are farmers. They live in tightly woven communes where property and income are shared among the members of the community. Interestingly, they are technologically savvy and employ the agricultural implements that characterize agribusiness, including huge diesel-powered tractors, sprayers, combines, and other tools of modern agriculture.

Undoubtedly better known than the Hutterites, the Amish share a number of characteristics with Hutterites, including distinctive dress, use of German, and rural isolation built around farming. Like the Hutterites, Amish view the entire non-Amish world as a corrosive and corrupting force. However, with very limited exceptions, the Amish eschew technology of all kinds. While their non-Amish neighbors farm with enormous tractors and farm implements, they continue to use draft animals and harvest some crops by hand. While even the most remote stretches of the Great Plains received electricity by the early 1940s, the Amish still operate without it, in keeping with their religious convictions. The Amish world is not without its contradictions. For example, they pay taxes but use very few public services, including not sending their children to public schools. Although only around 3,000 Amish dwell on the Great Plains today, most near the central Kansas town of Hutchinson, the Amish in this area, as is the case wherever they are found in the United States, are cultural icons who attract an inordinate amount of attention from tourists and curious locals.

Although the Hutterites and Amish are throwbacks culturally, most other Anabaptists make their homes in towns and live and work alongside those outside their religious tradition. Traditions that once presented obvious differences to the larger culture, such as distinctive dress and the German language, have all but faded.

Methodism and the United Methodist Church

Unlike Catholics, Lutherans, Anabaptists, and smaller denominations, Methodists on the Plains do not connect to a deeply rooted ethnic history. The United Methodist Church, the largest of a variety of Methodist bodies, was created in 1968. United Methodists are the second-largest Protestant denomination in the region, with 700,000 followers, and, unlike Southern Baptists, are represented in reasonably large numbers across the region. Throughout Kansas and Nebraska, seemingly every community has a large Methodist church, as these two states alone have approximately 1,100 Methodist congregations.[11]

Founded by John Wesley (1703–1791) in England in 1739, Methodism migrated west from the Mid-Atlantic states during the nineteenth century through the Ohio valley and across Missouri and Iowa. Wesley's vision of faith included church growth. Early Methodist ministers were to oversee a number of congregations within a region. The mounted Methodist pastor, the so-called circuit rider, raced from one congregation to the next, frequently ministering to a number of disparate gatherings of Methodists in a single day. However, Methodists gained a foothold in this region through constructing mission compounds aimed at Native Americans. The most famous of these is the Shawnee Methodist Mission, located in what today is bustling Johnson County, Kansas. Founded in 1830, this retraining school for Native youth also served as the Kansas Territory's capital. As Methodists came to the region from eastern states, the church's expansion on the Plains was greatly aided by a tradition of lay leadership and the fact that it was not tied to ethnicity. In general, once a congregation was established, its numbers swelled as it drew from a larger pool of potential members than other faiths more strongly associated with an ethnic tradition.

Currently, United Methodists on the Great Plains are found in the greatest numbers from northern Oklahoma to southern South Dakota. The faith is particularly robust in extremely rural stretches of the Plains, where towns are frequently very small and often in steep demographic decline. For example, the most recent Glenmary religious census shows that Methodists make up half the religious adherents in Jewell County, Kansas. As is the case for other counties on the Great Plains, the total population for this mostly rural north central Kansas county plummeted more than 75 percent during the twentieth century, and this decrease dramatically altered every aspect of life. Such population trends often plague the same areas where Methodists have long predominated. In part, this explains the denomination's activity in defending family farms and country churches throughout the Plains through agencies such as the Heartland Network for Town and Rural Ministries.

Church-related colleges were among the first institutions started by early Great Plains Methodists. Baker University in Baldwin City, Kansas, was inaugurated in 1858 and is the oldest four-year college in the state. United Methodists maintain connections with six other institutions of higher education on the Great Plains, including Southwestern University in Winfield, Kansas; Kansas Wesleyan University in Salina; Dakota Wesleyan University in Mitchell, South Dakota; Nebraska Wesleyan University in Lincoln; and Oklahoma City University in Oklahoma's capital city. Also a part of the United Methodist higher-education network, Omaha's Nebraska Methodist College is a vocational school whose sole focus for more than a century has been training health-care providers.

A number of smaller denominations are rooted in Wesley's teachings but consider themselves distinct from the United Methodist movement. The Wesleyan Church, which originated in the late nineteenth century, is one such example. Approximately 20,000 adherents live on the Plains. Part of what makes the Wesleyan Church's regional story interesting is its determination to have a college in an isolated part of the region. From 1909 until 1972, it supported Miltonvale Wesleyan College in the tiny Kansas farm community of the same name. The school then merged with Oklahoma's Bartlesville Wesleyan College. Today the institution is known as Oklahoma Wesleyan University.

The Church of the Nazarene is another offshoot of Methodism and a noteworthy part of the religious landscape in the southern Plains. This denomination, which split from the Methodists in 1908, has approximately 70,000 followers and nearly 350 congregations in Kansas and Oklahoma. Followers support two Church of the Nazarene–related colleges in these states, MidAmerica Nazarene University in Olathe, Kansas, and Southern Nazarene University in Bethany, Oklahoma.

In addition, the faith's headquarters and primary seminary are situated in Kansas City, Missouri. Apart from the Bible, the Nazarenes also look to the *Manual of the Church of the Nazarene* as a significant text. It includes the "Sixteen Articles of Faith," as well as descriptions of proper conduct.

Baptists, Southern and American

During the twentieth century, the Convention of Southern Baptists (SBC) solidified a hold on the southern United States. From Virginia to western Texas, no other organized faith challenges the SBC's dominance. Formed in Augusta, Georgia, in 1845, the group has seen continued growth despite a growing fissure between fundamentalist and more moderate factions inside the group over issues such as biblical inerrancy and the ordination of women. However, within the SBC there is little disagreement over other touchstone issues, such as the condemnation of homosexuality and abortion.

Aided by explosive growth during the last few decades of the twentieth century, the Southern Baptist Convention is the largest Protestant denomination in the United States. In terms of numbers of adherents on the Great Plains, the SBC is the largest Protestant group, and the SBC closely follows Catholicism in regard to total numbers on the Great Plains. The SBC has 1.1 million members in the region, the majority of whom live on the southern Plains, with approximately 900,000 Southern Baptists in Oklahoma alone.

The SBC's reach extends westward from the Deep South into Oklahoma, where the most recent Glenmary study reveals that there are more than 1,500 SBC congregations. Southern Baptists are the largest religious group in virtually every community, large and small, across the state. For example, more than 75 percent of the churched population of Atoka County in south central Oklahoma is Southern Baptist. Atoka, the county seat, with a population of approximately 4,000, has eight Baptist churches. Religion is of paramount importance here. The local high school even has a Bible Club.

Although Southern Baptists today dominate the Baptist dialogue across the country, the American Baptists USA, until 1950 known as the Northern Baptist Convention, are found in significant numbers on the Plains as well, especially in Kansas. The American Baptists USA (AB) is the largest and by far the most influential of several American Baptist (in essence, non–Southern Baptist) assemblies. This group has approximately 90,000 adherents on the Plains, about two-thirds of whom reside in the Sunflower State.

Historically, relations between these Baptist groups have been raw. The split between Northern and Southern Baptists dates back to the pre–Civil War era when the two groups divided over the issue of racial separation and slave ownership. The SBC formed largely because of the abolitionist sentiment of the Baptists who lived in the northern United States. Later, as the SBC matured, it began to hold fast to the notion of the autonomy of the local congregation. This has tended to weaken the SBC's institutional hold on congregations, but has done little to slow the growth of this strain of the Baptist faith. Local autonomy was one of several "landmarks" that gave Southern Baptists definition. Other such landmarks include the divinity of Jesus, his teachings, and scriptures; the acknowledgment of the fundamental nature of Christ before baptism; the act of baptism through total immersion in water;

and the ritual enactment of the Last Supper by baptized members of the faith. In general, Southern Baptists view the Bible as the precise words of God and hold that any overarching institutional or denominational structure is not biblically based and should always give way to the wishes of the local congregation.

Following the split, the Northern and Southern Baptists existed parallel to one another, separated as much by geography as by theology. The agreement struck in 1894 between the two groups at Fortress Monroe, Virginia, essentially created geographic areas of influence for the Northern and Southern Baptists. However, the SBC membership grew well past that of Northern Baptists, and the SBC quickly became synonymous with religion in the Deep South and began to expand beyond the bounds of the Fortress Monroe pact once the SBC brought several congregations in California into the fold during World War II. The Great Plains, and particularly the state of Kansas, are interesting in a geographic context because of the SBC's expansion north from Oklahoma, a state it had long dominated, following World War II, making Kansas a type of battleground, a state long the exclusive province of Northern (later American) Baptists.

Glenmary data suggest that the SBC now has more than 100,000 adherents in Kansas. This is 40,000 more than the AB, but predominance was not always the case. The growth of Southern Baptists in this state occurred during the last third of the twentieth century. Prior to this, Kansas was a Northern Baptist stronghold, in part anchored by the AB's Central Baptist Theological Seminary, constructed in 1901 in Kansas City, Kansas.

A few miles to the west of metropolitan Kansas City is the small town of Ottawa, Kansas, home to the AB's Ottawa University since 1865. The school's origins lie in the AB's missionary work with the local Ottawa tribe during the first half of the nineteenth century. In exchange for tribe-controlled land, the AB and college leaders promised a free college education to youth with a Kansas Ottawa heritage, and this commitment remains in place today.

While their numbers in Oklahoma are dwarfed by those of the SBC, the AB has an institutional presence of some note in Bacone College, once known as Indian Baptist University, located in Muskogee. Like Ottawa University, Bacone has strong links to Native culture. For example, its namesake, Almon Bacone (1830–1896), in the nineteenth century protested the federal government's policy of forced removal of Natives from the Deep South and relocating them into Indian Territory, as the state was then known. Also, on the college grounds is the Murrow Indian Children's Home, an AB mission project for homeless Indian youth that bears the name of missionary Joseph Samuel Murrow (1835–1929).

North of the Kansas-Oklahoma border, AB and SBC numbers on the rest of the Plains are generally fairly similar. For example, in Nebraska and the Dakotas, the SBC has approximately 27,000 adherents to the AB's nearly 20,000. However, Southern Baptist numbers continue to swell, unlike those of many other Protestant denominations. The SBC's expansion will likely continue to push north in the United States, and the Great Plains will be an important part of this growth.

Pentecostalism

In a region marked by understatement, humility, and modesty, it may come as a surprise that one of the most raucous forms of Christianity has its roots in Topeka,

Healing Hands Statue at Oral Roberts University, Tulsa, Oklahoma. Courtesy Oral Roberts University.

Kansas. The Pentecost in the Christian lexicon refers to the divine vision the apostles of Christ had fifty days following Christ's resurrection. In more common parlance, Pentecostalism refers to practices that involve zealous, emotion-filled worship services often punctuated by hand clapping, exuberant praying, worshipers speaking "in tongues," and spiritual healing.

At the beginning of the twentieth century, Pastor Charles Fox Parham's (1873–1929) Bethel Baptist Church in Topeka helped to spark the Pentecostal movement in the United States. A number of his students in the church were investigating Pentecost when they claimed to have been moved by the same spiritual impulse and began to speak in tongues. Soon Parham, too, had a similar experience. Parham's outspoken views on racial separation continue to make him a controversial character, but his role in helping to launch Pentecostalism is secure. The Bethel Baptist Church incident and, five years later, a similar period of religious intensity at a revival in Los Angeles at the Azusa Street mission are the touchstones that helped to spark the Pentecostal movement around the country and the world.

While the Pentecostal movement has influenced many denominations that do not necessarily identify with it, the principal groups that fully embrace the ideology include the Assemblies of God, International Church of the Foursquare Gospel, Church of God (Cleveland), Pentecostal Church of God, International Pentecostal Holiness Church, and the United Pentecostal Church. On the Plains, the Assemblies of God denomination, which originated in 1914, is the leading Pentecostal group. Glenmary data reveal more than 150,000 adherents in the region. With approximately 90,000 adherents and close to five hundred congregations, Oklahoma has the strongest Assemblies of God presence. It is important to note, however, that scores of Pentecostal congregations on the Great Plains are affiliated with a small band of like-minded churches or operate independent of denominational ties.

Many prominent religious leaders emerged from the Pentecostal movement. For the Plains, particularly Oklahoma, the most important figure is Oral Roberts (b. 1918). Exposed to the Pentecostal faith as a child in Ada, Oklahoma, Roberts eventually became a Methodist minister. However, his style of religious leadership is deeply steeped in Pentecostal practice, especially in terms of faith healing. Roberts began a barnstorming style of ministry centered on revival meetings during the 1940s and 1950s, and he eventually made the transition into radio and television. His ministry generated hundreds of millions of dollars, enabling Roberts to create an institutional stronghold in Tulsa. In addition to the headquarters of his ministries, he built a university that has a sixty-foot tall bronze praying-hands statue at its entrance and a six-story prayer tower in the heart of the campus. He also constructed a medical school and accompanying hospital, as well as a law school. Roberts' popularity peaked in the late 1970s, and a large drop in financial revenue ensued. Apart from the main offices for his ministries, only Oral Roberts University, with an enrollment of approximately 3,500, remains.

Other Protestant Movements

A unique and interesting feature of the Great Plains is that religious groups virtually unknown outside the region can have a large following in a localized area. For example, in rural Gray County in southwestern Kansas, the Church of God in Christ, Mennonite, known locally as Holdeman Mennonites, is by far the largest denomination. Few outside the county are familiar with this conservative group, but in Gray County, Holdeman Mennonites dominate the religious landscape. This Mennonite sect follows religious and cultural practices outlined by its founder, John Holdeman (1832–1900). Holdemans are Anabaptists, straddling the line between the secluded Amish and the more worldly Mennonites. Like the Amish, Holdemans wear distinctive clothes, educate their children in private schools under their control, and seek separation from the secular world. Unlike the Amish, Holdemans use technology, such as mechanized farm equipment, electricity, and telephones. Their homes, however, do not have televisions, and Holdemans remove the radios from their cars. At first glance, they would seem to have much in common with Hutterites, yet Holdeman Mennonites do not practice communal ownership.

Another example is the Disciples of Christ denomination. Congregations are found almost exclusively in the southern part of the region. Approximately 110,000 adherents live in Oklahoma and Kansas. However, the denomination's growth has stalled around the country, and it has also experienced financial difficulties in recent years. The lone Disciples college in the region, Phillips University of Enid, Oklahoma, declared bankruptcy and closed in 1998. To the north, another example is the Anglican Church. It has a pocket of relative strength in southern and central South Dakota. In this state, dominated by Catholicism and Lutheranism, the Anglican presence dates back to the missionary work in the nineteenth century with Native Americans.

One of the most recent additions to this Protestant potpourri is tied to population change. In the eastern region of the Great Plains, large cities such as Wichita, Overland Park, Tulsa, and Oklahoma City have a robust pace of growth. Here, so-called megachurches have taken root. In a region where churches have membership rolls in the hundreds (or less), megachurches boast membership totals of as many as 10,000. Most megachurches have several worship services per weekend in order to meet the demands of the large membership. Sometimes these churches are associated with conservative denominations. Often, however, megachurches operate as independent entities, often referring to themselves as "community churches." The megachurch successfully links traditional charismatic worship techniques with highly technical organization and outreach. Unlike many churches on the Great Plains where the paid staff consists of the minister and a part-time secretary, megachurches have a full-time team of paid and highly trained ministers and staffers involved with every aspect of church life, from the Sunday-morning music to specialized youth, family, singles, and retiree ministries. Generally, a head minister operates as much as a chief executive officer as a pastor. Additionally, the lay members take on positions of leadership and authority within the church. The massive membership rolls are generally sliced into small cell-like groups. These groups meet for informal worship and social gatherings, replicating the sensibilities of a rural church.

The worship facilities are typically new and very large, generally without steeples, bell towers, or other familiar features of church architecture. The exterior of a megachurch often resembles a hotel, including a vast parking space. Vehicle traffic flow is a consideration for megachurches because as soon as one service ends, another is set to begin. In addition, the worship services use the latest in sound and video systems. Services in a megachurch are a spectacle of sight and sound, along with an upbeat, nonjudgmental gospel message.

The numbers of participants in such churches are difficult to isolate. Their existence remains a phenomenon exclusive to only the few points of explosive population growth and suburban sprawl on the Great Plains. However, the techniques of these churches are being replicated by mainstream congregations across the region.

CULTURAL EXPRESSIONS OF FAITH

Ideological Landscapes

The sheer weight of church membership and the political and economic power religion wields in most towns on the Great Plains molds the ideological landscape of this region. For those with a religious tradition of European origin, their religion is largely marked by a combination of understatement and piety. For example, Lutherans on the Plains have been labeled the "frozen chosen." While great differences exist between expressions of, for example, Catholicism and Anabaptism, in general, religious fervor is not particularly zealous for any of the religions in the region. Especially on the northern Plains, denominations that practice a measure of religious fervor are generally viewed with suspicion. In all cases, however, religion deeply shapes the cultural landscape. Many communities on the Plains have a Church Street, some even a Christian Street. The second-tallest structure, after the grain elevator, is usually a church steeple, and the steeple often casts a bigger shadow.

The separation between church and state is relatively murky on the Plains, especially with regard to the church's influence on the activities and curriculum of the public schools. For example, the state of Kansas made international headlines in the late 1990s when the State Board of Education for a short time placed creationism on a par with evolution in its approved curriculum for primary schools. Although the relationship between public schools and local churches is slightly more subtle in the urban centers across the region, from Oklahoma City in the south to Fargo in the north, largely because of the greater religious and cultural diversity in these larger cities, public schools in small towns are tightly linked to the local religious communities.

Schools and churches are often the social hubs of small Plains communities, offering the facilities needed by groups, clubs, and even piano teachers. Virtually all athletic and cultural activity that takes place during a week occurs in one of these facilities. Tuesday, Friday, and Saturday evenings are often the exclusive domain of the school-sponsored events. However, Wednesday evenings are often set aside for church activities. Many denominations hold services, Bible study sessions, or youth-group events on Wednesday evening, and attendance is generally good. Consequently, many public school districts in smaller communities do not schedule events, including athletic team practices, on Wednesday evenings in order to avoid competing head-to-head with local church gatherings. Additionally, the school calendars of largely rural school districts dismiss students near the end of December for "Christmas Break." Before leaving school for the holiday, elementary and junior high schools hold holiday performances during which young musicians and choral groups play and sing an assortment of tunes, most of which reference either the cultural (Christmas) icon of Santa Claus or the tale of the birth of Christ. Few in the audience are aware of or concerned by this religious exclusivity.

Further evidence of the church's influence on the schools and, in this case, the school calendar is seen later in the school year when many public school districts are dismissed on the Christian Good Friday holiday. As with Christmas, elementary schools hold events in connection with the Christian celebration of Easter. The most popular of these activities, coloring eggs and having Easter-egg hunts, has its origins in paganism, a fact largely disregarded at the schools. At the same time, however, the story of Christ's resurrection is also not a big part of children's education at Easter time in the schools.

School districts across the Plains are not consciously intolerant or bigoted when it comes to faith-based influences on school activities and curricula. The way religion (Christianity) is articulated in public schools there is a function of regional religious demographics. For example, Columbus Day has been a federal holiday since 1971 and has been celebrated as an annual event in the northeastern United States since the 1920s. While virtually no school district on the Great Plains declares Columbus Day a school holiday, this is customary across the northeastern United States. Interestingly, Columbus Day is treated as a holiday with a strongly ethnic and religious component along the Atlantic coast, whereas schools on the Great Plains are as likely to broach the broader cultural problems that Columbus's presence thrust upon indigenous peoples. In this instance, a quasi-religious holiday in the eastern part of the country is not seen as such on the Plains. Religion on the Great Plains is an essential part of the fabric of life. On the Plains, religious faith equals Christianity. Public schools merely reflect their constituency.

Religion also influences the economic climate and business practices on the Plains. The prohibition of commercial activity on Sundays (so-called Blue Laws) once limited virtually every aspect of commercial activity on the Christian Sabbath. Municipalities, counties, and states on the plains all had laws regulating store openings, liquor sales, and even the showing of movies in theaters on Sundays. Such laws, often dating back to the nineteenth century, are rarely formally removed from statute books. Kansas, which prevented airlines from serving liquor to passengers while flying over the state in the early 1970s, engaged in a ferocious internal political struggle in 2003 to have its laws changed in order to allow Sunday liquor sales. Generally, however, support for implementing Blue Laws simply fades. The laws remain on the books throughout the Great Plains but rarely are enforced.

Temperance

A glass of sacramental wine is not unusual in a Catholic parish, nor is a visit to a beer garden during a summer festival. Wine and beer have a historical role in the faith. However, in many Protestant faiths, consumption of alcohol is frowned upon. The idea of a beer garden at a church-related event is simply unthinkable. This sentiment was embraced by legislators throughout large portions of the Great Plains. For example, until 2003 Kansas banned Sunday sales of alcohol of any kind, and Oklahoma still enforces this ban. On the southern Plains, in particular, temperance still has many allies.

Groups such as the Woman's Christian Temperance Union (WCTU) are relics of history, a memento of the country's flirtation with prohibiting alcohol manufacturing and consumption in the late 1920s. However, temperance was embraced in much of the Plains well before and long after the rest of the country turned its back on Prohibition in 1933, and the WCTU was a formidable political force in the region during this era. The WCTU emerged from a cultural landscape where alcohol was perceived as a cheap and easily obtainable "medicinal" agent that could also serve as a tonic against the harsh climate of the Plains. Generally pinning alcohol consumption solely on men, the WTCU viewed itself as the protector of women, children, and domestic life.

For a time at the beginning of the twentieth century, the notorious activities of the hatchet-wielding Carrie Nation (1846–1911) drew the attention of the temperance advocates to the small Kansas town of Medicine Lodge. Here Nation became involved in the activities of the local chapter of the WCTU. In an effort to generate publicity for temperance, Nation literally walked into saloons around the state. Rather than making speeches denouncing drink, often she instead used her trademark hatchet to wreak havoc inside the establishment. Her violent tactics were sustained for only two years, but she remains a cultural icon both of temperance supporters and of those who see her as an intolerant buffoon. Yet it was no accident that Nation's activities had their genesis in Kansas.

Kansas placed a prohibition law on the state books in the 1880s. Although the Twenty-first Amendment to the U.S. Constitution was instituted in 1933, Kansas waited an additional fifteen years to remove the ban from its books. However, in some cases, individual counties and cities continue to enforce tight controls over liquor sales and consumption. Other Plains states also struggled to regulate alcohol. For example, throughout Nebraska in the late nineteenth and early twentieth centuries, a robust debate surrounded Prohibition, often pitting Protestants against strongly "ethnic" faiths, such as Lutheranism and Catholicism. Eventually, Nebraska was a pivotal thirty-sixth state to endorse the Eighteenth Amendment supporting Prohibition in 1919, but summarily dismissed the era by striking it down in 1934. Oklahoma entered the union in 1907 as a "dry" state. Technically, until the late 1950s the mere possession of alcohol in the Sooner State was a misdemeanor. The history of the restriction on the sale and consumption of beer, wine, and spirits in the states on the Plains was strongly supported by many large Protestant denominations of the time, and alcohol continues to be largely taboo for these dominant religious groups.

Since the 1880s, the Southern Baptist Convention has remained firmly committed to abstinence from alcohol, a view that extends today to restricting alcohol advertising and the exportation of domestically manufactured beer and spirits. Some

Anabaptist groups also take a formal stand against drinking alcohol, and while other Anabaptist sects are officially silent on the matter, temperance is the norm for all. The United Methodists have long supported complete abstinence from alcohol and are active at home and abroad in eliminating its use, particularly among the youth.

By contrast, the ELCA has never supported a strict prohibition on alcohol consumption, although some Lutheran groups that predate the ELCA did offer limited support for temperance during the early twentieth century. Nevertheless, Lutheran culture is tolerant of drinking in moderation and incorporates wine into the Communion service. Like the ELCA, the Catholic Church on the Plains kept prohibition at arm's length, although it was not particularly enthusiastic in confronting political and legal leaders in defending parishioners' right to drink. Still, alcohol is a historical element of Catholic culture. While the Dakotas ratified the Eighteenth Amendment in 1918, today alcohol is, in measure, more accessible in both states than on the southern Plains. The regional distribution of faiths is a key component in this difference concerning alcohol.

The influence of these religious groups continues to be profound. Even today, many counties and localities totally prohibit the sale of alcohol, and virtually everywhere on the Plains, the public consumption of alcohol is either very closely regulated or wholly forbidden.

Rooted in Place

Undoubtedly, one of the most famous celluloid images of the Great Plains was created on a Hollywood sound stage in the late 1930s. The amazing tornado sequence in the film *The Wizard of Oz* still has the capacity to frighten. Those with even a cursory knowledge of the region know that such storms are an unfortunate reality in the heartland. From March through September, when the sky turns black and the wind grows wild, inhabitants take shelter. When the wind stops, rebuilding begins, and leading such efforts are the region's religious groups. Agencies such as Mennonite Disaster Service (MDS) and ELCA Domestic Disaster Response are just two of the denominationally affiliated relief units that arrive to assist communities following a natural disaster. MDS, for example, was founded in Hesston, Kansas, in 1950, and nearly forty years after its inception, scores of volunteers returned to this town to help it rebuild following a devastating storm in 1990.

A religious ethos fuels the desire to help, but adherents who work to put communities on the Great Plains back together are not necessarily hoping to evangelize. Instead, it is a chance simply to help a neighbor and put faith into action. It is this bond to neighbors, a region, and the land that motivated efforts in denominations across the spectrum to reach out to their rural constituency beginning in the early 1980s when the farm economy began a catastrophic downturn. While urban life is the norm in most parts of the country, the Great Plains remains a region of nearly endless countryside. Even those who live in the hearts of the large cities are only a few moments removed from the nearest farmstead. People involved in churches have known for many years that rural life and rural congregations are endangered, and they have been giving support to agencies within their respective denominations, such as the United Methodist Church's General Board of Church and Society, the ELCA's Rural Desk, and the Church of the Brethren's Eco-Justice and Rural Crisis Office, that provide aid to farmers and the congregations in farming areas.

During the initial years of the agricultural crisis, clergy and lay leaders from a variety of faiths set up counseling centers, mental health hot lines, and other efforts in order to meet the needs of struggling farm families. However, while an interfaith coalition in Nebraska still maintains a hot-line service to farmers, in general, the passion that sustained denominational agencies, help lines, and agriculture awareness conferences in the 1980s and early 1990s has been difficult to sustain. Many of the problems found in the region then are still in place, but it has been challenging for those closely affected by them to keep the attention of denominational leaders and adherents who do not live on the Great Plains.

Throughout the region, many of the smaller rural congregations cannot pay their bills through the income they receive from their membership. Consequently, their survival is linked to subsidies from denominational headquarters. However, most mainline Protestant denominations, such as the Presbyterian Church USA, the Disciples of Christ, the Lutheran Church–Missouri Synod, the Church of the Brethren, and the ELCA, have suffered budgetary setbacks in recent years. The level of support that a denomination can provide to a struggling congregation on the Great Plains is an open question. This is yet another challenge for churches across the region, especially those in areas that have endured painful consolidation in the agricultural economy.

CONCLUSION

Whether they are Protestant or Catholic, a majority of Great Plains inhabitants take religion quite seriously. Religion touches many aspects of daily life, including the school calendar, access to alcoholic beverages, and observance of the Sabbath by local shopkeepers. Church buildings are a unifying feature among communities across this region. Apart from the ubiquitous grain elevators, churches are the tallest and grandest structures in a typical Great Plains town. Because of their size, usually central location, and relative amenities (such as large kitchens and recreational facilities), churches often are open to community groups, hosting events unrelated to the denomination or to religion in general. From local day-care centers to community concert venues, church buildings are considered community assets for all residents. The church plays a social role in addition to a spiritual one, and in some cases this social function draws more people to the church on a Saturday evening than can be found there on a Sunday morning.

Especially in the more arid western half of the Great Plains, hundreds of communities have nearly vanished, the twenty-first-century equivalent of the ghost towns of a past century. Businesses have closed. Schools have consolidated, moving to larger towns. Because the population has dwindled to a precious few, one often finds as many abandoned homes as inhabited ones. However, very often, the churches live on, seemingly against all odds. Sometimes the building needs a new coat of paint, the sidewalk is crumbling, and the shingles on the roof should have been replaced years ago. However, it remains standing, and, as often as not, if the building is there, a congregation exists to use and support it.

Churches are among the last institutions to be abandoned in a Plains community. Congregations will go to great lengths to keep the doors of a church open. For example, the Enders Church of the Brethren in tiny Enders, Nebraska, now utilizes the long-abandoned school for its meeting house. While perhaps only one hundred people live in and around the unincorporated farm village near the Panhandle of the state, with the support of the larger denomination and determined leaders within the small congregation, this church continues to meet for weekly services on Sunday morning and evening.

Many Protestant congregations and Catholic parishes, however, struggle mightily in terms of clergy. The crisis in the Catholic Church over the declining of number of priests is well documented, and the many Protestant churches across the Great Plains with small congregations are simply unable to afford a full-time minister. Faiths with a tradition of lay (untrained) leadership can soldier on for years in the face of declining congregational numbers due to depopulation and economic deterioration. However, if a congregation needs a priest or pastor and is unable to find one, the result is frequently catastrophic, the closure of the church.

However, adherents across the Plains are beginning to adjust to the precarious population and economic trends that plague the region. The Catholic Diocese of Salina, Kansas, for example, oversees nearly one hundred parishes across the north central and western part of the state. Traditionally, this area was one of the most productive wheat-producing areas in the country, but this part of Kansas lost a significant part of its population during the latter half of the twentieth century. Also, this is one of the "oldest" parts of the entire country in terms of average age of the remaining inhabitants. Combine these realities with a chronic shortage of priests, and it is easy to see why many of the parishes in this area are on the edge of closing. However, they endure because parishes share priests and hold mass on a biweekly schedule. It is far from a perfect arrangement, but parishes there put up with it because the alternative is even more grim. Inhabitants of this rugged region want their churches to thrive. Few places in the United States can match the commitment to faith found on the Great Plains today.

RESOURCE GUIDE

Printed Sources

Alexander, Ruth Ann, ed. *From Idea to Institution: Higher Education in South Dakota*. Vermillion: University of South Dakota Press, 1989.

Bush, Perry. *Two Kingdoms, Two Loyalties: Mennonite Pacifism in Modern America*. Baltimore: Johns Hopkins University Press, 1998.

Carman, J. Neale, and Associates. *Foreign-Language Units of Kansas*. Vol. 1. Lawrence: University Press of Kansas, 1974.

Chiat, Marilyn J. *America's Religious Architecture: Sacred Places for Every Community*. New York: John Wiley and Sons, 1997.

Copeland, E. Luther. *The Southern Baptist Convention and the Judgment of History: The Taint of Original Sin*. Lanham, MD: University Press of America, 2002.

Deloria, Vine Jr. *For This Land: Writings on Religion in America*. New York: Routledge, 1999.

Eisenberg C. G. *History of the First Dakota-District of the Evangelical-Lutheran Synod of Iowa and Other States*. Trans. Anton Richter. Lanham, MD: University Press of America, 1983.

Emmons, David M. *Garden in the Grasslands: Boomer Literature of the Central Great Plains*. Lincoln: University of Nebraska Press, 1971.

Farnsworth, Arthur Emory II. *Southern Baptist Politics: Authority and Power in the Restructuring of an American Denomination*. University Park: Pennsylvania State University Press, 1994.

Feraca, Stephen E. *Wakinyan: Lakota Religion in the Twentieth Century*. Lincoln: University of Nebraska Press, 1998.

Gallup, George, Jr., and Timothy Jones. *The Next American Spirituality: Finding God in the Twenty-First Century*. Colorado Springs: Victor Cook Communications, 2000.

Harrell, David E. *Oral Roberts: An American Life*. Bloomington: Indiana University Press, 1985.

Harrod, Howard L. *The Animals Came Dancing: Native American Sacred Ecology and Animal Kinship*. Tucson: University of Arizona Press, 2000.

———. *Becoming and Remaining a People: Native American Religions on the Northern Plains*. Tucson: University of Arizona Press, 2002.

———. *Renewing the World: Plains Indian Religion and Morality*. Tucson: University of Arizona Press, 1987.

Henthorne, Mary Evangela. *The Career of the Right Reverend John L. Spalding as President of the Irish Catholic Colonization Association of the United States*. Urbana: University of Illinois Press, 1937.

Iorio, Sharon H. *Faith's Harvest: Mennonite Identity in Northwest Oklahoma*. Norman: University of Oklahoma Press, 1998.

Iverson, Peter, ed. *The Plains Indians of the Twentieth Century*. Norman: University of Oklahoma Press, 1985.

Johannes, Sister Mary. *A Study of the Russian-German Settlements in Ellis County, Kansas*. Washington, DC: Catholic University of America Press, 1946.

Jones, Dale E., Sherri Doty, Clifford Grammich, James E. Horsch, Richard Houssal, Mac Lynn, John P. Markum, Kenneth M. Sanchagrin, and Richard H. Taylor. *Religious Congregations and Membership in the United States, 2000: An Enumeration by Region, State and County Based on Data Reported for 149 Religious Bodies*. Nashville: Glenmary Research Center, 2002.

Kehoe, Alice B. *The Ghost Dance: Ethnohistory and Revitalization*. New York: Holt, Rinehart and Winston, 1989.

———. *North American Indians: A Comprehensive Account*. 2nd ed. Englewood Cliffs, NJ: Prentice-Hall, 1992.

Keillor, Garrison. *Lake Wobegon Days*. New York: Penguin, 1986.

Keller, Robert H., Jr. *American Protestantism and United States Indian Policy, 1869–82*. Lincoln: University of Nebraska Press, 1983.

Kraybill, Donald B., and C. Nelson Hostetter. *Anabaptist World USA*. Scottdale, PA: Herald Press, 2001.

Lindberg, Duane R. *Men of the Cloth and the Social Cultural Fabric of the Norwegian Ethnic Community in North Dakota*. Manchester, MN: Ayer Publishers, 1981.

Loewen, Royden K. *Family, Church, and Market: A Mennonite Community in the Old and New Worlds, 1850–1930*. Urbana: University of Illinois Press, 1993.

Lesser, Alexander. *The Pawnee Ghost Dance Hand Game: Ghost Dance Revival and Ethnic Identity*. Lincoln: Bison Books, 1996.

Matteson, Jean M., and Edith M. Matteson. *Blossoms of the Prairie: The History of the Danish Lutheran Churches in Nebraska*. Lincoln, NE: Blossoms of the Prairie, 1988.

McQuillan, D. Aidan. *Prevailing over Time: Ethnic Adjustment on the Kansas Prairies, 1875–1925*. Lincoln: University of Nebraska Press, 1990.

Miller, Mary. *Pillar of Cloud: The Story of Hesston College, 1909–1959*. North Newton, KS: Mennonite Press, 1959.

Miner, Craig. *West of Wichita: Settling the High Plains of Kansas, 1865–1890*. Lawrence: University Press of Kansas, 1986.

Nebraska: A Guide to the Cornhusker State. American Guide Series. New York: Viking Press, 1939.

Norris, Kathleen. *Dakota: A Spiritual Geography*. Boston: Houghton Mifflin, 1993.

Peterson, Peter L. *A Place Called Dana*. Blair, NE: Dana College, 1985.

Popper, Frank J., and Deborah E. Popper. "The Great Plains: From Dust to Dust." *Planning* (December 1987): 12–18.

Remple, Henry D., and Paul Toews. *From Bolshevik Russia to America: A Mennonite Family Story*. Sioux Falls, SD: Pine Hill Press, 2001.

Rølvaag, Ole E. *Giants in the Earth: A Saga of the Prairie*. New York: Harper and Brothers, 1927.

Rose, Marilyn P. *On the Move: A Study of Migration and Ethnic Persistence among Mennonites from East Freeman, South Dakota*. New York: AMS Press, 1988.

Sallet, Richard. *Russian-German Settlements in the United States*. Trans. Armand Bauer and La Verne J. Rippley. Fargo: North Dakota State University, 1974.

Schaller, Lyle E. *The Very Large Church*. Nashville: Abingdon Press, 2000.

Schnell, Stephen. "Little Sweden, U.S.A.: Ethnicity, Tourism, and Identity in Lindsborg, Kansas." Ph.D. diss., University of Kansas, 1998.

Shannon, James. *Catholic Colonization on the Western Frontier*. New Haven, CT: Yale University Press, 1957.

Sherman, William C. *Plains Folk: North Dakota's Ethnic History*. Fargo: North Dakota State University, 1986.

———. *Prairie Mosaic: An Ethnic Atlas of Rural North Dakota*. Fargo: North Dakota State University, 1983.

Shortridge, James. *Peopling the Plains: Who Settled Where in Frontier Kansas*. Lawrence: University Press of Kansas, 1995.

Sneen, Donald J. *Through Trials and Triumphs: A History of Augustana College*. Sioux Falls, SD: Center for Western Studies, 1985.

Stith, Marjorie. *Making a Difference: A Fifty-Year History of Kansas-Nebraska Southern Baptists*. Franklin, TN: Providence House, 1995.

Stump, Roger W. "The Geography of Religion: Introduction." *Journal of Cultural Geography* 7 (1986): 1–3.

Stumpp, Karl. *The German-Russians: Two Centuries of Pioneering*. Trans. Joseph Height. Bonn: Atlantic-Forum, 1967.

Szasz, Ferenc M. *Protestant Clergy in the Great Plains and Mountain West, 1865–1915*. Albuquerque: University of New Mexico Press, 1988.

———, ed. *Religion in the West*. Manhattan, KS: Sunflower University Press, 1984.

Treat, James, ed. *Native and Christian: Indigenous Voices on Religious Identity in the United States and Canada*. New York: Routledge, 1996.

Tucker, Cynthia G. *Prophetic Sisterhood: Liberal Women Ministers of the Frontier, 1880–1930*. Bloomington: Indiana University Press, 1994.

Wedel, Peter J. *The Story of Bethel College*. Ed. E. G. Kaufman. North Newton, KS: Bethel College, 1954.

Wheeler, Wayne. *An Analysis of Social Change in a Swedish-Immigrant Community: The Case of Lindsborg, Kansas*. New York: AMS Press, 1986.

Wigger, John H. and Nathan O. Hatch, eds. *Methodism and the Shaping of American Culture*. Nashville: Abingdon Press, 2001.

Web Sites

Native Americans

"Soul Wound: The Legacy of Native American Schools," Amnesty International http://www.amnestyusa.org/amnestynow/soulwound.html (accessed January 15–24, 2004)

Catholic

North Dakota Catholic Conference
http://ndcatholic.org/ (accessed January 15–24, 2004)

United States Conference of Catholic Bishops
http://www.nccbuscc.org/ (accessed January 15–24, 2004)

Lutheran

Evangelical Lutheran Church in America
http://www.elca.org/ (accessed January 15–24, 2004)

Lutheran Church–Missouri Synod
http://www.lcms.org/ (accessed January 15–24, 2004)

Anabaptist

Mennonites

Mennonite Church USA
http://www.mennoniteusa.org/ (accessed January 15–24, 2004)

Hutterites

Hutterite Brethren
http://www.hutterites.org/ (accessed January 15–24, 2004)

Church of the Brethren

Church of the Brethren
http://www.brethren.org/ (accessed January 15–24, 2004)

Baptist

American Baptist Churches-USA
http://www.abc-usa.org/ (accessed January 15–24, 2004)

Baptist General Convention of Oklahoma
http://www.bgco.org/ (accessed January 15–24, 2004)

Church of the Nazarene
http://www.nazarene.org/ (accessed January 15–24, 2004)

Southern Baptist Convention
http://www.sbc.net/ (accessed January 15–24, 2004)

Methodist/Wesleyan

Free Methodist Church
http://www.freemethodistchurch.org/ (accessed January 15–24, 2004)

United Methodist Church
http://www.umc.org/ (accessed January 15–24, 2004)

Pentecostalism

Assemblies of God USA
http://www.ag.org/ (accessed January 15–24, 2004)

Islam

Muslims in America: Historical Mosques
http://www.muslimsinamerica.org/ (accessed January 15–24, 2004)

State History Resources

Kansas

Kansas State Historical Society
http://www.kshs.org/ (accessed January 15–24, 2004)

Nebraska

Nebraska State Historical Society
http://www.nebraskahistory.org/ (accessed January 15–24, 2004)

North Dakota

State Historical Society of North Dakota
http://www.state.nd.us/hist/ (accessed January 15–24, 2004)

Oklahoma

Oklahoma Historical Society
http://www.ok-history.mus.ok.us/ (accessed January 15–24, 2004)

South Dakota

South Dakota State Historical Society
http://www.sdhistory.org/ (accessed January 15–24, 2004)

Historical Libraries, Historical Societies, and Research Institutions

American Catholic Historical Association
http://www.research.cua.edu/acha/ (accessed January 15–24, 2004)

American Historical Society of Germans from Russia
http://www.ahsgr.org/ (accessed January 15–24, 2004)

Center for the Study of Religion and Society, Creighton University
http://moses.creighton.edu/csrs/index.html (accessed January 15–24, 2004)

General Commission on Archives and History, The United Methodist Church
http://www.gcah.org/contact.htm (accessed January 15–24, 2004)

Germans from Russia Heritage Society
http://www.grhs.com/ (accessed January 15–24, 2004)

Glenmary Research Center
http://www.glenmary.org/grc/default.htm (accessed January 15–24, 2004)

Institute for Regional Studies, North Dakota State University
http://www.lib.ndsu.nodak.edu/ndirs/ (accessed January 15–24, 2004)

The Kansas Collection
http://www.kancoll.org/ (accessed January 15–24, 2004)

Online collection of Great Plains miscellany.

Lutheran Church Library Association
http://www.lclahq.org/ (accessed January 15–24, 2004)

Mennonite Library and Archives, Bethel College
http://www.bethelks.edu/services/mla/ (accessed January 15–24, 2004)

Southern Baptist Historical Library and Archives
http://www.sbhla.org/ (accessed January 15–24, 2004)

Other Resources

Association for the Sociology of Religion
http://www.sociologyofreligion.com/ (accessed January 15–24, 2004)

Girls and Boys Town (Boys Town, Nebraska)
http://www.girlsandboystown.org/home.asp (accessed January 15–24, 2004)

Interchurch Ministries of Nebraska's Rural Life Concerns
http://www.uccnebraska.org/mission/RuralLife.html (accessed January 15–24, 2004)

NebraskaStudies.org
http://www.nebraskastudies.org (accessed January 15–24, 2004)

The Religious Movements Homepage Project, University of Virginia
http://religiousmovements.lib.virginia.edu/ (accessed January 15–24, 2004)

Society for the Scientific Study of Religion
http://las.alfred.edu/~soc/SSSR/ (accessed January 15–24, 2004)

Woman's Christian Temperance Union
http://www.wctu.org/ (accessed January 15–24, 2004)

Religious and Ethnic Culture Festivals

Kansas

Emancipation and Homecoming Celebration, Downtown, Nicodemus
Annually in late July
http://www.washburn.edu/cas/art/cyoho/archive/KStravel/bigrocks/Nicodemus.html
(accessed May 31, 2004)

Messiah Festival of Art and Music, Bethany College, Lindsborg
Annually on Palm and Easter Sundays
http://www.bethanylb.edu (accessed May 31, 2004)

Mid-Kansas Mennonite Relief Sale, State Fairgrounds, Hutchinson
Annually in April
http://Kansas.mccsale.org/ (accessed May 31, 2004)

Nebraska

Annual Community Christmas Festival, Swedish Heritage Center, Oakland
Annually in December
http://www.ci.oakland.ne.us/events.htm (accessed May 31, 2004)

Kolach Days and Annual Polka Mass, St. Wenceslaus Catholic Church, Verdigre
Annually in June
http://ci.verdigre.ne.us/Kolach.html (accessed May 31, 2004)

Wilber Czech Festival, Downtown, Wilber
Annually in August
http://www.ci.wilbur.ne.us/festival.htm (accessed May 31, 2004)

North Dakota

Norsk Høstfest, State Fair Center, Minot
Annually in October
http://www.hostfest.com/index.html (accessed May 31, 2004)

St. Hildegard's Catholic Church Annual Fall Dinner, St. Hildegard's Catholic Church, Menoken
Annually on the first Sunday following Labor Day
http://www.plainsfolk.com/suppers (accessed May 31, 2004)

Scandinavian Hjemkomst Festival, Fargo Theater and Sons of Norway Lodge, Fargo
Annually in June
http://www.scandinavianhjemkostfestival.org (accessed May 31, 2004)

Oklahoma

Fall Inter-tribal Gourd Dance, Fairgrounds, Norman
Annually in October
http://www.integrate.com/~purseamy/alcs (accessed May 31, 2004)

Shalom Fest, Temple Israel, Tulsa
Annually in October
http://www.uahc.org/congs/ok/ok004/shalomfest99.htm (accessed May 31, 2004)

Wichita Annual Dance, Wichita Tribal Park, Anadarko
Annually in August
http://www.wichita.nsn.us/newsevents.html (accessed May 31, 2004)

South Dakota

Schmeckfest, Eureka Pioneer Museum, Eureka
Annually on the third weekend in September
http://www.eurekasd.com (accessed May 31, 2004)

Oglala Nation Powwow & Rodeo, Powwow Arena, Pine Ridge
Annually on the first full weekend in August
http://smokesignal.tripod.com/sioux-powwow.html (accessed May 31, 2004)

Taste of Denmark, Community Center, Viborg
Annually in December
http://www.southeastsouthdakota/events1.html (accessed May 31, 2004)

SPORTS AND RECREATION

Thomas A. Wikle and
John F. Rooney Jr.

There is no denying the overwhelming importance of sports and recreation in American culture. Along with architecture, food, and language, sport and recreation help define the character of regions and places. Pittsburgh is famous for Steelers football, and Orlando is known as a gateway to Disneyworld. Many larger regions are also known for unique sport or recreational qualities. The Midwest is renowned for the Big Ten Athletic Conference and the Rocky Mountains for outstanding skiing opportunities. The sports or recreational activities practiced in the Great Plains reveal a rich sense of both the culture and the natural environment.

This chapter examines sport and recreation in the five states that form the core of the Great Plains: North and South Dakota, Nebraska, Kansas, and Oklahoma. As a means of examining the evolution as well as the social and economic dimensions of sport and recreation, the discussion is divided into three sections. The first provides a historical look at sport among the area's early residents, including Native Americans, soldiers, cowboys, and homesteaders. The second section examines interest and participation in community-based sports, high-school and collegiate athletics, and the professional spectrum. Some unique factors have influenced the development of sport and recreation in Plains communities, especially settlement patterns and population density. The final section considers recreational facilities and heritage tourism.

The mix of sport and recreational activities established at any place is influenced by environmental, physical, demographic, and economic factors. Latitude, distance from a coastline, and the absence of high topographic relief combine to produce a Plains climate characterized by frequent wind, moderate precipitation, and rapid temperature changes. Climate influences the range of possible activities as well as the number of days with favorable weather for those activities. For example, cross-country skiing is dependent on adequate snowfall, while temperature, humidity, and cloud cover serve as controlling factors for activities such as golf and windsurfing. Many types of sport and recreation are dependent on specific terrain configurations.

Downhill skiing requires suitable topographic relief, while water skiing and sailing depend on the availability of lakes or reservoirs. With the exception of the Wichita and Ouachita Mountains in Oklahoma and the Black Hills of South Dakota, the Great Plains region offers few areas of significant topographic relief.

Demographic factors such as population density have important influences on the organization of team sports and the demand for recreational facilities. With few large cities, the Plains is overwhelmingly rural and one of the most sparsely populated areas in the United States. More than a third of its counties contain fewer than 2,500 persons. Plains settlement has been described as an archipelago of isolated cities surrounded by agriculture and connected by a network of highways. The type and quality of facilities that can be maintained for sport and recreational activities are also influenced by the economic viability of communities. In some areas, population decline has led to school consolidations and the closure of hospitals, movie theaters, and government offices. Such factors have impacted the tax base and have created challenges for small towns as they attempt to expand or even sustain sport and recreational facilities.

EARLY SPORT AND RECREATION IN THE GREAT PLAINS

Games and other forms of recreation were part of life on the Great Plains before the arrival of Europeans. Native American children were encouraged to participate in activities that developed strength and physical endurance. Boys hunted prairie dogs and birds with small bows and arrows or fought mock battles. Venturing from camp, they tested skills by hunting antelope, elk, deer, or bison. Young men also competed in games such as foot or horse races and tug-of-war. Girls engaged in activities that mimicked child rearing or household chores and sometimes played a game similar to hackeysack using a leather ball filled with antelope hair kept aloft by kicking.

Participation in adult sports was also separated by gender. Shinny was a men's game that resembled modern field hockey with the objective of driving a ball through an opponent's goal using a curved stick. Also popular was a game similar to lacrosse known among Indians as "game of ball" or "ball game" and among non-Indians as "Indian stick ball" in which players tossed a ball to teammates using a pole with leather webbing at one end. The goal was to heave the ball through the opposing team's goal. The game of "hoop and pole" involved throwing a pole, spear, or dart through a rolling hoop. Most villages had one or two well-worn hoop and ball tracks. Categories of players—small boys, young men, mature men, and old men—each had distinctive hoops and sticks for versions of the game. Other men's games included darts and archery. Women and girls played double ball, with teams of five to ten players. A curved stick was used to catch and throw the double ball, made from two pieces of leather tied together and weighted with sand. The object of the game was to carry the ball past a mark or hit a goal stake placed in the ground.

The first white occupants of the Plains included a succession of trappers, soldiers, hunters, and cowboys. Isolation meant that there were few opportunities to engage in organized sport or recreational activities. One of the earliest sports on the Plains was hunting buffalo (American bison) that once roamed the grasslands of North America in numbers exceeding 50 million. The animals were hunted from horseback or a fixed position. Eventually, hunting for food and sport was replaced by professional buffalo hunting financed by the federal government as a means of destroying the food source and pressuring nomadic Plains Indians into submission.

White travelers passing through the Great Plains on the Oregon, Santa Fe, and Mormon Trails had little time for sport or recreation. Music and dance around the evening campfire brought relief from the repetition of dust and monotonous meals that characterized prairie travel. In the rush to gain access to western lands, the railroad often preceded the influx of white settlers into the Plains. Steam-engine watering stops were needed along the tracks. Many of these small settlements grew into larger towns and cities such as Fargo, North Dakota.

To finance rail construction, companies such as the Northern Pacific Railway promoted settlement on lands received by the federal government. Newcomers soon discovered an unforgiving environment subject to dust storms, tornadoes, droughts, and bitter cold. Long hours of hard work were necessary to produce food, clothing, and shelter. However, despite the demands of frontier life, settlers found time for leisure pursuits by combining work, social interaction, and recreation. Anything that brought people together—quilting parties, harvests, barn raisings—was viewed with enthusiasm. As the population grew, farmers and townspeople gathered in larger numbers to socialize and participate in games.

Baseball, a sport that was entrenched in the East by 1870, spread rapidly through the Plains. Almost every small town had a team by 1920. The fortunes of the "local nine" were an important topic of conversation at church gatherings and in barbershops and saloons. Games sometimes became epic struggles. As early as 1871, the Blue Belts of Milford, Nebraska, played Seward, Nebraska, ten miles away. The four-hour marathon ended in a 97–25 win for Milford. Oklahoma's first organized baseball game was played in Krebs on July 4, 1882, by miners from Illinois, Ohio, and Pennsylvania who settled in Indian Territory. Sacks of hay or cans served as bases for the game, which pitted Krebs against a team from nearby Savanna. Playing before a crowd of three hundred, Krebs won the game 35–4.

Community picnics, surrey rides, and square dances were also a focus of social interaction. On holidays such as the Fourth of July, men competed in foot races or contests to climb greased poles or capture oiled pigs. Other events included tote-sack races, turkey shoots, horseback-riding competitions, and cow-pasture baseball games. Wild game provided a source of food as well as an opportunity for sport shooting. The high point of the week was the social dance on Saturday night.

Horse racing was popular as a spectator sport. Most races were held outside of town, but occasionally the town's main street was put into service as a makeshift track. Despite being condemned as immoral and damaging to the work ethic, gambling was part of almost every sporting event. Saloons served as retreats for sports enthusiasts to watch boxing matches, cockfights, or rat baitings or to wager on baseball games and horse races. Prizefights were often tests of endurance rather than exhibitions of skill. Sometimes their gruesomeness was exaggerated in local newspaper accounts.

Military personnel stationed at forts to protect transportation routes of settlers also played a role in shaping early sport and recreation on the Plains. Soldiers looked for activities to break the monotony of military life, and athletic competitions, especially baseball games, became important leisure outlets. Company- and battalion-level teams were organized for competitions within regiments or against nearby

Boxing match, circa 1915. Courtesy Kansas State Historical Society.

towns. Interest in baseball was further amplified in the 1880s by the introduction of the daily newspaper sports page and by the growing network of telegraph lines that transmitted baseball results. Football was sometimes played at military outposts but was less popular than baseball. Track-and-field competitions were also common. The training process for enlisted men included a monthly "field day" where civilian spectators watched individual as well as team competitions in track and field.

A spectator event that gained international popularity around 1900 was the Wild West show. Featuring Indian dances, horseback riding, shooting exhibitions, mock buffalo hunts, stage robberies, and battles, the shows were developed as entertainment, with themes nostalgic of Plains life. Two of the most popular Wild West shows originated in Oklahoma. Often cited as the first "cowgirl," Lucille Mulhall became one of the stars of her father's show, headquartered at the Mulhall Ranch north of Oklahoma City. Touring from 1900 to 1915, the Mulhall Wild West show was popular with President Theodore Roosevelt. One of the longest-running Wild West shows began on the Miller Brothers' 101 Ranch, near Ponca City. The 101 Ranch Show introduced "bulldogging" (steer wrestling) in 1905, invented and popularized by William Pickett.

Cowboys also played an important role in the evolution of sport and recreation on the Plains. After the Civil War, cattle were driven northward across Oklahoma, Kansas, Nebraska, and the Dakotas to be fattened on the open range. To occupy leisure time during drives and roundups, cowboys invented friendly competitions that showcased riding and roping skills. As increasing numbers of spectators came to watch, these informal contests evolved into the organized competitions known today as "rodeos." Col. W. F. "Buffalo Bill" Cody (1846–1917) is among those credited with helping make rodeo a sport. Cody was a frontiersman, rancher, vaudeville star, and admirer of cowboys and cowboy skills. In 1882, he convinced merchants to donate prizes for contestants at his July Fourth "Old Glory Blowout" in North Platte, Nebraska. Rodeo competitions in the 1920s were not the exclusive domain of men. With the decline in the popularity of Wild West shows after World War I, large numbers of women began competing in rodeo events.

THE CONTEMPORARY SCENE

The Great Plains is the core of what John Rooney and Richard Pillsbury have identified as the "Sports for Sports' Sake" region.[1] The strong interest in sports can be attributed to opportunities for high-school play that is sustained into adulthood. In contrast to urban areas, rural schools in the Plains have small enrollments and provide a playing opportunity for nearly every interested student. As a result, participation rates for almost every major team sport are significantly above the national average. Unlike Texas, where a town's prestige is often linked to high-school team success, athletics in Plains communities is more of an outlet for players and spectators. Though quality of play and success are important, the small enrollments of most high schools in the Plains place an emphasis on high levels of participation. Today there is considerable emphasis on women's athletics throughout the region, with high-school girls' basketball games often attract more media attention and spectators than boys' competitions.

Most significant in shaping community-based sports and recreation in the Plains is the region's widely dispersed population. Nonmetropolitan areas of the Great Plains are among the most rural in the nation, with large distances separating cities. Almost 60 percent of Plains counties have lost population within the last 10 years, due in part to young adults leaving for better employment opportunities in cities and metropolitan areas.[2] But even with this population loss, the Plains still has more than twice the U.S. per capita number of high-school competitors. However, opportunities are beginning to decline in some communities. Sherwood, North Dakota, with a population of 255, has three churches, a few retail stores, and a post office. Like other towns in rural North Dakota, Sherwood has experienced a gradual decrease in population. With only thirteen high-school boys enrolled during the 2002 school year, residents began discussions about merging the boys' basketball team with archrival Mohall High. Questions were raised, such as how team consolidation would impact seniors' playing time and which team name and school colors would be retained. The two schools had already combined football, baseball, track, and golf programs. Such stories are relatively common in the

Pawnee Wild West Show. Courtesy Oklahoma Tourism.

Plains, and teams continue to consolidate in portions of the Great Plains. There has been no reversal in this trend.

Football, Basketball, and Baseball

High schools serve as the backbone for organized sports in the Plains. They are the training ground for player development and the nexus of community involvement in sport. If a sport is not well represented at the high-school level, it has considerably less potential to be popular at youth or adult levels of play. Football, baseball, and basketball are the "holy trinity" of U.S. athletics because they generate the largest spectator base. Plains high schools mirror those found elsewhere in the United States in their emphasis on these three sports.

Because of the dispersed population and distance between towns, full-contact youth football programs such as Pop Warner are not well established in the Plains. A few independent organizations are based in Plains states, such as the Indian Nations Football Conference, based in Broken Arrow, Oklahoma. City recreation departments and local YMCAs also organize flag-football leagues. Tradition and rivalry are important concepts within high-school football. Often a large portion of a small town's population attends home or away football games. To compensate for differences in enrollment, high schools are grouped into several classes, and states have several football champions each year. Oklahoma has the largest number of divisions, six school classifications for eleven-man teams. The state's smaller schools are organized within two additional divisions that field eight-man teams. In contrast, North Dakota has three eleven-man classes and one nine-man class that includes the state's thirty-six smallest schools. The smallest schools in Nebraska compete in a six-man football class. Some schools form consolidated teams with players who come from two or more nearby schools.

Youth basketball came to the Plains shortly after its invention by James Naismith (1861–1939), who developed the game in 1891 to liven up his gym class at the International YMCA Training School in Springfield, Massachusetts. Basketball is organized through city recreation departments, schools, and private organizations such as local YMCAs. More selective traveling teams and summer camps are also popular. An attractive aspect of basketball for Plains towns is that once a suitable structure has been built, the game requires fewer players and is less costly than football. Basketball is played within many towns with high-school enrollments too small for a football team. It is the number one high-school sport in the Plains in terms of schools that field a team. In terms of players per capita, the northern Plains region has the highest rate of basketball participation in the nation. Though neighboring Iowa was the cultural hearth and epicenter of girl's basketball, it spread early to Oklahoma, Nebraska, and Kansas. One of the region's most successful coaches was Bertha Teague, who coached the Byng (Oklahoma) High School girl's basketball teams

Six-Man Football

Six-man football has its roots in the Plains. The game was invented in 1934 by Stephen E. Epler, who coached football at Chester High School in Nebraska. Epler hoped that his game would reduce the number of student injuries. Instead of using a 100-yard field, the game is played on an 80-by-40-yard field. An important difference in six-man play is that unless the ball is kicked or forward passed, it cannot pass the line of scrimmage until it has been exchanged with another player.

Little League baseball fans in Oklahoma gather to cheer on the kids as well as strengthen their community. Courtesy Harcourt Index.

from 1927 to 1969, compiling an unparalleled record of 1,152 wins and only 115 losses (a .909 average).

State-level Amateur Athletic Unions (AAUs) also sponsor basketball leagues. Tournaments and leagues offer opportunities for adult play, with divisions for commercial organizations, seniors, and women. Plains teams also compete in tournaments such as the Native American Basketball Invitational.

Like basketball, baseball is a game developed and perfected in the United States. The popularity of baseball within the Plains is due, in part, to the simple arrangement required for play: an infield with four bases and base paths, a pitcher's mound, two batter's boxes, and a grass outfield. Plains baseball at the youth level includes Little League and American Legion organizations. American Legion baseball was born in the Great Plains. First proposed in Milbank, South Dakota, in 1925, American Legion Junior Baseball is the oldest and largest teenage baseball program in the United States. Legion baseball was developed to promote American values, and teams often receive financial support from local businesses. Despite its success at the youth level, baseball is not as important in high schools as football and basketball. Facilities, publicity, and attendance generally fall off after Little League or American Legion play. Due to competition for players participating in other sports, baseball is often played as a fall sport in smaller high schools.

Intercollegiate Athletics

In the absence of "big-time" professional teams in the Great Plains, intercollegiate athletics has emerged as the most visible element of sports in the region. College sports bring traditions that transcend those of other competitions, such as marching bands, mascots, cheerleaders, and tailgate parties. In addition to individual colleges and universities, athletic conferences also provide identity for the region. The Big Eight Conference, expanded in 1996 to become the Big Twelve, is nearly synonymous with the Great Plains. The Big Twelve schools an Nebraska, Kansas, Kansas State, Missouri, Colorado, Iowa State, Oklahoma State, Oklahoma, Texas, Texas A&M, Texas Tech, and Baylor. Although intercollegiate sports such as baseball, hockey, and track are exciting to watch, only two sports, football and basketball, consistently draw large crowds.

The Football Cult of the Plains

The game of football was still young when it arrived on the Plains. The University of Nebraska Cornhuskers played their first game in 1890, beating the Omaha YMCA by a score of 10–0. Soon other universities began fielding football teams. The University of Oklahoma lost its first game to Oklahoma City in 1895, 34–0. Likewise, Kansas State lost its inaugural game to Fort Riley in 1896 (14–0) and Oklahoma A&M (now Oklahoma State) to Kingfisher in 1901 (12–0). Players on early teams played both ways, offense and defense. Once a game began, a man could not be substituted unless he was injured. No helmets or pads were worn, and there were frequent arguments over referee decisions.

In 1907, Kansas, Missouri, Nebraska, Iowa, and Washington University became charter members of the Missouri Valley Intercollegiate Athletic Conference, a precursor to the Big Eight/Big Twelve Conference. Plains teams soon became nationally recognized programs. Nebraska won notoriety in 1913 by beating Notre Dame. Under coach Fred Dawson, the Cornhuskers improved to become a major rival of Knute Rockne's Notre Dame teams of the 1920s. Plains teams also helped shape the modern game of football. For example, under Coach Bennie Owen, the University of Oklahoma helped popularize the forward pass.

Football stands out among intercollegiate sports as an activity that forges strong links between alumni and their alma mater. There is no better example of this bond than Nebraskans and Cornhusker football. Nebraskans love football, so much so that "Big Red" is a symbol of state identity. On game days, Memorial Stadium turns into a sea of red and white. Loyalty to school and team is represented in the words to a popular song:

> There is no place like Nebraska, dear old Nebraska U. Where the girls are the fairest and guys are the squarest of any old school I knew. There is no place like Nebraska, where they are all true blue. We'll all stick together in any old weather for dear old Nebraska U.

Nebraska's success on the field is demonstrated by three national championships during the last decade. Beginning with the 1967 season, the Cornhuskers have maintained an unbroken stream of sellout games, prompting author Michael Stein to describe fan loyalty as a "recreational cult."[3] Television and newspaper stories keep the team under a constant spotlight. From mid-August until the beginning of the season, there is an almost daily feature story about some aspect of Nebraska football. Various auxiliary and booster organizations such as the Touchdown Club work to raise financial support for the team. School spirit is displayed on hats, T-shirts, key chains, and spare-tire covers.

The situation in Oklahoma is similar to that in Nebraska. Under Bud Wilkinson, the Sooners won forty-seven straight games from 1953 to 1957. They have continued to win, with seven national championships under coaches Barry Switzer and Bob Stoops. Kansas State has also achieved national prominence in the last decade, giving other "doormat" teams a glimmer of hope. Oklahoma State and Kansas have had occasionally outstanding seasons and together have produced several great NFL stars, such as Barry Sanders, Thurman Thomas, John Riggins and Gayle Sayers. The Dakotas have no National Collegiate Athletic Association (NCAA) Division 1A football programs. However, North Dakota State has been one of the nation's best small-college teams during the last forty years.

The Oklahoma–Nebraska football rivalry is one of the nation's best-known college football contests. ESPN ranks it within the top 10 college rivalries along with Alabama–Auburn, Ohio State–Michigan, Army–Navy, and USC–UCLA.

Basketball

In 1898, James Naismith joined the faculty of the University of Kansas as a physical education professor. When his former student, Forrest "Phog" Allen (1885–1974), reported having been hired as basketball coach at Butler University, Naismith remarked, "Why, basketball is just a game to play. It doesn't need a coach."[4] Ironically, the inventor of basketball considered wrestling to be a better form of exercise than basketball. Allen went on to become a collegiate basketball legend. In thirty-nine seasons at the University of Kansas, he won 590 games and led KU to a 1952 NCAA championship.

Naismith went on to achieve later fame of his own. In 1899 he was coach of KU's first-ever basketball game. Naismith was the first inventor of a sport to see it played as an Olympic Medal event. The Naismith Memorial Basketball Hall of Fame in Springfield, Massachusetts, honors the inventor of basketball, a sport played in more than one hundred and forty countries.

The central Plains has become known for outstanding collegiate basketball players, teams, and coaches. The University of Kansas and Oklahoma State have each won national championships, Kansas in 1952 and 1988 and Oklahoma State the first back-to-back wins under coach Henry Iba (1904–1993) in 1945 and 1946. The University of Oklahoma and Kansas State have also appeared in basketball championship games and Final Four appearances. Oklahoma City's All College Tournament is the oldest college basketball tournament in the United States, attracting great players such as Pete Maravich, Karl Malone, and Bill Russell.

In recent decades, the University of Tulsa and Creighton University have made great strides nationally. They have become regulars in the NCAA Tournament and have been rated in the Associated Press Top 20 teams. Creighton began its rise in the late 1980s when Bob Harstad and Chad Gallagher were star players. Tulsa rose with great coaches, Nolan Richardson, Tubby Smith, and Bill Self. Other successful Plains basketball programs include Wichita State and Oral Roberts University.

Plains universities have also received visibility in women's basketball. Smaller schools have been successful in NCAA Division II and National Association of Intercollegiate Athletics (NAIA) basketball, as demonstrated through national cham-

Collegiate Football Stadiums

Among the most recognizable landmarks on college and university campuses are football stadiums. With a capacity of nearly 73,000 persons, the University of Oklahoma's Owen Field is the largest stadium in the Great Plains and the nineteenth-largest stadium used by a Division I university. Owen Field was named in honor of Bennie Owen (1875–1970), Sooners coach from 1905 to 1926 and a charter member of the National Football Hall of Fame. The push to build a modern stadium began in 1921 when OU students campaigned for the construction of a student union. This effort was later expanded to a combined football stadium and union. The first game was played at Owen Field on October 20, 1923. In 1929, the original 16,000 seats were expanded to 32,000, and in 1957 the seating capacity was increased to 55,000. The last major renovation took place in 1979.

Table 10. Major collegiate stadiums in the Plains

Stadium Name	University	Location	Capacity	Conference
Owen Field	University of Oklahoma	Norman, OK	72,765	Big 12
Memorial Stadium	University of Nebraska	Lincoln, NE	72,700	Big 12
Lewis Field	Oklahoma State University	Stillwater, OK	50,614	Big 12
Wagner Field	Kansas State University	Manhattan, KS	50,300	Big 12
Memorial Stadium	University of Kansas	Lawrence, KS	50,250	Big 12
Skelly Stadium	University of Tulsa	Tulsa, OK	40,385	WAC

The University of Kansas played its first two years of intercollegiate football (1890–1891) in Old Central Park on Massachusetts Street in Lawrence. In 1892, Mc-Cook Field, named after Colonel John McCook, was constructed with wooden bleachers on the sidelines. The Jayhawks played their first game at McCook on October 27, 1892, defeating Illinois, 26–4. The concept of a new and larger facility came at the urging of students, faculty, and fans in the years after World War I. Dr. F. C. "Phog" Allen (1885–1974), who in 1920 led KU to a 20–20 tie after trailing Nebraska 20–0 at halftime, helped push for the concept of a new stadium before going on to fame as KU basketball coach. Constructed in 1921, Memorial Stadium is the eighth oldest collegiate stadium in the nation and commemorates University of Kansas students who fought in World War I. When first constructed, the horseshoe-shaped stadium's capacity was 22,000. In 1927, the north bowl was completed to increase seating capacity to 35,000. Additional renovations were completed in 1963, 1966, and finally 1987, increasing capacity to 50,250. There is room for another 10,000 spectators on "the Hill" overlooking the south end zone.

The first grandstand on Oklahoma State's Lewis Field, named after Laymon Loweny Lewis, former dean of veterinary medicine and acting president of Oklahoma A&M University in 1914, was constructed in 1920 with 8,000 seats. Initially the bleachers were positioned with the traditional north-south orientation but were later changed to an east-west alignment to lessen the impact of prevailing winds. In 1924, the first concrete and steel section of the present stadium was built on the south side. During the 1929–30 season, the stadium's capacity was increased to 13,000, and in 1947 additional rows were added to increase capacity to 30,000. A permanent press box was also added at this time. Other renovations included the addition of end-zone bleachers that increased the stadium's capacity to 50,614.

A campaign to build a football stadium at the University of Nebraska was initiated in 1922, with students, faculty, alumni, and friends working to raise $430,000 needed for construction. The stadium was completed in 1923 and dedicated as a memorial to all Nebraskans who fought in overseas conflicts. The year 1997 marked the two hundredth straight "sold-out" game for Memorial Stadium. The stadium's capacity is 72,700, making it the second-largest stadium in the Big Twelve after Owen Field. In 1998, the university raised funds by selling luxury boxes near the fifty-yard line for $2 million each.

Kansas State's first football home was located a few blocks from campus on a site now occupied by Bluemont Elementary School. Its grandstand was built by Manhattan lumberyard owner and KSU graduate Emil Pfuetz. The present stadium at Wagner Field, named after Dave and Carol Wagner of Dodge City, Kansas, who donated $1 million to put artificial turf in the stadium, was financed through a combination of student fees, ticket sales, and contributions. On September 21, 1968, the Wildcats played their first game at Wagner Field, shutting out Colorado State, 21–0. During the summer of 1970, the stadium's original seating capacity of 35,000 was increased by the addition of permanent and temporary bleachers. The most recent renovation took place in 1998 when a deck and sky suites were added to the east side of the stadium. Wagner Field hosted the largest crowd (52,254) to witness a sporting event in the state when the Wildcats beat Kansas 50–9 on October 9, 1999, to win their seventh straight Governor's Cup.

NCAA Division II universities also maintain strong support from their fans. North Dakota State is among the top Division II schools in attendance for football, men's basketball, and volleyball. A football attendance record was set in 2000 at the Fargodome when 19,200 watched North Dakota State play North Dakota.

pionship wins by the University of North Dakota and North Dakota State University. Oklahoma City University has won the NAIA championship three times, while Southern Nazarene University's women have a 122-game winning streak at home.

Baseball

The central Plains has a long-standing tradition for outstanding collegiate baseball. Oklahoma State ranks fourth in the number of College World Series appearances with seventeen, while the University of Oklahoma is tenth with nine appearances. College World Series outstanding players include two from the University of Oklahoma (1994 and 1959), two from Oklahoma State (1961 and 1955), and one from Wichita State (1989). NCAA record holders from Plains states who went on to professional careers include Oklahoma State players Robin Ventura (fifty-eight-game batting streak) and Pete Incaviglia (forty-eight home runs in a seventy-five-game season). Each June the NCAA College World Series is played in Omaha's Rosenblatt Stadium, and single-game attendance often exceeds 20,000. The College World Series is an Omaha cultural fest and a rite of spring. All games of the double-elimination event, pitting the eight best collegiate nines in America, are televised on networks such as ESPN. Many participants have been drafted by major-league teams and have gone on to success at the professional level.

Professional Sports

Major professional sports are not well represented within the Great Plains. Given the limited base of fans, even large Plains cities are viewed as poor risks for establishing a major professional franchise that depends on attendance and television revenue. In the absence of "big-time" professional sports, minor-league and semiprofessional teams have established themselves in Plains states. At one time, minor-league baseball was well established in communities throughout the Plains. The Nebraska cities of Ord, Holdrege, McCook, Grand Island, Kastings, and Kearney once hosted minor-league baseball teams, as did thirty-seven cities and towns in Oklahoma at various times. The introduction of radio, which enables fans to follow games played in distant locations, contributed to declining interest in local minor league teams. As a result, interest in major league play increased at the expense of the minors.

Today's minor leagues serve as proving grounds for major-league programs. Within the Great Plains, the majority of teams are located in medium-sized cities. For example, the Omaha Royals is an AAA team associated with the Kansas City Royals organization. Another team, the AAA Oklahoma Redhawks, is an affiliate of the Texas Rangers and plays in Southwestern Bell Bricktown Ballpark in Oklahoma City. Class AA teams within the Texas League include the Tulsa Drillers and the Wichita Wranglers.

Professional baseball in the Plains is also represented by independent organizations. Spanning Minnesota to the Dakotas, the Prairie League includes the Dakota Rattlers (Bismarck, North Dakota) and the Grand Forks Varmints. Another independent organization, the Northern League, includes the Fargo-Moorhead Redhawks, the Kansas City T-Bones, the Sioux Falls Canaries, and the Lincoln Salt Dogs. The Northern League began in 1902, and Fargo had one of the founding franchises. Early in the league's development, a salary cap was enacted to protect teams that played in smaller towns from those in big cities that were capable of drawing larger crowds. Of note is Richard Brookings, who played on the 1908 Fargo team. Brookings was the first African American player to have a career outside of the Negro League until Jackie Robinson's minor league debut with Montreal in 1946. Over its history, the Northern League has experienced a number of ups and downs. The league's most recent rebirth took place in 1993 when a decision was made to resurrect independent, town-based teams rather than organization-grounded farm clubs. The names of some current Northern League teams are tied to local culture and history. For example, the Lincoln Salt Dogs is named for a salt flat now occupied by the city's Capitol Beach Lake that was a destination for settlers who sought to replenish their salt supplies.

Although semiprofessional football is less visible than baseball, it has become established in the Plains states. Unlike minor-league baseball, which prepares players for the majors, semiprofessional football is not a gateway to National Football League (NFL) teams. College stars accustomed to packed stadiums and television audiences must adjust to playing semiprofessional football for a few thousand fans. Most play because they love the game. The North American Football League (NAFL) includes the Nebraska Bears (Omaha), the Lincoln Renegades, the Tri-city Marshalls (Dodge City, Kansas), the Oklahoma Fire (Tulsa), and the Norfolk Thunderbirds (Norfolk, Nebraska). The Oklahoma Football League (OFL) includes the McAlester Bulls, the Wichita Aztecas, the Chickasha Predators, the Oklahoma City Fire, and the Tulsa Stampede. Several other teams play in the National Indoor Football League, including the Omaha Beef, the Oklahoma Crude (Enid, Oklahoma), the Rapid City Red Dogs, the Sioux City Bandits, and the Bismarck Roughriders. The Arena2 Football League includes the Tulsa Talons and the Wichita Stealth. Introduced in 1991, indoor football is played on a fifty-yard-long field with eight players on each team.

Two professional basketball leagues include teams in Plains states. The Dakota Wizards (Bismarck), the Fargo/Moorhead Beez, and the Sioux Falls Skyforce are part of the Continental Basketball Association (CBA), the oldest professional basketball organization in the United States. The league is made up of individually owned teams, a factor that reinforces local ties and community support. In 1988, the Fast Breakers, Tulsa's first professional basketball team, won the CBA championship. However, shortly after winning, the team disbanded because of financial troubles. The Oklahoma City Cavalry joined the CBA in 1990 but also fell on financial hard times and disbanded in 1997 after winning the league championship. Kansas and Oklahoma are home to three teams in the U.S. Basketball League, the Dodge City Legend, the Kansas Cagerz (Salina, Kansas), and the Oklahoma Storm (Enid, Oklahoma). Omaha was once the home of two professional basketball teams that have moved to other locations. The Kings played in Omaha from 1972 to 1974 before moving to Kansas City and then to their current location in Sacramento, California, while the Racers were based in Omaha from 1989 to 1996 before disbanding.

At one time Omaha hosted a professional hockey team, the Knights (1939 to 1975). Playing at Aksarben Coliseum, the Knights was a feeder team for the Detroit Red Wings and the New York Rangers. Professional hockey teams that are part of the Continental Hockey League are based in Kansas and Oklahoma and include the Oklahoma City Blazers, the Tulsa Oilers, the Topeka Scarecrows, and the Wichita Thunder. Professional soccer is represented by the Kansas City Comets, part of the Major Indoor Soccer League (MISL).

Great Players and Coaches

Over the years, the Plains states have produced dozens of outstanding college and professional athletes. One of the earliest inductees into the National Baseball Hall of Fame was Walter Johnson (1886–1946). A native of Allen County, Kansas, Johnson won 416 games as a pitcher for the Washington Senators, a record that is second only to that of Cy Young. During his career he threw 110 shutouts and struck out 3,508 batters. His trademark fastball was delivered with the speed of a locomotive, earning him the nickname "Big Train Johnson."

Jim Thorpe (1888–1953) is widely considered among the greatest athletes of all time. Born in Prague, Oklahoma, from Irish and Sac and Fox extraction, Thorpe attended the Indian Agency School near Tecumseh, Oklahoma. At age sixteen he was recruited to attend the Carlisle Indian School in Pennsylvania, where Glenn S. "Pop" Warner, the school's legendary football and track coach, asked him to try out for both the track and football teams. At that time, the Carlisle Indians were playing many of the best collegiate teams, often beating Chicago, Minnesota, Nebraska, Harvard, and Penn State. In 1912, Thorpe was selected to represent the United States in the decathlon and pentathlon at the Stockholm Olympic Games.

He earned a gold medal in the pentathlon by winning four of the five events: the broad jump, 200-meter dash, discus, and 1,500-meter race. He lost only in the javelin. Thorpe's gold-medal mark of 8,413 points in the decathlon stood for several decades. However, when it was revealed that he had been paid to play baseball in 1909 and 1910, Thorpe was asked to return his Olympic medals. He went on to play baseball for the New York Giants, Cincinnati Reds, and Boston Braves. In 1915, he played football for the Canton Bulldogs and in 1920 was appointed president of the American Professional Football Association, forerunner of the National Football League. Thorpe's football career included stints with the Oorang Indians, Cleveland Indians, Rock Island Independents, and Chicago Cardinals. In 1941, he left professional athletics. Over the years, there were several efforts to have Thorpe's gold medals returned, but it was not until 1982, twenty-nine years after his death, that his medals were finally reinstated. Jim Thorpe's reputation as an outstanding athlete has endured. In a 2000 Gallup poll, respondents were asked "What man or woman living anytime this century do you think was the greatest athlete of the century, in terms of athletic performance?" Thorpe ranked fourth behind Michael Jordan, Muhammad Ali, and Babe Ruth.[5]

Jim Ryun (b. 1947) achieved national acclaim as a high-school track star in Wichita, Kansas. In 1965, Ryun became the first high-school student to run the mile in less than four minutes (3:55.3), and in July 1966 he set the world record for the mile at 3:51.3. As a freshman at the University of Kansas, Ryun set a world record in the 880-yard run (1:44.9). In 1966, he received the Sullivan Award for being the top amateur athlete and was named "Sportsman of the Year" by *Sports Illustrated* magazine. Ryun was a member of the 1964, 1968, and 1972 U.S. Olympic teams and won a silver medal for the 1,500-meter run at the 1968 games. He was later elected to a seat in the U.S. House of Representatives, representing the Second District of Kansas.

An inductee into the National Basketball Hall of Fame, Wilt Chamberlain (1936–1999) gained national attention playing basketball for the University of Kansas and later as a professional. During his first game as a varsity player at Kansas, the seven-foot, one-inch Chamberlain set a school record of fifty-two points. Chamberlain's honors as a collegiate player include selection as a First Team All-American (1957, 1958), NCAA Tournament Most Valuable Player (1957), and All Big Seven player (1957, 1958). In two seasons at Kansas he averaged nearly thirty points and eighteen rebounds per game. After a brief stint with the Harlem Globetrotters, Chamberlain played for the Philadelphia (later San Francisco) Warriors (1959–1964), the Philadelphia 76ers (1964–1968), and the Los Angeles Lakers (1968–1973). As a professional, he was named NBA Rookie of the Year, All-Star Game Most Valuable Player, and NBA Most Valuable Player.

The University of Kansas also produced the man many consider to be the best running back in collegiate and NFL history, Gayle Sayers (b. 1943). After playing for the University of Kansas, Sayers was drafted by the Chicago Bears. His honors include NFL Rookie of the Year in 1965 and all-time NFL kickoff return leader in touchdowns and yardage. Sayers was the youngest player in NFL history to be inducted into the Pro Football Hall of Fame.

As a junior at Oklahoma State University, Wichita native Barry Sanders (b. 1968) won the Heisman Trophy after setting an NCAA record of 2,628 yards and 37 touchdowns. He later became one of the youngest running backs in NFL history. Sanders was the third player in NFL history to rush for over more than 2,000 yards in a season (2,053 in 1997) and was named the NFL's Offensive Player of the Year twice (1994 and 1997).

A native of Edmond, Oklahoma, Shannon Miller (b. 1977) was a member of the first U.S. Olympic gymnastics team to win a gold medal. Miller is the most decorated gymnast in U.S. history, having won two gold, two silver, and three bronze Olympic medals. Other honors include nine World Championship medals, fifty-eight international medals, and forty-nine national medals. She is also the only American gymnast in history to win two consecutive World Championship all-around titles. Miller is the youngest inductee into the Oklahoma Sports Hall of Fame.

Williston, North Dakota, native Phil Jackson (b. 1945) is the son of two fundamentalist preachers who swore an oath of poverty. At the University of North Dakota, Jackson received All-American honors as a basketball player. In 1967, he was drafted by the New York Knicks and contributed to their success in the NBA championship game in 1973. Jackson went on to coach the Chicago Bulls in 1989, leading the team to six national championships in nine years. His success has continued on the west coast as the head coach of the Los Angeles Lakers.

Other Community-Based Team Sports

While only a few athletes can ever play professional or collegiate sports, nearly anyone can participate in community-based team sports. Among these, softball is one of the most popular team games played in the Plains states. Two variants of softball are played: fast-pitch, where the pitcher tries to strike out the batter, and slow-pitch, where the ball is thrown so it can be hit. Slow-pitch softball is played throughout the Plains, while fast-pitch softball is popular mostly in the northern Plains. With an estimated 25,000 players on women's, men's, and youth teams, Omaha, Nebraska is sometimes referred to as the "softball capital of the world." During the month of January, die-hard Omaha residents participate in the annual "Sno-ball" softball tournament.

Amateur wrestling has continued to gain popularity throughout the Plains, particularly at the collegiate level. In 1928, the NCAA endorsed collegiate wrestling with rules and judging based on the awarding of points. Many communities sponsor youth wrestling programs in divisions that accommodate children as young as six. Younger children compete during two ninety-second periods, while matches for older participants (sixteen years and up) are played during two three-minute periods. In addition to being separated into age groups, youth wrestlers are divided into weight classes. Oklahoma State University's winning tradition in collegiate wrestling began under legendary coach Edward C. Gallagher (1887–1940). Between 1916 and 1940, Gallagher led the Cowboys to 138 dual-match wins with just 5 losses and 4 ties. Oklahoma State's thirty-one NCAA wrestling titles are the most collected by a school in a single sport. Oklahoma wrestlers have also been recognized at the international level. Former Oklahoma State wrestler and current coach John Smith (136.5 pounds) won his second gold medal at the 1992 Barcelona Olympics. Another OSU wrestler, Kendall Cross (125.5 pounds), won a gold medal for the United States during the 1996 Atlanta Olympic Games.

The historical roots of modern soccer can be found in England, where townspeople tried to force an inflated animal bladder into an opposing village. Teams sometimes included hundreds of men, and games were extremely rough. Although soccer has been a popular sport throughout Europe and South America for many years, it has not achieved the same stature in the United States. The sport is most popular in the Northeast and in western states and is less well established in the southern, midwestern, and Plains states. However, since the 1960s there has been considerable growth in the number of pre-high-school soccer leagues organized in the Plains states. Several private soccer organizations such as the American Youth Soccer Organization (AYSO) have become popular, notably in Kansas, Oklahoma, and South Dakota. In many communities, soccer is played as both an indoor sport during cooler winter months and as an outdoor sport during the spring and fall. An All American Girl's and Women's Soccer tournament is held each year for residents of northern Midwestern and Plains states.

Despite a nationwide decline in popularity, bowling remains a popular sport in the Plains. Bowling tournaments are offered in divisions for singles, seniors, doubles, and mixed doubles. Tournament play is especially popular in South Dakota, Nebraska, and Oklahoma. River Lanes in Tulsa is one of the largest bowling facilities in the United States.

In addition to opportunities for team play, many cities and towns sponsor athletic events ranging from ten-kilometer runs to golf tournaments. Bismarck's Prairie Rose Games is part of a national network of Olympic-style events for athletes of all ages and abilities. Male and female athletes participate in fifteen sports: baseball, figure skating, softball, basketball, gymnastics, swimming, bowling, ice hockey, tennis, diving, road race (five kilometers), track and field, field hockey, soccer, and wrestling. Nebraska's Cornhusker State Games is a similar event.

Winter Sports

Winter sports, including hockey, curling, downhill skiing, and cross-country skiing, are extremely popular in northern Great Plains states. Hockey is played as a high-school and college sport on a sheet of ice measuring two hundred feet by ninety feet. The popularity of hockey in North Dakota is illustrated by thirty-one separate hockey associations. Youth hockey organizations such as the American West Hockey League (AWHL) and the United States Hockey League (USHL) focus on preparing players for college scholarships. The Bismarck Bobcats and the Wichita Rustlers are part of the AWHL, while Omaha is the home city for the Lancers, a member of the USHL. The University of North Dakota remains an NCAA hockey powerhouse, having won seven NCAA hockey championships. In 2002, the North Dakota High School Activities Association added girls' hockey to its list of sanctioned activities with the stipulation that checking (intentional contact) was prohibited.

The sport of curling owes its beginnings to seventeenth-century Scotland, where it was played in nearly every parish. Scottish soldiers and emigrants helped spread the sport, and the first North American curling club was founded in Montreal in 1807. Within the Great Plains, curling is most established in North Dakota but is also played in South Dakota, Nebraska, and Kansas. Interest in curling is focused mostly in small towns and rural areas. Never well known in the United States, curling is a tradition passed down through families. Teams that compete in bonspiels (tournaments) are made up of four persons who play on a sheet of ice 145 feet long and 15 feet wide. Players from each team alternately slide stones toward the "house," a bull's-eye at the far end of the ice. As each stone is released, teammates use brooms to keep the pathway ahead of the stone clear of ice and snow. Points are based on the proximity of each stone to the house after all sixteen stones have been delivered.

Motor Sports

Several Plains cities maintain large facilities for automobile racing and smaller tracks for midget and go-cart racing. The I-70 Speedway in Kansas City, Kansas, hosts the Craftsman Truck series each year for sellout crowds of 10,000. Huset's Speedway in Sioux Falls, South Dakota, is home to the World of Outlaws Sprint Car Championship. Outlaw cars look like makeshift dune buggies with aerodynamic spoilers mounted above the driver's head that are nearly the size of the cars themselves. The class is named for drivers who are billed by promoters as unfair participants. Auto-racing tracks in the Plains serve as proving grounds for drivers who hope to qualify for high-prestige events such as Busch or Winston Cup races. Track layouts include semibanked ovals with dirt or clay surfaces and banked oval tracks for high-speed racing. Some examples of tracks are Heartland Park in Topeka, Dodge City Raceway Park, Sunset Speedway in Omaha, and the Hallett Motor Racing Circuit near Tulsa. River Cities Speedway in East Grand Forks, North Dakota, hosts super stock cars, late models, and sprint cars. There are also a few asphalt drag strips. The Dakota Flat Track in Minot, North Dakota, is a one-eighth mile track that hosts Pro Street, Super Trophy, Motorcycle, Junior Dragster, and Snowmobile class racing. Racing activities also take place away from tracks. Solo racing tests a driver's agility while navigating a clearly defined course such as a large parking lot. Speeds are limited to reduce hazards to spectators.

In the early 1940s, racing enthusiasts who could not afford cars for big-time speedway racing began building midgets. Initially, midget racing was held on dirt tracks at county fairgrounds. Later, specially designed midget tracks were built in Plains states. Some large companies became promoters of midget racing. The Maytag Washing Machine Company built an early midget racecar with a "Multi-Motor" engine, the same one used to power its washing machine. Midget auto racing in Belleville, Kansas, offers the "fastest ½ mile dirt track in the world."

Karting or go-cart racing is also popular, especially in Kansas and Oklahoma. Wooden Park Speedway in Wellington, Kansas, and the Oklahoma Motorsports Complex in Norman serve as homes for regional go-cart championships. Karts have small engines but can reach speeds of 65 to 140 mph. Two kinds of karts are most often raced, the Sprint kart and the Enduro kart. Sprint karts are characterized by a sitting-up position for drivers and are usually raced on tracks of a half mile or less in length. Enduro karts are designed so that drivers recline backwards, making the car design more aerodynamic. Enduro races are usually one hour in length and are staged at a larger motor sport complex. Classes are established according to driver age, car weight, size of engine, and other factors.

Equestrian Sports

During the 1920s, the U.S. Army held grueling rides as a means of evaluating cavalry and trail horses for their speed, strength, and endurance. These events helped generate renewed interest in riding for both recreation and sport. Riding competitions continue to be popular in the Plains. Western-style competitions are distinguished by the use of a heavy saddle. In comparison, the English style involves a lighter show saddle. Equestrian sports include show jumping, western pleasure, saddle seat, trail riding, and foxhunting. Show jumping involves horse and rider navigating a course made up of specially designed fences. The dressage (from the French word "dresser," to train) portion of an equestrian event consists of walks, trots, and canters, with each movement evaluated by judges. The object of dressage is to demonstrate the quality of the horse and rider's training.

Foxhunting has been popular in England, Ireland, and France since its origin as a sport in the 1700s. American foxhunting is thought to have originated in southern Kentucky in the late 1800s. The North Hills Hunt in Omaha, Nebraska, is an officially sanctioned hunt held on 10,000 acres of open land surrounding the Calamus Reservoir. For this event, a coyote is substituted for a fox. To riders, the longer the chase, the better. The leader of a foxhunt is the elected "master of foxhounds." One group of riders gives chase to the fox, while others are assigned to make sure the pack does not become too spread out. The "master" is assisted by the first "whipper-in," who is responsible for keeping the pack together, and the "earth stopper," who plugs holes where the fox may take refuge.

Horse and Dog Racing

Horse racing was the most organized sport in the United States before the Civil War. As a spectator event, it is sometimes referred to as the "sport of kings" because of its popularity during the reign of England's Charles II. The two major categories of horse racing are flat racing and steeplechase. Flat racing is held on oval-shaped, dirt tracks, while steeplechase requires that horse and rider navigate a series of fences. Initially, a flag was dropped to signify the beginning of a race, but it was later replaced with a mechanical signal to start all horses and riders at the same time. Horse-racing facilities within the Plains include Blue Ribbon Downs in Sallisaw, Oklahoma, which offers eighty-four race days each year for Appaloosas, quarter horses, thoroughbreds, and paints. Thoroughbred horses race over longer distances, while quarter horses are raced on a straightaway track 440 yards in length.

Because greyhound racing was once a favorite pastime of Queen Elizabeth I of England, it has been described as the "sport of queens." In the sport's early days, a rabbit was released for the dogs to follow, but this was replaced after 1900 by a mechanical rabbit. Greyhounds race in groups of eight over distances of five-sixteenths, three-eighths, seven-sixteenths, or nine-sixteenths of a mile and reach speeds up to forty-five mph. The Woodlands track in Kansas City is one of the premier greyhound-racing facilities in the United States. In 1987, the Woodlands featured the largest U.S. purse for a greyhound ($152,800). In recent years, the popularity of dog racing has declined, partly as a result of pressure from animal rights groups.

Golf

Golf had an early presence in the Plains. Between 1890 and 1920, the region experienced agricultural prosperity that led wealthy farmers, merchants and professionals to finance the construction of many courses. The initial investment in golf facilities was further enhanced during the 1960s and 1970s when many Plains cities and towns applied for federal grants to construct courses that were part of larger community recreation projects. Over the years, golf has become important within the social fabric of Plains cities and small towns. Many winter bowlers, curlers, and racquetball players switch to softball and golf during warmer months. Unlike other parts of the United States where transient golfers put significant pressure on courses, golf facilities in the Plains serve the resident population. Nearly every county in the Dakotas, Nebraska, and Kansas has a golf course. The majority of these are nine-hole courses, and a few still have sand greens.

Small courses are operated with little overhead, for example, in Bowbells, North Dakota, where a cashbox is found at the first tee to accommodate the "honor system" in effect for weekend play. Golf is inexpensive at such courses, often $10 or less for nine holes. Private golfing clubs are also less exclusive than those in other parts of the United States and therefore serve a broader spectrum of the local population. As a result of the availability of golf opportunities and player interest, Plains states have among the highest per capita levels of golf participation in the United States.

Several world-class golf courses are located in the Plains. Prairie Dunes was developed by the Carey family of Hutchinson, Kansas. The Careys were avid golfers who enjoyed traveling around the world to play outstanding courses. In 1937, they commissioned Golf Course architect Perry Maxwell to design a course comparable to those seen on their travels. After spending hours roaming the 480 acres, Maxwell remarked, "there are 118 golf holes here . . . and all I have to do is eliminate 100."[6] No modern equipment was used to build the first nine holes at Prairie Dunes. Teams of mules hauled soil to create the famous "Maxwell rolls." For more than twenty years, the original nine-hole course designed by Maxwell was rated among the top nine nine-hole courses in the country. During the 1950s, Maxwell's son developed the back nine holes. Prairie Dunes has been identified as among the best golf courses in the world by *Golf Magazine*. Several major events have taken place at Prairie Dunes, including the U.S. Women's Amateur (1964, 1980, 1991), the U.S. Mid-Amateur (1988), the Curtis Cup Match (1986), and the LPGA Championship (2002).

Built by Ben Crenshaw and Bill Coore in 1995, Sand Hills in Nebraska is another highly ranked course. Located in the rolling hills of north central Nebraska, the course follows natural contours of the landscape. Sand Hills does not have the cramped feel that plagues courses in urban and suburban areas. It is located in an entirely natural environment mostly unaffected by outside influences. Tulsa's Southern Hills has hosted seven major golf championships. With the exception of Augusta in Georgia, no other course in the United States has hosted as many major tournaments.

Youth Programs

Youth organizations in the Plains also provide opportunities to participate in competitive sports and recreation. 4H clubs offer training in shooting sports to promote safety and skill development in the use of rifles, shotguns, black-powder rifles, and pistols. Girl Scout and Boy Scout activities range from archery to bicycling, rock climbing, kayaking, gymnastics, and badminton. Older scouts participate in backpacking and canoeing excursions. Local scouting organizations operate permanent camps with pools, camping areas, cabins, and sport and recreation fields and facilities.

Mountain Biking, Chadron State Park, Nebraska. Photo by D. Curran. Courtesy Nebraska DED.

Heritage Events: Powwows, Rodeos, and Fast-Draw Shooting

Two great cultural events, the powwow and the rodeo, are important elements in the development of sport and recreation in the Plains. The Native American powwow began as a spring celebration of the renewal of life. The Sioux regarded the powwow as a prayer to Wakan-Tanka, the Great Spirit or Grandfather. Modern powwows continue to carry significance within Indian culture. Performers compete in dance competitions within categories, including Fancy, Traditional, Grass, Shawl, and Jingle Dress. The fancy dancer dons bustles and beads, while shawl dancers wear long-fringed garments over a beaded dress with moccasins and leggings. The Dakota "wacipi" involves dancers moving around a ring dressed in colorful regalia to a steady drumbeat. Powwows last from a few hours to a few days and may include craft displays, riding events, and cultural displays. Families often follow the powwow circuit during its peak season from June until September. The United Tribes Powwow in Bismarck, North Dakota, has been held every year since 1969. More than 1,500 dancers and 40 drum groups take part. The Ho-Chunk Powwow in Winnebago, Nebraska, is held over five days every July.

Rodeos remain extremely popular events in the Great Plains and for some communities serve as an important venue for celebrating western heritage. The "ballet" of bareback riding is so called because of the animal's natural desire to rid itself of whatever is on its back. Rodeo events fall into two categories. Rough stock includes bull riding, bareback, and saddle bronc, while timed events include calf roping, team roping and steer wrestling. Participation in women's rodeo has increased steadily and commonly includes barrel racing, goat tying, and breakaway tying. In barrel racing, riders compete for the fastest time navigating a triangular, cloverleaf pattern around three barrels. Success is tied to a rider's skill and training. Barrel racing began as a women's sport but has evolved into an amateur and professional event popular among both men and women.

Junior rodeo serves as a proving ground for later competitions and is divided into age groups for five- to twelve-, thirteen- to fifteen-, and sixteen- to eighteen-year-olds. Many junior rodeo participants come from second- and third-generation rodeo families. High-school rodeo includes separate competitions in bareback, saddle, bronc, bull riding, calf roping, cow cutting, and goat tying. There are also boys' and girls' all-around winners. Many Plains colleges and universities have rodeo teams that compete in events organized by the Intercollegiate Rodeo Association. The best amateur rodeo competitors participate in professional events.

Compared to other professional athletes, the prizes awarded to rodeo winners are relatively modest. Six-time world champion Larry Mahan described survival skills for rodeo competitors: "you have to learn to travel without a car, borrow clothes, and put up with ten men in your motel room."[7] Like other sports, rodeo has groupies known as "buckle bunnies" who follow winners. North Dakota's Brad Gjermundson is considered one of rodeo's great competitors, having won the World's Saddle Bronc Championship in 1981, 1983, 1984 and 1985. In 1995, he was inducted into the National Professional Rodeo Hall of Fame. Henryetta, Oklahoma, native Jim Shoulders is another rodeo legend and has won sixteen world championship titles.

Like powwows and rodeo, fast draw shooting is closely linked to the frontier

Rodeo. Courtesy South Dakota Tourism.

heritage. Fast draw involves reacting to a signal (a light or buzzer), firing, and hitting a target. Competitors fire full-powder blanks or wax bullets from .357- or .45-caliber single-action revolvers with barrels not less than $4\frac{5}{8}$ inches in length. Some events involve hitting balloons at distances ranging from eight to twelve feet. Events include the Wild Bill Hickock Days Championship for fast-draw shooting in Deadwood, South Dakota, and the Chisholm Trail Fast Draw Championship in Abilene, Kansas.

RECREATION ON THE PLAINS

The Great Plains has a rich endowment of lands suitable for recreation, ranging from cross-country ski trails, pristine lakes, and streams to forests suitable for hiking, camping, and hunting. Federal agencies maintain a variety of recreational facilities, including reservoirs, national forests, national park sites, and wildlife refuges. State park systems offer camping and recreation opportunities in parks, recreation areas, and resorts. These include horse trails, off-road recreational areas, nature centers, marinas, and picnic areas. Cities and towns in the Plains have also invested heavily in recreation facilities. Municipalities maintain public pools, tennis courts, fishing lakes, ice rinks, and golf courses. The sports complex, whether it is a hockey arena, ball field, or gymnasium, is often the most important gathering place in some small communities. This facility's location can affect other uses of open space such as parks, ball fields, and playgrounds, as well as influence traffic patterns and even property values. Local recreation facilities tend to be more developed and user oriented than federal or state recreation lands. In many cases, local sites are situated within the neighborhoods of the citizens they serve and are thus extremely accessible. In addition to public facilities, private organizations offer recreation facilities and programs through golf clubs, YMCAs, and fitness centers. Privately held farms and ranch lands are also part of the inventory of public lands in the Plains that are used for activities such as hunting, fishing, and snowmobile riding.

Water Recreation

Despite the common perception of the Plains as an arid environment, open water recreation opportunities are abundant. Large federally funded reservoir projects in states such as North Dakota, Nebraska, and Oklahoma provide hundreds of miles of shoreline and support fishing, waterskiing, sailing, and motorboating. Canoe trails are also available in some areas. In Nebraska, the Games and Parks Commission has established seven canoe trails with campsites spaced at one-mile intervals. A trip down 274 miles of North Dakota's Little Missouri River passes Sully Creek State Recreation Area, the Little Missouri Grassland, and Theodore Roosevelt National Park. Windsurfing and waterskiing are also popular on many lakes throughout the Plains, especially in Oklahoma, Kansas, and Nebraska.

Fishing

Fishing is extremely popular, especially within the northern Plains, where residents participate at nearly twice the U.S. average. Popular sport fish in the northern Plains include Chinook salmon, white bass, yellow perch, crappie, sauger, and brown trout. Also popular is winter ice fishing for yellow perch, northern pike, and walleye at destinations such as North Dakota's Spirit Lake. The Black Hills of South Dakota was a favorite fishing destination for Presidents Calvin Coolidge and Dwight Eisenhower. Reservoirs furnish the best fishing in Nebraska. Dozens of small lakes along the Platte River are stocked with largemouth bass, rock bass, and crappie. Fishing tournaments are popular throughout the Plains. A walleye tournament on Lake Sharpe in Pierre, South Dakota, offers professional anglers prizes up to $50,000 plus a fishing boat. Outstanding fishing areas in Oklahoma include Lake Texoma on the Oklahoma-Texas border, with abundant warm-water species, including white bass and crappie.

Sailboat on Lake Murray. Courtesy Oklahoma Tourism.

Hunting

Hunting is deeply ingrained in the culture of the Great Plains. Although the U.S. rate of hunting participation has declined since 1980, hunting participation has increased in the Plains. About 12 percent of Plains residents participate in hunting, compared to the national average of 6 percent. Hunting takes place on private land and within walk-in areas designated by state fish and game departments. Small-game hunting or "varmitting" is especially popular in the northern Plains. Small game animals include crows, groundhogs, coyotes, and prairie dogs. Although the hunting of these animals brings little prestige, it provides opportunities for sharpening shooting skills.

Each year thousands of people travel to the northern Plains to hunt waterfowl. The northern Plains are crossed by several migratory flyways, and tens of millions of geese and other birds stop on their way to wintering grounds in Louisiana and Texas. The Prairie Pothole region, extending from South Dakota to the forests of Saskatchewan and Alberta, is North America's largest duck area. Popular waterfowl include mallards, gadwalls, green- and blue-winged teals, widgeons, pintails, scaup, shovelers, and rednecks. Also hunted are Canada, snow, Ross, and white-fronted geese. Waterfowl hunters often find good duck and goose hunting on stock dams and adjacent to small lakes and ponds. A major threat to waterfowl hunting is the loss of grasslands and wetlands to agriculture. When water levels in the northern Plains began dropping in the late 1970s, most duck species began to decline in number. Initiated in 1995, the federally administered Conservation Reserve Program has helped protect millions of acres of grassland in the Plains for nesting cover, enabling duck populations to rebound. Other birds hunted in the northern Plains include pheasant, sharp-tailed grouse, Hungarian partridge, and wild turkey.

Hunting with rifles and bows is also popular for white-tailed deer, mule deer, and antelope. Wildlife losses due to hunting have brought concern among government agencies and conservation organizations. Overshooting and destruction of habitat have led to the disappearance of several Plains species, such as the greater prairie chicken in central South Dakota and the lesser prairie chicken in western Oklahoma. Large game animals have also disappeared. The Audubon bighorn sheep once ranged from the Rocky Mountains into the western part of the Dakotas and southwest Nebraska. The last bighorn sheep was killed in North Dakota in 1905. When white settlers first arrived on the Plains, the wapiti or American elk was found throughout the region. Today only a few wild wapiti are left, mostly on wildlife reservations. Prairie dogs, which once numbered in the millions, can still be found on the Plains, but their numbers have been severely depleted. Brought to the edge of extinction by uncontrolled hunting, the American bison is found in a few private herds and game preserves.

Bird Watching

The Northern Plains is extremely popular among birdwatchers for observing prairie species rare in other locations. Sample items on a birdwatcher's list may include Baird's sparrow, Sprague's pipit, the ferruginous hawk, and the least tern. Visitors also come to view the annual whooping crane migration. Whooping cranes are North America's tallest bird and migrate between northern Alberta and the Gulf coast of Texas each year between April and October. One of the world's largest nesting colonies of white pelicans can be found at North Dakota's Chase Lake. North Dakota has more national wildlife refuges (twenty-four) than any other state. In addition to managed refuges, the U.S. Fish and Wildlife Service maintains several unstaffed preserves on private land that provide sanctuaries for migrating waterfowl. Serving as a stopover for nearly half of North America's shorebirds, Cheyenne Bottoms, located near Great Bend, Kansas, is a wetland of international importance.

Winter Recreation

For most people, the word "skiing" implies the downhill kind. Only a few places in the Great Plains have topography suitable for downhill skiing. North Dakota's Huff Hills, Bears Den Mountain, and Frost Fire ski areas are small compared to those in Rocky Mountain states. With an elevation of more than 7,000 feet, South Dakota's Terry Peak Ski Area near Deadwood is one of the highest places between the Rocky Mountains and the European Alps. Several state parks and recreation areas in North and South Dakota offer cross-country ski trails. The origin of cross-country skiing in Plains states dates back to immigrants of the early nineteenth century who found it to be a faster and less fatiguing method of travel than snowshoeing for traversing long distances. Snowmobiling is also popular in the northern Plains. Some trails extend through forests of the Turtle Mountains and Pembina Gorge. More than three hundred miles of snowmobile trails crisscross Black Hills National Forest in South Dakota.

Recreational Tourism

Evidence of the Great Plains' frontier heritage has not been completely erased by time or human development. Wagon ruts from the Oregon and Mormon Trails can still be seen in places. Many visitors to the Plains come to gain a sense of the area's role in the westward expansion of the United States. Dressed in clothing of the period, a group of more than one hundred people meets each summer at Fort Seward near Jamestown, North Dakota, to reenact the pioneer wagon train experience. Outfitters offer camping trips built around nostalgic themes of the Oregon or Santa Fe Trails. Participants travel in wagons, camp each night, and cook over open fires. Evening campfire programs focus on storytelling and western singing.

Despite its important role in the settlement of the United States, the Great Plains is not a magnet for tourism. During his 1819 expedition, Major Stephen Long described the region as "the Great American Desert." More recently, descriptions have referred to the Plains as the "American Outback."[8] A 1988 survey of 1,000 college students from across the United States identified the Plains at the bottom of a list of regions preferred for recreation.[9] Plains residents themselves assigned a higher rating to the adjoining Rocky Mountains than to their own region. As a destination for international tourists, Oklahoma and Kansas are tied at thirty-eighth in the nation, and Nebraska, South Dakota, and North Dakota are ranked within the bottom five U.S. states.[10] The negative perception of the region as a destination is at least partly tied to the large distances that separate recreational amenities. For many Americans, the Plains is a region of transit rather than a destination. Most visitors do not venture far from interstate highways, as is demonstrated by the concentration of tourist amenities, especially private campgrounds and restaurants, within narrow corridors surrounding I-94 in North Dakota, I-90 in South Dakota, I-80 in Nebraska, I-70 in Kansas, and I-40 and I-44 in Oklahoma.

Public Recreation Areas

The Plains region has a comparatively small endowment of federal and state recreational lands. The Five Plains states rank within the bottom third in federal land acreage. Among these, Nebraska and Kansas are ranked forty-eighth and forty-ninth. Except for North and South Dakota, Plains states have relatively little U.S. Forest Service acreage and only a few federally designated wilderness areas.

National Park Lands

Despite having a smaller ratio of federal land than other regions, the Plains offers a diverse array of National Park Service sites. For example, Theodore Roosevelt National Park in North Dakota has eroded buttes, impassable badlands, and rolling hills across 70,000 acres divided between north and south units. Roosevelt first saw the area in 1883 and a year later purchased a ranch and shares in a herd of cattle. In 1949, land from Roosevelt's ranch was purchased to establish the park to recognize conservation efforts during his presidency that included designation of several national parks. Located just north of the Old West city of Medora, the South Unit experiences the heaviest recreation demand. In contrast, the North Unit is situated in a more remote setting and attracts visitors who prefer a primitive recreation experience.

Fort Union Trading Post National Historic Site is located in the far northwest portion of North Dakota. Established by the American Fur Company at the confluence of the Yellowstone and Missouri Rivers in 1829, the fort was an important site for the exchange of fur pelts and buffalo hides. Other national park units in the northern Plains include Wind Cave National Park and Jewel Cave National Monument, both in South Dakota. Wind Cave's prairie grasslands are home to pronghorn antelope, bison, elk, and prairie dogs. With more than 128 miles of surveyed passageways, Jewel is the world's third-longest cave. Underground "decorations" in Wind and Jewel Caves include stalactites, stalagmites, draperies, frostwork, and flowstone. Located in South Dakota, Badlands National Park encompasses 244,000 acres of eroded pinnacles, spires, and buttes. The Lakota Indians named the area "mako sica," meaning "bad land." In addition to protecting an area rich in fossil evidence dating to the Oligocene epoch, the park includes 64,000 acres of wilderness land. Agate Fossil Beds National Monument near Harrison, Nebraska, protects fossil beds formed 19 million years ago within mud that was compressed to form sedimentary rocks of the Carnegie and University Hills. Rising eight hundred feet above the North Platte River Valley, Scott's Bluff, the focal point of Scott's Bluff National Monument in western Nebraska, was an important landmark for westward travelers.

Only about 1 percent remains of the prairie ecosystem that once covered 400,000 square miles of North America. Discussions about establishing a national park to protect a representative sample of prairie land date back to the 1930s. However, Congress did not take action until 1996, when the Tallgrass Prairie National Preserve was created within the Flint Hills of Kansas. The preserve's 10,894 acres include a historic ranch house built in 1881, a limestone barn, several outbuildings, and a one-room schoolhouse. In south central Oklahoma, Chickasaw National Recreation Area protects mineral springs that were once considered important to therapeutic treatment of rheumatism and other ailments. The site encompasses the former Platt National Park, one of only two national parks to have been "decommissioned." The other, Sully's Hill National Park in North Dakota, is now managed as a game preserve.

U.S. Forest Service Lands

The U.S. Forest Service operates several recreation facilities within the Black Hills National Forest as well as three national grasslands within the Missouri Plateau. With an abundance of wildlife, Black Hills National Forest offers attractive scenic vistas and picturesque rock outcrops. Each year thousands of visitors come to see the granite carving of Presidents Washington, Jefferson, Lincoln, and Theodore Roosevelt on Mount Rushmore designed by sculptor Gutzon Borglum. The Black Hills is South Dakota's most important area for camping. During summer months, tourism increases the area's population by as much as 35 percent. Nearby, the cities of Hot Springs, Rapid City, and Deadwood are also important tourist attractions.

Located in southeastern Oklahoma and extending into southwestern Arkansas, the Ouachita National Forest is one of the largest national forests in the region. The forest's name comes from the Indian word "washitah," meaning "good hunting grounds." Within the forest is the 26,445-acre Winding Stair Mountain National Recreational Area established by Congress to offer recreation opportunities.

The U.S. Forest Service also manages several national grasslands in Plains states.

Nebraska's Oglala National Grassland is among North America's most complex ecosystems and offers outstanding opportunities for hiking and nature photography. Grassland wildlife includes sharp-tailed grouse, swift foxes, prairie falcons, golden eagles, and pronghorn antelope. Visitors to North Dakota's Little Missouri National Grassland can see a coal vein that has been smoldering several feet underground since before its discovery by white settlers. The fire burns at a rate of about ten feet per year, creating a "stairstep" appearance on the slope above.

Other Federal Lands Used for Recreation

Other federal agencies play a role in providing recreation facilities in Plains states. The U.S. Army Corps of Engineers is responsible for several water recreation areas. Among these is North Dakota's 575-square-mile Lake Sakakawea, created by the Missouri River's Garrison Dam. Other Corps reservoirs include Lake Ashtabula and Lake Darling in North Dakota, Patterson Lake in Kansas, and Lake Oahe in South Dakota. The U.S. Fish and Wildlife Service (USFWS), Bureau of Land Management (BLM), and Bureau of Reclamation (BOR) also control substantial acreage used for recreation. The USFWS operates dozens of wildlife refuges throughout the Plains, such as the Wichita Mountains National Wildlife Refuge in southern Oklahoma. Although BLM lands are used for wildlife viewing, hunting, and camping, they are often inaccessible and not managed strictly for recreation. The BOR manages large reservoirs that are used extensively for fishing, boating, and other water recreation.

State Parks

Because of frequently bitter winters, a saying among natives on the Plains is "forty below keeps the riffraff out." Indeed, state parks in Plains states are popular mostly among local residents. Cross Ranch State Park in North Dakota is located next to one of the few remaining wild sections of the Missouri River and provides habitat for coyotes, bald eagles and two endangered birds, the piping plover and the least tern. North Dakota's Metigoshe State Park offers year-round recreation. The Chippewa Indians called the region Metigoshe Washegum, meaning "clear lake surrounded by oaks." The park's wildlife include moose, bears, and an occasional wolf that wanders southward from Canada. With 73,000 acres, South Dakota's Custer State Park within the Black Hills is the second-largest state park in the United States. The Black Hills area was sacred to the Lakota Indians. Viewed from a distance, the park's rugged terrain acquires its dark color from thick stands of ponderosa pine.

Located at the base of the White River's rugged cliffs, Fort Robinson is Nebraska's largest state park. Occupation dates back to 1873, when a military fort stood on the site that was important in the nineteenth-century Indian Wars. The old parade grounds and officers' quarters are preserved. In 1887, Chief Crazy Horse was imprisoned at Fort Robinson following his surrender to the U.S. Army. In addition to camping facilities, the park offers a twenty-three-room lodge and thirty-two cabins. Situated on a narrow canyon flanked by bluffs that border agricultural land, Lake Scott State Park in western Kansas offers excellent crappie, bass, and channel catfish fishing opportunities. The park contains several archaeological sites, including what is believed to be evidence of the northernmost group of Pueblo Indians in North America. Representative of Oklahoma parks and resorts, the bouldered slopes of Oklahoma's Quartz Mountain State Park are situated within the Wichita Mountains near Lake Altus-Lugert.

Casino Gambling and Festivals

Casino gambling is a relatively new form of recreation in the Plains states. In 1988, Congress passed the Indian Gaming Regulatory Act, which enabled tribes to establish gaming facilities as long as the states where they are proposed have some form of legalized gambling. Casinos that operate on Indian land are equipped with tables for blackjack, roulette, craps, and poker as well as electronic gaming devices such as slot machines. In addition to nine casinos operated on tribal lands, the state of South Dakota permits bars and taverns to operate video poker, blackjack, keno, and bingo. In November 1989, the city of Deadwood, South Dakota, opened its first casino. Unlike destination resorts such as Atlantic City and Las Vegas, Deadwood's casinos attract mostly "day trippers" who are traveling within a hundred-mile radius of their homes. Casinos in Deadwood are required to conform to the city's 1800s architectural style. Many are located within historic structures such as the No. 10 Saloon. In addition to South Dakota, Indian gaming is permitted in North Dakota, Kansas, and Oklahoma, but not Nebraska.

The mix of cultures in the Plains is also represented in annual festivals held in cities and towns across the Plains. Since the 1950s, the frontier spirit of the Plains has been celebrated in the Oklahoma Panhandle as part of Guymon's annual Pioneer Days Celebration. Sodbuster Days is a two-day event held at North Dakota's Fort Ransom State Park to represent pioneer life during the early 1900s. Visitors can see demonstrations of corn grinding, quilting, and soap making. A number of festivals celebrate the heritage of European immigrants. Towns such as Wilber, Nebraska, and Tabor, South Dakota, host an annual Czech festival, while residents of Lindsborg, Kansas, celebrate their Swedish heritage during the Midsummer's Day Festival held in June.

During the first two weeks in August, thousands of motorcycle enthusiasts flock to Sturgis, South Dakota, for the Sturgis Rally, a series of races and other events that has been organized each summer since 1938. During May, the city of Wichita, Kansas, celebrates its River Festival, a ten-day event that includes raft and bathtub races, live entertainment, a fishing derby, and cook-offs. Sapulpa, Oklahoma, south of Tulsa, plays host to the Route 66 Blowout Festival in June to celebrate the transcontinental American highway important to many travelers prior to the advent of interstates.

CONCLUSION

The evolution of sports and recreation in the Great Plains has been a story of adaptation—to a challenging climate, to remoteness characterized by large distances between cities and towns, and to economic and social change brought about by urbanization. Leisure activities in the Plains evolved from rugged frontier individualism manifested in buffalo hunts to more sedate community-based activities such as baseball and golf. Sensing change at the end of the nineteenth century, a generation of Americans celebrated nostalgic themes of Plains frontier life through traveling Wild West shows. Economic hardship on farms and ranches led to decline in rural populations as the region became more urban in the years after the 1930s.

In contrast to more densely populated regions of the United States, per capita participation in sports and recreation in the Plains is very high. From youth to adult age groups, Plains residents participate in sport out of enjoyment. For most, the quality of play is less important than the goal of achieving high rates of involvement. However, many Plains communities struggle to maintain facilities in the face of population decline. In contrast to other U.S. regions, major professional teams are missing. Minor-league baseball and hockey teams can be found in larger cities, while a few others host semiprofessional baseball, football, and basketball teams with modest followings. Collegiate sports have emerged as the preeminent entertainment venue, and some teams have achieved national prominence. Residents of Kansas proudly identify with Jayhawk basketball, Oklahomans with Sooner football. A few programs have achieved cultlike loyalty from fans willing to travel hundreds of miles to attend games. Nebraska's "Big Red" football unites the farmer from Rushville with the attorney from Omaha and the car dealer from North Platte.

Plains communities maintain a commitment to providing sport and recreational facilities. Most have a high per capita number of golf courses, tennis courts, baseball diamonds, recreational trails, fishing lakes, and other public facilities. As a result of the region's isolation and modest tourist visitation, state parks and resorts cater mostly to local residents. Although not well endowed with national forest acreage, the region contains other federal lands that are used extensively for recreation, especially reservoirs and wildlife refuges. The region is known for interest in the outdoors. Residents of the northern Plains participate in hunting at twice the U.S. average and maintain high levels of interest in other outdoor activities such as fishing. Since the late 1970s, there has been a growing recognition within Plains states that sports and recreation constitute both an important stand-alone industry and a major influence on business decisions about the livability and investment appeal of a community. To attract new jobs and sources of income, Plains states have invested heavily in tourism, and restrictive "blue laws" have been liberalized, along with campaigns to legalize gambling. However, with large expanses of open range and cropland and few large cities, the Plains remains a destination with limited tourist appeal for most Americans. For most, the area is something to pass through rather than somewhere to go.

RESOURCE GUIDE

Printed Sources

Adams, Robert L., and John F. Rooney, "American Golf Courses: A Regional Analysis of Supply." *Sport Place* 3, no. 1 (1989): 3–17.

Anderson, Bob. *Sportsource*. Mountain View, CA: World Publications, 1975.

Buecker, Thomas R. 1996 "Prelude to Brownsville: The Twenty-fifth Infantry at Fort Niobrara, Nebraska, 1902–06." *Great Plains Quarterly* 16 (spring 1996): 95–106.

Burke, Bob, A. Franks, Royse Parr. *Glory Days of Summer: The History of Baseball in Oklahoma*. Oklahoma City: Oklahoma Heritage Association, 1999.

Krause, Kent M. "Changing the Pitch: Americanism, Athleticism, and the Development of Legion Baseball in Nebraska." *Great Plains Quarterly* 20 (winter 2000): 19–33.

LeCompte, Mary L. "Home on the Range: Women in Professional Rodeo: 1929–1947." *Journal of Sport History* 17, no. 3 (1990): 318–346.

Oxendine, Joseph B. *American Indian Sports Heritage*. Champaign, IL: Human Kinetics Books, 1988.

Rafferty, Milton. A *Geography of World Tourism*. Englewood Cliffs, NJ: Prentice Hall, 1993.

Raitz, Karl. "American Fox Hunting: Landscape Ensemble and Gratification." *Sport Place* 2, no. 3 (1988): 3–13.

Raitz, Karl, and Meftah Dakhil, "Physical Environment and Preferred Places for Recreation." *Sport Place* 2, no. 1 (1988): 25–33.

Reddin, Paul. *Wild West Shows*. Urbana: University of Illinois Press, 1999.

Rooney, John F. *A Geography of American Sport*. Reading, MA: Addison-Wesley Publishing Company, 1974.

Slatta, Richard W. *The Cowboy Encyclopedia*. New York: W. W. Norton and Co., 1994.

Stein, Michael. "Cult and Sport: The Case of Big Red." *Mid-American Review of Sociology 2*, no. 2 (1977): 29–42.

Welch, Paula D. *History of American Physical Education and Sport*. Springfield, IL: Charles C. Thomas, 1996.

Wheeler, Keith. *The Townsmen*. New York: Time-Life Books, 1975.

Wooster, Robert. *The Military and United States Indian Policy, 1865–1903*. New Haven, CT: Yale University Press, 1988.

Web Sites

O'Dell, Larry, *Encyclopedia of Oklahoma History and Culture*.
http://www.ok-history.mus.ok.us/enc/amuseparks.htm

Plains Folk: Six-man Football—the Game of the Plains
http://www.ext.nodak.edu/extnews/newsrelease/2000/102600/13plains.htm (accessed 2003)

Events

Family sports are important to these seasonal events:

Annual Sturgis Motorcycle Rally
The City of Sturgis
Rally Department
2030 Main St.
Sturgis, SD 57785
http://www.sturgismotorcyclerally.com/

Held in August each year.

Baseball College World Series
Rosenblatt Stadium Tickets and Seating Chart Map
1202 Bert Murphy Ave.
Omaha, Nebraska
http://www.cwsomaha.com/index.html

Played in June.

Midsummer's Day Festival
Midsummer's Committee

c/o Lindsborg Chamber of Commerce
104 E. Lincoln St.
Lindsborg, KS 67456
http://www.lindsborg.org/msommars/index.htm

Held on the third Saturday in June. A favorite holiday in Sweden, Midsummer's Day celebrates Swedish America.

Pioneer Days Celebration
Guymon Convention and Tourism Bureau
219 N.W. Fourth Street
Guymon, OK 73942
http://www.lasr.net/leisure/oklahoma/texas/guymon/att4.html

First weekend in May.

Sodbuster Days
Ft. Ransom State Park
5981 Walt Hjelle Parkway
Ft. Ransom, ND 58033
http://www.ndparks.com/Events/Sodbusters.htm

Held in July.

Organizations

National Cowboy and Western Heritage Museum
1700 Northeast 63rd Street
Oklahoma City, OK 73111
http://www.cowboyhalloffame.org/index2.html

National Softball Hall of Fame and Museum
2801 NE 50th Street
Oklahoma City, OK 73111-7203
http://www.softball.org/hall_of_fame/members.asp

Presents a history of the game and its greatest players and coaches.

Roger Maris Museum
West Acres Shopping Center
Fargo, ND 58103
http://www.rogermarismuseum.com

Presents the career of Fargo, North Dakota's, Roger Maris, who broke Babe Ruth's baseball home-run record in 1961.

TIMELINE

60 million B.C.E.	Last period of flooding of the region by a vast inland sea stretching from the Arctic to the Caribbean.
11,000 B.C.E.	Evidence of early Paleo-Indian life on the Plains along with dinosaurs such as mastodons and mammoths.
9000 B.C.E.	Increase in abundance of grasses and extensive herds of bison.
2000 B.C.E.	Bow and arrow technology revolutionized Plains hunting.
1400s C.E.	Large areas of the Plains abandoned by Native peoples due to increasingly arid summers, dust storms, and other adverse environmental conditions.
1540–1541	Francisco Vásquez de Coronado searches for the "Seven Cities of Cibola" on the Great Plains.
1682	Sieur de la Salle explores the Mississippi basin and claims the region drained by the Mississippi and its tributaries for France. The region is called Louisiana.
1700	Introduction of the horse and gun on the Great Plains.
1738	Pierre Gaultier de La Vérendrye, a French explorer, visits Mandan villages near the Missouri River. This is the first known Euro-American expedition into what is now North Dakota.
1762	All French territory west of the Mississippi is ceded to Spain.
1800	Louisiana is retroceded to France by Spain.
1803–1804	Napoleon sells all of Louisiana to the United States. President Thomas Jefferson proposes an exchange of land occupied by Native Americans in eastern states for "equivalent portions" in Louisiana.

1804–1806	Lewis and Clark exploratory expedition to the west coast up the Missouri River.
1806–1807	Zebulon Pike's exploratory expedition of the Mississippi River.
1807	Emanuel Lisa, Spanish fur trader, establishes trading stations above the headwaters of the Missouri River.
1808	Cherokee chiefs and headmen tell Jefferson that some of their tribe want to migrate to the West. This begins the move into what is now known as Oklahoma.
1814	Henry Brackenridge expedition for the Missouri Fur Company.
1819–1820	The Stephen Long expedition explores the Missouri River and pronounces it "uninhabitable" for agriculture.
1821	The route of the Santa Fe Trail is established.
1823	Boundary between Missouri and Kansas is created.
1838–1839	Trail of Tears.
1847	Mormons begin migrating in large numbers.
1849	California gold rush begins; 90,000 people travel west over Kansas trails.
1850s	Blacks began to settle in Kansas.
1854–1894	Sioux wars.
1860–1861	Pony express riders carry mail to the west coast.
1861	Kansas becomes a state.
1862	Homestead Act is passed.
1867	Nebraska becomes a state.
1869	Union Pacific Railroad is completed.
1870s–1880s	Decade of the Cattle Kingdom and the open range, known as the Empire of Grass.
1873	Timber Claim Act is passed.
1874–1877	Plague of grasshoppers damages crops; most serious damage is in 1874–1875.
1877	Desert Land Act is passed.
1878–1887	Decade of heavy rains that make the region bloom.
1880–1881	Severe blizzards cause deaths of thousands of cattle; many ranchers become bankrupt.
1881	Last cattle drive to Dodge City, Kansas.
1886	Severe blizzards destroy cattle, and cattlemen end their open range wars with farmers.
1887	Severe drought brings agricultural boom to an end. Dawes Act is passed, which allows the breakup of Indian reservations into individual allotments that white settlers can purchase for settlement.

1889	North Dakota and South Dakota become states.
1889	Oklahoma land rush.
1890	Wounded Knee Massacre of the Sioux by the U.S. Army.
1894	Drought; crops are destroyed by hot southwestern winds.
1907	Oklahoma becomes a state.
1912	Three-Year Homestead Act is passed.
1924	The Citizenship Act of 1924 makes all Indians born within the territorial limits of the United States full citizens.
1931	Record wheat crop in the Plains.
	The Great Plains by Walter Prescott Webb is published, the first history of the region.
1932	Beginning of dust storms.
1934	The Indian Reorganization Act accepts tribal governments as sovereign.
1934–1935	Lowest rainfall of the decade; dust storms with hurricane-force winds deposit soil on the ground in locations as far east as Washington, D.C.
1936	Severe drought on the Plains.
	Release of the federally funded documentary *The Plow That Broke the Plains.*
1939	Publication of *The Grapes of Wrath* by John Steinbeck.
1940	Movie of *The Grapes of Wrath* released, directed by John Ford.
1941	Mount Rushmore completed.
1942	Record wheat harvest on the Plains.
1944	Congress passes the Pick-Sloan Missouri Basin Project, authorizing the creation of flood-control dams, reservoirs, and hydroelectric plants in states drained by the Missouri River.
1950	Invention of the center-pivot irrigator that was able to tap the Ogallala Aquifer and bring fossil water to much of the Plains.
1950	Great Plains population peaks.
1950s	Little Dust Bowl.
1970s	Little Dust Bowl.
1973	Wounded Knee village is taken and occupied for seventy-one days by members of the American Indian Movement.
1976	The Center for Great Plains Studies (University of Nebraska) is chartered.
1987	The Buffalo Commons concept is introduced, which argues that the most distressed parts of the region should be taken out of agricultural production and turned into a national park.
1990	Since 1950, more than 40 percent of the counties, the most

rural, in the region have seen continuous decline in population. The region averages approximately six people per square mile.

1990s   Little Dust Bowl.

1995   Bombing of the Murrah Federal Building in Oklahoma City that killed 168 people.

Freedom to Farm Act is passed.

1999   Kansas State Board of Education removed evolution, cosmology and plate tectonic theories from high school curriculum.

2001   Kansas State School Board reversed its decision, about reinstating two other scientific theories of cosmology (the origin of the universe) and plate tectonics (the movement of vast plates across the earth's surface).

NOTES

Introduction

1. Sonja Rossum and Stephen Lavin, "Where Are the Great Plains? A Cartographic Analysis," *Professional Geographer* 52, no. 3 (2002): 543–552.

2. Walter Prescott Webb, *The Great Plains* (Boston: Ginn and Company, 1931), preface.

3. Harold E. Briggs, "An Appraisal of Historical Writings on the Great Plains since 1920," *Mississippi Valley Historical Review* (June 1947): 83–100.

4. Frederick C. Luebke, "Regionalism and the Great Plains: Problems of Concept and Method," *Western Historical Quarterly* (January 1984): 19–38.

5. Wright Morris, *The Territory Ahead* (New York: Harcourt, Brace, 1957), 22, cited in "Discovering a Dynamic Western Regionalism," in *Many Wests: Place, Culture, and Regional Identity*, ed. Michael C. Steiner and David M. Wrobel (Lawrence: University Press of Kansas, 1997).

6. Luebke, "Regionalism and the Great Plains," 38.

Architecture

1. While this were a notion so sound that it probably has several original authors, it was first introduced to me in the work of Allen Noble, longtime student of vernacular buildings. See Allen G. Noble, "The North American Settlement Landscape," in *Wood, Brick and Stone*, vol. 1 (Amherst: University of Massachusetts Press, 1984), pp. 1–9.

2. The ongoing life's work of Father William Sherman and a number of his professional colleagues to document the richly diverse and unexpected cultural traditions of the northern Plains is well summarized in William C. Sherman, et al., eds., *Plains Folk; North Dakota's Ethnic History* (Fargo: The North Dakota Institute for Regional Studies, 1988).

3. "The prairie eye looks for usefulness and plainness in art and architecture; the woods eye looks for the baroque and ornamental" (Bill Holm; quoted from his book *Prairie Days*). See David Erpestad and David Wood, *Building South Dakota: A Historical Survey of the State's Architecture to 1945* (Pierre: South Dakota State Historical Society Press, 1997), viii.

4. Most notably, see the excellent discussion of materials in Erpestad and Wood, *Building South Dakota*, pp. 19–36.

5. Peter Nabokov and Robert Easton, *Native American Architecture* (New York: Oxford University Press, 1989).

6. Michael H. Koop and Steven Ludwig, *German-Russian Folk Architecture in Southeastern South Dakota*, Video (Vermillion: South Dakota State Historic Preservation Center, 1984).

7. The characterization of the building's thermal and social comfort is a paraphrase based on an undocumented conversation between the author and an elderly visitor at the house site in 1995. The informant recalled having spent several days with the Hutmacher family after his car had become stranded in a snowstorm in the 1930.

8. This type of temporary dwelling has essentially disappeared from the landscape, but it is the central focus, discussed and illustrated throughout, in H. Elaine Lindgren, *Land in Her Own Name: Women as Homesteaders in North Dakota* (Fargo: North Dakota Institute for Regional Studies, 1991). See especially pp. 127–129.

9. See John N. Vogel, *Great Lakes Lumber on the Great Plains: The Laird, Norton Lumber Company in South Dakota* (Iowa City: University of Iowa Press, 1992); William Cronon, *Nature's Metropolis: Chicago and the Great Midwest* (New York: W. W. Norton and Co., 1991); and H. Roger Grant, *Living in the Depot: The Two-Story Railroad Station* (Iowa City: University of Iowa Press, 1993). The University of Iowa Press series American Land and Life has done an especially commendable job of highlighting cultural aspects of rural life in relationship to the built environment.

10. Richard Longstreth, *The Buildings of Main Street; a Guide to Commercial Architecture* (Washington, DC: Preservation Press, for National Trust for Historic Preservation, 1987).

11. David H. Sachs, and George Ehrlich, *Guide to Kansas Architecture* (Lawrence: University Press of Kansas, 1996), p. 311.

Art

1. Willa Cather, "The Sculptor's Funeral," in *The Troll Garden*, ed. James Woodress (Lincoln: University of Nebraska Press, 1983 [1905]), 39; Willa Cather, *My Antonia* (New York: Knopf, 1996 [1918]), 11; Wayne Fields, "Foreword," in *Plain Pictures: Images of the American Prairie*, Joni Kinsey, (Washington, DC: Smithsonian Institution Press, 1996), xvi.

2. Writers' Program of the Work Projects Administration in the State of Oklahoma, *The WPA Guide to 1930s Oklahoma* (Norman: University of Oklahoma Press, 1941; Lawrence: University Press of Kansas, 1986), 99; *A Survey of Nebraska Art: Exhibition, October 1–27, 1978, Kearney State College* (Omaha: Nebraska Arts Council, 1978), n.p.; *Kansas Centennial Historical Art Exhibition* (Topeka: Mulvane Art Center, 1961); Arthur Amiotte, "An Appraisal of Sioux Arts," in *An Illustrated History of the Arts in South Dakota*, ed. Arthur R. Huseboe (Sioux Falls, SD: Augustana College, 1989), 114.

3. Dorothy Dunn, *American Indian Painting of the Southwest and Plains Areas* (Albuquerque: University of New Mexico Press, 1968), 143; Janet C. Berlo and Ruth B. Phillips, *Native North American Art*, Oxford History of Art (Oxford: Oxford University Press, 1998), 112, 108.

4. Berlo and Phillips, *Native North American Art*, 112, 116; Dunn, *American Indian Painting*, 145.

5. Dunn, *American Indian Painting*, 145; Berlo and Phillips, *Native North American Art*, 117, 121–122.

6. Writers' Program of the Work Projects Administration for the State of Nebraska, *Nebraska: A Guide to the Cornhusker State*, sponsored by the Nebraska State Historical Society (New York: Viking, 1939), 120; John F. Helm Jr., "Artist Explorers," *Kansas Magazine* (1956): 103.

7. Roger B. Stein, "Packaging the Great Plains," *Great Plains Quarterly* 5 (1985): 9.

8. Dana Shostrom, *Study: Nebraska Artists of Merit* (Nebraska Federation of Women's Clubs, 1951), 2; Norman A. Geske, *Art and Artists in Nebraska: An Exhibition Presented February 11–March 28, 1982, Sheldon Memorial Art Gallery, University of Nebraska—Lincoln* (Lincoln: Sheldon Memorial Art Gallery, 1983), 9; Kinsey, *Plain Pictures*, 36; Oscar B. Jacobson and Jeanne d'Ucel, "Early Oklahoma Artists," *Chronicles of Oklahoma* 31 (1953): 123; James Nottage, *Prairie Visions: Art of the American West* (Topeka: Kansas State Historical Society, 1984), 10.

9. Kinsey, *Plain Pictures*, 77; Donald Bartlett Doe, "The Great Plains: The Land in the History of Nebraskan Art," in Geske, *Art and Artists in Nebraska*, 137.

10. Jacobson and d'Ucel, "Early Oklahoma Artists," 122; Helm, "Artist Explorers," 103; Geske, *Art and Artists in Nebraska*, 7.

11. *Arts and Crafts of Kansas Catalog: An Exhibition Held in Lawrence, February 18–22, 1948, in the Community Building* (Lawrence, 1948), 9; Robert Taft, "The Pictorial Record of the Old West, III. Henry Worrall," *Kansas Historical Quarterly* 14 (August 1946): 241.

12. South Dakota State College, *A Future for Art* (Brookings: South Dakota State College), 3; Angel Kwolek-Folland, "The Elegant Dugout: Domesticity and Moveable Culture in the United States, 1870–1900," *American Studies* 25 (1984): 21–38; C.A. Seward, "The Millet of the Prairies," *Kansas Magazine* 2.2 (August 1909): 1; Sarah Wool Moore, "History and Art," *Transactions and Reports of the Nebraska State Historical Society* 3 (1892; read before a meeting of the Society on January 10, 1888): 38.

13. Quoted in Huseboe, *Illustrated History of the Arts in South Dakota*, 382; Geske, *Art and Artists in Nebraska*, 7; Robert Taft, *Artists and Illustrators of the Old West, 1850–1900* (New York: Scribner's, 1953), 325n5; Doane Robinson, "John Banvard," *South Dakota Historical Collections* 21 (1942): 568, 591.

14. Florence Snow, "Kansas Art and Artists, III: Birger Sandzén," *Kansas Teacher* 26, no. 1 (November 1927): 11.

15. Clarissa Bucklin, ed., *Nebraska Art and Artists* (Lincoln: School of Fine Arts, University of Nebraska, 1932), 16; Frederick A. Olds, "Historians and Art: An Oklahoma Case Study," *Chronicles of Oklahoma* 52 (1974): 205; *WPA Guide to 1930s Oklahoma*, 100–101.

16. Florence L. Snow, "Kansas Art and Artists VI: John Noble," *Kansas Teacher* 26, no. 4 (February 1928): 20; Oscar B. Jacobson and Jeanne d'Ucel, "Art in Oklahoma," *Chronicles of Oklahoma* 32 (1954): 269; Huseboe, *Illustrated History of the Arts in South Dakota*, 255; *Survey of Nebraska Art*, n.p.; Geske, *Art and Artists in Nebraska*, 27; Bucklin, *Nebraska Art and Artists*, 18.

17. Quoted in Charles C. Eldredge, "William Dickerson's Kansas," in *The Regionalist Vision of William Dickerson*, ed. Bill North (Manhattan: Beach Museum of Art, Kansas State University, 1997), 1; Jacobson and d'Ucel, "Art in Oklahoma," 271.

18. *Nebraska: A Guide to the Cornhusker State*, 121; G.L. Brown, in *Ada B. Caldwell: A Tribute* (Brookings, SD: privately published, 1940), 32.

19. Nan Sheets, "In the Beginning," in *Widening Horizons in the Realm of Creative Arts, Oklahoma Edition: Commemorating 50 Years of Statehood* (Oklahoma City: Superior Printing Co., 1956), 29; quoted in William M. Tsutsui and Marjorie Swann, "'Open Your Eyes to the Beauty around You': The Art Collection of the Kansas Federation of Women's Clubs," in *Tallgrass Essays: Papers from the Symposium in Honor of Dr. Ramon Powers*, ed. Michael H. Hoeflich, Gayle R. Davis, and Jim Hoy (Topeka: Kansas State Historical Society, 2003), 62; South Dakota State Historical Society, "Capital and Capitol History of South Dakota," *South Dakota Historical Collections* 5 (1910): 240.

20. Quoted in Tsutsui and Swann, "'Open Your Eyes,'" 72; Ella C. Wittie, "Art in the Public Schools of Nebraska," in Bucklin, *Nebraska Art and Artists*, 72.

21. Fred N. Wells, *The Nebraska Art Association: A History, 1888–1971* (1972), 2, 13.

22. Norman A. Geske and Karen O. Janovy, eds., *The American Painting Collection of the*

Sheldon Memorial Art Gallery, University of Nebraska–Lincoln (Lincoln: University of Nebraska Press, 1988), xi; *WPA Guide to 1930s Oklahoma*, 101; Michael J. Harkins, "George Washington Lininger: Pioneer Merchant and Art Patron," *Nebraska History* 52, no. 4 (1971): 355.

23. Howard Roberts Lamar, "Seeing More than Earth and Sky: The Rise of a Great Plains Aesthetic," *Great Plains Quarterly* 9 (1989): 72; Joseph Stuart, *The Art of South Dakota, September 15–October 27, 1974, South Dakota Memorial Art Center* (Brookings: South Dakota State University, 1974), 19; Carleton Beals, "Kansas at the World's Fair," *Kansas Magazine* (1942): 23–24.

24. Joni Kinsey, "Cultivating the Grasslands: Women Painters in the Great Plains," in *Independent Spirits: Women Painters of the American West, 1890–1945*, ed. Patricia Trenton (Los Angeles: Autry Museum of Western Heritage in association with University of California Press, 1995), 243; Leonard Good, "Oklahoma's Art in the 1930s: A Remembrance," *Chronicles of Oklahoma* 70, no. 2 (summer 1992): 195; Lamar, "Seeing More than Earth and Sky," 74.

25. Eldredge, "William Dickerson's Kansas," 2; Karal Ann Marling, "The Prairie Print Makers: Five-Dollar Culture in the Great Depression," in *The Prairie Printmakers* (Kansas City: ExhibitsUSA, 2001), 8.

26. Quoted in Charles C. Eldredge, "Prairie Prodigal: John Steuart Curry and Kansas," in *John Steuart Curry: Inventing the Middle West*, ed. Patricia Junker (New York: Hudson Hills Press, 1998), 90; Thomas Craven, *Men of Art* (New York: Simon and Schuster, 1931), 511, 506, 508.

27. Quoted in Patricia Junker, "The Life and Career of John Steuart Curry: An Annotated Chronology," in Junker, *John Steuart Curry: Inventing the Middle West*, 212, 217, 219; Thomas Craven, "Introduction," in *Catalogue of a Loan Exhibition of Drawings and Paintings by John Steuart Curry* (Chicago: Lakeside Press Galleries, 1939), 6; quoted in Junker, "Life and Career," 219.

28. William M. Tsutsui and Marjorie Swann, "Kansans and the Visual Arts," *Kansas History* 25, no. 4 (Winter 2002–2003): 281; quoted in Junker, "Life and Career," 221.

29. Tsutsui and Swann, "Kansans and the Visual Arts," 284; Shostrom, *Study: Nebraska Artists of Merit*, 3.

30. Robert F. Karolevitz, *The Prairie Is My Garden: The Story of Harvey Dunn, Artist* (Aberdeen, SD: North Plains Press, 1969), 61; Edgar M. Howell, *Harvey Dunn, Painter of Pioneers*, Montana Heritage Series no. 15 (Helena: Montana Historical Society, 1968), n.p.

31. Barbara Kerr Scott and Sally Soelle, *New Deal Art: The Oklahoma Experience, 1933–1943* (Lawton, OK: Cameron University, 1983), 3; quoted in Bess England, "Artists in Oklahoma: A Handbook" (M.A. thesis, University of Oklahoma, 1964), 28; Carol Whitney, "A Place of Coming Together: The Historic Jacobson House," *Chronicles of Oklahoma* 78, no. 4 (winter 2000–2001): 448; see also Dunn, *American Indian Painting*, chapter 7.

32. Good, "Oklahoma's Art in the 1930s," 206; Wells, *Nebraska Art Association*, 23; quoted in Eldredge, "William Dickerson's Kansas," 3.

33. Birger Sandzén, "C. A. Seward—Promoter of Kansas Art," *Kansas Magazine* (1937): 4; Wells, *Nebraska Art Association*, 24–26.

34. Grant T. Reynard, *The Colors of My Life: Memoirs of a Nebraska Artist*, revised by Harry H. Hoffman (Kearney, NE: Kearney State College, 1986), 104; *WPA Guide to 1930s Oklahoma*, 355; quoted in Martin Wenger, "Thomas Gilcrease," *Chronicles of Oklahoma* 40, no. 2 (summer 1962): 96.

35. Good, "Oklahoma's Art in the 1930s," 195; Howard L. Meredith, "The Bacone School of Art," *Chronicles of Oklahoma* 58, no. 1 (spring 1980): 92.

36. Sandzén, "C. A. Seward," 2; on Seward, see also Barbara Thompson O'Neill and George C. Foreman, *The Prairie Print Makers* (Wichita: Gallery Ellington, 1984), 12–19; quoted in "A Patron of the Arts," *Widening Horizons*, 5; *Widening Horizons*, i; Edwin J. Deighton, "Oscar Brousse Jacobson: Oklahoma Painter," in *Oscar Brousse Jacobson: Oklahoma*

Painter, November 30, 1990–January 13, 1991 (Norman: University of Oklahoma Museum of Art, 1990), n.p.

37. Letter, Birger Sandzén to Charles Marshall, October 3, 1942, Charles Marshall Papers, University Archives, Kansas State University; Faye Davison, "What I Know about Kansas Artists," *Kansas Magazine* (1933): 43; John F. Helm Jr., "An Appraisal of Some Mid-Western Painters," *Kansas Magazine* (1936): 90.

38. Good, "Oklahoma's Art in the 1930s," 195.

39. England, "Artists in Oklahoma," 40; Marling, "The Prairie Print Makers," 12.

40. Quoted in Richard Lyons, *Paintings in Taxicabs: Characteristics of Certain Art Consumers* (Fargo: North Dakota Institute for Regional Studies, 1965), 108; Allan Nevins, "Kansas and the Stream of American Destiny" (1954) in *What Kansas Means to Me*, ed. Thomas Fox Averill (Lawrence: University Press of Kansas, 1991), 144; Lyons, *Paintings in Taxicabs*, 145.

41. Mabel Day O'Brian, "A Survey of Art in 388 North Dakota Homes" (M.A. thesis, University of North Dakota, 1931), 109–110; Lyons, *Paintings in Taxicabs*; Good, "Oklahoma's Art in the 1930s," 206; "Oklahoma City Art Museum History," Oklahoma City Museum of Art Homepage (Web site, cited June 25, 2003, http://www.okcmoa.com/press/history.htm); Wells, *Nebraska Art Association*, 36.

42. Mary A. Lierley, "Nebraska Interstate 80 Bicentennial Sculpture Project" (Ph.D. diss., North Texas State University, 1982), iii, 79, 75, 74; Joseph Stuart, *The South Dakota Collection* (Brookings: South Dakota Art Museum, South Dakota State University, 1988), 3.

43. Robert Pennington, *Oscar Howe: Artist of the Sioux* (Sioux Falls, SD: Dakota Territory Centennial Commission, 1961), 43, 41; John A. Warner, "The Sociological Art of Oscar Howe," in *Oscar Howe: A Retrospective Exhibition Catalogue Raisonné*, ed. Frederick J. Dockstader (Tulsa, OK: Thomas Gilcrease Museum Association, 1982), 13–14; Amiotte, "Appraisal of Sioux Arts," 140; Oscar Howe, quoted in Amiotte, "Appraisal of Sioux Arts," 140.

44. Paul E. Barr, *North Dakota Artists*, University of North Dakota Library Studies, no. 1 (Grand Forks: University of North Dakota Library, 1954), 6; quoted in Tsutsui and Swann, "'Open Your Eyes,'" 70; Mar Gretta Cocking, *My Story of Art in the Black Hills* (privately published, 1965), 31–54; Lyons, *Paintings in Taxicabs*, 123; Mary Jane Low, "Artists Gain Lasting Exhibit Place," *Bismarck Tribune*, March 18, 1955.

45. Robin S. Tryloff, "The Role of State Arts Agencies in the Promotion and Development of the Arts on the Plains," *Great Plains Quarterly* 9 (spring 1989): 121, 123.

46. Tsutsui and Swann, "Kansans and the Visual Arts," 287; Robert Smith Bader, *Hayseeds, Moralizers, and Methodists: The Twentieth-Century Image of Kansas* (Lawrence: University Press of Kansas, 1988), 141; *A Sense of Place: The Artist and the American Land, South Dakota Memorial Art Center, Brookings, South Dakota, April 7–28, 1974* (Brookings: South Dakota Memorial Art Center and the Mid-America Arts Alliance, 1974), n.p.

47. Quoted in Tryloff, "Role of State Arts Agencies," 119–120; Statistics from Robert C. Pierle, in *A Survey of Nebraska Art*, n.p.

48. Letter from Senator Tom Daschle to Terry Redlin, June 7, 2002, displayed in the Redlin Art Center, Watertown, SD.

49. Tsutsui and Swann, "Kansans and the Visual Arts," 289; Barbara Brackman et al., *Kansas Quilts and Quilters* (Lawrence: University Press of Kansas, 1993); Dorothy Cozart, "Camille Nixdorf Phelan, Oklahoma Quiltmaker," *Chronicles of Oklahoma* 72, no. 4 (Winter 1994–1995): 356–367.

50. Philip D. Jordan, "The People Paint the Plains," *Pacific Northwest Quarterly* 61, no. 2 (April 1970): 99; Jennie Chinn and Carl Magnuson, *Kansas Folk Arts Apprenticeship Program: Selected Portraits* (Topeka: Kansas State Historical Society, 1989), 3; Timothy J. Kloberdanz, "Foreword," in *Prairie Patterns: Folk Arts in North Dakota*, ed. Christopher Martin (Fargo: North Dakota Council on the Arts, 1989), viii; quoted in Elizabeth Broun, "Foreword," in *Backyard Visionaries: Grassroots Art in the Midwest*, ed. Barbara Brackman and

Cathy Dwigans (Lawrence: University Press of Kansas, 1999), vii; Tsutsui and Swann, "Kansans and the Visual Arts," 289.

51. John Carter, *Solomon D. Butcher: Photographing the American Dream* (Lincoln: University of Nebraska Press, 1985), 1; Joanne Jacobson, "Time and Vision in Wright Morris's Photographs of Nebraska," *Great Plains Quarterly* 7 (winter 1986): 3.

52. Geske, *Art and Artists in Nebraska*, 6–7; David Park Curry, "The Kansas Connection," in *The Kansas Art Reader*, ed. Jonathan Wesley Bell (Lawrence: Independent Study, University of Kansas, 1976), 327.

53. *Arts and Crafts of Kansas Catalog*, 8, 5; Governor Richard Kneip, State of the Arts address (1974), quoted in *20th Anniversary Report, 1966–1986* (Sioux Falls: South Dakota Arts Council, 1987), 15; Kinsey, "Cultivating the Grasslands," 243–244, 245.

54. Harvey Dunn, quoted in John E. Miller, *Looking for History on Highway 14* (Pierre: South Dakota State Historical Society Press, 2001), 65; Kathy Freise, "Native American Art," *Fargo Forum*, October 20, 1985; Jonathan Wesley Bell, "The Art of Kansas," in *Kansas Art Reader*, 6; Gertrude Dix Newlin, *Development of Art in Kansas* (Lawrence, KS: privately published, c. 1951), 35; Dora Hagge, ed., *Impact: The Art of Nebraska Women* (Columbus, NE: Impact, 1988), 3.

55. Davison, "What I Know about Kansas Artists," 43; C.M. Simons, "Andrew Standing Soldier," in *Andrew Standing Soldier: A Retrospective Exhibition* (Vermillion: University Art Galleries, University of South Dakota, 1990), 15–16; Good, "Oklahoma's Art in the 1930s," 196.

56. Doe, "Great Plains," 140; Florence L. Snow, "Kansas Art and Artists: Certain Conclusions," *Kansas Teacher* 27, 2–3 (June–July 1928): 13; William Allen White, "Introduction," in *In the Mountains: Reproductions of Lithographs and Wood Cuts of the Colorado Rockies*, by Birger Sandzén (McPherson, KS: Carl Smalley, 1925); Ross Shattuck, quoted in a letter from Edward W. Warwick to Mrs. K. Piper, June 21, 1949, "Ross Shattuck," Biography File, North Dakota State Library, Bismarck, James Yood, "Signe Stuart: An Essay," in *Signe Stuart: Retrospective, March 4–April 23, 1995, South Dakota Art Museum* (Brookings: South Dakota State University, 1995), 20–22; quoted in Lamar, "Seeing More than Earth and Sky," 75; Jani N. Sherrard, "Conversations," in *Kansas Art Reader*, 429.

57. Helm, "Appraisal of Some Mid-Western Painters," 90; Doe, "Great Plains," 138; Newlin, *Development of Art in Kansas*, 17; Stein, "Packaging the Great Plains," 7; See Reynard, *Colors of My Life*, 108.

Ecology and Environment

1. *History of the Expedition under the Command of Lewis and Clark*, ed. Elliott Coues (New York: Dover Publications, Inc., 1965, reprint of 1893 Harper edition), 1:120, 172, and 276, respectively.

2. Edward Hyams, *Soil and Civilization* (New York: Harper Colophon Books, 1976), 23; see also Chapter 10, "Oklahoma: Death of a Soil." See also William A. Albrecht, "Physical, Chemical, and Biochemical Changes in the Soil Community," in *Man's Role in Changing the Face of the Earth*, ed. William L. Thomas Jr. (Chicago: University of Chicago Press, 1956), 648–649, and Daniel Hillel, *Out of the Earth: Civilization and the Life of the Soil* (Berkeley: University of California Press, 1991).

3. William A. Albrecht, "Physical, Chemical, and Biochemical Changes in the Soil Community," in William L. Thomas, Jr., ed., *Man's Role in Changing the Face of the Earth* (Chicago: University of Chicago Press, 1956).

4. Edward Hyams, *Soil and Civilization* (New York: Harper Colophon Books, 1976; reprint from the original 1952 edition).

5. Peter Farb, *Living Earth* (New York: Harper Colophon Books, 1959), 103.

6. Robert G. Bailey, *Ecoregions Map of North America*. Miscellaneous Publication no. 1548 (Washington, DC: Forest Service, USDA, revised 1997), Reed F. Noss, and Robert L. Peters, *Endangered Ecosystems: A Status Report on America's Vanishing Habitat and Wildlife*. (Washington, DC: Defenders of Wildlife, 1995).

7. *Major Land Resource Area (MLRA) Boundaries*, Agricultural Handbook 296 (Washington, DC: USDA, Soil Conservation Service, 1981).

8. The H. John Heinz III Center for Science, Economics and the Environment, *The State of the Nation's Ecosystems* (Cambridge: Cambridge University Press, 2002).

9. John Opie, *Ogallala: Water for a Dry Land* (Lincoln: University of Nebraska Press, 1993, 2000), 20.

10. Theodore Binnema, *Common and Contested Ground: A Human Environmental History of the Northwestern Plains* (Norman: University of Oklahoma Press, 2002).

11. Walter Prescott Webb, *The Great Plains* (Lincoln: University of Nebraska Press, 1981; reprint of the 1931 edition).

12. Henry M. Brackerbidge, *Travels in the Interior of America* (Cleveland: Arthur H. Clark Co., 1904; reprint of 1819 original).

13. See discussion about various views in Opie, 1993, 54–59.

14. See the history of the negative and positive views of the Plains in Opie, *Ogallala*, 50–51.

15. Walter Prescott Webb, *The Great Plains* (Boston: Ginn and Company, 1931), 10.

16. Carl Ortwin Sauer, "Conditions of Pioneer Life in the Upper Illinois Valley," in John Leighly, ed., *Land and Life: A Selection from the Writings of Carl Ortwin Sauer* (Berkeley: University of California Press, 1963).

17. Josiah Gregg, *Commerce on the Prairies*, ed. Max L. Moorhead (Norman: University of Oklahoma Press, 1954).

18. Samuel Aughey and C. D. Wilbur, *Agriculture Begins at the 100th Meridian* (Lincoln: University of Nebraska Press, 1880).

19. Quoted in Gilbert C. Fite, *The Farmer's Frontier, 1865–1900* (New York: Holt, Rinehart, and Winston, 1966).

20. Willard D. Johnson, "The High Plains and Their Utilization," Twenty-first Annual Report of the United States Geologic Survey (Washington, D.C.: U.S. Government Printing Office, 1901), 4, 68.

21. John Wesley Powell, *Report on the Lands of the Arid Region of the United States*, reprint edition (Boston: Harvard Common Press, 1983; originally published 1879), 38–39.

22. Frederick H. Newell, "Irrigation on the Great Plains," *Yearbook of the United States Department of Agriculture, 1896* (Washington, DC: USDA, 1897), 167.

23. For further discussion, see Opie, *Ogallala*, 94–98.

24. Paul Bonnifield, *The Dust Bowl: Men, Dirt, and Depression* (Albuquerque: University of New Mexico Press, 1979), 64.

25. John Borchest, "The Dust Bowl in the 1970s," *Annals of the Association of American Geographers* 61 (March 1971): 13.

26. Quoted in R. Douglas Hurt, *The Dust Bowl: An Agricultural and Social History* (Chicago: Nelson Hall, 1981), 141.

27. William E. Splinter, "Center-Pivot Irrigation," *Scientific American* (June 1976): 49–55.

28. Opie, 2000, 137.

29. Ibid.

30. Ibid.

31. The above discussion among ranchers, rangers, and officials about the future of the Plains is based on *High Country News* 32 (June 5, 2000) 11: 1, 11.

32. Jon K. Piper, "Prairie Patterns and Their Relevance to Sustainable Agriculture," *Land Report* (of the Kansas Land Institute) 22 (Summer 1998): 3.

33. Deborah Epstein Popper and Frank J. Popper, "The Great Plains: From Dust to Dust," *Planning* 53 (December 1987): 12–18; see also Frank Popper and Deborah Popper, "The American Frontier, the Great Plains and the Buffalo Commons," *WildEarth* 2 (spring 1992): 1–17; and Anne Matthews, "The Poppers and the Plain," *New York Times Magazine*, June 24, 1990, esp. 24–26, 41, 48–49, 53.

34. Anne Matthews, "The Popper and the Plains," *New York Times Magazine* (June 24, 1990): 24.

35. Jon K. Piper, "The Prairie as a Model for Sustainable Agriculture: A Preliminary Study," *The Land Report Research Supplement* 3 (1986): 3.

Ethnicity

1. John E. Farley, *Majority-Minority Relations*, 4th ed. (Upper Saddle River, NJ: Prentice Hall, 2000), 526. The definition of ethnicity is complex. I will follow the one used by David Gradwohl and the theoretical stance of George DeVos "Ethnic Pluralism: Conflict and Accommodation," in George DeVos and Lola Romanucci-Ross, *Ethnic Identity: Cultural Continuities and Change* (Palo Alto, CA: Mayfield Publishing Company, 1975), 5–41. Here DeVos contends: "An ethnic group is a self-perceived group of people who hold in common a set of traditions not shared by others with whom they are in contact. Such traditions typically include folk religious beliefs and practices, language, a sense of historical continuity, and common ancestry or place of origin. The group's actual history often trails off into legend or mythology, which includes some concept of an unbroken biological-genetic generational continuity, sometimes regarded as giving special characteristics to the group . . . the ethnic identity of a group of people consists of their subjective symbolic or emblematic use of any aspect of culture in order to differentiate themselves from other groups. These emblems can be imposed from the outside or embraced from within. Ethnic features such as language or clothing or food can be considered emblems, for they show others who one is and to what group one belongs. A Christian, for example, wears a cross; a Jew, the Star of David (page 9). See David Mayer Gradwohl, "Intra-Group Diversity in Midwest American Jewish Cemeteries: An Ethnoarchaeological Perspective," in James B. Stoltman, *Archaeology of Eastern North America: Papers in Honor of Stephen Williams* (Jackson Archaeological Report no. 25, Mississippi Department of Archives and History, 1993), 364–382.

2. This is a relatively conservative date for the occupation of the Plains. Waldo R. Wedel, *Central Plains Prehistory: Holocene Environments and Cultural Change in the Republican River Basin* (Lincoln: University of Nebraska Press, 1988), 49, places an early date at 11,550 to 11,000 BP. George Frison, *Prehistoric Hunters of the High Plains* (San Diego: Academic Press, 1991), 25, has as his earliest radiocarbon 11,570 ± 170 BP. Jeffery L. Eighmy and Jason Label, "Radiocarbon Dating of Twenty-seven Plains Complexes and Phases," *Plains Anthropologist* 41, no. 155 (February 1966): 64, bracket the Clovis (i.e., the earliest period) at 12,040–9750 BP. Earlier dates have been reported on the Plains, but here we will simply use the conservative age and note that some sites place the entry of humans into North America as early as 17,000 BP.

3. For examples of this, see Wedel, *Central Plains Prehistory*; W. Raymond Wood and Margot Liberty, eds., *Anthropology of the Great Plains* (Lincoln: University of Nebraska Press, 1980). On the surface, it would appear that the Great Plains has little ethnic or racial diversity. This is far from the fact. While oftentimes the numbers of a given group of people are not high, the diversity is great. Cherokee, Choctaw, Chickasaw, Osage, and Sioux all lived on a land where blacks, Hispanics, and Vietnamese have settled. Books have been written on these various groups. In fact, more has been written about the Cherokee than any other First Nation (the Iroquois and Navajo also have a large body of literature dealing with tribal history and culture, and some say that these two groups have the largest body of history written about them). This chapter simply highlights significant trends and does not

exhaust the wealth of primary and secondary research dealing with the various groups discussed. This chapter highlights and outlines what is considered a rich and varied cultural tradition that has been and is part of the American Plains.

4. Charles C. Royce, *The Cherokee Nation of Indians* (Smithsonian Institution Press Book: Fifth Annual Report to the Bureau of Technology, 1888; reprint ed., Chicago: Aldine Publishing Co., 1975), 2–3. See also James Mooney, *Sacred Myths of the Cherokee and Sacred Formulas of the Cherokee* (Nashville, TN: Charles and Randy Elder Booksellers, 1982), 98, 94, 63, and 96, and Walter Lowrie and Walter Franklin, eds., *American State Papers: Indian Affairs*, vol. 2 (Washington: Gales and Seaton Pub., 1834), 129, 204.

5. Mooney, *Sacred Myths of the Cherokee*, 130–131. See also H. T. Malone, *Cherokees of the Old South: A People in Transition* (Athens: University of Georgia Press, 1956) and Royce, *Cherokee Nation of Indians*, 2–3.

6. Mooney, *Sacred Myths of the Cherokee*, 132–133.

7. Theda Perdue, *Slavery and the Evolution of Cherokee Society 1540–1866* (Knoxville: University of Tennessee Press, 1979); Annie Heloise Abel, *The American Indian as Slaveholder and Secessionist* (Lincoln: University of Nebraska Press, 1992), 3.

8. Abel, *American Indian as Slaveholder*, 3.

9. Anthony McGinnis, *Counting Coup and Cutting Horses: Intertribal Warfare on the Northern Plains, 1738–1889* (Evergreen, CO: Cordillera Press, 1990), 71.

10. Alan D. McMillan, *Native Peoples and Cultures of Canada* (Vancouver: Douglas and McIntyre, 1988), 273–278. All quotes regarding the Métis come from McMillan, *Native Peoples*, 273–278. This excellent work is often overlooked but provides great insight into the northern Plains of the United States and Canada.

11. McMillan, *Native Peoples*, 277.

12. David M. Emmons, *The Butte Irish: Class Ethnicity in an American Mining Town, 1875–1925* (Urbana: University of Illinois Press, 1989), 1–12

13. U.S. census, 1860, Dakota Territory.

14. Howard Palmer and Tamara Palmer, eds., *Peoples of Alberta: Portraits of Cultural Diversity* (Saskatoon, Saskatchewan: Western Producer Prairie Books, 1985), 108–109.

15. T. M. Devine, ed., *Scottish Emigration and Scottish Society: Proceedings of the Scottish Historical Studies Seminar University of Strathalyde* (Edinburgh: John Donald Publishers, 1992), 15–17; U.S. census, 1860, Dakota Territory.

16. Quintard Taylor and Shirley Ann Wilson Moore, *African American Women Confront the West, 1600–2000* (Norman: University of Oklahoma Press, 2003), 4.

17. William Loren Kutz, *The Black West*, 3rd ed., rev. and exp. (Seattle: Open Hand Publishing, 1987), 11–13.

18. W. Sherman Savage, *Blacks in the West* (Westport, CT: Greenwood Press, 1976), 5, 7–9. Savage notes that York possibly lived with the Crows in the 1830s (9).

19. Nat Love, *The Life and Adventures of Nat Love* (New York: Arno Press, 1968), 40–41; Bertha W. Calloway and Alonzo Nelson Smith, *Visions of Freedom on the Great Plains: An Illustrated History of African Americans in Nebraska* (Virginia Beach, VA: Donning Publishers, 1998).

20. Kenneth Marvin Hamilton, *Black Towns and Profit: Promotion and Development in the Trans-Appalachian West, 1877–1915* (Urbana: University of Illinois Press, 1991), 5, 6, 7, 99, and 101.

21. Juanita Brooks, *History of the Jew in Utah and Idaho* (Salt Lake City: Western Epics, 1973), 1.

22. David Mayer Gradwohl and Hanna Rosenberg Gradwohl, "That Is the Pillar of Rachel's Grave unto This Day: An Ethno Archaeological Comparison of Two Jewish Cemeteries in Lincoln, Nebraska," in *Persistence and Flexibility: Anthropological Perspectives on the Jewish Experience*, ed. Walter P. Zenner (Albany: State University of New York Press, 1988), 230–231. For additional reading regarding this topic, see Paul Olson, ed., *Broken Hoops and*

Plains People: A Catalogue of Ethnic Resources in the Humanities: Nebraska and Surrounding Areas (Lincoln: University of Nebraska Press, 1976).

23. Sophie Trupin, *Dakota Diaspora: Memoirs of a Jewish Homesteader* (Berkeley, CA: Alternative Press, 1984), i, 5, 31, 35; David Mayer Gradwohl, personal communication, February 1, 2004.

24. U.S. census, 1860, Dakota Territory.

25. Palmer and Palmer, ed. *Peoples of Alberta*, 174–179. See also D. Jerome Tweton and Theodore Jellif, *North Dakota: The Heritage of a People* (Fargo: North Dakota Institute for Regional Studies, 1976), and Francie M. Berg, ed. *Ethnic Heritage in North Dakota* (Washington, DC: Attigeh Foundation, 1983).

26. *Villages*, American Historical Society of Germans from Russia, http://www.ahsgr.org/villages.htm (accessed January 30, 2004).

27. Tweton and Jellif, *North Dakota*, 114–115; Berg, *Ethnic Heritage in North Dakota*, 94, 95, 100, 101.

28. Royden K. Loewen, *Family, Church, and Market: A Mennonite Community in the Old and New Worlds, 1850–1930* (Urbana: University of Illinois Press, 1993), 71, 118.

29. Kenneth S. Davis, *Kansas: A Bicentennial History* (New York: W. W. Norton and Co., 1976), 115–116.

30. Frederick C. Luebke, *Immigrants and Politics: The Germans of Nebraska, 1880–1900* (Lincoln: University of Nebraska Press, 1969), 16, 19, 21.

31. Ibid. In Lincoln, Nebraska, the American Historical Society of Germans from Russia has an excellent archive and museum.

32. Laura Wilson, *Hutterites of Montana* (New Haven, CT: Yale University Press, 2000); Palmer and Palmer, *Peoples of Alberta*, 349–356, 354; "The Hutterian Brethren," http://www.hutterites.org/groups.htm (accessed January 30, 2004). The quotes in this section are from Wilson's *Hutterites of Montana*. Discussions on the present location of Hutterite groups comes from "The Hutterian Brethren" Web site.

33. Joseph G. Svoboda, "Czechs: The Love of Liberty," in *Broken Hoops and Plains People: A Catalogue of Ethnic Resources in the Humanities Nebraska and Thereabouts* (Lincoln: University of Nebraska Curriculum Development, 1976), 160–173; Rose Rosicky, *A History of Czechs (Bohemians) in Nebraska* (Omaha: Czech Historical Society of Nebraska, 1929).

34. Ken Adachi, *The Enemy That Never Was: A History of the Japanese Canadians* (Toronto: McClelland and Stewart, 1991), 5, 8. For a broader historic context, see Marias B. Jansen, *The Making of Modern Japan* (Cambridge, MA: Belknap Press of Harvard University Press, 2002), for an overview of changes in Japan in the nineteenth century. See also John Curtis Perry, *Facing West: Americans and the Opening of the Pacific West* (Westport, CT: Praeger, 1994), 25–53; Gordon G. Nakayama, *Issei: Stories of Japanese Canadian Pioneers* (Toronto: NC Press, 1984), 15; and Paul A. Kamatsa, *Meiji 1868: Revolution and Counter-Revolution in Japan* (New York: Harper and Row, 1972), 240–259. For additional information on the Japanese in the New World, see Nakayama, *Issei* 15; John Modell, "Tradition and Opportunity: The Japanese Immigrant in America," *Pacific Historical Review* 40, no. 2 (1971); Takeo Yazaki, *Social Change and the City in Japan: From Earliest Times through the Industrial Revolution* (New York: Japan Publications, 1969); Gordon Hirabayashi, "Japanese Canadians: A New Awareness," *Canadian Ethnic Studies* 9, no. 2 (1977): 101–105, and W. Thomas White, "Race, Ethnicity, and Gender in the Railroad Workforce: The Case of the Far Northwest, 1883–1918," *Western Historical Quarterly* 16 (July 1985).

35. Mee Her, Ge Lor, Sirathra Som, and Salouth Soman, "Hmong and Cambodian Voices, 1970s—Present," in Sucheng Chan et al., *People of Color in the American West* (Lexington, MA: D.C. Health and Co., 1994) 576.

36. Ibid., 576, 579. For information used in this section see Sucheng Chan, *Asian Americans: An Interpretive History* (Boston: Twayne, 1991), 155–159.

37. "Kansas: Emerging Asian American and Pacific Islander Communities," Association of Asia Pacific Community Health Organizations, http://www.aapcho.com/draft/vs_draft. htm, (accessed January 30, 2004) 1.

38. *Omaha World Herald*, May 13, 2002. All quotes come from this article.

39. Benny Joseph Andres, "Power and Control in Imperial Valley, California: Nature, Agribusiness, Labor, and Race Relations, 1900–1940" (Ph.D. dissertation, University of New Mexico, 2003); Ronald T. Takaki, *Strangers from a Different Shore: A History of Asian Americans* (Boston: Little, Brown, 1989); H. Brett Melendy, *Asians in America: Filipinos, Koreans, and East Indians* (Boston: Twayne, 1977). Benny Andres' efforts have provided insight into the historic and present nature of Filipino immigration into the United States. Dr. Andres graciously provided the background data regarding Filipinos in the United States. For 2000 Census Records see the U.S. Census Bureau http://www.census.gov/main/ (accessed February, 2004).

40. "Iraqi Dissidents' American Dream and Nightmare," *Washington Post*, December 28, 2000.

41. Robert E. Pierre, "In Nebraska, 'Spanish Now Spoken Here,'" *Washington Post*, September 2, 2003, p. A03.

42. "Oklahoma Towns Try to Embrace Hispanics," *Amarillo Globe-News*, December 4, 2000.

43. The information here comes from a series of newspaper articles. Specifically, see "Hispanics Fuel Population Jump," *Lawrence Journal-World*, March 14, 2001; "Illegal Workers Swell Population of State Hispanics," *Topeka Capital-Journal*, June 4, 2001; "Store to Mark *Cinco de Mayo* with Poetry, *Topeka Capital-Journal* May 4, 2003; and *"Cinco de Mayo* Parade Attracts 15,000, *Grand Island Independent*, May 4, 2003.

44. Juan Gonzales Jr., *Racial and Ethnic Families in America*, 2nd ed. (Dubuque, IA: Kendall/Hunt, 1994), 288–289.

45. "Dakota Comment," *Argus Leader*, Sioux Falls, July 7, 2003.

Fashion

1. R. Peter Winham and Edward J. Lueck, "Cultures of the Middle Missouri," in *Plains Indians, A.D. 500–1500*, ed. Karl H. Schlesier (Norman, OK: University of Oklahoma Press, 1994) 149–175.

2. Carol Lynn MacGregor, ed., *The Journals of Patrick Gass* (Missoula, MT: Mountain Press Publishing Company, 1997), 55.

3. Barbara A. Hail, *Hau, Ko'la!* (Bristol, RI: Haffenreffer Museum of Anthropology, 1980), 68.

4. George Catlin, *Letter and Notes on the Manners, Customs, and Conditions of North American Indians, Volumes 1 and 2* (New York: Dover Publications, Inc., 1973), 51.

5. Ibid., 224.

6. Florence M. Montgomery, "1984." *Textiles in America 1650–1870* (New York: W. W. Norton), 353.

7. Randy Steffen, *The Horse Soldier 1776–1943, Volume II, The Frontier, the Mexican War, the Civil War, the Indian Wars 1851–1880* (Norman, OK: University of Oklahoma Press 1978), 6.

8. Douglas C. McChristian, *The U.S. Army in the West, 1870–1880: Uniforms, Weapons, and Equipment* (Norman, OK: University of Oklahoma Press, 1995), 164.

9. Carol Coburn, "'Well, I Wondered When I Saw You, What All Those New Clothes Meant': Interpreting the Dress of Norwegian-American Immigrants," in *Material Culture and People's Art Among the Norwegians in America*, ed. Marion John Nelson (Northfield, MN: Norwegian-American Historical Association, 1994), 125–126.

10. John A. Hostetler and Gertrude Enders Huntington, *The Hutterites in North America* (New York: Holt, Rinehart and Winston, 1967), 51.

11. Ann Marie Low, *Dust Bowl Diary* (Lincoln, NE: University of Nebraska Press, 1984), 13.

12. Ibid., 14.

Film and Theater

1. Frederick C. Luebke, "Regionalism and the Great Plains: Problems of Concept and Method," *Western Historical Quarterly* 15 (January 1984): 38, 31. For more general information concerning regionalism, see Merrill Jensen, ed., *Regionalism in America* (Madison: University of Wisconsin Press, 1952), and James E. Wright and Sarah Z. Rosenberg, eds., *The Great Plains Experience: Readings in the History of a Region* (Lincoln: University of Nebraska Press, 1978).

2. Luebke, "Regionalism and the Great Plains," 31.

3. Henry Nash Smith, *Virgin Land: The American West as Symbol and Myth* (Cambridge, MA: Harvard University Press, 1950), xi.

4. See also Gerald D. Nash, *Creating the West: Historical Interpretations, 1890–1990* (Albuquerque: University of New Mexico Press, 1991), and two books by Richard Slotkin, *Regeneration through Violence: The Mythology of the American Frontier, 1600–1860* (New York: Harper Perennial, 1996) and *Gunfighter Nation: The Myth of the Frontier in Twentieth-Century America* (New York: Atheneum, 1992), for the cultural significance of the American West.

5. Peter Stanfield, *Hollywood, Westerns, and the 1930s: The Lost Trail* (Exeter: University of Exeter Press, 2001), 7.

6. Frederick Jackson Turner, *The Frontier in American History* (New York: H. Holt, 1920).

7. Scott Simmon, *The Invention of the Western Film* (New York: Cambridge University Press, 2003), xiii.

8. George MacDonald Fraser, *A Hollywood History of the World* (New York: Fawcett Columbine, 1988), 201.

9. Stanfield, *Hollywood, Westerns, and the 1930s*, 146.

10. John C. Tibbetts, "Riding with the Devil: The Movie Adventures of William Clarke Quantrill," *Kansas History: A Journal of the Central Plains* 22, no. 3 (autumn 1999): 186.

11. Ibid., 196.

12. Richard M. Barsam, *Nonfiction Film: A Critical History* (Bloomington: Indiana University Press, 1992), 153.

13. Willa Cather, *O Pioneers!*

14. Jane Tompkins, *West of Everything* (New York: Oxford University Press, 1992), 71.

15. Thomas J. Harris, *Bogdanovich's Picture Shows* (Metuchen, NJ: Scarecrow Press, 1990), 139.

16. J. Hodgman, "The Bard of Omaha," *New York Times Magazine*, December 8, 2002, 91.

17. Vivian Sobchack, *Screening Space: The American Science Fiction Film*.

18. William J. Palmer, *The Films of the Eighties: A Social History* (Carbondale: Southern Illinois University Press, 1993), 190.

19. Arthur F. McClure, *Memories of Splendor: The Midwestern World of William Inge* (Topeka: Kansas State Historical Society, 1989), 71.

20. William Inge, *Picnic*.

21. Ralph F. Voss, *A Life of William Inge: The Strains of Triumph* (Lawrence: University Press of Kansas, 1989), 273.

22. John Opie, *Ogallala: Water for a Dry Land* (Lincoln: University of Nebraska Press, 1993), xvi.

23. *Oread*, April 19, 1996, 7.

Folklore

1. Elliott Oring, *Folk Groups and Folklore Genres: An Introduction* (Logan: Utah State University Press, 1986).

2. Barre Toelken, *The Dynamics of Folklore* (Logan: Utah State University Press, 1996.)

3. *WPA Guide to 1930s Oklahoma* (Lawrence: University Press of Kansas, 1986), 114.

4. Jim Hoy and Tom Isern, *Plains Folk* Web site, www.plainsfolk.com/youmust/accessed May 28, 2004.

5. Plains Folk Web site, http://www.plainsfolk.com/youmust/ accessed January 11, 2004.

6. Keith H. Basso, " Stalking with Stories: Names, Places, and Moral Narratives among the Western Apache." in *On Nature: Nature, Landscape, and Natural History*, ed. Daniel Halpern (San Francisco: North Point Press, 1987).

7. "The End of the World: The Buffalo Go," told to Alice Marriott by Old Lady Horse (Spear Woman) in *American Indian Mythology*, by Alice Lee Marriott and Carol K. Rachlin (New York: Thomas Crowell, 1968), 138–139.

8. "How and Why: Why the Bear Waddles When He Walks," told to Carol K. Rachlin by Marie Cox, in Marriott and Rachlin, *American Indian Mythology*, 129.

9. "Saynday and Smallpox: The White Man's Gift," told to Alice Marriott by Frank Givens (Eagle Plune, Kiowa) in ibid., 143–146.

10. *WPA Guide to 1930s Kansas* (Lawrence, Kansas, University Press of Kansas, 1984), 101.

11. Richard M. Dorson, "Folklore and Fake Lore," *American Mercury* 70 (1950): 335–343.

12. Paul R. Beath "Frebold Feboldson *Nebraska Folklore Pamphlets* 5 (1937).

13. *WPA Guide to 1930s Kansas*, 115.

14. Ibid., 102.

15. *WPA Guide to 1930s Oklahoma*, 116.

16. Jim Hoy, *Cowboys and Kansas* (Norman: University of Oklahoma Press, 1995), 54.

17. Ibid., 55.

18. *WPA Guide to 1930s Oklahoma*, 115.

19. *WPA Guide to 1930s Kansas*, 101

20. American Folklore Web site, http://www.americanfolklore.net/folktales/ok.html, accessed January 9, 2004.

21. The American Folklore Web site, http://www.americanfolklore.net/folktales/ne.html accessed January 9, 2004.

22. *WPA Guide to 1930s Kansas*, 101.

23. State of South Dakota Web site, http://www.state.sd.us/governor/Kids/legends.htm, accessed January 9, 2004

24. Jim Hoy and Tom Isern, *Plains Folk: A Common Place of the Great Plains* (Norman: University of Oklahoma Press, 1987).

25. Jim Hoy, *Cowboys in Kansas* (Norman: University of Oklahoma Press, 1995).

26. Ibid.

27. *WPA Guide to 1930s Kansas*, 100.

28. Ibid., 101.

29. American Folklore Web site, http://www.americanfolklore.net/folktales/ks1.html, accessed January 9, 2004.

30. Hoy and Isern, *Plains Folk*, 8–9.

31. Phone interview with author, January 2004.

32. National Public Radio, *Morning Edition*, http://www.npr.org/programs/morning/features/patc/homeontherange/index.html, accessed January 6, 2004.

33. Ibid.

34. This stanza is from Jim Hoy's grandmother's ballad book, located on his Plains Folk Web site, http://www.plainsfolk.com/songs/song6.htm, accessed January 15, 2004.

35. *WPA Guide to 1930s Kansas*, 103.

36. *WPA Guide to 1930s Oklahoma*, 116.

37. Ibid., 116–117.

38. Information on cowboy poetry and its performance can be gleaned from the Cowboy Poetry Web site, http://www.cowboypoetry.com.

39. Oklahoma History Museum Web site, http://www.ok-history.mus.ok.us/folk/charm_strings.html, accessed January 8, 2004.

40. Ibid.

41. John Dorst, "Roadside Attractions," in *Encyclopedia of the Great Plains*, ed. David J. Wishart (Lincoln: University of Nebraska Press, 2004).

42. Jim Hoy, *Cowboys in Kansas* (Norman: University of Oklahoma Press, 1995).

43. *Wrong Side*, retold by S. E. Scholooser, American Folklore Web site, http://www.americanfolklore.net/folktales/nd.html, accessed on January 9, 2004.

44. Hoy, *Cowboys and Kansas*, 131.

45. Ibid., 138–139.

46. Ibid., 61.

Food

1. Author survey, unpublished.

2. "Harvey House Gong," http://www.kshs.org/cool3/harveygong.htm (originally published: Minnie Dubbs Millbrook, "Fred Harvey and the Santa Fe," in *The Santa Fe in Topeka*, Shawnee County Historical Society Bulletin 56 [1979]).

3. Barbara M. Burgess, *Kansas Historical Markers Guide* (Topeka: State Historical Society and Kansas Department of Transportation, 2001), 29.

4. United States Department of Agriculture, National Agriculture Statistics Service, "All Cattle and Beef Cows: Inventory for Nebraska," 2001, http://www.nass.usda.gov.81/ipedb.

5. Carrie Young, *Nothing to Do but Stay: My Pioneer Mother* (Iowa City: University of Iowa Press, 1991), 70–72.

6. Tom Isern, *Dakota Circle: Excursions on the True Plains* (Fargo: Institute for Regional Studies, North Dakota State University, 2000), 87.

7. Kathleen Norris, *Dakota: A Spiritual Geography* (New York: Ticknor and Fields, 1993), 136.

8. Roger Welsch, *It's Not the End of the Earth, but You Can See It from Here: Tales of the Great Plains* (New York: Villard Books, 1990), 84.

9. Jane Winge, *Ritzy Rhubarb Secrets Cookbook* (Litchville, ND: Litchville Committee, 2000).

10. "Annual Church Suppers in North Dakota," http://www.webfamilytree.com/annual_church_suppers_in_north_dakota.htm (originally published: *Hannaford Enterprise*, November 1947, 1).

Language

1. Harold B. Allen, ed., *The Linguistic Atlas of the Upper Midwest*, 3 vols. (Minneapolis: University of Minnesota Press, 1973–1976).

2. Raymond J. DeMallie, ed., *Handbook of North American Indians: Plains* (Washington, DC: Smithsonian Institution, 2001).

3. The numbers of speakers for many of the languages discussed here are taken from the Ethnologue Web site, maintained by the Summer Institute of Linguistics (SIL), www.ethnologue.org. Numbers for the following languages are taken from other sources: Assiniboine, Raymond J. DeMallie and David Reed Miller, "Assiniboine," in DeMallie, *Handbook*, 572, 588; Crow, Fred W. Voget, "Crow," in DeMallie, *Handbook*, 713; Mandan,

Michael Krauss, "The World's Languages in Crisis," *Language* 68, no. 1 (1992): Teton, Raymond J. DeMallie, "Teton," in DeMallie, *Handbook*, 794; Ponca, Donald N. Brown and Lee Irwin, "Ponca," in DeMallie, *Handbook*, 416; Omaha, Margot P. Liberty, W. Raymond Wood, and Lee Irwin, "Omaha," in DeMallie, *Handbook*, 411–412; Iowa and Otoe, Marjorie M. Schweitzer, "Otoe and Missouria," in DeMallie, *Handbook*, 447; Kansa, Garrick A. Bailey and Gloria A. Young, "Kansa," in DeMallie, *Handbook*, 474; and Osage, Garrick A. Bailey, "Osage," in DeMallie, *Handbook*, 492.

4. This classification system is drawn from Ives Goddard, ed., *Handbook of North American Indians: Languages* (Washington, DC: Smithsonian Institution, 1996), 3. Krauss, "World's Languages in Crisis," 4, uses a slightly different, but similar system. Despite the difference in terminology for the varying levels of maintenance status, the classification levels of the languages discussed here and the indications of the likelihood of maintaining each language into the future are consistent with both Goddard's and Krauss's findings.

5. The numbers of speakers of the non–Native American languages discussed here are taken from reports produced from 1970, 1980, 1990, and 2000 census data.

6. The 1970 census data comes from U.S. Bureau of the Census (1973).

7. U.S. Bureau of the Census (1943a), 172–173; U.S. Bureau of the Census (1943b), 1–2.

8. More information about the regional diffusion of these dialects can be found in Allen, *Linguistic Atlas of the Upper Midwest*, vol. 1, and Craig M. Carver, *American Regional Dialects: A Word Geography* (Ann Arbor: University of Michigan Press, 1987). Both works provide good detail about the ways in which linguists determine dialectal variation and its geographic extent, as well as a discussion of the historical factors that led to the formation of the different dialects of U.S. English.

9. The vocabulary items presented here, among others, also may be found in Allan Metcalf, *How We Talk: American Regional English Today* (Boston: Houghton Mifflin, 2000).

10. The etymology for this term is presented by Metcalf, *How We Talk*, 113.

11. Carver, *American Regional Dialects*, 161–203; Hans Kurath, *Word Geography of the Eastern United States* (Ann Arbor: University of Michigan Press, 1949), 37.

12. Hans Kurath, *Linguistic Atlas of New England*, 3 vols. (Providence, RI: Brown University, 1939–1943).

13. Kurath, *Word Geography of the Eastern United States*.

Literature

1. Willa Cather, *My Antonia* (New York: Mariner Books, 1918, 1954), 12.

2. Lee Clark Mitchell, in his work *Westerns: Making the Man in Fiction and Film*, defines the western's obsession with the problem of what it means to be a man, and usually, but not always, a white man.

3. Clark, August 25, 1804.

4. "Zebulon Pike Explores Nebraska and the West," rpt. of Zebulon Pike's "Account of Expeditions" (1910), accessed January 17, 2004, http://www.nebraskastudies.org/0400/stories/0401_0110.html.

5. Edwin James, *From Pittsburgh to the Rocky Mountains: Major Stephen Long's Expedition, 1819–1820*, ed. Maxine Benson (Golden, CO: Fulcrum, 1988), 287.

6. Ibid.

7. James Fenimore Cooper, *The Prairie* (Oxford University Press, 1989), 13.

8. Hamlin Garland, *Main-Travelled Roads* (1891; rpt. Lincoln: University of Nebraska Press, 1993), 99.

9. Kathleen Norris, *Dakota: A Spritual Geography* (Boston: Houghton Mifflin, 1993, 2001), 13.

10. Sarah Raymond Herndon, *Days on the Road: Crossing the Plains in 1865* (Guilford, CT: Globe Pequot Press, 2003), 30.

11. Catherine Haun, "A Woman's Trip across the Plains in 1849," in *Women's Diaries of the Westward Journey*, ed. Lillian Schlissel (New York: Schocken Books, 1982, 1992), 177.

12. Linda Hassels, *Between Grass and Sky: Where I Live and Work* (Reno: University of Nevada Press, 2002).

13. Schlissel, *Women's Diaries of the Westward Journey*, 9–10.

14. Sharon Butala, *The Perfection of the Morning: An Apprenticeship in Nature* (Toronto: HarperCollins, 1994), 76–92.

15. Paul Gruchow, *Journal of a Prairie Year* (Minneapolis: University of Minnesota Press, 1985), 37–40.

16. John Madson, *Where the Sky Began: Land of the Tallgrass Prairie* (San Francisco: Sierra Club Books, 1982), 62, 67, 69, 76, 78, 79.

17. Mari Sandoz, *Love Song to the Plains* (Lincoln: University of Nebraska Press, 1961), 2.

18. Mildred Walker, *Winter Wheat* (Lincoln: University of Nebraska Press, 1992), 3.

19. Katherine Wood, "Plains Preponderance," in *Leaning into the Wind*, ed. Linda Hasselstrom, Gaydell Collier, and Nancy Curtis (Boston: Houghton Mifflin, 1997), 197.

20. John Steinbeck, *The Grapes of Wrath* (1939; rpt. New York: Penguin Books, 1992), 5.

21. William Least Heat-Moon, *PrairyErth* (Boston: Houghton Mifflin, 1991), 120.

22. Ibid., 81–82.

23. Landon Y. Jones, ed., *The Essential Lewis and Clark* (New York: Ecco Press, 2000), 9–10.

24. Walker, *Winter Wheat*, 145.

25. Ian Frazier, *The Great Plains* (New York: Farrar, Straus and Giroux, 1989), 7.

26. Wallace Stegner, *Wolf Willow*, 1995 (rpt. the Viking Press, 1962; rpt. Penguin Books with an intro by Page Stegner, 2000).

27. N. Scott Momaday, *The Way to Rainy Mountain* (University of New Mexico Press, 1976).

28. Frazier, *Great Plains*, 7.

29. Kenneth Porter, *No Rain in These Clouds: Poems, 1927–1945*. (New York: John Day and Company, 1946), 125–128.

30. William Stafford, *The Darkness around Us Is Deep: Selected Poems* (New York: Harper-Perennial, 1993), 85–86.

31. Linda Hogan, *Red Clay* (Greenfield Center, NY: Greenfield Review Press, 1991), 8–9.

32. Linda Hogan, *Book of Medicines* (Minneapolis: Coffee House Press, 1993), 28–29.

33. Marjorie Saiser, "Adios, Goodbye," online selections from *Plains Song Review*, http://www.unl.edu/plains/publications/psr-selections.html, accessed on October 10, 2003.

34. Frazier, *Great Plains*.

35. Wallace Stegner, "Living Dry," in *Where the Bluebird Sings to Lemonade Springs* (New York: Random House, 1992), 72.

36. Walter Prescott Webb, *The Great Plains* (Lincoln: University of Nebraska Press, 1931, 1959), 273–280.

37. Louise Erdrich, *The Beet Queen* (New York: Perennial, 1986), 1.

38. Ibid., 49.

39. This is a summary of the introduction to *My Antonia* (New York: Houghton Mifflin, 1918), 1–2.

40. Heat-Moon, *PrairyErth*, 228.

41. George Becker, "Realism: An Essay in Definition." *Modern Language Quarterly*, Vol. X (1949): 186–187. For a more thorough discussion, see George Becker's *Realism in Modern Literature* (New York: Frederick Ungar Publishing Co., 1980).

42. Mark Twain, *The Adventures of Huckleberry Finn*, in *The Works of Mark Twain*, vol. 8 (Berkeley: University of California Press, 2003), 23.

43. Morris Wright, *The Home Place* (Lincoln: University of Nebraska Press, 1948, 1998), 1.

44. Ibid.

45. Roland Flint, *Stubborn* (Urbana: University of Illinois Press, 1990), 7.

46. Gretel Ehrlich, *The Solace of Open Spaces* (New York: Penguin Books, 1985), 79.

47. Mari Sandoz, *Miss Morissa: Doctor of the Gold Trail* (Lincoln: University of Nebraska Press, 1955, 1980), 27.

48. Becker, "Realism," 195.

49. Stephen Crane, "The Maggie Inscription to Hamlin Garland" (1893), *The Portable Stephen Crane*, ed. Joseph Katz (New York: The Viking Press, 1969).

50. Stephen Crane, *The Red Badge of Courage*, rpt. in *The Anthology of American Literature*, 7th ed., ed. George McMichael (Upper Saddle River, NJ: Prentice Hall, 2000), 789.

51. Donald H. Ringe, *Introduction Essay to the Prairie* (New York: Oxford World Classics, 1992), xix.

52. Kroke qtd. in Jack Sullivan, "Senators Aim to Revive Plains Towns." *Denver Post*, April 27, 2003, 4A.

53. Willa Cather, *O Pioneers!* (Boston: Houghton Mifflin, 1913, 1941), 3.

54. Ibid., 9.

55. O. E. Rølvaag, *Peder Victorious: A Tale of the Pioneers Twenty Years Later* (New York: Harper and Brothers, 1929, 1956), 186.

56. Cather, *O Pioneers!*, 179.

57. Cather, *My Antonia*, 77.

58. Linda Hasselstrom, *Feels Like Far* (Boston and New York: Houghton Mifflin, 1999), 226.

59. Wallace Stegner, *Wolf Willow* (New York: Penguin Books, 1955, 1962), 202–203.

60. Ibid., 219.

61. Joy Harjo, *Mad Love and War* (Middletown, CT: Wesleyan University Press, 1990), 1.

62. William Least-Heat Moon, "About the Red Buffalo," *PrairyErth* (Boston and New York: Houghton Mifflin, 1991), 77.

63. William Allen White, "A Story in the Highlands," in *The Real Issue: A Book of Kansas Stories* (Chicago: Way and Williams, 1897), 77.

64. Linda Hasselstrom, Gaydell Collier, and Nancy Curtis, ed., *Leaning into the Wind: Women Write from the Heart of the West* (Boston: Houghton Mifflin, 1997), 33, 114, 229, 182.

65. Linda Hasselstrom, Gaydell Collier, and Nancy Curtis, eds. *Crazy Woman Creek* (Boston and New York: Houghton Mifflin, 2004).

66. Joy Harjo, *Mad Love and War*.

67. Norris, *Dakota*, 61.

68. Ibid.

69. Wes Jackson, "Matfield Green," in *Rooted in the Land: Essays on Community and Place*, ed. William Vitek and Wes Jackson (New Haven, CT: Yale University Press, 1996), 95–103.

70. Cather, *O Pioneers!* 21.

71. Diane Quantic, *The Nature of the Place: A Study of Great Plains Fiction* (Lincoln: University of Nebraska Press, 1995), 24.

72. Linda Hasselstrom, *Land Circle: Writings Collected from the Land* (Golden, CO: Fulcrum Press, 1991).

73. Butala, *Perfection of the Morning*, 77.

74. Ted Kooser, *Weather Central* (Pittsburgh: University of Pittsburgh Press, 1994), 43, 19, 7.

75. Ted Kooser, *Winter Morning Walks: One hundred Postcards to Jim Harrison* (Pittsburgh: Carnegie Mellon Press, 2000).

76. Ted Kooser, *Local Wonders: Seasons in the Bohemian Alps* (Lincoln: University of Nebraska Press, 2002).

77. Walter Prescott Webb, *The Great Plains* (Lincoln: University of Nebraska Press, 1931, 1959), 52–53.

78. Zitkala Ša (Gertrude Simmons Bonnin), "When the Buffalo Herd Went West," in *Dreams and Thunder: Stories, Poems, and the Sun Dance Opera*, ed. P. Jane Hafen (Lincoln: University of Nebraska Press, 2001), 13–19.

79. John Neihardt, *Black Elk Speaks* (1932; rpt., Lincoln: University of Nebraska Press, 1988), 16.

80. Luther Standing Bear and Herbert Morton Stoops, *Stones of the Siovx* (Lincoln: University of Nebraska Press, 1988).

81. Louise Erdrich, *Love Medicine* (New York: HarperCollins, 1984, 1993), 367.

82. Linda Hogan, *Mean Spirit* (New York: Atheneum, 1990).

83. Linda Hogan, "What I Think," in *Savings* (Minneapolis: Coffee House Press, 1988), 55.

84. Charles Baudelaire, *The Flowers of Evil* (Oxford and New York: Oxford University Press, 1993; page numbers and stanza numbers are in parentheses following quotes).

85. Annie Proulx, "The Governors of Wyoming," in *Close Range: Wyoming Stories* (New York: Simon and Schuster, 1999), 216.

86. Louise Erdrich, *The Beet Queen* (New York: Harper Collins, 1986), 58.

87. William Kloefkorn, "Free Cheese," in selections from the *Plains Song Review*, http://www.unl.edu/plains/publications/psr-selections.html, accessed October 27, 2003.

88. Henry Taylor, "Landscape with a Tractor," in *The Flying Change: Poems by Henry Taylor* (Baton Rouge: Louisiana State University Press, 1985), 3.

89. E. I. Pruitt, in "Comn," *South Dakota Review* (spring/summer 2003), 42–43.

90. Timothy Egan, "Great Plains Ailing as Livelihoods Dry Up, Poverty Soars," *The Denver Post*, December 1, 2003: 7A.

91. *Oklahoma Today Magazine*, accessed February 25, 2004, http://www.oklahomatoday.com.

92. "The Center for Great Plains Studies," Emporia State University, accessed July 20, 2004. http://www.emporia.edu/cgps/center.htm.

Music

1. Charlotte Heth, ed., *Native American Dance: Ceremonies and Social Traditions* (Golden, CO: Fulcrum Publishing, 1992).

2. Jennie A. Chinn and Carl R. Magnuson, "Don Lipovac: Button Box Accordion," in *American Musical Traditions*, ed. Jeff Todd Titon and Bob Carlin (New York: Schirmer Reference, 2002), 86–90.

3. "Pisnicka Ceska," performed by the Masopust Polka Band on August 2, 2003, sung in Czech by Carla Maltas. Translation by LaVerne Benda.

4. Kansas City Jazz Museum, www.americanjazzmuseum.com, accessed June 4, 2004.

5. Ibid., 20.

6. Tara Browner, "Transposing Cultures: The Appropriation of Native North American Musics, 1980–1990" (Ph.D. diss., University of Michigan, 1995; Ann Arbor: University Microfilms, 1997).

7. "Biography: Howard Hanson," *New Music Box: The Web Magazine from the American Music Center*, http://www.newmusicbox.org/first-person/nov99/howardhanson.html, accessed June 1, 2004 (no author listed).

8. Ibid.

Religion

1. Dale E. Jones, Sherri Doty, Clifford Grammich, James E. Horsch, Richard Houseal, Mac Lynn, John P. Marcum, Kenneth M. Sanchagrin, and Richard H. Taylor, *Religious Congregations & Membership in the United States, 2000: An Enumeration by Region, State and County*

Based on Data Reported for 149 Religious Bodies (Nashville: Glenmary Research Center, 2002), pp. 23, 29, 34, 37, and 33. In each decade since the 1970s, the Glenmary Research Center of Nashville, Tennessee, has conducted a census surveying nearly 150 religious bodies across the United States.

2. *North Dakota: A Guide to the Northern Prairie State*, American Guide Series (Fargo: Knight Printing Company, 1938), 256–257.

3. See http://www.glenmary.org/grc/default.htm for more information about the work of the Glenmary Research Center. It is the standard-bearer for those interested in the spatial implications of religion in the United States.

4. George Gallup Jr. and Timothy Jones, *The Next American Spirituality: Finding God in the Twenty-First Century* (Colorado Springs: Victor Cook Communications, 2000), 180.

5. *Nebraska: A Guide to the Cornhusker State*, American Guide Series (New York: Viking Press, 1939) 177.

6. Alice B. Kehoe, *North American Indians: A Comprehensive Account*, 2nd ed. (Englewood Cliffs, NJ: Prentice-Hall, 1992), 328–335. Also see Kehoe, *The Ghost Dance: Ethnohistory and Revitalization* (New York: Holt, Rinehart and Winston, 1989), and Alexander Lesser, *The Pawnee Ghost Dance Hand Game: Ghost Dance Revival and Ethnic Identity* (Lincoln: Bison Books, 1996).

7. Robert H. Keller Jr., *American Protestantism and United States Indian Policy, 1869–82* (Lincoln: University of Nebraska Press, 1983), 219.

8. Ibid., 149–166.

9. *The Evangelical Lutheran Church in America Home Page*, accessed November 27, 2003, http://www.elca.org/findachurch.html.

10. One such example: South Dakota's worst air disaster occurred earlier today when a crop duster crashed into a local Norwegian cemetery. Ole and Sven, the area's search and rescue squad, have recovered 450 bodies so far. They expect these numbers to rise as they continue to dig for survivors.

11. *The United Methodist Church Home Page*, accessed December 1, 2003, http://www.find-a-church.org/fac/.

Sports and Recreation

1. John F. Rooney and Richard Pillsbury, *The Atlas of American Sport* (New York: Macmillan Publishing, 1992).

2. Marvin Duncan, Dennis Fisher, and Mark Drabenstott, "Planning for a Sustainable Future in the Great Plains," Planning a Sustainable Future: The Case of the North American Great Plains, Proceedings of the Symposium, http://www.iisd.org/Agri/Nebraska/duncan.htm.

3. Michael Stein, "Cult and Sport: The Case of Big Red," *Mid-America Review of Sociology*, no. 2 (1977): 29–42.

4. Kansas State Historical Society,

5. *Gallup Monthly Poll*, Gallup Organization, Princeton, NJ, January 4, 2000.

6. Seth Jones, "A Midwestern Welcome. Prairie Dunes Golf Course, 2003," http://www.gcsaa.org/gcm/2002/july02.pdfs/07midwestern.pdf.

7. Richard W. Slatta, *The Cowboy Encyclopedia* (New York: W. W. Norton and Co., 1994), 319.

8. Kathleen Norris, *Dakota: A Spiritual Geography* (New York: Ticknor & Fields, 1993).

9. Karl Raitz and Meftah Dakhil, "Physical Environment and Preferred Places for Recreation," *Sport Place* 2, no. 1 (1988): 25–33.

10. Ibid.

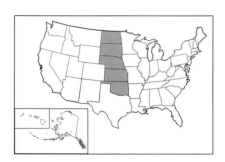

BIBLIOGRAPHY

Blouet, Brian W., and Merlin P. Lawson, eds. *Images of the Plains: The Role of Human Nature in Settlement*. Lincoln: University of Nebraska Press, 1975.

Blouet, Brian W., and Frederick C. Luebke, eds. *The Great Plains: Environment and Culture*. Lincoln: University of Nebraska Press, 1980.

Briggs, Harold E. "An Appraisal of Historical Writings on the Great Plains since 1920." *Mississippi Valley Historical Review* (June 1947): 83–100.

Jones, Dale E., Sherri Doty, Clifford Grammich, James E. Horsch, Richard Houseal, Mac Lynn, John P. Marcum, Kenneth M. Sanchagrin, and Richard H. Taylor. *Religious Congregations and Membership in the United States 2000: An Enumeration by Region, State, and County Based on Data Reported for 149 Religious Bodies*. Cincinnati: Glenmary Research Center, 2000.

Hoy, Jim, and Tom Isern. *Plains Folk: A Commonplace of the Great Plains*. Norman: University of Oklahoma Press, 1987.

Isern, Tom. *Plains Folk* column, self-syndicated in numerous Plains newspapers; can also be found on the Plains Folk Web site along with numerous folklore and foodways items. http://www.plainsfolk.com.

Kinsey, Joni. *Plain Pictures: Images of the American Prairie*. Washington, DC: Simthsonian Institution Press, 1996.

Luebke, Frederick C. "Regionalism and the Great Plains: Problems of Concept and Method." *Western Historical Quarterly* 15, no. 1 (January 1984): 38.

———, ed. *Ethnicity on the Great Plains*. Lincoln: University of Nebraska Press, 1980.

Luebke, Frederick C., Frances W. Kaye, and Gary E. Moulton, eds. *Mapping the North American Plains: Essays in the History of Cartography*. Norman: University of Oklahoma Press; Lincoln: Center for Great Plains Studies, University of Nebraska–Lincoln, 1987.

Opie, John. *Ogallala: Water for a Dry Land*. Lincoln: University of Nebraska Press, 1993.

Quantic, Diane Dufva. *The Nature of the Place: A Study of Great Plains Fiction*. Lincoln: University of Nebraska Press, 1995.

Quantic, Diane D., and P. Jane Hafen, eds. *A Great Plains Reader*. Lincoln: University of Nebraska Press, 2003.

Rossum, Sonja, and Stephen Lavin. "What Are the Great Plains? A Cartographic Analysis." *Professional Geographer* 52, no. 3 (August 2000): 543–552.

Steiner, Michael, and Clarence Mondale. *Region and Regionalism in the United States: A Source Book for the Humanities and Social Sciences.* New York: Garland Publishers, 1988.

Steiner, Michael C., and David M. Wrobel. *Many Wests: Place, Culture, and Regional Identity.* Lawrence: University Press of Kansas, 1997.

Webb, Walter Prescott. *The Great Plains.* Boston: Ginn and Company, 1931.

Worster, Donald. *Dust Bowl: The Southern Plains in the 1930s.* New York: Oxford University Press, 1979.

ACADEMIC CENTERS FOR GREAT PLAINS REGIONAL STUDIES

Canadian Plains Research Center, University of Regina
http://www.cprc.ca/ (accessed May 27, 2004)

Center for Great Plains Studies, Emporia State University
http://www.emporia.edu/cgps/ (accessed May 27, 2004)

Center for Great Plains Studies, North Dakota State University
http//www.lib.ndsu.nodak.edu/ndirs/ (accessed May 27, 2004)

Center for Great Plains Studies, University of Nebraska
http://www.unl.edu/plains/ (accessed May 27, 2004)

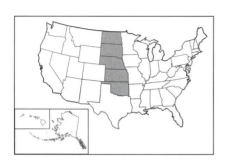

INDEX

ABOUT THE EDITOR AND CONTRIBUTORS

Editor and contributor AMANDA REES is visiting assistant professor in the Department of Geography at the University of Wyoming, on the western side of the Great Plains. A cultural geographer, Rees has recently published essays on the future of the Great Plains and the possibilities and perils of new urbanism, a recent architectural and planning movement that is reshaping some of the West's urban and suburban landscape. Her other interests involve regions, in particular the American West, American landscapes, and tourism, in particular dude ranching.

T. CHRIS APLIN graduated from the University of Oklahoma School of Music in 2002 with a master's in ethnomusicology. As an Oklahoma resident, scholar, and performer, he has conducted research on the Fire Dance of the Fort Sill Chiricahua/Warm Springs Apache tribe of Oklahoma, as well as various regional popular musics. He continues to pursue his interests in traditional and popular music forms at UCLA, where he is currently working on a doctorate in ethnomusicology.

PAULA CONLON is assistant professor of ethnomusicology in the School of Music at the University of Oklahoma. She has completed a biography of noted Comanche flutist/artist Doc Tate Nevaquaya, and is researching the Creek Stomp Dance for her next publication. Conlon is a frequent presenter at national and international professional conferences and gives Native American flute lecture-recitals in Oklahoma and the surrounding area.

STACY COYLE received a B.S. in foreign service and an M.A. in English from Georgetown University and both an M.F.A. in creative writing and a Ph.D. in American literature from the University of Maryland. She is a lecturer in the Core Humanities program at the University of Denver, where she designs and teaches interdisciplinary courses focused on the Great Plains and the American West.

ADDIE DeHILSTER is a graduate student at the University of Oklahoma. In 2002, she earned a master's degree in flute performance and is now pursuing a second master's in musicology/ethnomusicology. Her thesis is on the music and dance of the Kiowa Black Leggings Warrior Society, which was the topic of her presentation at the 2003 Society for Ethnomusicology national conference.

STEVE FOULKE, a native Kansan, is an assistant professor of history at Ottawa (Kansas) University and received his Ph.D. in geography from the University of Kansas. His dissertation, "Shaping of Place: Mennonitism in South-Central Kansas," details how faith influences the cultural landscape. He writes about faith and ethnicity on the Great Plains and participates in the Kansas Humanities Council's Talking about Literature in Kansas (TALK) program.

A. DUDLEY GARDNER is the division chair of the Social Science Fine Arts Department at Western Wyoming Community College. He earned his Ph.D. from the University of New Mexico and his M.A. from Colorado State University. He has published several books and articles, including *Forgotten Frontier: A History of Wyoming Coal Mining*, which he coauthored with Verla Flores. He is a professional historical archaeologist and historian who specializes in ethnic and social history. He has conducted archaeological excavations of historical Chinese, Japanese, and eastern European communities throughout the Rocky Mountain West.

PAMELA INNES is an assistant professor of linguistic anthropology at the University of Wyoming. She is currently working with two members of the Seminole Nation on an advanced textbook on Mvskoke, the language spoken by members of the Muskogee and Seminole Nations of Oklahoma. Her first textbook about Mvskoke, written with the same coauthors, was published in 2004.

STEVE MARTENS is an architect, preservationist, and architectural historian who earned his postprofessional M.Arch. degree from the University of Minnesota. He was cocurator for the exhibit "Seeking Connections/Comparing Visions" interpreting the Plains Art Museum's renovated historic building and has been involved in design and consulting for more than a dozen successfully preserved historic buildings. He has led grant-supported research projects for German Russian farmsteads, WPA fieldstone buildings, rural cemetery landscapes, and cooperative creameries and is currently coauthoring a book on buildings of North Dakota. He serves on the Board of Preservation North Dakota and is contributing to its pending book on Prairie churches.

JOHN OPIE, who holds a Ph.D. from the University of Chicago, is the author of *Nature's Nation: An Environmental History of the United States* (1998) and the prizewinning *Ogallala: Water for a Dry Land* (1993/2000). Other publications include *Energy and American Values* (1981) and *The Law of the Land: 200 Years of American Farmland Policy* (1987/1994). He is a distinguished professor emeritus of environmental history and policy from the New Jersey Institute of Technology. Recent publications include essays on moral geography, irrigation history, and environmental aesthetics. Forthcoming is *Virtual America: Sleepwalking through Paradise*. He is currently a lecturer at the University of Chicago.

RONALD L. M. RAMSAY earned university degrees with an emphasis in architectural history from the University of Oklahoma and University of Texas at Austin. He has done postgraduate study at the University of Delaware and was the 1995 recipient of the deMontquin Prize for colonial-era history research. As an educator for more than twenty-six years, he has motivated broad interest in architecture on the Great Plains. He developed gallery exhibits celebrating the work of regionally important architects Milton Earl Beebe and the Hancock Brothers, as well as "In the Architect's Eye: 100 Years of North Dakota Building" and "Seeking Connections/Comparing Visions." He is currently coauthoring a book on buildings of North Dakota and is developing separate manuscripts on the emergence of the architectural profession on the Great Plains and relationships between Victorian society and key personalities of the Episcopal Church on the northern Plains.

JOHN F. ROONEY JR. is Regents Professor Emeritus and former head of the Geography Department at Oklahoma State University. He is the author of several books on the geography of sport, including *Recruiting Game* and *Atlas of American Sport*. Rooney is president of the Rooney Golf Group and cofounder of Longitudes LLC, a leading research company in geodemographic dimensions of the American sports industry.

BARBARA SHORTRIDGE is an assistant professor in the Department of Geography at the University of Kansas. She is the author of *Atlas of American Women* (1987) and editor of *The Taste of American Place* (1998). Her most recent publications related to food are a chapter in *Culinary Tourism* (2004) on "Ethnic Heritage Food in Lindsborg, Kansas and New Glarus, Wisconsin" and "Not Just Jello and Hot Dishes: Representative Foods of Minnesota" in the *Journal of Cultural Geography* (2004): She recently received an Anne U. White Research Grant from the Association of American Geographers to explore "Local Foodways Knowledge in the Cutover Lands of the Upper Midwest." She is a board member of the interdisciplinary Association for the Study of Food and Society.

MARJORIE SWANN is associate professor of English at the University of Kansas, where she teaches courses in Renaissance literature and material culture studies. She is the author of *Curiosities and Texts: The Culture of Collecting in Early Modern England* (2001). She and William Tsutsui have cowritten several articles on the history of the visual arts in Kansas.

WILLIAM M. TSUTSUI is associate professor of history at the University of Kansas and director of the Kansas Consortium for Teaching about Asia. A specialist in modern Japanese history, he is the author of numerous books and articles, including *Manufacturing Ideology: Scientific Management in Twentieth-Century Japan* (1998), and currently serves as president of the Kansas State Historical Society. He has cowritten several articles on the history of the visual arts in Kansas with Marjorie Swann.

THOMAS A. WIKLE is professor of geography and associate dean in the College of Arts and Sciences at Oklahoma State University. His past research has focused on topics ranging from the distribution of volunteer organizations to impacts of wireless telephone technology on the American landscape. Wikle's projects have been funded by the National Geographic Society, the U.S. National Park Service, and the National Science Foundation.

LAUREL E. WILSON is an associate professor at the University of Missouri at Columbia. She is most recognized for her research about the dress of American cowboys. She is a member of the Scholars Roundtable of the Costume Society of America and Associate Editor for *Clothing and Textile Research Journal*. She has received several awards for teaching including the University of Missouri's Kemper Fellowship for Excellence in Teaching.

RONALD W. WILSON received his Ph.D. in Film Studies at the University of Kansas. He currently has a chapter in the *Columbia Companion to American History on Film*. He has written reviews for *Literature/Film Quarterly*, *Journal of Popular Film & Television*, *Film International*, *Film Quarterly*, and *Scope: An Online Journal of Film Studies*.

The Greenwood Encyclopedia of American Regional Cultures

The Great Plains Region, *edited by Amanda Rees*

The Mid-Atlantic Region, *edited by Robert P. Marzec*

The Midwest, *edited by Joseph W. Slade and Judith Yaross Lee*

New England, *edited by Michael Sletcher*

The Pacific Region, *edited by Jan Goggans with Aaron DiFranco*

The Rocky Mountain Region, *edited by Rick Newby*

The South, *edited by Rebecca Mark and Rob Vaughan*

The Southwest, *edited by Mark Busby*